ENGLISH G

| G9 |

access 6

Cornelsen

English G Access
G9 Ausgabe 2019 · Band 6
Schulbuch

Im Auftrag des Verlages herausgegeben von
Prof. Jörg Rademacher, Mannheim

Erarbeitet von
Peadar Curran, Berlin; Laurence Harger, Wellington,
Neuseeland; Cecile Niemitz-Rossant, Berlin

unter Mitarbeit von
Dr. Annette Leithner-Brauns, Dresden; Birgit Ohmsieder,
Berlin; Mervyn Whittaker, Bad Dürkheim

in Zusammenarbeit mit der Englischredaktion
Filiz Bahsi (koordinierende Redakteurin),
Bonnie Glänzer, Michelle Fridman, Graeme Garson
(Redaktionsleitung), Georg Raspe, Dr. Philip Devlin,
Ralph Williams *und* Lothar Teworte (digitales Schulbuch),
Sophie Dupiech (Lizenz- und Medienmanagement)

Beratende Mitwirkung
Friederike von Bremen, Hannover; Peter Brünker,
Bad Kreuznach; Anette Fritsch, Dillenburg; Uli Imig,
Wildeshausen; Bernd Koch, Marburg; Thomas Neidhardt,
Bielefeld; Wolfgang Neudecker, Mannheim;
Dr. Andreas Sedlatschek, Esslingen; Sieglinde Spranger,
Chemnitz; Marcel Sprunkel, Köln; Sabine Tudan,
Reichenau; Britta Weber, Aachen;
Harald Weißling, Mannheim

Illustrationen
Tobias Dahmen, Utrecht/NL;
Burkhard Schulz, Düsseldorf; Michael Fleischmann,
Waldegg *sowie* Eric Gira, Berlin

Umschlaggestaltung
hawemannundmosch, Berlin

Layout und technische Umsetzung
Eric Gira, Berlin

Soweit in diesem Buch Personen fotografisch abgebildet
sind und ihnen von der Redaktion fiktive Namen, Berufe,
Dialoge und Ähnliches zugeordnet oder diese Personen in
bestimmte Kontexte gesetzt werden, dienen diese
Zuordnungen und Darstellungen ausschließlich der
Veranschaulichung und dem besseren Verständnis des
Buchinhaltes.

Begleitmaterial zu English G Access 6

978-3-06-036009-3	Workbook mit Audios online
978-3-06-036010-9	Workbook mit Audios online und interaktiven Übungen
978-3-06-036015-4	Vokabeltaschenbuch
978-3-06-036287-5	Wordmaster Band 5 + 6
978-3-06-036013-0	Klassenarbeitstrainer
978-3-06-033864-1	*Mr Penumbra's 24-Hour Bookstore* (Lektüre)
978-3-06-036000-0	E-Book

www.cornelsen.de

Die Webseiten Dritter, deren Internetadressen in diesem
Lehrwerk angegeben sind, wurden vor Drucklegung
sorgfältig geprüft. Der Verlag übernimmt keine Gewähr für
die Aktualität und den Inhalt dieser Seiten oder solcher, die
mit ihnen verlinkt sind.

Dieses Werk berücksichtigt die Regeln der reformierten
Rechtschreibung und Zeichensetzung.

Alle Drucke dieser Auflage sind inhaltlich unverändert und
können im Unterricht nebeneinander verwendet werden.

Druck und Bindung: Mohn Media Mohndruck, Gütersloh

1. Auflage, 1. Druck 2023
ISBN 978-3-06-036248-6 – broschiert

1. Auflage, 1. Druck 2023
ISBN 978-3-06-036288-2 – gebunden

ISBN 978-3-06-036000-0 – E-Book

PEFC zertifiziert
Dieses Produkt stammt aus nachhaltig
bewirtschafteten Wäldern und kontrollierten
Quellen.
PEFC
PEFC/04-31-1033
www.pefc.de

English G Access · G9 · Band 6 enthält folgende Teile:

Units	die drei Kapitel des Buches
Access to cultures	andere Kulturen kennenlernen und verstehen
Text Challenge	Vorbereitung auf die Oberstufe
Grammar & Practice (GAP)	Grammatikerklärungen und Übungen zum Wiederholen
Skills & Media Competence (SMC)	eine Beschreibung wichtiger Lern- und Arbeitstechniken
Vocabulary	das Wörterverzeichnis zum Lernen der neuen Wörter jeder Unit
Dictionary	ein alphabetisches Wörterverzeichnis zum Nachschlagen

In den Units findest du diese Überschriften:

Looking at language	Beispiele sammeln und sprachliche Regeln entdecken
Language help	Hilfe in Form von sprachlichen Regeln
Practice	Aufgaben und Übungen
Access to words	Wortschatz systematisch ausbauen
Listening course	Hörverstehen gezielt trainieren
Study skills	Einführung in Lern- und Arbeitstechniken
Background file	Informationen über Land und Leute
The world behind the picture	vom Bild in den Film – Videoclips mit Aufgaben

Du findest auch diese Symbole:

🔊	Audios zum Herunterladen: *www.cornelsen.de/codes (Webcode niwijo)*
www	zusätzliche Materialien, die du unter *www.cornelsen.de/codes* finden kannst *(Webcode: bajeki;* Videos: *novetu)*
▪▪ ▪ ▪	Übungssequenz: neue Grammatik intensiv üben und dann anwenden
Early finisher ▸	zusätzliche Aktivitäten und Übungen für Schüler/innen, die früher fertig sind
More help ▸	zusätzliche Hilfen für eine Aufgabe
You choose ▸	zwischen zwei Aufgaben auswählen
EXTRA	zusätzliche Aktivitäten und Übungen für alle
MY BOOK	schöne und wichtige Arbeiten sammeln
Your task ▸	Was du gelernt hast, kannst du in der Lernaufgabe am Ende jeder Unit noch mal zeigen und dich auch selbst einschätzen.
👂 💬 📖 ✏	Hören Sprechen Lesen Schreiben
EN/DE 💬	Mediation (zwischen zwei Sprachen vermitteln), Thinking about language (Sprachreflexion)
MK	auch mit digitalen Medien lernen
👥 👥 👥 🧩	Partnerarbeit Partnercheck Gruppenarbeit Kooperative Lernform

	You learn about …	**Your task** *(Lernaufgabe)*	**Texts**

Introduction

Unit 1
Who are you?

- Photo and image
- Identity in poetry
- Imagery in literature
- Gender and history
- Cultural and genetic identity
- Technology and privacy

Write an opinion piece for a class magazine (pp. 30–31)

A Poems by Kae Tempest, Langston Hughes, Dean Atta and Katy Perry

B Gender and equality (an opinion piece)

C *The seven daughters of Eve* by Brian Sykes (non-fiction: an excerpt)

Background file
Tech identity
(p. 28)

www
Find out more about
Langston Hughes (p. 13)
Find out about three other flags
(p. 26)
Find out more about Amazonian
tribes (p. 36)

Unit 2
What makes a community?

- The characteristics of communities
- Everyday life in an Amazon community
- Behavioural differences
- How music connects
- Collective protest
- Social and political involvement

Prepare an electronic presentation (p. 53)

A *Go and come back* by Joan Abelove (excerpt from a novel)

B New Yorkers in the jungle (review of the novel *Go and come back*)

C Community projects (blog, non-fiction text)

Background file
Political systems in the USA and the UK
(pp. 50–51)

www
Find out more about the British
and American voting systems
(p. 50)

Access to cultures   Appropriate behaviour

Skills

Language

8

🔖 **Study skills**
Improving your electronic texts
(p. 17)

Access to cultures
Flags and identity
(p. 26)

Viewing
Advertisement: *The DNA journey*
Making the film: Influencing an
audience
(p. 27)

Listening course
Connected speech: weak pronunciation
(p. 29)

MyBook
Writing an opinion piece
(pp. 19, 30)

Access to words
talking about identity
adverb and adjective collocations

Grammar
the simple present (revision);
the simple past (revision);
modal verbs (revision);
the passive (progressive);
adverbial clauses

Pronunciation
Weak pronunciation in normal speech
(p. 29)

10

Part A 12
Part B 18
Part C 22

Skill in focus: Writing

Viewing
Documentary: *Joe's violin*
Making the film: Elements of
a documentary
(p. 40)

Listening course
Understanding different accents
(p. 41)

MyBook
Writing a book review
(p. 43)

Study skills
Analysing a text – Part 1
(p. 37)

Access to words
Refining your presentation
techniques
(p. 52)

Grammar
indirect speech (revision);
participle clauses (revision);
emphatic structures;
the gerund after prepositions

Pronunciation
Accent variation
(p. 41)

32

Part A 34
Part B 42
Part C 46

Skill in focus: Reading

54

You learn about ...	**Your task** (Lernaufgabe)	**Texts**
Unit 3 **How is the world changing?** · Technology and change · About AI · Our future without bees · Native American traditions in a changing world · Imagining the future (www) *Find out about the history of "The news" (p. 66)*	Take part in a panel discussion (p. 75)	A Artificial intelligence (feature article) B When the bees buzz off (feature article) C *Mr Penumbra's 24-hour-bookstore* by Robin Sloan (excerpt from a novel) **Background file** Energy for the future (p. 67)

Text Challenge	**Introduction**
	Finding Nevo Excerpt from an autobiographical text
	Messy Roots Excerpt from a graphic novel
	The Crowdfunded Conservationist Who Wants to Save the World Non-fictional text

More help	
Early finisher	
Partner pages	
Grammar & Practice	Overview and explanation of grammar points with exercises for practice
Skills & Media Competence	· Your companion to working techniques end methods · Exam Skills

202 Vocabulary	274 English sounds	276 Countries and continents
228 Dictionary English – German	275 List of names & False friends	278 Irregular verbs

Pro Unit können mehrere Klassenarbeiten vorgesehen werden, die Schwerpunkte sowohl im Bereich der Beherrschung der sprachlichen Mittel als auch der kommunikativen Kompetenzen bilden können.
(Weitere Hinweise in *Vorschläge zur Leistungsmessung*)

Skills	Language		

Skills

MyBook
Writing a feature article
(p. 63)

Using digital tools
Doing internet research
(p. 63)

Viewing
News clip
(p. 66)

Listening course
Dealing with listening tasks
(pp. 72–73)

Study skills
Analysing a text – part 2 (p. 71)
Preparing for a panel discussion (p. 74)

Language

Access to words   **56**
information and communication
technology   Part A   58
collocations   Part B   62
                              Part C   68
Grammar
the definite article (revision);
the sequence of adverbials (revision);
defining and non-defining relative
clauses (revision);
relative clauses to comment

Skill in focus: Speaking

76

77

80

84

88

94

98

104

162
195

280 Early finisher · Lösungen
282 Operatoren

284 Quellenverzeichnis
286 Giving feedback to your classmates

Describe the picture and discuss
what ideas it expresses.

Say how you think these ideas
are linked to the topics
of Units 1–3.

8

Who are **you?**

3

6

9

1 Profile pictures

a) Describe the people in the pictures.
Point to similarities and differences.
- This photo looks as if it was taken in a park/…
- It shows
  - someone (maybe) in their late teens / …
  - someone standing/sitting/smiling/…
- He/She has dreadlocks / curly hair / kinky hair / …
  - … is dressed casually/formally/…
  - … is wearing …

> blazer · cap · denim jacket · face paint ·
> glasses · headscarf · scarf · tie · …

- Like/Unlike most of the others, she is/isn't smiling/
looking directly at the camera/…

b) 👥 💬 Discuss how you think the people in the
photos would like to be seen.
- I think he wants to come across as mysterious/
patriotic/serious/…
- Her expression/hairstyle/… suggests that
she wants to look thoughtful/traditional/…

c) 👥 Choose a person you would like to meet.
Describe your first impression of them and explain
why you would like to meet them.
- I think I'd like to meet …
- To me she seems easy-going/friendly/…
- Even though he looks a bit conservative/shy/…,
I still think …

2 Choosing your profile picture

Discuss the points you consider when you post a photo
of yourself, e.g. on social media.
- I like to use a photo where I look friendly/…
- I'd like people to see me as funny/original/…
- I'd prefer people not to think I'm …
- I use any photo. I never think about how I look.

> **Your task**

At the end of this unit:
You will make a magazine in which you express
your opinion on an important issue.

1 Tiresias (excerpt by Kae Tempest)

Picture the scene:
A boy of fifteen.
With the usual dreams
And the usual routine.

5 Heading to school with a dullness inside
Borne of desires left unsatisfied.

Is he stifled or is he just
Learning the ways of his times?
Give him limbs that are awkward
10 But know how to climb.

Give him a gait that you know.
Give him hopes.
His days are so painfully slow,
But he copes.

15 This morning
He wakes to the same old alarm.
Slumps in the shower
Like a frog in the rain.
Winks at the mirror – does cool, does charm.
20 Shaves soft skin.
Nods at the pain.
No hair yet. Soon though.

Headphones on.
Last half of last night's joint in his lips.
25 Bass so loud it feels like a movie.
Scuffing his trainers.
Swinging his hips.

They're always laughing,
The kids at the bus stop.
30 He tries to ignore them,
But it doesn't help.

Hood up, he walks past them.
Blowing out smoke rings.
Singing out Wu-Tang.
35 Hating himself.

---

dullness Mattigkeit **borne of ...** geboren aus …
unsatisfied unbefriedigt **stifle** unterdrücken;
ersticken **limbs** Glieder **gait** Gang
slump zusammensacken **do charm** auf Charme machen

Kae Tempest (born 22.12.1985, pronouns: *they/them*) is an award-winning British poet, spoken word performer, rap singer, playwright and novelist.

a) Read the excerpt from the poem to yourself. Read it twice if you need. Do you like it? Explain why or why not.

b) Look at these words from ll. 1–17: 'the usual routine', 'a dullness inside', 'stifled', 'the same old alarm', 'slumps'. What mood or atmosphere do these words create? Read the last three stanzas again. Is the mood the same or does it change? 👥 Discuss.

c) 👥 💬 Describe the protagonist's character and emotions. Give evidence from the excerpt to support your description.

> **TIP** When quoting lines from a text, use quotation marks and give the line number (a single 'l.' for one line, 'll.' for more), e.g. "Give him a gait that you know." (l. 11). If you quote one word or part of a line, you can use single quotation marks, e.g. 'dullness' (l. 5).

➡ *SMC 10: Writing an article (p. 170)*

d) 👥 🎧 Listen to a live recording of the excerpt performed in 2015. How does listening to the poet read their work affect your understanding of the excerpt? Does it change any of your answers to a) or c)? If so, explain how.

EXTRA ✏ Imagine you are the protagonist from the excerpt. You arrive home from school on the day the poem describes. Write a short diary entry describing how your day was and how you feel.

2 Theme for English B (by Langston Hughes)

The instructor said,

> Go home and write
> a page tonight.
> And let that page come out of you—
> 5   Then, it will be true.

I wonder if it's that simple?
I am twenty-two, colored, born in Winston-Salem.
I went to school there, then Durham, then here
to this college on the hill above Harlem.
10 I am the only colored student in my class.
The steps from the hill lead down into Harlem,
through a park, then I cross St. Nicholas,
Eighth Avenue, Seventh, and I come to the Y,
the Harlem Branch Y, where I take the elevator
15 up to my room, sit down, and write this page:

It's not easy to know what is true for you or me
at twenty-two, my age. But I guess I'm what
I feel and see and hear, Harlem, I hear you.
hear you, hear me—we two—you, me,
20 talk on this page.
(I hear New York, too.)   Me—who?
Well, I like to eat, sleep, drink, and be in love.
I like to work, read, learn, and understand life.
I like a pipe for a Christmas present,
25 or records—Bessie, bop, or Bach.
I guess being colored doesn't make me not like
the same things other folks like who are other races.
So will my page be colored that I write?

Being me, it will not be white.
30 But it will be
a part of you, instructor.
You are white—
yet a part of me, as I am a part of you.
That's American.
35 Sometimes perhaps you don't want to be a
part of me.
Nor do I often want to be a part of you.
But we are, that's true!
As I learn from you,
40 I guess you learn from me—
although you're older—and white—
and somewhat more free.

This is my page for English B.

a) 👂 Follow the text of the poem on this page as you listen to a recorded reading of it.

b) Choose one or two lines of the poem that spoke to you strongly.

👥 💬 Compare the lines you chose and discuss your ideas about the text.

EXTRA Using the link below, read more information about the poet and the poem. Say whether this information changes your understanding of the message of the poem.

🔗(www) Find out about Langston Hughes.

c) 👥 💬 Discuss how life changes between the ages of 15 and 22. Say what you think are important influences during these years.

The Y (YMCA, Young Men's Christian Association)
Bessie (Bessie Smith) amerik. Bluessängerin
(1894–1937) **bop (bebop)** Jazzstil

3 Identity – two perspectives

a) 👥 Read the two poems. In pairs, describe what kind of person each narrator is, giving examples from the text to explain your answer.

b) How would you describe the tone of each poem? Choose adjectives from the box and quote some lines from each poem to support your opinion.

> aggressive · bright · depressed ·
> light-hearted · melancholic · nostalgic ·
> positive · serious · uplifting

4 A poetry circle 💬

a) 👥 In groups of three, working in one of these roles, examine the poems again.

WORD EXPERT: Choose a few words or phrases from the poems which speak to you.

ARTIST: Draw a picture or make a diagram which reflects the content of the poems.

QUESTIONER: Write down questions for a discussion about the content of the poems.

b) 👥 Present your results to your group. Then, using the ideas you have collected, discuss how the poems explore the theme of identity.

c) 👥 Compare your initial reaction to the poems with your understanding of them now. Refer to any insights you gained from the discussion with your partners.

· When I first read the poems, I thought …
· Now that we've discussed the poems, I think …
· The discussion made me realize that …

Early finisher ▸ p. 94

From **I Come From** (by Dean Atta)

I come from shepherd's pie and Sunday roast
Jerk chicken and stuffed vine leaves
I come from travelling through my taste buds but loving where I live

5 I come from a home that some would call broken
I come from D.I.Y. that never got done
I come from waiting by the phone for him to call

I come from waving the white flag to loneliness
I come from the rainbow flag and the union jack
10 I come from a British passport and an ever-ready suitcase

Roar (Text and music by Katy Perry and others)

I used to bite my tongue and hold my breath
Scared to rock the boat and make a mess
So I sat quietly, agreed politely
I guess that I forgot I had a choice
5 I let you push me past the breaking point
I stood for nothing, so I fell for everything

You held me down, but I got up (hey!)
Already brushing off the dust
You hear my voice, you hear that sound
10 Like thunder, gonna shake your ground
You held me down, but I got up
Get ready 'cause I've had enough
I see it all, I see it now

I got the eye of the tiger, a fighter
15 Dancing through the fire
'Cause I am the champion, and you're gonna hear me roar
Louder, louder than a lion
Cause I am a champion, and you're gonna
20 hear me roar!

Chorus:
Oh … You're gonna hear me roar!
Now I'm floating like a butterfly
Stinging like a bee I earned my stripes
25 I went from zero, to my own hero

---

jerk chicken karibisches Gericht mit mariniertem Huhn   **stuffed vine leaves** gefüllte Weinblätter   **taste buds** Geschmacksknospen
D.I.Y. (do-it-yourself) Heimwerken   **wave the white flag** die weiße Fahne hochhalten   **suitcase** ['suːtkeɪs] Koffer
roar [rɔː] brüllen   **I bite my tongue** [tʌŋ] ich beiße mir auf die Zunge; ich halte den Mund   **rock the boat** Ärger machen
make a mess *etwa:* Mist bauen   **fall for sth.** auf etwas hereinfallen   **brush sth. off** [brʌʃ] abbürsten, abklopfen   **float** schweben
sting stechen   **bee** Biene   **stripe** (Ärmel-)Streifen *(milit. Rangabzeichen)*

5 Painting with words

a) Match each image to a line (or lines) in one of the poems on p. 14.
Then, in your own words, write down what you think each image means.
👥 Compare your ideas.

TIP Imagery

To create images in their readers' minds, writers use special language called imagery.
Common types of imagery are similes and metaphors, two devices for making comparisons.

- **Similes** compare things by using the words *as* or *like*.
  He was as gentle as a dove. · *She was like a dove among pigeons.*

- **Metaphors** are often considered stronger than similes because they <u>do not</u> use *as* or *like*.
  Instead they suggest that one thing <u>is</u> another, often by using a form of the verb *be*.
  She was a dove that shone in the night. · *Be a dove and not a hawk.*
- Other verbs can also be used as metaphors, e.g. *fly* to mean *go fast* or *hurry*.
  She came out of the building and flew down the street.
- Metaphors are often combined with similes.
  She flew from the room like a dove from a storm.

---

b) Read the tip above and then go back to the poems on p. 14.
Decide how often each poem uses imagery and what kind of imagery is used.
Think about the words and describe the images they create in your mind.

More help ⟩ p. 88

6 Create your own images 🖉

You choose ⟩ a) or b).

a) Similes often describe character or appearance:
She was as wise as an owl / as white as a ghost / …

Using these or other adjectives, make similes to describe people. Collect them in class.

> angry · blind · brave · clever · fast · hungry · large · mad · peaceful · pretty · proud · tall

b) Find a photo of someone you find interesting, and write a few lines describing how you think they look, sound, smell, etc. Use imagery.

The man in this photo looks as sweet as a lamb. His smile lights up the room and his voice is music in people's ears.

Early finisher ⟩ p. 94

On this page you will work with words and phrases people use to talk about identity.
Then you will write a short personal profile.

1 Word field: Talking about identity

Look at these figures and think about how they might describe themselves. Using phrases from below, write four sentences for each person. You can use ideas from the box or your own ideas.

1   I'm the sort of person who wants to achieve something in life ...

- I'm ...   • People / My friends say I'm ...
- I'm proud to be ... / I'm proud of ...
- I like ...   • I'm a fan of ...
- I'm the sort of person who likes / tries to ...
- ... is important to me / is a big part of my life.
- One person/place that has influenced me is ...
- One thing I value is ...
- I'm hoping to become ... / study ... / travel to ...

good-looking · +athletic · +gay · +straight ·
gentle · aggressive · ambitious · easy-going ·
hard-working · reliable · patriotic · creative ·
musical · talented · passionate · +conventional ·
conservative · +liberal · +religious ·
+African-American · British · ...
climbing · cycling · opera · ...
family · +upbringing · teacher · hometown ·
local +dialect · region · environment · ...

+ = new words

2 Collocations (Adverbs and adjectives as modifiers)

Rewrite some sentences from 1 to make the meaning stronger or weaker. Use words from the box.

1 My friends say I'm extremely creative.
  I'm not particularly creative.

big · great · huge
extremely · quite · fairly · somewhat
a lot · a bit
(not) really · (not) very · (not) particularly

More help ▶ p. 88   ➡ GAP 27: Emphasis (p. 158)

TIP

Use adverbs or adjectives to modify statements (make them stronger or weaker).
I'm a great / ... fan of ...
I'm fairly/not very / ... proud to be ...
One thing that I value a bit / a lot is ...
I'm particularly / really hoping to ...

Test collocations using a search engine, e.g. compare 'extremely musical' with 'extremely talented'. If you only get a few results, the collocation may not be very common.

✎ Write a profile for a website – either for yourself or for a character you create.

On this page, you will learn basic rules about the layout, formatting and checking of electronic texts. This will help you to make your own electronic texts visually more inviting and easier to read.

a) Read the guidelines on text layout and formatting. Then examine the text on Kae Tempest. Decide if it follows the guidelines. Then tell your partner what you would change, and why.

Partner A: Focus on text layout.

Partner B: Focus on text formatting.

Text layout

1 Do not put too much text on one page. Use proper margins (top, bottom, left, right).
2 Indent paragraphs or leave an empty line.
3 Consider using headings to guide your reader.
4 Think about the best place for images. Make sure they are neither too big nor too small in relation to your text. If you use images or if you quote text, <u>always add the source</u>.

Text formatting

1 Use a standard font that is easy to read, e.g. Arial, Times New Roman, etc.
2 Use a different style (*italics*, **bold**, etc.) for greater clarity, e.g. for book or song titles.
3 Use <u>one</u> font for the body of the text. You can use other fonts for headings, captions, etc., but more than three can make a text look untidy.
4 Make sure the font size is legible, e.g. 12 pt.

KAE TEMPEST

Kae <u>tempest</u> is a <u>british</u> poet, spoken-word performer, rap singer, playwright and novelist. Kae was <u>been</u> born in 1985 and grew up <u>inin</u> south London. In 2020, they came out as non-binary and use the pronouns they/them. They are widely seen as Britain's leading
5 spoken-word poet.
Kae started performing when they were only 16 <u>yera</u> old, going to open mic nights, but have since worked with the Royal Shakespeare Company and performed at festivals such as Glastonbury and Edinburgh. Across the <u>atlantic</u>, they have won poetry slams in New York.
Kae Tempest's poetry collections *Hold your own* and *Everything speaks in its own way* mix word play and
10 street slang and are so full of emotion they must touch the hart of any reader. Hold your own is a series of connected poems who fueture the figure of the gender-changing, blind prophet Tiresias from Greek mythology. Tempest has also written several pieces for the stage, includeing the award-winning *Brand new ancients*.
MUsic
15 Of course, it's through their music that Kae Tempest is reaching most people and they have toured the world with their hip-hop band **Sound of Rum.** Their first album, Everybody down (2014), was shortlisted for the Mercury music prize and Let them eat chaos (2016) has been called an uncomparable musical novel in 13 chapters.
However, poetry, theatre and hip-hop are not enough for this multi-talent. They have also wrote
20 a novel, *The bricks that built the houses*, which retells the story told in the songs of her album *Everybody down*.
Tempest has received much acclaim for their work in all therse fields. The Huffing Post called Tempest "Britain's leading young poet, playwright and rapper... – the complete package of lyrics and delivery... the most exciting young writers working in Britain today." Above all, Kae Tempest is a
25 performer andthese lines from the first line of their poem These things I know (2017) could be their motto: "Language lives when you speak it / Let it be heard."

b) Read the tip carefully. Then agree on what needs to be corrected in the text above.

EXTRA Using an electronic version of the text, improve the text layout and formatting and correct any mistakes.

➡ SMC 15: *Revising and improving electronic texts (p. 174)*
➡ SMC 28: *Creating a good layout for a page or poster (p. 185)*

TIP Using the check function
The check function underlines spelling, typing and grammar mistakes, but remember
· it sometimes underlines correct words.
· it doesn't always recognize a mistake.
So before you correct a word, make sure you understand <u>why</u> it was underlined.
And check the text yourself for mistakes the check function may not have found.

Gender and equality: An opinion piece

a) In one minute, name and write on the board the names of famous men and women from history.

Women need to be recognized as a part of our history *Shari Boiskin*

Women make up 50.8 percent of the world's 7,404,976,783 person population.

That means that there are 3,761,728,205 women. Yet, for some reason, women, throughout time have
5 been, and still are, treated like a nonexistent part of our history.

Yes, men and women differ biologically. When it comes to representation in academia, where it should be equal, it is also different. Women are
10 dropped. I had my nine-year-old brother try to name some important women from history – he was able to list Betsy Ross, Harriet Tubman and Rosa Parks. When asked to list some
15 important men, he was able to go on for at least ten minutes – I had to stop him. Where are women in history? It's not like women just recently decided to show up and
20 start doing things. Angela Merkel is not the first woman to have thought of going into government. Malala Yousafzai is not the first to have thought of
25 advocating for women's right to education.

In 1777, Sybil Ludington went on a midnight ride similar to, but actually twice as long as Paul Revere's. In the 1920s, Zelda Fitzgerald's
30 dancing, writing, and musical talents were always overshadowed by those of her husband, the author of *The Great Gatsby*, Scott Fitzgerald. I never learned about these women in school. I had to discover them on my own.
35 Abigail Adams sent a letter to her husband John Adams while he was at the Constitutional Convention, in which she wrote, "remember the ladies." Yet, so many women are forgotten in the annals of history.

My sister is in Israel, spending her 10th grade Spring 40 semester abroad. She called me from Israel on International Women's Day to tell me that one of the male counselors from her program had just said that International Women's Day is irrelevant and Women's History Month is neither important nor necessary. 45 She didn't understand why he would say that, and asked me what I would've said if I had been there.

I told her that I would have said yes, and told the counselor that I agree with him. I would have continued to say that I also believe 50 that having an International Women's Day and Women's History Month is pretty ridiculous. I believe that every day should be women's day! 55

Women should be acknowledged for their role in society not just during one day of the year, and their contributions to the world for not just one month, but for the 60 entire year, every year. After all, men are acknowledged constantly. We study men's history in school. That's why there's no need for an International Men's Day or Men's 65 History month. I would also add that I believe that both International Women's Day and Women's History Month should be eliminated – as soon as women are treated as complete equals to men. 70

That will take some time. So, in the meantime, my sister's counselor should crack open a book on Elizabeth Cady Stanton or Rosalind Franklin, or perhaps read more blogs and articles about the importance of women's history. Women need to be 75 recognized as a part of our history.

(*From **Eastside**, the school newspaper of Cherry Hill High School East, Cherry Hill, New Jersey*)

b) Look at the names you wrote in a). Do they support the opinion Shari expresses? Explain why or why not.

---

academia die akademische Welt **advocate for** sich einsetzen für **overshadow sth.** etw. in den Schatten stellen **Constitutional Convention** verfassunggebende Versammlung **annals** Annalen **acknowledge** anerkennen **crack sth. open** etw. öffnen

Writing an opinion piece ✏️

Each unit of this book will focus on writing a different type of text.
*In this unit, the text in focus is an **opinion piece**. In an opinion piece, you express your view on an issue you feel strongly about. Opinion pieces often appear online, e.g. in blogs or newspapers.*
Over the next three pages, you will work through the following steps to produce your opinion piece.

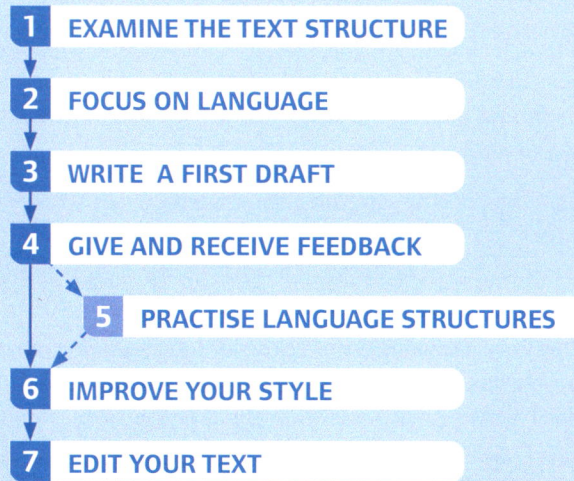

1 EXAMINE THE TEXT STRUCTURE

2 FOCUS ON LANGUAGE

3 WRITE A FIRST DRAFT

4 GIVE AND RECEIVE FEEDBACK

5 PRACTISE LANGUAGE STRUCTURES

6 IMPROVE YOUR STYLE

7 EDIT YOUR TEXT

1 EXAMINE THE TEXT STRUCTURE

 Read about the structure of an opinion piece. Then discuss whether Shari follows these tips.

> **OPINION PIECE: STRUCTURE**
> · Headline Catch your readers' attention. Make a clear statement, ask a provocative question, promise a solution to a problem.
> · First paragraph Keep it short. State your topic <u>and</u> opinion clearly. Keep readers interested.
> · Supporting paragraphs Use statistics, other facts or quotes to back up your main statement.
> · Conclusion Restate your opinion. Suggest a solution, or call for action.

2 FOCUS ON LANGUAGE

a) Read Shari's text again. Identify the two main tenses and collect examples.
   Compare your results. Explain why each of the tenses is used.

b) Scan lines 54–75. Find and note down four examples of the use of *should*.
   Discuss why Shari uses the word *should* so often.

3 WRITE A FIRST DRAFT

a) Discuss why topics like these can be important for people's identities:
women's rights, same-sex marriage, fashion, language, social media, sport, hometown, …

b) Choose a topic from a). Express your view in a sentence or two, e.g.
   · *Sport should not be separated by sex.* · *You don't need to follow fashion. Be yourself.*
   Then write a first draft of your opinion piece. Consider the points you discussed in 1 and 2.

4 GIVE AND RECEIVE FEEDBACK

 Give your text to a partner to read. Get feedback on the structure and grammar.

> *I think you need a paragraph break here.*

> *Nice conclusion! You expressed your opinion very clearly.*

> *Great! You used the simple present every time you …*

5 PRACTISE LANGUAGE STRUCTURES

1 **REVISION** **Statements and arguments** (Simple past and present, present perfect)

> *In an opinion piece, you often need the **simple present** to make general statements.*
> *You use the **simple present** or **simple past** to support your argument with examples from your personal experience, from history, research, etc.*

a) Read these paragraphs, looking carefully at the verbs.
   Correct the mistakes you find.

 **More help** *p. 88*

1 Equal pay for equal work is a basic right. If a woman doesn't earns as much as a man doing the same job, this is discrimination. It exist in many countries.

2 Here in the UK we have a long history of discrimination at the workplace. In 1970, the Equal Pay Act has made it illegal to discriminate on pay. But my grandma has worked in a factory in the 1970s and 80s. And she don't earned as much as men in the same job.

3 So is the situation better today? Sadly, discrimination against women are still found. Today, the average woman earn 18.1 percent less than the average man. And the pay gap is even bigger for a woman who take time off to have children. Twelve years after she is having her first baby, the gap between her and a man can reaches 33 percent!

4 Where do I got these facts? I didn't made them up. I found them in a report from the Office of National Statistics that has come out just last year, half a century after the Equal Pay Act has became law.

5 So the question is: why exists still a pay gap between men and women?
   If you're thinking this question is important, you should raise your voice in protest.

b) Explain the corrections you made. Then check the verbs in your first draft again.

➡ *GAP 2: Talking about the present (p. 108);* ➡ *GAP 3: Talking about the past (I) (p. 110)*

2 **REVISION** **Stressing your point** (Modals)

> *When you write an opinion piece, you can use modals (and their substitutes) to*
> *· say clearly what you think is right (should, shouldn't, ought to, …).*
> *· express more strongly what you think is important or necessary (must, mustn't, have to, …).*

Decide which of these statements express support for equal pay for women and men.
Rewrite the other sentences so that they also express support for equal pay.

1 Any company that pays women less should have to pay a fine.
2 We must give up our protests against equal pay.
3 Women should earn less than other workers.
4 We mustn't take protests against unequal pay very seriously.
5 These are the facts – we needn't consider them.
6 The government ought to do something – immediately.
7 We have to accept the situation as it is.
8 Women protesting against unequal pay must be supported.

➡ *GAP 11–13: Modal auxiliaries (pp. 126–131)*

6　**IMPROVE YOUR STYLE** Persuasion techniques

Using persuasion techniques will improve your style and help to win over your readers.
Read these tips based on techniques used in Shari's text (p. 18) and do tasks a)–e).

Use personal pronouns
· *I* shows how strongly you feel　· *you* shows readers you are speaking to them
· *we* suggests that you have something in common with your readers

a) Scan Shari's text (p. 18). Say which pronoun she uses most, and where in the text.
　Comment on how her use of this pronoun affects her message.

Tell anecdotes about your experience
Anecdotes are short stories about real events. Writers use them to get closer to their readers.
Shari, for example, tells anecdotes about members of her family.

b) Identify the anecdotes in Shari's text. Comment on their effect on you as a reader.

Include statistics, historical facts and quotes
· *Statistics* suggest that your arguments are based on facts.
　Dramatic or unexpected statistics help you to catch your readers' attention or
　to underline important points.
　Be careful not to overuse statistics – your readers might begin to get bored.
· Like statistics, *examples from history* also suggest that your argument is factual.
　If you want to surprise your readers, you could use less well-known facts.
· A *quote* in support of your argument shows that other people agree with you.
　Remember to use quotation marks ("…") and include the source.

c) In Shari's text, find examples of her use of statistics, historical facts and quotes.
　Comment on how these techniques affect you as a reader.

Use expressive language
Use words that touch your readers' emotions, i.e. make them feel angry, happy, etc.

d) Find these words in Shari's text: *nonexistent, dropped, overshadowed, forgotten,
　irrelevant* (p. 18, ll. 1–45). **Explain who or what they refer to.**
　Then comment on how they affect you as a reader.

Use rhetorical questions
Rhetorical questions don't expect answers. They're often really statements.
For example, *Who can deny this?* is an emphatic way of saying *This is true*.

Who can deny this?

e) Read the second paragraph of Shari's text. Identify the rhetorical question and discuss its meaning.

7　**EDIT YOUR TEXT**

a) Read your first draft again and consider
　· your partner's feedback on it.　· any relevant points you have covered in steps 5 and 6.
　Think of improvements you could make. Then edit your text and read it again.

b) 👥 Exchange your edited texts. Read them and give feedback on the changes.
　Make suggestions for any further improvements.　➡ *SMC 8: Writing an opinion piece / a comment (p. 168)*

1 Identity: A question of choice?

Look at the illustration. Say what you think it shows.
Look at the title of the book the excerpt is taken from. Say who *Eve* might be.

The seven daughters of Eve (by Bryan Sykes)

Where do I come from?

How often have you asked yourself that question? We may know our parents, even our grandparents; not far beyond that, for most of us the train begins to
5 disappear into the mist. But each of us carries a message from our ancestors in every cell of our body. It is in our DNA, the genetic material that is handed down from generation to generation. Within the DNA is written not only our histories as individuals but the
10 whole history of the human race. With the aid of recent advances in genetic technology, this history is now being revealed. We are at last able to begin to decipher the messages from the past. Our DNA does not fade like an ancient parchment; it does not rust in the
15 ground like the sword of a warrior long dead. It is not eroded by wind or rain, nor reduced to ruin by fire and earthquake. It is the traveller from an antique land who lives within us all.

This book is about the history of the world as
20 revealed by genetics. It shows how the history of our species, *Homo sapiens*, is recorded in the genes that trace our ancestry back into the deep past, way beyond the reach of written records or stone inscriptions. These genes tell a story which begins over
25 a hundred thousand years ago and whose latest chapters are hidden within the cells of every one of us.

It is also my own story. As a practising scientist, I am very lucky to have been around at the right time and able to take an active part in this wonderful
30 journey into the past that modern genetics now permits. I have found DNA in skeletons thousands of years old and seen exactly the same genes in my own friends. And I have discovered that, to my astonishment, we are all connected through our
35 mothers to only a handful of women living tens of thousands of years ago.

In the pages that follow, I will take you through the excitement and the frustrations of the front-line research that lies behind these discoveries. Here you
40 will see what really happens in a genetics laboratory. Like any walk of life, science has its ups and downs, its heroes and its villains.

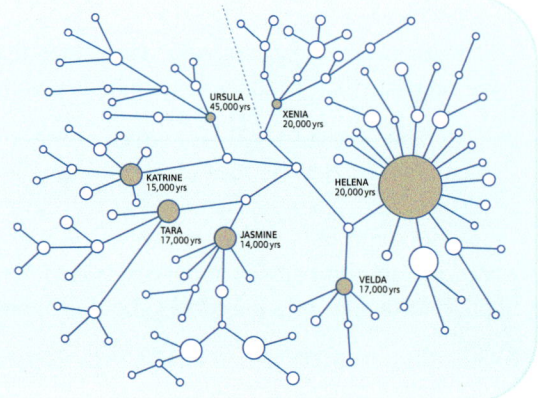

2 Comprehension

Read the text and say if the following statements are true or false. Give a piece of evidence from the text to support your answers.
1 DNA only records the history of each individual.
2 DNA helps us to learn about human history further back in time than any man-made texts.
3 Homo sapiens, our human species, appeared 100,000 years ago.
4 The author was not surprised to find that we are all related to each other.

3 Discussion 💬

a) 👥 Find out more about the scientific research the book describes. Explain the link between the title of the book, the text of the prologue on this page and the illustration.

b) 👥 Discuss the difference between personal and genetic identity. **More help** *p. 89*

EXTRA 🖊 Write a comment on the title of the book "The seven daughters of Eve".
Include aspects such as whether you think it is a good title and if you would like to read the book.

---

advances Fortschritte **decipher** entschlüsseln **fade** verblassen, ausbleichen **parchment** Pergament **warrior** Krieger/in **trace sth. back** etwas zurückverfolgen; etwas zurückführen **ancestry** Abstammung **inscription** Inschrift **chapter** Kapitel **villain** Schurke, Schurkin

4 What if we could rewrite the book of life?

Look at the title and the illustration. What do you think the article is about?

DNA is often called the book of life because the four chemical compounds inside it are known by four letters , C-G-A-T, and it contains the 'instructions' for building its host organism. That
5 does not mean that the book of life is easy to read, however. The DNA packed into a human cell has six billion letters and is two metres long, so it took nearly twenty-five years for an international team of scientists to identify and list every gene
10 in human DNA.

Over the last fifty years, the study of DNA has led to techniques for directly modifying or editing the genes in some organisms. However, it has always been a very expensive and difficult task, as
15 well as very controversial. Whereas the US allows many GM (genetically modified) plants and food, EU countries have been much slower and more cautious about allowing them.

In the last decade, a new development in
20 genetic science could revolutionize medicine and maybe change humanity's future: Crispr (pronounced 'crisper'). Crispr is a piece of DNA itself – bacteria DNA. It was discovered twenty years ago when researchers were studying how
25 some bacteria defend themselves against viruses. They realized that Crispr can identify the dangerous genes in the virus DNA, cut the DNA open where those genes are located and remove and replace them with harmless genes.

30 While that was extraordinary itself, the real breakthrough came ten years ago. Scientists discovered how to 'program' Crispr so that it could edit DNA in the precise way they wanted. This new technique is much more accurate, cheaper
35 and easier than other methods.

Today, gene therapies are being developed using Crispr to treat diseases with genetic causes, including dementia, diabetes and some cancers. The huge advantage of gene therapies is that
40 they are short and the effects are permanent. In the future, it may even be possible to take a Crispr gene therapy as a pill.

Although many have high hopes for Crispr, others have raised fears about the technology.

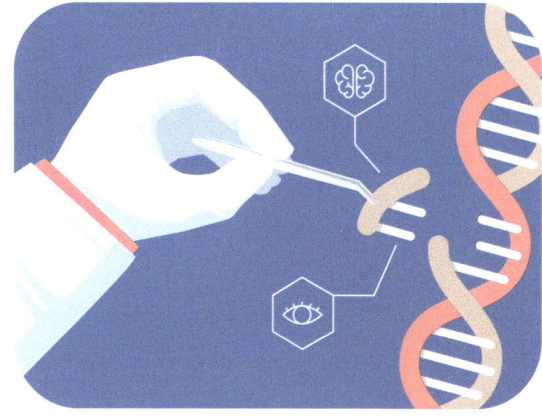

45 They say that it could open the door to so-called 'designer babies', where parents choose their child's eye colour, height and even intelligence as though they were ordering pizza toppings from a menu. Even if the technology made that possible,
50 such uses are illegal in almost every country in the world and generally considered unethical.

5 Comprehension

Write short answers to the following questions.

1 Why is DNA called the 'book of life'?
2 In what way are EU countries different to the US with regard to GM plants and food?
3 What was the most important discovery involving Crispr?
4 What fear do some people have about Crispr?

6 Discussion 💬

You choose a) or b).

a) 👥 After reading the text, discuss whether you think Crispr is a positive or negative development.

b) "Humanity is acquiring all the right technology for all the wrong reasons."
👥 Discuss the quote and its relevance to the text.

> **Language help** ▶
>
> a) You have already learned how to form passive sentences like these:
>
> … the genetic material that **is handed down** from generation to generation.
> It shows how the history of our species … **is recorded** in the genes.
>
> Find another example of the passive in the text (p. 22).
>
> b) There is one passive form in the text that you haven't learned before:
> Find this sentence in the text and say why the author uses the progressive form.
>
> … this history **is now being revealed**.   ➡ *GAP 9–10: The passive (pp. 122–125)*

1 On the radio (The passive: present progressive form)

a) Some journalists are watching scientists examining a mummy.
Complete their sentences using the present progressive passive.

1 We *are being led* (lead) into the lab now.
2 And now the mummy … (weigh).
3 Hundreds of photos … (take) as I talk to you.
4 A scanner … (set up) next to the mummy.
5 The mummy … (scan) now.
6 It … (carry) into the next room as we watch.
7 An MRI of the body … (make) in there.
8 The images on the monitors … (examine) by scientists.

b) Complete a newsreader's sentences in the present progressive. Use the passive form if needed.

1 1,000 homes are still without power after last night's storm as power lines … (still · repair).
2 The power company … (hope) to finish the repairs by mid-afternoon.
3 Work is difficult as the area … (still · hit) by high winds.
4 The new rail link to Dorking has not opened yet as a bridge over the River Mole … (still · complete).
5 Railway engineers … (plan) to finish the work by next weekend.
6 New rail links … (also · plan) to Guildford and Haslemere.   **Early finisher** ▶ *p. 95*

2 You are your phone

a) You and a student at a British partner school are doing a project
together on new ways that science can help fight crime.
You do some research and find a report online.

👥 Before you listen, explain these German words in English:
chemische Signatur · Indizien · Massenspektrometer · Pharmazeut
Then listen. Take notes on the kind of information a phone reveals.

b) Write an email in English to your project partner.
Summarize what you have learned and explain:

· who the researchers are   · how the method could help the police   · other possible uses of the methods

c) 👥✓ Compare emails with a partner. Give each other feedback.

➡ *SMC 16: Mediating written or spoken information (p. 175)*

> **Language help**
>
> You have already learned about some **types of adverbial clause**.
> Look at the examples from the text on p. 23: **Type:**
>
> ll. 1–2: *DNA is ... called the book of life **because the four chemical compounds inside it are** ...* reason
> ll. 6–8: *The DNA ... is two metres long, **so it took nearly twenty-five years** ...* result
> ll. 15–17: ***Whereas the US allows many GM plants and food**, EU countries have been ...* contrast
> ll. 23–25: *It was discovered twenty years ago **when researchers were studying how** ...* time
> ll. 26–28: *Crispr can ... cut the DNA open **where those genes are located** ...* place
>
> Here are two more you haven't learned:
> **Main clause** **Adverbial clause of purpose**
> ll. 31-33: *Scientists discovered how to 'program' Crispr* **so that** *it could edit DNA ...*
>
> Unlike an adverbial clause of result, there is no comma before 'so'.
> In informal speech or writing, 'that' can be left out.
>
> **Main clause** **Adverbial clause of manner**
> ll. 46-48: *... parents choose their child's features,* **as though** *they were ordering pizza ...*
> With this type of clause, we give more information on how something is done by comparing it to
> another action. For this reason, it is also described as an adverbial clause of comparison.
> We can introduce this type of clause also with: 'as', 'as if' or in informal speech or writing with 'like'.
>
> ➜ *GAP 28: Adverbial clauses (p. 160)*

3 REVISION My parents have blue eyes, so mine are blue too. (Adverbial clauses)

a) Complete the sentences using a conjunction from the box.

    because · even though · everywhere · so · when

1 There would be less racism in the world if people knew that there's someone related to you ... you go.
2 ... genes and DNA are important, I don't think they decide who you are as a person.
3 I want to go to sleep ... people start talking about science.
4 My dad wanted to know his genetic background, ... he got a DNA test and found out his genes come
   from Ireland, France, England and Turkey!
5 My sister and I were asked to take part in genetic research ... we are twins.

b) Now say what kind of adverbial clause is used in 1-5 in a).

4 She looked as if she had seen a ghost. (Adverbial clauses of manner/purpose)

Complete the sentence pairs with the conjunctions given.

1 a) My brother acts ... he knows everything.
  b) My brother is studying ... he can do well in the exam.
2 a) The government minister visited our school ... she could see our new sports hall.
  b) The government minister talked to us ... she was a teenager too.
3 a) You're just being nice to me ... you can borrow my favourite jeans.
  b) You want me to be nice to you ... you hadn't stolen my favourite jeans!
4 a) You treat your dog ... he is a person.
  b) You should train your dog ... he behaves better.

like · so

as if · so that

like · so

as though · so that

1 Flying flags

Identify the flags in the photos on the right
and describe each situation. Say how you think the flags are
being used in each situation.

· In the picture with the … flag, it looks as if …
· The flag is there because it expresses/stands for …

2 What do flags mean? 💬

🧩 In groups of three, each student chooses one of the
three flags on the right.

a) Make notes on what you know about
  · the flag's history and symbolism (the meaning of the
    crosses, stars, stripes, colours, …).
  · rules and traditions about flying the flag (e.g. when and
    where it is flown, who flies it, …).

b) Read more about your flag.
  A ➡ p. 98, B ➡ p. 100, C ➡ p. 102
  Correct and add to the information in your notes if necessary.

c) Share your information with other groups.
  Comment on any similarities or differences.

d) Discuss your feelings about the flags flown in your country
  (national, European, regional …)

🖐www Find out about three other flags.

3 Germany and the USA 🔤

a) A student from your school's partner school in the US sends you an email. Read it and then use the
  information on p. 103 to write an email in English with answers to his/her questions.

> **Subject:** My class project on flags of the world
>
> F K U T ▤ ▤ ▤ ▤ ▤ ▤ ▤ ▤ IA ⬥ ·—
>
> Hi!
> My class is doing a project about flags of the world. I have some questions about the German flag, and I hope
> you can help me. Can you tell me: – when it became the national flag?
>   – what the colours are and what they stand for?
>   – when the flag is used?
> One last thing – in the US, you can see our flag everywhere. Lots of people hang it outside their homes. Is it
> the same in Germany?
> Thanks a lot for your help! 🙂

b) 👥 Compare your email with a partner. Give each other feedback.

EXTRA 👥 Before you can send your email, imagine the American student video calls you to get the
answers to his/her questions. Prepare your dialogue and then take turns to act out both roles.

➡ *SMC 16: Mediating written or spoken information (p. 175)*

1 The DNA journey

a) Look at the film stills above and speculate on what the film is about.

b) Watch the film. Compare your ideas from a) with what happens in the film.

c) 👥 💬 Work in groups of three. Each student chooses one person from the film stills.
Watch the film again and take notes on your person's attitudes and statements
· before the test. · after the test.

d) 👥 💬 Discuss the film's message about our relationship with other human beings.

e) 👥 💬 Many people have criticized the film. Here are some typical criticisms.
· "It's not real. Those people are actors."
· "It's impossible to link people by DNA tests to individual countries like Britain or Germany."
Discuss whether these criticisms make the film's message less valid.

2 Making the film: Influencing an audience

a) The DNA journey is an advertisement. Watch a short scene again.
Discuss who you think the advertisement is aimed at.

b) Watch two scenes again. Describe the different music and sounds in each scene.
Then say how such differences can affect a viewer's feelings. The words in the box may help.

> applause · climax · crescendo · laughter · quiet · relaxed ·
> single instrument · tension · whistling

More help *p. 89*

c) The DNA journey went viral on the internet. Discuss why so many people wanted to share the link.

d) Discuss similarities and differences between this advertisement and others you know.
· Normally, advertisements show where/what/…
· This advertisement is/isn't typical because …

Early finisher *p. 95*

In many countries, people carry ID cards to prove who they are. But new technology is now also able to identify people and their location, and even to assess their feelings. Is this progress?

It's in the DNA

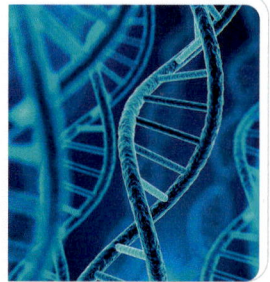

Every cell in your body contains a complete set of your DNA, the molecule that carries your genetic code. 99.9% of your DNA is the same as anyone else's, but, unless you have an identical twin, whose DNA is exactly the same
5   as yours, 0.1% is unique to you. This means DNA testing can be used to prove if someone was involved in a crime or is the parent of a child. For example, if you compare a sample of DNA from someone's cells, from their hair or blood or saliva, with DNA from skin cells found under an attack victim's fingernails, this can show if the cells are from the same person.

They recognize faces

10 How do you lock your phone or laptop? With a PIN, a pattern or your face? Facial recognition software uses 'deep learning', a field of artificial intelligence, to identify people and match photos with astounding accuracy. When this technology was first developed, companies used it without directly asking people for permission. It also gave rise to 'deep fake' technology, computer programs that
15 can generate disturbingly realistic fake images and even videos of people. These developments and concerns about people's privacy rights have led to many countries adopting stricter laws on the whole field of facial recognition.

Who's tracking what?

20 What is there not to like about a fitness tracker? These little gadgets help you to lead a healthy lifestyle by counting the steps you take, measuring how far you walk or run or bike, and how many calories that burns. They'll measure your heart rate and blood pressure and they work all night too, recording how long and how well you sleep. The trackers store this useful medical information online, but the downside is that maybe it isn't as safe there as you think. Some
25 of your data might get shared with health insurance companies, or stolen. Some might even be found through a public online search. The consequences could be enormous.

It all comes together

30 You head for the mall, biking to the station with your fitness tracker on your wrist and your smartphone in your pocket. You swipe your smartcard to get on the train and out of the station at your destination. The transport company now knows where your smartcard is, and cameras on the street and in the station, linked to facial recognition software, confirm it's you. The wi-fi sensors
35 in the mall log your movements too when your smartphone and fitness device connect to them. Another app is watching. It captures all this information, combines it with your social media profile and sends an app user nearby a Google map with a photo of you (and any other people the user might find interesting) showing your current location. Scary or not? You decide …

a) Think: List advantages and disadvantages of being able to identify people easily using technology.

b) 👥 Pair: Compare your lists and add any other ideas you have.

c) 👥 Share: Discuss ideas with another pair. Explain why you **are/are not** worried by this technology.

On this page you will learn to recognize certain words that are not pronounced clearly in spoken English.

Step 1
a) The captions below are written as spoken in normal speech. Listen and repeat them a few times.

| a paira shoes ana bag | Try aneat more fruit! | Wyzee growna beard? | Izza hair blacka brown? |

b) Rewrite the sentences in normal spelling. Listen again. Now repeat them in spoken English.

Step 2
a) Listen to each sentence. Focus on the pronunciation of the underlined words.
Listen again and repeat the underlined words as you heard them.
1 Jake said <u>you were going to</u> help me.
2 I <u>can help you</u> tonight.

b) You will hear the underlined words spoken individually and in natural speech.
Listen and compare.
1 Where <u>does he</u> go to school?
2 If you like, you can give it <u>to us</u>.
3 <u>We'll have to</u> go soon.
4 You <u>can tell him</u> when he gets here.
5 <u>Are you</u> going to <u>eat your</u> breakfast?
6 Everyone says <u>she should have been</u> an actor.
7 Actually, <u>there were over</u> a hundred people there.
8 <u>She's as</u> tall <u>as her</u> brother.

c) 👥 Now listen to the sentences in natural speech and repeat them.

Step 3
Listen to these sentences spoken at normal speed and write down the missing words.
1 … much too tired to go out.
2 … late for class.
3 And he was so helpful – … really?
4 I'll …, I promise.
5 … when we left Scotland.
6 … was so upset about it.
7 Are you going … or am I?
8 He's late – he … the bus.

Reflection
a) Collect examples of the words you have heard that are not pronounced clearly in spoken English.
What kind of words are they?

b) Now listen and compare your observations with what the speaker says.

➡ *SMC 26: Listening strategies (p. 182)*

Workbook 1
Checkpoint 1
(pp. 12–15)

Your task

A class magazine

Make a magazine using the opinion pieces written by your class in this unit.

STEP 1 Get your text ready
Work with the version of your text from p. 21.

a) Check your text one final time for grammar, spelling or typing mistakes.

b) Find a good photo or illustration (drawing, chart, …) and add it to your text.

c) Prepare a short summary of your text, about two sentences. Add your name.

 Keep a copy of your opinion piece.

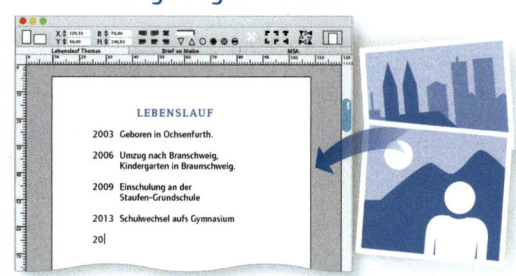

TIP Inserting images in a text

For internet tips on adding images, use a search term like **insert images document** in English or in your language.

STEP 2 Put your magazine together 💬
Divide the class into four groups. Each group will work on a different aspect of the magazine. Read your group task. Decide if you need to pass on your results to another group. If so, agree with them on when to do this.

1 Editors

- Collect and read all the summaries. Decide how to arrange the opinion pieces. Alphabetically? By topic? Some other way? Prepare a table of contents.
- Then choose a title for the magazine and write a short introduction (not more than 200 words) to get people interested in it.

2 Copy editors

- Read the texts and agree on a maximum length. If necessary, suggest shortening a text with the author.
- Review any changes, checking for mistakes or typos. Your group are the final readers!

3 Layout and art directors

- Make one document with all the articles. Choose the font and font size for each opinion piece.
- Lay out the text on each page. Decide on the final size and position of the illustrations.

4 Logistics

- Discuss who you would like to read your magazine: just your classmates, or other students, teachers, parents, … ?
- Discuss the pros and cons of printing versus publishing online, e.g. amount of paper used, binding, method of distribution (by hand, email, school website, …).
- Decide on your medium and make the magazine available to your readers.

STEP 3 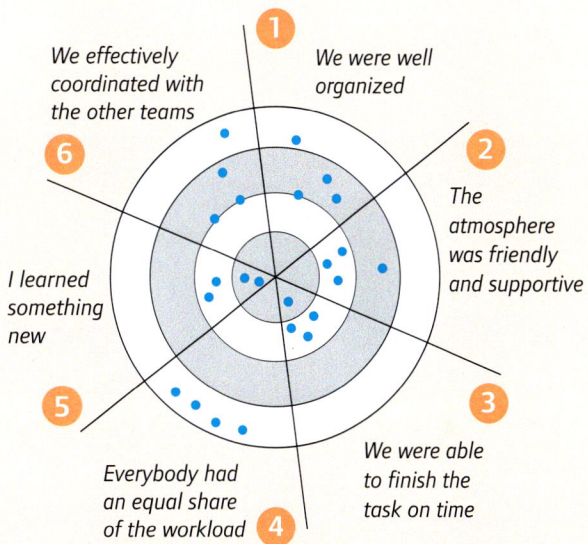 Evaluate your group work

a) In the same groups, work with the evaluation target your teacher gives you. Discuss criteria 1–6 and decide if they are helpful for evaluating your work. Make changes if you consider it necessary.

b) Each group member evaluates the team's work by putting dots in the target circles (inner circle = highest evaluation).

c) Look at each section of your target. Think about the position of the dots and what it says about your teamwork. Make notes for a discussion.

d) Discuss what went well and what you could do better next time.

1 We were well organized

2 The atmosphere was friendly and supportive

3 We were able to finish the task on time

4 Everybody had an equal share of the workload

5 I learned something new

6 We effectively coordinated with the other teams

STEP 4 **EXTRA** Discuss your opinions

a) Form new groups of four or five.
Read your partners' opinion pieces, making notes on your response to each piece.

b) Each partner opens the discussion for their opinion piece and explains briefly why the issue is important to them.

> The topic of my opinion piece is …

> Before we start our discussion, I'd like to sum up why I think …

> So that's why I feel so strongly about this topic.

The other members of the group use their notes to react to each opinion piece.
They can also comment on each other's views on each of the topics.

> I found all/most/… of your arguments convincing.

> One point I agree with is …

> You pointed out that …

> You didn't mention that …

> Jana made a point which I think is …

> I agree more with Jasper than with Jana.

What makes a **community?**

A

B

1

2

1 Coming together 💬

a) 👥 Look at photos A – D. Describe the setting, the people, and what they are doing. Say why you think they have come together. Make notes on your ideas for each photo.

b) 👥 Match each photo from the bottom row to one in the top row. Discuss the connections and differences you see between the photos you have matched.

 More help ▶ *p. 90*

2 Defining a community 💬

a) 👥 Tell your group which photos you matched in 1. Explain why. Then discuss whether each photo depicts a community.

b) 👥 Discuss different characteristics that make a community. Agree on a definition of "community" and write it down.
People make up a community when …

c) Present your group's definition to the class.

C

D

3

4

3 Your communities

a) Make a list or draw a network – like the one on the right – of the communities you are part of.

Note down things that connect the people in each of your communities.

b) 🧩 When you have finished, go to a bus stop. Compare and explain your list or network.

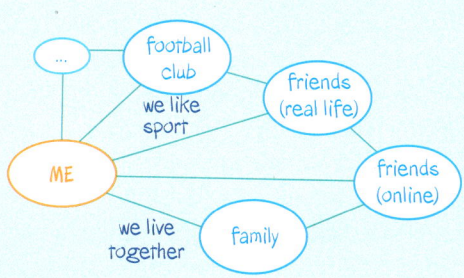

Your task

At the end of this unit:
You will give an electronic presentation calling for action on an important issue in your local community.

1 A meeting of two Americas (excerpts from a novel by Joan Abelove)

The novel *Go and come back* is set among a tribe in the Peruvian rainforest.
What do you think life in their community might be like?

Joanna and Margarita, two young white anthropologists from New York, arrive in a Peruvian jungle village to study the lifestyle of the Isabo people. To the locals, they are known as the 'old ladies'. The villagers promise to build a house for them, but until it is finished, they live with Chawa, who also prepares their food. Alicia, an Isabo teenager, observes everything and tells the story of how life in the village is affected by the strange behaviour of the 'old ladies'.

EXCERPT 1

[…] But nothing was simple with these old ladies. They brought a big bottle of sugarcane liquor, enough to keep the whole village drunk
5 for a day and a half, and they didn't want to open the bottle. They were saving it. What was the matter with them? Did they think it would get better with age? When you have liquor, you drink it. When you have food, you eat it. It's only
10 natural. When you have food, you make sure to be generous and give some to all your relatives, so when they have some, they will share it with you. That is how you "save" food. The same with liquor. Where did these people come from? How
15 did they live with such stupid ideas? I was upset. We were all upset. The whole village. Nonti tried to talk to the old ladies.
"I see the village is very sad," he began.
"Sad?" asked Joanna. "What do you mean?"
20 "They are all sad. Very sad. They want to have a party to welcome you to your new home and now they cannot do so. Therefore I see that they are very sad."
The old ladies looked around at everyone.
25 Then they jabbered at each other in their own language. The tall one was really mad. Joanna kept on turning the fish ring on her hand. Nonti looked up at them sadly. Then he looked at the whole village and sighed again. Finally, they told
30 him yes, they would have a party, but they wanted to save half of the sugarcane liquor for a party when their house was finished. They would only have half a party. Well, that was better than no party. […]

[…] First, they told everyone to come and ask for 35
medicines. They had eyedrops for infected eyes, aspirina for pain, paregorico for diarrhea, a white cream and some blood-red liquid that burned for sores, and antibióticos for very bad sores. They would wait in Chawa's house each morning, and 40 people could come and get medicine. That was good. They started to walk through the village every evening to visit every house. They visited all eighteen houses. They didn't seem to notice that no one else ever did that. No one visits 45 everybody. You visit someone. You don't stroll through the whole village. These women knew nothing about manners. They just burst into someone's house, no matter if it was mealtime. For normal people, if you happen to arrive at 50 someone's house when they were starting to eat, they invited you to join the meal. But if that happened, or if you arrived at mealtime on purpose, you knew you had to pay them back. You expected to see these people who had fed 55 you arrive at your house for a meal. That is the way things are done. But these women! They wandered through the village at a time when everyone was eating, and they said, "No, thank you. We're not hungry." Then why were they 60 walking around when people are eating?
Juanita and her sister decided to teach them a lesson. They found out that Margarita had traded some bullets with Nimeran so when he went hunting the next time he would bring the old 65 ladies a piece of whatever he got. And Nimeran had just returned with a nice big deer. The old ladies got a leg.

---

anthropologist Anthropologe, Anthropologin **sugarcane liquor** Zuckerrohrschnaps **jabber** schnattern, plappern **eyedrops** Augentropfen **diarrhea** [ˌdaɪəˈrɪə] Durchfall **sore** Wunde **stroll** schlendern **mealtime** Essenszeit

Chawa cooked it for them, and when they were
70 shooing the chickens out of their kitchen so
they could sit down and eat, Juanita and her
sister arrived to "visit". Chawa, of course, knew
what was going on. She also knew that
Margarita and Joanna were starving. They
75 hadn't eaten meat for at least a week.
"Hohue," Joanna said to Juanita and Paulita.
At least she had learned the appropriate
greeting.
"Hoho," they both responded, leaning up
80 against the kitchen posts, looking down at the
bowls full of wonderful-smelling deer stew.
"I don't know if they'll invite you to eat or
not," said Chawa. "When they're hungry, they
are animals. Joanna practically grabbed the last
85 piece of turtle meat from my little one the
other day. They have no manners and very little
sense. And they give me and my children
nothing."
"Well, we'll just see what happens," said
90 Paulita. And they both continued to lean up

against the kitchen poles. Joanna started to
look uncomfortable and said something to
Margarita, who seemed to be thinking it over,
whatever it was. Then they both came to some
understanding, and Margarita said to Juanita 95
and Paulita, "Sit, eat. Pihue!"
"Maybe they are beginning to learn
something," Chawa said to Juanita, as Juanita
dipped her fingers into the big stew bowl.
Joanna got two more spoons from the kitchen 100
shelf and handed one to each of the visitors.
The old ladies never ate with their fingers and
seemed not to understand why we did. Some
of us had a few spoons, but we hardly ever
used them. Fingers are so much easier, and 105
none of us mind the heat of the stew.
"I guess they're not always as stingy as they are
most of the time," my mother said.
"At least they're interesting. And they are fun
to watch," said Chawa. "And the whole village 110
seemed to agree. They were fun to watch. [...]

shoo [ʃuː] verscheuchen   **dip sth. into sth.** etwas in etwas eintauchen

2 Comprehension

Choose the correct ending for each statement.
Give evidence from the text to support your answers.

1 *The Isabo 'save' food and drink by*

a) keeping some for a later time.
b) eating it quickly while it is fresh.
c) sharing it with their wider family.

2 *The villagers can't understand why the 'old ladies'*

a) won't share the sugarcane liquor.
b) insist on having two small celebrations.
c) think that the Isabo have stupid ideas.

3 *Joanna and Margarita do not realize that during mealtime it is rude to*

a) refuse an offer of food when you visit.
b) accept an offer of food when you visit.
c) visit somebody without bringing food.

4 *Juanita and Paulita visit the 'old ladies' during their mealtime because*

a) they haven't eaten meat in a week.
b) they want to learn American manners.
c) they want the ladies to learn Isabo ways.

In this later excerpt from Abelove's novel, some American missionaries come to the Isabo village.

EXCERPT 2

[…] They had brought a lot of stuff. Most of it was food – bacon, a cake called Betty something, bags and bags of candy, mattresses to sleep on, and bread. Joanna and Margarita had brought lots of
5 stuff – but these women brought things that even Joanna and Margarita hadn't seen before, at least not here, in the jungle.

Joanna, Margarita, Elena and I waited until the missionaries got settled in Angel's house and then
10 went over to visit.

"They better give us some of that candy," said Joanna. "They brought so much. And one of those bags is filled with white chocolate bars. Big, thick chocolate candy bars. They better offer us some."
15 Joanna and Margarita sat on Angel's porch, chatting with the missionary ladies. We sat on the ground nearby. As they talked, the missionary ladies kept on eating the cooked bacon they had brought.
20 Joanna's eyes never left the plate of bacon, and the missionary ladies didn't offer her any. They just kept talking and eating. Joanna was almost drooling.

"So all of your people are stingy," I whispered to Joanna.
25 She took her eyes off the bacon and looked at me.

"It seems so, doesn't it?" Joanna whispered back.

Then one of the missionaries went looking through one of their boxes and brought out a big bag of chocolate. Each missionary lady took a bar and then
30 they put the bag back in the box. I thought Joanna was going to grab the bag out of the box and run. But she just kept chatting calmly, although her eyes never left the box that the bag of candy was in. Her hands were busy turning her ring.
35 Finally, one of the missionaries reached for the bag again – those women ate constantly – and she finally noticed that Joanna kept staring at the chocolate. She gave Joanna and Margarita each a chocolate bar and ate a few more bars herself.
40 Joanna and Margarita unwrapped their candy, each took a tiny piece, and Joanna gave me hers and Margarita gave hers to Elena to divide up among all of us who were watching.

---

drool sabbern

"Yohuashi biris," said Joanna to me, indicating the missionary ladies. "They have so much chocolate, 45 and they are so stingy with it."

Joanna looked at me and then looked at everyone sharing that one bar of chocolate, and something happened to her. I could see the thought go through her body – the way she was being with 50 the missionaries was the way we had been with her, wanting everything they had and not understanding why they were so stingy. I just nodded at her.

3 Analysis

Examine how the two anthropologists' behaviour and their understanding of community has changed between the first excerpt and the second. Give quotes from the novel to support your answer.

> **Early finisher** Joan Abelove, a US anthropologist and author of *Go and come back*, lived for two years in the Amazon jungle.

Explain why you think she decided not to write the novel from the perspective of Joanna or Margarita, the US anthropologists.

4 Comment ✏

> **You choose** a) or b).

a) Imagine you are staying with the Isabo. Write an email to a friend comparing the Isabo attitude to possessions with the attitude of the community you come from.

b) Imagine you are the narrator, Alicia. Write your diary entry after the end of excerpt 2. Include
   • what your opinion of Joanna and Margarita was at the beginning.
   • what your opinion of them is now.

(www) Find out more about Amazonian tribes.

1 Identifying the type of text

a) Match the texts and extracts below with the correct type. Look at the pages in your student's book.

Title	Page	Type
1 Excerpt from *Tiresias*	12	a) Newspaper article: opinion piece
2 *Roar*	14	b) Narrative prose: fiction
3 "Women need to be recognized …"	18	c) Poetry
4 Excerpt from *The seven daughters of Eve*	22	d) Graphic novel
5 Excerpts from *Go and come back*	34–36	e) Non-fiction: science
6 Excerpt from *Messy Roots*	84–87	f) Song

b) 👥 Discuss the different purposes authors have when writing the types of text a) – f).
Example: In an opinion piece, the writer wants to appeal to readers and persuade them.

2 Analysing narrative technique

Narrative technique: This refers to how a story, is told and, importantly, who tells it.

First-person narrator: The story is usually told through the eyes of the protagonist, the main character, but not always. Knowing how the protagonist thinks and feels can make the reader feel like the character's companion during the story and we may feel sympathy for them and want them to succeed.
With this technique, the narrator's observations of other characters and the dialogue between characters are very important because they are our only way of knowing what other characters are thinking.

Third-person narrator: This narrator is not involved in the story and can be omniscient or limited.
An omniscient narrator knows everything that happens and can take us inside the minds of different characters, hearing their thoughts and seeing the story from their perspective. A limited narrator may follow an individual character and only knows what that character experiences. As with a first-person narrator, the behaviour of other characters and dialogue tell us what those characters may be feeling.

a) Look back at the excerpts from *Go and come back* (pp. 34–36). You have already thought about why the author chose Alicia as the narrator. Now describe what narrative technique is used.

b) *"These women knew nothing about manners. They just burst into someone's house …"* (Excerpt 1, ll. 47–49)
👥 What effect does seeing the anthropologists through Alicia's eyes have on you as a reader?

c) 👥 What are the advantages and disadvantages of using this kind of narrative technique? Discuss.

3 Over to you 🖉

Choose a piece of writing that you like. It could be an excerpt from a short story, novel or play.
a) Identify the type of text and find out about why the author wrote it.
b) Identify the narrative technique used.
c) Analyse the effects the narrative technique has on you as a reader. Mark up a copy of the text and identify good quotations you can use.
d) Write up your analysis, along with the background information, in poster form.
e) Hang your posters up in the classroom and do a gallery walk. Give feedback on your classmates' posters.

➡ *SMC 34: Giving feedback (p. 189)*

Looking at language

a) You already know different ways to report speech and commands, requests, suggestions, etc.

Nonti: *"**They wanted** to have a party to welcome **you** to your new home **and now** they **cannot** do so"*
*Nonti **told** Joanna / **said to** Joanna that the villagers **had wanted** to have a party to welcome **them** …*
***but then** they **couldn't** do so.*

Margarita to Juanita: *"Sit, eat."*

*Margarita **asked/told/advised** Juanita to **sit and eat**.*
*Margarita **suggested sitting** and **eating** (to Juanita).*

b) Look at these *wh*-questions and how they are reported.

Alicia: *"**Where did** these people **come** from?"*

Joanna to Nonti: *"**What do you mean**."*

*Alicia **asked where** the people **had come** from.*

*Joanna **asked** Nonti **what he meant**.*

TIP We can also use the verb *wonder* or the phrase *want to know*.

Alicia **wondered** where the people **had come** from.   Joanna **wanted to know** what Nonti **meant**.

c) Look at these *yes/no* questions and how they are reported.

Juanita: *"**Will** Joanna invite **us** to eat?"*

Alicia to Joanna: *"**Are** all Americans so stingy?"*

*Juanita **asked if** Joanna **would** invite **them** to eat.*

*Alicia **asked whether** all Americans **were** so stingy.*

*Juanita **wondered if** Joanna **would** invite …*

*Alicia **wanted to know whether** all Americans **were** …*

d) Explain the changes to *wh*-questions and *yes/no* questions when we report them.

➡ *GAP 17: Indirect speech (I) (p. 138)*

---

1 **REVISION** **In another country** (Indirect speech)   ▪ ▪ ▪ ▪ ▪

Lauren is a British exchange student in Frankfurt. She is talking to Nawal, her host sister.
Report what the girls say.

1 Nawal: "I'm so glad to have you here. It will be awesome."
   Nawal said she was so glad to have Lauren there and that it would be awesome.
2 Lauren: "I'm glad too. But I'm a bit tired. I need a rest after my journey."
3 Nawal: "I understand. The bedroom is ready. You can sleep if you need to."
4 Lauren: "That's nice. Everybody has been so nice and friendly to me."
5 Nawal: "You haven't met my brother yet. He's at handball practice. He will be home later."
6 Lauren: "I'm going to have a rest now. You may need to wake me up when your brother comes home."

2 **REVISION** **Meeting the host family** (Indirect speech: *advise, promise, suggest, …*)   ▪ ▪ ▪ ▪ ▪

Use a verb from the box to report what the people say. Use each verb only once.

1 Host mum: "Please take your shoes off in the house, Lauren."
   The host mum asked Lauren to take …
2 Host dad: "Let me take your suitcase upstairs."
3 Nawal: "We should go into the living room."
4 Host mum: "Come on a tour of Frankfurt with us tomorrow."
5 Host dad to host mum: "Miriam, we should speak German to Lauren."
6 Lauren: "No, no. I don't want to speak any German today. I'm too tired!"
7 Nawal: "OK, Lauren. Have a rest now. I will wake you up in two hours."

> advise · ask ·
> invite · offer ·
> promise · refuse ·
> suggest

More help ▸ *p. 90*   **Early finisher** ▸ *p. 96*

3 Lauren asked Nawal a lot of questions (Indirect speech: *wh*-questions) ▪▪▪▫▫

Lauren and Nawal talked in Nawal's room. Report their questions and answers. Use the verbs *ask* and *tell*.

1 Lauren: Where is your school?
   Lauren asked Nawal where her school was.
2 Lauren: What is the uniform like?
3 Lauren: How many subjects do you study?
4 Nawal: Why did you only bring one suitcase?
5 Lauren: Why are there two beds in your room?
6 Lauren: Where did your sister go?
7 Lauren: Which bed is mine?

Nawal: It's not far from my house. We can walk there.
   Nawal told Lauren (that) it wasn't far from …
Nawal: We don't wear school uniforms.
Nawal: I study thirteen subjects.
Lauren: My parents will bring another one when they visit.
Nawal: I shared my room with my big sister before she left.
Nawal: She moved to Berlin to study at university.
Nawal: The one on the left is yours.

4 Are you enjoying your stay? (Indirect speech: *yes-no* questions) ▪▪▪▪▫

a) One evening, Lauren made a video call to her friend in the UK. Read these parts of their conversation.

1	Did you have a good journey there?	My plane was delayed so it took six hours! I was really tired when I arrived.
2	Are you enjoying your stay?	It's been great so far. Everyone is really helpful and friendly.
3	Is your host family nice?	They're cool. Their English is pretty good.
4	Do you speak English with them?	I know I shouldn't. I'm going to try and speak more German.
5	Can you understand people when they speak in German?	If they speak slowly. The accent here is different from what we hear in our schoolbooks.
6	Have you seen much of the city?	Yes, I have. Yesterday, we went on a tour. It was interesting.
7	Do you like the food over there?	It's nice. They eat a lot of dark bread though. I don't like it very much.
8	Will you post some photos on social media?	I don't want to put any photos on the internet. I'll send you some on our messaging app.

b) **Take turns to play Lauren's friend. Tell a classmate about the conversation you had yesterday.**
I asked Lauren if she … · Then I wanted to know whether she … · I wondered whether her host family … ·
She told me … · She explained that … · She said … · She promised …

5 I have some questions for you … (Indirect speech: questions) 💬 ▪▪▪▪▪

 Make groups of three: A, B and C.
Think of a topic you can ask each other questions about: *last weekend, plans for next weekend*, etc.
Student A writes four questions to ask **student B**, **student B** writes four questions to ask **student C**, and
student C writes four questions to ask **student A**.
When you are all ready, **student A** can begin by asking **B**.
The student who is not talking should note down the questions asked and the answers given.
After all the questions have been asked, report what was said. Take turns.

1 *Joe's violin:* A documentary

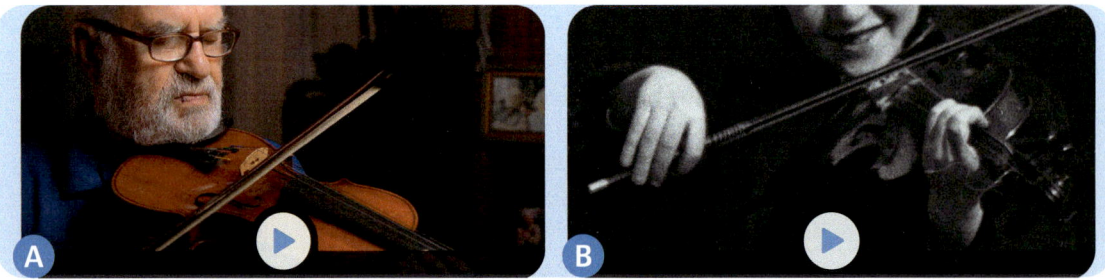

a) 👥 Describe these two stills from the film. Speculate on how they might be related.

b) Watch an excerpt from the film. Take notes on what Joe says about his life.
👥 Compare your notes. Then describe Joe's relationship with the violin – in the past and now.

c) Watch a second excerpt from the film. Find out what happens to Joe's violin.

d) 👥 Watch two more excerpts. Then explain what the stills below are about – and what links them.

e) In the last excerpt, Brianna's teacher said: "Music has connected everyone here today."
In class, discuss in what way music has created a community.

2 Making the film: Elements of a documentary

a) A documentary uses different kinds of "document" or material, e.g.:
interviews · narration · filmed action · old footage · music · photos · maps or diagrams · text
Watch the extracts from the film again. Note down examples of different "documents".
👥 Compare your results. Discuss the reasons why different documents are used.

b) Watch part of an excerpt again. You will see an example of a match cut.
Then explain what a match cut is and why the film-maker uses it. You can refer to these stills.

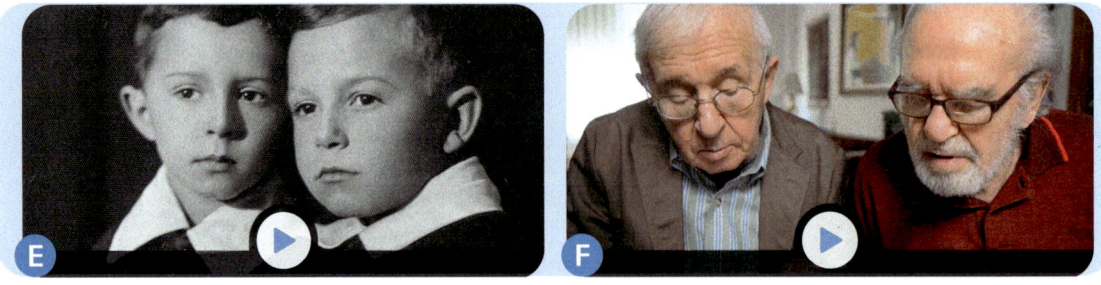

EXTRA 👥 💬 Discuss ideas for a film about an important event in each of your lives.
Decide which documents you would use. Try to think of a match cut you could make.

On this page you will learn about how the same words sound different in different English accents.

1 Standard British and American English

a) You will hear the sentences below. Listen to the **t** in the words in bold print.

weak **t** (North America)	I **wrote** him a **letter**. Is this dress **cotton**? This is much **better**. **What** a **lot** of **potatoes**!	strong **t** (Britain)	I **wrote** him a **letter**. Is this dress **cotton**? We need some more **butter**. **What** a **lot** of **pretty** toys.

b) You will hear the sentences below. Listen to how the **r** is pronounced in the words in bold print.

weak **r** (south of England)	Are the shops **near here**? New **York** has three **airports**. You **aren't** being **fair**. What **perfect weather**!	strong **r** (North America)	Are the shops **near here**? New **York** has three **airports**. I don't **care where** we go. Did you **hear** the **thunder**?

c) 👥 Repeat the sentences from a) and b) to show the difference between BE and AE pronunciation.

2 Standard British and American English

a) You will hear six pairs of sentences. One speaker is British and the other is American.
In each pair, one word is the same. Write it down.

b) Listen again. Repeat the two pronunciations of the word in common.

c) Say the following words as you think they are pronounced in BE and AE. Then listen and check.
coffee · glass · fast · honest · new · passport · possible · task · top · tune

3 Different British accents

a) You will hear six sentences spoken twice.
The first speaker has a regional accent. The second speaker uses standard pronunciation.
Listen and focus on the words listed below. The regional accents are given (in brackets).

1 about (London/southeast)
2 phone (Scotland)
3 house (Northern Ireland)
4 writes (Scotland)
5 grass (England: north)
6 farmers (England: west)

b) Listen again. After each sentence pair suggest other words where a similar difference might be heard.
· *A Londoner might pronounce the word **better** like …*
· *Someone from Scotland might pronounce **home** like …*

4 Listening for detail

a) You will hear three people discussing what colour to paint a community centre recreation room.
Listen and identify the accents.

b) Listen again. Note down the colours they discuss and their arguments for or against them.

5 Reflection 💬
👥 Discuss your own experience of different accents (films, songs, people you know, …).
Describe the differences you have noticed.
Think of tips you could give to help people to understand different accents better.

➡ *SMC 26: Listening strategies (p. 182)*

1 *Go and come back*: A book review

a) Read the review, collect new information about the novel and identify the writer's opinion about the book.

NEW YORKERS IN THE JUNGLE

In a remote village in the Peruvian jungle, two American women live as guests of the local people, studying their customs and way of life. Joanna and Margarita, anthropologists from New York, are
5 *doing research on the Isabo, a (fictional) tribe of Amazonian Indians. The Isabo are just as curious about their unusual guests, the "two old white ladies" as they call them (although they are really just in their twenties).*

10 *In her first novel,* Go and come back, *Joan Abelove describes the relationship between the tribespeople and their visitors, exploring their many everyday misunderstandings. The story is narrated by Alicia, an Isabo teenage girl, allowing us to see the two*
15 *white women through the eyes of the village community. To the Isabo, Joanna and Margarita are impossibly stingy. Although they offer the villagers medicines and brightly coloured jewellery, they keep almost everything else they have for themselves.*
20 *They also seem unclean, bathing in the river only once a day and using the jungle as their toilet instead of the river. To Alicia, the women are also ignorant. They don't even know that washing sand off a turtle in the river will bring rain!*

25 *Alicia also tells her own story, showing us how the Isabo see community relationships. She has been promised as wife to her sister's husband. Wanting to enjoy her teenage years, she hopes to put off the marriage for as long as possible. For now she has*
30 *adopted the abandoned child of a non-Isabo woman. Hoping to keep it alive, she persuades her mother and other village women to breastfeed it and think of it as their own. Although Isabo families live in separate houses, looking after children is*
35 *everyone's responsibility. Growing closer to Joanna over time, Alicia explains these customs to her.*

Thanks to Alicia's help, the American women eventually "become caibo, caibo raibirai. Real people, kinsmen, or whatever they would be". And
40 *through her explanations, Alicia too achieves a deeper understanding of her own community. She also has the chance, literally, to see her village from a different perspective. Before returning to the States, Joanna takes her up in a small plane.*
45 *Looking down from above, Alicia sees her village grow smaller and smaller with only the tops of the houses and the kitchens along the river still in view: "And then we could see how far the jungle stretched beyond the village, and it was so big and so*
50 *beautiful and our village was such a small spot compared to the enormous forest."*

Abelove is herself an anthropologist who spent two years among Amazonian Indians. Writing with such rich experience, she tells a very credible story which is not just informative, but also sometimes
55 *very funny. I strongly recommend this engaging work of young adult fiction, especially to anyone curious about the cultural differences between distant communities.*

b) You have already read some excerpts from this book. Describe how the review has influenced you. Has it made you *more* or *less* interested in reading the whole novel? Explain why.

c) Give reasons why you read/don't read book or film reviews. Describe the kind of information about a book or a film that would interest you most.

Writing a book review

*In this unit, the text in focus is a **review** of a novel. In a review, you inform your reader about the content or plot. You can also give a personal opinion. Reviews can appear in print or online.*
Over the next three pages, you will work through the following steps to produce a review of a novel.

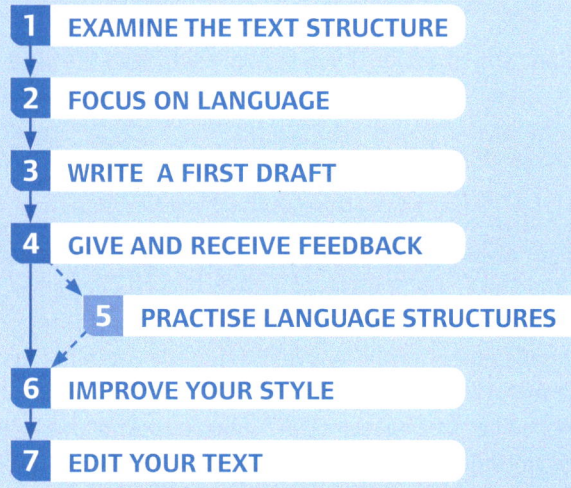

1	EXAMINE THE TEXT STRUCTURE
2	FOCUS ON LANGUAGE
3	WRITE A FIRST DRAFT
4	GIVE AND RECEIVE FEEDBACK
5	PRACTISE LANGUAGE STRUCTURES
6	IMPROVE YOUR STYLE
7	EDIT YOUR TEXT

1 EXAMINE THE TEXT STRUCTURE

Read about the structure of a review. Then identify the four main parts of the review on p. 42.
Check to what extent the review follows the tips below.

> **REVIEW OF A NOVEL: STRUCTURE**
> · Headline Catch your reader's attention. Hint at the content of the book and/or your opinion of it.
> · Introduction Give key information on some of these points: setting, theme, author.
> · Main body Summarize the plot of the novel (using the present tense). Cover the main events, characters and conflicts without going into too much detail or revealing too much about the plot.
> · Conclusion Give your opinion of the novel. Explain why you think it is/isn't worth reading and say if you would recommend it, who to, and why.

2 FOCUS ON LANGUAGE

Some of the more advanced grammar structures you have learned are suitable for texts like a review.

a) Read these three sentences. Then find how they are expressed in the text on p. 42.
   1 Two American women live as guests of the local people and study their customs and way of life. *(ll. 1–3)*
   2 They also seem unclean because they bathe in the river only once a day. *(ll. 20–22)*
   3 Before she returns to the States, Joanna takes her up in a small plane. *(ll. 43–44)*

   Write down the sentences from the text and underline the structure they have in common.
   Say why you think the author chose to use this structure.

b) The text on p. 42 contains ten more sentences that use the same structure.
   Find as many as you can and paraphrase them to show that you understand their meaning.

3 **WRITE A FIRST DRAFT**

Choose a novel. Make notes on the author, themes, plot, characters, etc. Organize your notes in line with the structure on p. 43. Then write a first draft. ➡ *SMC 12: Writing a review (p. 171)*

4 **GIVE AND RECEIVE FEEDBACK**

👥 Read your partner's first draft. Give feedback on the structure of the review. In addition, consider
· whether the review gives you a good idea of what the book is about.
· whether it has helped you to decide if you would like to read the book.
Comment on the language. If possible, suggest where your partner could use a participle clause.

5 **PRACTISE LANGUAGE STRUCTURES**

1 Talking about time (Participle clauses with *after, before, since, …*)

Make one sentence out of two. Use participle clauses with the conjunction given.
1 Joanna returns to the States. Before that, she takes Alicia up in a small plane. (before)
   Before returning to the States, Joanna takes Alicia up in a small plane.
2 Joan Abelove returned home. Twenty-five years later, she wrote her first novel. (after)
   Twenty-five years after …
3 J. K. Rowling published her first novel in 1997. She has sold over 450 million books. (since)
4 Harry Potter travels to Hogwart's School. He makes friends with Ron Weasley. (while)
5 Jake, the hero, leaves home one morning. He sees a strange box on the steps. (when)
6 Sue invites Alex for a goodbye drink. Then she leaves England for Australia. (before)

More help ▶ p. 91

2 Explaining why (Participle clauses meaning *because …*)

Decide which sentence gives a reason: a) or b). Then make them into one sentence. To give the reason, use a participle clause (-ing …/Not -ing …) at the beginning of the longer sentence.
1 a) Joan Abelove writes with rich experience.   b) She tells a very credible story.
   Writing with rich experience, Joan Abelove tells a very credible story.
2 a) Joan Abelove wanted to share her experience.   b) She decided to write about her time in Peru.
3 a) J. K. Rowling's novels quickly became bestsellers.   b) They appealed to children everywhere.
4 a) Harry Potter loses his parents at the age of one.   b) He goes to live with his aunt and uncle.
5 a) Jake decides that he has to escape.   b) He realizes that his life is in danger.
6 a) Alex doesn't know that Sue is planning to leave.   b) He is shocked when she tells him the news.

3 Talking about connected actions (Participle clauses meaning *and …*)

Using participle clauses, rewrite each sentence in two different ways.
1 The women live with the local people **and** study their way of life.
   The women live with the local people, studying their way of life.
   Living with the local people, the women study their way of life.
2 The author describes small-town life **and** paints a fun picture of local characters.
3 The plot develops quickly **and** holds the reader's interest.
4 The hero wanders around the town **and** looks for a place to eat.
5 The two girls travel through the jungle **and** sleep in trees as they go.
6 Jake stood at the top of the ladder **and** tried to open the window.

More help ▶ p. 91   ➡ *GAP 21-23: Participles (pp. 146–151)*

6 IMPROVE YOUR STYLE Description techniques

You can use different *description techniques* to help you to make your review as informative as possible.

Name the genre
The terms used to describe novels often refer to
· the type of story: *fantasy novel · (semi-)autobiographical novel · crime fiction · thriller · ...*
· the intended audience: *children's book · young adult fiction · gay fiction · ...*
Readers who know what genre a book belongs to may find it easier to decide if it interests them.

a) 👥 Comment on the reference to genre in the review on p. 42 (ll. 56–59).
   Does it come in a good place? Why (not)? Could the review mention other genres? Which?

b) 👥 Note down and compare different ways to describe the category of the book you reviewed, e.g.
   [Name of book] by [author] is a brilliant/powerful/... work of *young adult fiction*.
   [Name of book] by [author] is a must-read for lovers of *crime fiction*.
   [Author]'s latest *fantasy novel* is set in the land of ...

Use effective phrases
· Include informative adjective-noun collocations: an action-packed thriller, a hilarious page-turner, ...
· Combine different adjectives: an exciting, fast-moving adventure, a heartbreaking but funny account, ...
· Use adverbs for emphasis: a highly readable novel, an extremely entertaining read, ...

c) Using words from the boxes below, make collocations that would fit in your review.

readable · enjoyable · engaging · entertaining · slow-moving · fast-moving · action-packed · funny · hilarious · heartbreaking · heart-warming · moving · lifelike · gripping · thought-provoking	book · novel · read · account · story · thriller · page-turner

Refer to the author
· Give <u>relevant</u> background information about the author, e.g. Abelove is herself an anthropologist ...
· If the author has written other well-known novels, compare them with the novel you are reviewing.

As in Compared with In contrast to	her his	first earlier ...	novel, novels,	this book ... the author ...

Use meaningful quotations
When quoting from a book, choose lines that express a key point you wish to make.

d) 👥 Comment on the quotations in the review on p. 42. Explain whether you find them effective.

e) Check your text. Consider whether you could change or add quotations.

TIP Quote exactly. Use quotation marks. Avoid extremely long quotations. ➜ *SMC 10: Writing an article (p. 170)*

7 EDIT YOUR TEXT

a) Read your first draft. Consider your partner's feedback and any relevant points from steps 5–6.
   Then edit your text, making improvements where you can.

b) 👥 Read each other's edited texts and comment on the changes. ➜ *SMC 12: Writing a review (p. 171)*

1 Community and diversity

Mt. Rainier student's photos now on display outside Des Moines Theater

The outside of the old Des Moines Theater is now an exhibition space for a photography show titled 'Harmony within Diversity' by Rahel Ambachew, a sophomore at Mount Rainier High School. Rahel is from Ethiopia, and her display is part of a worldwide movement called 'The Inside Out
5 *Project,' … The following is a statement by the artist:*

Hello, my name is Rahel Ambachew. I am a sophomore at Mount Rainier High School. …
People in our community are not often encouraged or given the space to express themselves. Our goal
10 should be to, every day, embrace what makes us different, instead of hiding or shaming others for celebrating who they are. The reason I did this project is because although we may seem harmonized living in a community with such great
15 diversity, we as individuals are not harmonized. We cannot be accepting of each other when there are derogatory stereotypes present. I decided to photograph twenty-seven Mount Rainier High School students holding up a sign with a short state-
20 ment and/or one word that captures their diversity …

http://waterlandblog.com/2016/05/05/mt-rainier-students-photos-now-on-display-outside-des-moines-theater/

About the Inside Out Project

Started by the French artist JR, INSIDE OUT offers everyone the opportunity to paste their portraits in public places and make a statement about what
5 they stand for.
You send your portraits online to the INSIDE OUT team; they print them and send the posters back to you to paste and install.

"I wish for you to stand up for what you care about
10 *by participating in a global art project, and together we'll turn the world … INSIDE OUT."* **JR**

2 Working for harmony

a) Describe Rahel's view of her community and how she would like to make it a better place. Explain how the *Inside Out* project helped her to spread her ideas.

b) 👥 Discuss ideas for improving harmony in your community. Agree on one good idea and share it with the class.

3 Explaining your view 🖉

You choose ▶ a) or b).

a) Imagine you wrote one of the signs above. Write a short text explaining your statement.

b) Take a photo you would like to upload to the *Inside Out* project. Write a text explaining where you would hang the poster, and why.

4 Taking a stand: Collective action

👥 Brainstorm different kinds of actions that groups can take to raise awareness of issues.

Da-Xia, 16, Taipei, Taiwan – *'Flash mobber'*

I'm part of a group of young people who want to raise awareness of climate change. We organize different kinds of events ourselves. For example,
5 we organized a flash mob on a busy street in Taipei, Taiwan, my home city. Each person wore part of a sign which read: "Save the Antarctic. Young people rise up".

Only when something affects your daily life, do
10 you really pay attention and even though climate change is real and it's happening, it's not touching a lot of people's daily lives yet. That's why we chose this form of protest and interrupted people's normal routine.
15 I think our protest did make a difference: Not only did a large crowd stop to read our signs, the media also reported on it. It's true that we do cause some disruption, and some people react angrily, but we try to keep it as short as possible
20 and we're absolutely non-violent.

It's our message that's important and that's what we want people and the media to focus on. Public opinion does matter. Frightening people or making them very angry only stops them hearing
25 our message.

Caitríona, 15, Bracora, Scotland – Online activist

I live in a small town in Scotland. Seldom do I have the chance to take part in marches myself, but, online, it doesn't matter where I am. I work with other young people all over the world as part of a 5 community called EcoTok. It's our aim to encourage people to live more sustainably, so we share short videos that give people practical ideas and tips that they can use themselves. The group even supported my email writing campaign to improve 10 public transport in rural areas of Scotland.

The climate crisis is scary, and I do think it's easy to get depressed about it all. The best thing about our group is that we don't focus on the doom and gloom – we concentrate on being 15 positive and practical. After all, the challenge of climate change means each one of us must take action ourselves to reduce our impact on the environment.

I think our group is succeeding. We started off 20 with just 17 members a couple of years ago, but now we have over 115,000 followers. Our posts are getting more than 260 million views!

5 A flash mob

a) Watch a video of another flash mob on the internet. Say what impression it makes on you.

b) 👥 One of you is a flash mob organizer and the other is a person who cannot go to school/work/an important appointment because of the flash mob. Have a discussion about the event, its reasons and effects.

6 Discuss 💬

👥 Your local council plans to build new apartments on a large park in your town and you want to take collective action against it.

a) Discuss what actions you can organize, e.g. online activities, marches, flash mobs, etc. and decide on one or a mix of actions. Write a brief plan and outline your reasons.

b) Present your plans to the class.

1 It does matter (Different forms of emphasis)

Language help

To emphasize a particular idea when speaking or writing you can use these options:

1 Use *do, does* or *did* in positive sentences.
   - *Our protest **did** make a difference.*
   - *We **do** cause some disruption.*
   - *Public opinion **does** matter.*

2 Use *It's … / It was … + relative clause*
   - ***It's** our message that's important.*
   - ***It was** our protest that made a difference.*
   - ***It's** all of us who can make a difference.*

3 Use adverbs such as *absolutely, definitely,* etc.
   - *… we're **absolutely** non-violent …*
   - *We are **totally** committed to changing …*

4 Use reflexive pronouns.
   - *… practical ideas that people can use **themselves**.*
   - *… each one of us must take action **ourselves**.*
   - *The protest **itself** was short.*

5 Use inversion
   - *A large crowd stopped to read …, and the media also reported on it.*
     → ***Not only did** a large crowd **stop** to read …, the media also reported on it.*
   - *You only really pay attention when something affects your daily life.*
     → ***Only when** something affects your daily life, **do you** really **pay** attention.*
   - *I seldom have a chance to take part …*
     → ***Seldom do I have** a chance to take part …*
   - *I have never felt so motivated to do something.*
     → ***Never have I felt** so motivated …*

➡ *GAP 27: Emphasis (pp. 158-159)*

a) 🎧 💬 You will hear the first sentence from each set of examples above.
Listen carefully and read out the other sentences, using the same stress pattern.

b) Then listen and check.

c) 👥 Work in groups of four.
The example sentence has been rewritten using the techniques to add emphasis from 1 to 4 above.

Each student should rewrite one of the sentences 1-4 in the same way.

Example: We need to solve this problem. ➡

We need to solve this problem.

a We do need to solve this problem.
b It's this problem that we need to solve.
c We absolutely need to solve this problem.
d We need to solve this problem ourselves.

1 We have to save our environment.
2 I want to change my lifestyle.
3 The government promised to help with the problem.
4 Polluters need to take action.

d) 👥 Each student reads out their sentences one by one.
After each sentence, comment briefly on the stress and intonation and discuss where the emphasis lies.

2 I did take part in the protest (Emphatic *do* when disagreeing)

We often use *do, does* or *did* in positive sentences when we disagree with something somebody has said.
People are discussing ways of improving their local area.
Make the responses (B, D, F, etc.) stronger using *do, does* or *did*.

1 A People don't cycle in town.
   B They cycle. We just need more cycle paths.

2 C The park is lovely. It doesn't need improving.
   D It is lovely, but it needs a skatepark for teenagers.

3 E The council doesn't care what we think.
   F It cares – that's why it wants to hear our ideas.

4 G Nobody reacted when the trees were cut down.
   H People reacted – there was a big protest.

5 I Why didn't Rob go on the climate march?
   J He went. He was with Sam and Maria.

6 K You didn't tell me that you signed a petition.
   L I told you and I emailed you a link to it.

➡ *GAP 27.2: Emphatic do/does/did (p. 158)*

3 Not only will it help the environment, you'll also save money! (Inversion for emphasis)

These sentences are from student presentations. Rewrite them using inversion to give them more impact. Begin the sentences using the word(s) in **bold**.

1 We **not only** reduced our waste, we saved money also.
2 We will **only** succeed **when** we work together.
3 I have **never** been so convinced about anything in my life.
4 You will **not only** agree with me, you'll want to take action also.
5 We **rarely** see governments take real action on the climate crisis.
6 The climate crisis is **not only** real, its effects can also be seen now.

➡ *GAP 27.6: Inversion (p. 158)*

4 Instead of using your car … (The gerund after prepositions)

After prepositions (e.g. *as well as, instead of, by, for, …*), we use a gerund, not the infinitive of a verb.
Complete these sentences from a local council brochure on cycling. Use gerunds.

> combine · cycle (2x) · get · improve · make · save · spend · take part · use

1 Instead of … your car, why not go by bike?
2 Just think about all the advantages of …
3 You'll save time by … exercise and transport.
4 You'll reduce the cost of … to work or school.
5 Instead of … money on petrol, you could buy something nice for yourself!

6 As well as … money, you'll help our planet.
7 By … in our project, you'll make a difference.
8 The council has spent a lot on … cycle paths.
9 Check our website for advice on … safely.
10 If you have ideas for … cycling safer and more attractive, get in touch with the council.

➡ *GAP 15: The gerund II (p.134)*

5 Youth projects in Germany 🔲EN/DE

a) You're taking part in a youth project and want to post information about it on an international youth-in-action platform. Go to p. 99. Read about the project and write a short description in English for the internet platform. Mention the workshop, the '*Skate-Olympiade*' and the skateboard contest in your text.

b) 👥 Compare your text with a partner.

Before you read, watch two short clips on the American and British political systems. While you watch, take notes on the main political institutions in both countries and the powers they have. 👥 Use your notes to compare the two systems.

Voting and elections

In the **US** you can vote from age 18
· in local elections (e.g. for mayor, local law enforcement).
· at state level (Governor, state Senators and Representatives).
5 · at federal level (President, Senators and Representatives in Congress).

In the **UK**, you can vote from age 18 (in Scottish elections from 16)
· in local elections (e.g. for mayor).
· for regional parliaments (in Northern Ireland, Scotland and Wales).
· in UK-wide elections to the House of Commons. (The House of Lords is
10 not elected.)
The head of state in the UK, the King, is of course not elected.

The Capitol, Washington, D.C.

Referendums and initiatives

In a referendum, the people are asked by the legislature to vote on a single issue. In an initiative, citizens who want to change the law collect signatures. If
15 *they collect enough, a vote is held.*

In the **USA**, referendums and especially initiatives are common at state level, but there are none at federal level. Examples of initiatives include votes on abortion rights, on the minimum wage and on legalizing marijuana.

In the **UK**, there are no initiatives, and referendums are only held on major
20 issues. In the last 50 years, there were UK referendums in 1975, to join the EEC (later the EU), in 2011, to keep the existing voting system, and in 2016, to leave the EU.

Supporters of Leave in the 2016 EU referendum

Polarization in the US and the UK

Both the UK and US use a 'first-past-the post' system. This means politics in both countries is
25 dominated by two large parties: the Republican Party and Democratic Party in the US and the Conservative Party and Labour Party in the UK.
In contrast to other European countries, coalition governments are seldom formed in the UK, and in the US there has never been anything other than a one-party government. Nevertheless, when the American president and the majority in the House or Senate are from different parties,
30 effective laws can only be passed through bipartisan (meaning both parties) cooperation.
Since 2015, bipartisan cooperation has become very rare and instead US politics has become very polarized – with Republicans and Democrats disagreeing on many issues, including immigration, police violence, gun laws and abortion. Both sides often accuse the other of trying to unfairly 'fix' elections. Despite winning in 2016, President Trump claimed there was election fraud by the Democrats, a lie which he repeated even more strongly when he
35 lost in 2020. On January 6th, 2021, around 2,000 Trump supporters violently broke into the US Capitol to try and stop Joseph Biden becoming president, an event which shocked the country and the world.
In the UK, issues such as Brexit, the handling of the Corona pandemic and Scottish independence have led to divisions in British politics and society since 2014. Sometimes this has led to great political instability – in the summer of 2022 the country had three different prime ministers! Fortunately, British society has not seen the
40 same level of violence or social unrest as the United States.

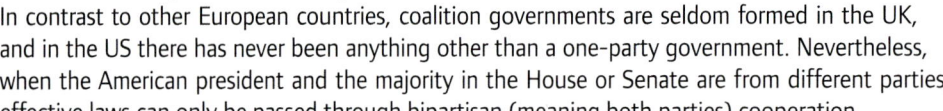

Compare the right to vote in Germany with that in the UK and the USA.
 Find out more about the British and American voting systems.

The most important thing you can do in a democracy is vote. In many countries, however, the percentage of young people who vote is often lower than older age groups.

In the 2019 UK general election, only 47% of all British 18 to 24-year-olds cast their election vote compared to 74% of over-65s. In the 2016 US general and presidential
5 *elections, the number was similar to the UK: 49% of 18 to 34-year-olds voted. In 2020, this number rose to 57%.*

Some young people say they do not vote because politicians do not care about young people's issues – but politicians need votes to get elected. In 2013, Scotland lowered the voting age to 16 but only in elections to the Scottish parliament and in Scotland-only referendums.

👥 Discuss why you think fewer young people than older people tend to vote.
Find out what percentage of young people voted in Germany's last federal election. Is it higher, lower or similar to the UK and US? Discuss why.

10 **Joining a party**

If you join a political party, you can shape its policies and help to get its candidates elected. Young people can join a UK party from the age of 15 or 16 and around 1 million people (under 2% of the population) are members of a political party. In contrast, the two big parties in the US have over 70 million
15 members (about a quarter of the population). One reason for this is you often need to register with a party to vote in primaries (the first round in an American election).

Standing for election

If you're a party member and old enough, you could try to get elected yourself.

Look at the table and say how well young people are represented.*

	House of Commons (UK)	House of Representatives (US)	Senate (US)
Average age	51	59	63
Members under 30	21 (of 650)	1 (of 435)	0 (of 100)
Youngest member	23	25	33
Minimum candidate age	18	25	30

*UK figures are for 2019; US figures are for 2021

20 **Fighting for causes**

If you prefer to support a particular cause, you can join a pressure group. Unlike political parties, pressure groups do not usually put up candidates in elections. Instead they try to win over public opinion with petitions, demonstrations or other activities. Many of the big pressure groups like
25 Greenpeace or Amnesty International operate in different countries. However, some groups fight for local causes, e.g. saving a forest or historic building, etc.

Find out
• the names of the UK Prime Minister and Leader of the Opposition and the parties they belong to.
• the names of the US President and the Senate and House majority leaders and their parties.

You have already learned signposting phrases to help your audience follow a presentation. On this page, you will learn two special techniques that will help you to refine your introduction and summary.

1 Strong openers

If you grab your audience's attention at the beginning, there's a good chance they will listen more carefully.

a) Match 1–4 to a–d below to make openers that will help you to create a stronger first impression.

1	The climate crisis is kind of ironic: dinosaur fossils	a	Is that what you think?
2	The UN says, "Climate change is the defining issue	b	million chickens are killed for food every day.
3	Animal rights – I don't have a pet, so I don't care.	c	could make humans go extinct!
4	You love chicken? You're not alone. In the US, 24	d	of our time and we are at a defining moment."

b) Copy the table below and add 1–4 from a) under the correct heading.

a surprising/ shocking statistic	a question to challenge	a joke or funny story	a relevant quote
...	...	...	...

c) Now add examples from the box under the right headings in your table. There are three for each.

> Have you heard the joke about ...? · Have you ever asked yourself ...? Why not? ·
> Here's a number for you: one out of every three ... · "The longest journey begins with the first small step." ·
> A wise woman once said, "..." · Numbers don't lie. · Let me ask you something ... ·
> Knock, knock. · Have you ever wondered ...? ·
> To make this plastic shopping bag, one kilo of carbon is released into the air. ·
> Three men are standing at the bar, one says ... · The Irish have a saying, "..."

d) Write some more openers, one of each type, for a presentation on the climate crisis or animal rights.

e) 👥 Take turns to read out your openers. Give each other feedback.

2 Ending with a bang

Find a special way to end your talk. This will help your audience to remember your message afterwards.

a) Match the examples a–f with the type of ending 1–3.

1	An appeal or a call to action	a	As I finish, I think this photo sums up my message better than any words could.
		b	In conclusion, I have one request – no, a demand! I urge you to ...
2	A final question to provoke further thought	c	I've posed many questions in my talk. You've heard my answers. What are yours?
		d	If you don't believe your ears, trust your eyes. Look!
		e	When all is said and done, ask yourself this: Am I doing enough?
3	A memorable image	f	I'll end my talk now, but I don't want you to clap – I want you to act!

b) For each of the openers you wrote in 1 d), think of a good ending with a 'bang' and write it down.

c) 👥 Work in the same group. Share your ideas and give each other feedback.   `Early finisher` ▸ p. 96

Workbook
Checkpoint 2
(pp. 32–35)

Your task

A call for action

You're attending a European conference on young people's ideas for making your community more environmentally friendly. Prepare a four-minute electronic presentation with a proposal for action in your local community

Work in small teams.

➡ *SMC 33: Working in a team (p. 188)*

STEP 1 Agree on what action to take

Collect ideas. If necessary, check out your local newspaper or council website.

For example, you could

· support an existing community project <u>or</u> come up with your own.

· focus on a local controversy and suggest how to resolve it.

Discuss why each idea would be valuable to the community and agree on the best one.

STEP 2 Develop your idea

Work out the content of your presentation and make notes. For example, you could deal with

· the key points showing what you plan to do.

· how much it will cost and how it will be paid for.

· whose support you will need, and how to get it.

· who you can involve in your action, and how.

· who will benefit.

· …

STEP 3 Prepare your slides

· Using your notes, prepare the slides.

· Keep the four-minute time limit in mind. If necessary, agree on what to shorten or leave out.

· Then decide how many are going to speak and plan the transitions, e.g.

 And now we'd like to explain how the project will be financed. Alex will tell you something about that.

STEP 4 Practise your presentation ⬭

a) Practise giving your presentation out loud. Concentrate on speaking directly to your audience, using your slides just for reference.

b) Pay attention to your opening and closing. Is your opening strong? Do you end with a 'bang'?

REDUCE TRAFFIC IN OUR DISTRICT

· less noise and pollution

· safer, healthier streets

STEP 5 Present and give feedback ⬭

Give your presentation to the class.

Then listen carefully to the other presentations.

Take notes to help you give feedback.

STEP 6 Give feedback ⬭

· Using your notes, give feedback on each presentation you heard and say whether the opening and closing were effective.

· Say whether you would like to join in the proposed action and explain why.

➡ *SMC 29: Making good slides for an electronic presentation (p. 185); SMC 30: Giving a presentation (p. 186); SMC 34: Giving feedback (p. 189)*

Appropriate behaviour

1 Communication across cultures 💬

Describe how you greet your friends, your parents' friends, or someone you meet for the first time.

a) 👥 Divide the class into groups **A** and **B**.

A: Government officials: You are at a reception for foreign diplomats.
Talk to different diplomats and ask them about their countries.
Make them feel as welcome as possible.

B: Foreign diplomats: You are at a government reception in your host country.
Talk to the host country officials.
Answer all their questions and be as polite as you can.

Before starting, each group should read the information the teacher gives them.

b) 👥 In mixed groups, comment on anything that surprised you about the behaviour of the people you spoke to. Say what you learned about
· yourself.
· interacting with people from other cultures.

c) 👂 Read the tips below about typical behaviour in some English-speaking countries.
· You will now hear three short dialogues. Listen and match two of them to the tips below.
· Listen to the other dialogue again.
· Decide what the situation is and write a tip based on the way the people behave.

> **TIP**
> Meeting and greeting in the USA
>
> 1 If you pass someone in an uncrowded area like a park or on a country road, it is polite to lift your head, catch their eye, smile and nod hello.
>
> 2 People make small talk with the staff in shops. An assistant might ask *How are you today?*
> It is enough to reply *Fine, thanks. And you?* But people often share personal information too.
>
> 3 If people like something, or if they share or receive good news, they react enthusiastically, using adjectives that express how they feel, e.g. *awesome, incredible, amazing, great, …*

d) 👥 Discuss whether the scenes in c) might develop differently where you live.

2 Different German-speaking cultures 🔲

a) Kim is a New Zealander exchange student in your class. She is going on a skiing holiday to Switzerland for a week with her host family and she would like to know more about the country. You offer to help.

During a break at school, you talk to Kim and she asks you some questions about Switzerland. Look at p. 98, read her questions and make notes.

b) Later, you find this article online. Read it and find the answers to Kim's questions.

Ein kurzer Leitfaden für Deutsche, die die Schweiz besuchen

Deutsche und Schweizer teilen die Liebe zur Pünktlichkeit, aber es gibt einige Unterschiede, die Deutsche, die das Land besuchen oder sogar dort leben möchten, kennen sollten.

- Glaube nicht, dass alles in Ordnung ist, nur weil
5 du Deutsch sprichst. Während das deutschsprachige Gebiet recht groß ist und 62% der Schweizer Deutsch sprechen, sprechen nur 11% der Schweizer Hochdeutsch. Von den 38% der Schweizer, die kein Deutsch sprechen, sprechen über 20%
10 Französisch, 8% Italienisch und unter 1% Rätoromanisch.

- Im Allgemeinen sind Schweizer freundlich und höflich und vermeiden es, negative Dinge direkt zu sagen – darin ähneln sie eher den Englisch-
15 sprechenden. Sie können sich auch Zeit lassen, wenn sie reden, und es gilt als unhöflich, sie zu unterbrechen.

- Deutschschweizer sind weniger formell als Deutsche und das Sie/Du ist nicht so streng. In man-
20 chen Gegenden verwenden die meisten Menschen unter 50 Jahren die meiste Zeit das Du.

- Der schweizerdeutsche Akzent ist sehr musikalisch, mit Höhen und Tiefen, und wenn zwei Einheimische miteinander sprechen, kann es für Deutsche schwierig sein, zu folgen. 25

- Zum Akzent kommt noch der Wortschatz hinzu. Es gibt viele schweizerdeutsche Wörter, die es im Standarddeutsch nicht gibt oder die anders geschrieben/gesprochen werden, z.B. *Grüezi* oder *Guete Daag* (Guten Tag), *En Guete!* (Guten 30 Appetit), *poschte* (einkaufen), *gäbig* (praktisch), und oft sind Wörter aus dem Französischen übernommen worden, z.B. *Billett* (Fahrkarte), *merci* (danke), *Glace* (Eis).

- Nicht-EU-Reisende können in die Schweiz reisen, 35 wenn sie ein Visum für Deutschland haben, aber das Land ist nicht in der EU, also vergiss nicht, dass du die schweizer Währung brauchst: den Schweizer Franken.

- Nimm zusätzliches Taschengeld mit: Die Lebens- 40 haltungskosten in der Schweiz sind viel höher als in Deutschland, also lass dich nicht von den Preisen schocken.

---

c) Write an email in English to Kim. Answer her questions and give her any tips from the article that might be useful for her trip. You can also add any information that you may have from your own experience.

d) 👥 Compare your email with a partner. Give each other feedback.

EXTRA 👥 It is the evening before Kim goes to Switzerland. As you are browsing the internet, you come across some tips for first-time skiers (p. 100). You decide to phone Kim to pass on the tips. Make notes in English and then take turns to role-play the telephone dialogue.

➡ SMC 19: Cultural differences (p. 176)

How is the world changing?

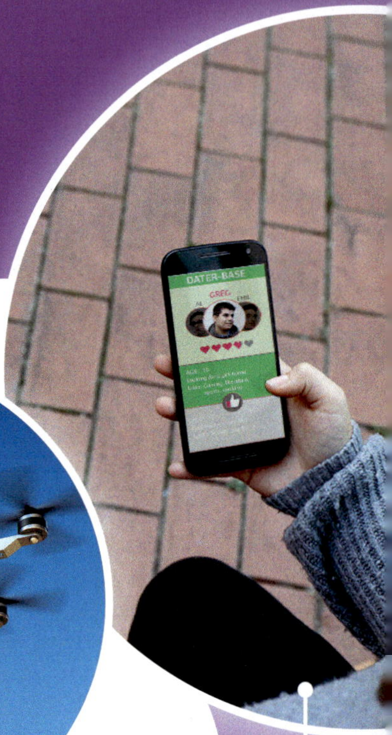

A

B

C

D

1 Past, present, future 💬

a) **Think:** Describe each pair of images on the left using words from the box. You can also look up words in a dictionary if you need them.

> globe · planet · technological progress ·
> delivery · package · interaction · automation ·
> communication · computer chip · digital device ·
> drone · robot · artificial intelligence ·
> bee · insect · pollinate · agriculture ·
> food · production

b) **Pair:** Discuss how the image pairs reflect our world as we have known it and how this could change in the future.
Say what role you expect machines to play.
· The first pair shows ... This suggests that ...
· I can imagine machines replacing ...

c) **Share:** Join up with another pair and compare your ideas.
Imagine each image pair illustrates an article.
Agree on a headline for each article.
Read out your headlines to the class.

2 Your world – your future ✏️

a) Think of another pair of images to illustrate the present and the future.

b) 👥 Write a description of your idea and read it to your partner.

EXTRA Find images to fit your description. Hang them on the wall with your description. In a gallery walk, discuss what the images suggest about the future of the world.
· I think these images are optimistic/pessimistic about the future of the world because ...

Your task ▶

At the end of this unit:
You will prepare for and take part in a panel discussion on a global issue.

1 A newspaper article: *Four things you need to understand about AI*

Read the headlines below. Do you think they are positive or negative stories about AI?
👥 Imagine an older relative is confused about AI. Think of four things you can tell them.
Read the text and see what four things the author wants us to understand.
Does he mention any of your ideas? On your first reading, ignore gaps A – D.

This excerpt is from an article written by Gary Marcus, a scientist and an author.
It was published in *The Observer* newspaper in August 2022.

A new discovery (or debacle) is reported practically every week, sometimes exaggerated, sometimes not. Should we be exultant? Terrified? Policymakers struggle to know what to make of AI and it's hard
5 for the lay reader to sort through all the headlines, much less to know what to be believe. Here are four things every reader should know.

First, …A… . And it matters. If you care about the world we live in, and how that world is likely to
10 change in the coming years and decades, you should care as much about the trajectory of AI as you might

was "quite obvious that we should stop training radiologists", given how good AI was getting, adding that radiologists are like "the coyote already over the edge of the cliff who hasn't yet looked 30 down". Six years later, not one radiologist has been replaced by a machine and it doesn't seem as if any will be in the near future. [...]

The third thing to realise is that …C… . Take the much-heralded GPT-3, which has been featured in 35 the *Guardian*, the *New York Times* and elsewhere for its ability to write fluent text. Its capacity for

Robot artist Ai-Da tells MPs AI is threat and opportunity problem

Google fires engineer who says AI is sentient

Chess robot breaks finger of 7-year-old child

DeepMind solves biology's biggest problem

about forthcoming elections or the science of climate breakdown. What happens next in AI, over the coming years and decades, will affect us all.
15 Electricity, computers, the internet, smartphones and social networking have all changed our lives, radically, sometimes for better, sometimes for worse, and AI will, too. [...]

Second, …B… . Which means that you can't –
20 and shouldn't – believe everything you read. Big corporations always seem to want us to believe that AI is closer than it really is and frequently unveil products that are a long way from practical; both media and the public often forget that the road from
25 demo to reality can be years or even decades. [...] in 2016 Geoffrey Hinton, a big name in AI, claimed it

fluency is genuine, but its disconnection with the world is profound. Asked to explain why it was a good idea to eat socks after meditating, the most 40 recent version of GPT-3 complied [...] by creating a wholesale, fluent-sounding fabrication, inventing non-existent experts in order to support claims that have no basis in reality: "Some experts believe that the act of eating a sock helps the brain to come out 45 of its altered state as a result of meditation." [...] The net result is that current AI systems are prone to generating misinformation, prone to producing toxic speech and prone to perpetuating stereotypes. They can parrot large databases of human speech 50 but cannot distinguish true from false or ethical from unethical. [...]

exultant jubelnd   **trajectory** Entwicklungsverlauf   **forthcoming** bevorstehend   **unveil** enthüllen   **"the coyote …"** Anspielung auf *eine alte Zeichentrickfigur, die oft ins Unglück stolpert*   **much-heralded** viel gepriesen   **genuine** echt   **profound** tiefgründig   **comply (with sth./sb.)** etwas gehorchen   **wholesale** umfassend   **fabrication** Fälschung   **net result** Nettoergebnis   **be prone to sth.** für etwas anfällig   **perpetuate** verewigen   **parrot** nachäffen   **distinguish** unterscheiden

The fourth thing to understand here is this: …D…. It's really just a motley collection of
55 engineering techniques, each with distinct sets of advantages and disadvantages. […] Current AIs are like idiots savants, fantastic at some problems, utterly lost in others. DeepMind's AlphaGo can play go better than any human ever
60 could, but it is completely unqualified to understand politics, morality or physics. Tesla's self-driving software seems to be pretty good on the open road but would probably be at a loss on the streets of Mumbai, where it would be likely
65 to encounter many types of vehicles and traffic patterns it hadn't been trained on. While human beings can rely on enormous amounts of general knowledge ("common sense"), most current systems know only what they have been trained
70 on and can't be trusted to generalise that knowledge to new situations (hence the Tesla crashing into a parked jet). AI, at least for now, is not one size fits all, suitable for any problem, but, rather, a ragtag bunch of techniques in
75 which your mileage may vary.

Where does all this leave us? For one thing, we need to be sceptical. Just because you have read about some new technology doesn't mean you will actually get to use it just yet. For another, we need
80 tighter regulation and we need to force large companies to bear more responsibility for the often unpredicted consequences (such as polarisation and the spread of misinformation) that stem from their technologies. Third, AI literacy is probably as
85 important to informed citizenry as mathematical literacy or an understanding of statistics.
Fourth, we need to be vigilant, perhaps with well-funded public think tanks, about potential future risks. […]

90 Finally, we should think seriously about whether we want to leave the processes – and products – of AI discovery entirely to megacorporations that may or may not have our best interests at heart: the best AI for them may not be the best AI for us.

---

motley zusammengewürfelt **idiot savant** Idiotengenie **utterly**
vollkommen **be at a loss** in Verlegenheit sein **encounter sb./**
sth. jdm./etwas begegnen **rely on sb./sth.** sich auf jdn./etwas
verlassen **hence** deshalb **ragtag** zusammengewürfelt **mileage**
hier Zuverlässigkeit **vary** abweichen **literacy** *hier* Kompetenz
citizenry Bürgerschaft **vigilant** aufmerksam

2 Comprehension

Read the text again and do tasks a) and b).

a) Match the phrases 1–5 with the correct topic sentence in the article A–D. There is one phrase you do not need.
  1 … a great deal of current AI is unreliable.
  2 … have faith in science.
  3 … AI is not magic.
  4 … AI is real and here to stay.
  5 … promises are cheap.

b) Are the following statements true or false? Give evidence from the text to support your answer.
  1 It is difficult for ordinary people to understand the topic of AI.
  2 We can already see that AI is taking jobs away from people.
  3 Some AI systems have deliberately created lies and harmful texts.
  4 So far, we have not developed an AI that is good at a wide variety of tasks.
  5 We need to stop large companies doing AI research because of the potential risks.

3 Comment ✏

Write a letter to the editor of *The Observer* in which you express your reaction to the article.

a) Include the author and the date of publication.

b) Read the article again, noting down your opinion on the 'four things' and the article's conclusion.

c) Plan your letter first, then write a first draft. Use paragraphs and a formal style.

d) 👥 Exchange your letters, proofread and give feedback.

e) Write a final draft.

➡ *SMC 9: Writing a letter / an email to the editor (p. 169)*

1 REVISION *People* or *The people* (The definite article)

Decide where you need to add a definite article to the sentences below.
Discuss your answers, referring to rules in the *Language help* box.

1 Will … people soon be replaced by … machines?
2 Do you like … people you work with?
3 It's important for us to protect … nature.
4 A man has been sent to … prison for water pollution.
5 Was … life in the past more difficult than … life today?
6 … life of a bee only lasts a few weeks.
7 … most smartphones are expensive, but … most expensive ones are not always … best.
8 … teachers in Britain have voted to go on strike.
9 Not everyone is interested in … politics.
10 Our family goes to … church on Sundays.
11 I love the windows in … church in Clyde Road.
12 I'm really interested in … history.

> **Language help**
>
> In English, the definite article **the** is left out in certain cases where it is used in German.
> Do <u>not</u> use *the*
> · before uncountable nouns (*history, life, nature,* …) or plurals (*books, train drivers,* …) if talking about things or people <u>in general</u>.
> · before *most* when it is followed by a <u>noun or noun phrase</u>.
> · before certain buildings (*school, hospital, church,* …) if talking about their usual function.
> ➡ *GAP 26: The definite article (p. 156)*

2 REVISION The right position (Sequence of adverbials)

Rewrite the sentences including the adverbials.
Compare your answers with a partner.

1 I attend music classes. (twice a week, usually)
2 You should read the label before buying a product. (always, carefully)
3 I have read such nonsense. (in a book, in my whole life, never)
4 You can come if you'd like to. (of course, really, to the party)
5 Tom and Jane have arrived, but we're waiting for Jake. (just, still, unfortunately)
6 We don't have hurricanes. (in the British Isles, luckily, often)

➡ *GAP 1: Word order (p. 106)* More help p. 92

3 REVISION Building complex sentences (Sequence of adverbials)

a) Arrange the puzzle pieces into meaningful sentences.

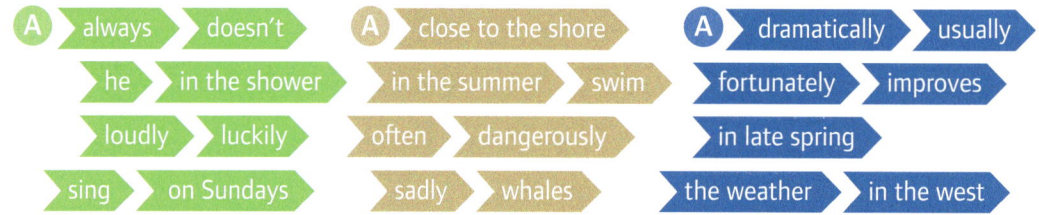

b) Label each puzzle piece using terms from the box.

> subject · main verb · auxiliary verb · sentence adverb · adverb of frequency · adverb of manner · adverb of place · adverb of time

➡ *GAP 1: Word order (p. 106)* Early finisher p. 97

On this page you focus on collocations for talking about information and communication technology. At the end you will describe an app you like to a partner.

1 Managing your device

Make collocations using a verb from box A with words from box B. Structure the collocations (e.g. in a Venn diagram) under *getting connected* and *navigating*.

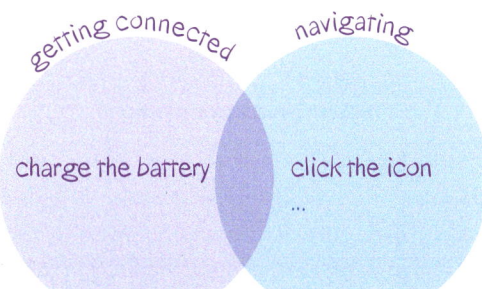

A

charge · click · connect to · enter · join · open · scroll · swipe · tap

B

the battery · the button · the icon · the internet · a local network · the menu · the search bar · the tab · your username · the web · wifi · down the page · right · left · on the screen

getting connected   *navigating*

charge the battery   click the icon
...

2 Software and data

Say what you can do in the situations below. Use a verb from box A and a noun from box B. More than one answer may be possible.

1 You want to play a game on your phone.
2 You want a friend to read an online article you saw.
3 The memory on your device is full.
4 You don't want to lose data.
5 You want to know what's on at the cinema.
6 You want to send your homework by email.
7 You have a new phone. You want to hear text messages arriving.

A download · install · run · create · make · save · delete · import · export · share · browse · search for · customize · add · take

B app · program · settings · backup file · photos · selfies · music · attachment · the internet · the web · a link · a page

EXTRA 👥 Make six more phrases using boxes A and B. Then make a list of situations, one for each phrase. Give your list of situations to a partner and ask them to guess your phrases.

3 Communication and social media

a) Copy the list of verbs on the left. For each verb, make collocations using nouns from the box.

A

accept · block · choose · create · enter · invite · log in/on to · send

B

account · chat group · contacts · friend · friend request · friends to a conversation · password · text message · username

b) 👥 Compare your results. Check your collocations on the internet.

➡ *SMC 37: Using online translators (p. 191)*

c) 👥 💬 Describe one of your favourite apps to your partner. Say what it's for and how you use it. Use words or collocations from this page.

Early finisher ▶ p. 97

1 A feature article

a) Name things that would be missing at your meal times if there were no bees.

WHEN THE BEES BUZZ OFF

MEL FERAPIS, APRIL 24, 2022

For over 25 years, scientists have been collecting insects in traps in the same place in Germany. Traps which held 1,400 grams of insects in 1989 contained only 295 grams in 2016. Great, you think, fewer insects to bite or sting me. But without some of those insects, you might go hungry in future.

5 Imagine the scene. You're walking through the supermarket. You have coffee, tomatoes, fruit and sunflower oil on your shopping list, but you cannot find any of them. What's happened? Is it just a weird dream? No, you're definitely awake. But, of course – all those 10 products you're looking for are pollinated by bees, and the bees are dying. Without bees, harvests of many crops will be much smaller, and some crops won't grow at all.

Since the beginning of the century, bee colonies 15 have been disappearing around the world. Some years are worse than others. In 2015, for example, 42 percent of colonies in the USA collapsed. Although there is no single reason for this colony collapse disorder (CCD), scientists have identified several factors that play a 20 role.

The use of particular kinds of pesticides called neonicotinoids – or neonics – has increased greatly during this century. It seems that neonics are especially good at killing bees.

25 Just like humans, who do best on a varied diet, bees are healthiest when they get pollen from a variety of sources. This is more difficult in times of industrial farming, which often covers huge areas with a single crop. In addition, cities and suburbs are spreading into 30 the country, which destroys the wild flowers bees also rely on for food.

Parasites like the Varroa mite, which weaken the bees' immune system and make them more prone to disease, are another problem.

New research shows that climate change is also 35 affecting bee populations. Flowers bloom earlier in the spring and by the time bees come out of their winter hibernation, the flowers they feed on have already bloomed and died. In addition, in southern Europe and the south of the US, the bees' habitat is shrinking, as 40 higher temperatures make it too warm for them to survive. Unlike other plants and animals, bees are not moving north to compensate, which might seem worrying.

Yet not all experts are so worried. Some say the worst 45 years of CCD are over – global bee populations are no longer falling – and new laws in the US and Europe have limited the use of the pesticides which were contributing to the problem. With queens that lay 1,500 eggs a day, bee populations can also recover very 50 quickly, even after 30–40 percent die off in any year.

What everyone agrees on is that we need to do all we can to ensure the survival of the bees – the world's food supply depends on it. Nearly all fruits and non-grain vegetables are pollinated by bees, so although we might 55 still be able to eat muesli for breakfast, we'd have no fruit to go with it. Who would want to live in a world like that?

b) After reading the article, how would you change what you said in a)?

c) ✜ In groups of three, read these lines again:
   Partner A: ll. 25–34   **Partner B:** ll. 35–44   **Partner C:** ll. 45–58.
   Then: **Partners A and B:** Take notes on why the bee population has been falling.
         Partner C: Take notes on why some people are not worried about the fall in the number of bees.

d) ✜ 💬 Explain what you have found out. Discuss the issues presented in the article.

EXTRA ✏ Write a tweet expressing your opinion about the bee population.

 Writing a feature article

*In this unit, the text in focus is a **feature article**. Feature articles look at topics that have often been in the news for some time, exploring the background or causes. They appear in newspapers and magazines, in print or online. Over the next three pages, you will take the following steps to write a feature article.*

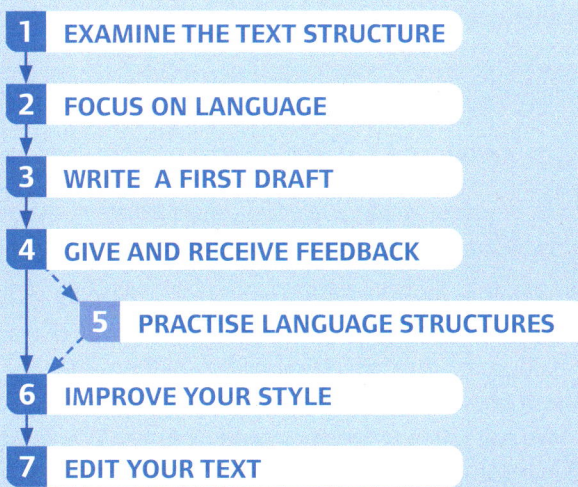

1 EXAMINE THE TEXT STRUCTURE
2 FOCUS ON LANGUAGE
3 WRITE A FIRST DRAFT
4 GIVE AND RECEIVE FEEDBACK
5 PRACTISE LANGUAGE STRUCTURES
6 IMPROVE YOUR STYLE
7 EDIT YOUR TEXT

---

1 **EXAMINE THE TEXT STRUCTURE**

Match the different elements of a feature article to the definitions.
1 headline · · presents the topic and shows that it is relevant or interesting
2 summary · · announces the topic in a catchy way
3 introduction · · finds a strong way to finish
4 main body · · sums up what the article will be about
5 conclusion · · presents facts in a logical series of paragraphs

Compare your results. Then, on a copy of the article, identify and highlight the different parts.

---

2 **FOCUS ON LANGUAGE**

a) In texts like feature articles, the author will often wish to define or describe, explain or comment. Find these words in the text on p. 62:
traps (l. 2) · products (l. 10) · humans (l. 25) · compensate (l. 43)
Identify the structure that follows them and say what it is used for.

b) Find other examples of these structures and say why the author uses them.

➡ *GAP 20: Relative clauses (p. 144)*

---

3 **WRITE A FIRST DRAFT**

a) Choose a topic that interests you, e.g. *climate change, local power generation, pilotless planes, …*

b) Research your topic on the internet and take notes.

c) Organize your material in an outline. Find images to go with your text.

d) Write your first draft, using a similar structure to the text on p. 62.

➡ *SMC 6: Making an outline (p. 167); SMC 10: Writing an article (p. 170); SMC 27: Finding information online (p. 183); SMC 41 Making and taking notes (p. 195)*

4 GIVE AND RECEIVE FEEDBACK

👥 Read your partner's first draft. Give feedback on
· the overall structure of the feature article (e.g. Does it have all the elements described in 1?)
· the effectiveness of different elements (e.g. Is the headline catchy? etc.)

Comment on the use of language in your partner's text.
If possible, suggest where they could improve their text by using relative clauses.

➡ *SMC 34: Giving feedback (p. 189)*

5 PRACTISE LANGUAGE STRUCTURES

1 REVISION Products that depend on bees ... (Defining relative clauses)

Use the information in brackets to add a relative clause where it makes sense in each sentence.
Use relative pronouns (*who, which, that*) where necessary. Leave them out where possible.

1 Products (...) fill the shelves of our food stores (...). (*They depend on bees.*)
   Products that/which depend on bees fill the shelves of our food stores.
2 Bees (...) help to produce the fruit and vegetables (...). (*We eat them.*)
3 The disappearance of bees (...) is a problem (...). (*It needs to be solved.*)
4 The experts (...) have pointed to different causes (...). (*They have investigated the problem.*)
5 Pesticides (...) are a big threat to bees (...). (*They are made to kill other insects.*)
6 The green spaces (...) are being eaten up by growing cities (...). (*Bees need them to survive.*)
7 One of the many problems (...) are the mites (...). (*They infect bees with disease.*)
8 Scientists (...) say the dangers (...) are not so great. (*They take a different view.*)

➡ *GAP 20.1–20.2: Relative clauses (p. 144)*

2 REVISION Global warming (Non-defining relative clauses)

Using a relative clause, rewrite each pair of sentences as one sentence,

1 Global warming has to be taken seriously. It is a huge threat to our future.
2 The world's oceans are under threat from rising temperatures. They are a source of food for millions.
3 Human beings must try to change their behaviour. They have already damaged our planet so much.
4 We should build a better infrastructure for cyclists. They help to reduce the levels of pollution.
5 Electric cars can also help to reduce air pollution. They are becoming more and more popular.
6 Wind energy is now being used in millions of homes. It is a clean source of power.

More help ▸ p. 92 ➡ *GAP 20.3: Relative clauses (p. 144)*

3 ..., which is bad news for polar bears (*which* referring to the main clause)

Add a relative clause to comment on each of the sentences.
1 Sea ice is melting.
2 Many people prefer holidays close to home.
3 Quite a few jobs could be done by robots.
4 A lot of younger people are eating less meat.
5 It costs more to produce organic food.
6 Some students volunteer before going to uni.

More help ▸ p. 92 Early finisher ▸ p. 97

➡ *GAP 20.4: Relative clauses (p. 144)*

Sea ice is melting, which is bad news for polar bears.

6 IMPROVE YOUR STYLE CONCISE LANGUAGE

A well-written article uses language economically, so try not to be too wordy.
Concise sentences are more readable and often have a stronger impact.

a) Read the first six lines of an earlier draft of the article on p. 62. Say how you think the author wants to change the highlighted parts.

b) Read the tips below. Explain which of them refer to the highlighted parts of the text.

> **TIP** Concise sentences
> To write more concise sentences …
> 1 Consider cutting parts of the text that give information that is already known.
> 2 Use contact clauses instead of relative clauses wherever possible.
> 3 If possible, include extra information in a clause instead of adding it in a separate sentence.
> 4 Find a single word with the same meaning to replace a group of words.

c) On a copy of the text, highlight the parts *you* would change. Note down your reasons.

d) Compare your ideas for changing the text.

e) Look at lines 5–20 of the text on p. 62. Compare your ideas for changes to the text with the changes the author made.
Discuss whether you wish to revise any of your changes.

Imagine the scene. You're walking through the supermarket. You have coffee, tomatoes, strawberries, oranges, apples and sunflower oil on your shopping list,
5 but you cannot find any of them in the supermarket. What's happened? Is it a weird dream, a nightmare perhaps? You pinch yourself and let out a cry. You're awake. Then you remember: all those
10 products that you are looking for are pollinated by bees, and the bees are dying. Without our friends the bees, harvests of many crops will be so much smaller and some crops that we need won't grow at all.

15 Since the beginning of the century, bee colonies have been disappearing around the world. Some years are worse than others. Quite a good example of a really bad year is 2015, when 42 percent of all
20 the colonies in the USA collapsed. There seems to be no single reason for this colony collapse disorder. Scientists call it CCD for short. They have identified several important factors and say that they all play
25 a role.

7 EDIT YOUR TEXT

a) Read your first draft again and consider
· your partner's feedback on it (step 4).
· relevant points from steps 5–6.
Make improvements where possible.

b) Mark two parts of your text you think could still be improved.
Ask one or two other students for advice.
Then make your final changes.

SMC 14: Revising texts (p. 173);
SMC 15: Revising and improving electronic texts (p. 174)

1 In the news

a) Describe the stills above. Explain who/what you think the news clip is about.

b) Watch the clip. Takes notes on
- the issue the report is about.
- the people shown in the report.
- why the issue is important to these people.

c) Watch the clip again. Take notes on the solutions that the people in the report want.

d) Say whether you think the people in the report will achieve their goals and explain why / why not.
- *Maybe a report like this will influence public opinion.*
- *Don't forget social media.*
- *…*

(www) Find out about the history of 'The news'.

2 Making the film: Elements of a news clip

a) 👥 Make a list of the different types of communication that are used in a news report.
- news reporters explain a situation
- music for atmosphere
- …

More help ▶ *p. 93*

b) 👥 💬 Watch the clip again. Say whether it uses the same types of communication as you listed in a). Add to your list if necessary.
Say if you think these different elements are important for understanding a report and explain why.

c) Read the two statements and say if they match the news clip.
"A news clip should always show both sides of an argument without emotion. A news reporter's job is to inform the public, not to comment."

"A news clip should speak to the viewer's emotions. It is acceptable to report only one side of an argument if it is the right side."

d) 👥 💬 Discuss your views of the statements in c).

EXTRA 🖊 Describe the sources you get news from. Are the reports you watch similar to the clip you've just watched? Explain why / why not.

ENERGY FOR THE FUTURE

The sun is already an important source of clean, solar energy, but the process which powers the sun itself, nuclear fusion, could hold the key to meeting humanity's energy needs.

Today's nuclear power is produced by nuclear fission – a dangerous, explosive process which splits atoms, creating heat and radioactive waste. Fusion, however, uses tremendous heat to force atoms together.

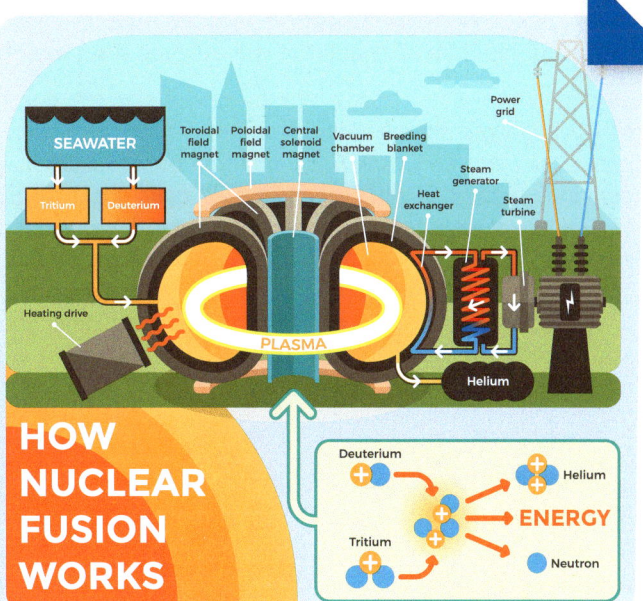

HOW NUCLEAR FUSION WORKS

THE BENEFITS

- The fuel for nuclear fusion can be obtained from seawater.
- The main waste from nuclear fusion is helium, which is harmless. The process itself makes the reactor radioactive but only for 100 years, not thousands of years like the waste from current nuclear power.
- As well as producing less dangerous waste, fusion does not carry the same risks as typical nuclear power plants – fusion cannot go out of control or melt down. A fusion power plant could be located in a city centre.
- Once the technology has been developed and perfected, fusion power will be a cheap, clean and endless source of power.

THE DRAWBACKS

- Fusion power is still in development; it will not help meet the urgent challenges of climate change which we are now facing.
- At the moment, fusion is not economical: it takes more energy to create fusion than the energy we get from it. Huge experimental reactors are being built and tested in France, Britain, the US and Japan, but the costs are huge. Cost effective fusion power could still be decades away.
- Climate campaigners argue the time and money spent on developing fusion now would be better spent increasing our use of solar, wind and hydro energy today.
- The costs and technology of fusion power mean it may always remain out of reach for the majority of our planet, who live in poorer countries.

Germany and nuclear power

👥 As part of a project on energy sources, you are working virtually with a student in Ireland.

Partner A: Turn to p. 103.

Partner B: Turn to p. 101.

Over to you

You choose 👥 Research topic a), b) or c). Then report back to your group.

a) Green hydrogen
b) Tidal power
c) Geothermal energy

1 **Maximum happy imagination** from *Mr. Penumbra's 24-Hour Bookstore* by Robin Sloan

a) Say what you think Clay and Kat will talk about on their first date.

> *Clay Jannon loses his job as a web designer when his company goes bankrupt. New jobs in IT are hard to find, so Clay is now working nights as a clerk in Mr. Penumbra's 24-hour bookstore in San Francisco. The strange thing is that the bookstore has few books for sale but many books that members come to borrow at all hours of the night. Clay's job is to record the details of the members' visits in a log book – why, he does not know.*
>
> *Clay sets up some Google ads to try and attract other customers and in this way meets Kat Potente, who works for Google. Later during the night, after she has left, Clay emails Kat and asks her out to lunch the next day.*

"… CALLED SINGULARITY SINGLES," Kat Potente is saying. She's wearing the same red and yellow BAM! T-shirt from before, which means (a) she slept in it, (b) she owns several identical

5 T-shirts, or (c) she's a cartoon character – all of which are appealing alternatives.

Singularity Singles. Let's see. I know (thanks to the internet) that the Singularity is the hypothetical point in the future where technology's

10 growth curve goes vertical and civilization just sort of reboots itself. Computers get smarter than people, so we let them run the show. Or maybe they let themselves …

Kat nods. "More or less."

15 "But Singularity Singles …?"

"Speed-dating for nerds," she says. "They have one every month at Google. The male-to-female ratio is really good, or really bad. Depends who – "

"You went to this."

20 "Yeah. I met a guy who programmed bots for a hedge fund. We dated for a while. He was really into rock-climbing. He had nice shoulders."

Hmm.

"But a cruel heart."

25 We are in the Gourmet Grotto, part of San Francisco's gleaming six-floor shopping mall. It's downtown, right next to the cable-car terminus, but I don't think tourists realize it's a mall; there's no parking lot. The Gourmet Grotto is its food

court, probably the best in the world: all locally 30 grown spinach salads and pork belly tacos and sushi sans mercury. Also, it's below ground, and it connects directly to the train station, so you never have to walk outside. Whenever I come here, I pretend I'm living in the future and the 35 atmosphere is irradiated and wild bands of biodiesel bikers rule the dusty surface. Hey, just like the Singularity, right?

Kat frowns. "That's the twentieth-century future. After the Singularity, we'll be able to solve those 40 problems." She cracks a falafel in two and offers me half. "And we'll live forever."

"Come on," I say. "This is just the old dream of immortality – "

"It is the dream of immortality. So?" She pauses, 45 chews. "Let me put it a different way. This is going to sound strange, especially because we just met. But, I know I'm smart."

That's definitely true –

"And I think you're smart, too. So why does that 50 have to end? We could accomplish so much if we just had more time. You know?"

I chew my falafel and nod. This is an interesting girl. Kat's utter directness suggests homeschooling, yet she is also completely charming. It helps, I 55 guess, that she's beautiful. I glance down at her T-shirt. You know, I think she owns a bunch that are identical.

"You have to be an optimist to believe in the

---

singularity *Theorie aus der Zukunftsforschung (Zeitpunkt, zu dem der technologische Fortschritt sich so beschleunigt hat, dass die Zukunft der Menschheit nicht mehr abgeschätzt werden kann)* **growth curve** *Wachstumskurve* **gleaming** *schimmernd, glänzend* **cable-car terminus** *Endhaltestelle der (gezogenen) Straßenbahn* **pork belly** *Schweinebauch* **sushi sans mercury** *quecksilberfreies Sushi* **irradiated** *verstrahlt* **smart** *schlau, intelligent* **immortality** *Unsterblichkeit* **chew** *kauen* **utter directness** *vollkommene Offenheit*

Singularity," she says, "and that's harder than it seems. Have you ever played Maximum Happy Imagination?"

"Sounds like a Japanese game show."

Kat straightens her shoulders. "Okay, we're going to play. To start, imagine the future. The good future. No nuclear bombs. Pretend you're a science fiction writer."

Okay: "World government … no cancer … hover-boards."

"Go further. What's the good future after that?"

"Spaceships. Party on Mars."

"Further."

"Star Trek. Transporters. You can go anywhere."

"Further."

I pause a moment, then realize: "I can't."

Kat shakes her head. "It's really hard. And that's, what, a thousand years? What comes after that? What could possibly come after that? Imagination runs out. But it makes sense, right? We probably just imagine things based on what we already know, and we run out of analogies in the thirty-first century."

I'm trying hard to imagine an average day in the year 3012. I can't even come up with a half-decent scene. Will people live in buildings? Will they wear clothes? My imagination is almost physically straining. Fingers of thought are raking the space behind the cushions, looking for loose ideas, finding nothing.

"Personally, I think the big change is going to be our brains," Kat says, tapping just above her ear, which is pink and cute. "I think we're going to find different ways to think, thanks to computers. You expect me to say that" – yes – "but it's happened before. It's not like we have the same brains as people a thousand years ago."

Wait: "Yes we do."

"We have the same hardware, but not the same software. Did you know that the concept of privacy is, like, totally recent? And so is the idea of romance, of course."

Yes, as a matter of fact, I think the idea of romance just occurred to me last night. (I don't say that out loud.)

"Each big idea like that is an operating system upgrade," she says, smiling. Comfortable territory. "Writers are responsible for some of it. They say Shakespeare invented the internal monologue."

Oh, I am very familiar with the internal monologue.

ROBIN SLOAN

Mr. Penumbra's 24-Hour Bookstore

CORNELSEN SENIOR ENGLISH LIBRARY

"But I think the writers had their turn," she says, "and now it's programmers who get to upgrade the human operating system."

I am definitely talking to a girl from Google. "So what's the next upgrade?"

"It's already happening," she says. "There are all these things you can do, and it's like you're in more than one place at one time, and it's totally normal. I mean, look around."

I swivel my head, and I see what she wants me to see: dozens of people sitting at tiny tables, all leaning into phones showing them places that don't exist and yet are somehow more interesting than the Gourmet Grotto.

"And it's not weird, it's not science fiction at all, it's …" She slows down a little and her eyes dim. I think she thinks she's getting too intense. (How do I know that? Does my brain have an app for that?) Her cheeks are flushed and she looks great with all her blood right there at the surface of her skin.

---

straighten straffen **cancer** Krebs *(Krankheit)* **physically straining** körperlich anstrengend **rake** absuchen **operating system upgrade** Update des Betriebssystems **internal monologue** innerer Monolog **swivel** drehen **dozen** Dutzend **dim** sich verdunkeln **intense** ernst **flushed** gerötet

"Well," she says finally, "it's just that I think the Singularity is totally reasonable to imagine."

150   Her sincerity makes me smile, and I feel lucky to have this bright optimistic girl sitting with me here in the irradiated future, deep beneath the surface of the earth.

2 Comprehension

a) Look at the questions below. Write short answers.

1 What is the Singularity?
2 What does Clay like about the shopping mall? Mention two points.
3 According to Kat, why is it difficult for people to imagine longer than 1,000 years into the future?
4 What change does Kat say is happening to humanity now and who is responsible for it?

b) Choose the correct answer a, b or c. Give evidence from the text to support your choice.

1 About the Singularity, Clay
   a) is more optimistic than Kat.
   b) has the same opinion as Kat.
   c) is a little pessimistic.
2 There aren't many tourists in the mall because
   a) they do not know it's a shopping mall.
   b) it's too far from the public transport.
   c) it's too far from the city centre.
3 Kat compares changes in human society to
   a) replacing old IT equipment with new equipment.
   b) installing new versions of computer programs.
   c) learning new concepts like privacy or romance.
4 Clay thinks people are staring at their phones
   a) because they don't want to talk to each other.
   b) because they are addicted to them.
   c) because they are dreaming of being somewhere else.

EXTRA 👥 💬 Play *Maximum happy imagination*.
👥 Share your predictions with another group.

3 Analysis

a) Look at the quotation below from the excerpt. Collect arguments for and against Kat's opinion that technology and maybe even the Singularity are an 'upgrade [to] the human operating system' (ll. 123–124).

"… dozens of people sitting at tiny tables, all leaning into phones showing them places that don't exist and yet are somehow more interesting than the Gourmet Grotto." (ll. 136–141)

b) 👥 Compare your arguments and add new arguments to your list.

4 Comment ✏

You choose ▶ a) or b).

Based on the arguments you collected in 3, write a blog entry for your school website explaining what the Singularity is, your view on it and your reasons. Depending on your personal opinion, your blog has the title:

a) The Singularity is coming, and we should be afraid

b) The Singularity is coming, and we should welcome it

c) EXTRA Post your blog on a class website. Read your classmates' blogs and have a class discussion.

1 Characterization

Authors can describe characters directly or indirectly.

- Direct characterization involves a straightforward description of a character's physical appearance, speech and actions, for example:
  Tom lost his temper. He hit the table with his hand. "Be quiet!" he shouted angrily.

- Indirect characterization allows us to see 'into' a character's inner feelings, personality or motivations. This can include the character's speech, their internal monologue (their inner thoughts) or descriptions of their body language:
  "That's enough", thought Tom to himself and, slamming his hand on the table, roared "Be quiet!"

Look at two quotations from the novel excerpts in this book. Say whether they are direct or indirect characterizations. For the indirect characterization, say what you learn about the character's inner feelings.
"[Joanna] just kept chatting calmly, although her eyes never left the box that the bag of candy was in. Her hands were busy turning her ring." (*Go and come back*, p. 36, ll. 32–34)

"She's wearing the same red and yellow BAM! T-shirt from before … she is also completely charming. It helps, I guess, that she's beautiful." (*Mr. Penumbra's 24-Hour Bookstore*, p. 68, ll. 2–3, ll. 55–56)

2 Atmosphere, tone and mood

A well-written text or well-drawn graphic novel will make you react emotionally, and these feelings can change as you read. Atmosphere can be generated by many things: descriptions of the weather and physical surroundings may be very detailed, making you feel like you are actually there; long sentences can convey a relaxed atmosphere and slow pace, short sentences can convey action and speed; the tone of the narrator can influence how you feel: a first-person narrator may 'talk' to the reader, making you feel like a friend, experiencing the same emotions as they do; a third-person narrator who knows more than the characters themselves may make you worry about the character because you know what could happen, but they don't.

3 Examining a text for evidence of characterization and atmosphere

Find and read these lines from the excerpt *Maximum happy imagination* on pp. 68–70.
Match the lines with the correct description.

1 ll. 25–39	a) The narrator uses rhetorical questions and metaphorical language to convey how hard he is trying to imagine the far future.
2 ll. 7, 57–58 and 118–119	b) The narrator's positive tone makes us feel that the date has gone well and that both characters are nice, optimistic people.
3 ll. 60–76	c) The description of the physical surroundings – it sets the scene and gives the text a futuristic atmosphere.
4 ll. 89–98	d) The back-and-forth dialogue between the characters conveys the speed of their talk and shows the characters are getting on well.
5 ll. 150–153	e) The narrator addresses the reader in a relaxed, informal way and even makes a joke about stylistic techniques in writing.

You choose a) or b). For both tasks, give evidence from the text to support your answers.
a) Describe your impression of Clay and say whether you would like him as a friend.
b) Imagine you are Kat. Describe your impression of Clay. Do you think you will go on another date with him?
c) 👥 💬 Work with a partner who did the other task. Decide how your impressions of the character were influenced by the narrative technique and stylistic elements such as characterization, atmosphere, etc.

Listening is a very important skill. In exams, your listening skills are tested by different types of task. On these two pages, you will practise four kinds of listening exercise.

1 You are going to listen to a news report on farming in New Zealand.
Before you do each task, read the tips.

a) **Listen to a news report. Choose the correct answer a, b or c. You can listen to the recording twice.**

> **TIP** Multiple choice tasks
>
> - Always read the task <u>carefully</u>. You will have some time (90–120 seconds) to do this before the audio begins.
>
> - On your first listen, mark the answers you are sure of. Use your second listen to focus on the answers you do not know. After your second listen, if you still do not know – guess!
>   Do not leave any task unanswered.
>
> - The audio text often uses synonyms of words in the task questions. Before you do the task below, think of synonyms for the following words:
>   *farming, important, half, three-quarters, discotheque, countryside, typical.*

Factfile

New Zealand – Aotearoa
Capital: Wellington
Pop.: 5 million
Languages: English, Māori

1 For New Zealand's economy, farming is
  a the most important industry.
  b more important than tourism.
  c the second most important industry.

2 Farming in New Zealand also
  a protects half of the country's wetlands.
  b produces half of the country's greenhouse gases.
  c provides half of the country's food.

3 Mark's farm is located
  a in an old discotheque in Auckland.
  b in his home in Auckland city centre.
  c in the countryside outside Auckland.

4 Per square metre, Mark's farm can grow
  a six times as many strawberries as a typical farm.
  b two times as many strawberries as a typical farm.
  c fewer strawberries than a typical farm.

b) **Listen to the second part of the report and complete the sentences in your exercise book.
You can listen to the recording twice.**

> **TIP** Sentence completion tasks
>
> - Think about the meaning of the sentence parts you are given. On your first listen, make short notes.
>
> - After your second listen, check your notes. Complete the sentences <u>using as few words as possible</u>.
>
> - Make sure your completed sentence makes sense.

1 Professor Highsmith says that once students see Mark's farm, they … .

2 She thinks that farming won't become more environmentally friendly unless … .

3 She takes her students to the farm because the activity there is forty percent farming knowledge … .

4 Professor Highsmith believes that farms like Mark's could solve global food issues and … .

2 You are going to listen to a podcast made by two British teens, Pete and Nawal.
Before you do each task below, read the tips.

a) Listen to the first part of the podcast. Complete the statements below by filling in the missing word(s). You can listen to the recording twice.

> **TIP** Gap filling tasks
> - Read the task for information on the topic of the audio. Knowing the topic can help you activate vocabulary you might need.
> - Read each statement, look for key words and their synonyms and say them to yourself.
> - Examine the gaps – predict what type of words or information could fill them, e.g. phrasal verbs, -*ing* forms, nouns, numbers, etc. Remember: a gap may need only one word or more.

1 The [1]... survey compared how [2]... younger and older people were about the world today and the future.

2 The results showed that [3]... were the more positive group.

3 However, in addition to climate change, they were concerned about [4]... and [5]....

4 Despite being positive about a world connected by the internet, less than a [6]... of young people trusted social media as a source of [7]....

5 While [8]... of younger people viewed themselves as global citizens, the percentage for older people was only [9]....

b) Listen to the second part of the podcast. You will hear five people expressing their views on the present and future. While listening, match five of the descriptions a–f with the speakers 1–5. There is one description more than you need. You can listen to the recording twice.

> **TIP** Matching tasks
> - It is very difficult to read and listen at the same time, so make sure to read the task very carefully <u>before</u> you listen. Identify the general themes you need to listen for and think of key vocabulary you might hear.
> - On your first listen, do not try to understand every single word. Try to understand the gist – the general meaning or 'bigger picture' instead. After your first listen, note the answers you are confident about and decide which of the alternatives you can ignore.
> - On your second listen, check your answers and concentrate on the parts you are less sure of.

a Prefers the present to the past, but is pessimistic about the future.

b Depressed by the fact that young people seem to care more about being popular than solving today's problems.

c Uncertain about the future and believes life has become more difficult and often overwhelming.

d Confident that humanity will make progress despite the challenges in today's world.

e Determined to improve the world and believes in the ability of youth to achieve it.

f Angry because young people have to live with the consequences of other people's actions.

Copy the table and write in your answers.

Speaker	1 Tim	2 Tina	3 Sunita	4 Alun	5 Seán
Description	...	...	...	...	

In a panel discussion, a small group of people discuss a topic of interest in front of an audience. The discussion is chaired by a moderator.
On this page, you will focus on skills that will help you to hold a good panel discussion.

1 The topic

Choosing a good topic will help to make a panel discussion successful. A good topic is one that
· appeals to the audience (e.g. it is interesting, relevant, controversial, …).
· is practical to research (e.g. it is focused, not too general; facts and arguments are available online; …).
Look at these four topics and discuss how well they meet the criteria above.
Then agree on a topic for a panel discussion.
· *We need to reduce air pollution.*   · *We should limit families to one child.*
· *Private cars should be banned.*   · *Overpopulation should concern us all.*

2 The roles

a) 🎧 Listen to three excerpts from a panel discussion.
   Decide which speaker is the moderator and which are panellists. Explain your answer.

b) 👥 Read these twelve tips. Make two lists of tips, one for panellists, one for the moderator.
   Some of the tips are good for both roles.

1 When presenting your position, refer to views already expressed.
2 Show respect when referring to the views of others, even if you disagree with them.
3 Introduce the topic and the panellists.
4 React to other panellists during the discussion, e.g. to support or to disagree with them.
5 Present your position in a structured way.
6 Make sure that all important aspects of the topic are discussed.

7 Make sure that everyone stays on topic.
8 State your position briefly in a provocative or catchy sentence.
9 Sum up and maybe comment, but without taking sides, and thank everyone at the end.
10 Make sure that everyone has an equal chance to speak.
11 If you prefer not to be interrupted with a question, say so firmly, but politely.
12 Invite questions from the audience.

3 The language

a) 🎧 Listen to six short excerpts from a panel discussion. Match each excerpt to a situation in 2b).

b) 🎧 Listen to each excerpt again. Write down a key phrase or sentence for each situation.
   1 I would like to remind you that our topic today is …   2 …

c) 👥 In groups of four collect key sentences for the situations in 2b).
   Partners A and B: Collect sentences for panellists.
   Partners C and D: Collect sentences for the moderator.
   TIP You can organize your sentences in a discussion fan.

4 The arguments

👥 💬 Discuss these tips. Explain why they might be important for panellists and/or the moderator.
1 Research the topic thoroughly.
2 Find arguments for your position and rank them from strong to weak.
3 Think of how the others may argue and what counter-arguments you could use.
4 During the discussion, take notes while you're listening.

➡ *SMC 23: Preparing and taking part in a panel discussion (p. 179)*

Workbook
Checkpoint
(pp. 52–5

Your task

Let's discuss this! 💬

The whole class will set up, take part in and give feedback on one or more panel discussions.

STEP 1 Advance planning
Make decisions on the following points:
· whether to invite an audience from outside your class (another class, other teachers, parents, …).
· the date, time and venue (classroom, school hall, …).
· furniture and seating (Where will the moderator, panellists and audience sit?).
· equipment (Will you need a microphone? A timer for the moderator? An internet connection?).
· how many topics to discuss; which topic(s).
Plan how to share responsibility for any arrangements you need to make.

STEP 2 Preparing for the discussion
a) Agree on a topic (or topics). Perhaps choose the topic you agreed on in 1 on p. 74.

b) Choose panellists and a moderator for each discussion you have planned.

c) Prepare for your roles on one or more panel discussions.

Panellists	Moderators
· Brainstorm aspects of your topic that might come up, and how best to research them. · Research your topic. · Rank your main arguments and decide how to structure your contribution. · Think about how to answer possible arguments from other panellists or questions from the audience.	· Decide what information you need as the moderator and research your topic. · Form a group with other moderators and discuss how to introduce your topic and the panellists. · Then discuss how you could summarize at the end.

d) 👥 At the end, you will give feedback on each discussion. Before the event, use a placemat to choose feedback criteria for the moderator or panellists.
Consider the tips from 2b) on p. 74 when discussing your criteria.
Then compare your ideas in class. For each role, make one final list for the whole class.

STEP 3 On stage
Hold your panel discussion(s).
· During the discussion(s), students in the audience should make notes for giving feedback.
· They can also note down any questions they wish to ask the panellists at the end of the discussion.
· At the end, the moderator questions the panellists before inviting questions from the audience.

STEP 4 Feedback
Using the list of criteria you prepared, give feedback on the discussions you watched.
Reflect on the feedback you receive and suggest anything you could improve next time.

➡ *SMC 23: Preparing and taking part in a panel discussion (p. 179); SMC 34: Giving feedback (p. 189)*

In exams and when you are in the *Oberstufe*, you will often have to work with a variety of challenging texts:

· **literary** texts, like excerpts from novels, short stories, poetry, drama, many autobiographies, …
· **image-based** texts, like graphic novels, posters, adverts, graffiti, …
· **non-fiction** texts, like news articles, comments, reviews, biographies, …

When working with these texts, you will be asked to:

· demonstrate that you understand them generally and in detail (**comprehension**)
  – *Tick the correct box and give evidence from the text by quoting short passages from the text.*
  – *Summarize what you get to know about the character's life and situation.*

· study how they are written and what effects this has on the reader (**analysis**)
  – *Analyse how the main character's feelings change over the course of the story and look at the way the story is told (narrative technique, use of language, etc.).*
  – *Explain why the character's relationship with his friends changes during the story.*

· Write a particular type of text giving an opinion, a reaction, or going beyond the text (**comment**)
  – *Comment on the title of the book and say whether you would like to read it. Explain why or why not.*
  – *You are the main character at the end of the excerpt:*
    Write a letter to your friend, Maria, telling her what has happened and what you plan to do.

On the following pages, you will read three different types of text. At the end of each text, there are tasks to help you practise the skills you need for exams now and in the *Oberstufe*.

---

literary [ˈlɪtərəri]   **biography** [baɪˈɒɡrəfi]

Text 1

What's in a name? (from *Finding Nevo* by Nevo Zisin)

When I was born, I was named Liat. Liat is a Hebrew name that my mum felt very strongly about, one that I grew to feel a deep connection with. It translates loosely into English as "You're mine". It was a special message from my mother to me. Those series of letters somehow became defining to who I was as a person.

Some trans people hate their birth names. There is a lot of associated trauma and distress and many refer to it as their "deadname". It is considered an act of transphobia to use someone's birth name without their consent. I have had mine used many times without consultation, in interviews and articles and by people who have decided it is too difficult to adjust to a new name. That name being used as a way of invalidating my identity has caused a bitter rift in my relationship with those people. Though truthfully, I love my birth name. Revealing that name to people is a recognition of closeness. So by choosing to include my birth name at this point in my book, I am allowing you to see a very guarded part of me.

There will always be a part of me that is Liat. I think of her almost as a little sister, and sometimes I miss her. When I refer to my past self, sometimes I use "she" pronouns and sometimes I use my old name. By no means does that give permission to anyone else to do the same. I exclusively use they/them and he/him pronouns now, and that is what I expect people to use when referring to me in the past. I know this sounds confusing, but I think it's okay to have a different set of rules for myself in relation to my gender and past than I do for others.

There is a part of me that wishes I could have kept my birth name. But as time went on, my name felt distant. I started to see it as a "girl's name" rather than my name. Out of the mouths of those I knew would not accept me it felt like a slur, an insult and total invalidation. When people said that I would always remain Liat to them, it felt like they would never see me for who I truly was, just merely the performance I had been. Once my name became my insult, there was no getting it back.

I spent a long time deciding on a name for the new me. It's difficult to choose your own name. I started making lists and searching Hebrew baby-name books. It was important to me that the name would be Hebrew as my Israeli heritage is central to my identity. I thought about Lior – close to my name; maybe too close. It would feel strange correcting people. Also, it's a gender-neutral name and it was very important to me to have a masculine name (whatever that means!). I read my list of new names to Tia. She didn't like any of them. But they were Hebrew and probably sounded very foreign and strange to her. I would have loved my mum to be a part of my name-choosing process, except she was not ready to face the reality of my transition.

I went away for the weekend to a Hebrew camp organised by my school, in which Israeli leaders came to teach us about topics relating to Israel. I asked one of them what her favourite Hebrew boy's name was and she said Nevo. And something about it felt right. I also loved that it could be shortened to Nev for those who

---

Hebrew [ˈhiːbruː] hebräisch   **associated** [əˈsəʊʃieɪtɪd] verbunden, zugehörig   **distress** Leid, Verzweiflung, Schmerz   **consultation** Absprache   **adjust to** sich einstellen auf, sich anpassen an   **invalidate** annullieren, entwerten   **rift** Kluft; Krise   **recognition** Anerkennung   **closeness** Nähe   **by no means** keinesfalls   **remain** bleiben   **truly** wirklich, wahrhaft(ig)   **merely** lediglich   **once** (*conj*) sobald   **heritage** [ˈherɪtɪdʒ] Erbe   **Tia** *an old and very close friend of Nevo's*   **transition** Wandel; Übergang

couldn't correctly pronounce it. I told my close friends and Tia and I started living more comfortably with myself.

75 But my mother didn't know my name. I left the house and was Nevo, authentically and truthfully, and at home I was Liat, quiet, sad and hidden. Eventually my mum found out my new first name, and I gave her the opportunity to choose my middle name. That is how 80 I became Nevo Amiel Zisin.

* * *

With the tension with my mum over gender issues, I avoided telling my dad I was trans. Similar to when I came out as a lesbian, I offered myself adjustment time between par-85 ent coming outs. We were at lunch when I decided to tell him. I could barely hear the conversation over the sound of my thumping heart. It was time.

Dad and I had always had a relationship that 90 might be described more stereotypically as father-son. We used to wrestle, go fishing and fly kites. Those aren't activities restricted to boys but I told myself becoming his son wouldn't change our relationship very much. At 95 the end of our meal, I quickly blurted out how I had been feeling. He took a moment, looked at me, and said something along the lines of, "I'd be lying if I said I was completely surprised. I will always support you no matter what. I just 100 want my kids to be happy." I couldn't believe the relief that followed. I thought he would understand but I didn't quite expect the degree.

It did however become clear that his initial reaction was perhaps more accommodating than he was feeling. He struggled with the new 105 reality, especially in conversations over medical intervention and he often tried to tell me how supportive he was, in a way that felt to me like he was congratulating himself.

People often tell my parents how incredible 110 they are for supporting me. While this is true, it certainly doesn't make me feel very good about what a "burden" I have been to my parents and how much they've had to "overcome" to accept me. This reinforced the feelings I had that I was 115 consciously bringing this selfish and hugely difficult transition onto my family as a way of being destructive. I had no choice in the matter; this was survival. Believe me, I am grateful for their support, but that doesn't mean I shouldn't 120 have expected it.

Accepting your child for who they are and being there for them, regardless of how difficult it may be, should not be placed on a pedestal.

* * *

---

authentic(ally) [ɔːˈθentɪk] echt, authentisch **adjustment** Anpassung **thump** klopfen **barely** kaum **wrestle** [ˈresl] ringen, kämpfen **fly kites** Drachen steigen lassen **restricted to** beschränkt auf **blurt sth. out** mit etwas herausplatzen **lie, lied, lied** lügen **relief** Erleichterung **accommodating** entgegenkommend **struggle with** ringen mit, sich abmühen mit **medical intervention** medizinische Eingriffe **congratulate** gratulieren **burden** Bürde, Last **reinforce** [ˌriːɪnˈfɔːs] verstärken **consciously** wissentlich, bewusst **selfish** egoistisch **grateful** dankbar **pedestal** Sockel

STEP 1 Comprehension

Task: Outline the process Nevo goes through while transitioning from Liat to Nevo.

· Look at aspects like parents' attitudes, gender pronouns, …
· Describe how Nevo gets his new full name.

STEP 2 Analysis

Task: Explain how the author influences your impression of Nevo in this passage.

· Take account especially of the narrative technique used.
· Illustrate your findings with quotations from the text.

STEP 3 Comment

You choose ▶ a), b) or c).

a) *Nevo says, "It was important to me that the name would be Hebrew as my Israeli heritage is central to my identity."* Reflect on what else can influence a person's identity.

b) You are Nevo and you have just finished the talk with your father at lunch (see ll. 85–102). Write an email to your friend, Ben, about the conversation.
Include the following aspects
· how you felt before the talk and why.
· your father's reaction.
· your feelings.

c) Comment on how important your own name is to you.
· Explain why you would or would not want to have a different name. What name might you choose? What would change for you if your name was different?

EXTRA 👥 Think about what can define a person's identity, e.g. nationality, fashion, taste in music, etc.
Then discuss this question:
If we don't share someone's identity, to what extent should we respect it?
How can we show respect for that identity?

take account of sth. etwas beachten

Text 2 **Excerpt from a graphic novel**

Working with graphic novels

Graphic novels tell stories just as prose novels do but with the added visual medium of illustrations. This means there are some features you will not find in traditional prose.

Panels: These divide the page into different parts and can be small or large.

Visual elements: Artists choose colour, shade, perspective or style of drawing as carefully as prose authors choose their words. Every visual element can add to the story being told.

Text: Captions contain scene-setting information such as time, location, etc., as well as the voice of the narrator if present. Characters' speech and thoughts are usually contained in bubbles. Sound effects are normally expressed with onomatopoeic words such as *bang, splash, chirp, screech*, etc.

Athlete to Mathlete (from *Messy Roots* by Laura Gao)

Laura Gao was born Yuyang Gao in Wuhan, China, and moved with her parents to Texas, USA, when she was four years old. The link between the Covid-19 pandemic and Gao's native Wuhan led to a rise in anti-Chinese racism in the United States. In response Gao published a short comic on Twitter called 'The Wuhan I know', describing her relationship with the city. The huge positive response to her comic inspired her to write and draw Messy Roots, *her memoir. The novel describes her experience growing up and coming of age in Texas as a Chinese American immigrant and also as a queer woman.*

Look at the first two pages of the excerpt. What is your first impression of Laura?

👥 Compare. (Note: Blue speech bubbles indicate the characters are speaking Chinese.)

---

messy chaotisch, unordentlich **roots** Vorfahren / Haarwurzeln **pick up sth.** etwas lernen **elementary school** Grundschule **unique** einzigartig **nainai** Chinesisch für Großmutter **short-lived** von kurzer Dauer **middle school** Mittelschule (Klassen 6–8) **chink** rassistische Bezeichnung für Menschen chinesischer Abstammung

MVP *(Most valuable player)* bester Spieler **attaboy** guter Junge **crickets** Grillengezirpe **snicker** Kichern **Yang Yang** *Spitzname in der Familie für Yuyang/Laura* **barely** kaum
** *Der rote Knoten, der im Auto hängt, ist ein chinesischer Glücksbringer.*

fit in einfügen   **How dare you!** Was fällt dir ein!   **butt heads with sb.** mit jdm. aneinandergeraten   **stubborn** stur
YMCA *gemeindebasierte Wohltätigkeitsorganisation*   **kick off** beginnen   **trade in sth. for sth.** etwas für etwas in Zahlung geben
TI-84 *Taschenrechner*   **Jordans** *Basketball Schuhe*   **run laps** Runden laufen   **fweet** *Pfeifton*

flawless makellos

STEP 1 Comprehension
Task: Outline the challenges Laura faces as she begins middle school and how she deals with them.
Look at aspects such as the differences between her old and new schools, her new schoolmates' and her parents' attitudes, Laura's reactions, …

STEP 2 Analysis
Task: Analyse how Laura's feelings change over the course of the story and how they are conveyed.
Look at aspects such as the narration in the captions, dialogue and visual aspects including close-ups, long shots, use of colour, …

STEP 3 Comment
You choose ▸ a) or b).

a) You are Laura. Write your diary entry after you get home from the 6th grade awards ceremony.
   Look at aspects such as why you didn't collect your award, your feelings towards your schoolmates and your parents, and mention your plan for dealing with the situation.

b) You are Laura at the end of the excerpt. Write an email to an old friend from McCoy Elementary.
   Include the following aspects: explain your decision to play basketball and your hopes for the future.

EXTRA 👥 In some ways Laura changes herself to fit in at Coppell.
Discuss how important you think it is to fit in?
How much would you change about yourself if you had to move to a new school, city or country?

Text 3

The Crowdfunded Conservationist
Who Wants to Save the World

*Has a young Dutchman found the solution
to all that plastic in our oceans?*

Ten miles from the Dutch coast, near the top of a concrete high-rise in downtown Delft, is a palatial glass-walled office better suited to Silicon Valley than a 13th-century city. The building is
5 home to the Ocean Cleanup, a foundation created in 2013 that is hoping to deploy a giant 62-mile-wide filtration device in the Pacific Ocean, the initial step in an effort to rid the seas of plastic. When I visited the Netherlands last June for the
10 launch of a scaled-down prototype, I found the CEO, 22-year-old Boyan Slat, slumped in a cubicle. His shaggy hair gave him the look of either a boy-band star or an eccentric genius, depending on your opinion of him – and these
15 days there are a few.

Slat is a new breed of environmentalist: young, crowdfunded, and tired of waiting around for government solutions. Still, he's less a traditional ocean conservationist than a natural engineer.

When he was 12, he set a Guinness World Record 20 for the most water rockets launched simultaneously: 213.

Slat's inner environmentalist didn't come alive until he was 16, when he began scuba diving on a trip to Greece. Expecting to see an array of sea 25 creatures, he instead saw a slew of plastic trash. The experience was life changing. Slat, who would soon drop out of Delft University of Technology to focus on the issue full-time, remembers thinking, *This plastic problem, I want to know more about it.* 30

The news was grim. About nine million tons of plastic waste makes its way into the oceans each year – by 2050, plastic will outweigh fish. Making matters worse, much of the debris has been broken down by wind, waves, and sun into tiny 35 microplastics, which are extremely difficult to remove.

---

conservationist Umweltschützer/in   **a concrete high-rise** ein Betonhochhaus   **palatial** [pəˈleɪʃl] palastartig   **suited to** geeignet für, passend zu   **foundation** Stiftung   **deploy** stationieren, installieren   **filtration** Filterung   **rid sth. of sth.** etwas von etwas befreien   **scaled-down** verkleinert   **CEO (chief executive officer)** Hauptgeschäftsführer/in   **slump** zusammensacken   **cubicle** Bürozelle   **shaggy** struppig, zottelig   **either … or …** entweder … oder …   **genius** Genie   **breed** Art, Sorte   **rocket** Rakete   **scuba diving** Sporttauchen, Gerätetauchen   **array** [əˈreɪ] Ansammlung, Anordnung   **slew** *(infml)* Menge   **grim** düster   **outweigh sth.** etwas übertreffen *(an Gewicht)*   **debris** [ˈdebriː] Abfall

As Slat's obsession grew, he gravitated to the infamous Great Pacific Garbage Patch, a vast area between Hawaii and the North American continent, where it has been estimated that 170,000 tons of plastic rubbish swirl in the currents. He contacted marine engineers, scientists, and experts to talk about cleaning up the Garbage Patch. Everyone told him the problem was unsolvable. Dozens of other entrepreneurs were also searching for a solution, to no avail.

A breakthrough came when he discovered the work of American oceanographers Curtis Ebbesmeyer and Jim Ingraham, who, in the 1990s, tracked the movement of a lost consignment of 29,000 rubber bath toys as they floated across the Pacific, corralled by the current. If ocean flotsam remained grouped together, says Slat, "why can't you just stay put and let the plastic come to you?"

In 2013, Slat developed the Ocean Cleanup Array, a moored, 62-mile V-shaped floating barrier (think of a giant pool noodle with a five-foot fin extending below the water's surface), which will lie across a plastic-laced stretch of Pacific current and funnel the trash to its vertex, where a silo-like receptacle will then catch and store the debris. The barrier, Slat says, will reduce the Garbage Patch by half in less than a decade. Early estimates put the cost of the array at $330 million.

After a TED Talk Slat gave in 2013 went viral, he launched his first crowdfunding campaign, raising $80,000 in 15 days. A second effort, in 2014, brought in $2.1 million from 38,000 donors, including $600,000 from the Dutch government.

At his office in Delft, no one seemed concerned that, apart from the prototype, the barrier remains conceptual (its launch is scheduled for late 2020), nor were they bothered by the Ocean Cleanup's partnership with fossil-fuel giants Boskalis and SBM Offshore, which are contributing materials and engineering expertise. "We're trying to get the point across that we can't just not talk to them," said 31-year-old Bruno Sainte-Rose, the project's lead computation modeler, referring to other big industry players. "If they come with a couple of million dollars, we're interested."

Not surprisingly, the Ocean Cleanup's funding philosophy and lofty goals have met with criticism. Kim Martini, a University of Washington oceanographer who often satirizes what she sees as Slat's boyish naiveté on the blog Deep Sea News, has written the project off as unfeasible, due to concerns about the prototype. Marcus Eriksen goes even further, suggesting that the Ocean Cleanup could do more harm than good, diverting resources from efforts to keep plastics out of the ocean in the first place.

Eriksen cofounded the 5 Gyres Institute, a Culver City, California, nonprofit that focuses on activism, research, and education, to fight plastic pollution at the corporate and government level. He says the problem has been described inaccurately, thanks in part to organizations like the Ocean Cleanup. "It's not a patch, and it's not a soup either," Eriksen told me. "It's a plastic smog. And like the smog in our atmosphere, just cleaning it up is not a viable solution." He believes money and effort should go toward policy instead of what he considers pie-in-the-sky innovation. "When the Clean Air Act came into play, it set high standards for what's tolerable in terms of emission controls. You saw gasguzzlers come off the roads, standards for coal-burning plants, corporations innovate. There was no one saying, 'Let's suck carbon out of the atmosphere.' "

---

gravitate to sich angezogen fühlen von   **infamous** [ˈɪnfəməs] berüchtigt   **patch** Fleck   **estimate** (v) schätzen; (n) Schätzung   **swirl** wirbeln   **current** Strömung   **entrepreneur** [ˌɒntrəprəˈnɜː] Unternehmer/in   **to no avail** vergeblich, erfolglos   **consignment** Sendung **float** treiben   **corralled** [kəˈrɑːld] eingefangen, eingepfercht   **flotsam** Treibgut   **stay put** an Ort und Stelle bleiben   **moored** vertäut **a plastic-laced stretch** ein plastikhaltiger Abschnitt   **funnel** *(durch einen Trichter)* leiten   **vertex** Scheitelpunkt   **receptacle** Behältnis **donor** Spender/in   **apart from** abgesehen von   **be bothered** [ˈbɒðəd] beunruhigt sein, sich gestört fühlen   **lofty** stolz   **unfeasible** nicht durchführbar   **divert** ablenken   **suck** saugen   **computation modeler** *jemand, der für Berechnungsmodelle zuständig ist*

Slat regards his critics the way a teenager greets parents who just don't get it. "Even if we stopped producing plastics today, ocean-born microplastics will still increase twentyfold or more over the next few decades if we don't do anything," he told me. We were in the galley of the Estrella, a battered fishing boat hired for the day to ferry a scrum of journalists out to witness the 328-foot prototype's mooring in the North Sea, 14 miles from the Dutch coast. It was dawn, and the faint silhouettes of wind turbines were visible on a stormy horizon. Slat apologized for the plastic cup that held my steaming coffee. "It's everywhere," he said, wringing his hands.

"Human history is a list of things that couldn't be done and then were done," he continued. "The way you advance a technological society is to try things – to be controversial and contrarian in your thinking in order to get to something that eventually people say, 'I told you it was a great idea.'"

Three months later, the prototype was pulled from the water for maintenance after engineers detected damage from heavy wind and waves. "When ideas are confronted with reality," Slat wrote on the Ocean Cleanup's website, "there will always be surprises."

satirize satirisch verspotten   write sth. off as unfeasible etwas als undurchführbar abtun/abschreiben   harm Schaden   divert resources [daɪˈvɜːt] Mittel/Ressourcen umlenken   corporate Unternehmens-   level Ebene   viable realisierbar, brauchbar   pie-in-the-sky Luftschlösser   Clean Air Act Gesetz zur Luftreinhaltung (USA)   in terms of ... was ... betrifft   gasguzzler (AE, infml) Benzinfresser   plant Werk, Fabrik   regard betrachten   twentyfold zwanzigfach   galley Kombüse, Bordküche   battered ramponiert   scrum Gedränge   witness sth. etwas miterleben, Zeuge bei etwas sein   dawn Morgengrauen   faint blass   apologize sich entschuldigen   steam dampfen   advance sth. etwas vorantreiben, voranbringen   contrarian nonkonformistisch   maintenance Wartung

STEP 1 Comprehension

Task: Write a profile of Boyan Slat and explain his mission.
- Read the task carefully. You will need to write about two things: Boyan Slat the person and his project.
- Scan the text to identify the relevant content.
- Pay attention to the adjectives and nouns the author uses to describe Slat. These words can help you better understand what kind of person he is. They might also help you describe him.

STEP 2 Analysis

Task: Analyse whether or not the author of the article has presented a balanced view of Boyan Slat's project, its supporters and critics.
- First, identify the place in the article where the author presents criticism of the project.
- Then list the arguments for and against Slat's project and the ways the author of the article presents these arguments.
- Support your analysis with quotations.

STEP 3 Comment

You choose a), b) or c).

a) Comment on Slat's Ocean Cleanup project. Explain why you would or wouldn't support his project.

b) Comment on the role the internet and crowdfunding has played in the realization of the Ocean Cleanup project. Discuss the potential advantages and disadvantages of this type of fundraising and consciousness-raising.

c) Not everyone can start a project like Boyan Slat. However, as individuals we constantly make decisions that affect our environment.
Discuss different ways in which we, as consumers, can take on responsibility for the environment.

EXTRA 🖵 Watch a video about the Ocean Cleanup.
- Summarize what you see. Say
  - who is speaking and what their message is.
  - what audience they want to reach.
  - what the aim of the video is.

- Give examples of the film techniques in the video and explain why they are used.
  Describe the effect the video has on you.

- If you were making a video about a cause you support, which techniques would you borrow from this video? What would you do differently?

---

consciousness-raising Bewusstseinsbildung, Sensibilisierung

5 Painting with words

◀ *p. 15* **Part A**

b) Read the tip on p. 15. Then look at these images and decide if they are similes or metaphors.

From "I Come From" — *I come from shepherd's pie and Sunday roast*

Roar — *You hear my voice ... like thunder · I got the eye of the tiger · I'm floating like a butterfly · [I'm] stinging like a bee · I went from zero, to ...*

Read the poems on p. 14 again. Look for other examples of imagery.
Think about the words and describe the images they create in your mind.

2 Collocations (Adverbs and adjectives as modifiers)

◀ *p. 16* **Access to words**

Read these sentences about the people in 1. Use an adjective/adverb to make the meaning stronger, and one to make it weaker. The third adjective/adverb doesn't fit.

The man:
- *I'm proud to be Scottish.* ——————— extremely · little · quite
- *I'm a fan of Manchester United.* ——————— great · large · not particularly
- *People say I'm ambitious.* ——————— not really · really · unfortunately

The woman:
- *I am passionate about the environment.* ——————— fairly · really · sadly
- *One place that has influenced me is Paris.* ——————— carefully · particularly · somewhat
- *I'm hoping to study the violin.* ——————— extremely · not particularly · really

1 REVISION Statements and arguments (Simple present, simple past)

◀ *p. 20* **Part B Practice**

a) Correct the highlighted mistakes.

1 Equal pay for equal work is a basic right. If a woman doesn't earns as much as a man doing the same job, this is discrimination. It exist in many countries.

2 Here in the UK we have a long history of discrimination at the workplace. In 1970, the Equal Pay Act has made it illegal to discriminate on pay. But my grandma has worked in a factory in the 1970s and 80s. And she don't earned as much as men in the same job.

3 So is the situation better today? Sadly, discrimination against women are still found. Today, the average woman earn 18.1 percent less than the average man. And the pay gap is even bigger for a woman who take time off to have children. Twelve years after she is having her first baby, the gap between her and a man can reaches 33 percent!

4 Where do I got these facts? I didn't made them up. I found them in a report from the Office of National Statistics that has come out just last year, half a century after the Equal Pay Act has became law.

5 So the question is: why exists still a pay gap between men and women?
If you're thinking this question is important, you should raise your voice in protest.

3 Discussion (Adjectives and nouns)

◀ p. 22 **Part C**

b) Discuss the difference between personal and genetic identity. These ideas might help you:

Think of twins (with identical DNA) who are adopted by two different families, in different parts of the world, with a different education, different amounts of money, different religions, …

Are they still identical?

Which of these characteristics are connected to personal identity and which to genetic identity? Group the words in a mind map.

culture · development · education · environment ·
eye colour · growth · hair colour · health ·
language · money · religion · skin ·
way of life · where you live

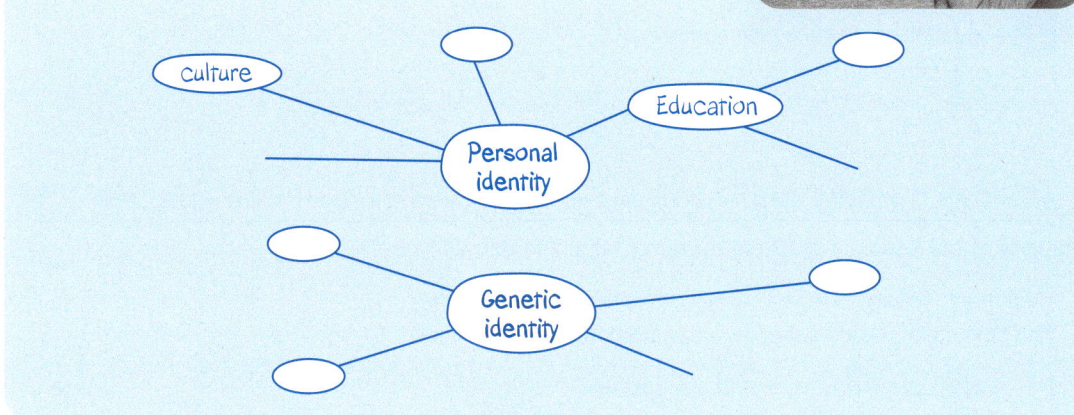

2 Making the film: Influencing an audience

◀ p. 27 **The world behind the picture**

b) Watch two scenes again. In which scene do these things happen, and in which order?

The music:

creates tension · fades out ·
grows louder in a crescendo ·
is relaxed · is quieter again when
the people speak · is simple and slow ·
moves us and perhaps makes us cry ·
reaches a climax · reflects the
mood of the people

What we see and hear:

happy faces · cheering ·
whistling · applause · laughter ·
the same slow music, but much louder ·
a single instrument, perhaps
a synthesizer · You don't really
notice the background.

1 Coming together

← p. 32 **Lead in**

b) 👥 These words might help you. Look them up in the Dictionary if you are unsure of their meanings.

> **A** market · buy/sell · +trader · +customer

> **B** hang out · +socialize

> **C** have a debate · +House of Commons (+lower house in the UK parliament)

> **D** +carols · Christmas · choir

> **1** +participate · religious · +ritual · +Holi (the Hindu festival of colours)

> **2** protester · march · fight for a +cause · take a +stand

> **3** buy/sell · +shares · goods · +stock · +stock market · trade · +traders

> **4** social media · online community

2 Meeting the host family (Indirect speech: advise, promise, suggest)

← p. 38 **Part A Practice**

Use one of the words in brackets to report what the people say.

1 Host mum: "Please take your shoes off in the house, Lauren." (ask · offer)
The host mum asked Lauren to take her shoes off in the house.

2 Host dad: "Let me take your suitcase upstairs." (invite · offer)

3 Nawal: "We should go into the living room." (suggest · promise)

4 Host mum: "Come on a tour of Frankfurt with us tomorrow." (refuse · invite)

5 Host dad to host mum: "Miriam, we should speak German to Lauren." (advise · ask)

6 Lauren: "No, no. I don't want to speak any German today. I'm too tired!" (suggest · refuse)

7 Nawal: "OK, Lauren. Have a rest now. I will wake you up in two hours." (ask · promise)

> **REMEMBER**
> · change pronouns (e.g. I => she/he)
> · most of the verbs are followed by a to-infinitive, but suggest is followed by a gerund

1 Talking about time (Participle clauses with *after, before, since, …*) ← *p. 44* | **Part B Practice**

Complete with verbs in the right form. Use participle clauses with the conjunction given.

1 Joanna **returns** to the States. Before that, she **takes** Alicia up in a small plane.
   Before returning to the States, Joanna … Alicia up in a small plane. (return, take)

2 Joan Abelove **returned** home. Twenty-five years later, she **wrote** her first novel.
   Twenty-five years **after** … home, Joan Abelove … her first novel. (return, write)

3 J. K. Rowling **published** her first novel in 1997. She **has sold** over 450 million books.
   Since … her first novel in 1997, J. K. Rowling … over 450 million books. (publish, sell)

4 Harry Potter **travels** to Hogwart's School. He **makes** friends with Ron Weasley.
   While … to Hogwart's School, Harry Potter … friends with Ron Weasley. (travel, make)

5 Jake, the hero, **leaves** home one morning. He **sees** a strange box on the steps.
   When … home one morning, Jake, the hero, … a strange box on the steps. (leave, see)

6 Sue **invites** Alex for a goodbye drink. Then she **leaves** England for Australia.
   Sue … Alex for a goodbye drink **before** … England for Australia. (invite, leave)

3 Talking about connected actions (Participle clauses meaning *and* …) ← *p. 44* | **Part B Practice**

Using participle clauses and verbs in the correct form, rewrite the sentences in two different ways. Then go back to p. 44 and try sentences 5 and 6.

1 The women **live** with the local people **and** **study** their way of life.
   a) The women live with the local people, studying their way of life.
   b) Living with the local people, the women … their way of life.

2 The author **describes** small-town life **and** **paints** a fun picture of local characters.
   a) The author … small-town life, … a fun picture of local characters.
   b) … small-town life, the author … a fun picture of local characters.

3 The plot **develops** quickly **and** **holds** the reader's interest.
   a) The plot … quickly, … the reader's interest.
   b) … quickly, the plot … the reader's interest.

4 The hero **wanders** around the town **and** **looks for** a place to eat.
   a) The hero … around the town, … a place to eat.
   b) … around the town, the hero … a place to eat.

3 More help

2 REVISION The right position (Sequence of adverbials) ← p. 60 | Part A Practice

Rewrite the sentences including the adverbials in the correct position.
👥 Compare your answers with a partner.

1 I ... attend music classes ... .   (twice a week, usually)
2 You should ... read the label ... before buying a product.   (always, carefully)
3 I have ... read such nonsense ... .   (in a book, in my whole life, never)
4 ... you can come ... if you'd ... like to.   (of course, really, to the party)
5 Tom and Jane have ... arrived, but ... we're ... waiting for Jake.   (just, still, unfortunately)
6 ... we don't ... have hurricanes ... .   (in the British Isles, luckily, often)

2 REVISION Global warming (Non-defining relative clauses) ← p. 64 | Part B Practice

Using a relative clause in the gap, rewrite each pair of sentences as one sentence.

> **REMEMBER**
> Only use *who* or *which* in a non-defining relative clause. Don't use *that*.
> Separate the non-defining relative clause from the main clause with commas.

1 Global warming ... has to be taken seriously.   It is a huge threat to our future.
2 The world's oceans ... are under threat from rising temperatures.   They are a source of food for millions.
3 Human beings ... must try to change their behaviour.   They have already damaged our planet so much.
4 We should build a better infrastructure for cyclists ...   They help to reduce the levels of pollution.
5 Electric cars ... can also help to reduce air pollution.   They are becoming more and more popular.
6 Wind energy ... is now being used in millions of homes.   It is a clean source of power.

3 ..., which is bad news for polar bears (*which* referring to the main clause) ← p. 64 | Part B Practice

Add a relative clause to comment on each of the sentences.
You can choose some of the ideas in brackets.

1 Sea ice is melting.
   (bad news for polar bears / water levels are rising / can cause climate change)
2 Many people prefer holidays close to home.
   (better for the environment / make travel cheaper / good for local business)
3 Quite a few jobs could be done by robots.
   (more free time for people / people lose jobs / fewer mistakes)
4 A lot of younger people are eating less meat.
   (positive effect on health / we need less land to produce food / good for the environment)
5 It costs more to produce organic food.
   (reason why some farmers haven't changed to organic farming / more expensive for shoppers)
6 Some students volunteer before going to uni.
   (useful experience/ older when they start work / benefits lots of people)

2 Making the film: Elements of a news clip ← p. 66   **The world behind the picture**

a) Look at the stills below. For each still, note down the way information was communicated.
Think about
  • camera work (long shot, medium shot, close-up, etc.).
  • film material (e.g. Does the report use footage of earlier events?).
  • the spoken word (the reporter explains a situation, people are interviewed, etc.).
  • other sounds (e.g. music, singing, etc.).
  • the use of text (captions on screen, shots of text).

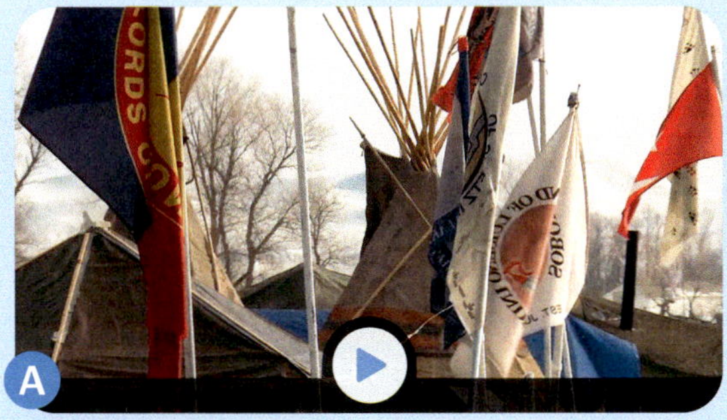

Writing a limerick

← p. 14, exercise 4 **Part A**

a) A limerick is a traditional form of funny (sometimes rude) rhyme which follows certain rules. Read this example by Edward Lear (1812-1888) to yourself and answer the questions.

> There was an Old Man with a beard,
> Who said, 'It is just as I feared!
> Two Owls and a Hen,
> Four Larks* and a Wren*,
> Have all built their nests in my beard!

· Lines 1, 2 and 5 must rhyme, how many syllables are there in each line?
· Lines 3 and 4 must rhyme, how many syllables are there in each line?

b) Rewrite the following limerick with the words in order so that they follow the rhyming rules:

> was there from a man young Cologne
> the called his best on phone who friend:
> let's walk for a go,
> have talk and a good,
> better much alone being than it's.

c) Now compose your own limerick, keeping in mind the stress and rhyming rules. You can choose your own beginning or start with *"There once was a student called …"*

Similes

← p. 15, exercise 6 **Part A**

Create pairs using the expressions in the box to make English similes and match them with their definitions.

Example: This describes someone who has a very high opinion of themselves ⟶ as proud as a peacock

1 This describes someone who is extremely worried and nervous
2 Behaving carelessly and clumsily
3 Someone who refuses to change their mind
4 To be so confident that you don't care what others think
5 To be calm even in stressful and difficult situations
6 Describes a task that is very simple to achieve
7 An expression used mainly to describe children who behave very well

peacock · like a cat · as cool as a · pie · like a bull · as stubborn as a · brass · in a china shop · as proud as a · gold · as bold as · mule · as good as · as easy as · cucumber · on a hot tin roof · like a bull

---

lark Lerche **wren** Zaunkönig **bold** wagemutig **brass** Messing **china** Porzellan **clumsily** tollpatschig **cucumber** Gurke
mule Maultier **peacock** Pfau **stubborn** stur **tin** Blech

DNA manipulation

← p. 24, exercise 1 | Part C Practice

a) Choose a verb from the box to complete the sentences.

1. New methods of manipulating DNA ... by scientists every day, it seems.
2. Here, genetic material ... from a human cell.
3. DNA sequences ... by a scientist looking for damaged genes that can lead to disease.
4. The disease-causing gene ... with a good copy from a healthy cell.
5. The question of whether we should change our genetic code ... still ... today.

discover ·
replace ·
extract ·
discuss ·
examine

b) Match the sentences to the pictures below.

Advertising slogans

← p. 27, exercise 2 | **The world behind the picture**

a) Write these mixed-up slogans in the order you think best and match them with their product.

1. to fresh success leads breath
2. a journey getting than A is just more from to B
3. pocket life your whole in your keep
4. your healthy way day the start

b) Create your own slogans for the two pictures that don't have one.

Where was it said?

← p. 38, exercise 2

Part A Practice

a) Match each statement with the place where it might be said or written, for example *H9*.

A	B	C
I think Tim needs some extra maths lessons.	If you do that again, you'll get a red card!	Dear passengers, the next service to London will be delayed by ten minutes.
D	**E**	**F**
No, it's my toy – I won't give it to Linda, it's mine.	Madam, our pasta is homemade and very tasty, I think you'll like it.	Take this medicine and rest at home for three days.
G	**H**	**I**
Mark and Robert, please concentrate on the task.	Mel & Leo, We would be delighted if you could attend our wedding.	We will give you €50 for your old phone, when you buy a new model.

1	2	3
A football pitch	A classroom	A parent-teacher meeting
4	**5**	**6**
A restaurant	A doctor's clinic	A kindergarten
7	**8**	**9**
A train platform	An advertisement	A formal invitation

b) Use the following verbs to report the statements in the light blue squares.

1 invite · 2 offer · 3 warn · 4 announce · 5 advise · 6 tell · 7 refuse · 8 suggest · 9 recommend

Example: 1 *The couple invited Mel and Leo to their wedding.*

Presentation tips

← p. 52, exercise 2

Access to words

Match two boxes to make a presentation tip. Write the tips in your exercise book.

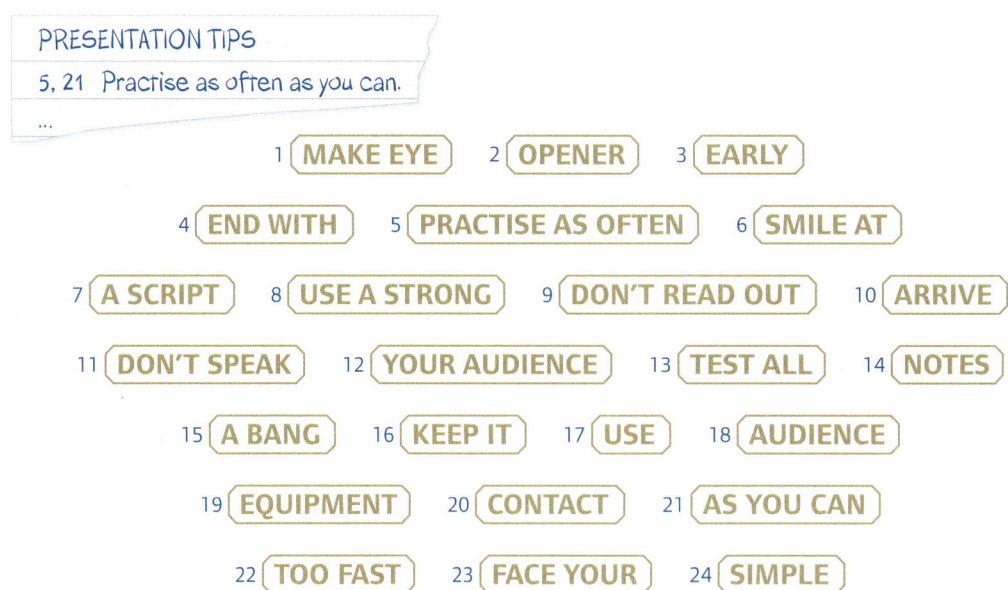

PRESENTATION TIPS

5, 21 Practise as often as you can.

...

1 MAKE EYE   2 OPENER   3 EARLY
4 END WITH   5 PRACTISE AS OFTEN   6 SMILE AT
7 A SCRIPT   8 USE A STRONG   9 DON'T READ OUT   10 ARRIVE
11 DON'T SPEAK   12 YOUR AUDIENCE   13 TEST ALL   14 NOTES
15 A BANG   16 KEEP IT   17 USE   18 AUDIENCE
19 EQUIPMENT   20 CONTACT   21 AS YOU CAN
22 TOO FAST   23 FACE YOUR   24 SIMPLE

Adjectives to adverbs

← p. 60, exercise 3 **Part A Practice**

Rewrite the sentences using adverbs instead of the highlighted adjectives.
Make any necessary changes. One example has been done for you.

1 I wish my dog wasn't so noisy in the morning, barking at me for her walk.
   I wish my dog wouldn't bark at me so noisily in the morning.

2 We're very lucky to have such good weather on the day of our football.

3 It's quite normal for us to watch two films in a row on Saturdays.

4 Frank told Sally the bad news in a very gentle way.

5 Ben and Kevin are both allergic to nuts and milk.

6 Try not to use such a glum voice when you're giving your presentation.

7 Anish is a popular student and his classmates have a high opinion of him.

8 He came into the room and gave us an awkward smile.

9 She is always so passionate when playing the piano.

10 Try to be more respectful when you speak to your parents.

11 The rain was so heavy that it caused serious flooding.

Communication and social media

← p. 61, exercise 3 **Access to words**

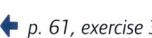

c) What would you say are the features of a good app? Rank these features according to how
   important they are to you, and add more features if you like.

> · it does something cool   · it's secure   · it looks attractive   · it's cheap/free
>
> · it's easy to navigate   · it's fast   · it works offline

Change one letter

← p. 64, exercise 3 **Part B Practice**

Change one letter of each word to get a word that matches the definition.
Write the new words on a piece of paper and underline the changed letters.
The underlined letters make up a three-word sentence. What is it?

1 JOG   Some students have one in the school holidays.

2 RISK   Move higher.

3 PAT   Don't do this with your hands, use a knife and fork.

4 TEA   This is salty.

5 MEET   Vegetarians don't like this.

6 GLOW   As you do this, you become taller.

7 HUGS   Extremely large

8 PAUSE   This has an effect.

9 PRINT   Use your finger to show where.

10 SAME   Not all

11 LEVER If you play well, you'll get to a higher one.

2 What do flags mean?

◄ *p. 26*

United Kingdom: The Union Flag

The Union Flag (or Union Jack) is one of the world's oldest national flags. It combines three different symbols.

England: Red cross on white field

5 Scotland: White diagonal cross on blue field

Ireland: Red diagonal cross on white field

The flag stands for the unity of the different nations of the United Kingdom.

Original Union Flag (1606–1800)

Irish Flag (1800)

The Union Flag is over 400 years old, going back to the year 1606. It was created because Scotland and England had united under one king. In 1801, the flag of
10 Ireland was added when the Irish and British parliaments voted to unite, and the United Kingdom was formed.

Originally, the flag was used only by ships. It was not until the 19th century that it became common to fly a national flag from public buildings.

Today there are about 20 "flag days" (e.g. birthdays of members of the Royal
15 Family) when the flag is flown from government buildings. In many places, it is often flown on other public or commercial buildings during the year. In most parts of the UK, however, it is unusual for people to fly the flag from their homes.

Union Flag (since 1801)

In most countries, national flags play a big role in international sport events, but this is not always true of the Union Flag. In football, for example, there is no UK
20 team. Teams from England, Northern Ireland, Wales and Scotland use their own national flags at international matches.

Since the 1960s, the Union Flag has become a fashion icon across the world and can be found on T-shirts, bags, umbrellas and many other products.

Union Flag travel bag

unity Einheit   **commercial** [kəˈmɜːʃl] kommerziell; Geschäfts-

2 Different German-speaking cultures

◄ *p. 55*

a) Kim asks you some questions about Switzerland.
Make notes, then turn back to p. 55 and continue the task.

- "My German is quite good now. I won't have any problems communicating with people in Switzerland, will I?"

- "I suppose as neighbouring cultures with the same language, there aren't many differences between the cultures, are there?"

- "When we went on holiday for a week to the Baltic Sea, I had €75 spending money. That should be enough. What do you think?"

- "I don't need to bring my passport and visa when I travel to Switzerland, do I? It's part of the EU, after all."

← p. 49

CREATE YOUR SKATEPLAZA 2.0

Ergebnisse der Workshops, Skaten am U und Contest

15. Aug 2016 | Kunst im öffentlichen Raum, Upcycling & Do-It-Yourself   0 Kommentare

Ende Juli starteten 21 TeilnehmerInnen in den Workshops zum Skaterampenbau des Vereins „Die Urbanisten e.V." und kreierten mehrere skatebare Elemente für den Vorplatz des Dortmunder U. An zwei Wochenenden wurden die Rampen geplant, die Materialien gründlich vorbereitet und schlussendlich zusammengebaut. Dafür war jede Menge Fleißarbeit notwendig, doch der Spaß kam auch nicht zu kurz. In lockerer Atmosphäre lernten sich die TeilnehmerInnen kennen und tauschten sich aus, z.B. beim gemeinsamen Grillen. Nebenbei wurden noch T-Shirts mit dem Create your Skateplaza 2.0 *Logo* bedruckt, alle TeilnehmerInnen durften sich eines der T-Shirts mitnehmen.

Nach Fertigstellung der Rampen wurden die Rampe dann vom Dietrich-Keuning-Haus mit einem Transporter des Jugendamtes zum Dortmunder U gebracht. Hierfür waren aufgrund des hohen Gewichts der Rampen zahlreiche Helfer notwendig, auch die WorkshopteilnehmerInnen packten kräftig mit an. Nachdem die Rampen am Dortmunder U ihren Standort gefunden hatten, wurden sie in den letzten Wochen ausgiebig befahren. Die Rampen laden an allen Wochentagen zum freien Skaten ein, zudem bietet die Skateboardinitiative bis Ende August an drei Tagen in der Woche eine Skateboardschule an. Pro Termin haben in den letzten Wochen bis zu 20 interessierte SkaterInnen mitgemacht. Die weiteren Daten in diesem Monat findet ihr unter Termine. Den Abschluss der Skateboardschule markiert die Skate-Olympiade am Sonntag, den 21.08.2016 von 12:30 bis 15:00 Uhr. Jeder kann mitmachen, die Anmeldung ist kostenlos und es gibt Sachpreise zu gewinnen.

Der Höhepunkt des Projektes folgt allerdings erst noch, denn am 27.08.2016 geht es richtig rund: Ein Skateboard-Contest mit mehreren Disziplinen und ein Longboardcontest locken ab 12:00 Uhr SkaterInnen und Neugierige zum Dortmunder U. Unsere Contest-Sponsoren Titus Dortmund, S.P.O.T Bochum, und Obtain sorgen für schöne Sachpreise. Das tagesfüllende Programm wird abgerundet vom zeitgleich stattfindenen Oneness Festival im Rahmen des Sommer am U.

2 What do flags mean?

← *p. 26*

The European Union: The Flag of Europe

The EU flag is made up of a circle of 12 gold stars on a blue field. The number of stars has nothing to do with the number of countries in the EU. Twelve is traditionally a number that stands for something
5 complete or perfect, e.g. twelve months in a year, the twelve apostles, etc. The stars stand for the unity and harmony of people in Europe.

The Flag of Europe was designed in 1955 as a symbol for the whole of Europe. It has been used by different European institutions and, in
10 1985, the European Union (at that time known as the European Communities) adopted it as its official symbol.

The European flag is flown at EU institutions and events, usually together with all the national flags. In many EU countries, it is also flown next to the national flag on public buildings.

15 You also see the twelve stars on little things – on car number plates and on euro notes and coins.

For some people, the Flag of Europe has become a symbol of European identity. It has been carried at demonstrations by supporters of more European integration. During the 2016 British
20 referendum, it was widely used by people who were against the United Kingdom leaving the EU.

The Flag of Europe

The Flag of Europe with European national flags

The EU and French flags outside a public building

number plate Autokennzeichen, Nummernschild   **referendum** Volksentscheid

2 Different German-speaking cultures

← *p. 55*

Ein paar Tipps für Skianfänger

· Ziehe dir Skikleidung an und trage mehrere Schichten Kleidung darunter, um dich warm zu halten.

· Die meisten Skiausrüstungen können ausgeliehen werden, aber keine Skibrillen. Es wäre gut, wenn du eine Skibrille mitbringst.

· Benutze Sonnencreme für dein Gesicht und deine Lippen. Man kann in den Bergen sehr schnell einen Sonnenbrand bekommen.

· Bleibe immer in speziell für Anfänger ausgewiesenen Gebieten und fahre niemals alleine los.

· Gehe es ruhig an und fahre langsam – und habe keine Angst zu stürzen.

· Viel Spaß! Genieße deinen Aufenthalt!

Germany and nuclear power

← *p. 67*

Partner B: Read the text and have a look at partner A's task (p. 103). Then make short notes in English so that you can answer your partner's questions in English.

1969 wurde in Deutschland das erste Kernkraftwerk eröffnet. Bis 1989 wurden sowohl in West- als auch in Ostdeutschland Anlagen gebaut. Nach 1990 wurden alle
5 Kernkraftwerke in der ehemaligen DDR geschlossen, weil man sich Sorgen um die Sicherheitsstandards beim Bau machte. Von 1990 bis 2011 lieferten die 17 bestehenden Atomreaktoren rund 25% des deutschen
10 Stroms.

Atomkraft war in Deutschland nie ein angenehmes Thema, und von Anfang an haben sich Umweltgruppen wegen der Sicherheitsrisiken und der Auswirkungen auf
15 die Umwelt, vor allem wegen des langfristigen Problems des Atommülls, gegen sie eingesetzt. Die Sorge um die Sicherheit und die Auswirkungen der Atomkraft auf die Umwelt nahm nach der Atomkatastrophe in
20 Tschernobyl (Ukraine) im Jahr 1986 stark zu. Aus diesem Grund wurden nach 1989 keine neuen Kernkraftwerke mehr gebaut. Unterschiedliche Regierungen verfolgten in den folgenden Jahren eine wechselnde Politik
25 hinsichtlich der bestehenden Anlagen.

Im Jahr 2011 hat die Atomkatastrophe in Fukushima, die durch ein Erdbeben und dem daraus resultierenden Tsunami verursacht wurde, das Thema der nuklearen Sicherheit
30 wieder neu aufgeworfen. Die deutsche Regierung beschloss daraufhin, die Hälfte der Atomkraftwerke des Landes sofort abzuschalten und die restlichen Anlagen bis 2022 stillzulegen.

Im Jahr 2021 deckte die Kernenergie aus 35 den sechs verbleibenden Kraftwerken 13% des deutschen Strombedarfs ab, während die erneuerbaren Energien (Wind, Wasser, Sonne und Biomasse) fast 50% abdeckten. Der Rest des Stroms wurde aus fossilen Energieträgern 40 wie Kohle und Erdgas erzeugt. Im selben Jahr wurden, dem Plan folgend, drei der letzten sechs Atomkraftwerke geschlossen.

2022 hätte das Jahr sein sollen, in dem die drei letzten verbliebenen Atomkraftwerke in 45 Deutschland abgeschaltet werden. Doch im Februar 2022 marschierte Russland in die Ukraine ein und begann einen Krieg gegen das Land. Daraufhin beschloss die Europäische Union, den Import von Erdgas 50 aus Russland zu reduzieren und einzustellen. Um die Auswirkungen der Reduzierung des Gases aus Russland abzumildern, beschloss die deutsche Regierung auch, die Abschaltung der Kernkraftwerke zu verschieben. 55

Zum Zeitpunkt der Erstellung dieses Artikels ist immer noch unklar, wann Deutschland die Kernenergie endgültig abschaffen wird.

2 What do flags mean?

← *p. 26*

United States: The Stars and Stripes

The American flag is made up of 13 horizontal stripes and 50 stars. Each stripe stands for one of the thirteen colonies that broke away from Great Britain in 1776. The 50 stars represent the
5 50 states that today make up the USA.

As well as having 13 stripes, the original US flag also had 13 stars, one for each state in the Union. At that time, there was no fixed way of arranging the stars. Sometimes they were in rows, sometimes in a circle. It depended on the flagmaker.

10 At first, when a new state joined the USA, a new star and stripe were added. But as more states joined, it became difficult to add more stripes. So in 1818 it was decided to go back to thirteen stripes, and only to increase the number of stars. The 50th star was added in 1960, for Hawaii.

15 In the United States, the flag plays a very important role in everyday life. It is flown daily on most public buildings and on many other buildings too. Many citizens fly the flag outside their homes. And at school, children face the flag every day and, with their right hand on their heart, swear allegiance to it and to the
20 United States.

The flag is widely seen as a symbol of liberty and justice, and for this reason is often seen at political demonstrations. Sometimes, as a form of protest, people fly it upside down. This is a way of saying that something in the country is not in order.

The US flag today

An early version of the US flag

The US flag with 35 stars

---

stripe Streifen **be made up of** bestehen aus; sich zusammensetzen aus **depend on** abhängen von **daily** täglich
citizen Bürger/in **swear allegiance** [əˈliːdʒəns] Treue schwören **justice** Gerechtigkeit **upside down** verkehrt herum

3 Germany and the USA

← *p. 26*

Deutschland: Schwarz – Rot – Gold

Die schwarz-rot-goldene Trikolore wurde 1949 zur Nationalflagge der Bundesrepublik Deutschland. Die Flagge ist jedoch viel älter: Sie wurde z. B. im 19.
Jahrhundert im Zusammenhang von demokratischen Bewegungen mitgeführt.

5 1832 wurde sie von Demonstranten auf dem Hambacher Schloss getragen.
Und während der Revolution von 1848 bis 1849 wurde die Trikolore als
Deutschlands Nationalflagge eingesetzt.

Obwohl wir wissen, dass die Flagge seit dem 19. Jahrhundert verwendet wird,
ist nicht klar, wofür die Farben stehen oder woher sie stammen. Eine der vielen
10 Theorien ist, dass die deutsche Trikolore die Farben der Flagge des Heiligen
Römischen Reiches übernommen hat. Aber das ist nur eine Theorie. 1950 wurde
geregelt, dass die drei Querstreifen der Nationalflagge gleich groß sein müssen.

Im Vergleich zu anderen europäischen Ländern ist die Nationalflagge in
Deutschland sehr selten zu sehen. Sie wird vor offiziellen Gebäuden wie z. B.
15 dem Bundestag oder Rathäusern gehisst. Seit dem Zweiten Weltkrieg sind
Begriffe wie ‚Nationalstolz', patriotische Äußerungen oder das Hissen der
Flagge negativ belegt. Solche Dinge werden mit Rechtsnationalismus assoziiert.
Der Zweite Weltkrieg hat das Verhältnis der Deutschen zu ihrer Flagge sehr
geprägt.

20 Mit der Zeit hat sich das jedoch verändert. Ereignisse wie die Austragung der
Fußballweltmeisterschaft im Jahr 2006 in Deutschland und die positive Rolle
Deutschlands in Europa und der Welt haben bewirkt, dass die Deutschen ihren
Stolz und ihre Liebe zu ihrem Land durch das Schwenken der Nationalflagge
bei wichtigen Ereignissen, vor allem beim Sport, immer mehr zum Ausdruck
25 bringen. Dennoch gibt es Deutsche, die das Schwenken oder Hissen der
Flagge immer noch kritisch sehen.

Die deutsche Flagge heute

Flagge des Heiligen Römischen Reiches

Schwarz, Rot und Gold in Frankfurt während der Revolution von 1848

Germany and nuclear power

← *p. 67* **Background file**

Partner A: You are the Irish student. As Ireland has never had any nuclear power plants, you have some questions to ask your German partner. Prepare questions in English about:

the beginnings of nuclear power in Germany	its importance, including some statistics	and its future

When your partner answers your questions, ask follow-up questions spontaneously.

Grammar and practice

Der **Grammar and practice**-Teil dieses Buches (S. 104 – 161) fasst die wichtigsten grammatischen Themen der Sekundarstufe I zusammen.

Auf den linken Seiten stehen Erklärungen und Beispielsätze, auf den rechten Seiten findest du passgenaue Übungen zu den grammatischen Punkten. Erledige die Aufgaben in deinem Englisch-Heft oder -Ordner.

Unter cornelsen.de/webcodes (Webcode: midifa) kannst du nachsehen, ob du die Übungen richtig bearbeitet hast. Dort findest du auch eine Übersicht grammatischer Fachbegriffe.

Inhalt

				Seite
1	Word order	1.1	S – V – O	106
		1.2	Adverbs / Adverbials of place and time	
2	Talking about the present	2.1	The simple present	108
		2.2	The present progressive	
		2.3	Simple present or present progressive?	
3	Talking about the past (I)	3.1	The simple past	110
		3.2	*used to* + infinitive / *would* + infinitive (German "früher")	
		3.3	The past progressive	
4	Talking about the past (II)	4.1	The past perfect (simple)	112
		4.2	The past perfect progressive	
5	Linking the past and the present	5.1	The present perfect (simple)	114
		5.2	The present perfect progressive	
		5.3	*since* and *for* (German "seit")	
		5.4	Present perfect or present perfect progressive?	
6	Talking about the future (I)	6.1	The *going to*-future	116
		6.2	The *will*-future	
		6.3	The future perfect	
7	Talking about the future (II)	7.1	The future progressive	118
		7.2	The present progressive	
		7.3	Overview: *going to*-future, future progressive and present progressive	
		7.4	The simple present	
8	Aspect: the simple form and the progressive form	8.1	Simple and progressive form compared	120
		8.2	Activity verbs and state verbs	
9	The passive (I)	9.1	Active and passive	122
		9.2	The passive: use	
10	The passive (II)	10.1	The passive: form	124
		10.2	The passive of verbs with two objects	
11	Modal auxiliaries	11.1	Use	126
		11.2	Form	
12	Modals and their substitutes (I)			128
13	Modals and their substitutes (II)			130
14	The gerund (I)	14.1	Verbs followed by a gerund	132
		14.2	Verbs followed by a gerund <u>or</u> infinitive	
		14.3	Verbs that change their meaning	
15	The gerund (II)	15.1	The gerund after prepositions	134
		15.2	The gerund with its own subject	

16	The *to*-infinitive	16.1	Verb + object + *to*-infinitive	136
		16.2	Question word + *to*-infinitive	
		16.3	The *to*-infinitive instead of a relative clause	
17	Indirect speech (I)	17.1	Direct and indirect speech	138
		17.2	Indirect speech: backshift of tenses and other changes	
18	Indirect speech (II)	18.1	Indirect speech: questions	140
		18.2	Indirect speech: requests, commands, advice, suggestions	
19	Conditional sentences	19.1	Conditional 1: *if* + simple present	142
		19.2	Conditional 2: *if* + simple past	
		19.3	Conditional 3: *if* + past perfect	
		19.4	Other conditional sentences	
20	Relative clauses	20.1	Defining relative clauses	144
		20.2	Contact clauses	
		20.3	Non-defining relative clauses	
		20.4	Relative clauses with *which* to refer to a whole clause	
21	Participles (I)	21.1	Participle forms	146
		21.2	Participle clauses instead of relative clauses	
		21.3	Verb of perception + object + present participle	
22	Participles (II)	22.1	Participle clauses to describe connected actions	148
		22.2	Participle clauses instead of adverbial clauses of time	
23	Participles (III)	23.1	Participle clauses instead of adverbial clauses of reason	150
		23.2	Other participle clauses	
24	The comparison of adjectives	24.1	Forms	152
		24.2	The adjective in comparisons	
25	Countable and uncountable nouns	25.1	Characteristics	154
		25.2	Quantifiers: *some, a lot of, many, much, a few, a little*	
26	The definite article	26.1	Things in general – specific things	156
		26.2	Buildings and institutions	
27	Emphasis	27.1	Word stress	158
		27.2	Emphatic *do/does/did*	
		27.3	Emphasizing pronouns	
		27.4	Adverbs	
		27.5	*It's … / It was …* + relative clause	
		27.6	'Negative' adverbials + inversion	
28	Adverbial clauses	28.1	Clauses of place; clauses of time	160
		28.2	Clauses of reason; clauses of result	
		28.3	Clauses of contrast	
		28.4	Clauses of manner; clauses of purpose	

1 Word order

1.1 S – V – O

The S – V – O rule is the most important rule in **positive** and **negative** statements, and in **questions**.

		Subject	Verb	Object	
positive		Emily The Martins	likes have bought	popcorn. a house	in France.
negative		Jacob My parents	didn't like can't speak	the film. English	very well.
question	Can Do	you the Martins	play speak	chess? French?	

The S – V – O rule means that English word order is often different from German word order:

1 An **object** cannot go between the <u>parts of a verb</u>.
  · <u>We're going to have</u> a big party. Wir <u>werden</u> eine große Party <u>veranstalten</u>.
2 **Adverbs** or **time phrases** cannot go between <u>verb and object</u>.
  · We **often** <u>have fish</u> on Fridays. Wir <u>essen</u> **freitags oft** <u>Fisch</u>.
3 The order **subject** – **verb** stays the same when a sentence begins with a <u>time phrase</u> or a <u>subordinate clause</u>.
  · <u>Today</u> we**'re visiting** our grandparents. <u>Heute</u> **besuchen wir** unsere Großeltern.
  · <u>When Jake arrived</u>, he **opened** the door. <u>Als Jake ankam</u>, **öffnete er** die Tür.
4 <u>Subordinate clauses</u> also follow the **subject** – **verb** (– **object**) rule.
  · Why don't you go to bed <u>if **you're** tired</u>? Warum gehst du nicht ins Bett, <u>wenn **du** müde **bist**</u>?
  · Sue told me <u>that **she** likes Jake</u>. Sue sagte mir, <u>dass **sie** Jake **mag**</u>.

1.2 Adverbs / Adverbials of place and time

Different kinds of adverbials have different positions in a sentence or clause:

1	**Sentence adverbs**	**front position**
	(luckily, unfortunately, maybe, of course, at first, suddenly, at last, finally, …)	**Unfortunately** it started to rain, but **luckily** I had an umbrella. **At first** the rain was light, but **suddenly** it got very heavy.
2	**Adverbs of**	**mid-position**
	· **frequency** (always, often, sometimes, …) · **indefinite time** (already, ever, just, still, …)	I don't **often get up** early on Sundays. I **usually stay** in bed till 10. I've **just come** downstairs. Mum and Dad are **still having** breakfast.
3	**Adverbs of**	**end position**
	· **manner** (quickly, well, politely, …) · **place** (outside, in the garden, to Bristol) · **time** (tomorrow, a year ago, in 2008)	Try to **speak slowly** and **clearly** – then you'll **do well**. They **went outside** and **played in the park**. We're **leaving tomorrow** and we hope to **arrive the following day**.
	❗ The word order at the end of the sentence is usually **place** – **time**: We were **in Italy** **last summer**.	
4	**Adverbs of degree**	**before the word they refer to**
	(very, quite, too, really, nearly, almost, …)	That phone looks **very/quite** expensive. I'd **really** love one of those.

If an adverb does not come in its usual position, this is often because it is given special emphasis:
· **Sometimes** I see foxes in the garden. **In cities,** you didn't use to see foxes, but **now** this is beginning to change.

German summary

Die wichtigste Wortstellungsregel lautet **S – V – O** (subject – verb – object). Diese Wortstellungsregel hat zur Folge, dass die englische Wortstellung oft anders ist als die deutsche (siehe oben Abschnitt 1.1, Beispiele 1–4).

Bei Adverbien und adverbialen Bestimmungen unterscheidet man zwischen **front position** (Satzadverbien wie luckily, at first), **mid-position** (Adverbien der unbestimmten Zeit/Häufigkeit wie always, ever) und **end position** (Adverbien der Art und Weise – Ortsangaben – Zeitangaben).
Gradadverbien wie very, quite, extremely, really stehen gewöhnlich direkt vor dem Wort, auf das sie sich beziehen.

1 Exercises

1.1 S – V – O

These aliens' vocabulary is perfect, but they need help with their sentence structures.
Rewrite their conversation with the correct word order. Use all of the words.

Example: Alien Budi: Hello Bobo! How are you?

Alien Budi: Bobo hello! Are you how?
Alien Bobo: Thanks, fine. Yesterday visited I the Earthlings.
Alien Budi: The Earthlings like you did?
Alien Bobo: Yes, did I. Going to them see tomorrow I'm. With me to come want you do?
Alien Budi: Know I don't. When their television watch I, often see I that each other eat they.
Alien Bobo: Worry don't. Sure I'm that in 7 series Rick them all save will.
Alien Budi: Sure you are?
Alien Bobo: Must he. The last series of The Zombies Walking it's.

1.2 Adverbs / Adverbials of place and time

a) Copy and complete the table below with the words and phrases from the box.

> really · often · obviously · quite · straight · still · loudly · now · recently ·
> downstairs · pretty · there · any time · everywhere · fortunately ·
> on the moving day · as easily as before · of course

sentence adverbs	adverbs of frequency / indefinite time	adverbs of manner	adverbs of place	adverbs of time	adverbs of degree
fortunately					

b) Rewrite the sentences, including the adverbs in brackets. Sometimes different word order is possible.

Example: 1. We recently moved to a new flat. / We moved to a new flat recently.

1. We moved (to a new flat / recently).
2. We said goodbye to our ground-floor flat and hello to a bigger one (on the third floor / sadly).
3. I liked our old place because we went and played (in the garden / quite / often).
4. Our cat, Felix, liked being able to go and hunt (any time / outside / really).
5. We can't go (now / as easily as before / outside).
6. It was busy (pretty / on the moving day).
7. Poor Felix was confused and got in the way (all the time / very / not surprisingly).
8. Dad broke his neck when he fell over Felix and shouted at him (really / loudly / nearly).
9. Felix ran and disappeared. (away)
10. Felix hadn't come back and we searched for him. (everywhere / after a few hours / still)
11. I went and looked. (below / on the balcony)
12. There he was! I ran to get him. (downstairs / at last)
13. He ran to me, and he wasn't hurt. (amazingly / straight)
14. He didn't know how high our new flat was. (obviously)
15. Cats have nine lives and Felix has eight left. (still / fortunately)
16. I leave the balcony doors open after what happened. (never / of course)

2 Talking about the present

2.1 The simple present

We use the **simple present** to say that something happens **regularly, often, always** or **never**.
We often use it with phrases of time like *always, never, often, sometimes, usually, every week, on Fridays, after school*, etc.
· Jack **usually gets** the bus to school.   *Jack **nimmt** meistens den Bus zur Schule.*
· **On Fridays** his mother **takes** him in the car.   *Freitags **bringt** ihn seine Mutter mit dem Auto.*
· He **never cycles** because it's too far.   *Er **fährt** nie mit dem Fahrrad, weil es zu weit ist.*

We also use the **simple present** to make **general statements**.
· Olivia **lives** in Chester.   *Oliva **wohnt** in Chester.*
· She **plays** tennis and **collects** old computer games.   *Sie **spielt** Tennis und **sammelt** alte Computerspiele.*
· Her mother is Polish, so she **speaks** two languages.   *Ihre Mutter ist Polin, daher **spricht** sie zwei Sprachen.*
· Her parents **work** for a computer company.   *Ihre Eltern **arbeiten** für eine Computerfirma.*

2.2 The present progressive

We use the **present progressive** to say that someone **is doing** something **now** or that something **is happening now**.
The action or event is **not finished yet**. Common phrases of time are *at the moment, now, just* and *still*.

· What**'s** Dan **doing**? – He**'s cleaning** his bike.
*Was **macht** Dan? – Er **putzt** sein Rad.*
· Dan (on the phone): "I**'m** busy, Oliver. I**'m** still **cleaning** my bike."
*„Ich bin beschäftigt, Oliver. Ich **bin** noch **dabei**, mein Rad **zu putzen**."*

We also use the **present progressive** for actions that are repeated over a limited period of time.
Olivia has a holiday job.
· She**'s working** as a waitress in a small café in Devon.   *Sie **arbeitet** als Kellnerin in einem kleinem Café in Devon.*
· She**'s living** with her aunt while she's there.   *Während sie sich dort aufhält, **wohnt** sie bei ihrer Tante.*

2.3 Simple present or present progressive?

In German, ***Harry und Ben spielen Hockey*** can mean two things:

a) Playing hockey is Harry and Ben's hobby.
b) They are in the middle of a hockey match.

In English, we use the **simple present** for meaning **a)**:
· Harry and Ben **play** hockey every Friday.

We use the **present progressive** for meaning **b)**:
· Harry and Ben **are playing** hockey at the moment.

Simple present	· wenn etwas **regelmäßig, oft, immer** oder **nie** geschieht (oft mit *always, never, often, sometimes, usually, every week, on Fridays, after school* u.Ä.) · wenn man über Dauerzustände spricht (Wohnorte, Hobbys, Berufe, …)
Present progressive	· wenn etwas **gerade im Gange** – also noch **nicht abgeschlossen** – ist (oft mit *at the moment, now, just, still*) · wenn man über vorübergehende Zustände spricht (Zustände, die nur für einen begrenzten Zeitraum gelten)

2 Exercises

2.1 The simple present

a) How often does Matilda do these things?
   Put the adverbs in the correct place in the sentences.

   1. She meets her boyfriend near her home. **xx**
   2. She remembers to charge her smartphone. **+++**
   3. She and her friends hang out in the park. **++**
   4. She goes to poetry slam events. **x**
   5. She asks other people for advice. **xxx**
   6. She doesn't change her profile picture. **+**

never:	**xxx**
hardly ever:	**xx**
sometimes:	**x**
often:	**+**
usually:	**++**
always:	**+++**

b) Complete these English proverbs and expressions with the correct verbs.
   Use the simple present.

   1. Still waters ... deep.
   2. ... a book by its cover.
   3. He who ... last ... longest.
   4. What ... around ... around.
   5. ... your chickens before they hatch.
   6. Sophia and Orla ... like peas in a pod.
   7. Everybody ... mistakes.
   8. People who ... in glass houses shouldn't throw stones.

> be · come ·
> not count · go ·
> laugh (x 2) · live ·
> make · run ·
> not judge

2.2 The present progressive

Complete the sentences with the verbs in the present progressive.

1. Steven ... (save) money to buy a new scooter.
2. ... Ralph still ... (write) his English essay?
3. Julie texted. She ... (get) on the plane right now.
4. I ... (not joke) – that's what really happened.
5. Dana ... (work) in summer camp for the holidays.
6. Annika and I had a fight. We ... (not talk).
7. I can't come right now. We ... (have) our dinner.
8. Why ... you ... (look) at me like that? Is there something on my face?

2.3 Simple present or present progressive?

Complete the sentences with the verbs given. Put one in the simple present and the other in the present progressive.

1. My baby brother often ... but he's quiet at the moment because he ... . (cry, sleep)
2. Why ... you ... a dress? You never ... dresses. (wear, wear)
3. On Friday afternoons, Seán normally ... his friends but not today – he ... for an exam. (meet, study)
4. Mum and Dad, you always ... for us. Today though, you ... a meal that we've prepared. (cook, have)
5. Abdul ... to school this week because the tram which he usually ... is out of service. (cycle, take)
6. You must be very hungry. You ... even ... the broccoli. You usually ... it on your plate. (eat, leave)
7. Why ... Krsysztof ... so early? He normally ... until the end of every party. (leave, stay)
8. If you ... anything now, come over to my house. It's Saturday and we always ... a movie. (not do, watch)

3 Talking about the past (I)

3.1 The simple past

We use the **simple past** to say that something happened **in the past** (it is now over).
- Olivia's mother *moved* to England **ten years ago**.
  *Vor zehn Jahren ist Olivias Mutter nach England **gezogen** / **zog** Olivias Mutter nach England.*
- **Last Friday** Olivia's family *flew* to Italy.   *Letzten Freitag ist Olivias Familie nach Italien geflogen.*

Time phrases like *last Friday, yesterday, last week, in 2012, ten years ago* and *an hour ago* are often used.

We use the simple past in **reports** about past events and in **stories** (often with *first …, then …, after that …*).
- Yesterday Olivia *went* to town with her friend Sue. First they *looked* round the shops, and Sue *bought* a CD.
  Then they *tried on* shoes in four shops, but they *didn't buy* any. After that they *had* an ice cream.

> **!** In **German**, you can report past actions in the *Perfekt* and in the *Imperfekt*.
> In **English**, you cannot use the present perfect instead of the simple past.

3.2 *used to* + infinitive / *would* + infinitive (German "früher")

With ***used to* + infinitive** we can talk about things that were true in the past but are not true any more.
- We *used to live* in Manchester.   *Wir **wohnten früher** in Manchester.*
- Manchester United *used to be* my favourite team.   *Früher war Manchester United meine Lieblingsmannschaft.*
- I *used to spend* lots of money on sweets.   *Ich **habe früher** immer viel Geld für Süßigkeiten **ausgegeben**.*

We can also use ***would* + infinitive** (without *to*) to talk about **regular actions** in the past.
- Grandpa *would visit* us every Sunday after church.
  *Opa **besuchte** uns jeden Sonntag nach der Kirche. / Opa **pflegte** uns jeden Sonntag nach der Kirche **zu besuchen**.*
- We *would* often *go* for long walks in the woods.
  *Wir **haben** oft lange Spaziergänge im Wald **gemacht**. / Wir **pflegten** lange Spaziergänge im Wald **zu machen**.*

3.3 The past progressive

We use the **past progressive** to talk about actions that were **not yet finished** at a particular time in the past.
- Yesterday at 3.30 Olivia *was waiting* for her bus.   *Gestern um 15.30 **wartete** Olivia noch auf ihren Bus.*
- It *was raining*, so people *were carrying* umbrellas.   *Es **regnete** (gerade), daher **trugen** die Leute Regenschirme.*

The simple past is used with the past progressive when a short action interrupts a longer action.
- Sally *was cycling* home when a dog *ran out* in front of her bike.
  *Sally **radelte** (gerade) nach Hause, als ihr ein Hund vors Fahrrad **lief**.*

> **!** Note the difference in meaning:
> 1 Jan *was making* tea when his dad came home.
>   (First Jan started making tea. Then his dad came home.)
> 2 Jan *made* tea when his dad came home.
>   (First Jan's dad came home. Then Jan started making tea.)

Simple past	· wenn etwas **in der Vergangenheit** stattfand (oft mit genauen Zeitangaben wie *last Friday, yesterday, last week, in 2012, ten years ago, an hour ago* u. Ä.)
	· wenn man über **vergangene Ereignisse** berichtet oder eine **Geschichte** erzählt (oft mit *first …, then …, after that …*)
Past progressive	· wenn etwas zu einem bestimmten Zeitpunkt in der Vergangenheit noch im Gange (noch nicht abgeschlossen) war
	· wenn man beschreiben will, was gerade vor sich ging (*past progressive*), als ein bestimmtes Ereignis eintrat (*simple past*)

German summary

3 Exercises

3.1 The simple past

Complete these sentences about the history of phones.
Put the verbs into the simple past and choose the correct year.

1. Alexander Graham Bell ... (invent) the telephone in 1836/1876/1916.
2. The Motorola company ... (produce) the first commercial handheld mobile telephone in 1973/1983/1993.
3. Neil Papworth, a software engineer, ... (send) the first ever SMS in 1992/2002/2012.
4. Steve Jobs, the founder of Apple, ... (launch) the first iPhone in January 1987/1997/2007.
5. In the UK, the number of mobile calls ... (not overtake) the number of landline calls until 2011/2016/2022.

3.2 used to and would

Which is correct – *used to* or *would*? Or are both correct?

Example: 1. Both are correct because 'hunt' is an activity verb, not a state verb.

1. Our old cat used to / would hunt mice in the garden and bring them to us.
2. My first rabbit used to / would like sleeping on my bed, but Bugs – my new rabbit – doesn't.
3. We didn't use to / wouldn't have a dog – until last summer when we moved into our house.
4. I used to / would take Rex for long walks in the park at the weekends. I miss that.
5. My cousin used to / would have a pony that used to / would eat strawberries.

3.3 The past progressive

a) Match the sentence halves and put the verbs into the past progressive.

1. I fell as
2. We decided not to go to the park
3. I couldn't answer the teacher's question
4. Although the sun ... (shine),
5. We ... (do) a maths test
6. Mary ... (talk) about Gary when

a) because it ... (rain) so heavily.
b) when the fire alarm went off.
c) I ... (get) off the bus.
d) because I ... (laugh) so hard.
e) he walked into the room.
f) the water was too cold to swim in.

b) Matilda and Jim went on a date to an art gallery. Matilda is telling her friend how it went.
Complete her story with the verbs in the simple past or past progressive.

"Our date at the art gallery [1] ... (not begin) well. Jim [2] ... (talk) to his ex-girlfriend when I [3] ... (arrive)! She [4] ... (say) she [5] ... (be) there because she [6] ... (do) research for a school project. Luckily, she [7] ... (not stay) for long. Things [8] ... (not get) any better though. As we [9] ... (go) into the gallery, Jim [10] ... (hit) his head on the door and [11] ... (fall) over. Then he [12] ... (bump) into an old lady as he [13] ... (get up)! The gallery [14] ... (be) was nice though. We [15] ... (see) a lot of lovely paintings. As we [16] ... (finish) our tour, Jim [17] ... (want) to take a selfie of the two of us. While he [18] ... (hold) his phone up, a security guard [19] ... (come) over to us and [20] ... (tell) us that photos [21] ... (not be) allowed. Embarrassing. After the gallery, we [22] ... (go) to an Italian restaurant, but the problems [23] ... (not stop). As Jim [24] ... (take) his pizza, the toppings [25] ... (fall) off onto his lap! Poor Jim!"

4 Talking about the past (II)

4.1 The past perfect (simple)

To talk about a past action, we use the simple past, e.g.
· *Emily got home.*
· *It started to rain.*

To say what happened *before* a past action, we use the **past perfect**.
· *When Emily got home, her parents **had** already **eaten**.*
  Als Emily nach Hause kam, **hatten** *ihre Eltern* **schon gegessen**.
· *We **had** already **arrived** home when it started to rain.*
  Wir **waren schon** *zu Hause* **angekommen**, *als es anfing zu regnen.*

 Note the difference in meaning:
  1 *Jason **had made** tea when his father came home.*   *Jason* **hatte** *(bereits) Tee* **gekocht**, *als sein Vater heimkam.*
  2 *Jason **made** tea when his father came home.*   *Jason* **kochte** *Tee, als sein Vater heimkam.*

  ▶ In **1** *(past perfect)*, the tea **was ready** when Jason's father came home.
  ▶ In **2** *(simple past)*, the tea **wasn't ready** when his father came home. Jason only started making it then.

4.2 The past perfect progressive

We use the past perfect (simple) to say what happened before a past action.
· *We **had** already **arrived** home when it started to rain.*

We use the **past perfect progressive** for *continuous* actions that ended at (or just before) a past point of time.
· *We **had been playing** tennis for half an hour when it started to rain.*
  Wir **hatten** *eine halbe Stunde Tennis* **gespielt**, *als es anfing zu regnen.*
· *Olivia was very tired when she arrived home. She **had been studying** for a test all day.*
  Olivia war sehr müde, als sie nach Hause kam. Sie **hatte** *den ganzen Tag für einen Test* **gelernt**.

We had been waiting for over an hour when the bus finally appeared.

Past perfect	· wenn etwas noch vor etwas anderem in der Vergangenheit stattgefunden hatte
Past perfect progressive	· wenn eine Handlung vor einem Zeitpunkt in der Vergangenheit begonnen hatte und bis (oder fast bis) zu jenem Zeitpunkt andauerte

4 Exercises

4.1 The past perfect

Complete the sentences with the correct verb from the box in the past perfect.

> be · do · eat · explain · have · hear · see · not win

1. Before Barack Obama, there ... never ... a Black American president.
2. I didn't laugh at Maria's joke because I ... it before.
3. Although Julia ... already ... the movie, she enjoyed watching it a second time.
4. When we got our new dog, we had to learn a lot – we ... never ... any pets before.
5. After Paul ... dessert, he felt ill and went to the bathroom.
6. During the exchange, Neil had the chance to do things he ... never ... before.
7. Until yesterday's game, our team ... any of our last five matches.
8. The students began the exam after the teacher ... the instructions.

4.2 The past perfect progressive

a) Put the verbs into the past perfect progressive.

1. Sophia couldn't answer the teacher's question because she ... (not listen).
2. The activist ... (speak) for only five minutes when the police came to stop the demonstration.
3. Fatima needed a break – she ... (study) since early in the morning.
4. The birdwatchers ... (not wait) long when they spotted a rare Capercaillie bird.
5. Jim ... (tell) me about his date with Matilda when Alan came over and interrupted him.
6. My dad ... (search) for his glasses for an hour when he found them – on top of his head.

b) Complete the story with the verbs in the past perfect simple or past perfect progressive.

Last night on the way to the cinema, I realized that I [1] ... (leave) my money at home. I [2] ... (look forward to) the film for weeks and I didn't want to miss it, so I got off the bus and ran home. When I arrived, I realized that I [3] ... (forget) my keys too, so I couldn't get in. I rang the doorbell, but everybody [4] ... (go) out. So I ran as fast as I could to my friend Jeremy's place. His mother opened the door, but Jeremy wasn't in. He [5] ... (not come) home yet. His mother saw that I [6] ... (run), so she asked me to sit down and gave me a drink. I started playing a game on my phone. I [7] ... (play) for twenty minutes when Jeremy finally arrived. He lent me some money, and I ran back to the bus stop. When I finally got to the cinema, the film [8] ... (already start).

Grammar

5 Linking the past and the present

5.1 The present perfect (simple)

We use the **present perfect (simple)** when a **past** action has a connection with *now*.
1 *Mel **has lost** her mobile. She can't phone anyone.*   *Mel **hat** ihr Handy **verloren**. Sie kann niemanden anrufen.*
2 *I think Matt Damon is great. I**'ve seen** all his films.*   *Ich finde Matt Damon toll. Ich **habe** alle seine Filme **gesehen**.*
3 *Luke must be hungry. He **hasn't eaten yet** today.*   *Luke muss hungrig sein. Er **hat** heute noch **nichts gegessen**.*
4 ***Have** you **ever been** to Paris? – No, I**'ve never been** there, but I'd like to go.*
   Warst du schon (mal) in Paris? – Nein, ich war noch nie dort, aber ich würde gern hinfahren.

> **!** If we use <u>time phrases</u>, they have a **present meaning** *(today, this week, always, often, never, just, so far, not … yet)*.
> We never use past time phrases *(yesterday, last week,* etc.) with the present perfect.

5.2 The present perfect progressive

We use the **present perfect progressive** for actions that **began in the past** and have continued till **now**.
1 *Ella **has been writing** letters **all afternoon**.*   *Ella schreibt (schon) den ganzen Nachmittag Briefe.*
2 *My brother **has been playing** the piano **since** 2013.*   *Mein Bruder spielt seit 2013 Klavier.*
3 ***How long have** you **been learning** French now?*   *Wie lange lernst du jetzt (schon) Französisch?*

The **present perfect progressive** in these sentences corresponds to the German *Präsens*:
· *He**'s been playing** … since/for …   Er **spielt** seit …*
Some common time phrases are *all afternoon, all day, the whole morning, since …, for …*

> **!** You <u>cannot</u> use the present perfect progressive with **state verbs** (e.g. *be, have, know, like, hate, …*).
> *Leon **has been** a member of the chess club **for** ten years.   Leon **ist** seit zehn Jahren Mitglied im Schachklub.*
> *How long **have** you two **known** each other?   Wie lange **kennt** ihr zwei euch schon?*
> *I**'ve had** a dog since my childhood.   Ich **habe** seit meiner Kindheit einen Hund.*   ➡ *State verbs: 8.2*

5.3 *since* and *for*: German "seit"

since + **Zeitpunkt** (wann etwas begann)	*for* + **Zeitraum** (wie lange etwas andauert)
*I've been playing the drums **since 2015**.* … seit 2015	*I've been playing the piano **for three years**.* … seit drei Jahren

5.4 Present perfect or present perfect progressive?

When we say *how long* something has been happening: present perfect progressive.

When we talk about the *result* of an action: **present perfect (simple)**.

· *Ella **has been writing** letters **all afternoon**.   Ella **schreibt** (schon) den ganzen Nachmittag Briefe.*
· *Ella **has written** three letters since lunch.   Ella **hat** seit dem Mittagessen drei Briefe **geschrieben**.*

5 Exercises

5.1 The simple past and the present perfect

a) Copy the table and put the signal words/phrases from the box under the correct tense.
NB: one phrase can go under both tenses.

> already · always · at 9am · ever · for six weeks · four weeks ago · how long …? ·
> in 2021 · just · last Sunday · never · since 2018 · so far · this year · when …? · yesterday · yet

signal words/time phrases for the simple past	signal words/time phrases for the present perfect
at 9am	already

b) Complete the sentence pairs with the verbs given.
Use the simple past for one sentence and the present perfect for the other.

1. a) Linda … in hospital since Tuesday.
   b) Linda … in hospital three weeks ago.
2. a) That girl's name is Rebecca – I … her since we were in kindergarten together.
   b) That girl's name is Rebecca – I … her when we were in kindergarten together.
3. a) JK Rowling … seven books in the original Harry Potter series between 1997 and 2007.
   b) JK Rowling … seven books, a play and several movie screenplays so far in her career.
4. a) How long … you … in this house?
   b) How long … you … in your last house?
5. a) I … the book, but now I have to write a report on it for school.
   b) I … the book yesterday but I still have to write a report on it for school.
6. a) Liam sent Miriam a message on Snaptalk last week, but she … until two days later.
   b) Liam sent Miriam a message on Snaptalk two days ago, but she … yet.

be

know

write

live

finish

not answer

5.2 The present perfect progressive

Put the verbs into the present perfect progressive.

1. Are they ever going to finish the new sports hall? It seems like they … (build) it for years.
2. How long … you and Helen … (see) each other?
3. My parents … (talk) to my teacher for forty-five minutes! I wonder what they're talking about.
4. Orla … (not practise) her violin often enough recently – she really has to make more of an effort.
5. Philip, your hands are really dirty. What … you … (do)?
6. Stefan … (study) for hours – he should take a break and have something to eat.

5.4 Present perfect simple or present perfect progressive?

Use the four verbs in the box to complete the four sentence pairs. One verb per pair.
Use the present perfect simple for one sentence and the present perfect progressive for the other.

1. a) I … six bookshops so far but not one has the book that I'm looking for.
   b) I … the bookshop since this morning but nobody answers the phone.
2. a) We … for hours. Can't we have a break?
   b) We … only five kilometres so far. We need to run five more.
3. a) How many times … you … the pain in your back?
   b) How long … you … pain in your back?
4. a) I … model cars since I was six years old.
   b) I … over 350 different kinds of model car since I was six years old.

call ·
collect ·
feel ·
run

6 Talking about the future (I)

6.1 The *going to*-future

We use the *going to*-future to talk about **intentions** or **plans** for the future.
· *After school I'm going to study architecture.*
  *Nach der Schule **werde** ich Architektur **studieren** / **habe** ich **vor**, Architektur **zu studieren**.*
· *The Millers are going to move to New Zealand.*
  *Die Millers **werden** nach Neuseeland **ziehen** / **wollen** nach Neuseeland **ziehen**.*

We use the *going to*-future to make predictions about the future,
especially when you can already see the signs.
· *Look at those clouds. There's going to be a storm.*
  *Schau dir die Wolken an. Es **wird** ein Gewitter **geben**.*

· *Oops! It looks like I'm going to be in trouble.*
  *Huch! Ich glaube, das **wird** Ärger **geben**.*

6.2 The *will*-future

We use the *will*-future to make statements or predictions about the future.

We often use it when talking about things that we **cannot control** (e.g. our age, the weather).
· *I'll be 16 next October.*   *Nächsten Oktober **werde** ich 16.*
· *It will be cool tomorrow.*   *Morgen **wird** es kühl **sein/werden**.*
· *There will be showers in the west.*   *Im Westen **wird** es Schauer **geben**.*

When we make predictions, we often use these expressions: *I think, I'm sure, I suppose, I expect, I hope, maybe, probably.*
· *I suppose Ella will arrive late again as usual.*   *Ich nehme an, Ella kommt wie üblich wieder zu spät.*
· *Dan will probably feel tired when he gets in.*   *Dan wird wahrscheinlich müde sein, wenn er nach Hause kommt.*

We use the *will*-future when we decide something in the moment we speak, e.g. when we make a **promise** or an **offer**.
· *I won't tell anyone what's happened.*   *Ich **sage** niemandem / **werde** niemandem **sagen**, was passiert ist.*
· *One moment – I'll open the door for you.*   *Moment. Ich **mache** Ihnen die Tür **auf**.*

6.3 The future perfect (*will + have + past participle*)

We use the **future perfect** to say something will be **complete at a future point of time** (e.g. next Friday, by the end of
the month, etc.). We use the future perfect progressive when we want to express that an ongoing action will be
complete at some time in the future.
· *Next Friday we will have finished the exams.*   *Nächsten Freitag **werden** wir die Prüfungen **geschafft haben**.*
· *Next year I will have been working here for 5 years.*   *Nächstes Jahr **werde** ich hier 5 Jahre **gearbeitet haben**.*

Going to-future	· wenn man über Vorhaben und Pläne für die Zukunft spricht
	· wenn man sicher ist, dass etwas gleich geschehen wird (es gibt bereits deutliche Anzeichen)
Will-future	· wenn man Vorhersagen über die Zukunft machen will (oft geht es um Dinge, die man nicht beeinflussen kann, z. B. das Alter oder das Wetter)
	· wenn man Vermutungen zum Ausdruck bringen will (oft mit *I think, I suppose, maybe, u. Ä.*)
	· wenn man sich spontan – also ohne es im Voraus geplant zu haben – zu etwas entschließt (oft geht es dabei um Hilfsangebote oder Versprechen)
Future perfect	· wenn etwas zu einem zukünftigen Zeitpunkt geschehen oder getan sein wird

6 Exercises

6.1 The *going to*-future

Use the *going to*-future and a verb from the box to complete the sentences.
Then say if each one is referring to a plan or a prediction.

> answer · be · do · not look for · spill · stay in · switch off · take

1. My parents ... angry when I tell them I failed another test.
2. Chris has decided that he ... a job this summer.
3. Be careful! You ... the milk.
4. What ... Siobhán ... in the summer holidays?
5. I'm tired. I ... and relax this evening.
6. ... you ... Linda's text message?
7. 2% battery! My phone ... in a minute.
8. Ann and Jo ... the bus and meet us at the mall later.

6.2 The *will*-future

Find B's reactions to A's statements and complete them with the *will*-future.

A	B
1. There's somebody at the door.	a) I just have water, thanks.
2. I can't do this exercise.	b) I check my team calendar and let you know.
3. Be careful with that glass – it was expensive.	c) I see who it is.
4. Orla mustn't find out.	d) I help you.
5. Tea or coffee?	e) I not tell her.
6. Do you know if you're playing handball this weekend?	f) I not drop it

6.3 The future perfect simple and progressive

Complete the sentences with the verbs given. Put the verbs into the right form:
future perfect simple or future perfect progressive.

1. My dad is German and next year we're celebrating because he ... (live) here for twenty-five years.
2. Call me after four o'clock because by then my lessons ... (finish).
3. We don't need to go to the airport yet – Grandma's plane ... (land) yet.
4. I started my violin lessons when I was five. Next month, I ... (learn) the violin for exactly eleven years.
5. By the time we have our exams, do you think we ... (study) everything we need to pass them?
6. After we visit the Brandenburg Gate, we ... (see) every important sight in Berlin.
7. Ben is addicted to that game – at six o'clock, he ... (play) for three hours!
8. When I finish this sentence, I ... (complete) all eight sentences in this exercise.

7 Talking about the future (II)

7.1 The future progressive (will + be + -ing form)

We use the **future progressive** for actions that will be **in progress at a point of time in the future**.
We often use it with phrases of time like *a week today* („heute in einer Woche") and *this time next week*.
· *A week today Jana will be in Spain – and I'**ll be doing** my maths exam.*
  *Heute in einer Woche wird Jana in Spanien sein – und ich **werde dabei sein**, meine Mathe-Prüfung **zu machen**.*

We often use the **future progressive** when we **expect** something to happen or **know** that it will happen.
· *We'**ll be playing** football again next Friday.   Nächsten Freitag **spielen** wir **(wie immer)** Fußball.*
· *I'**ll be going** shopping later. Do you need anything?   Ich **gehe (ohnehin)** nachher einkaufen. Brauchst du etwas?*

We also use the **future progressive** to ask politely about somebody's plans.
· *What **will** you **be doing** over the next couple of days?   Was **werden** Sie die nächsten Tage **unternehmen**?*
· *How long **will** you **be staying** in Washington?   Wie lange **werden** Sie (denn) in Washington **bleiben**?*
· ***Will** you **be travelling** alone?   **Werden / Wollen** Sie allein **reisen**?*

7.2 The present progressive

We use the **present progressive** to say that something is **definitely planned or arranged** for the future. (This use of the present progressive is sometimes called the **diary future**, because arrangements are often written down in a diary.)
· *I'**m meeting** a friend in town **tomorrow** at 12.*
· *All my friends **are coming** to my party **on Friday**.*

We need a future time phrase *(tomorrow, on Friday)* unless the context shows that a sentence is about the future.
· *Can we meet up at the weekend? – Sorry, but we'**re driving** to Scotland to see my mum.*

7.3 Overview: *going to*-future, future progressive and present progressive

There are many situations in which the differences between these verb forms do not matter.
However, there are small differences in meaning, and these may be important sometimes. Compare:
· *I feel a bit tired so I'**m going to stay** at home this evening. ▶ (You want to stress that you've decided.)*
· *I'**ll be staying** at home this evening – my favourite TV series is on. ▶ (You're talking about a routine.)*
· *I can't meet you this evening. We've invited some friends to dinner, so I'**m staying** at home. ▶ (You want to stress you have an arrangement.)*

7.4 The simple present

We use the **simple present** when a future event is part of a **timetable**, **schedule** or **programme**.
Verbs like *arrive, leave, go, open, close, start, stop* are often used in this way.
· *When **does** the next train to Liverpool **leave**?   Wann **fährt** der nächste Zug nach Liverpool?*
· *The film **begins** at 8 o'clock.   Der Film **beginnt** um 20:00 Uhr.*
· *Our cookery course **starts** on 2 September.   Unser Kochkurs **startet** am 2. September.*

German summary	
Future progressive	· wenn etwas in der Zukunft im Gange (noch nicht abgeschlossen) sein wird
	· wenn man erwartet oder weiß, dass etwas geschehen wird (Routinen)
	· wenn man sich höflich nach den Plänen anderer erkundigen will
Present progressive	· wenn etwas für die Zukunft fest verabredet ist *(diary future)*
Simple present	· wenn ein zukünftiges Geschehen durch einen Fahrplan, ein Programm oder Ähnliches festgelegt ist *(timetable future)*

7 Exercises

7.1 The future progressive

Ada and her father (who is English) are discussing when her parents can call during a class trip to London next week. Choose the correct future form for each sentence: *will*-future or future progressive.

Example: 1. *You'll be unpacking or relaxing in the hotel then.*

1. Dad: We could call you on Wednesday evening at 9pm. You will be unpacking or relaxing / will unpack or relax in the hotel then.
2. Ada: No, don't call me then – I will send / will be sending a text instead to let you know I'm okay.
3. Dad: Thursday morning isn't so good. You will enjoy / will be enjoying your ride on the London Eye.
4. Ada: And in the afternoon we will be doing / will do something in the West End.
5. Dad: *H.P and U.C.* sounds like a play at a theatre – that will be taking / will take a whole afternoon.
6. Dad: What about Friday morning? I will be calling / will call at 7am before you go shopping.
7. Ada: Okay, Friday morning. But not at 7am – that's 6am British time, I will still be sleeping / will still sleep at that time.

7.2 & 7.4 The present progressive and the simple present

Put the highlighted verbs into the correct future form – simple present or present progressive.

Example: 1. *... in two days we're going on ...*

Miss Zobel: Well children, in two days we ¹go on our class trip. Does anyone have any questions about our itinerary?

Max: The flight only takes an hour and ten minutes – that's fast!

Miss Zobel: No, Max – the plane ²land at twenty-five past six but that is British time. We actually ³arrive at twenty-five past seven German time. The flight takes two hours and ten minutes in real time.

Frederika: Miss, is the hotel where we ⁴stay nice? Is it 5-star?

Miss Zobel: 5-star?! No, I'm afraid not. It's a 2-star, but very nice.

Joshua: Maria ⁵come with us, Miss?

Miss Zobel: I'm sorry, Joshua, but she can't – her parents told me she ⁶spend the next three weeks at home because of her broken leg. Ada, do you want to ask something?

Ada: What we ⁷do in the West End on Thursday?

Miss Zobel: Well, on Thursday morning, we ⁸go on the London Eye and in the afternoon, we ⁹go to the A. K. Grayling play 'Harriet Popper and The Unlucky Child' in the West End. The play ¹⁰start at 4pm.

Matilda: Miss, on Friday it says 'HoP'. What is that?

Miss Zobel: That means 'Houses of Parliament'. The public gallery ¹¹open at two o'clock each afternoon – next Friday they ¹²discuss the European Union – it should be interesting.

- - - - - - - - - - - - - - - - - - - -

WOLKENSTEIN GYMNASIUM

Klassenfahrt Klasse 7A nach London
Mittwoch 15. April – Montag 20. April

REISEABLAUF / ITINERARY

Wednesday 15th

Flight GB142   17:15 – 18:25
Heathrow London
20:00 Check-in Britannia Hotel, Notting Hill

Thursday 16th

Morning – London Eye
Afternoon – West End (H.P. & U.C.)

Friday 17th

Morning – Trocadero Shopping Centre
Afternoon – H.o.P.

Saturday 18th

Morning – Madame Tussaud's / H.M.S. Belfast
Afternoon – National Museum

Sunday 19th

Morning – Tower of London
Afternoon – Walking tour City of London

Monday 20th

Morning – Check-out & flight DE871 10:30 – 13:40.

8 Aspect: The simple form and the progressive form

8.1 Simple and progressive form compared

In contrast to German, English verbs have **simple forms** and **progressive forms**.

Tense	Simple form	Progressive form
Present tense	sing(s)	am/are/is singing
Past tense	sang	was/were singing
Present perfect	have/has sung	have/has been singing
Past perfect	had sung	had been singing
will-future	will sing	will be singing

We use the **simple form** to say that
· someone does something regularly or repeatedly ▶ *Tom **plays** basketball on Saturdays.* ▶ (it's his hobby)
· an action is long-lasting or permanent ▶ *Mr Clark **works** as an editor.* ▶ (it's his job)
· an action is complete. ▶ *Sue **has written** four letters today.* ▶ (she has finished)

We use the **progressive form** to say that
· an action is in progress at the moment of speaking ▶ *Tom isn't in. He's **playing** basketball.* ▶ (right now)
· an action is going on for a temporary period of time ▶ *This week Mr Clark **is working** in London.* ▶ (just this week)
· an action is not yet complete. ▶ *Sue **has been writing** letters all day.* ▶ (she's still writing)

8.2 Activity verbs and state verbs

Activity verbs refer to **activities** (*do, go, make, read, …*) or **events** (*become, happen, …*).
They can be used both in the **simple form** and in the **progressive form**.
· *(in a shop window) We **make** the best pizza in town!*   · *(on the phone) I'm **making** pizza. I'll call you back.*
· *It **gets** dark very early here in winter.*   · *At 5 o'clock it **was** already **getting** dark.*

State verbs do not refer to **activities.** They refer to **states**.
State verbs are used only in the **simple form**. They can refer to
1 **characteristics and ownership:** *be, exist, include, seem, sound, mean ("bedeuten"), cost, need, own, belong, …*
   · *Emily **seems** happy at her new school now.*   *not … is seeming …*
   · *The price **doesn't include** breakfast.*   *not … isn't including …*
   · *Jake's uncle **owns** a house in the country.*   *not … is owning …*
2 **thinking and knowing:** *believe, know, mean ("meinen"), remember, imagine, realize, recognize, understand, …*
   · *Do you **believe** their story? not … Are you believing …*
   · *I **don't know** the answer to question 5.*   *not … I'm not knowing …*
   · *Anna **didn't understand** what Julie **meant**.*   *not … wasn't understanding … was meaning*
3 **liking, disliking** and **wishing:** *like, love, dislike, hate, mind, prefer, want, wish, …*
   · *Lucy **doesn't like** people who talk a lot.*   *not … isn't liking …*
   · *I **don't mind** waiting for you here.*   *not … I'm not minding …*
   · *We **prefer** brown bread to white bread.*   *not … are preferring …*

Simple form: für regelmäßige/wiederholte Handlungen   **Progressive form:** für Handlungen, die im Verlauf sind
für Dauerzustände   für vorübergehende Zustände
für abgeschlossene Handlungen   für nicht abgeschlossene Handlungen

· **Tätigkeitsverben** *(activity verbs)* bezeichnen **Tätigkeiten** oder **Vorgänge** und können sowohl in der *simple form* als auch in der *progressive form* verwendet werden.

· **Zustandsverben** *(state verbs)* bezeichnen **Zustände**. Sie werden in der Regel nur in der *simple form* verwendet.
Zu den Zustandsverben gehören
   1 Verben, die Eigenschaften, Besitz oder Zugehörigkeit ausdrücken *(be, exist, include, mean ("bedeuten"), own, …)*
   2 Verben des Meinens und des Wissens *(believe, know, mean ("meinen"), remember, imagine, understand, …)*
   3 Verben des Mögens und Wollens *(like, love, dislike, hate, mind, prefer, want, …).*

8 Exercises

8.1 Simple and progressive forms compared

Complete these sentences using the verb given. Decide on the correct tense: past, present or future.
Use a simple verb form in one sentence and a progressive verb form in the other.

1. a) The students ... carefully to the instructions from their teacher and then started the test.
    b) I didn't hear the doorbell because I ... to music.

    listen

2. a) Oh no! We've missed the bus! What ... we ... ?
    b) This time next week, I ... my work experience at a computer factory.

    do

3. a) I can't talk right now – we ... dinner.
    b) Every Friday, we order a takeaway and ... it while watching a movie.

    have

4. a) ... you ever ... GTA on the gamestation?
    b) How long ... you ... that video game? You should stop now and take a break from it.

    play

8.2 Activity and state verbs

Match the sentence halves and put the verbs into the correct form.

1. A: What's that smell? ... you ... (wear) aftershave?
    B: Yes. ... you ... (like) it?
    A: I ... (think) it ... (smell) really nice.

2. A: I ... (make) dinner now. ... you ... (want) pasta or homemade pizza?
    B: I ... (not mind). Which ... you ... (prefer)?
    A: Mm. I ... (think) I'm in the mood for pizza. With lots of cheese and mushrooms.
    B: That ... (sound) great.

3. A: I ... (need) a new phone. It ... (not matter) how much it costs.
    B: What ... you ... (mean)? You ... (have) a great phone.
    A: It's two years old! They ... (bring) out the new S25Plus next week.
    B: I ... (not believe) it. You are never happy with what you have.
    A: You just ... (not understand).

9 The passive (I)

9.1 Active and passive

Verbs can be active or passive. Which one you use depends on the focus of your sentence.

· **Active:** *In 1971, **John Lennon** wrote "Imagine".*   *Im Jahr 1971 schrieb John Lennon „Imagine".*

· **Passive:** *"Imagine" was written in 1971.*   *„Imagine" wurde im Jahr 1971 geschrieben.*

▶ The active sentence is about **John Lennon**. It tells us what he did in 1971.

▶ The passive sentence is about **"Imagine"**. It tells us when the song was written.

 The subject of an English passive sentence is sometimes a dative object in German.
· ***She** was paid £12 an hour.*   *Ihr wurden £12 die Stunde bezahlt. / Sie erhielt £12 die Stunde.*

➡ 10.2, The passive of verbs with two objects, p. 124

9.2 The passive: use

We use the passive to say what is done or what happens to something or someone.
Who does the action is often unknown or unimportant (1 and 2) or obvious (3 and 4).

1 *The match **was cancelled** because of rain.*   *Das Spiel **wurde** wegen Regen **abgesagt**.*
2 *A new sports centre **has been opened** in Chelsea.*   *In Chelsea **ist** ein neues Sportzentrum **eröffnet worden**.*
3 *Breakfast **is served** from 7 to 10.30am.*   *Frühstück **wird** von 7 bis 10.30 **serviert**.*
4 *The thieves **have been sentenced** to two years.*   *Die Diebe **sind** zu zwei Jahren Haft **verurteilt worden**.*

The passive is often found in reports of accidents, crimes or natural disasters and in technical or scientific writing.

> Yesterday a drunk driver hit a 15-year-old boy in Lichfield Road. The boy was taken to hospital, where he was treated for shock. He is now recovering. The driver was taken to Horton Road police station. He is answering police questions.

Often, we change between active and passive so that we can focus on one person or thing over several sentences (here: the 15-year-old boy).

> Yesterday a drunk driver hit a 15-year-old boy …. The boy was taken to hospital, where he was treated … He is now recovering.

If you want to say who or what does the action, you can use the preposition *by*.
· *The driver **was questioned by** the police.*   *Der Fahrer wurde **von** der Polizei verhört/befragt.*
· *The house **was damaged by** a falling tree.*   *Das Haus wurde **von** einem umstürzenden Baum beschädigt.*

German summary

Das Passiv (I)
· Vorgänge können (je nach Blickwinkel) mit Aktiv- oder mit Passivsätzen beschrieben werden. Das Subjekt des Passivsatzes entspricht dem Objekt des Aktivsatzes.
· Mit einem Passivsatz kann man eine Handlung beschreiben, ohne zu sagen, wer die Handlung ausführt.
· Das Subjekt des englischen Passivsatzes kann auch einem deutschen Dativobjekt entsprechen: ***She** was paid £12. – **Ihr** wurden £12 bezahlt.*
· Das Passiv wird oft in Nachrichten und Zeitungsartikeln (z.B. über Unfälle, Verbrechen, Naturkatastrophen) sowie in technischen und wissenschaftlichen Schriften verwendet.
· Wenn man in einem Passivsatz „Täter" oder „Verursacher" nennen will, kann man die Präposition *by* verwenden.

9 Exercises

9.1 Active and passive

Look at these sentences. Decide which ones would be better in the passive form and rewrite them.

1. Somebody told me that Gary and Elaine are breaking up.
2. Peter sent me a text message.
3. Somebody has uploaded a picture of the accident onto Instagraph.
4. Somebody cleans the hotel rooms every day.
5. A teacher will put the exam results on the noticeboard.
6. Mr Patterson sent an email to everyone about the physics homework.
7. Somebody took this photo when we were in 8th class.
8. A construction company is building a new shopping centre near my home.
9. My English teacher always tells us such interesting stories.
10. By the time I took out my phone, somebody had already called the police.

9.2 The passive: *use*

a) Rewrite the answers to the questions in the passive form.

1. Was Tom's accident bad? – He broke his leg.
2. Where are all the students? – A teacher has sent them home.
3. Why did you take the bus? – Because they are repairing my bicycle.
4. What's Gaelic? – It's a language. People in Ireland and Scotland speak it.
5. When did this parcel arrive? – The postman has just delivered it.

b) Complete this news report with the right passive forms of the simple present, simple past, present perfect and present progressive.

A search [1]... (carry out) right now in the Sydney Harbour National Park for a missing 16-year-old student, Leon Schmidt. The boy, who is an exchange student from Germany and was camping with a youth group, [2]... (not see) since yesterday. The alert [3]... (raise) late last night by one of the group's leaders who said Leon had gone for a walk alone and hadn't returned. They were unable to contact Leon and his mobile phone [4]... (find) in his tent. Police say that the boy's parents in Germany [5]... (inform) last night but, due to the warm, dry weather last night, they are not overly concerned. Leon [6]... (hear) talking about 'sleeping under the stars' by another group member during dinner yesterday afternoon. Police say at the moment every effort [7]... (make) to find Leon and a helicopter [8]... just ... (call) to help assist in the search. The youth group leader said Leon – like all group members – [9]... (give) tips and advice on staying safe in the bush before the trip.

10 The passive (II)

10.1 The passive: form

In German, the passive is a form of "werden" + past participle. In English, it is a **form of *be* + past participle**.

Simple present	English *is spoken* in many countries.
Simple past	The match *was talked about* all over Britain.
Present perfect	All the biscuits *have been eaten*.
Past perfect	I didn't go to the party because I *hadn't been invited*.
***going to*-future**	Look, the lions *are going to be fed* soon.
***will*-future and modal auxiliaries**	The last match of the season *will be played* next Friday. Mobile phones *should be turned off* during lessons. Concert tickets *can be bought* online.
Future perfect	I'm sure lots of new planets *will have been discovered* by 2050.

The **passive progressive** is formed with ***being***.

Present progressive	Three new blocks of flats *are being built* in King Street.
Past progressive	The museum was closed. The rooms *were being painted*.

10.2 The passive of verbs with two objects

Some verbs can have **two objects**, e.g.
· give/promise/send/show **somebody** **something**   *jemandem etwas* geben/versprechen/schicken/zeigen

In English, **passive sentences** with verbs like these usually begin with the person (*She* …).
This structure is called **personal passive** ("persönliches Passiv").

	object object	**object** object
Active	The manager promised *her* *a job*.	*Der Manager versprach **ihr** **eine Stelle**.*
Passive	*She* (subject) *was promised **a job*** (object).	***Ihr** (indirect object, dative)* wurde **eine Stelle** (subject) *versprochen.*

Personal passive sentences are very common in English. In German, you have to use other constructions.
· *She **was paid** a lot of money for her book.*
 Ihr wurde eine Menge Geld gezahlt für ihr Buch. / Sie bekam eine Menge Geld für ihr Buch.
· *He **was given** the key and went up to his room.*   *Ihm wurde der Schlüssel gegeben … / Er bekam den Schlüssel …*
· *I**'ve been told** she has lost her job.*   *Mir wurde erzählt, dass sie ihre Stelle verloren hat.*

Das Passiv (II) · Das Passiv bildet man mit einer Form von ***be*** und der 3. Form des Verbs (Partizip Perfekt). Bei den *progressive forms* wird das Passiv mit ***being*** gebildet.

· Passivsätze von **Verben mit zwei Objekten** beginnen im Englischen meist mit der Person. Diese Art des Passivs wird ***personal passive*** („persönliches Passiv") genannt. (Im Deutschen kann dagegen nur das direkte Objekt (das Sachobjekt) zum Subjekt des Passivsatzes werden. Die Dativform des Personenobjekts bleibt im deutschen Passivsatz erhalten.)

10 Exercises

10.1 The passive: form

Julia and Robert are discussing the organization of their garden party on Saturday.
Use the passive to complete the sentences in blue. Think carefully about which tense you need.

Example: 1. *So what still has to be done?*

Julia

Robert

¹ *So what / still have to / do?*

² *Well, the decorations / already hang up.*

Yes, they look nice, don't they? What about the chairs and tables?

³ *They / still have to / arrange. Maybe we could ask Jake and Paula to do that?*

Good idea. What about the drinks?

⁴ *They / order / last Monday.*

⁵ *And when / they / deliver?*

Tomorrow afternoon, I think.

And the food?

⁶ *It / deliver / on the day of the party.*

Of course, that makes sense. And the karaoke machine?

⁷ *It / should deliver / yesterday. But it didn't arrive, unfortunately.*

We'd better phone up about it. And talking about music: ⁸ *the neighbours / have to / tell.*

I know. I don't feel like telling them. Do you?

OK. How loud do you think it will be? How many guests are we actually expecting?

⁹ *Well / the invitations / send out / three weeks ago. So far 50 people have said they're coming.*

10.2 The passive of verbs with two objects

Alice and Mike are talking about some problems Mike had when he went on holiday.
Read their conversation. Rewrite 1–7 in the passive.

Alice: Your flight was seven hours late? How awful!
Mike: Yes, it was a long wait. (1) But the ground staff gave us a £10 voucher for food and drink.
Alice: That's not much for seven hours. (2) Didn't they offer you anything else?
Mike: (3) Well, they promised us a 20 percent reduction on our next flight.
Alice: I don't think that's very generous. (4) They should have offered you a free flight!
Mike: That would have been nice.
Alice: Well, I hope the rest of your holiday was OK.
Mike: Actually, it wasn't. When we finally arrived (5) someone handed a note to our tour guide. It seems our hotel was overbooked and we had to stay somewhere else.
Alice: You must have been disappointed about that.
Mike: I certainly was. I couldn't believe my eyes (6) when they showed me my room. It was small and dirty and it smelled awful.
Alice: You poor thing.
Mike: Yes, I won't use that travel agent again – (7) not if they paid me a million pounds.

1. *But we were given ...*   2. *Weren't ...*   3. *Well, we ...*   4. *You ...*   5. *our tour guide ...*   6. *when I ...*   7. *not if I ...*

11 Modal auxiliaries

11.1 Use

The modal auxiliaries are *can, could, may,* etc.

can	could	may	might	must	mustn't
needn't	ought to	shall	should	will	would

We use modals to talk about whether something is allowed, possible or necessary.
- *You can take the car. I can go by bike.*   *Du darfst das Auto nehmen. Ich kann mit dem Rad fahren.*
- *Do you think we should invite Jake to the party?*   *Meinst du, dass wir Jake zur Party einladen sollten?*
- *I must go shopping. The fridge is nearly empty.*   *Ich muss einkaufen gehen. Der Kühlschrank ist fast leer.*

 Note the difference between ***mustn't*** and ***needn't***.

mustn't = it is not allowed   *needn't = it is not necessary*

We also use modals to say if we think something may happen, or that something is likely or certain to happen.
1 *There's somebody at the door.*
   - *It could be the postman.*   *Es könnte der Briefträger sein.*
   - *It must be the postman.*   *Es muss der Briefträger sein.*
   - *It will be the postman.*   *Es wird der Briefträger sein.*
   - *It can't be the postman.*   *Es kann nicht der Briefträger sein.*
2 *Julie should be here by now.*   *Julie sollte jetzt (eigentlich) hier sein.*
3 *I must have fallen asleep.*   *Ich muss eingeschlafen sein.*

11.2 Form

1 There is **one form of modal for all persons** (no -*s*-forms, no -*ing*-forms). It is used with an infinitive.
   - *I/We* **can**/**could** /... **help** *you with those bags now.*
   - *He/She/They* **can**/**could** /... **help** *you ...*
2 We do not use *do/does/did* to make negative sentences or questions. In short answers, modals can stand on their own.
   - ***Jack* can't help** *you today.* – ***Can** he* **help** *me tomorrow?* – *Yes, he* **can***.* / *No, he* **can't***.*
3 Modals cannot form most of the verb tenses. There is no -*ed*-form. That is why we have to use **substitute forms**.

➡ *12, Modals and their substitutes (I), p. 128*

German summary

Modale Hilfsverben drücken aus, was jemand tun **kann, darf, muss, soll** usw.

Mit **modalen Hilfsverben** kann man auch zum Ausdruck bringen, für wie **gewiss, wahrscheinlich** oder **möglich** man etwas hält (z.B. wenn man Annahmen oder Schlussfolgerungen formuliert).

Modale Hilfsverben
- werden zusammen mit dem Infinitiv eines Vollverbs verwendet; nur in Kurzantworten können sie allein stehen;
- haben nur eine Form, es gibt also keine Endungen auf -*s*, -*ing* oder -*ed*;
- bilden Frage und Verneinung ohne *do/does/did*;
- können nicht alle Zeitformen bilden; daher gibt es zu bestimmten modalen Hilfsverben Ersatzverben.

11 Exercises

11.1 Modal auxiliaries – use

a) Before Brian can have his first mobile phone, his parents want him to agree to some rules.
   Look at the rules and complete the sentences with the right modal verb.

1. He ... let his parents have the password.
   (should / must / could)
2. He ... turn the phone off at 8pm on school nights.
   (must / can / might)
3. At weekends, he ... turn the phone off at 8pm. He ... use it until 10pm.
   (mustn't / ought to / needn't) – (might / needn't / may)
4. During family time, he ... use his phone.
   (needn't / can't / may)
5. He ... answer messages or calls from unknown numbers.
   (needn't / must / mustn't)

> **Brian's phone rules**
> - Let Mum & Dad have the password
> - Phone off at 8pm school nights / 10pm weekends
> - No phone during family time – meals, etc.
> - Messages or calls from strangers – NO!!!

b) Brian has had his phone for a week now. Rewrite the sentences below using a modal verb from the box.
   Careful: there is one modal in the box that you don't need!

> must · must · needn't · might · ought to · can't

Example: 1. *That must be Mark – he said he would call me around now.*

1. *(Phone ringing)* "That ... be Mark – he said he would call me around now."
2. *(Phone ringing)* "That ... be my phone – I have a different ringtone."
3. "My phone says I only have 66 cents credit left! That's strange – there ... be at least €5 left."
4. "I have a missed call from my mother. I'm going to call her back, she ... worry about me if I don't."
5. Brian: "Whose phone is this?" – Mark: "It's David's – he ... have forgotten it."

11.1 & 11.2 Modal auxiliaries – use and form

a) Correct any mistakes you find in the sentences. Not all sentences have mistakes.

1. She can speaks French and a little German. – *She can speak French and a little German.*
2. Coud you please be quiet?
3. You mussn't take photographs inside the museum.
4. I can't get in – the door wont open.
5. Would like your friend to have dinner with us?
6. Shall we eat first and go shopping later?
7. You needent pay – my ticket covers both of us.
8. I think you ought tell him the truth.
9. Let's go to the shop now – it might still be open.

b) Match the corrected sentences in a) to the meaning expressed by the modal verb they contain.
   You have more options than you need.

a) request
b) ability
c) ability
d) (lack of) permission
e) deduction

f) refusal
g) necessity
h) suggestion
i) advice
j) offer

12 Modals and their substitutes (I)

Some modals have **substitute forms**, which we need to form the **infinitive**, the **-ing-form** and **other tenses**.
· I'd love **to be able to** play the piano.   Ich würde liebend gern Klavier spielen **können**.
· **Being able to** play the piano must be great.   Es muss großartig sein, Klavier spielen **zu können**.
· We **weren't allowed to** play the piano after 9pm.   Wir **durften** nach 21 Uhr **nicht** Klavier spielen.
· You **won't be allowed to** play the piano after 9pm.   Nach 21 Uhr **wirst** du **nicht** Klavier spielen **dürfen**.

Here is an overview of modals and their substitutes in different tenses.

German "können": modal auxiliary _can_ – modal substitute _(to) be able to_

Present	My little brother **can** / **is able to** swim. My cousins **can't** / **aren't able to** swim.
Past	**Were** you **able to** visit the British Museum when you were in London? I **could** smell fire, but I **couldn't** see any smoke.
	❗ We use the past form **could** mainly with verbs of perception (_smell, see, hear_) and in negative sentences.
Present perfect	I **haven't been able to** contact Jack yet. Do you think he **has been able to** check his mails?
will-future	I'm taking driving lessons, so next year I**'ll be able to** drive.

German "dürfen": modal auxiliary _can_ / _may_ – modal substitute _(to) be allowed to_

Present	**Can** / **May** I have a sleepover on Friday, Mum? Jake **is allowed to** stay up late in the week, but we **aren't** (**allowed to**).
Past	Under-12s **couldn't** / **weren't allowed to** see the film without an adult.
Present perfect	I've always **been allowed to** have pets.
will-future	**Will** you **be allowed to** go to the party?
	❗ When something is **forbidden**, we use **must not** (mustn't) or **(to) be not allowed to**. · Jeans **must not** be worn at this school. · At my school we**'re not allowed to** wear jeans.

German "müssen": modal auxiliary _must_ – modal substitute _(to) have to_

Present	Teacher: You **must** work harder, Noah. Noah's teacher says he **has to** work harder. I **needn't** get up at 6 tomorrow. / I **don't have to** get up at 6 tomorrow.
	❗ The negation of **must** is **needn't**, not mustn't.
Past	I **had to** rewrite my essay, but we **didn't have to** do any maths homework.
Present perfect	Lauren **has had to** go to the dentist's a lot recently.
will-future	You **will have to** go to the dentist's too if you don't look after your teeth better.
	❗ We also use the full verb **(to) need to** to say that it is necessary for someone to do something. · Everyone **needs to** take a break from time to time. But I **don't need to** take a break right now. · I **didn't need to** tell her. She already knew it. **Do** we **need to** tell anyone else?

German summary

Modale Hilfsverben können nicht alle Zeitformen bilden – daher gibt es zu bestimmten modalen Hilfsverben Ersatzverben mit ähnlicher Bedeutung, von denen man den Infinitiv, die -ing-Form und alle Zeitformen bilden kann.

„können" Modalverb **_can_** – Ersatzverb **(to) be able to**
 Die Vergangenheitsform **_could_** steht vor allem in verneinten Sätzen und mit Verben der Wahrnehmung wie _smell, see, hear_.

„dürfen" Modalverb **_can_ / _may_** – Ersatzverb **(to) be allowed to**
 Für ausdrückliche **Verbote** wird **must not (mustn't)** oder **(to) be not allowed to** verwendet.

„müssen" Modalverb **_must_** (Verneinung: **_needn't_**) – Ersatzverb **(to) have to**
 Auch das Vollverb **(to) need to** drückt aus, dass jemand etwas tun muss oder nicht zu tun braucht.

12 Exercises

12.1 *(to) be able to / be allowed to*

a) Rewrite the sentences replacing *can/could* with a past or present form of *(be) able to* or *(be) allowed to*.

1. I phoned Kevin, but he couldn't hear me because he was at a concert.
2. In Paris we saw the Mona Lisa, but we couldn't take photos because of the security guards.
3. Mary can't come shopping with us – her mum is still angry with her for coming home late on Friday.
4. Most of the exam questions were okay, but I couldn't answer the last one.
5. This French homework is difficult – can you understand it?
6. Don't walk there! Only cyclists can go there.

b) Now use a future form of *(be) able to* or *(be) allowed to* to complete these sentences.

1. One day people ... live on Mars.
2. I'd love to see Duo Libra in concert, but ... we ... get tickets for it or are they sold out?
3. I think in a few years' time they'll change the rules so 16-year-olds ... vote in elections.
4. Motorists ... drive on the main street from 1 January because of a new law.
5. The minister plans to change the rules so that only over-18s ... use social media.
6. Some scientists say in ten years' time we ... swallow a pill to cure even serious diseases.

12.2 *(to) have to*

Match the sentence halves and complete the sentences with *(not) have to* in the correct tense.

1. Peter ... go to extra maths lessons every week
2. Our new teacher is very relaxed, so
3. We've got special VIP tickets for next week's concert,
4. Since my dad's accident,
5. I'm sorry, sir, your dog ... stay outside
6. When we fly to Spain,

a) ... we ... wear medical masks in the plane?
b) because pets are not allowed in the store.
c) he ... wear a special boot on his foot.
d) we ... do any homework since the start of term.
e) because his marks are so bad.
f) so we ... queue like other people.

13 Modals and their substitutes (II)

German "sollen"

Here is an overview of how to express the different meanings of German "sollen" in English.

should and **ought to**
We use the modals **should** and **ought to** to talk about an **obligation** or to give **advice**.
· Dogs **should** be left outside.   Hunde **sollten** draußen gelassen werden / draußen bleiben.
· You **should** tell him / You **ought to** tell him the truth.   Du **solltest** ihm die Wahrheit sagen.
· We **should** have asked our parents.   Wir hätten unsere Eltern fragen **sollen**.

We also use **should** and **ought to** to say that we expect something to be true.
· They **should** / They **ought to** be here by 8pm.   Sie **sollten** (eigentlich) bis 20 Uhr hier sein.

be supposed to and **had better**
We use **be supposed to** to say that you should do something because **others expect** it (because it is a **rule** or **tradition**, or because you **agreed to do it**).
· You**'re not supposed to** use mobiles in the theatre.   Man **soll** im Theater keine Handys benutzen.
· Men **are supposed to** take off their hats in church.   Männer **sollen** in der Kirche den Hut abnehmen.
· We **were supposed to** be back at six .   Wir **sollten** um 6 Uhr zurück sein.

We use **had better** (short form: **'d better**) to say what **somebody should do in a specific situation.**
· I**'d better** go now. It's late.   Ich **sollte** jetzt (lieber) gehen. Es ist spät.
· It's cold. You**'d better** stay at home.   Es ist kalt. Du **solltest** lieber zu Hause bleiben.

Compare:

A You**'re not supposed to** use mobiles here.
(general rule)

B Yes, I**'d better** turn it off now.
(specific situation)

We're not supposed to fish here.

We'd better go somewhere else then.

be supposed to and **be said to**
We can use **be supposed to** or **be said to** to say that people believe something is true.
· They **are supposed to** be very rich.   Sie **sollen** sehr reich sein. / **Man sagt**, sie seien sehr reich.
· They**'re said to** have six houses.   Sie **sollen** sechs Häuser haben. / **Man sagt**, sie hätten sechs Häuser.
· Carrots **are supposed to** be good for your eyes.   Mohrrüben **sollen** gut für die Augen sein.

„sollen":	
should und **ought to**	· zum Ausdruck von **Verpflichtungen** und **Ratschlägen** · wenn etwas **wahrscheinlich der Fall ist** oder **eigentlich der Fall sein sollte**
be supposed to	· wenn etwas von jemandem erwartet wird, z.B. weil etwas **vereinbart** ist, oder weil **Regeln**, **Traditionen** oder **Gesetze** es verlangen
had better	· um zu sagen, was jemand **in einer bestimmten Situation** tun sollte
be supposed to und **be said to**	· wenn etwas **angeblich der Fall** ist („die Leute sagen", „man sagt")

13 Exercises

13 Modals and their substitutes (II)

a) Correct any mistakes that you find. (Not every sentence contains a mistake!)

Example: 1. *He ought to be here by now.*

1. Robert texted 20 minutes ago that he was on the bus. Normally it takes 15 minutes. He ought be here by now.
2. If that guy in Year 10 is bullying you, I don't think you shouldn't ignore it – tell someone.
3. I really ought to stop playing this game and do my homework, but I'm nearly at the end of the level!
4. Oh no! I have no power left in my tablet – I should charged it before I left.
5. Mary was screaming at Jill. I don't think she should have react like that. It was a misunderstanding.
6. Tomorrow's weather looks bad. We will ought to pack some rain clothes before we go.

b) Look at the examples. Then complete the sentences using the correct option:
be supposed to or *had better*.
Be careful with the tenses. And sometimes you need a negative form.

Examples: 1. *People often cycle on the pavement even though they're not supposed to.* (general situation)
2. *We'd better not cycle in the pedestrian zone. We could get a fine of £75.* (specific situation)

1. People often cycle on the pavement even though they ... .
2. We ... cycle in the pedestrian zone. We could get a fine of £75.
3. You ... tidy your room if you want to watch that movie this evening.
4. We ... look at the answers in the back of the book, but I always do.
5. We ... clean up before your parents come home or they'll never let us have a party again!
6. You ... clean up the kitchen before you started watching TV – turn off the TV and do it now, please.
7. Students ... leave the school grounds during break.
8. We ... get back to school – somebody might notice that we're gone.

c) Rewrite the sentences. Use *should* or *be said to* instead of *be supposed to*.

Example: 1. *You shouldn't be playing computer games now.*

1. You aren't supposed to be playing computer games now.
2. Jake is supposed to be really good at computer games.
3. You're supposed to be doing your homework now.
4. What are you doing here? You're supposed to be in bed.
5. Try milk with honey! It's supposed to be good for a cold.
6. Lily is supposed to be very good at acting.
7. I'm supposed to be at a meeting, but I didn't feel like going.
8. I wouldn't go into that house. It's supposed to have a ghost.
9. He's supposed to be a distant cousin of the Royal Family.
10. When you meet the King, you're only supposed to say "Your Majesty" once.
11. You aren't supposed to swim here. The water isn't very clean.
12. There's a little lake not far from here which is supposed to be good for swimming.

14 The gerund (I)

You can use the -ing form of a verb like a noun.
· *I love* **holidays**. ▶ (= *I love* + noun)   · *I love* **travelling**. ▶ (= *I love* + -*ing* form of the verb *travel*)

This -*ing* form is called a **gerund**. It can be the **subject** or the **object** of a sentence.
· **Travelling** *is fun.*   *Reisen macht Spaß.*
· *I love* travelling.   *Ich liebe das Reisen. / Ich reise gern.*

The gerund can be **followed by an object** or **by an adverbial phrase**. In this way, it is like a verb.

gerund + <u>object</u>	*I love* **playing** <u>board games</u>.	*Ich spiele sehr gern Brettspiele.*
gerund + <u>adverbial phrase</u>	**Cycling** <u>in the rain</u> *can be fun too.*	*Radfahren im Regen kann auch Spaß machen.*

14.1 Verbs followed by a gerund

In contrast to German, some verbs **<u>cannot</u> be followed by an infinitive**. We use a **gerund** instead, e.g.
· *Nobody* **enjoys** ~~to go~~ **going** *to the dentist.*   *Niemand geht gern zum Zahnarzt.*
· *I can't* **imagine** ~~to live~~ **living** *in the country.*   *Ich kann mir nicht vorstellen, auf dem Land zu leben.*

These are some of the other verbs that take a gerund:
admit, consider, deny, discuss, dislike, fancy, finish, give up, keep, mind, miss, practise, regret, risk, suggest

14.2 Verbs followed by a gerund <u>or</u> infinitive

The verbs **begin/start, continue, hate, like, love, prefer** can be followed by a gerund or a *to*-infinitive:

· *When it* **started** **raining,** / **to rain,** *we all went home.*   · *I* **hate** / *I* **don't like** **getting up** / **to get up** *when it's still dark.*

After **would like, would love, would hate** (short form: *'d like*, etc.) we usually use the *to*-infinitive, not the gerund.
· *My mother* **would like** **to move** *to a small village, but I* **would hate** **to leave** *London.*

14.3 Verbs that change their meaning

Some verbs have **different meanings**, depending on whether they are followed by a **gerund** or a *to*-infinitive:

forget *doing sth.*	· *I'll never* **forget** **meeting** *the Queen.* *vergessen, dass/wie man etwas getan hat*
forget *to do sth.*	· *I* **forgot** **to phone** *him. I'm sorry.* *vergessen, etwas zu tun*
remember *doing sth.*	· *I* **remember** **meeting** *her.* *sich daran erinnern, dass/wie man etwas getan hat*
remember *to do sth.*	· *I must* **remember** **to phone** *him.* *daran denken (nicht vergessen), etwas zu tun*
stop *doing sth.*	· *I've* **stopped** **eating** *hamburgers.* *aufhören, etwas zu tun*
stop *to do sth.*	· *I* **stopped** **to buy** *a hamburger.* *anhalten, um etwas zu tun*
try *doing sth.*	· *It's very sour.* – **Try** **using** *more sugar.* *etwas (aus)probieren*
try *to do sth.*	· *I* **tried** **to open** *the door, but I couldn't.* *versuchen, etwas zu tun*

· Wenn die -*ing*-Form eines Verbs die **Funktion eines Nomens** hat, wird sie **Gerundium (gerund)** genannt. Das Gerundium kann Subjekt oder Objekt eines Satzes sein.
· Wie ein Verb kann das Gerundium durch ein Objekt oder eine Orts- oder Zeitangabe erweitert werden.
· Nach einigen englischen Verben darf kein *to*-Infinitiv stehen. Stattdessen muss man ein Gerundium verwenden.
· Auf *begin/start, continue, hate, like, love, prefer* kann – bei gleicher Bedeutung – ein Gerundium <u>oder</u> ein *to*-Infinitiv folgen.
· Bei *forget, remember, stop, try* verändert sich die Bedeutung, je nachdem, ob ein Gerundium oder ein *to*-Infinitiv folgt.

14 Exercises

14 The gerund (I)

a) The subjects and objects in the sentences below are not complete.
   Make plausible sentences using the words and phrases from the boxes.

For the subjects

I · listen to · ~~father~~ · little brother · walk · wear

For the objects

Brian · parents · sister · ~~smoke~~ · take · throw

Example: 1. My father wants to give up smoking.

1. My … wants to give up …
2. My … loves … snowballs.
3. … shoes in the flat really annoys my …
4. … music helps … to concentrate on his homework.
5. … the dog gives my … a chance to meet her boyfriend.
6. … hate … the bus to school, especially on Mondays.

b) The Student Council met yesterday. Complete the text with the correct forms of the verbs in brackets –
   infinitive or gerund.

Example: 1. The Student Council met yesterday to discuss organizing a money-raising event …

The Student Council met yesterday to discuss ¹… (organize) a money-raising event for refugees. Alex suggested
²… (have) a funny costume day – students could dress in costumes when they came to school and pay £5 each.
David said it was because Alex enjoys ³… (dress up) and it was a stupid idea. Alex asked David what he would like
⁴… (do) instead. Alex and David started ⁵… (argue). Peter then said we should consider ⁶… (organize) a student
concert. Everyone agreed this was a good idea. Alice said her father wouldn't mind ⁷… (print) the tickets in his shop
– for free of course. Daniel said he'd like ⁸… (ask) the local music shop to lend them the sound equipment. There
were a lot of ideas but some members disliked ⁹… (plan) too much too soon and said they'd prefer ¹⁰… (wait) and
get permission from the school management first. Peter asked who would talk to the head teacher because he
didn't fancy ¹¹… (do) it. David offered ¹²… (do) it. The Student Council is going to meet again in two days after we
know what the school management thinks.

c) Complete these short dialogues with the correct forms of the verbs from the box – infinitive or gerund.

have · shout · take (2x) · change (2x)

1. Lucy: Did you remember ¹… photos at Uncle Pete's birthday party?
   Mum: Of course – you can see them on my mobile.
   Lucy: Oh look Mum – the last photo is a selfie of you and Dad.
   Mum: Oh God, I look terrible. I don't remember ²… it. It must have been very late.

2. Son: What are you doing, Dad?
   Dad: I'm trying ³… the channel on the TV. The TV isn't working, or the remote control isn't.
   Son: Maybe the batteries are low. Have you tried ⁴… them?
   Dad: Good idea. I'll try that.

3. Child 1: Daddy, can we stop ⁵… a burger or something? I'm so hungry.
   Child 2: Yes, Daddy – I'm hungry too, I want a cheeseburger, pleeeaase!
   Dad: Girls! Stop ⁶… – I'm trying to drive. We'll stop at the next café, OK?

15 The gerund (II)

15.1 The gerund after prepositions

Verbs take the **gerund** form after a **preposition** (*about, at, by, for, in, instead of, of, without, …*).
· *The man left the shop **without paying**.*   Der Mann verließ den Laden, ohne zu bezahlen.
· *You can save petrol **by driving** more slowly.*   Man spart Benzin, wenn/indem man langsamer fährt.

The prepositions are often linked to an <u>adjective</u>, a <u>noun</u> or a <u>verb</u>.
· *My little brother is **<u>afraid</u> <u>of</u> sleeping** in the dark.*   Mein kleiner Bruder hat Angst davor, im Dunkeln zu schlafen.
· *What were his **<u>reasons</u> <u>for</u> leaving** school?*   Was waren die Gründe dafür, dass er die Schule verlassen hat?
· *They **<u>decided</u> <u>against</u> moving** to Italy.*   Sie entschieden sich dagegen, nach Italien zu ziehen.

The following box has an overview of some of the most common combinations.

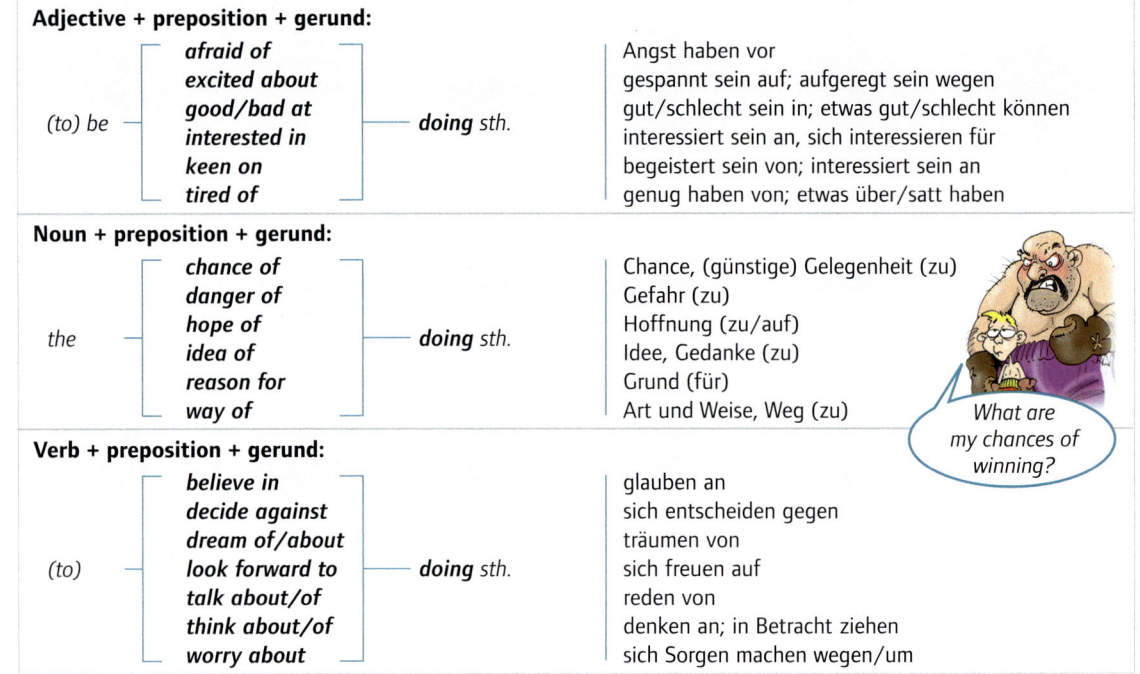

Adjective + preposition + gerund:

| (to) be | *afraid of*
excited about
good/bad at
interested in
keen on
tired of | *doing* sth. | Angst haben vor
gespannt sein auf; aufgeregt sein wegen
gut/schlecht sein in; etwas gut/schlecht können
interessiert sein an, sich interessieren für
begeistert sein von; interessiert sein an
genug haben von; etwas über/satt haben |

Noun + preposition + gerund:

| the | *chance of*
danger of
hope of
idea of
reason for
way of | *doing* sth. | Chance, (günstige) Gelegenheit (zu)
Gefahr (zu)
Hoffnung (zu/auf)
Idee, Gedanke (zu)
Grund (für)
Art und Weise, Weg (zu) |

What are my chances of winning?

Verb + preposition + gerund:

| (to) | *believe in*
decide against
dream of/about
look forward to
talk about/of
think about/of
worry about | *doing* sth. | glauben an
sich entscheiden gegen
träumen von
sich freuen auf
reden von
denken an; in Betracht ziehen
sich Sorgen machen wegen/um |

15.2 The gerund with its own subject

Compare these sentences:
1 *Ava can't imagine **moving** to Wales.*   Ava kann sich nicht vorstellen, nach Wales zu ziehen.
2 *Ava can't **imagine** **her family** moving to Wales.*   Ava kann sich nicht vorstellen, dass ihre Familie nach Wales zieht.

❗ In the second sentence, the gerund (*moving*) has its <u>own subject</u> (*her family*). *Ava* is the subject of the whole sentence.

If the gerund's own subject is a **personal pronoun**, it takes the **object form** (e.g. *me* instead of *I*).
· *Do you **mind me leaving** early today?*   Macht es Ihnen etwas aus, wenn ich heute früher gehe?

· Wenn auf eine **Präposition** (*about, at, for, in, instead of, of, without, …*) **ein Verb folgt**,
  dann steht dieses Verb als **Gerundium**.
  Die Präposition kann allein stehen oder mit einem anderen Wort (einem Adjektiv, Nomen oder Verb) verbunden sein.

· Das Gerundium kann ein **eigenes Subjekt** haben.
  Wenn das Subjekt des Gerundiums ein **Personalpronomen** ist, dann steht es in der **Objektform** (z.B. *me* statt *I*).

15 Exercises

15.1 The gerund after prepositions

Complete the blue sentences. Use a verb from the original sentence plus a preposition from the box. (Look at the example sentence for help.)

> about · against · at · by · for · in · of · on · to · without

Example: 1. *Open the door by pressing the X button.*

1. Press the X button. This will open the door.
   Open the door ...
2. I asked John to taste the crab meat. He didn't really want to.
   John wasn't keen ...
3. I have a ticket to go to the Bad Uncles concert and Elaine wants to go too.
   Elaine is interested ...
4. Peter said we should organize a student concert to raise money for refugees.
   Peter had the idea ...
5. David said it was my fault Julia broke up with him. I don't know why.
   I can't explain David's reason ...
6. We're going to the seaside next weekend. I can't wait to relax on the beach.
   I'm looking forward ...
7. Mum doesn't want us to have fireworks because she thinks they'll scare our dog.
   Mum is worried ...
8. I was going to buy a Gamestation 5 but changed my mind.
   I decided ...
9. Alice cooked spaghetti again. As usual, it was much too soft.
   Alice is really bad ...
10. Wash your face first, then you can go.
    My mother told me not to go ...

15.2 The gerund with its own subject

Complete the sentences using the gerund of the highlighted verb.
Remember: If there is a personal pronoun before a gerund, it takes the object form.

Example: 1. *My little brother and sister hate me telling them what to do all the time.*

1. *I* tell my little brother and sister what to do all the time.
   My little brother and sister hate ...
2. *My older sister* tells me what to do all the time.
   I don't like ...
3. *My father* used to take me out on Saturday mornings but he doesn't have the time any more.
   I miss ...
4. *My brother and I* eat too much chocolate, so Mum often hides it.
   Mum often hides the chocolate to stop ...
5. My uncle visited us on his brand-new mountain bike. I asked if *I* could ride it, but he said no.
   My uncle didn't fancy ...
6. My mother said that *Grandma* was really angry, but Grandma is always so quiet and calm.
   I can't imagine ...
7. My teacher was sure that *he* had said my presentation was on Wednesday, but I forgot about it.
   I didn't remember ...

Grammar

16 The *to*-infinitive

In English, we sometimes use infinitive structures where German *does not* use the infinitive

16.1 Verb + object + *to*-infinitive

We can use an object + *to*-infinitive after *cause, expect, tell, want, would like, would love*.
· His parents **expect him to be** home by ten.   *Seine Eltern erwarten, **dass** er bis zehn Uhr zu Hause ist.*
· The police officer **told us to wait** outside.   *Die Polizeibeamtin sagte, **dass** wir draußen warten sollten.*
· I**'d like you to sit** down in a circle now.   *Ich möchte, **dass** ihr euch jetzt im Kreis hinsetzt.*

> **!** After the German verbs, there is usually a clause with "**dass**". In English, a *that*-clause is **not possible.**

Other verbs that can take an object + *to*-infinitive include *allow, ask, help, invite, teach*.
(After the German verbs, you use "**zu**" + infinitive.)
· Our teacher **allows us to use** mobiles.   *Unser Lehrer erlaubt uns, Handys **zu benutzen**.*
· My sister **asked me not to wear** her T-shirts.   *Meine Schwester bat mich, nicht ihre T-Shirts **zu tragen**.*
· Pictures can **help you to learn** new words.   *Bilder können dir helfen, neue Wörter **zu lernen**.*

16.2 Question word + *to*-infinitive

After question words (*what, who, ...*), we can use subordinate clauses with modal auxiliaries (*can, must, ...*).
· I don't know   **what I can do** | **who I must ask** | **where I should go**.
  Ich weiß nicht,   *was ich tun kann* | *wen ich fragen muss* | *wohin ich gehen soll.*

> **!** However, a *to*-infinitive is the more usual structure in English. (It is not possible in German.)
> · I don't know   *what **to do*** | *who **to ask*** | *where **to go***.

16.3 The *to*-infinitive instead of a relative clause

We often use a *to*-infinitive instead of a relative clause.
It can come after a **superlative** (1) and after **the first, the last, the next, the only** (2–4).
1 **Sophie was the youngest (girl) to take part.** ▶ (... the youngest (girl) who took part.)
2 The **first/last person to arrive** was Jonathan. ▶ (The first/last person who arrived ...)
3 We're the **only shop to offer** this service. ▶ (... the only shop that offers this service.)
4 I was **the only person/the only one to win** a prize. ▶ (... the only person/the only one who won a prize.)

> **!** **the only** must be followed by a noun (*shop, person, ...*) or one/ones.

The *to*-infinitive can also come after a **noun** (especially **person, place, way**). It replaces a relative clause with a modal.
· Luigi's is **the place to go** for a good pizza. ▶ (... the place that you must/should go for ...)
· I'm looking for **someone to share** a flat with. ▶ (... someone who I can share a flat with.)

It can also replace a relative clause after **someone, anybody, something, anything, nothing, nowhere**, etc.
· There's **nothing to do** and **nowhere to go**. ▶ (There's nothing that I can do and nowhere that I can go.)

· Nach bestimmten Verben kann ein **Objekt + *to*-Infinitiv** stehen. Im Deutschen steht meist „zu" + Infinitiv.

· Auch nach *cause, expect, tell, want, would like, would love* kann ein Objekt + *to*-Infinitiv stehen.
  Nach den entsprechenden deutschen Verben steht meist ein Nebensatz mit „dass", aber auf die englischen Verben darf kein *that*-Satz folgen.

· Der *to*-Infinitiv steht oft nach einem Fragewort (*what, who, how, when, where* usw.). Er entspricht in der Regel einem Nebensatz mit modalem Hilfsverb (*can, could, should* usw.).

· Der *to*-Infinitiv wird oft anstelle eines Relativsatzes verwendet, und zwar nach Superlativen und nach *the first, the last, the next, the only* sowie nach Nomen (*person place, way*) und *someone, anything, nowhere* usw.

German summary

16 Exercises

16.1 Verb + object + *to*-infinitive

Use the verbs from the box to express the meaning of sentences 1–7 with a *to*-infinitive form.

> allow · ask · help · ~~invite~~ · teach

1. Lucy: I'm going to a Robin Hood festival, Rosie. Do you want to go too?
   Lucy invited Rosie to go to a Robin Hood festival.
2. Rosie: My parents said I can go! Rosie's parents ... go to the festival.
3. Festival worker: Can you each take a corner of the tent, girls? A worker ... help him with a tent.
4. Maid Marian: Wait here for a moment, girls. I'll get Robin. Maid Marian ... wait for a moment.
5. Robin Hood: This is how you shoot a bow and arrow, Rosie. Robin Hood ... shoot a bow and arrow.
6. Lucy: I'm going to help Maid Marian gather firewood. Lucy ... gather firewood.
7. Rosie: Robin, can you take a photo of us with Maid Marian? Rosie ... take a photo.

16.2 Question word + *to*-infinitive

Cecilia has just arrived in New Zealand on an exchange and has a lot of questions.
Use a question word and the *to*-infinitive to write about her questions.

1. **What** should I **do** if I don't like my host family? *Cecilia doesn't know what to do if she doesn't like ...*
2. **When** should I **phone** my family in Germany?
3. **Where** can I **buy** an adapter for my phone?
4. **How** can I **get** to the city centre?
5. **Who** can I **talk** to if I am homesick?
6. **Which** wild animals should I **avoid** in New Zealand?

16.3 The *to*-infinitive instead of a relative clause

a) Look at the boxes and the example sentence. Think of your family – who is the first / the last / the only one to do these things? (You can add *always, usually, often*, etc.).

I		*get up*	1. *My ... is (usually) the first to get up.*
My parents		*have a shower*	2. *I'm (always) ...*
My mother	*the first*	*have breakfast*	3. ...
My father	*the last*	*leave home*	4. ...
My sister	*the only one(s)*	*come home*	5. ...
My brother		*go to bed*	6. ...

b) Melinda is unhappy. But why?
Choose verbs from the box and complete her sentences. Example sentence 1 can help you.

1. I'd like to go dancing tonight. The Funk House would be
   the perfect place *to go*, but it's a long way from where I live.
2. And there are no buses after 11,
   so I'd need someone ... me a lift back home.
3. Jacob would be the person ..., but he's away on holiday.
4. And I've got nobody ... anyway.
5. I wish I had some new music ...
6. I guess it'll be another evening at home with nothing ... but watch a film.

> ask · do ·
> give · go ·
> go with ·
> listen to

17 Indirect speech (I)

17.1 Direct and indirect speech

To tell somebody else what Norah has said you can use her exact words (**direct speech**):
· Norah says, "I **love** music. I **go** dancing every Saturday."

You can also use **indirect speech**:
· Norah says that she **loves** music and that she **goes** dancing every Saturday.

 In English there is no comma before indirect speech.
We often leave out the word **that** (especially after *say, tell sb.* and *think*):
Norah **says she loves** music and she **goes** dancing every Saturday.

*I **love** music – I **go** dancing every Saturday.*

17.2 Indirect speech: backshift of tenses and other changes

If a **reporting verb** is in the **simple past** (e.g. *said* and *told*), the verb in indirect speech usually moves back a step in the past (= **backshift of tenses**): *Norah **said** she **loved** music and she **went** dancing every Saturday.*

Backshift of tenses	direct speech	indirect speech
present → past	"I **don't like** musicals." "We'**re** just **having** dinner."	She **told** us she **didn't like** musicals. He **said** they **were** just **having** dinner.
past → past perfect [1]	"I **arrived** on Friday evening." "Alex **was waiting** for Olivia."	She **said** she **had arrived** on Friday evening. Bobby **said** Alex **had been waiting** for Olivia.
present perfect → past perfect	"I'**ve seen** that film before."	I **told** her that I **had seen** the film before.
will-future → would + infinitive	"I'm sure you'**ll qualify**."	Mr Jones **said** he **was** sure I **would qualify**.
going to-future → **was/were going to + infinitive**	"We'**re going to fly** to Italy in July."	They **said** they **were going to fly** to Italy in July.
can → could	"You **can** use my laptop."	Her dad **said** she **could** use his laptop.

[1] Simple past forms in direct speech often stay the same in indirect speech (i.e. are not changed to the past perfect):
*I **arrived** on Friday evening. → She told us she **arrived** on Friday evening.*

As in German, other words also change to show the point of view of the person who is reporting:

pronouns (*I, you, …*) **possessive determiners** (*my, your, …*)	Norah Norah reports Ava reports	"*I* can lend *you my* bike, Ava." I told Ava *I* could lend *her my* bike. Norah said *she* could lend *me her* bike.
time phrases (*tomorrow, yesterday, last week, …*) **phrases of place** (*here, …*)	On a postcard from Alex Alex's mother (to a friend, a week later)	*I like it a lot here in France. I'm flying to Paris tomorrow.* *He wrote that he liked it a lot there, and that he was flying to Paris the next day.*

· Wenn das die indirekte Rede **einleitende Verb im *simple past*** steht (*said, told, …*),
  dann werden die Zeitformen der direkten Rede meist um eine Zeitstufe in die Vergangenheit
  „zurückverschoben" **(*backshift of tenses*)**.

· Wie im Deutschen werden in der indirekten Rede die Pronomen und Possessivbegleiter sowie
  die Orts- und Zeitangaben so angepasst, dass sie der Sicht des Berichtenden entsprechen.

· Im Englischen steht vor der indirekten Rede kein Komma, und die Konjunktion *that* wird oft weggelassen.

17 Exercises

17.1 Direct and indirect speech

Write complete sentences. There is only one correct ending for each sentence beginning.

Examples: 1. + j Every night Mum tells me to sleep well.
2. + c Every night Mum says, "Good night, my little princess."

1. Every night Mum tells	a) I should ask Mum.
2. Every night Mum says,	b) to you?" asked Martha.
3. My teacher told	c) "Goodnight, my little princess."
4. My teacher said	d) told the student.
5. "That's not right, Mr Roberts,"	e) you?" asked Martha.
6. "That's not right," Mr Roberts	f) I was making progress.
7. "What did she say	g) "Ask your mum."
8. "What did she tell	h) me I was making progress.
9. Dad says	i) said the student.
10. Dad says,	j) me to sleep well.

17.2 Indirect speech: backshift of tenses and other changes

Read the phone conversation. Then write sentences 1–9 to report what Mary and Julia said.
Be careful to make any necessary changes.

Example: 1. Julia told Mary that the karaoke machine hadn't arrived yet.

Mary: Hi Julia, where are you?
Julia: Mary! Hi! I'm in the garden preparing for the party.
Mary: Cool. Has the karaoke machine arrived yet?
Julia: (1) No, it hasn't arrived.
Mary: Oh, dear. Do you think it will arrive in time?
Julia: (2) I'm expecting it soon.
Mary: Have you told your neighbours about the party yet?
Julia: (3) Robert is going to do it.
Mary: Knowing Robert, he'll probably forget. You should do it yourself.
Julia: OK. Later.
Mary: Can I help with anything?
Julia: Yes, actually, you can. One of the spotlights is broken.
Mary: That's annoying.
Julia: (4) I need to replace it. Do you know where you can get one?
Mary: Well, (5) I would order one online. If you order from Jungle Instant, they deliver the same day.
Julia: That would be fantastic, thanks Mary … There's just one more thing. It's about David.
Mary: What's the problem with David?
Julia: (6) I don't know if he's coming to the party.
Mary: Did you invite him?
Julia: Of course, but (7) he seemed angry when I spoke to him a few days ago.
Mary: So what do you want me to do?
Julia: Could you speak to him, please?
Mary: Of course. And don't worry about David, Julia. (8) I'm sure he doesn't want to miss your big party.
Julia: I hope you're right.
Mary: (9) I'll call him right away.
Julia: I think it would be better if you didn't mention Alex. It's a very sensitive topic. …

1. Julia told Mary that …
2. She said that …
3. Mary: Julia told me …
4. Mary: Julia told me …
5. Mary: I said …
6. Julia told Mary …
7. Julia explained that …
8. Mary said that …
9. Julia: Mary said that …

18 Indirect speech (II)

18.1 Indirect speech: questions

If the reporting verb is in the <u>simple past</u> (e.g. *asked, wanted to know, wondered*), you backshift the verb in the question.

direct	*"Why **don't** you **like** musicals?"* *"What**'s going** on?"*	indirect	I <u>asked</u> her why she **didn't like** musicals. Miss Hall <u>wanted to know</u> what **was going** on.

If the direct question is a **yes/no question**, we use *whether* or *if* (= "ob") in the indirect question.

direct	*"**Do** you **want** to join us?"* *"**Are** you **going to** stay long?"*	indirect	She <u>asked</u> **whether** I **wanted** to join them. Jake <u>asked</u> me **if** I **was going to** stay long.

The word order in indirect questions is the same as in statements: **S – V – …**

			S	V	
statement			"We	live	in Hamburg."
direct questions		"Do "Where do	you you	live live?"	in Hamburg?"
indirect questions	I asked I asked	if where	they they	lived lived.	in Hamburg.

(!) We do <u>not</u> use *do/does/did* before the subject in <u>indirect</u> questions.

Note the **position of the preposition** in direct and indirect questions in English.

direct	*"What are you waiting **for**?"*	indirect	He asked me what I was waiting **for**. (…, *worauf* ich wartete.)

18.2 Indirect speech: requests, commands, advice, suggestions

We usually use **infinitive constructions** to report **requests**, **commands** and **advice**.
· requests: *ask sb. to do sth.* (or *ask sb. not to do sth.*)
· commands: *tell sb. to do sth.* (or *tell sb. not to do sth.*)
· advice: *advise sb. to do sth.* (or *advise sb. not to do sth.*)

direct	*"Can you lend me your pen?"* *"Don't touch the paintings."* *"I'd get a holiday job if I were you."*	indirect	A man **asked** me **to lend** him my pen. The guide **told** us **not to touch** the paintings. Mr Williams **advised** Grace **to get** a holiday job.
			Grace **was advised to get** a holiday job.

We often use **passive constructions.** ➡ *Passive: 9 and 10, pp. 122–125*

Never use an infinitive after *suggest* – you can use the following structures to report **suggestions**:

direct	*"Let's go for a pizza."*	indirect	He **suggested going** for a pizza. He **suggested that we go** for a pizza. He **suggested we should go** for a pizza.

Indirekte Rede: Fragen
· *backshift of tenses* bei einleitendem Verb im *simple past*
· direkte Frage ohne Fragewort --> ***whether/if*** in der indirekten Frage
· **kein** *do/does/did* in indirekten Fragen

Bitten, Aufforderungen, Ratschläge, Vorschläge
· Bitten: ***ask*** sb. (not) to do sth.
· Aufforderungen: ***tell*** sb. (not) to do sth.
· Ratschläge: ***advise*** sb. (not) to do sth.
· Vorschläge: ***suggest*** doing sth.
    suggest that we/you/… do sth.
    suggest we/you/… should do sth.

18 Exercises

18.1 Indirect speech: questions

Read Mary and Julia's phone conversation.
Then write sentences 1–7 to report the questions.

Mary: Hi Julia, where are you?
Julia: Mary! Hi! I'm in the garden preparing for the party.
Mary: Cool. (1) Has the karaoke machine arrived yet?
Julia: No, it hasn't.
Mary: Oh, dear. (2) Do you think it will arrive in time?
Julia: I'm expecting it soon.
Mary: (3) Have you told your neighbours about the party yet?
Julia: Robert is going to do it.
Mary: Knowing Robert, he'll probably forget. (8) You should do it yourself.
Julia: OK. Later.
Mary: (4) Can I help with anything?
Julia: Yes, actually, you can. One of the spotlights is broken.
Mary: That's annoying.
Julia: I need to replace it. (5) Do you know where you can get one?
Mary: Well, (9) I would order one online. If you order from Jungle Instant, they deliver the same day.
Julia: That would be fantastic, thanks Mary … There's just one more thing. It's about David.
Mary: What's the problem with David?
Julia: I don't know if he's coming to the party.
Mary: (6) Did you invite him?
Julia: Of course, but … he seemed angry when I spoke to him a few days ago.
Mary: (7) So what do you want me to do?
Julia: (10) Could you speak to him, please?
Mary: Of course. (11) And don't worry about David, Julia. I'm sure he doesn't want to miss your big party.
Julia: I hope you're right.
Mary: I'll call him right away.
Julia: (12) I think it would be better if you didn't mention Alex. It's a very sensitive topic …

Example: 1. *Mary wanted to know if the karaoke machine had arrived yet.*

1. Mary wanted to know if …
2. Mary asked Julia if …
3. Mary asked Julia whether …
4. Mary asked Julia …
5. Julia asked Mary …
6. Mary wanted to know …
7. Mary asked Julia …

18.2 Indirect speech: requests, commands, advice, suggestions

Read the phone conversation again and complete sentences 8–12.

Example: 8. *Mary advised Julia to tell her neighbours about the party herself.*

8. Mary advised Julia …
9. Mary suggested …
10. Julia asked Mary …
11. Mary told Julia …
12. Julia advised Mary …

19 Conditional sentences

A conditional sentence tells us what must happen so that something else can happen too.
If you give me your number, **I'll call you**.   *Wenn du mir deine Nummer gibst, rufe ich dich an.*

Conditional sentences have a subordinate clause with *if* <u>and</u> a **main clause**. (Be careful: We use **when** to refer to the time of a future situation. **When** *I'm older, I would like to go to university.*) There are three common types:

19.1 Conditional 1: *if* + simple present

In the main clause we can use

the **will**-future	If I **miss** the bus, I**'ll take** a taxi.
	Wenn ich den Bus verpasse, <u>nehme</u> ich ein Taxi.
a **modal**	If Dan **misses** the bus, he can/should/must take a taxi.
an **imperative**	If you **miss** the bus, **take** a taxi.

19.2 Conditional 2: *if* + simple past

We use *if + <u>simple past</u>* when we imagine what **might or might not** happen now or in the future.

In the main clause we can use

would + infinitive	If I **missed** the bus, I**'d take** a taxi.
	Wenn ich den Bus verpasste/verpassen würde, <u>würde</u> ich ein Taxi <u>nehmen</u>.
could/might + infinitive	If Dan **missed** the bus, he could/might take a taxi.

19.3 Conditional 3: *if* + past perfect

We use *if + <u>past perfect</u>* when we imagine situations that <u>did not</u> happen in the past.
You say *If I had missed the bus …* only when you <u>did not</u> miss it.

In the main clause we can use

would have + past participle	If I **had missed** the bus, I would have taken a taxi.
	Wenn ich den Bus verpasst hätte, <u>hätte</u> ich ein Taxi <u>genommen</u>.
could have **might have** + past participle	If Dan **had missed** the bus, he could have taken a taxi. / he might have taken a taxi.

19.4 Other conditional sentences

As in German, there can be situations where we use **other combinations of verb forms** in conditional sentences.
· If we **had gone** by car, we **would be** there now.
  Wenn wir mit dem Auto gefahren wären, wären wir schon da.
· If I **knew** her better, I **would have asked** her.
  Wenn ich sie besser kennen würde, hätte ich sie gefragt.
· If you**'ve been** here before, you**'ll know** the rules.
  Wenn du schon mal hier warst, dann kennst du (ja) die Regeln.
· If they **left** at seven, they **won't be** here until twelve.
  Wenn sie um 7 Uhr losgefahren sind, werden sie erst um 12 hier sein.

If we **had gone** by car, we **would be** there now.

· Bedingungssatz **Typ 1** (*if* + simple present): „<u>Was ist, wenn …</u>"; im Hauptsatz steht das *will-future* oder ein Modalverb oder ein Imperativ

· Bedingungssatz **Typ 2** (*if* + simple past): „<u>Was wäre, wenn …</u>"; im Hauptsatz steht *would/could/might* + Infinitiv

· Bedingungssatz **Typ 3** (*if* + past perfect): „<u>Was wäre gewesen, wenn …</u>"; im Hauptsatz steht *would have/could have/might have* + Partizip Perfekt

Beachte, dass – wie im Deutschen – je nach Situation auch andere Kombinationen von Zeitformen in Bedingungssätzen vorkommen können.

19 Exercises

19.1 Conditional 1

If or *when*? Make complete sentences using *if* or *when* in one clause and *will* + verb in the other.

1. ... I ... (get) home,
2. ... the weather ... (be) is nice tomorrow,
3. ... you ... (not go) to sleep now,
4. ... Orla ever ... (go) to Paris one day,
5. You ... (not eat) your dinner
6. We ... (have) a big party

a) ... you ... (have) that snack now.
b) she ... definitely ... (visit) the Louvre.
c) I ... (text) you.
d) you ... (be) tired tomorrow.
e) ... my grandmother ... (arrive) tomorrow.
f) we ... (go) to the beach.

19.2 Conditional 1 or 2

Decide if the sentences are realistic or hypothetical.
Then write them in conditional 1 or 2, according to your choice.

1. If you ... (buy) fewer things online, you ... (help) reduce packaging and emissions from delivery trucks.
2. We ... (limit) or even reverse global heating if we all ... (become) vegetarian.
3. People ... (reduce) the rubbish they throw away if they ... (be charged) for waste collection by weight.
4. You ... (save) money and plastic if you ... (keep) a cloth shopping bag with you all the time.
5. If the government ... (make) public transport free, far fewer people ... (drive) their cars.
6. If we ... (repair) electronic devices instead of buying new ones, we ... (save) resources and money.

19.3 Conditional 3

Read the situations below. Write conditional 3 sentences to express what could, would or might have happened if the situations had been different.

Example: I didn't lock my bicycle. It was stolen.
　　　　　If I had locked my bicycle, it wouldn't have been stolen.

1. I didn't see your text message. I didn't reply to it.
2. Matilda studied hard for her exam. She got an A.
3. You didn't listen to what I said. You made that mistake.
4. We didn't leave on time. We missed our train.
5. Orla practised her violin piece. She played it so beautifully.
6. My parents didn't have social media years ago. They don't understand it.
7. You didn't write down the homework. You forgot it.
8. My mum visited Dublin. That's where she met my dad.

Grammar

20 Relative clauses

20.1 Defining relative clauses

A **defining relative clause** gives **important information** about a noun. (It *defines* the noun.)
In these examples, the <u>relative clauses</u> tell us which girl and which shop we are talking about.
· *Do you know* the girl <u>who works at the Oxfam shop</u>?   … *das Mädchen, <u>das im Oxfam-Shop arbeitet?</u>*
· *It's* the shop <u>which sells old clothes and books</u>.   …*der Laden, <u>der alte Kleidung und Bücher verkauft</u>.*

We use the relative pronoun *who* for people and *which* for things. We can also use *that* for people <u>and</u> things.
… the <u>girl who</u> works / … the <u>girl that</u> works …   … the <u>shop which</u> sells … / … the <u>shop that</u> sells …

In English there is **no comma** between the main clause and a defining relative clause.

20.2 Contact clauses

When the **relative pronoun** is the **object** of the relative clause, we often **leave it out**. This is called a **contact clause**.
You cannot make contact clauses when the relative pronoun is the **subject** of the relative clause.

	Relative clause			Contact clause
Mr Jones is <u>the teacher</u>	**who** I **like the most**.		*Mr Jones is* <u>the teacher</u>	I **like the most**.
These are <u>the photos</u>	**that** Dad **took in Wales**.		*These are* <u>the photos</u>	Dad **took in Wales**.
Do you know <u>the girl</u>	**who works at the Oxfam shop?**			

The **relative pronoun** is the subject when the next word is a <u>**verb**</u>, e.g. *the girl* **who** <u>works</u> … / *the shop* **which** <u>sells</u> …

20.3 Non-defining relative clauses

Non-defining relative clauses give **additional information** about a noun. They are used mainly in written English.
· *Agatha Christie*, **who died in 1976,** *wrote about 70 detective novels.*
· *John Lennon*, **whose mother taught him to play the banjo,** *later became famous as a member of the Beatles.*
· *At 11.35 we landed at Atlanta International*, **which is one of the world's busiest airports**.

Without a non-defining relative clause, the main clause still makes sense: *At 11.35 we landed at Atlanta International.*

 In non-defining relative clauses: · you **must** use commas between the relative clause and the main clause
                                  · you **cannot** leave out the relative pronoun
                                  · you **cannot** use the relative pronoun *that*.

20.4 Relative clauses with *which* to refer to a whole clause

We can use relative clauses with *which* to **comment on** the statement in the main clause.
These are like German relative clauses with "was". There is a comma between the main clause and the relative clause.
· *Jane helped us to tidy up*, **which was very good of her**.   …, *was ich sehr nett von ihr fand.*
· *I'm late*, **which means I'm going to miss the train**.   …, *was bedeutet, dass ich den Zug verpassen werde.*
· *In 1980, John Lennon was murdered*, **which shocked the world**.   …, *was die Welt schockierte.*

German summary

· **Bestimmende Relativsätze** bestimmen das Nomen näher, auf das sie sich beziehen, und geben damit Informationen, die zum Verständnis des Hauptsatzes notwendig sind. Sie werden nicht durch Kommas abgetrennt.
Bei **Personen** verwendet man die Relativpronomen *who* oder *that*; bei **Dingen** *which* oder *that*.

· Wenn das Relativpronomen **Objekt des Relativsatzes** ist, wird es oft weggelassen *(contact clause)*.
Beachte: Wenn das Relativpronomen direkt vor dem Verb steht, ist es Subjekt und darf nicht weggelassen werden.

· **Nicht bestimmende Relativsätze** geben Zusatzinformationen, die zum Verständnis des Hauptsatzes nicht zwingend notwendig sind. Sie kommen vorwiegend in geschriebenem Englisch vor und werden durch Kommas abgetrennt.

· **Satzbezogene Relativsätze** kommentieren die Aussage des Hauptsatzes. Sie entsprechen deutschen Relativsätzen mit „was" und werden durch Kommas abgetrennt.

20 Exercises

20.1 Defining relative clauses

Choose a phrase from the right and make clues to describe the person or thing on the left.
Use *This is someone who … / This is something which … .*

Example: 1. *This is someone who you can borrow clothes from. (an older sister)*

1. an older sister	tells you the time
2. a suitcase	helps you to learn how to surf
3. a memory card	you can borrow clothes from
4. a police officer	is good to have at parties
5. a surfing instructor	you can carry clothes in
6. a watch	you can store files on
7. a karaoke machine	protects you and your family

20.2 Contact clauses

Rewrite 1–6. In each sentence, take out one *that* and replace the other with *which* or *who*.

Example: 1. *The boy I like most is Henry, but the boy who likes me most is Robert.*

1. The boy that I like most is Henry, but the boy that likes me most is Robert.
2. Some of the apps that I use are free, but most apps that are free are full of advertisements.
3. Some people that I know think I am confident, but people that know me very well know I am shy.
4. We used to live in a house that had lots of character, but the house that we live in now is nothing special.
5. This isn't the book that I wanted. This is the book that doesn't have the answers.
6. I need to see the woman that sells the tickets. The ticket that she sold me was for the wrong concert.

20.3 Non-defining relative clauses

Rewrite the sentences on the left including the correct extra information from the right.
Don't forget to use commas.

Example: 1. *E-readers, which I don't often use, can never replace real books.*

1. E-readers can never replace real books.	who loves crime novels
2. *The Little Hero* was the last book I read.	who reminded me of my grandfather
3. The main character is a young girl from Scotland.	which is around the corner from my house
4. I went to the library to take back the books.	who has the same first name as me
5. My mother is writing her own detective story.	which I don't often use
6. I was sad that Old Mr Bumblebore died in the end.	which is the first part of a series

20.4 Relative clauses with *which* to refer to a whole clause

Read sentences 1–5. Choose a suitable comment from a) to e) and rewrite the sentences as in the example.

Example: 1. *We're moving to Leeds in the summer, which means I'll have to change school.*

1. We're moving to Leeds in the summer.	a) It means I'll be able to buy a new computer soon.
2. Emily won the 100 metres.	b) It shocked people all over the world.
3. Jonathan offered to help with the dishes.	c) It means I'll have to change school.
4. In 1968, Martin Luther King was killed.	d) That was very nice of him.
5. I'm going to get a pay rise next month.	e) It surprised everybody.

21 Participles (I)

21.1 Participle forms

There are two main participle forms:

1 **Present participles** (*-ing*-ending)	work → **working** dance → **dancing**	try → **trying** plan → **planning**
2 **Past participles** (*-ed*-ending with regular verbs)	work → **worked** dance → **danced**	try → **tried** plan → **planned**

Irregular verbs have special past participle forms.

➡ *Unregelmäßige Verben: S. 278–279*

build → **built**	grow → **grown**
make → **made**	see → **seen**
teach → **taught**	write → **written**

21.2 Participle clauses instead of relative clauses

To make sentences shorter, you can often use **participle clauses** instead of **relative clauses**.

Present participle (for active verbs)	*The city is always full of people looking for a parking space.* (*The city is always full of people **who are looking for a parking space**.*) *The man **driving the red car** waved at us.* (*The man **who was driving the red car** waved at us.*)
Past participles (for passive verbs)	*The Eurovision Song Contest is an international event **watched by millions of people**.* (*The Eurovision Song Contest is an international event **which is watched by millions of people**.*)

21.3 Verb of perception + object + present participle

After verbs like *feel*, *hear*, *listen to*, *notice*, *see*, *smell*, *spot* and *watch* we can use an **object + present participle**.
1 We **heard a baby** crying.   *Wir hörten ein Baby weinen.*
2 He **watched the band** practising.   *Er beobachtete, wie die Band übte. / Er beobachtete die Band beim Üben.*
3 She **saw someone** climbing on the roof.
   Sie sah jemanden auf das Dach klettern. / Sie sah, wie/dass jemand auf das Dach kletterte.
4 I **noticed two women** arguing outside.
   Ich bemerkte, dass sich zwei Frauen draußen stritten. / Ich bemerkte zwei Frauen, die sich draußen stritten.

! This structure is used in English for a number of <u>different</u> German structures, e.g. the infinitive (1), a subordinate clause with "wie" or "dass" (2, 3, 4) or sometimes a relative clause (4).

We can also use an **infinitive** after these verbs. The infinitive expresses the idea that **the complete action is perceived from beginning to end**.
· We **saw him** grab the money and run away.   *Wir sahen, wie er sich das Geld schnappte und davonlief.*

· Das **Partizip Präsens** (*present participle*) endet auf *-ing*: working, trying, dancing, planning.
  Das **Partizip Perfekt** (*past participle*) endet bei regelmäßigen Verben auf *-ed*: worked, tried, danced, planned; unregelmäßige Verben haben eigene *past participle*-Formen.

· Relativsätze werden oft zu **Partizipialsätzen** verkürzt. Das *present participle* entspricht dabei einem Relativpronomen + Verb im Aktiv, das *past participle* entspricht einem Relativpronomen + Verb im Passiv.

· Auf **Verben der Wahrnehmung** wie *feel, hear, listen to, notice, see, smell, spot, watch* kann ein Objekt + Partizip Präsens folgen. Mit solchen Sätzen sagt man, dass man etwas wahrnimmt, das gerade im Gang ist (bzw. war).

21 Exercises

21.1 Participle forms

Find and correct any mistakes which you can find in the participle forms.

1. The girl wearring the white T-shirt is Irish – her name is Orla.
2. Schools builded years ago are always really cold.
3. The tablet found on the school bus belongs to Jamal.
4. The protesters lieing on the motorway are campaigning against fossil fuels.
5. Cars drove by intelligent computers are no longer science fiction.
6. Students taught at home by their parents often do better in exams.
7. The Tom Bolland fans hopeing to meet their hero waited for hours outside his hotel.
8. The next movie staring the actor is Spiderboy III and it will be in cinemas next month.

21.2 Participle clauses instead of relative clauses

Use participle clauses to shorten the relative clauses.

Example: 1. The line of fans waiting to buy the latest book in the Harriet Popper series ...

1. The line of fans who are waiting to buy the latest book in the Harriet Popper series stretches for a mile.
2. *Harriet Popper and the Alchemist* – the first in the series which was published in 2012 – was an unexpected success.
3. It is one of those books that are loved by people of different age groups.
4. One of the young fans shouts out, "Who is that woman who is standing at the door?!"
5. It's a woman who is wearing a purple coat and who is carrying a magic lamp. Could it be the author, A. K. Grayling?
6. Every single fan would love to get a copy of the book which is signed by the author herself.

21.3 Verbs of perception + object + present participle

Put one of the verbs from the box into each pair of sentences.
Use the present participle form if the action is in progress or the infinitive form if it is complete.

~~walk~~ · come · drop · look · play · tell

Examples: 1 a) Do you know where Julia is going? I saw her walking down the road.
b) I saw Trevor walk into the bookshop five minutes ago ...

1 a) Do you know where Julia is going? I saw her ... down the road.
b) I saw Trevor ... into the bookshop five minutes ago – if you go now, he should still be there.

2 a) Brian, I heard you ... Suzy a joke – what was the last part? I missed it.
b) Oh Dad, not that story about the huge fish that got away, we've heard you ... that a million times!

3 a) I saw you ... football and wanted to ask if I can join in.
b) Dad and I saw Manchester United ... against Chelsea last year.

4 a) Mum: "Oh hi darling! I didn't hear you ... in." Son: "Hi Mum!"
b) Quick kids, hide your father's present, I can hear him ...!

5 a) On the bus, I noticed a girl ... at me. I asked her if she knew me – it was Molly, our ex-neighbour!
b) Alice: "Did you notice David ... at Julia when someone mentioned Alex?" Mary: "Yeah! What a look!"

6 a) While I was talking to Molly, I saw a lady ... her mobile. I shouted to her and she picked it up.
b) My mother didn't see my five-year-old brother ... little stones behind him on our walk – like Hansel.

22 Participles (II)

22.1 Participle clauses to describe connected actions

We often use **present participle clauses** to talk about different actions which are connected to each other.
In German sentences like these, we use a main clause with ***und*** or a subordinate clause with ***wobei*** or ***indem***.

· *It rains a lot here, **sometimes flooding** the roads.*
  *Hier regnet es viel, **und** manchmal überschwemmt es (dabei) die Straßen.*
· *Last Sunday morning, we stayed in bed, **reading** and **listening** to the radio.*
  *Letzten Sonntagmorgen sind wir im Bett geblieben **und** haben gelesen und Radio gehört.*
· *Charlotte ran down the stairs, **losing** a shoe.*
  *Charlotte rannte die Treppe hinunter, **wobei** sie einen Schuh verlor.*
· ***Using** a knife, she was able to open the door.*
  ***Indem** sie ein Messer benutzte, konnte sie die Tür öffnen.*

22.2 Participle clauses instead of adverbial clauses of time

After the conjunctions ***after***, ***before***, ***until***, ***when***, ***while*** you can use **participle clauses** instead of **adverbial clauses of time**.

Present participle (for active verbs)

*Jack decided to go on a world tour **after winning** the lottery.*
*(Jack decided to go on a world tour **after he (had) won** the lottery.)*
Jack beschloss, eine Weltreise zu machen, nachdem er im Lotto gewonnen hatte.
***While walking** down the street, Emily saw a huge dog.*
*(**While she was walking** down the street, Emily saw a huge dog.)*
Während Emily die Straße hinunterging, sah sie einen riesigen Hund.

The conjunctions *while* and *when* can be left out if you put the participle clause at the beginning of a sentence.
***Walking** down the street, Emily saw a huge dog.*

❗ If you start with the main clause, do <u>not</u> leave out the conjunction.

Compare:
1 *Emily saw a huge dog **while walking** down the street.* ▶ <u>Emily</u> was walking down the street.
2 *Emily saw a huge dog **walking** down the street.* ▶ <u>The dog</u> was walking down the street.

Past participles (for passive verbs)

***When asked** why he had left school so early, he said he had wanted to earn money.*
*(**When he was asked** why he had left school so early, he said he had wanted to earn money.)*
Als er gefragt wurde, warum er so früh die Schule verlassen hat, …

The participle clause normally comes before the main clause.
The conjunction (*when*, *while*) can be left out.
***Asked** why he had left school so early, he said he had wanted to earn money.*

These past participle structures are typical of written English.

· ***Present participle clauses*** werden oft verwendet, wenn man über miteinander verbundene Vorgänge spricht (z.B., um Begleitumstände oder Konsequenzen einer Handlung / eines Vorgangs zu beschreiben).
  Im Deutschen steht meist ein Hauptsatz mit „und", manchmal auch ein Nebensatz mit „wobei" oder „indem".

· ***Participle clauses***, die mit ***when*** oder ***while*** eingeleitet sind, entsprechen Nebensätzen der Zeit.
  Das *present participle* entspricht dabei einem Verb im Aktiv, das *past participle* einem Verb im Passiv.
  Solche Partizipialsätze können auf den Hauptsatz folgen oder vor dem Hauptsatz stehen.
  Wenn sie vor dem Hauptsatz stehen, kann die Konjunktion (*while*, *when*) weggelassen werden.
  (Vorsicht: Wenn der Partizipialsatz auf den Hauptsatz folgt, führt das Weglassen der Konjunktion zu einer Bedeutungsveränderung!)

22 Exercises

22.1 Participle clauses to describe connected actions

Add the information given in brackets to sentences 1–9. Use present or past participle clauses.

Example: 1. Thomas walked through the school gate, saying he had bought something cool.

1. Thomas walked through the school gate. (He said he had bought something cool.)
2. The boys came over to Thomas. (They were trying to see what he had.)
3. He took out a firework and lit it. (The other boys encouraged him.)
4. The firework exploded sooner than he had expected. (The firework burned his hand badly.)
5. One boy ran towards the school. (He was looking for help.)
6. Thomas was driven to hospital. (The emergency services helped him.)
7. The teachers calmed down the other students. (They told them Thomas would be well taken care of.)
8. The next day, the head teacher spoke to the students. (He reminded them about the safety risks of fireworks.)
9. When Thomas returned to school, he said sorry to everyone. (He promised to be more responsible in future.)

22.2 Participle clauses instead of adverbial clauses of time

a) Complete the sentences with a participle clause. Use *after*, *before* or *while* with one of the ideas from the box.

> arrive in London · enter the restaurant · cycle over 40 miles · fly over the Alps ·
> move to another country · eat his salad · climb up the ladder · finish her book

Example: 1. Before entering the restaurant, he checked he had enough money to pay for the meal.

1. ... he checked he had enough money to pay for the meal.
2. ... he noticed an insect under one of the leaves.
3. ... she put it back in its place on the shelf.
4. ... we looked down at the mountains below us .
5. ... you should find out something about its customs and way of life.
6. ... they decided it was time for a break.
7. ... we headed straight for Buckingham Palace.
8. ... I fell off and broke my leg.

b) First decide which conjunction to use in each sentence: *when* or *while*.

Examples: 1. When Julia told him Alex was invited to the party, David said he didn't want to go.
2. While he was doing his homework, Jack fell asleep.

1. ... Julia told him Alex was invited to the party, David said he didn't want to go.
2. ... he was doing his homework, Jack fell asleep.
3. ... I was running to catch the bus, I fell and hurt my leg.
4. ... he was asked to help, David immediately agreed.
5. ... Dad was preparing breakfast, he dropped all the eggs on the floor.
6. The 'Where's my phone?' function uses GPS to record its location ... you turn it on.
7. ... I was cleaning my teeth, I suddenly remembered the homework I hadn't done.
8. ... you learn a foreign language, it is important to practise a little every day.
9. I didn't notice the bus come and go ... I was texting my friend.
10. ... he was informed that he hadn't passed the exam, Jo felt very disappointed.

c) Rewrite your sentences and replace the adverbial of time (*while* ... / *when* ...) with a participle clause.

Examples: 1. When told Alex was invited to the party, David said he didn't want to go.
2. While doing his homework, Jack fell asleep.

23 Participles (III)

23.1 Participle clauses instead of adverbial clauses of reason

You can use participle clauses as an <u>alternative</u> to **adverbial clauses of reason** (clauses with *because*).
This is more usual in written English than in everyday spoken English.

Present participle (for active verbs)

· <u>**Feeling** tired</u>, I decided to go to bed early.
(I decided to go to bed early <u>because I was feeling tired</u>.)
Weil/Da ich müde war, beschloss ich, früh schlafen zu gehen.

· <u>**Being** a doctor</u>, she knew exactly what to do.
(She knew exactly what to do <u>because she's a doctor</u>.)
Weil/Da sie Ärztin ist, wusste sie genau, was zu tun ist.

· <u>**Not knowing** what to do</u>, she asked for advice.
(She asked for advice <u>because she didn't know what to do</u>.)
Weil/Da sie nicht wusste, was sie tun sollte, bat sie um Rat.

Not being able to swim, he almost drowned.

🛈 You cannot use the conjunction *because* in participle clauses.

~~*Because feeling very tired*~~, …   ~~*Because being a doctor*~~, …   ~~*Because not knowing what to do*~~, …

Past participles (for passive verbs)

<u>**Warned** by his wife</u>, the man was able to escape.
(The man was able to escape <u>because he had been warned by his wife</u>.)
Von seiner Frau gewarnt, konnte der Mann entkommen. / Weil er von seiner Frau gewarnt wurde/worden war, …

23.2 Other participle clauses

Participle clauses can begin with other conjunctions, e.g. **although**, **if**, **unless**, **whether**.

· It is forbidden to enter the building site <u>**unless wearing** a hard hat</u>.
(It is forbidden to enter the building site <u>unless you are wearing a hard hat</u>.)
…, außer man trägt einen Schutzhelm.

· <u>**Although asked** to stop by the police</u>, he drove on.
(<u>Although he was asked to stop</u> by the police, he drove on.)
Obwohl er von der Polizei aufgefordert wurde, …

· <u>**If posted** before 12 o'clock</u>, the letter should arrive tomorrow.
(The letter should arrive tomorrow <u>if it is posted before 12 o'clock</u>.)
Wenn der Brief vor 12 Uhr eingeworfen wird, …

· Everyone should have access to a garden, <u>**whether living** in the city or the countryside</u>.
(Everyone should have access to a garden, <u>whether they live in the city or the countryside</u>.)
…, egal, ob er oder sie in der Stadt oder auf dem Land lebt.

· **Partizipialsätze** können auch anstelle von Nebensätzen des Grundes stehen.
(Beachte, dass die Konjunktion *because* nicht in Partizipialsätzen verwendet werden kann.)

· **Partizipialsätze** können auch durch andere Konjunktionen eingeleitet werden,
z. B. durch *although*, *if*, *unless*, *whether*.

23 Exercises

23.1 Participle clauses instead of adverbial clauses of reason

a) Match the main clauses on the left to a reason on the right.

Example: 1 + e) Leo didn't ask Mel out on a date because he was too shy.

1. Leo didn't ask Mel out on a date	a) she didn't have the money for the bus ticket.
2. I sat next to the new student	b) he thought the man was his father.
3. Joe easily got a job as a tour guide	c) he noticed that it had got colder.
4. Cilla decided to explore the city	d) I saw how sad and lonely she looked.
5. He jumped on the man's back	e) he was too shy.
6. Peter put on a second pair of socks	f) she had plenty of time before her train left.
7. Jane had to walk home from school	g) he knew a lot about the town's history.

because

b) Rewrite the sentences you matched in a), using a present participle clause. Start your sentences with the participle clause.

Examples: 1 + e <u>Being</u> too shy, Leo didn't ask Mel out on a date.

23.2 Other participle clauses

Make participle clauses from the phrases in the box to complete the sentences.
You will need present and past participle clauses.

> eat raw or cooked · expect a phone call · offer a lot of money · sign by a parent ·
> stay in central London · use a hands-free device · use carefully · work or not

Example: 1. It's illegal for drivers to make phone calls unless using a hands-free device.

1. It's illegal for drivers to make phone calls **unless** …
2. Applications for the exchange programme will not be accepted **unless** …
3. **Although** still …, he felt tired and went to bed.
4. **Although** …, she decided not to accept the job.
5. This product is safe **if** …
6. **If** …, why not start your visit with a trip on the London Eye?
7. Many vegetables are tasty, **whether** …
8. You can sell your old computer in this shop, **whether** …

24 The comparison of adjectives

24.1 Forms

We can compare people and things by using the **comparative** and **superlative** forms of adjectives.
- **Comparative** *Emily is 13 years old. Her sister Sophie is younger – she's ten.*
- **Superlative** *Ava is the youngest, and Lily is the oldest.*

We use **-er/-est** for adjectives with		comparative	superlative
one syllable	small	**smaller**	(the) **smallest**
	big	**bigger**	(the) **biggest**
two syllables <u>with</u> a **y**-ending	busy	**busier**	(the) **busiest**
	easy	**easier**	(the) **easiest**

We use **more/most** for adjectives with			
two syllables (without a y-ending)	boring	**more boring**	(the) **most boring**
	careful	**more careful**	(the) **most careful**
three (or more) syllables	exciting	**more exciting**	(the) **most exciting**
	difficult	**more difficult**	(the) **most difficult**

❗ With some adjectives we can use **-er/-est** or **more/most**, e.g. *clear, clever, polite, safe, simple, stupid, sure*.	simple	**simpler**	(the) **simplest**
		more simple	(the) **most simple**

There are also some **irregular** forms.	good	**better**	(the) **best**
	bad	**worse**	(the) **worst**
	much/many	**more**	(the) **most**
	(a) little	**less**	(the) **least**

24.2 The adjective in comparisons

When people or things **differ** in size/age/speed/…, we use the **comparative + *than*** (German "als"):
- *The Millers' dog is **bigger than** their youngest son.*   *Der Hund der Millers ist **größer als** ihr jüngster Sohn.*
- *Do you think that English is **harder than** French?*   *Findest du, dass Englisch **schwieriger als** Französisch ist?*

When saying whether size/age/speed/… are the **same**, we use ***as … as***:
- *I'm almost **as tall as** my mother now.*   *Ich bin jetzt fast **so groß wie** meine Mutter.*
- *Jake isn't **as old as** Sarah.*   *Jake is nicht **so alt wie** Sarah.*
- *My cat is **as fast as** your rabbit.*   *Meine Katze is **so schnell wie** dein Kaninchen.*

❗ In comparisons we normally use the **object form** of personal pronouns: ***me/him/her/us***, etc. (<u>not</u> *I/he/she/we*, etc.).
  - *My sister is ten. I'm **older than her**.*   *Meine Schwester ist zehn. Ich bin **älter als sie**.*

German summary

- Man kann Dinge und Personen **vergleichen**, indem man Adjektive steigert:
  Man verwendet einen **Komparativ** (*bigger; more careful*) oder einen **Superlativ** (*biggest; most careful*).

  Mit **-er/-est** werden gesteigert: **einsilbige** Adjektive;
  zweisilbige Adjektive, die auf **-y** enden.

  Mit ***more/most*** werden gesteigert: **zweisilbige** Adjektive, die <u>nicht</u> auf **-y** enden;
  Adjektive mit **mehr als zwei Silben**.

- Wenn Dinge und Personen **unterschiedlich** groß/alt/schnell/… sind, verwendet man den **Komparativ + *than***.
  Wenn man sagen will, ob Dinge und Personen **gleich** groß/alt/schnell/… sind, verwendet man ***as … as***.

24 Exercises

24.1 The comparison of adjectives – forms

Brian (14) and his father are looking at information about three mobile phone service providers.
Rewrite the sentences with the correct forms of the adjectives.

Example: 1. Calls with Cell UK are cheaper than with Oxygen, but with Portaphone they are the cheapest.

	Portaphone	Cell UK	Oxygen
Customers	15.5m	22m	13m
Calls (pence/min)	14	15	25
Text messages (pence/text)	10	12	16
Monthly data (GB)	1.5	1.5	3
5G LTE network	85%	97%	75%
Customer experience	★ ★ ★ ☆ ☆	★ ★ ★ ★ ☆	★ ★ ★ ★ ★

1. Calls with Cell UK are (cheap) than with Oxygen, but with Portaphone they are (cheap).
2. Getting a good signal is important – Cell UK's coverage is (wide).
3. Texting with Oxygen is (expensive) than with Portaphone and Cell UK.
4. Cell UK's customers are (happy) with their service than Portaphone's customers.
5. Oxygen's data allowance is 3GB – that's (big) and (good) than the other two networks.
6. Oxygen's signal network is the (bad) of the three networks.
7. Of the three providers, Portaphone is (good) for people who prefer calling to texting.

24.2 The adjective in comparisons

Brian and his father are deciding which mobile network they should choose for Brian.
Change the adjectives in brackets into their correct comparative or superlative forms.
Add *than* or *as … as* where necessary.

Examples: 1. cheaper than - 2. older than me

Dad: Let's compare the pay-as-you-go providers. Calls and text messages with Portaphone are (1. cheap) the other two.
Brian: You're (2. old – I). And you call (3. often – I do). My apps use a lot of data and Cell UK's data allowance is
        (4. not – big – Oxygen's) – they offer 3 gigabytes. Oxygen would be (5. good) Cell UK for me.
Dad: Yes, Brian, but just look at the prices! Calls and texts with Oxygen are (6. expensive)! Plus, their network is
        (7. small – the other two). Maybe you won't get a good signal.
Brian: Oxygen is (8. new – Portaphone and Cell UK) and I'm sure they'll grow (9. large). Anyway, look at their customer
        experience results – their customers are (10. happy). Though that's probably because they give (11. late) phone
        to new customers.
Dad: You don't need a new phone, you can have my old one …
Brian: DAD! No way! That phone is nearly (12. old – you)!
Dad: Brian, don't forget who's paying for this. Can you be a little (13. polite), please?
Brian: Sorry, Dad.

25 Countable and uncountable nouns

25.1 Characteristics

Most nouns are countable. That means that we can use them in the **singular** and in the **plural**.
· *a boy* ▶ *two boys*   *ein Junge – zwei Jungen*   · *a book* ▶ *lots of books*   *ein Buch – viele Bücher*
· *one hour* ▶ *many hours*   *eine Stunde – viele Stunden*

Some nouns are uncountable. We cannot form a plural. Many food words and many abstract nouns are uncountable.
· *bread* Brot · *butter* Butter · *luck* Glück · *milk* Milch · *money* Geld · *music* Musik · *plastic* Plastik · *time* Zeit
We **cannot use** *a/an* or *one/two/three*, etc. with uncountable nouns: *not:* ~~a bread, two breads~~; ~~a butter, two butters~~.

To talk about a quantity or number, we use phrases like *a glass of* …, *a kilo of* …, *a piece of* …, *two packets of* …
· *Would you like a glass of milk?*   *Möchtest du ein Glas Milch?*
· *Two pounds of butter*, please.   *Zwei Pfund Butter, bitte.*
· *There's a piece of plastic in my cornflakes.*   *Da ist ein Stück Plastik in meinen Cornflakes.*

In contrast to German, the following nouns are uncountable.

advice	Rat; Ratschläge	*furniture*	Möbel	*knowledge*	Kenntnis(se)
equipment	Ausrüstung(en)	*homework*	Hausaufgabe(n)	*news*	Nachricht(en)
experience	Erfahrung(en)	*information*	Information(en)	*progress*	Fortschritt(e)

The determiners, verbs and pronouns they combine with are **singular**.
· *Where did you get this information? It's very helpful.* ▶ Not: *… ~~these informations. They're~~ very helpful.*
· *Can you be quiet, please? The news is on.* ▶ Not: *The news ~~are~~ on.*
· *Let me give you a piece of advice/some advice.* ▶ Not: *Let me give you ~~an advice~~.*

25.2 Quantifiers: *some, a lot of, many, much, a few, a little*

We use *some* and *a lot of* (or *lots of*) with the **plural of countable nouns** <u>and</u> with **uncountable nouns**.

Countable (plural)		Uncountable	
some students	*einige* Schüler/in	*some* cheese	*etwas* Käse
some books	*einige* Bücher	*some* information	*einige* Informationen
a lot of students	*viele* Schüler/in	*a lot of* cheese	*viel* Käse
a lot of books	*viele* Bücher	*a lot of* information	*viele* Informationen

❗ We use *many* and *a few* with the **plural of countable nouns**, but *much* and *a little* with **uncountable nouns**.

Countable (plural)		Uncountable	
how *many* students?	wie *viele* Schüler/innen?	how *much* cheese?	wie *viel* Käse?
not *many* books	nicht *viele* Bücher	not *much* information	nicht *viel(e)* Information(en)
a few students	*einige* Schüler/innen	*a little* cheese	*etwas/ein bisschen* Käse
a few books	*einige* Bücher	*a little* information	*wenig(e)* Information(en)

❗ We usually use *a lot of* in **positive** statements. In **negative** statements and **questions** *much / many* are more common.
· *There were a lot of pedestrians in town this morning, but there wasn't too much traffic.*
· *Do many people travel by bike where you live?*

German summary

· Die meisten Nomen sind **zählbar**: Sie bezeichnen etwas, das wir zählen können, und werden im Singular und Plural verwendet.
  Nicht zählbare Nomen haben keinen Plural und werden nicht mit *a/an* oder *one/two/…* verwendet.
  Sie stehen oft mit Wendungen wie *a glass of* …, *a kilo of* …, *a piece of* …, *two packets of* …
· Mit dem **Plural von zählbaren Nomen** stehen die Mengenbezeichnungen *some, a lot of* (oder *lots of*), *many, a few*.
  Mit **nicht zählbaren Nomen** stehen *some, a lot of* (oder *lots of*), *much, a little*.
· In bejahten Aussagesätzen wird in der Regel *a lot of* verwendet, in verneinten Aussagesätzen eher *many* bzw. *much*.

25 Exercises

25.1 Countable and uncountable nouns - characteristics

a) Write two headings – countable and uncountable.
Then write the nouns from the box under the correct heading.

> advice · bar · beer · bottle · butter · chocolate · cup ·
> glass · milk · packet · piece · spoonful · sugar · tea

Example:

countable	uncountable
bar	advice

b) Now combine the countable nouns with a suitable uncountable noun – like this: a bottle of beer.

c) Choose the correct words to complete the two dialogues.

Example: 1. Have you made any progress on our presentation?

1. Student 1: There you are. Have you made any progresses / progress on our presentation?
2. Student 2: I was in the school library – there isn't / aren't a lot of information about Germany there.
3. Student 1: Not in the books maybe, but we can do research / a research about the *Kulturkampf* on the PCs.
4. Student 2: Those computers are too slow. Anyway, this homework is / these homeworks are very difficult – we didn't do anything in our history class about Bismarck. And now Mr Roberts wants a presentation?!

5. Teacher 1: The school IT equipment is / are being replaced.
6. Teacher 2: Those are / That's good news.
7. Teacher 1: I hope they replace the furniture too. It's / They're so old and uncomfortable.
8. Teacher 2: In my experiences / experience the school never thinks about our comfort.

25.2 Quantifiers: *some, a lot of, many, much, a few, a little*

Oliver and Brian are shopping for food and drinks for Julia's party.
Choose the correct place for these quantifiers:
many – much – some – a little – a few – lots of (or *a lot of*)
(Note: In some cases, there is more than one correct solution.)

Example: 1. ... how many things ...

Oliver: Okay, let's see how (1) ... things we have to buy – Linda got (2) ... snackfood and drinks yesterday but she didn't think of the fruit smoothies. So, we need (3) ... ingredients – (4) ... kiwis, for example, and bananas.
Brian: How (5) ... do we need? What does the recipe say?
Oliver: One and a half kiwis and one banana per smoothie.
Brian: And we also need to get (6) ... orange juice.
Oliver: How (7) ... orange juice do we need? Or should I say how (8) ... bottles?
Brian: One bottle is enough for four smoothies.
Oliver: What about (9) ... beer?
Brian: Hey! How (10) ... times did Julia tell you?! We're not supposed to get alcohol.
Oliver: Not for us – I know that, but if (11) ... adults come – they might like (12) ... beer, don't you think?
Brian: Okay, okay. Now, come on – for 30 people we need to get (13) ... meat for the barbecue. We'd better hurry up, we don't have (14) ... time.
Oliver: Don't forget Theresa and Alice – they're vegetarians. We should get (15) ... veggie burgers for the vegetarians.

26 The definite article

26.1 Things in general – specific things

In English, the definite article (*the*) is used differently from German.

When we talk about things or people **in general**, we do **not** use *the*.		However, we **do** use *the* when we talk about **specific** things or people.

· **Life** in London is extremely expensive.
  Das Leben in London …
	Compare
	◄ ►
		· It's a film about **the life of teenagers** in London.
		  … *das Leben von Jugendlichen* in London.

· What will happen if we run out of **oil**?
  …, wenn uns *das Öl* ausgeht?
		· **The oil they found there** made them rich.
		  Das Öl, das sie dort gefunden haben, …

· **People** are worried about climate change.
  Die Menschen machen sich Sorgen …
		· **The people who live here** all help each other.
		  Die Menschen, die hier leben, …

· Fruit **prices** have gone up again.
  Die Preise für Obst sind wieder gestiegen.
		· **The prices you pay in this shop** are shocking.
		  Die Preise, die man … bezahlt, …

Here are some more common examples of where we do **not** use the definite article *the* when talking **in general**.
· The title is "Woman's role in modern **society**".   … in *der* modernen *Gesellschaft*
· We discussed **American politics** in school today.   … *die* amerikanische *Politik*
· Do you think **world peace** is in danger?   … *der Weltfrieden*
· **Medical progress** helped to save millions of lives.   *Der medizinische Fortschritt* …
· **Space travel** is a chance and a challenge.   *Die Raumfahrt* …
· I'm very interested in **nature** and **wildlife**.   … *die Natur* … *die Tierwelt*
· You need money to fight **unemployment**.   … *die Arbeitslosigkeit*

 Note that we also use *most* ("die meisten") without *the*.
  · **Most boys** had long hair in the 1970s.   *Die meisten Jungen* …
  · **Most of us** went home after the match.   *Die meisten von uns* …

26.2 Buildings and institutions

In British English we do **not** use *the* with *church, hospital, prison, school, college, university* when we are thinking of the normal use of the building.
In American English, *the* is used with *university* and *hospital*.
· We go to **church** every Sunday.   … in *die Kirche* (zum Gottesdienst)
· He spent two years in **prison**.   *im Gefängnis* (um eine Strafe zu verbüßen)
· I know her from **school**.   … aus *der Schule* (vom gemeinsamen Unterricht)
· My sister studies at **university**. (AE: at **the university**)   … an *der Universität* (zu Ausbildungszwecken)
· Dad's ill. He's in **hospital**. (AE: in **the hospital**)   … *im Krankenhaus* (zur Behandlung)

We **do** use *the* when we are thinking of the **place** / the **building**. Here, there is no difference between English and German.
· There's a concert in **the church / the university** on Friday.
· He works in one of the shops behind **the prison**.
· Go straight on till you get to **the school**, then turn left.

26 Exercises

26.1 Things in general – specific things

a) Rewrite the incorrect sentences. Add or take away *the* where necessary. Three of the sentences are correct.

Examples: 1. Incorrect - The school day in Ireland begins at 9am.   2. Correct

1. School day in Ireland begins at 9am.
2. There should be more modern technology in German schools.
3. The education is important to improve your chances in the life.
4. At my friend's school, they have latest technology.
5. British students have to wear school uniforms.
6. Menus in school canteens should give students healthy but tasty choices.
7. At our school, menu in canteen is always same.
8. The stress doesn't help you to learn.
9. The stress of exams can really affect the students' health.

b) John Harries, a writer, has just celebrated his 97th birthday, and is in the best of health.
Read this interview in which he talks about how the world has changed since he was born.
Decide where it is necessary to add *the*.

Examples: 1. Correct - "the" is not necessary   2. What would you say is the biggest change?

Interviewer: You must have seen a lot of change since you were born.
Harries: Yes, (1) … life has changed a lot in the last 100 years.
Interviewer: What would you say is (2) … biggest change?
Harries: Well, one of (3) … the biggest changes is in life expectancy. When I was born, (4) … life expectancy of a male was about 55 years. Today it is over 75 years. And I've been very lucky – I have lived over 20 years longer than (5) … average male.
Interviewer: Obviously (6) … health has improved a lot over the years.
Harries: And not just (7) … health: (8) … education has improved too. When I was a boy, most children left (9) … school when they were 14. Today 85 percent of 16-year-olds still attend (10) … lessons.
Interviewer: Would you say that (11) … technological progress has made (12) … things easier for (13) … people?
Harries: Oh yes, take (14) … travel, for example. When I was a boy, (15) … journey from New York to London took five days. Today you do it in five hours – well, almost.
Interviewer: Anything else?
Harries: Well, there's (16) … telephone. When I was young, not even 10 percent of (17) … population had a telephone. Now everyone has one. And you can carry it around with you, and do so much with it.
Interviewer: What is the most important change for you?
Harries: Well, I think it's (18) … peace. Since (19) … war ended in 1945, we've had (20) … peace here in the UK. Although, of course, it's sad that there is still (21) … war in so many other parts of the world.

26.2 Buildings and institutions

Are the following sentences correct or incorrect? Rewrite the wrong sentences correctly.

Example: 1. Excuse me, do you know where the church is?

1. Excuse me, do you know where church is?
2. College in our district is closing down.
3. Hurry up, Michael, or you'll be late for school!
4. I heard his older brother was sent to prison for stealing a car.
5. I want to go to university when I am older.
6. Dad: Where are you going? Mum: I have to go to school for the parent/teacher meeting.
7. My mum's a doctor – today she went to prison in Birmingham to examine a prisoner.
8. What time do you go to church on Sundays?
9. How long do you have to stay in hospital?
10. My sister told me President Smith spoke at university yesterday.

Grammar

27 Emphasis

27.1 Word stress

Any word in an English sentence can be emphasized if you <u>stress</u> it when speaking.
· *I* *think he'll help you.* · *I think he'll help you.* · *I think he'll help you.* etc.

❗ We use the long form of auxiliaries (e.g. *is, have, will, would*) if we stress them: *I think he will help you.*

27.2 Emphatic *do/does/did*

In simple present and simple past sentences we can use stressed *do*, *does* or *did* to add emphasis.

without emphasis	with emphasis	
I think you should talk to your dad.	*I **do** think you should talk to your dad.*	*Ich denke wirklich …*
You promised to help me.	*You **did** promise to help me.*	*Du hast doch versprochen …*

27.3 Emphasizing pronouns

The *-self/-selves* **pronouns** can be used to emphasize nouns or pronouns that come earlier in the sentence.

without emphasis	with emphasis	
The work isn't difficult.	*The work **itself** isn't difficult if you have the tools.*	*Die Arbeit selbst …*
I can repair this.	*I can repair this **myself**. I don't need help.*	*Ich kann es selbst …*

27.4 Adverbs

We often use certain **adverbs** to add emphasis, e.g. *really, fairly, pretty, completely, absolutely, extremely, particularly, somewhat, so, such, never, ever*: · *I couldn't answer the interviewer's questions – I felt **pretty/really/so/extremely** stupid.*
· *I was **such** a mistake not to prepare – I won't **ever** do that again.*

27.5 *It's … / It was …* + relative clause

We can emphasize a **noun**, a **pronoun** or an **adverbial** using *It's … / It was … + that/who …*
We use this structure to express a contrast.
· *It was **my grandparents** who/that gave me the money.* ▶ (not my parents or somebody else)
· *It's **me** who/that doesn't eat meat.* ▶ (not somebody else)
· *It was **in the shopping mall** that I first met my boyfriend.* ▶ (in that place, not somewhere else)

27.6 'Negative' adverbials + inversion

Some **adverbials** with a **negative** or **restrictive** meaning can go at the beginning of the sentence for special emphasis.
Examples: *never, rarely (selten), hardly (kaum), only later, under no circumstances (unter keinen Umständen).*
· ***Never** had we seen so many people.*   *Noch nie hatten wir so viele Leute gesehen.*
· ***Only much later** did they realize who the woman was.*   *Erst viel später haben sie realisiert, wer die Frau war.*

❗ Note the <u>change</u> in word order (inversion): · *Never **had we** seen …* · *Only much later **did they** realize …*

German summary

· Man kann beim Sprechen einzelne Wörter oder Satzteile **stark betonen**, um sie hervorzuheben.
· Im *simple present* und *simple past* kann man **betontes *do/does/did*** vor das Vollverb stellen, um der Aussage des Satzes Nachdruck zu verleihen.
· Mit den **Pronomen auf *-self/-selves*** kann man Nomen oder Pronomen besonders hervorheben.
· Mit **Adverbien** wie *really, pretty, absolutely, so, ever* u. Ä. kann man einzelne Wörter oder Satzteile hervorheben.
· Mit *It's … / It was …* + **Relativsatz** kann man Nomen, Pronomen und adverbiale Bestimmungen hervorheben.
· Einige adverbiale Bestimmungen mit **verneinender oder einschränkender** Bedeutung (*never, hardly, only later, …*) können zu Betonungszwecken an den Satzanfang rücken. In diesem Fall ändert sich die Wortstellung (Inversion).

27 Exercises

27.1 Word stress

Look at this sentence: *She said it was a great idea.*
Decide which word should be stressed strongly to express the meanings below.
Example: 1. *She* said it was a great idea. ('She' is stressed to show that I have a different opinion.)
1. My sister's opinion was that it was a very good idea, but I don't agree.
2. She thinks it was a very good idea before, but it's not such a good idea now.
3. She doesn't think it's just a good idea, but a fantastic idea!
4. I heard her say that it was a great idea, but I'm not sure that's what she really thinks.
5. She thinks that the idea is very good in theory, but it's not very practical.

27.2 Emphatic *do/does/did*

There is only one emphatic auxiliary in each sentence. Decide which verb the speaker wants to emphasize and write the sentences correctly.
Example: 1. ... I did do the homework but I forgot to bring it today.
1. I promise, Mr Roberts, I did / did do the homework but I forgot / did forget to bring it today.
2. I can't understand why the plant died / did die. I remembered / did remember to water it, honestly.
3. I like / do like you, Jake, really – it's just that I think / do think we're too young for a serious relationship.
4. You needn't worry, Mum – you packed / did pack the sunscreen. I saw / did see you pack it.
5. The last time you did buy / bought a skirt without trying it on, it was the wrong size. So please, do try / try this one on.

27.3 Emphasizing pronouns

Rewrite the sentences below and add the correct *-self/-selves* pronouns.
1. I want to do it ... .   4. You can do it ... – it's not very difficult.
2. She wants to do it ... .   5. The teacher, said we didn't have to do it ... .
3. He wants to do it ... .   6. The teacher said they could do it ... .

27.4 Adverbs

Rewrite the sentences using **two** of the three adverbs.
1. The weather was bad – it was a disappointing holiday. (completely / so / such)
2. The film was terrible. We were disappointed. (absolutely / really / such)
3. The charity concert was a success. It went well. (completely / such /so)
4. Never let your baby brother do that again – it's dangerous! (ever / such / really)
5. I forgot about your birthday. I am embarrassed. (so / absolutely / completely)

27.5 *It's ... / It was ...* + relative clause

Rewrite the sentences in this way: *It's ... / It was ...* + relative clause
1. They stole Brian's bike, not mine.   4. I didn't suggest it, Peter did.
2. She doesn't like pork, but she eats beef or chicken. 5. The Wi-Fi connection was the problem, not the
website.
3. I don't like his friends – I think he is OK.   6. I prefer the blue blouse, not the red one.

27.6 'Negative' adverbials + inversion

Rewrite these sentences. Begin with the negative adverbials in **blue**. Be careful with the word order.
Change the verb forms when needed.
Example: 1. *Never* in all my years as a teacher *have I taught* ...
1. In all my years as a teacher, I have never taught such good students.
2. We had hardly begun to eat our meal when Inspector Lastrade burst into the restaurant.
3. Godfrey understood only then that he loved her. But it was too late – she had left forever.
4. You can find better prices nowhere than at MediaMagic – sale now on!

28 Adverbial clauses

An adverbial clause is a subordinate clause which adds information to what is said in the main clause. The two clauses are joined by conjunctions (linking words). Depending on the type of information contained in the adverbial clause, we use names such as clauses of place, time, reason, result, etc.

Adverbial clauses can usually be written before or after the main clause. If the adverbial clause introduces the main clause, you need to put a comma between it and the main clause.

28.1 Clauses of place; clauses of time

We can use the following conjunctions in **clauses of place** to give information about location and direction: **where, wherever, everywhere**.
· Crispr can identify individual genes and cut the DNA open **where** they are located. ▶ (in this specific location)
· **Wherever** you go in the USA, you will see the Stars and Stripes flying. ▶ (the specific location does not make a difference)

We can use the following conjunctions in **clauses of time** to give information about the timing, order of events, frequency, duration, beginning or end: **when, whenever, before, after, as, while, since, until**.
· Crispr was discovered **when** scientists were studying bacteria. ▶ (at this specific time)
· **Whenever** I see the rainbow flag, I smile. ▶ (each/every time)
· Read the tasks **before** you read the text. ▶ (order of events)

28.2 Clauses of reason; clauses of result

We can use the following conjunctions in **clauses of reason** to give information about the reason for or the cause of a situation: **as**, **because**, **since**, **so**.
❗ Note: As and since are usually used at the beginning of a sentence.
· DNA is often called the book of life **because** it contains four chemical compounds known by four letters C-G-A-T.
· **As/Since** both my parents have blue eyes, they were surprised when I was born with brown eyes.

We can use the following conjunction in **clauses of result** to give information about the result or consequences of a situation: **so**
❗ Note: When we use **so** in this sense, it always comes in the middle of a sentence after a comma.
  · Human DNA has six billion letters, **so** it took scientists years to identify and list each gene.

28.3 Clause of contrast

We can use the following conjunctions in **clauses of contrast** to compare situations or express some difference between situations: **although**, **even if/though**, **whereas**, **while**.
· **Although/Even though** genetics is a complex topic, Brian Sykes explains it in an easy-to-understand way.
· **Whereas/While** the US allows many GM food products, the EU takes a much stricter approach.

28.4 Clauses of manner; clauses of purpose

We can use the following conjunctions in clauses of manner (or comparison) to show how something is done by comparing it to another action/situation: **as, as if, as though, like**.
❗ Note: These clauses usually follow the main clause and in informal or spoken English, like is used more often.
· Critics of gene-editing fear a future of parents choosing their child's features **as though/as if/like** they were ordering pizza.

We can use the following conjunctions in **clauses of purpose** to express the reason or intention behind an action: **so, so that**
❗ Note: In informal use, that may be left out. Note also that no comma is needed before so.
  · Scientists can 'program' Crispr **so that** it can edit single genes in the DNA.

German summary

· Adverbialsätze sind Nebensätze, die durch unterordnende Konjunktionen (z.B. where, when, because, etc.) mit Hauptsätzen verbunden werden.
· Ein Adverbialsatz kann vor oder nach dem Hauptsatz stehen.
  Wenn er vorangestellt ist, wird meist ein Komma gesetzt.
· Es gibt Adverbialsätze, des Ortes, der Zeit, des Grundes, des Gegensatzes, der Art und Weise, des Zwecks usw.

28 Exercises

28.1 Clauses of place; clauses of time

a) Make the sentences more natural by replacing the bold words with a word from the box.

> everywhere · where (2 x) · wherever (2 x)

1. **At all the places** the tourists went in Sydney Harbour, hungry seagulls followed them.
2. If you have to write a password down, never leave it **in a place that** people could see it.
3. **It doesn't matter to which place** my brother goes, he always has to have his phone with him.
4. We misunderstood the man's directions and after 20 minutes arrived back **in the place** we'd started from.
5. The police announced that **it didn't matter in which places** the thieves hid, they would be caught.

b) Complete the sentences using one of the two words given.

1. … the students stopped talking, the teacher explained the activity. (once, until)
2. The fans crowded the streets … the concert had finished. (since, while)
3. … politicians talk and talk, the climate crisis is getting worse. (until, while)
4. … I see Jane, she seems to be wearing something new. (while, whenever)
5. How have you been … I last saw you? (since, when)

28.2 Clauses of reason; clauses of result

a) Join each clause 1–6 with a suitable clause a–f. Put *As* at the beginning or *because* in the middle. Remember to use capital letters at the beginning and add a comma after the *As …* clauses.

1. my parents took my keys away
2. I was out of school ill for a week
3. my aunt is afraid of dogs
4. Sarah often borrows her sister's clothes
5. Adrian is building a model of a Spitfire plane
6. Krzysztof's family often go on holiday to Poland

a) both girls are the same size.
b) his father's side of the family live there.
c) I had to work hard to catch up on the things I missed.
d) she hasn't visited us since we got our new labrador.
e) they say I'm not responsible enough.
f) he went to the museum to take photos of a real one.

b) Complete the clauses of result in a suitable way. Use the information in a) to help you.

1. I forgot to close our front door one day, so my parents …
2. The class test was on a topic I had missed, … my teacher …
3. Aunt Julia came to visit us, … Rex had to …
4. Sarah and her sister are the same size, … they …
5. Adrian lost a very important part of his model, … he …
6. Krzysztof is in Poland very often, … his Polish …

28.3 Clauses of contrast

a) Join the sentence halves using the adverbials given. Be careful where you place the adverbials.

1. a) it was a cold day / the sun was shining brightly
   b) it was a cold day / we still went to the beach for a swim
2. a) the new phone is expensive / Barry has to have it
   b) the new phone is expensive / they reduce the price by 10%
3. a) Steven was tired / he hadn't done anything all day
   b) Steven was tired / he stayed up late watching a movie

> although
>
> even if
>
> even though

b) Write sentences comparing the twins Anna and Lily. Use *while* and *whereas*.
Anna and Lily are identical twins, but they are not exactly the same.
Anna has short hair, eats meat and loves fashion. Lily has short hair, is vegetarian and hates fashion.

28.4 Clauses of manner; clauses of purpose

Complete the sentences using the words in the box.

> as if · as though · like · so (2 x) · so that

1. My parents treat me … I was still six years old.
2. I took a photo of her … I wouldn't forget her face.
3. You need to study … you are ready for the exam.
4. Tom sounded … he had a cold.
5. Please arrive early … we can start on time.
6. You should sing … nobody was listening.

Skills and Media Competence

Inhalt

			Seite
READING SKILLS	SMC 1	Ordering and structuring vocabulary	163
	SMC 2	Taking notes	163
WRITING SKILLS	SMC 3	Structuring texts	164
	SMC 4	Writing good sentences	165
	SMC 5	Writing a formal letter or email	166
	SMC 6	Making an outline	167
	SMC 7	Writing an argumentative essay	167
	SMC 8	Writing an opinion piece / comment	168
	SMC 9	Writing a letter/email to the editor	169
	SMC 10	Writing an article	170
	SMC 11	Writing a report	171
	SMC 12	Writing a review	171
	SMC 13	Writing a summary	172
	SMC 14	Revising texts	173
	SMC 15	Revising and improving electronic texts	174
MEDIATION SKILLS	SMC 16	Mediating written or spoken information	175
	SMC 17	Selecting relevant information	175
	SMC 18	Paraphrasing	176
	SMC 19	Cultural differences	176
SPEAKING SKILLS	SMC 20	Communicating in everyday situations	177
	SMC 21	Having a discussion	178
	SMC 22	Agreeing and disagreeing with people's opinions	178
	SMC 23	Preparing and taking part in a panel discussion	179
	SMC 24	Taking part in an interview	180
VIEWING SKILLS	SMC 25	Viewing	181
LISTENING SKILLS	SMC 26	Listening strategies	182
PROJECT AND PRESENTATION SKILLS	SMC 27	Finding information online	183
	SMC 28	Creating a good layout for a page or poster	185
	SMC 29	Making good slides for an electronic presentation	185
	SMC 30	Giving a presentation	186
	SMC 31	Talking about statistics	187
	SMC 32	Describing and presenting pictures	188
	SMC 33	Working in a team	188
	SMC 34	Giving feedback	189
STUDY SKILLS	SMC 35	Understanding new words	189
	SMC 36	Using a dictionary	190
	SMC 37	Using an online translator	191
	SMC 38	Using the internet to improve your vocabulary	192
	SMC 39	Ordering and structuring vocabulary and ideas	193
	SMC 40	Working with a grammar	194
	SMC 41	Making and taking notes	195
EXAM SKILLS	SMC 42	Preparing for a written exam	195
	SMC 43	Preparing for a speaking exam	198
	SMC 44	Preparing for a listening exam	200

Die mit diesem Symbol gekennzeichneten Abschnitte enthalten Hinweise und Tipps, die dir dabei helfen, elektronische Medien beim Englischlernen einzusetzen.

READING SKILLS

1 Skimming and scanning

Skimming *(reading for gist)* und Scanning *(reading for specific information)* sind Lesetechniken, die viel Zeit sparen, v. a. beim Lesen von langen Texten.

SKIMMING

Skimming hilft, schnell zu sehen, ob ein Text für deinen Zweck geeignet ist.

Step 1: Sieh dir diese Textteile an, um zu sehen, worum es im Text geht:
- Überschrift und Unterüberschriften
- Bilder und Bildunterschriften
- den ersten Satz jedes Absatzes – dieser Satz ist meist der *topic sentence*, der die Hauptidee des Absatzes nennt
- den letzten Absatz des Textes, der oft eine Zusammenfassung des Textes enthält

Step 2: Fasse für dich selbst den Text in ein paar Worten zusammen. Wenn dir das ohne Probleme gelingt, dann weißt du, um was es in dem Text geht – und dass dein Skimming erfolgreich war.

> **TIPP**
> Mache dir um unbekannten Wortschatz erstmal keine Gedanken – dafür ist Zeit, wenn du feststellst, dass der Text für dich geeignet ist.

SCANNING

Scanning hilft, in einem Text schnell nach bestimmten Informationen zu suchen.

Step 1: Überlege dir *keywords*. Suchst du z. B. die Öffnungszeiten eines Museums, könnten das Wörter sein wie *open, hours* oder *days*.

Step 2: Überfliege den Text und suche nach den *keywords*. Du kannst dabei mit dem Finger in einer "S-Form" durch den Text gehen.

Step 3: Lies die Textstelle, die dein *keyword* enthält, um zu sehen, ob sie die gewünschten Informationen enthält. Wenn nicht, scanne weiter.

> **TIPP**
> Wenn du mit Texten im Internet arbeitest, kann dein Browser dir viel Arbeit abnehmen.
> Mit Strg+F (Cmd+F am Mac) kannst du nach deinen *keywords* suchen und nur die Textstellen lesen, in denen ein *keyword* markiert ist.

2 Marking up a text

Auf Kopien von Texten kannst du Informationen markieren, um sie einfacher wiederzufinden, z. B. wenn du eine Zusammenfassung schreiben sollst.

Step 1: Lies die Aufgabe genau und überlege, welche Informationen du zur Beantwortung brauchst. Behalte dies beim Lesen des Textes im Kopf.

Step 2: Markiere nur Informationen, die wichtig sind (z. B. durch Unterstreichen, Einkreisen oder Markieren mit einem Textmarker). Oft reicht es, nur ein oder zwei Wörter in einem Satz zu markieren.

Step 3: Mach dir kurze Notizen am Rand – z. B. kurze Überschriften oder Stichwörter –, die den Inhalt kurz zusammenfassen. (➜ *SMC 41*)

> **TIPP**
> 1. Verwende unterschiedliche Farben für unterschiedliche Aufgaben/Fragestellungen.
> 2. Markiere wirklich nur Stichwörter, sonst wird es unübersichtlich.

Fifty years ago today, Rudy Lombard, who is black, and his friend Lanny Goldfinch, who is white, walked into a diner in downtown New Orleans. With two other black friends, they took Many of those who took part were students, both white and black. Today, not everyone realizes how dangerous it was to stand up against segregation. Through their actions, the protesters

WRITING SKILLS

3 Structuring texts

STRUCTURE

Ein guter Text besteht in der Regel aus den folgenden drei Teilen:

- Einleitung *(introduction)*:
  Hier steht, worum es in dem gesamten Text geht. An dieser Stelle kann auch ein Problem genannt werden, das in dem Text erörtert werden soll.

- Hauptteil *(main body)*:
  Dieser Teil ist in mehrere Absätze gegliedert und präsentiert die Details (Fakten, Beispiele etc.) zu deinem Thema.

- Schluss *(conclusion)*:
  Hier gibst du deinem Text ein passendes, interessantes Ende.

PARAGRAPHS

Längere Texte sind einfacher zu lesen und schneller zu verstehen, wenn sie in Absätze eingeteilt sind. Dabei solltest du folgende Dinge beachten:

- Fange für jeden neuen Aspekt einen neuen Absatz an.

- Beginne mit einem interessanten *topic sentence*.

- Beende deinen Text im letzten Absatz mit einer Zusammenfassung oder etwas Persönlichem.

TOPIC SENTENCES

Jeder Absatz sollte mit einem Einleitungssatz beginnen.

Dieser topic sentence beschreibt, worum es in dem Absatz geht. Wichtige Dinge, die du in einem *topic sentence* ansprechen kannst, sind z. B.

- **Orte:** *My trip to Berlin was exciting.*

- **Personen:** *The Beatles are one of the most famous bands in the world.*

- **Aktivitäten:** *Lots of people ride their bike every day.*

My Trip to New Orleans

Last summer I wanted to go to New Orleans because I like big cities.

First I had to find some information on New Orleans. So I went online and looked for websites about things to do in New Orleans. I found a website with some interesting information on the sights and I also found a list of hostels for New Orleans. I saved about five cool websites in my favourites list.

At home I started to plan for my trip. I read all the websites and took notes on museums, the sights and the best cheap cafes in the city. After a few days I knew where I wanted to go and what I wanted to do there.

I did not want to go to New Orleans alone, so I had to find someone to go with me. I called most of my friends and told them about my plan. Some of them did not want to spend their holidays in a big city and others had no money for the trip. But my friend Judith agreed to go with me. We decided to go in late August.

Judith and I spent two lovely weeks in New Orleans. We went to the French Market and enjoyed the fantastic food there. We stayed in a lovely hostel and met lots of really nice people. Before we went home we spent a whole afternoon in the French Quarter where we listened to music while we walked around.

This was one of the best summer holidays I ever had. Go to New Orleans – it's fantastic!

4 Writing good sentences

Gute Texte bestehen aus gut formulierten, abwechslungsreichen Sätzen. Die folgenden Techniken helfen dir, dich gut auszudrücken und damit den Stil deiner Texte zu verbessern.

ADJEKTIVE
Verwende Adjektive, wenn du Dinge, Orte und Menschen näher beschreiben möchtest:
- *a bright face*
- *a fantastic trip*

Stell aber sicher, dass du die Adjektive good, bad and nice nicht zu häufig einsetzt.
Ersetze sie durch andere Adjektive mit einer ähnlichen bzw. genaueren Bedeutung:
- *a nice teacher: a friendly teacher, a helpful teacher, …*
- *a good book: an interesting book, a funny book, …*

ADVERBIEN
Verwende Adverbien, um Handlungen näher zu beschreiben:
- *They walked home slowly.*
- *She talked quietly.*

Verwende Ausdrücke wie really, very, a bit etc., um Aussagen zu verdeutlichen oder zu verstärken:
- *It was a really sad story.*
- *The houses are very high.*

KONJUNKTIONEN
Konjunktionen wie and, but oder because geben deinen Sätzen eine klare, gut nachvollziehbare Struktur:
- *We went to the London Eye but it was very expensive.*

RELATIVSÄTZE
Relativsätze verbinden Sätze oder geben mehr Informationen zu einer Sache oder einer Person:
- *This is the shop which sells the best ice cream in Berlin.*

ZEITANGABEN
Time markers / adverbiale Bestimmungen der Zeit helfen dem Leser, sich in einem Text oder einer Geschichte zeitlich zurechtzufinden. Verwende *time markers*, um …
- die Reihenfolge von Ereignissen zu verdeutlichen:
  at first, next, finally, …

- zu zeigen, wie viel Zeit zwischen einzelnen Ereignissen vergeht:
  for half an hour, just two minutes later, …

- zu verdeutlichen, wie langsam oder schnell etwas passiert:
  immediately, it took hours, faster than I could look, …

- zu sagen, wenn etwas zeitgleich passiert:
  while I was waiting, during the lesson, as we came round the corner, …

- die Ereignisse eines Textes/einer Geschichte zeitlich einzuordnen:
  two summers ago, last Halloween, on my way home from school yesterday, …

5 Writing a formal letter or email

Wenn du einen Brief oder eine Mail an eine Organisation, einen potenziellen Arbeitgeber oder Ähnliches schreibst, sollte dein Schreiben gewissen formalen Regeln folgen.

Schreibe deine Adresse (ohne Namen) oben rechts. Verwende keine typisch deutschen Buchstaben wie ä, ö, ü oder ß.

> Kruemelstrasse 12
> 12345 Berlin
> Germany

Schreibe die volle Anschrift (mit Namen, wenn du ihn weißt) des Adressaten auf die linke Seite.

> John Keats
> Donne House
> Ipswich IP3 4BA
> United Kingdom

Schreibe das Datum auf die rechte Seite.

> 3 March 2019

Sage kurz im Betreff, worum es geht.

> Enquiry about exchange programme

Beginne deinen Brief/deine Mail mit *Dear Sir or Madam* wenn du keinen genauen Ansprechparntner hast. Ansonsten schreibe *Dear Mr/Mrs/Ms …* (mit Komma danach, in den USA auch oft mit Doppelpunkt). Fange danach immer groß an.

> Dear Mr Keats,

> I am writing to enquire about the exchange programme which I saw advertised in The English Magazine.

Nenne den Grund des Schreibens im ersten Absatz.
- Ergänze weitere Informationen in den folgenden Absätzen.
- Verwende Langformen (*I am/We are/I would*) statt Kurzformen (*I'm/We're/I'd*) und Abkürzungen.

> I have been studying English at school for six years now and I would like to take part in an exchange programme to improve my English.

> Could you please tell me if you offer any exchange programmes for one month in the summer? It would be helpful to know about dates, application procedures and the cost of such an exchange. Any additional information would be very welcome.

Wenn du den Adressaten um etwas bittest (z.B. Informationen), bedanke dich im Voraus.

> Thank you for your help. I look forward to hearing from you soon.

Beende das Schreiben mit *Yours sincerely* wenn du den Namen des Ansprechpartners kennst; ansonsten schreibe *Yours faithfully* (wenn du an einen amerikanischen Kontakt schreibst, kannst du in diesem Fall auch *Yours truly* schreiben). Tippe deinen Namen am Ende des Briefes, aber lasse ausreichend Platz für deine Unterschrift.

> Yours sincerely,
>
> *Paul Panther*
>
> Paul Panther

TIPP

Bei einer formellen E-Mail brauchst du Datum und Adressaten nicht zu nennen. Ansonsten gelten dieselben Regeln wie bei einem formellen Brief. Liste am Ende der Mail deine Kontaktdaten auf (Name, Adresse, ggf. Telefonnummer). Ganz wichtig: verwende auf keinen Fall Emoticons oder Smileys.

6 Making an outline

Jede Art von Text profitiert davon, wenn du dir vorab überlegst, was du in welcher Reihenfolge schreiben willst.

- Für eine Erörterung (➡ SMC 7) kannst du in deiner Outline schon die Argumente sortieren, die du im Text bringen möchtest.

- Bei einer Zusammenfassung (➡ SMC 13) kannst du hier die wichtigsten Punkte festhalten.

Damit leistest du schon eine Menge Vorarbeit und erleichterst dir das Schreiben.

```
Outline

1. Title

2. Introduction
   keywords

3. Main body
   Sub-heading
   keywords

4. Conclusion
   keywords
```

7 Writing an argumentative essay

Wenn du eine Erörterung schreibst – also schriftlich für oder gegen etwas argumentierst – solltest du deinen Text gut strukturieren und deine Argumente klar und schlüssig präsentieren, um deine Leser zu überzeugen.

PLANUNGSPHASE

Step 1: Lies die Aufgabe sorgfältig durch.

Step 2: Sammle Ideen und mache erste Notizen. Schreibe alle Argumente pro *und* contra auf, die dir einfallen.

Step 3: Ordne deine Argumente, z. B. in Form einer Outline. (➡ SMC 6) Hebe das Argument hervor, das deine Position am besten unterstreicht – damit solltest du deinen Hauptteil beenden, denn das merken sich die Leser am ehesten.

SCHREIBPHASE

Step 1: Schreibe deine Einleitung: sage kurz, um welches Thema es geht, ohne deine eigene Meinung dazu zu äußern.

Step 2: Im Hauptteil präsentierst du die Argumente, die du dir überlegt hast. Dabei helfen folgende Redemittel:

- Presenting arguments:
  One of the main reasons why … • It is often said that … • Some people think … • In addition to these points …

- Ordering arguments:
  To start with, … • Firstly,/Secondly,/Thirdly, … • Finally, … • First of all …

- Contrasting arguments:
  On the one hand … on the other hand • Contrary to what most people believe, … • While / Although …

- Giving examples:
  For example, … • This is clear because …

```
Outline / Notes

1. Introduction
   introduce the topic

2. Main body
   1. paragraph: arguments contra
      - argument 1
      - argument 2 etc
   2./3. paragraph: arguments pro
      - argument 1
      - argument 2 etc
      end with strongest argument!

4. Conclusion
   sum up your arguments
   give your opinion
```

8 Writing an opinion piece / a comment

Im Gegensatz zu einer Erörterung (➡ SMC 7), in der du beide Seiten eines Themas vorstellst und dann zu einer Schlußfolgerung kommst, geht es bei einem *opinion piece* (Kommentar oder Meinungsartikel) darum, deine persönliche Meinung zu präsentieren und mit Argumenten zu stützen.

PLANUNGSPHASE

Step 1: Sammle Ideen und mache erste Notizen. Was willst du sagen? Was willst du erreichen? Welche Fakten oder Zitate unterstützen deine Meinung? Hast du schon eine Lösungsidee, von der du andere überzeugen möchtest?

Step 2: Überlege dir eine gute Überschrift. Sie sollte die Aufmerksamkeit der Leser wecken und sie neugierig machen.

Step 3: Erstelle eine Outline. (➡ SMC 6) Überlege, wie du deine Argumentation/Meinung unterstützen kannst (Fakten, Statistiken, Zitate etc.).

Step 4: Recherchiere passendes Material. (➡ SMC 27)

SCHREIBPHASE

Step 1: Beginne dein *opinion piece* mit einem kurzen Absatz zu dem Thema und deiner Meinung dazu.

Step 2: Präsentiere Argumente für deine Meinung in den folgenden Absätzen und ergänze sie mit weiteren Fakten, Beispielen oder Zitaten. Dabei kannst du viele der Redemittel verwenden, die du auch bei einer Erörterung nutzt. (➡ SMC 7)

- Benutze das simple present für generelle Aussagen und das simple present oder simple past für die Beispiele, Anekdoten etc., die deine Meinung stützen.

  - Verwende Überzeugungstechniken. Das sind z.B
    – Personalpronomen, um den Text persönlicher zu machen: mit you sprichst du Leser direkt an, mit we stellst du eine Gemeinsamkeit her und mit I unterstreichst du, dass es sich um deine Meinung handelt.
    – Zitate, Anekdoten, Statistiken stützen deine Meinung: Zitate zeigen, dass andere Menschen deine Meinung teilen, Anekdoten bringen deine Punkte den Lesern näher und Statistiken belegen, dass deine Meinung auf Fakten beruht.
    – Ausdrucksstarke Sprache: schreibe abwechslungsreich (➡ SMC 4) und verwende Wörter, die emotional ansprechen, wie z. B. Adjektive und Adverbien, die den Leser wütend oder glücklich, traurig oder fröhlich machen
    – Rhetorische Fragen: mit Fragen, auf die eigentlich keine Antwort erwartet wird, kannst du deine Aussage nochmal unterstreichen: Is climate change real? Is killing wrong? Who can deny this?

Step 3: Im letzten Absatz, der *conclusion*, wiederholst du noch einmal deine Meinung und schlägst entweder eine Lösung vor (wenn es sich z. B. um ein Problem handelt) oder forderst deine Leser auf, etwas zu tun.

Outline / Notes

1. Headline
   - catch your readers' attention (clear statement, provocative question etc.)

2. First paragraph
   - state your topic AND your opinion clearly (keep it short!)
   - keep your readers interested

3. Supporting paragraphs
   use statistics, facts, quotes etc. to back up your main statement

4. Final paragraph / Conclusion
   - restate your opinion
   - suggest a solution or call for action

TIPP

Übertreibe es nicht mit den Statistiken, Anekdoten und Zitaten, sondern konzentriere dich auf besonders interessante oder spannende Punkte wie z. B. Zahlen, die dich in einer Statistik selber überrascht haben.

9 Writing a letter/email to the editor

Ein Leserbrief (oder heutzutage meist eine Leser-Mail) ist eine Reaktion auf einen Artikel in einer Zeitung oder einem Magazin und ist im Aufbau eine Mischung aus einem formellen Brief und einem *comment*.

VORBEREITUNG
- Lies den Artikel, auf den du reagieren willst, noch einmal gründlich durch. Mach dir dabei Notizen zu den Punkten, auf die du dich beziehen willst.

- Ordne deine Notizen in einer Gliederung (SMC 6). Notiere dir auch gleich deine Argumente und Belegstellen/Beispiele dafür.

FORMELLES
- Für einen Brief hältst du dich an dieselben Regeln wie bei einem formellen Brief (SMC 5). Bedenke bei der Adresse, dass du das Schreiben an den Autor oder die Autorin des Artikels richtest sowie an die Adresse der Zeitung.

- Wenn du den Namen nicht kennst, schreibe an *The Editor*. Die Adresse für Leserbriefe findest du in der Regel im Impressum der Zeitung.

- Die Email-Adresse für Leserbriefe findest du oft auf der Webseite unter *Contact*.

SCHREIBEN
- Beginne deinen Brief/deine Mail mit *Dear Sir or Madam* wenn du keinen genauen Ansprechparntner hast. Ansonsten schreibe *Dear Mr/Mrs/Ms …* (mit Komma danach, in den USA auch oft mit Doppelpunkt). Fange danach immer groß an.

- Einleitung: Im ersten Absatz nennst du den Artikel und die Ausgabe, in der er erschien, damit dein Leserbrief einfach zugeordnet werden kann. Du kannst hier auch schon sagen, wie du auf den Artikel reagieren wirst (*agreeing/ disagreeing/commenting/criticizing*):
  I have read your article "Into the future", published in The Newspaper on 27 September 2022, which deals with … I am writing to you in order to … / I agree/disagree with you on …

- Im Hauptteil gehst du auf einen oder mehrere Punkte des Artikels und deine Meinung dazu ein. Du bringst hier nur Argumente an, die deine Perspektive stützen.

- Nutze für jedes neue Argument einen neuen Absatz, aber halte dich relativ kurz. Ein Leserbrief ist kein Aufsatz, sondern ein Schreiben, in dem du kurz und klar deine Meinung zu einem Artikel gibst.

- Bleibe sachlich und möglichst neutral, auch wenn es um deine Meinung geht. Verwende formale Sprache und vermeide Kurzformen.

- Schluss: Beende deinen Brief oder deine E-Mail mit *Yours sincerely* wenn du den Namen des Ansprechpartners kennst; ansonsten schreibe *Yours faithfully* (wenn du an einen amerikanischen Kontakt schreibst, kannst du in diesem Fall auch *Yours truly* schreiben). Bei einem Brief tippe deinen Namen am Ende, aber lasse ausreichend Platz für deine Unterschrift.

LANGUAGE HELP
Hier sind ein paar Redemittel, die du in deinem Leserbrief verwenden kannst:

Agreeing	Disagreeing	Commenting/Criticizing
• *First of all, I would like to approve/ agree with you/…* • *You are right in writing/saying/…* • *You have a point in saying/ mentioning/writing that …*	• *I am afraid I do not quite agree …* • *I am not convinced that …* • *You have a point in saying …, but I would like to point out that …* • *However/Nevertheless, it could also be said that …*	• *I would like to add that …* • *Moreover, I would like to point out that …* • *It is true that …, but on the other hand it should be made clear that …*

10 Writing an article

Artikel sind Texte, die in der Regel zur Veröffentlichung in einer Zeitung, Zeitschrift oder einem Blog geschrieben werden. Es gibt verschiedene Arten von Artikeln wie z. B. Nachrichten, Berichte (➡ SMC 11), Kommentare (➡ SMC 8) oder Rezensionen (➡ SMC 12).

Für einen guten Artikel solltest du folgende Punkte beachten:

PUBLIKUM

Für wen schreibst du? Wer ist die Zielgruppe deines Artikels? Wenn du z. B. einen Artikel über politische Demonstration in deiner Stadt schreibst, hast du möglicherweise andere Leser als bei einem Artikel über das letzte Spiel des lokalen Fußballvereins. Das Wissen über die Zielgruppe hilft dir, sie richtig anzusprechen und z. B. eine Überschrift zu wählen, die das Interesse dieser Leser weckt.

AUFMERKSAMKEIT

Wie erregst du die Aufmerksamkeit möglicher Leser? Dein Artikel kann noch so gut sein – wenn ihn keiner liest, nützt das nichts. Eine gute Überschrift hilft, ebenso wie ein interessanter Einstieg. Beides kann z. B. provokant sein oder witzig – wichtig ist, dass es Leser dazu bringt, bei deinem Artikel "hängen zu bleiben".
Ein gutes Mittel sind z. B. rhetorische Fragen oder ein Zitat zum Thema (ähnlich wie bei Präsentationen, ➡ SMC 30).

INTERESSE

Ein Artikel funktioniert nur, wenn deine Leser auch bis zum Ende interessiert bleiben und nicht nach ein oder zwei Absätzen aussteigen. Halte das Interesse hoch, indem du deinen Text z. B. mit Beispielen, Anekdoten und Zitaten anreicherst.

ZITATE

Wenn du in deinem Artikel Zitate einbauen möchtest, denke daran, dass diese immer als solche erkennbar sein müssen:

· Setze wörtliche Zitate immer in Anführungszeichen („..." im Deutschen, "..." im Englischen).
  Für ein Zitat innerhalb eines Zitats setzt du einfache Anführungszeichen (s. u.).
· Gib die Quelle des Zitats an, entweder in Klammern direkt nach dem Zitat oder in einer Fußnote auf der Seite. Das gilt auch für Zitate innerhalb von Zitaten:
  Johnson says, "You have to name your sources even if it's a 'quote within a quote' (Smith, Using quotes, p. 25)." (Johnson, How to quote, p. 12)
· Verändere den Wortlaut des Zitats nicht. Du kannst Wörter auslassen, musst dies aber durch drei Punkte (…) deutlich machen.

LESBARKEIT

Erleichtere das Lesen des Artikels, indem du ihn mit Zwischenüberschriften in Abschnitte unterteilst und gut strukturierst. (➡ SMC 3) Wichtig ist eine gute Planung mithilfe einer Outline, mit der du den Artikel schon vorstrukturierst. (➡ SMC 6) Überlege, wie du in deiner Einleitung das Interesse der Leser wecken kannst, ohne schon vorwegzunehmen, was im Rest des Artikels kommt.

ABSCHLUSS

aEin guter Artikel regt die Leser auch über die Zeit des Lesens hinaus noch zum Nachdenken an. Der letzte Absatz bestimmt entscheidend den Gesamteindruck mit – der Schluss ist das, was deinen Lesern in Erinnerung bleibt und sie im besten Fall weiter beschäftigt.

Dies kannst du erreichen, in dem du z. B. nochmal auf ein Zitat in deiner Einleitung zurückkommst oder hier ein weiteres anbringst. Wenn du im ersten Absatz eine rhetorische Frage gestellt hast, kannst du im letzten Absatz diese beantworten oder noch einmal stellen. Oder du stellst eine weiterführende Frage, die sich aus dem Informationen in deinem Artikel ergibt.

TIPP
Aufmerksamkeit erregende Überschriften heißen im Internet *"clickbait"*, also Klick-Köder. Wenn du das nächste Mal Artikel suchst, achte darauf, *warum* du bestimmte Artikel liest und andere nicht: Was an den Überschriften hat dich gereizt, weiterzulesen oder den Link anzuklicken?

TIPP
Quellenangaben machst du so:
· Bücher: Autor, Titel, Seitenangabe, also z. B. A. Meier, Buch ohne Titel, S. 15
· Webseiten: URL und ggf. Titel, z. B. www.wikipedia.de: William Shakespeare

TIPP
Ein Artikel ist kein Aufsatz, bei dem du in der Einleitung die Fragestellung wiederholst und andeutest, wie du sie lösen willst. Bei einem Artikel geht es eher darum, in der Einleitung das Interesse der Leser zu wecken und sie zum Weiterlesen oder Nachdenken zu bewegen.

11 Writing a report

In einem Bericht stellst du übersichtlich und gut verständlich Fakten dar, z. B. zu einem Ereignis oder einem Vorfall.

STRUKTUR

Wie jeder Text sollte ein Bericht aus einer Überschrift, einer Einleitung, einem Hauptteil und einem Schluss bestehen. (→ SMC 3)

In einer Gliederung (→ SMC 6) kannst du die Struktur schon anlegen und für jeden Textteil eine Überschrift notieren sowie Stichwörter dazu ergänzen. Wenn du viele Informationen im Hauptteil unterbringen willst, verwende auch Unterüberschriften.

STICHWÖRTER

In der Einleitung sagst du kurz, was passiert ist. Dabei kannst du schon knapp die wichtigsten wh-Fragen beantworten, bevor du im Hauptteil näher darauf eingehst. In deiner Gliederung (→ SMC 6) solltest du deswegen für die Einleitung deine Stichworte auf die Fragen Who?, What?, When?, Where? und Why? konzentrieren.

Im Hauptteil eines Berichtes stehen die Details des Ereignisses, meist in chronologischer Reihenfolge. Hier werden die wh-Fragen genauer beantwortet, weswegen du in der Gliederung für den Hauptteil weitere Stichworte zu den einzelnen Fragen sammeln solltest.

Im Schlussabsatz bringst du deinen Bericht zum Abschluss, indem du z. B. kurz das Ergebnis oder die Folgen des beschriebenen Ereignisses darstellst.

> **TIPP**
> Ein Bericht soll objektiv sein und Fakten darstellen. Konzentriere dich bei deinen *keywords* in der Gliederung darauf, die 5 *wh*-Fragen zu beantworten:
>
> • What happened?
> • Who did what?
> • When did it happen?
> • Where did it happen?
> • Why did it happen?
>
> Denk daran, dass ein Bericht im *simple past* geschrieben wird. Du solltest also deine Stichworte auch gleich so notieren.

12 Writing a review

In einer Rezension zu einem Buch oder einem Film gibst du dem Leser standardmäßig folgende Informationen: Autor/Regisseur, Darsteller, Charaktere, Handlung etc. Am Ende gibst du deine persönliche Meinung zum Film oder Buch ab.

VORBEREITUNG

Step 1: Lies das Buch bzw. gucke den Film. Notiere dir, was dir besonders auffällt – positiv, negativ oder einfach als bemerkenswert.

Step 2: Ergänze deine Notizen mit Informationen über das Buch bzw. den Film. Am besten strukturierst du die Notizen gleich, z. B. in einer Tabelle. Folge dabei schon der Struktur der Rezension (siehe rechts).

SCHREIBPHASE

Step 1: Schreibe einen ersten Entwurf.
- Verwende das simple present.
- Beginne mit der Einleitung, die die grundlegenden Informationen enthält.
- Im Hauptteil schreibe mithilfe deiner Notizen eine kurze Zusammenfassung des Inhalts (ohne zuviel zu verraten – besonders nicht das Ende) und gib mehr Informationen zu den Charakteren.
- Am Schluss gib deine Meinung zum Buch oder Film. Sage, weshalb du glaubst, dass man das Buch lesen/ den Film sehen sollte (oder nicht). Eventuell erwähne, für welche Zielgruppe das Buch/der Film gedacht ist.
- Falls du es noch nicht getan hast, überlege dir eine Überschrift, die das Interesse der Leser weckt.

Step 2: Überarbeite deinen Text. (→ SMC 14, 15)

Headline	• catch your readers' attention • hint at your opinion or the book's/movie's content
Introduction	• title, author/director, year, length (pages/ minutes), setting • basic information: genre/type of movie/ book (action, drama, comedy), characters, one-sentence summary of plot
Main part	• short summary of the plot (but don't reveal too much!) • more information about characters (and cast if you're writing about a movie)
Conclusion	• your opinion, e.g. on characters, plot, actors, dialogue, special effects, the message of the book/movie, … • recommendation; who is the target group? (e.g. young adults, comedy fans, people who like drama/romance)

> **TIPP**
> Verwende starke Adjektive und Adverbien, um deine Leser entweder von dem Buch/Film zu überzeugen oder abzuschrecken (an action-packed thriller, a hilarious comedy, a highly entertaining movie, a boring drama with one-dimensional characters …).

13 Writing a summary

Wenn du eine Zusammenfassung schreiben sollst, ist es wichtig, den Text gut zu kennen. Erst dann kannst du entscheiden, welche Aspekte so wichtig sind, dass sie in deiner Zusammenfassung erwähnt werden sollten – und welche nicht.
Die folgenden Schritte können dabei helfen:

PLANUNGSPHASE

Step 1:   Lies den Text genau. Mach dir Notizen (➡ SMC 41) oder markiere wichtige Stellen im Text (➡ SMC 2).

Step 2:   Beantworte die *wh*-Fragen Who? What? Where? When? Why? zum Text.
Du kannst dir dazu Stichworte am Rand machen.

Who?   *Who does something? Who is the text about?*

What?   *What happens? What does person X do?*

Where?   *Where does it take place?*

When?   *When does it take place?*

Why?   *Why does person X act this way? Why does something happen?*

Step 3:   Entscheide, welche Textteile wichtige Informationen enthalten.
Beispiele, Vergleiche, direkte Rede oder Zahlen und Ähnliches gehören nicht in eine Zusammenfassung.

> **TIPP**
> Du kannst Teile, die für deine Zusammenfassung überflüssig sind, im Text einklammern.

SCHREIBPHASE

Step 1:   Schreib einen ersten Entwurf deiner Zusammenfassung:

- Beginne mit einer Einleitung, in der wichtige Informationen wie z. B. Titel, Autor/in, Thema und Hauptaussage des Textes stehen. Wenn du einen Zeitungsartikel zusammenfasst, solltest du hier auch die Quelle nennen.

- Verwende immer das simple present.
  Ausnahme hiervon: Wenn der Autor etwas beschreibt, das in der Vergangenheit oder der Zukunft liegt, z. B. in einem Zeitungsartikel, kannst du das auch so wiedergeben. Beispiel:
  The writer describes the festival in New York, which started on Saturday, 4th April. She gives details about the opening event, where the mayor gave a speech to the large crowd. She also writes about New Orleans, where next year's festival will take place.

- Kopiere nicht den Text, sondern benutze deine eigenen Worte.

Step 2:   Überarbeite deine Zusammenfassung:

- Hast du alle wichtigen Aspekte genannt?

- Hast du unwichtige Details weggelassen?

- Ist dein Text durchgängig im *simple present*? (außer in den oben genannten Ausnahmen)

- Hast du deine Textteile gut verbunden? Ist dein Text logisch aufgebaut und gut zu verstehen?

- Vergiss auch nicht, den Text auf Rechtschreibung und Zeichensetzung zu checken. (➡ SMC 14, 15)

> **LANGUAGE HELP**
> Folgende *phrases* können dir bei der Einleitung helfen:
> - The story/text is about …
> - The text deals with …
> - The topic of the text is …
> - The article/text shows …

14 Revising texts

Egal, ob du eine Rückmeldung von einem Partner/einer Partnerin bekommen hast oder nicht – einen Text solltest du auf jeden Fall noch einmal gut prüfen, bevor du ihn deinem Lehrer/deiner Lehrerin übergibst.

TEXTÜBERARBEITUNG

1. Stimmt die Struktur?
Jeder Text braucht
- eine Einleitung, die in das Thema einführt,
- einen Hauptteil, der das Thema ausführt,
- einen Schluss, der alles auf den Punkt bringt.
(➡ SMC 3)

2. Stimmt der Aufbau der Absätze?
Jeder Absatz
- befasst sich mit einem zusammenhängenden Gedanken,
- beginnt mit einem **topic sentence**, der diesen Gedanken einführt.
(➡ SMC 3)

3. Stimmen die Verknüpfungen?
Gute *linking words*
- schaffen Verbindungen zwischen Sätzen oder Satzteilen,
- helfen, Zusammenhänge besser darzustellen und verständlich zu machen.
(➡ SMC 4)

4. Sind die Zeitangaben richtig gesetzt?
Time markers
- helfen, sich z. B. in einer Geschichte zurechtzufinden,
- machen das Geschehen anschaulicher.
(➡ SMC 4)

Today I wanted to do somthing different.

because

and

Two minutes later

good

slowly

5. Enthält der Text Adjektive und Adverbien?
Adjektive und Adverbien
- erlauben nähere Beschreibungen von Personen und Dingen,
- machen Texte anschaulicher.
(➡ SMC 4)

6. Hat der Text sprachliche/grammatikalische Fehler?
Überprüfe deinen Text
- auf Rechtschreibung und Satzzeichen,
- auf grammatische Formen, z. B. Verbformen, Satzbau (*word order*) usw.

AUF WAS SOLLTEST DU SONST NOCH ACHTEN?

Zeichensetzung
- Überprüfe die Zeichensetzung im Text. Sind die Kommas richtig gesetzt, z. B. bei *non-defining relative clauses* oder wenn ein Satz mit dem Nebensatz beginnt (*If he …, …*)? Enden alle Sätze mit den richtigen Satzzeichen?
- Doppelpunkt: nach einem Doppelpunkt geht es klein weiter, außer es handelt sich beim ersten Wort um eins, das immer großgeschrieben wird (Namen, Wochentage usw.).
- Abkürzungen: wenn du in deinem Text Abkürzungen verwendest, überprüfe die Schreibweise. "E.g." (*for example*) und "i.e." (*in other words*) enthalten z. B. Punkte und danach folgt ein Komma: *There are many kinds of birds, e.g., falcons, ravens or parrots.*

TIPP
Häufige Fehlerquellen sind z. B.
- Groß-/Kleinschreibung,
- Wörter, die gleich klingen, aber unterschiedlich geschrieben werden: *your/you're, their/they're/there,*
- Verwendung des Apostrophs,
- Zeichensetzung,
und du kannst sie z. B. in *online dictionaries* überprüfen.

15 Revising and improving electronic texts

Viele deiner Texte schreibst du nicht mit der Hand, sondern am Computer, sei es für eine Hausaufgabe, ein Referat oder ein Projekt.

Bei der Überarbeitung dieser Texte gelten dieselben Grundsätze wie beim Überarbeiten aller Texte (➜ SMC 14), aber es kommen auch noch ein paar Besonderheiten dazu. Diese findest du im Folgenden:

KORREKTUR
- Nutze die Überprüfungsfunktion deines Textverarbeitungsprogramms. Aber: sieh dir alle gemeldeten Fehler genau an, denn nicht alles, was als falsch angezeigt wird, ist auch wirklich falsch.
- Lies deinen Text trotz der Überprüfung durch das Programm noch einmal Korrektur, denn nicht alle Fehler werden auch als solche erkannt (z.B. wenn ein Tippfehler zu einem anderen korrekten Wort führt, das aber im Kontext nicht passt wie *the win in the trees* statt *the wind in the trees*).

TIPP

Denk dran, vor der Überprüfung deines Textes die Rechtschreibüberprüfung auf "Englisch (Großbritannien)" einzustellen.

LAYOUT
- Lass genügend Abstand an den Rändern (normalerweise reichen die voreingestellten Ränder in deinem Textverarbeitungsprogramm, also 2,5 cm).
- Richte den Text linksbündig aus, denn das ist am besten lesbar (Ausnahme: die Überschrift kann zentriert sein, ebenso wie z.B. ein Zitat zum Einstieg).
- Zwischenüberschriften lockern den Text auf und machen das Lesen leichter, weil sie größere Textblöcke unterteilen.
- Überlege dir gut, wo du Bilder einbaust und welche Größe sie haben sollen: Bilder, die einen Inhalt im Text veranschaulichen, sollten auch möglichst nah an dieser Textstelle platziert werden. Die Größe solltest du so wählen, dass die der Inhalt gut zu erkennen ist. Gib immer die Quelle an, wenn du ein Bild verwendest, v.a. wenn möglich auch den Namen des Urhebers/der Urheberin. (➜ SMC 27, 28, 29)

TIPP

Wenn dein Text der Öffentlichkeit zugänglich gemacht wird, z.B. auf der Schulwebseite, musst du vor der Verwendung von Bildern die Urheber um Erlaubnis fragen. (➜ SMC 27. 28, 29)

ZITATE
Wenn du Zitate verwendet hast, überprüfe, ob sie als solche erkennbar sind:
- Sind sie in Anführungszeichen gesetzt?
- Hast du die Quelle des Zitats angegeben?
- Ist der Wortlaut des Zitats genau wie im Original? Wenn nicht, hast du Auslassungen kenntlich gemacht? (➜ SMC 10)

FORMATIERUNG
- Wähle eine gut lesbare Schriftart. Benutze diese Schrift für den kompletten Text. Für Überschriften oder Bildunterschriften kannst du eine andere Schrift verwenden (aber nie mehr als drei verscheidene Schriftarten).
- Die Schriftgröße sollte so groß sein, dass der Text gut lesbar ist (z.B. 12 pt). Das gilt auch für den Zeilenabstand.
- Zur Hervorhebung bestimmter Textstellen, z.B. Zitaten, Songtiteln, Buchtiteln, Namen etc., kannst du Schriftstile wie **fett**, *kursiv* oder <u>unterstrichen</u> verwenden. Du solltest aber sparsam damit umgehen, damit der Text nicht unübersichtlich wird und auch nicht alles gleichzeitig verwenden.

TIPP

Bei Schriften unterscheidet man zwischen serifen (z.B. Times New Roman) und serifenlosen (z.B. Arial). Für längere, gedruckte Texte nimmt man in der Regel serife Schriften. Kürzere Texte und solche, die vor allem am Bildschirm gelesen, wirken durch serifenlose Schriften oft lesbarer.

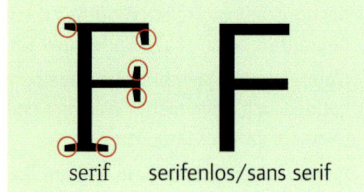

serif   serifenlos/sans serif

MEDIATION SKILLS

16 Mediating written or spoken information

Nicht jeder spricht und versteht sowohl Deutsch als auch Englisch; daher kann es vorkommen, dass du in bestimmten Situationen für Andere zwischen den Sprachen vermitteln musst – das nennt man dann Mediation.

Wie und was genau du vermitteln musst, hängt von der Situation ab und auch davon, ob du den Inhalt eines geschriebenen Textes wiedergeben oder zwischen zwei Sprechern vermitteln sollst.

Sprachmittlung bedeutet nicht Übersetzen (von Texten) oder Dolmetschen (bei Unterhaltungen), sondern das sinngemäße Übertragen von Inhalten in die andere Sprache.

MEDIATION VON SCHRIFTLICHEN ODER MÜNDLICHEN INFORMATIONEN

Wenn du Informationen in einer anderen Sprache wiedergeben sollst, geht es nicht darum, alles zu übersetzen, sondern es kommt darauf an, die wichtigsten Informationen herauszusuchen. Oft stellt dir die Person, für die du die Informationen wiedergibst, gezielte Fragen – so weißt du, worauf du achten musst.

Schriftliche Informationen

- Scanne den Text gezielt nach den geforderten Informationen. (➡ SMC 1)

- Mach dir keine Sorgen, wenn du nicht jedes Wort verstehst. Das ist oft nicht nötig, um die wichtigen Punkte zu verstehen und wiederzugeben.

- Wenn der Text länger ist und du viele Informationen im Blick behalten musst, markiere die wichtigsten Textstellen. (➡ SMC 2)

- Mach dir Notizen in deinen eigenen Worten. (➡ SMC 41)

Mündliche Informationen

- Achte beim Hören gezielt auf die gesuchten Informationen. (➡ SMC 26)

- Mach dir Notizen. (➡ SMC 41)

- Überlege, wie du deine Notizen am besten in der anderen Sprache wiedergeben kannst.

> **TIPP**
>
> Bei Mediation im Unterricht hast du in der Regel eine Aufgabenstellung, die dir sagt, worauf du beim Lesen oder Hören achten musst bzw. welche Stellen du wiedergeben sollst. Konzentriere dich beim Lesen des Textes auf diese Stellen (scanning) bzw. mache dir gezielt zu diesen Stellen Notizen.

> **TIPP**
>
> Wenn du den Inhalt eines Texts schriftlich in einer anderen Sprache wiedergeben sollst, achte darauf, dass deine Mediation nicht länger ist als ca. 35-40% des Originaltextes, ähnlich wie bei einer summary. (➡ SMC 13)

17 Selecting relevant information

Manchmal gibt es keine gezielten Fragen oder Aufgabenstellungen, die dir sagen, welche Informationen du aus einem Text heraussuchen und wiedergeben sollst. In der Regel hast du aber trotzdem Anhaltspunkte, die sich aus der Situation ergeben oder aus dem, was dir dein Gegenüber erzählt hat.

Wenn du in einer solchen Situation bist, helfen folgende Hinweise:

- Analysiere die Situation, um abzuschätzen, um welche Informationen es gehen könnte (Restaurant, Bahnhof, Flughafen usw.).

- Wenn du unsicher bist, frage nach.

- Übersetze wichtige Stichworte direkt, wenn du die Wörter kennst.

- Umschreibe Begriffe, die du nicht kennst.

> **TIPP**
>
> Wenn du Informationen wiedergibst, kannst du oft Details zu einem Begriff zusammenfassen. Wenn z. B. in einem Text twitter, Facebook, tumblr und Pinterest vorkommen, kannst du social media sagen anstatt alle aufzuzählen.

18 Paraphrasing

Es fällt dir eventuell manchmal schwer, mündliche Aussagen oder Texte in Englisch wiederzugeben, z. B. weil

- dein Wortschatz nicht ausreicht

- dir bekannte Wörter „im Stress" der Situation nicht einfallen

- oder spezielle Fachbegriffe auftauchen.

Wenn dir das passiert, dann solltest du versuchen, diese Wörter zu umschreiben, z. B. mithilfe von Relativsätzen

It's somebody/a person who
It's something that you use to
It's an animal that …
It's a place that/where …

Oh, sure. There's a drugstore down the street. Come on, I'll show you.

Ich hab Kopfschmerzen. Kannst du Marcus mal fragen, wo hier eine Apotheke ist?

Apotheke? Er … OK … Marcus, is there a place nearby where Lukas can buy something for his headache?

> **TIPP**
>
> Oft helfen beim Umschreiben auch Synonyme (gleiche Bedeutung) oder Antonyme (gegenteilige Bedeutung). Wenn du die weißt, kannst du z. B. sagen:
> - It's the same as …
> - It's the opposite of …

19 Cultural differences

Wenn du anderen Menschen hilfst, Texte oder Gehörtes zu verstehen, kann es neben Wortschatzproblemen auch noch andere Schwierigkeiten geben. Diese sind häufig in kulturellen Unterschieden begründet. Um hier helfen zu können, musst du dir beim Sprachmitteln bewusst machen, dass dein Gegenüber evtl. bestimmte Dinge nicht weiß, die für dich selbstverständlich sind, oder dass er/sie dich nicht sofort versteht, obwohl du den Inhalt korrekt übertragen hast.

Dinge, die häufig zu Missverständnissen führen, sind z. B.
- Temperaturen: 30 Grad bei uns sind heiß, in den USA eher kalt, weil in den USA Temperaturen in Fahrenheit angegeben werden, nicht in Celsius.

- Längenangaben/Geschwindigkeit: Bei uns wird das metrische System verwendet (Meter, Kilometer usw.), in den USA das *imperial system* mit *inch*, *yard* und *mile*. Das kann auch bei Geschwindigkeitsangaben zu Verwirrung führen, denn 75 *mph* (Meilen pro Stunde) sind z. B. ca. 120 km/h.

Am besten ist es, wenn du immer noch mal höflich nachfragst, ob dein Gegenüber alles verstanden hat. Wenn du dann feststellst, dass es zu einem Missverständnis gekommen ist, dann kannst du folgende Dinge probieren:
- Frage höflich nach, wo das Missverständnis ist.

- Versuche, das Missverständnis durch eine neue Erklärung zu beseitigen.

- Ergänze deine Erläuterung evtl. mit Hintergrundinformationen: Es kann sein, dass du bestimmte Dinge, die für dich völlig normal sind, erklären musst (wie z. B. Mülltrennung oder das Benutzen des Nahverkehrs).

- Sei auch offen für die Erklärungen, die du evtl. im Gegenzug bekommst – hier kannst du Dinge über das Land deines Gegenübers lernen.

SPEAKING SKILLS

20 Communicating in everyday situations

Es ist nicht immer einfach, sich mit Menschen aus anderen Ländern zu unterhalten. Neben der Sprachbarriere gibt es oft auch kulturelle Unterschiede, wie das folgende Beispiel zeigt.

Lies dieses Gespräch zwischen Paul, einem deutschen Schüler, und seinem Austauschpartner Jack in den USA:

Jack: How's your school at home?
Paul: It's okay.
Jack: Oh … good. What are your favorite subjects?
Paul: Er, I don't know.
Jack: Oh, well. Maybe you'll enjoy our school too.
Paul: Maybe.
Jack: Er … want to play a game?

Das Gespräch kommt nicht so richtig in Gang, und Jack gibt irgendwann auf. Wenn man aber einige Regeln beachtet, werden Unterhaltungen einfacher und für beide Parteien erfreulicher. Vergleiche das folgende Gespräch mit dem obigen

Jack: How's your school at home?
Paul: I like it … but of course I don't like all my teachers.
Jack: Yeah, I think that's normal. What are your favorite subjects?
Paul: I'm not sure. I like history and maths, but art and German are okay too.
Jack: Ah, my favorite subject is English. Anyway, I'm sure you'll enjoy our school too. Our history teacher is pretty cool. Have you met any of the teachers yet?
Paul: No, not yet, but I think …

Die folgenden Schritte helfen dir, wenn du dich freundlich und flüssig unterhalten willst:

Step 1: Beginne freundlich, z. B. mit etwas, was beide Gesprächspartner verbindet (der Ort, die Situation usw.).

Step 2: Halte die Unterhaltung am Laufen:
- zeige dein Interesse, indem du Fragen stellst
- vermeide einsilbige Antworten, um nicht desinteressiert oder unfreundlich zu wirken
- wenn du etwas nicht verstehst, frage nach
- wenn du etwas nicht sagen kannst, versuche es zu umschreiben oder bitte deinen Gesprächspartner um Hilfe

Step 3: Beende das Gespräch so freundlich, wie du es angefangen hast:
- bedanke dich, wenn du um Hilfe gebeten hast
- verabschiede dich freundlich

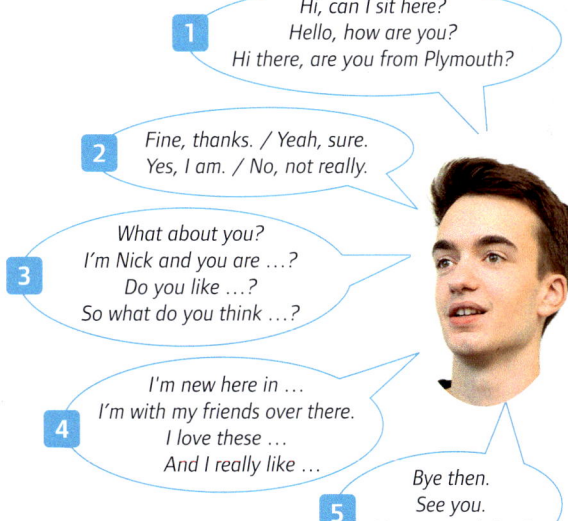

1 Hi, can I sit here?
Hello, how are you?
Hi there, are you from Plymouth?

2 Fine, thanks. / Yeah, sure.
Yes, I am. / No, not really.

3 What about you?
I'm Nick and you are …?
Do you like …?
So what do you think …?

4 I'm new here in …
I'm with my friends over there.
I love these …
And I really like …

5 Bye then.
See you.
Have a good time!

TIPP Aussprache und Satzmelodie (z.B. bei *question tags*) sind wichtig im Englischen. Da es aber mitten in einem Gespräch nicht immer einfach ist, darauf zu achten, solltest du das Sprechen regelmäßig üben, indem du dich aufnimmst (etwa mit der Diktierfunktion deines Handys) und dich dann anhörst, um deine Aussprache zu überprüfen. Das funktioniert am besten, wenn du einen Text liest, den du auch als Audio vorliegen hast, also etwa ein Text aus dem Schülerbuch oder dem Workbook oder ein Audiobook, denn dann kannst du deine Aussprache gut mit der korrekten vergleichen.

21 Having a discussion

In einer Diskussion tauscht man Meinungen und Ideen zu einem bestimmten Thema aus.

VORBEREITUNGSPHASE

Step 1: Bereite dich auf das Thema vor: Recherchiere Fakten und Beispiele. Überlege, was deine Meinung zu dem Thema ist. Mache dir Notizen.

Step 2: Halte deine Notizen für die Diskussion bereit – z.B. auf kleinen Zetteln – damit du darauf zugreifen kannst, falls du sie brauchst.

Step 3: Überlege dir vorher ein Statement, das deine Meinung zum Thema gut ausdrückt; das erleichtert den Einstieg in die Diskussion.

DISKUSSION

Step 1: Starting the discussion: Sage deine Meinung (z.B. mithilfe der Eröffnung, die du dir überlegt hast).

Step 2: Continuing the discussion: Tausche deine Meinung mit anderen aus. Bleibe höflich und sachlich. Hör den anderen zu und lass sie ausreden.

- Wenn du sprichst, beziehe dich auf die Anderen und sage, weshalb du ihren Argumenten zustimmst (oder nicht).

- Stütze deine Meinung mit Fakten und Beispielen.

Step 3: Ending the discussion:

- Fasse deinen Standpunkt noch einmal knapp zusammen.

- Versuche, Gemeinsamkeiten festzustellen (v.a. wenn es darum geht, sich auf etwas zu einigen) oder einigt euch darüber, dass es nicht *eine* gemeinsame Lösung gibt *(agree to disagree)*.

- Falls gefordert, einigt euch auf eine Lösung oder einen Kompromiss.

> **TIPP**
>
> Bei Rollenspielen musst du manchmal eine Meinung vertreten, die anders ist als deine eigene. Dann kannst du in deinen Notizen z.B. versuchen, Argumente und Gegenargumente einander gegenüberzustellen, um dann in der Diskussion schnell und gut reagieren zu können.

> **TIPP**
>
> Im Englischen ist man häufig weit weniger direkt als im Deutschen. Das bedeutet, dass du bei Diskussionen
> - besonders gut zuhören musst, weil du sonst evtl. nicht genau mitbekommst, ob man dir zustimmt oder widerspricht;
> - kurze, zu direkte Antworten wie *"No."* vermeiden solltest, weil sie unhöflich wirken.

22 Agreeing and disagreeing with people's opinions

Wenn du mit Anderen diskutierst, wirst du anderen Gesprächsteilnehmern zustimmen oder widersprechen. Wie im Deutschen, gibt es dafür auch im Englischen bestimmte Redewendungen, die du dafür gut verwenden kannst.

> **LANGUAGE HELP**
>
> Es ist bei Diskussionen hilfreich, einige Standard-Redewendungen parat zu haben. Wenn du die beherrscht, kannst du dich mehr auf deine Argumente konzentrieren. Folgende Phrasen solltest du dir aufschreiben und sie lernen:
>
> | Stating your opinion | Agreeing | Disagreeing |
> |---|---|---|
> | · In my opinion … | · I agree … | · I'm afraid I don't quite agree … |
> | · Well, I'd say … | · Exactly./Absolutely./… | · I'm not sure about that. |
> | · It's a fact that … | · You're quite right. | · Do you really think so? |
> | · Personally, I think… | · I think so too. | · I'm not convinced that … |
> | · If you ask me … | · You've got a good point there. | · I doubt that (very much). |
> | · I think/feel/believe … | · That's exactly how I see it. | · I don't agree with you at all. |
> | · First of all, I'd like to point out… | · That's true/right. | · I disagree (completely). |
> | · I'm certain that … | · I couldn't agree with you more. | · It's not as simple as that. |

23 Preparing and taking part in a panel discussion

Eine Podiumsdiskussion ist eine Sonderform der Diskussion, bei der 3–5 Vertreter unterschiedlicher Meinungen/Gruppen vor Zuhörern unter der Leitung eines Moderators ein Thema diskutieren.

VORBEREITUNGSPHASE

Step 1:   Bereite dich auf die Diskussion vor wie auf andere Diskussionen auch: Recherchiere Fakten und überlege, was deine Meinung zu dem Thema ist. Mache dir Notizen.

Step 2:   Halte deine Notizen für die Diskussion bereit – z. B. auf kleinen Zetteln – damit du darauf zugreifen kannst, falls du sie brauchst.

Step 3:   Bereite dich auf deine Rolle in der Diskussion vor – Moderator, Diskussionsteilnehmer oder Zuhörer. Jede Rolle hat andere Aufgaben. Nützliche Redemittel (➡ SMC 22) können auf einem discussion fan notiert werden, damit sie schnell zur Hand sind.

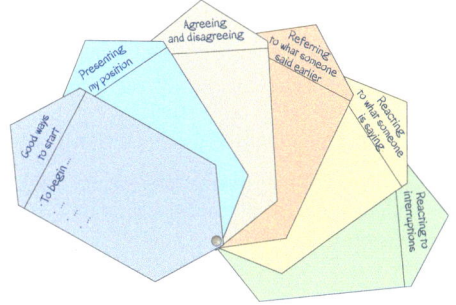

MODERATOR/IN

Die Moderatorin/Der Moderator einer Podiumsdiskussion
- überlegt sich im Vorfeld der Diskussion mögliche Fragen für die Teilnehmer
- stellt kurz die Diskussionsteilnehmer vor
- leitet die Diskussion und stellt Fragen, wenn die Diskussion stockt
- sorgt dafür, dass sich alle Beteiligten an die Regeln halten und dass alle Teilnehmer etwa gleich viel Redezeit haben
- achtet auf die Zeit oder bestimmt einen timekeeper, der dies tut
- ermuntert die Zuhörer, Fragen zu stellen und moderiert diese.

DISKUSSIONSTEILNEHMER/IN

Die Teilnehmer einer Podiumsdiskussion
- sind gut vorbereitet: sie haben sich ihre eigenen Argumente notiert und sich Gedanken zu den möglichen Argumenten der anderen Teilnehmer gemacht
- geben zu Beginn der Diskussion ein kurzes Statement, das ihre Meinung knapp zusammenfasst
- folgen der Diskussion aufmerksam und notieren sich Argumente der anderen Teilnehmer, um darauf reagieren zu können.

ZUHÖRER/IN

Die Zuhörer bei einer Podiumsdiskussion
- überlegen sich im Vorfeld, welche Argumente sie zu bestimmten Themen erwarten und überlegen sich entsprechende Fragen/Kommentare
- können sich im Anschluss an die Diskussion dazu äußern, welche Argumente sie am überzeugendsten fanden
- machen sich während der Diskussion Notizen, um im Anschluss Fragen zu stellen oder die Argumente kommentieren zu können.

DURCHFÜHRUNG

Eine Podiumsdiskussion sollte einen vorher vereinbarten Zeitrahmen nicht überschreiten (z.B. 30 Minuten). Im Anschluss daran sollte Zeit für Fragen und Kommentare der Zuhörer eingeplant werden.

Für die Einhaltung der Zeit und der Diskussionsregeln ist der Moderator/die Moderatorin verantwortlich.

24 Taking part in an interview

Interviews sind häufig Bestandteil von Prüfungen oder Bewerbungen. Es ist wichtig, gerade wenn es um Bewerbungsgespräche oder Prüfungen geht, dass du dich gut darauf vorbereitest.

Bei Bewerbungsgesprächen helfen die folgenden 4 Ps:

PREPARE
- Finde so viel wie möglich über den Job und den Arbeitgeber heraus.
- Notiere mögliche Fragen, die du dem Arbeitgeber stellen kannst.
- Überlege dir aber auch, welche Fragen man dir stellen könnte und bereite Antworten darauf vor.

PRACTISE
- Übe das Bewerbungsgespräch mit einem Partner/einer Partnerin.
- Gib deinem Übungspartner die Fragen, die du von deinem Arbeitgeber erwartest und beantworte sie. Sage deinem Übungspartner auch, dass er/sie dir ruhig unerwartete Fragen stellen soll. So übst du, auf unvorbereitete Fragen zu antworten.

PRESENT
- Überlege dir im Vorfeld, was du zu dem Bewerbungsgespräch anziehen möchtest. Besprich das ruhig auch mit einem Freund/einer Freundin oder deinen Eltern. Die Auswahl der Kleidung hängt vom Arbeitgeber ab.
- Stelle sicher, dass du pünktlich bist. Suche dir vorher heraus, wie du zum Ort des Gespräches kommst. Plane Zeit für Unvorhergesehenes ein. Es ist immer besser, zehn Minuten zu früh als zu spät zu sein.

PARTICIPATE
- Stelle dich am Anfang vor, am besten mit einem freundlichen Lächeln.
- Lass dir Zeit, Fragen zu beantworten, besonders wenn es unerwartete Fragen sind. Antworte nicht mit "Yes." oder "No.", sondern versuche, Fragen ausführlich und höflich zu beantworten.
- Wenn du eine Frage nicht verstehst, frag nach.
- Am Ende des Gespräches, verabschiede dich mit einem freundlichen Lächeln und bedanke dich für das Gespräch.

> **TIPP**
> Achte auch auf deine non-verbale Kommunikation – wie du stehst, gehst, sitzt – und siehe deinem Gegenüber in die Augen.

> **LANGUAGE HELP**
> Folgender Wortschatz hilft dir ...
>
> - bei der Begrüßung: *Nice to meet you too.* • *Thank you for inviting me today.* • *I'm fine, thank you.*
> - über dich selbst zu sprechen: *Well, I'm 16 years old and …* • *Actually, one of my main strengths is …*
> - zu erklären, was du meinst: *What I mean is …* • *What I'm really trying to say is …* • *I'm glad you asked that question because …* • *… is very important to me, as is …*
> - weitere Punkte anzubringen: *Another point I should mention is …* • *There's something else I'd like to say.* • *Let me explain that in some more detail.*
> - aufmerksam zu wirken: *I see.* • *Right.* • *Uhuh.*
> - bei Unklarheiten nachzufragen: *Sorry, I don't quite understand.* • *Sorry, but do you mean …* • *I am not sure I have understood your question correctly.* • *Sorry, could you rephrase that?*
> - bei der Verabschiedung: *Thank you for the chance to speak to you.*

VIEWING SKILLS

25 Viewing

Wenn du verstehst, wie Filmtechniken eingesetzt werden, um beim Zuschauer z. B. Angst, Freude, Spannung oder Lachen auszulösen, bekommst du ein besseres Verständnis dafür, wie Filme funktionieren.

Es gibt viele verschiedene Elemente, die die Atmosphäre und die Wirkung eines Filmes beeinflussen:

- Genre: Handelt es sich um einen Dokumentarfilm (documentary), einen Spielfilm (feature film) wie z. B. thriller, science-fiction/sci-fi movie, comedy oder ein drama? Oder ist es ein Videoclip oder ein Werbefilm?

- Story: Wo und wann spielt der Film (setting)? Besetzung der Rollen (cast), Schauplatz (location), Handlung (plot).

- Camera: Erst durch die Bilder der **Kamera** ist der Zuschauer in der Lage, einen Film wahrzunehmen. Die Kamera stellt das Blickfeld her und begrenzt es gleichzeitig, z. B. hinsichtlich der Beziehung der Charaktere zueinander. Auch die Stimmung oder Spannung in einer Szene wird von der Kameraführung beeinflusst. Dafür gibt es z. B. folgende Mittel:

  - Shots: Die **Kameraeinstellung** beeinflusst, wie man Szenen wahrnimmt, ob z. B. Personen oder Objekte als Nahaufnahme (close-up), aus der mittleren Distanz (medium shot) oder als Totale (long shot) gefilmt sind.

  - Editing: Filme werden in der Regel nicht chronologisch gedreht und auch nicht nur mit einer einzigen Kamera, d. h. am Ende der Dreharbeiten müssen viele einzelne Shots zu einem Film zusammengefügt werden. Dieser **Filmschnitt** bestimmt, wie eine Szene wirkt. Er bestimmt den Rhythmus – lange Einstellungen mit wenigen Schnitten wirken eher ruhig, können aber auch große Spannung erzeugen, während schnelle, harte Schnitte eher actiongeladen wirken. Wie genau eine Szene wirkt, hängt oft auch vom Zusammenspiel von Schnitt und Musik ab.

- Soundtrack: Die **Musik**, die für eine Szene gewählt wird, hat großen Einfluss darauf, wie man die Szene wahrnimmt. Eine Actionszene wird meist mit schneller, lauter Musik unterlegt, eine romantische Szene eher mit ruhiger, leiser Musik. Dies geschieht, um die Wirkung des Gesehenen zu verstärken.

long shot

medium shot

close-up

`Workbook` Wordbank 6

VIEWING LOG

Wenn du eine Szene oder einen ganzen Film sehr intensiv analysieren möchtest, hilft es, ein Filmtagebuch (viewing log) anzulegen, in dem du die Handlung oder einzelne wichtige Szenen sowie deine Reaktion darauf festhältst.

Das Filmtagebuch kann z. B. eine simple, zweispaltige Tabelle sein:
Spalte 1: What you noticed – images, sounds, dialogue, lighting, costumes, mood, characterization, plot, etc.
Spalte 2: Your reaction – What did you think? How did the scene make you feel?

TIPP
Wenn du über Filme sprechen möchtest, können dir folgende Redewendungen helfen:

- *The film is about … / shows … / tells the story of …*
- *The music creates/builds/supports tension/ suspense/joy …*
- *The actor's body language helps to create a feeling of happiness/joy/anger/suspense …*

- *In this scene the music/effects/camera angle … supports the plot /mood of the scene / …*
- *The camera movement creates a feeling of …*
- *The camera work/soundtrack helps to …*
- *The close-ups show his/her feelings.*

LISTENING SKILLS

26 Listening strategies

Wenn du Englisch hörst, kann es sein, dass du entweder Details heraushören musst (listening for detail), z.B. bei Ansagen am Bahnhof, oder generell verstehen musst, um was es geht (listening for gist) wie z.B. bei einem Film. Dazu kannst du verschiedene Hörverstehenstechniken anwenden.

LISTENING FOR DETAIL

- Überleg dir vorher, auf welche Informationen du achten musst.
  - Bei einem Wetterbericht sind das z.B. Beschreibungen wie sunny, cloudy, chance of rain etc., bei Bahnhofsansagen z.B. Wörter wie platform oder Orte und Zeiten.
  - Höre dann gezielt auf solche Wörter und notiere sie. (➜ SMC 41)

- Manchmal können dir Signalwörter helfen, dem Inhalt zu folgen und dich auf die Details zu konzentrieren:
  - Gründe, Folgen: because, so, so that, …
  - Vergleiche: larger/older/… than, as … as, more, most, …
  - Reihenfolge: before, after, then, next, later, …

LISTENING FOR GIST

- Mache dir keine Sorgen, wenn du nicht jedes Wort verstehst – das brauchst du nicht, um dem Inhalt oberflächlich folgen zu können. Überlege dir anhand der Aufgabe, um was es gehen könnte und konzentriere dich darauf.

- Versuche, von den Sachen, die du verstehst, auf Inhalte zu schließen, die noch kommen könnten.

HÖRVERSTEHENSTECHNIKEN

Es gibt zwei verschiedene Techniken beim Hörverstehen:
- Bei der bottom-up-Technik gehst du vom Gesprochenen an das Hören heran: Konzentriere dich darauf, *was* gerade gesagt wird und beachte dabei z.B die Besonderheiten verschiedener Akzente. Wie gut du das verstehst, was du in der Fremdsprache hörst, ist eine Frage der Übung.

  Du solltest beim Hören folgende Dinge beachten:
  - Chunks/connected speech: Im Englischen spricht man oft mehrere Wörter als Einheit aus, bei der Wortgrenzen verschwinden. Das findet man verstärkt bei
    - Ausdrücken mit Modalverben: she'd've told me · you shouldn't've bought it · you mustabin asleep
    - häufigen Alltagsphrasen: Whatcha think o'that? · Howdju feel? · Dincha see it? · Whatchadoin'?

  - Wörter, die gesprochen gleich klingen, sich in der Bedeutung aber unterscheiden:
    We'd like ice in our drinks. – We like ice in our drinks.
    I can't see them now. – I can see them now. (besonders im AE)
    Hier schafft im Gespräch gezieltes Nachfragen Sicherheit: Sorry, was that can or can't?

- Bei der top-down-Technik gehst du von der Gesprächssituation aus an das Hören heran und versuchst, mögliche Inhalte vorherzusagen:
  - Du kannst Gesprächsinhalte erschließen und das Verstehen erleichtern, wenn du dir Gedanken über die Situation machst:
    - Wer redet in dieser Situation?
    - Über was wird in dieser Situation eventuell gesprochen?
    - Wie sprechen die Personen in dieser Situation miteinander?
    - Werden die Personen eher freundlich, höflich oder verärgert sein?

> **TIPP**
>
> Im Unterricht kannst du Texte oft zweimal hören und hast weitere Hilfen:
> - Sieh dir die Aufgabenstellung an: Was sollst du heraushören?
> - Sieh dir Titel und Bilder an.
> - Vergleiche nach dem Hören mit einem Partner, was ihr verstanden habt.
> - Vervollständige deine Notizen sofort.

> **TIPP**
>
> Beim Hörverstehen hilft vor allem Übung, v.a. wenn es um Chunks/connected speech oder verschiedene Dialekte und Akzente geht.
> Höre dir deshalb so oft du kannst Originaltexte an, z.B Audiobooks oder in Videos online, um ein Gefühl dafür zu entwickeln.
>
> Um dich in unterschiedliche Akzente reinzuhören und sich an sie zu "gewöhnen", kannst du z.B Filme und Serien im Original gucken, bei denen du zur Hilfe englische Untertitel einblenden kannst.

- Sprechen sie in der gegeben Situation eher schnell oder langsam, eher formell oder informell?

  – Diese Vorüberlegungen helfen dir vorherzusagen, was im Gespräch gesagt wird (prediction), selbst wenn du nicht jedes Wort verstehst oder durch äußere Umstände wie z. B laute Nebengeräusche nicht hören kannst: It's very warm in here, isn't it? Should I open …? · It's my brother's birthday next week. I don't know what to …

  – Häufig kannst du das Thema eines Gespräches erkennen, auch wenn du nicht hörst, worum es genau geht (inference). Du hörst dabei die Situation sozusagen "zwischen den Zeilen" heraus. Im folgenden Kurzdialog geht es z. B um Essen und sehr wahrscheinlich um Pizza, ohne dass davon direkt gesprochen wird: Hey, do you want one slice or two? – I'll have two. Ham and extra cheese.

PROJECT AND PRESENTATION SKILLS

27 Finding information online

Das Internet ist voller Informationen und es ist nicht einfach, genau die Informationen zu finden, die du benötigst.

Wie finde ich die Informationen, die ich brauche?

- Überlege, was die wichtigsten **Stichwörter** für dein Thema sind. Für das Thema "The Beatles in Hamburg" wären *Beatles* und *Hamburg* ein guter Start.

- Gib deine Stichwörter in eine **Suchmaschine** ein. Je mehr gute Stichwörter du eingibst, desto genauer sind die Ergebnisse. In der Infografik rechts kannst du sehen, wie du an ganz spezielle Informationen kommen kannst. Achte darauf, dass die Suchmaschine keine Informationen über deine Suchen trackt und Nutzerinformationen speichert oder verwende zumindest den privaten Modus deines Browsers.

- Verwende möglichst Suchmaschinen, die deine Suchen nicht tracken, um deine Privatsphäre zu schützen.

- Sieh dir mehrere **Suchergebnisse** an, um zu sehen, ob sie passen. Wenn du schnell ein bestimmtes Wort wie z. B. *Hamburg* finden willst, dann kannst du mit der Tastenkombination **Strg + F** danach suchen. Das Wort wird dann bei den meisten Browsern auf der Seite markiert und du kannst schnell sehen, ob die Information relevant ist.

- Achte darauf, wer die Webseite erstellt hat, um die **Qualität** der Suchergebnisse einzuschätzen. Sind sie eher zuverlässig (Online-Lexikon, bekannte Medien, …) oder eher persönliche Meinungen (Forum, Fan-Seite, soziale Medien…)?

- Überlege, wer etwas für wen und aus welchem Grund geschrieben hat: Wer ist Autor? Wer is Zielgruppe? Was bezweckt der Text/die Webseite? Ist es z. B. ein Zeitungsartikel oder eine optisch als Artikel dargestellte Werbung? Sieh dir Seiten genau an, um zu erkennen, wer dahintersteht.

- Setze dir ein Zeitlimit für deine Recherche und ordne dann dein Material. Prüfe, ob dir etwas fehlt und suche ggf. gezielt nach nur noch diesen Informationen.

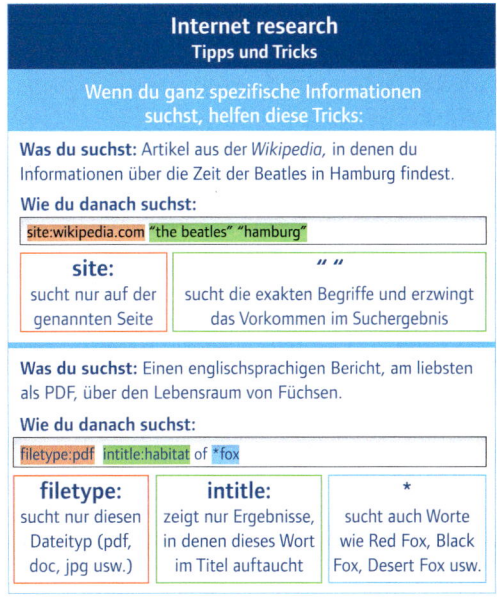

Internet research
Tipps und Tricks

Wenn du ganz spezifische Informationen suchst, helfen diese Tricks:

Was du suchst: Artikel aus der *Wikipedia*, in denen du Informationen über die Zeit der Beatles in Hamburg findest.

Wie du danach suchst:

site:wikipedia.com "the beatles" "hamburg"

site:	**" "**
sucht nur auf der genannten Seite	sucht die exakten Begriffe und erzwingt das Vorkommen im Suchergebnis

Was du suchst: Einen englischsprachigen Bericht, am liebsten als PDF, über den Lebensraum von Füchsen.

Wie du danach suchst:

filetype:pdf intitle:habitat of *fox

filetype:	**intitle:**	*****
sucht nur diesen Dateityp (pdf, doc, jpg usw.)	zeigt nur Ergebnisse, in denen dieses Wort im Titel auftaucht	sucht auch Worte wie Red Fox, Black Fox, Desert Fox usw.

TIPP
Du kannst bei einfachen Suchanfragen auch direkt die Frage ins Suchfeld eingeben, z. B. *What is 20 oz in grams?* Die Suchmaschine sucht sich dann selbst die relevanten Stichworte heraus – hier *20 oz* und *grams* – und liefert die Antwort. Bei komplexeren Suchanfragen sind die Antworten oft besser, je genauer du dir Suchbegriffe überlegst.

- Leg alle interessanten Materialien zu deinem Thema in einem eigenen Ordner ab. Dann kannst du sie dir später genauer ansehen und auswählen, was du nutzen möchtest.

- Kopiere nicht einfach ganze Artikel aus dem Internet. Mach dir Notizen und verwende deine eigenen Worte, um die Inhalte wiederzugeben.

> **TIPP**
> Denk dran, dass du deinen Dateien und Ordnern Namen gibst, die es dir leicht machen, sie hinterher wiederzufinden. Dasselbe gilt für Lesezeichen im Browser.

Bildsuche im Internet

Die folgenden Hinweise helfen dir, wenn du für eine Aufgabe online Bilder suchen sollst, denn dabei gibt es einiges zu beachten. Zum Glück haben fast alle Suchmaschinen eine Bildsuche, die du in der Regel entweder schon vor der Suche oder bei den Ergebnissen durch das Klicken auf den "Bilder"-Knopf erreichen kannst.

Wie finde ich die richtigen Bilder?

Auch hier kommt es vor allem auf die richtigen **Suchbegriffe** an. Je genauer du suchst, d.h. je enger deine Suche ist, desto besser werden deine Ergebnisse sein und desto weniger Zeit brauchst du.

Nehmen wir an, du suchst etwas zum Eton College:

- *eton college* findet alle Bilder zu *eton* und *college*, wird aber in der Regel schon gute Ergebnisse liefern, weil die Schule berühmt ist; suchst du nach *"eton college"* bekommst du nur Ergebnisse, bei denen diese Wörter genau so in den Bildinformationen hinterlegt sind

- suchst du z. B. Bilder zu Sport und speziell Rugby am Eton College, kannst du die Suche weiter einschränken:
  eton college sports findet Bilder zu allen Sportarten und -teams an der Schule
  eton college rugby findet bevorzugt Bilder zu Rugby an der Schule
  eton college "rugby team" findet Bilder zur Rugbymannschaft der Schule
  eton college sports -rugby hingegen zeigt dir alle Sportarten *außer* Rugby an

Bedenke bei der Suche zu Orten wie Städten, Parks, Flüssen usw., dass es die mehrfach geben kann, d.h. hier musst du ggf. deine Suche um ein *UK*, *USA* oder *Canada* ergänzen, je nachdem, wonach du suchst. Städte namens Plymouth z. B. gibt es in GB, USA und Kanada.

Wie speichere ich die Bilder und wie darf ich sie nutzen?

Bilder, die du im Internet findest, haben einen **Urheber**, d.h. du darfst sie nicht so ohne Weiteres einfach speichern und verwenden.

- **Was du darfst**: Bilder speichern (rechte Maustaste -> Bild speichern unter ...) und in Präsentationen oder Postern für den Unterricht verwenden, **aber:** du musst die Quelle angeben, am besten direkt am Bild und auf diese Weise: *Quelle: Adresse der Webseite (URL)* oder im Idealfall *Name des Fotografen (+ URL)*

- **Was du nicht darfst**: Präsentationen mit fremden Fotos auf die Schulwebseite laden oder sie anderweitig veröffentlichen. Dazu brauchst du immer die Erlaubnis des Urhebers.

> **!** Wenn du ein Bild gespeichert hast, aber nicht mehr weißt, wo es herkommt, ist das noch kein Grund zur Sorge: Du kannst bei vielen Suchmaschinen eine Suche anhand des Bildes starten.
>
>
>
> Dazu klickst du auf das kleine Kamerasymbol in der Suchleiste und lädst dann das Bild hoch. Als Ergebnis kommt dann eine Liste mit Webseiten, auf denen das Bild verwendet wurde und du kannst gucken, wo du es gefunden hast und dir dann die Quelle kopieren/notieren.

28 Creating a good layout for a page or poster

Wenn du einen Text gestalten möchtest, z. B. für einen Vortrag, einen Blog oder als Poster für eine Präsentation, können dir folgende Hinweise helfen:

- Sortiere die Informationen, die du vermitteln willst: Was ist wichtig? Was ist ein Unterpunkt? Hast du Beispiele für Thesen/Argumente?

- Gib deinem Produkt eine klare Struktur: Texte haben meist drei Teile (Einleitung, Hauptteil, Schluss), während Poster häufig aus Aufzählungen wichtiger Punkte bestehen. Beginne für jeden neuen Gedanken einen neuen Absatz bzw. einen neuen Stichpunkt.

- Eine Überschrift verdeutlicht, worum es in deinem Text geht. Sie soll Leser auch neugierig machen auf das, was kommt. Wenn es in deinem Produkt um mehrere Themen/Aspekte eines Themas geht, dann kannst du für einzelne Abschnitte auch Zwischenüberschriften verwenden. Das gibt dem Ganzen eine klare Struktur und hilft dem Leser, sich schnell zu orientieren.

- Ergänze dein Produkt mit passenden Fotos, Videos, Audios, Statistiken etc. Vergiss nicht anzugeben, woher die Medien stammen (➡ SMC 27, 29).

- Wenn nicht auf den ersten Blick erkennbar ist, was z. B. ein Bild zeigt, füge Bildunterschriften ein.

- Formatiere dein Produkt so, dass es gut lesbar ist. Dabei ist das Medium wichtig – für einen ausgedruckten Handzettel kannst du andere Schriftarten wählen als für einen Text, der am Bildschirm gelesen wird. (➡ SMC 15) Für ein Poster (z.B. für einen *gallery walk*) muss die Schriftgröße größer sein als für einen Ausdruck. Eine große Schriftgröße hilft dir auch, nicht zu viele Punkte auf dem Poster unterzubringen – hier ist weniger mehr.

29 Making good slides for an electronic presentation

Vieles, was für das Layout von Texten/Postern gilt, kannst du auch auf Folien für Präsentation anwenden. Es gibt aber einige Besonderheiten zu beachten. Generell gilt: gut ist, was deine Folien übersichtlich und leicht zu lesen macht.

TEXT
- Verwende möglichst wenige Folien.
- Nutze Aufzählungen mit *keywords*, keine ganzen Sätze und schreibe nicht mehr als sechs Zeilen auf eine Folie.
- Wähle eine ausreichende Schriftgröße (mindestens 30pt, gerne mehr) und eine gut lesbare Schrift und gehe sparsam mit Texthervorhebungen wie fett, kursiv, Unterstreichung um; lass einen ausreichend großen Abstand zwischen den Zeilen.
- Richte den Text linksbündig aus, außer du verfolgst ein ganz besonderes Ziel damit (z.B. zentriert zum Herausheben eines Zitats), aber mische die Ausrichtung nicht auf einer Folie. Zitate z. B. wirken oft am besten, wenn sie zentriert alleine auf einer Folie stehen.

FARBE UND KONTRAST
- Du kannst einzelne Wörter in einer anderen Farbe setzen, um sie hervorzuheben. Aber auch hier gilt: weniger ist mehr – mehrere Wörter in unterschiedlichen Farben zu setzen, kann beim Lesen eher hinderlich sein.
- Wenn du mit farbigem Untergrund oder Fotos als Hintergrund arbeitest, solltest du darauf achten, dass dein Text in einer Farbe ist, die ausreichend Kontrast zum Hintergrund bietet – je stärker der Kontrast, desto besser die Lesbarkeit.

TIPP
- Eine gute Faustregel lautet **6 x 6**: pro Folie maximal 6 Zeilen mit je maximal 6 Wörtern
- Bedenke: Folien sind eine **visuelle Unterstützung** für eine Präsentation, keine Zusammenfassung. Die Zuhörer sollen hören, nicht lesen – die Texte sollten daher auf das Wichtigste reduziert sein.
- **Vermeide Spezialeffekte** wie verspielte Übergänge, tanzende Buchstaben etc. Sie kosten viel Zeit und helfen den Zuhörern nicht.

ABBILDUNGEN

- Ein Bild sagt mehr als tausend Worte – das gilt auch für Folien: manche Inhalte kannst du ebenso mit einem passenden Bild oder einer Grafik ausdrücken.

- Suche ein Bild, dass die Aussage deines Vortrages unterstreicht: z. B. ein Foto, das eine Fragestellung gut illustriert oder eines, das das Problem gut darstellt. Es muss auch kein Foto sein – manchmal ist eine passende Grafik genauso gut, um z. B. statistische Aussagen auf den Punkt zu bringen.

- Wichtig: bei allen Bildern, die du verwendest, musst du die Quelle angeben, d.h. der Fotograf/die Fotografin, Illustrator/Illustratorin etc. sowie der Ort, wo du das Bild gefunden hast (eine Suchmaschine im Internet ist keine Quellenangabe!).

> **TIPP**
>
> Wenn du deine Folien/Poster nur vor der Klasse zeigst, darfst du Bilder verwenden, ohne die **Urheber** um Erlaubnis zu fragen, weil es sich um eine begrenzte Öffentlichkeit handelt. Wenn die Folien aber öffentlich zugänglich sind (z.B. auf einer Webseite oder der Schulzeitung), musst du die Urheber unbedingt um **Erlaubnis** fragen.
> Als Faustregel gilt: veröffentliche kein Bild ohne Erlaubnis, das du nicht selbst gemacht hast.

30 Giving a presentation

Wie halte ich eine gute Präsentation?

Vorbereitung
- Sammle Informationen zu deinem Thema.

- Wähle eine Form der Präsentation aus, die das Thema gut veranschaulicht (Poster, Folie, Tafel, …).

- Mach dir Notizen, z. B. auf nummerierten Karteikarten oder in einer App.

- Bereite deine Medien vor (Poster, Folie, Tafelanschrieb, …). Schreibe groß und für alle gut lesbar.

- Übe deine Präsentation zu Hause vor einem Spiegel oder vor einem kleinen Publikum (Eltern, Großeltern, Freunde).

- Sprich laut, deutlich und langsam.

Durchführung
- Warte, bis es ruhig ist. Schaue die Zuhörer/innen an.

- Beginne mit einem prägnanten Einstieg, z. B. einem Zitat oder einer Frage, die das Interesse der Zuhörer weckt.

- Erkläre, worüber du sprechen wirst und wie deine Präsentation aufgebaut ist.

- Lies nicht von deinen Karten ab, sondern sprich möglichst frei.

- Erkläre unbekannten Wortschatz, besonders, wenn er zum Verständnis deines Themas wichtig ist.

Schluss
- Komme am Ende noch einmal auf deinen Einstieg zurück, indem du z. B. die Frage aus dem Einstieg wieder aufgreifst und beantwortest.

- Bei längeren Präsentation solltest du am Ende die wichtigsten Punkte noch einmal zusammenfassen und das Wichtigste herausheben.

- Bedanke dich am Ende fürs Zuhören.

- Frag die Zuhörer/innen, ob sie Fragen haben und beantworte diese.

31 Talking about statistics

Statistiken können auf unterschiedliche Weise dargestellt werden: Tortendiagramm (pie chart), Säulendiagramm (bar chart), Kurvendiagramm (line graph) oder in einer Tabelle (table). Wenn du Statistiken analysieren und vorstellen sollst, gehst du am besten wie folgt vor:

Step 1: Identifiziere, welche Art von Diagramm du vor dir hast – pie chart, bar chart, line graph oder Tabelle – und sieh dir die Quelle an:

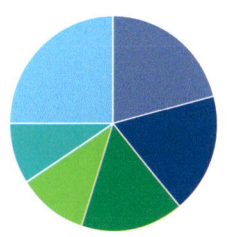

pie chart

- Ist die Quelle verlässlich?
  Ist der Herausgeber z. B. ein Ministerium/eine Behörde oder eine Organisation wie *amnesty international*?

- Sind die Angaben/Zahlen im Diagramm aktuell?
  Wenn du z. B. eine Statistik zu Kinderarmut in Großbritannien vor dir hast, ist es ein wichtiger Unterschied, ob die Zahlen von 1973 oder 2013 sind.

Step 2: Beschreibe das Diagramm/die Tabelle:

- Worum geht es? Welche Informationen gibt das Diagramm?
  The bar chart / pie chart / line graph / table … shows the different … / compares the size/number of … / is about … / contrasts … with …

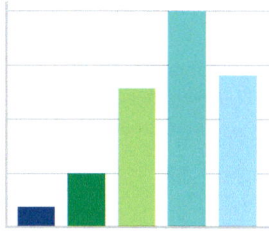

bar chart

- Zeigen die Daten eine Entwicklung oder werden verschiedene Zeitpunkte miteinander verglichen?
  It shows … in contrast to…
  The chart gives us information about who/what/how many/…

- Werden absolute Zahlen oder Prozentangaben verwendet?
  The chart/table shows us the number of/percentage of …
  It shows which percentage of …

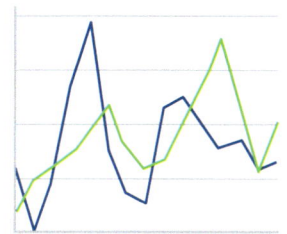

Step 3: Ziehe deine Schlussfolgerungen aus dem Diagramm/der Tabelle:
  My main conclusion is that …
  The most imporant thing I've learned is that …
  One thing that I hadn't realized before is …

line graph

LANGUAGE HELP
Wenn du über Diagramme sprichst, können dir folgende Redewendungen helfen:

Pie chart
- *The pie chart is divided into … segments, which show/represent …*
- *The smallest/biggest segment …*
- *The segments representing … and … constitute the majority …*
- *A huge majority/minority is …*

Bar chart
- *The bars are arranged horizontally/vertically.*
- *There are big/vast/surprising differences between …*
- *At the top/bottom of the ranking comes…*
- *… is first/last in rank*
- *… has the largest / second largest …*

Line graph
- *The graph shows the relationship between … and …*
- *… is twice/three times as high as …*
- *There are more than / nearly twice as many … as there are …*
- *… increase/decrease / reach a high point / rise/fall/drop/ grow steadily*

32 Describing and presenting pictures

Manchmal sollst du ein Foto vor der Klasse vorstellen und es dabei beschreiben. Hier sind ein paar Hilfen.

Wie stelle ich ein Foto vor?

1 Stelle das Foto vor und sage, woher es kommt.

2 Beschreibe das Foto:

– Sage, was wo zu sehen ist: *at the top/bottom · in the foreground/background · in the middle · on the left/right*

– Diese Präpositionen sind auch hilfreich: *behind · between · in front of · next to · under · over*

– Geh bei der Beschreibung in einer bestimmten Reihenfolge vor, z. B. von links nach rechts oder von oben nach unten.

3 Sage, was dir an dem Foto gefällt oder nicht.

4 Wenn du mit der Vorstellung des Fotos fertig bist, bedanke dich fürs Zuhören und frage, ob noch jemand Fragen hat.

1 *I'd like to talk about this photo of … I found it on the internet/in a magazine/…*

2 *In the foreground you can see … I think the people in the photo are talking about …/having fun/ celebrating/…*

3 *I really like/don't like the photo because … It's interesting/boring/exciting/ … because …*

4 *Thank you for listening. Do you have any questions?*

33 Working in a team

Bei Projekten arbeitet ihr oft im Team. Dabei solltet ihr eure unterschiedlichen Fähigkeiten und Talente einbringen und bestimmte Regeln beachten. Folgende Schritte können helfen, die Arbeit zu organisieren:

Step 1: Legt Regeln für die Arbeit in der Gruppe fest, z. B. gegenseitige Unterstützung, pünktliches und zügiges Arbeiten, einander zuhören oder verschiedene Lösungen diskutieren usw.

Step 2: Sammelt Ideen für die Bearbeitung eures Themas (z. B. in einer Mindmap). Wählt gemeinsam Unterthemen aus und legt die Arbeitsschritte fest, die für die Bearbeitung nötig sind.

Step 3: Verteilt Rollen und Aufgaben nach euren Interessen und Fähigkeiten. Wenn ihr euch nicht einigen könnt, hilft Auslosen oder Würfeln. Folgende Rollen solltet ihr auf jeden Fall verteilen:
– coordinator
– writer
– researcher

Step 4: Macht einen Zeitplan für eure Arbeiten, an den sich alle halten.

Step 5: Am Ende der Arbeit sollte ein Rückblick stehen: Besprecht, was gut war und wo ihr Verbesserungsmöglichkeiten seht.

34 Giving feedback

Manchmal sollst du im Unterricht Partnern/Partnerinnen eine Rückmeldung zu einer Aufgabe geben.
Das nennt man *peer feedback*.

Wozu ist *peer feedback* gut?

Gegenseitige Rückmeldungen sind für dich und deine Partner *(peers)* wichtig, denn du kannst
· jemanden loben für etwas, das er/sie gut gemacht hat,
· Hinweise geben, wo deine Partner noch Probleme haben,
· durch die Rückmeldungen selbst lernen, was du schon gut kannst und was du anders machen solltest.

Was muss ich beachten?

Bei deiner Rückmeldung solltest du drei Dinge beachten:

· Halte dich an die Punkte, zu denen du Rückmeldung geben
  sollst, z. B. die Aussprache, Betonung und Verständlichkeit bei
  einem Dialog, die Rechtschreibfehler in einem Text, das
  Einhalten eines roten Fadens in einer Geschichte usw.
  Begründe deine Einschätzungen.
· Gib deine Rückmeldung mit Respekt – niemand soll sich
  angegriffen fühlen. Nenne zuerst Gelungenes und mache dann
  Verbesserungsvorschläge zu Punkten, die noch nicht so
  gelungen sind.
· Wenn du eine Rückmeldung bekommst, überdenke die
  Vorschläge gut. Korrigiere die Fehler, die andere gefunden
  haben, und arbeite an den Stellen nach, wo du eventuell
  Probleme hattest.

What I liked	What you could do better
You chose a great photo. ☺ You spoke clearly and looked at us. …	Next time, say what is happening in the photo. Sometimes you stood in front of the photo. …

STUDY SKILLS

35 Understanding new words

Das Nachschlagen unbekannter Wörter kostet Zeit und ist auch nicht immer nötig. Oft geht es auch ohne den Einsatz eines
Wörterbuches.

Immer gleich im Wörterbuch nachschlagen?

· Viele englische Wörter werden ähnlich wie im Deutschen geschrieben oder
  klingen ähnlich (z.B. *brochure, statue, insect*). Manche sehen auch einem
  Wort aus anderen Sprachen ähnlich, z.B. *voice (French: voix; Latin: vox)*.

· In manchen Wörtern stecken bekannte Teile, z.B. *bottle opener, snowshoe*.

· Präfixe und Suffixe wie *un-, re-* und *-er* helfen beim Erschließen:
  listener (sb. who listens), **un**happy <> happy, **re**pay (pay sb. back).

· Bilder zum Text zeigen oft Dinge, die du im Text vielleicht nicht verstehst.

· Der Kontext, also die Wörter und Sätze um das Wort herum, kann beim
  Verstehen helfen, z.B. *Let's hurry. The train **departs** in ten minutes.*

> **TIPP**
> Nicht alle Wörter, die im
> Deutschen und Englischen
> ähnlich sind, haben auch dieselbe
> Bedeutung.
> Achte daher auf false friends:
> *handy* = praktisch, *nicht* Handy

36 Using a dictionary

Es gibt unterschiedliche Wörterbücher, in denen du nachschlagen kannst. Wenn du die Bedeutung eines unbekannten Wortes nachschlagen willst, dann benutzt du am besten ein zweisprachiges Wörterbuch (Englisch-Deutsch bzw. Deutsch-Englisch). Wenn du mehr Informationen zu englischen Wörtern haben möchtest, etwa Beispielsätze, Definitionen oder Alternativen, dann bietet sich ein einsprachiges Wörterbuch an.

ZWEISPRACHIGE WÖRTERBÜCHER

Die Leitwörter *(running heads)* oben auf der Seite helfen dir, schnell zu finden, was du suchst. Auf der linken Seite steht das erste Stichwort, auf der rechten Seite das letzte Stichwort der Doppelseite.

- *resign* ist das Stichwort *(headword)*. Stichwörter sind alphabetisch geordnet: *r* vor *s, ra* vor *re, rhe* vor *rhi* usw.

- Die kursiv gedruckten Hinweise helfen dir, die für deinen Text passende Bedeutung zu finden.

- Die Ziffern 1, 2 usw. zeigen, dass ein Stichwort unterschiedliche Bedeutungen haben oder unterschiedlichen Wortarten angehören kann (z. B. Adjektiv, Nomen, Verb).

- Beispielsätze und Redewendungen sind dem Stichwort zugeordnet.

- Unregelmäßige Verbformen, besondere Pluralformen, die Steigerungsformen der Adjektive und ähnliche Hinweise stehen oft in Klammern oder sind kursiv gedruckt.

- Die Lautschrift gibt Auskunft darüber, wie das Wort ausgesprochen und betont wird.

resort

resign /rɪˈzaɪn/
1 BERUF • *als Vorsitzender usw* zurücktreten: *He* **resigned from** *the company.* Er verließ das Unternehmen.
2 *(job, post)* aufgeben *(Stelle, Posten)*
3 resign oneself to something sich mit etwas abfinden
resignation /ˌrezɪɡˈneɪʃn/
1 BERUF • *bei Unternehmen* Kündigung; *von Minister usw* Rücktritt
2 hand in one's resignation *von Angestelltem* kündigen; *von Minister usw* sein Amt niederlegen
3 *Gemütszustand* Resignation
resigned /rɪˈzaɪnd/ *(look, sigh)* resigniert

resit¹ /ˌriːˈsɪt/ *Verb* (→ *sit*) *BE (exam)* wiederholen *(Prüfung)*
resit² /ˈriːsɪt/ *Substantiv • BE* Wiederholungsprüfung
resolution /ˌrezəˈluːʃn/
1 POLITIK Beschluss, Resolution
2 *bei Problem, Streit* Lösung
3 ≈ *Entschiedenheit* Entschlossenheit

TIPP

Wenn du ein Online-Wörterbuch oder eine App verwenden möchtest, weil das schneller geht oder du dein Handy gerade zur Hand hast, erkundige dich vorher bei deiner Lehrerin/deinem Lehrer, welche zu empfehlen sind, denn nicht alle sind gleich gut. Fast alle funktionieren aber nach den gleichen Prinzipien wie gedruckte Wörterbücher. Nur kannst du dir online auch gleich die Aussprache anhören. Am besten probierst du beides aus und siehst, was für dich das Beste ist. Bevor du allerdings ein Online-Wörterbuch im Unterricht verwendest, klärt am besten in der Klasse ab, wann und wie du das einsetzen darfst. Bei den Hausaufgaben sieht das evtl. anders aus als bei einer Klassenarbeit oder im Unterricht.

EINSPRACHIGE WÖRTERBÜCHER

Wenn du selbst einen englischen Text schreibst, kannst du ein einsprachiges englisches Wörterbuch zu Hilfe nehmen. Hier findest du mehr über ein englisches Wort heraus als in einem zweisprachigen Wörterbuch:

- Ein einsprachiges Wörterbuch erklärt die Bedeutung eines englischen Wortes auf Englisch. Da manche Wörter mehrere Bedeutungen haben, ist es wichtig, alle Einträge und Beispielsätze zu einem Wort zu lesen und mit deinem englischen Text zu vergleichen, um die korrekte Bedeutung herauszufinden.

- Das Wörterbuch hilft dir, die passende Verbindung mit anderen Wörtern zu finden, z. B. zu Verben, Präpositionen oder in bestimmten feststehenden Wendungen. Das ist nützlich, wenn du selbst einen englischen Text schreiben willst und nach den richtigen Wörtern suchst.

deadly [ˈdedli] *adj*
1 *able or likely to kill people* {= lethal}: This is no longer a deadly disease.
deadly to The HSN virus is deadly to chickens.
a deadly weapon The new generation of biological weapons is more deadly than ever.
2 *(only before noun)* {= complete}:
deadly silence There was deadly silence after his speech.
a deadly secret Don't tell anyone – this is a deadly secret.
deadly serious *completely serious:* Don't laugh – I am deadly serious!
3 *(informal)* very boring: Many TV programmes are pretty deadly!

37 Using an online translator

Wenn du ein englisches Wort nicht kennst, kannst du die deutsche Bedeutung oft aus dem Kontext ableiten oder nachschlagen. Wenn du die korrekte englische Entsprechung für ein deutsches Wort suchst, hilft dir der Kontext in der Regel nicht, das Wort zu erschließen, aber er hilft dir, im Wörterbuch das korrekte Wort zu finden, denn oft gibt es mehrere mögliche Wörter.

Kann ich mir die Wörter nicht online übersetzen lassen?

Für einzelne Wörter kannst du auch *online translators* verwenden – sie funktionieren dann im Prinzip wie Wörterbücher. Das geht schnell, kann aber auch ein paar Nachteile haben:

· ein Wörterbuch (egal ob online oder als Buch) gibt dir wesentlich mehr Informationen, wie z.B. Beispielsätze, in denen das gesuchte Wort verwendet wird.

· Übersetzungsmaschinen geben dir oft nicht alle möglichen Übersetzungen, sondern nur ein oder zwei Möglichkeiten oder die gängigsten.

· Übersetzungsmaschinen bieten dir keinen Kontext, was es dir schwerer macht, das richtige Wort zu finden.

> **TIPP**
> Wenn du dir nicht sicher bist, ob dir auch die korrekte Übersetzung angezeigt wird, dann mache einen Gegentest: lass das englische Wort ins Deutsche übersetzen und schaue, was dir als deutsches Wort angeboten wird.

Was ist denn dann mit ganzen Sätzen?

Ganze Sätze oder gar Texte mit Übersetzungsmaschinen vom Deutschen ins Englische zu übertragen, ist keine gute Idee, weil die automatische Übersetzung dazu immer noch zu viele Fehler macht. Das liegt daran, dass die künstliche Intelligenz, die dahintersteckt, in der Regel die Frequenz bestimmter Wortkombinationen analysiert und dann die wahrscheinlichste Übersetzung ausgibt, aber die konkrete oder implizite Bedeutung nicht erkennen kann.

Das funktioniert bei Einzelwörtern und einfachen Sätzen – mit Einschränkungen – noch ganz gut, stößt aber bei komplexeren Satzstrukturen, Absätzen oder ganzen Texten an Grenzen.

Vor allem bei folgenden Dingen haben Übersetzungsmaschinen Probleme:

· **Grammatik**: da die Übersetzungsmaschinen von Worten ausgehen und nicht von der Satzstruktur, entstehen gerade bei komplexeren Sätzen hier schnell Fehler.

· **Idiome**: aus demselben Grund sind auch Idiome und geflügelte Worte ein Problem, denn die Maschine kann die oftmals nicht-wörtliche Bedeutung nicht erkennen. Hier ein Beispiel:

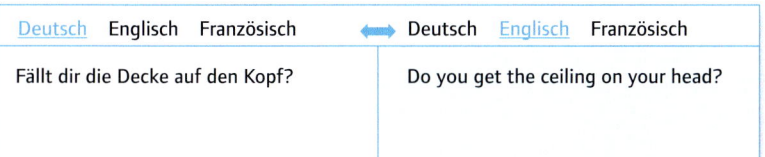

Deutsch Englisch Französisch ⬌	Deutsch Englisch Französisch
Fällt dir die Decke auf den Kopf?	Do you get the ceiling on your head?

· **Regionale Sprachbesonderheiten**: manche Wörter und Ausdrücke sind regionalspezifisch (oder heute weniger gebräuchlich) und werden vom *online translator* nicht erkannt. Sie geben dann das identische Wort als Übersetzung an, ohne das zu kommentieren (eine korrekte Übersetzung wäre *floor-cloth* gewesen, aber die Maschine hat dieses Wort nicht als eine Variante für "Scheuerlappen" erkannt):

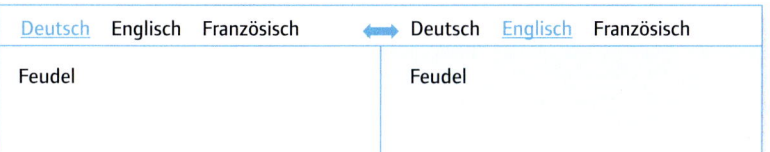

Deutsch Englisch Französisch ⬌	Deutsch Englisch Französisch
Feudel	Feudel

38 Using the internet to improve your vocabulary

Das Internet bietet dir neben allen erdenklichen Informationen auch die Möglichkeit, dein Englisch zu verbessern und deinen Wortschatz zu erweitern.

Lesen und Schreiben

Englisch ist die am weitesten verbreitete Sprache im Internet, d.h. wo immer du auch hinsurfst, du wirst englischen Texten begegnen. Das ist grundsätzlich schon hilfreich, aber du kannst noch gezielter vorgehen:

- Lies regelmäßig Blogs/Webseiten zu Themen, die dich interessieren. Damit erweiterst du deinen Wortschatz, weil du darin idiomatischen Ausdrücken, Vokabeln, Kollokationen etc. begegnest, und du bekommst ein Verständnis vom Aufbau von z.B. Artikeln, was dir beim Schreiben eigener Texte hilft.

- Lies Nachrichten online, z.B. auf den Seiten von Zeitungen wie dem *Guardian (GB)* oder der *New York Times (USA)*.

- Lade dir freie Ebooks herunter. Das *Project Gutenberg* z.B. hat eine große Auswahl an Büchern, die man umsonst herunterladen kann.

- Starte einen eigenen Blog und/oder kommentiere Artikel in anderen Blogs und tausche dich auf diese Weise mit anderen Nutzern aus.

Hören und Sehen

Internetradio, Podcasts und Videos schulen dein Verständnis von gesprochenem Englisch in unterschiedlichsten Akzenten und Dialekten.

- Finde Radiostationen online (mit gesprochenen Reportagen und Interviews) wie z.B. *NPR, BBC World Service* oder *Voice of America*. Oder suche Podcasts zu Themen, die dich interessieren.

- Seiten wie *YouTube* bieten jede Menge Clips aus Nachrichtensendungen oder auch komplette Dokumentationen. Sieh dir regelmäßig Clips und Filme an.

- Webseiten wie die des *British Council* oder der *BBC* bieten gute Podcasts zum Thema Englisch und Englisch lernen.

- Auf Seiten wie z.B. *LibriVox* kannst du kostenlose Audiobücher herunterladen und anhören.

Wortschatz

Suchmaschinen sind eine gute Hilfe, wenn du deinen Wortschatz erweitern willst oder überprüfen möchtest, ob z.B. die Redewendung, die du in einem Text verwendet hast, korrekt ist.

- Verwende Suchmaschinen als Ergänzung zum Rechtschreibcheck deines Schreibprogramms: gib ein, was du geschrieben hast und suche danach. Wenn du kaum Ergebnisse bekommst, solltest du deine Kollokation nochmal checken. Bekommst du viele Ergebnisse, sieh dir einige davon an, um zu sehen, ob der Zusammenhang auch zu deiner Verwendung passt.

- Wenn du online nach Wörtern und Redemitteln suchst, ist eines der ersten Ergebnisse häufig ein Online-Wörterbuch, bei dem du dann weitere Bedeutungen und häufige Kollokationen nachlesen kannst.

- Suchmaschinen versuchen, deine Suche vorherzusagen (siehe Beispiel rechts). Dies kannst du nutzen, um gängige Kollokationen und Wortkorrelationen zu finden. Notiere dir solche, die du interessant oder hilfreich findest, dann kannst du sie nutzen, wenn sich die Gelegenheit ergibt. Stelle aber sicher, dass du auch genau weißt, was sie bedeuten und in welchem Zusammenhang sie verwendet werden.

> **TIPP**
> Gib die Kollokationen oder idiomatischen Ausdrücke in Anführungszeichen ein, damit die Suchmaschine auch nach genau diesem Ausdruck sucht, z.B. "between a rock and a hard place".

shower
shower **curtains**
shower **heads**
shower **thoughts**

39 Ordering and structuring vocabulary and ideas

Warum Wortschatz sammeln und strukturieren?

Wenn du einen Text zu einem bestimmten Thema schreiben sollst, kann es helfen, vorab Vokabeln dazu zu sammeln, damit dein Text einen abwechslungsreichen Wortschatz hat und sich gut liest. Oft wird auch schon beim Sammeln eine Gliederung des Themas erkennbar. Dadurch merkst du auch schnell, welche Wörter du ggf. noch nachschlagen musst.

Diese Art, Wortschatz zu ordnen, hilft dir auch, neue Vokabeln zu lernen und sie zu vernetzen, so dass sie besser in deinem Gedächtnis bleiben.

Die gleichen Methoden kannst du auch anwenden, um Ideen zu sammeln und zu ordnen, wenn du z. B. eine Präsentation vorbereitest oder einen Text zu einem bestimmten Thema schreiben willst.

Welche Methoden gibt es?

Für das Ordnen der Wörter gibt es verschiedene Möglichkeiten. Du solltest unterschiedliche Formen ausprobieren und dann diejenige verwenden, die am besten zu dir oder der Aufgabe passt.

Einige der Formen, die du nutzen kannst, sind:

· Tabellen (*tables*)

· Diagramme (z.B. *tree diagrams*)

· Mindmaps

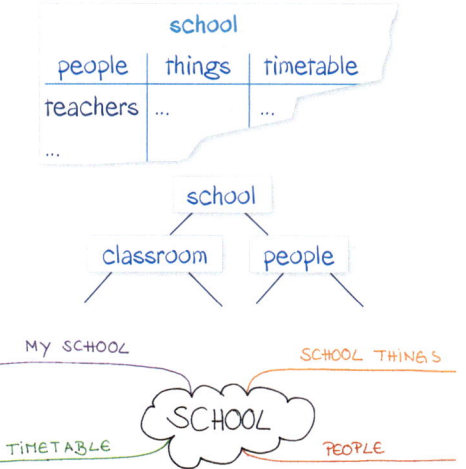

> **TIPP**
> Wenn du Wortschatz für einen Text zusammenstellst, solltest du daran denken, dass du nicht nur Nomen, sondern auch Verben, Adverbien, Adjektive etc. brauchst, sowie Varianten für Ausdrücke, die häufig vorkommen.

Synonyms and antonyms

Eine andere gute Möglichkeit zur Organisation sind Synonyme und Antonyme, die du in einer Tabelle zusammenstellst, evtl. mithilfe eines Wörterbuches oder eines Thesaurus. Mit dieser Methode kannst du nicht nur deinen bestehenden Wortschatz organisieren, sondern ihn auch erweitern. Siehe dir aber immer die Beispielsätze im Wörterbuch an, bevor du die Wörter selbst vernwendest.

word	synonym	antonym	example sentence
difficult	hard	easy	The test was very difficult.
safe	...	dangerous	Don't be afraid, this area is quite safe.
scenic	beautiful	...	We took the scenic tour along the coast.

> **TIPP**
> Wenn du ein neues Adjektiv lernst, schlag es nach, entweder online oder in einem Wörterbuch, um zu sehen, ob es Antonyme oder Synonyme mit Präfixen oder Suffixen gibt, so dass du nicht nur z. B. das Adjektiv "legal" lernst, sondern auch gleich "illegal".

40 Working with a grammar

Grammatik ist das System, das eine Sprache strukturiert. Grammatik bildet dabei die Regeln und Konventionen ab, sozusagen das Grundgerüst, und ohne Grammatik kannst du keine Sprache wirklich beherrschen und gut sprechen.

Die Grammatik lernst du im Schulbuch, sowohl in den Units – schrittweise aufgebaut und mit Übungen – als auch in *Grammar and Practice*, aber es gibt natürlich auch eigenständige Grammatiken, die du zur Ergänzung nutzen kannst. Der Aufbau einer Grammatik ist dabei meist relativ ähnlich wie die Grammatik in diesem Buch und sieht oft so aus:

Überschrift
Hier steht, worum es auf der Seite geht.

Zwischenüberschrift
Wenn ein Thema mehrere Unterthemen hat, gibt es meist entsprechende Unterüberschriften.

Erklärung/Regeln
Hier wird das Thema erklärt mit allem, was man dazu beachten muss. Oft gibt es hier auch noch einmal Unterteilungen.

Beispiele
Neben den Erläuterungen (oder darunter) sind Beispiele und Beispielsätze zu finden.

Zusammenfassung
Oft findet sich am Ende eines Themas oder Unterthemas noch einmal eine Zusammenfassung.

Weitere Dinge
Je nach Grammatik und/oder Thema kann es z.B. auch noch nützliche Tipps oder Warnungen vor besonders häufigen Fehlerquellen geben.

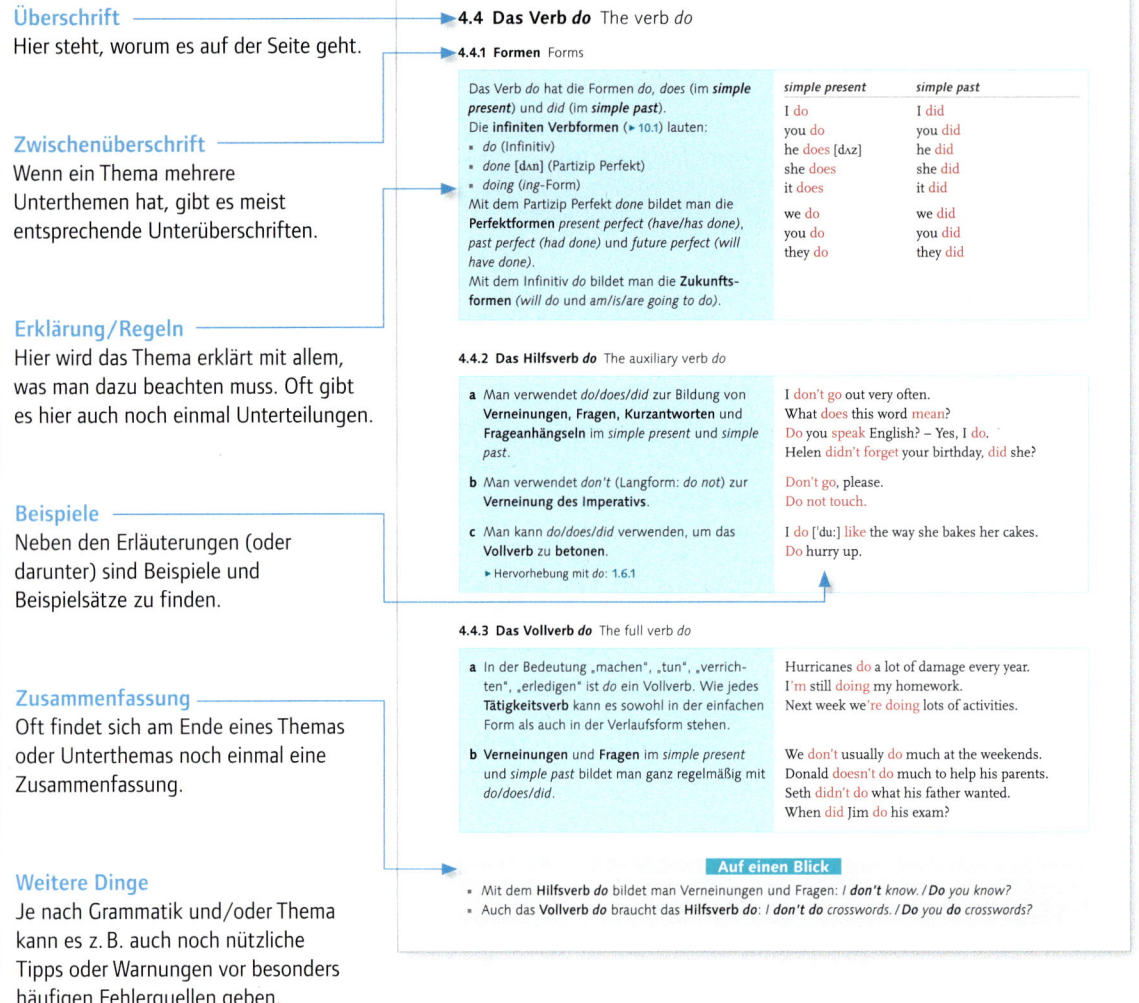

4.4 Das Verb *do* The verb *do*

4.4.1 Formen Forms

Das Verb *do* hat die Formen *do, does* (im *simple present*) und *did* (im *simple past*).
Die **infiniten Verbformen** (▸ 10.1) lauten:
- *do* (Infinitiv)
- *done* [dʌn] (Partizip Perfekt)
- *doing* (ing-Form)
Mit dem Partizip Perfekt *done* bildet man die **Perfektformen** *present perfect (have/has done), past perfect (had done)* und *future perfect (will have done)*.
Mit dem Infinitiv *do* bildet man die **Zukunftsformen** *(will do* und *am/is/are going to do).*

simple present	simple past
I do	I did
you do	you did
he does [dʌz]	he did
she does	she did
it does	it did
we do	we did
you do	you did
they do	they did

4.4.2 Das Hilfsverb *do* The auxiliary verb *do*

a Man verwendet *do/does/did* zur Bildung von **Verneinungen, Fragen, Kurzantworten** und **Frageanhängseln** im *simple present* und *simple past*.

I don't go out very often.
What does this word mean?
Do you speak English? – Yes, I do.
Helen didn't forget your birthday, did she?

b Man verwendet *don't* (Langform: *do not*) zur **Verneinung des Imperativs**.

Don't go, please.
Do not touch.

c Man kann *do/does/did* verwenden, um das **Vollverb** zu **betonen**.
▸ Hervorhebung mit *do*: 1.6.1

I do ['du:] like the way she bakes her cakes.
Do hurry up.

4.4.3 Das Vollverb *do* The full verb *do*

a In der Bedeutung „machen", „tun", „verrichten", „erledigen" ist *do* ein Vollverb. Wie jedes **Tätigkeitsverb** kann es sowohl in der einfachen Form als auch in der Verlaufsform stehen.

Hurricanes do a lot of damage every year.
I'm still doing my homework.
Next week we're doing lots of activities.

b **Verneinungen** und **Fragen** im *simple present* und *simple past* bildet man ganz regelmäßig mit *do/does/did*.

We don't usually do much at the weekends.
Donald doesn't do much to help his parents.
Seth didn't do what his father wanted.
When did Jim do his exam?

Auf einen Blick
- Mit dem **Hilfsverb** *do* bildet man Verneinungen und Fragen: *I **don't** know. / **Do** you know?*
- Auch das **Vollverb** *do* braucht das **Hilfsverb** *do*: *I **don't** do crosswords. / **Do** you do crosswords?*

TIPP
Wenn du bei bestimmten Themen Schwierigkeiten hast, kannst du dir zu denen auch eine eigene Grammatik anlegen. Dazu nimmst du dir eine große Karteikarte oder ein Blatt Papier und notierst zunächst die Regel. Dann ergänzt du diese Regel mit deinen eigenen Beispielsätzen – diese kannst du dir leichter merken und dann fällt es dir auch nicht mehr so schwer, die Regeln und die Anwendung zu erinnern. Nimm dir deine Grammatik einmal die Woche vor und teste, ob du anhand deiner Beispielsätze noch die Regel formulieren kannst.

41 Making and taking notes

Wenn du Informationen oder eigene Gedanken kurz für dich notierst – z. B. als Vorbereitung auf einen eigenen Vortrag oder eine Präsentation –, heißt das im Englischen making notes. Wenn du dir Notizen beim Lesen oder Zuhören machst, heißt das taking notes. Für beide Varianten gelten aber die gleichen Grundsätze.

Step 1: Achte auf keywords, die die wichtigsten Informationen enthalten, um deine Frage/Aufgabe zu beantworten oder den Inhalt eines Textes grob zu verstehen.

Step 2: Notiere nur die wichtigsten Informationen. Verwende Abkürzungen und Symbole, aber achte darauf, dass du ein System hast und immer dieselben verwendest, damit du deine Notizen auch später noch verstehst. Markiere offene Fragen.

Step 3: Geh im Anschluss an das Lesen oder Hören nochmal durch deine Notizen und ergänze evtl. noch fehlende Informationen.

TIPP

Wenn du kein eigenes System von Abkürzungen hast, kannst du z. B. auch diese verwenden:

· the same as	=	· between	b/w	· not	x
· not the same as	≠	· in other words	i.e.	· with	w/
· about the same as	≈	· for example	e.g.	· without	w/o
· and	+	· important	!	· open question	??
· becomes/will be	->				

EXAM SKILLS

42 Preparing for a written exam

Aufgaben in schriftlichen Tests lassen sich in geschlossene (closed) und offene (open) Testformate unterteilen. Es ist bei Klassenarbeiten oder Prüfungen auch möglich, dass es eine Mischung aus geschlossenen und offenen Formaten gibt.

GESCHLOSSENE AUFGABEN

VORBEREITUNG

Step 1: Übe die unterschiedlichen Formate wie z. B. multiple-choice tasks, true/false statements, matching tasks oder gapped texts (Lückentexte), z. B mit dem Klassenarbeitstrainer oder mithilfe dieses SMC. Mache dich mit den verschiedenen Formaten vertraut.

DURCHFÜHRUNG

Step 1: Lies die Arbeitsanweisungen gut durch. Stelle sicher, dass du genau verstanden hast, was du tun sollst.

Step 2: Konzentriere dich auf die Informationen, die du benötigst, um die Aufgaben zu bearbeiten und mache dir Notizen dazu (➜ SMC 41).
- Bei Höraufgaben versuche so viel wie möglich beim ersten Hören zu verstehen und nutze das zweite Hören, um die Informationen zu vervollständigen. (➜ SMC 26)
- Bei Textaufgaben lies den Text gründlich (wenn es um Details gehen soll) bzw. skimme/scanne ihn (wenn es um den groben Inhalt geht oder um bestimmte Informationen, ➜ SMC 1). Beantworte dann zuerst die Fragen, bei denen du dir sicher bist, und dann die, bei denen du länger nachdenken musst.
- Beantworte immer alle Aufgaben. Wenn du die Antwort nicht weißt, versuche die Antwort zu erschließen.

Hier sind noch einige Tipps, worauf du bei den einzelnen Testformaten besonders achten solltest:

Multiple-choice tasks

Bei *multiple-choice*-Aufgaben sollst du aus mehreren Antwortmöglichkeiten die korrekte auswählen.

· Lies die gegebenen Optionen sehr genau, denn manchmal sind Fallen darin versteckt: sie können z. B Stichwörter aus dem Text enthalten, aber das genaue Gegenteil vom Textinhalt aussagen.
· Wenn du unsicher bist, was die richtige Antwort ist, gehe alle Antwortoptionen durch und überlege, warum sie falsch sein könnten.

True/false statements

Bei *true/false*-Aussagen geht es darum, jede gegebene Aussage hinsichtlich ihres Wahrheitsgehaltes zu überprüfen.

· Um falsche oder wahre Aussagen zu identifizieren, gehe durch den Text und finde Belege dafür. In der Regel kannst du Textstellen finden, die den Inhalt der Aussage widerspiegeln bzw. genau das Gegenteil sagen.
· Manchmal sollst du belegen, weshalb du eine Aussage für wahr oder falsch hältst. Nenne dann Textstellen, die du gefunden hast.

Matching tasks

Bei *matching*-Aufgaben werden Dinge einander zugeordnet, also z. B Absätze und Überschriften oder Satzhälften.

· Ordne Dinge nicht einander zu, nur weil sie sich ähneln oder weil sie Wörter mit ähnlicher Bedeutung enthalten. Zur Sicherheit solltest du den Inhalt für dich umschreiben und nur Dinge mit passendem Inhalt einander zuordnen.

Gapped texts

Bei *gapped texts* müssen Lücken im Text sinnvoll befüllt werden.

· Achte besonders auf Wörter, die Sätze oder Gedanken verbinden wie z. B *linking words* oder Pronomen sowie den Zeitablauf im Text. Diese Stellen können dir gute Hinweise geben, wie Lücken sinnvoll gefüllt werden sollten.
· Wenn du den Text vervollständigt hast, lies ihn nochmal gut durch, um sicher zu stellen, dass die Grammatik passt (Zeiten, Aktiv/Passiv etc.) und dass der Text logisch ist (kausale Zusammenhänge).

OFFENE AUFGABEN

In den meisten Prüfungen wirst du mit Texten konfrontiert – dies können gedruckte Texte verschiedener Textsorten sein, aber auch visuelle Impulse wie Bilder, Cartoons oder Filmclips – oder mit Kombinationen von Texten wie z. B ein Text und ein Bild, zu denen du Aufgaben bearbeiten sollst.

VORBEREITUNG

Step 1: Erkundige dich, ob Hilfsmittel erlaubt sind (wie z. B Wörterbücher).
Step 2: Übe mit alten Prüfungen, um zu sehen, was auf dich zukommen könnte.
Step 3: Lerne die wichtigsten Arbeitsanweisungen und was von dir dabei erwartet wird (siehe unten).

DURCHFÜHRUNG

In der Regel werden die Aufgaben zum Text drei Anforderungsbereiche abdecken, zu denen du dich äußern musst. Diese Anforderungsbereiche sind:

· Anforderungsbereich I: Textverständnis
· Anforderungsbereich II: Analyse und Interpretation
· Anforderungsbereich III: Transfer

Die unterschiedlichen Anforderungsbereiche haben verschiedene Arbeitsanweisungen, an denen du sie erkennen kannst. Im Folgenden kannst du sehen, was sie bedeuten und was von dir verlangt wird.

Anforderungsbereich I: Textverständnis

Diese Aufgaben befassen sich mit dem Inhalt des Textes. Hier sollst du zeigen, dass du den Text verstanden hast. Textverständnisaufgaben können entweder geschlossene Aufgaben oder offene Aufgaben sein.

> **TIPP**
>
> Für die Bearbeitung dieser Aufgaben brauchst du unterschiedliche Techniken wie z. B · *skimming/ scanning* (➜ SMC 1)
> · Texte markieren (➜ SMC 2)
> · Notizen machen (➜ SMC 41)

> **TIPP**
>
> Auf diese Dinge solltest du bei den einzelnen Arbeitsaufträgen achten:
> · outline: Strukturiere deine Antwort in Haupt- und Unterpunkte (➜ SMC 6)
> · state: Sei präzise und erkläre einen oder mehrere Punkte
> · summarize: Fasse dich kurz und gehe nicht ins Detail (➜ SMC 13)

Im Folgenden findest du Beispiele für typische Aufgaben zur Überprüfung des Textverständnisses. Wichtige Signalwörter für diesen Aufgabenbereich sind outline, state sowie summarize/sum up/write a summary of.

- Nenne die wichtigsten Punkte oder grundsätzliche Aspekte eines Themas:
  Outline the writer's views on … · Outline/Say why this topic is important.

- Erläutere einen bestimmten Punkt oder ein bestimmtes Thema im Text:
  State the author's opinion on … ·

- Gib eine knappe Darstellung eines Ereignisses oder Themas im Text oder fasse Inhalte des Textes knapp zusammen: Summarize the event described in the text. · Sum up the role of person X in this scene. · Write a summary of …

- Es kann auch Kombinationen geben: Summarize the first scene and state why it is important for the rest of the text.

Anforderungsbereich II: Analyse/Interpretation

Bei diesen Aufgaben geht es um ein tieferes Verständnis des Textes. Hier sollst du zeigen, dass du nicht nur den Inhalt, sondern auch die Intention des Autors verstehst. Fragen, die du dir stellen solltest, sind z. B: Warum hat der Autor etwas genau so beschrieben? Was will er/sie damit erreichen? An wen richtet sich der Text? Was sagt die Beschreibung eines Charakters über ihn/sie aus?

Lies die Arbeitsanweisungen genau, damit du weißt, was von dir verlangt wird. Signalwörter für diesen Aufgabenbereich sind analyse, examine oder explain:

- Beschreibe und erkläre bestimmte Aspekte eines Textes im Detail:
  Analyse the main elements of the poster/scene/text.

- Erläutere einen bestimmten Punkt oder ein bestimmtes Thema im Text:
  Examine how the main character is characterised.

- Beschreibe und definiere ein Ereignis/Thema oder einen bestimmten Punkt im Detail: Explain the main character's reaction to …

Anforderungsbereich III: Über den Text hinaus

Aufgaben aus diesem Anforderungsbereich fordern dich oft auf, dich kreativ mit einem Text oder einem Thema auseinanderzusetzen, z. B indem du ein Ende für einen Text oder eine Szene aus der Perspektive eines anderen Charakters schreiben sollst. Hier solltest du darauf achten, dass dein Stil zum Ausgangstext bzw. zu dem Charakter passt. Manchmal ist dir die Textsorte freigestellt, manchmal ist eine bestimmte Textsorte vorgeschrieben.

Beachte auf jeden Fall immer die Grundsätze für das Schreiben guter Texte (➜ SMC 3ff.).

Im Folgenden findest du Beispiele für typische Aufgaben in diesem Anforderungsbereich. Wichtige Signalwörter in den Arbeitsaufträgen sind z. B comment on, discuss oder justify.

- Gib deine Meinung zu einem Thema und begründe sie mit Belegen aus dem Text:
  Comment on the author's belief that … · Comment on the question of …

- Erörtere ein Thema. Bringe dabei Argumente pro und contra ein:
  Discuss why it is important for minorities to be represented in films/on TV.

- Finde Gründe und Belege für deine Meinung/Entscheidung/Schlussfolgerung:
  Justify your answer. · Justify why …

TIPP
Auf diese Dinge solltest du bei den einzelnen Arbeitsaufträgen achten:
- analyse: Stelle immer eine Verbindung zwischen verwendeten Stilmitteln und ihrer Wirkung her
- examine: Achte auf das, was im Text konkret steht ebenso wie auf Dinge, die sich "zwischen den Zeilen" befinden.
- explain: Beschreibe nicht nur, sondern begründe anhand des Textes, weshalb Dinge deiner Meinung nach so dargestellt sind, wie sie sind.

TIPP
Textsorten, die du in diesem Anforderungsbereich produzieren sollst, können z. B sein:
- Brief/E-Mail (➜ SMC 5)
- Erörterung (➜ SMC 7)
- Kommentar (➜ SMC 8)
- Leserbrief (➜ SMC 9)
- Artikel (➜ SMC 10)
- Bericht (➜ SMC 11)
- Review (➜ SMC 12)

TIPP
Auf diese Dinge solltest du bei den einzelnen Arbeitsaufträgen in der Vorbereitung achten:
- comment on: Bevor du schreibst, sammle Textbelege und strukturiere sie.
- discuss: Wäge beide Seiten des Themas ab und komme zu einer begründeten Schlussfolgerung.
- justify: Markiere Textstellen, die deine Aussage stützen oder begründen.

43 Preparing for a speaking exam

Auf Sprechprüfungen/Kommunikationsprüfungen kannst du dich ebenso vorbereiten wie auf schriftliche Prüfungen.

WIE SIEHT DIE PRÜFUNG AUS?

Step 1: Als erstes solltest du herausfinden, um welche Art von Prüfung es sich handelt. Es gibt zwei Formen: monologisches Sprechen oder dialogisches Sprechen (oder eine Kombination von beidem, z. B zuerst ein Monolog, gefolgt von einem Dialog zu einem bestimmten Thema).

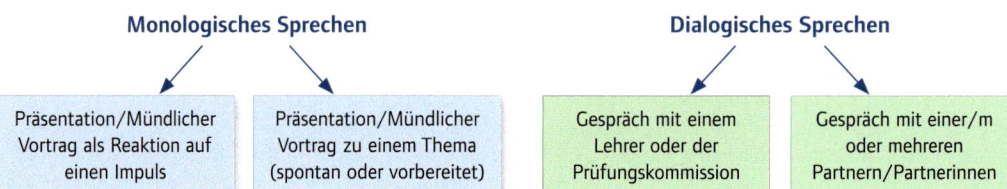

Monologisches Sprechen		**Dialogisches Sprechen**	
Präsentation/Mündlicher Vortrag als Reaktion auf einen Impuls	Präsentation/Mündlicher Vortrag zu einem Thema (spontan oder vorbereitet)	Gespräch mit einem Lehrer oder der Prüfungskommission	Gespräch mit einer/m oder mehreren Partnern/Partnerinnen

Step 2: Informiere dich über weitere Aspekte:

- Partner: Kannst du eine/n Partner selbst wählen oder wird er/sie zugeteilt? Könnt ihr vor der Prüfung gemeinsam üben?

- Format: Welche Form hat die Prüfung? Freies Sprechen zu einem Thema oder bekommst du einen Impuls (Text, Bild etc.)?

- Dauer: Wie lange dauert die Prüfung/die einzelnen Teile?

- Vorbereitung: Wann erfährst du das Thema? Kannst du dich zu Hause vorbereiten oder erst direkt vor dem Test?

- Medien: Sollst du Medien (Computer, Folien etc) verwenden? Wieviel Zeit hast du, diese vorzubereiten?

- Benotung: Wie wird die Prüfung benotet? In der Regel setzt sich die Note aus Inhalt und sprachlicher Kompetenz zusammen.

Step 3: Sammle alle Informationen wie z. B auch Musterprüfungen und Informationen zur Benotung in einem Ordner, so dass du schnell darauf Zugriff hast.

MONOLOGISCHES SPRECHEN

PRÄSENTATION/MÜNDLICHER VORTRAG ZU EINEM IMPULS

Wenn du in deinem mündlichen Vortrag auf einen Impuls reagieren sollst, kann das z. B ein Bild oder Text sein, aber auch ein Zitat, eine Statistik, ein Cartoon oder eine oder mehrere Fragen. Oft erfährst du das erst kurz vor oder in der Prüfung selbst.

Aber auch wenn du nicht genau weißt, mit welcher Art von Impuls du konfrontiert wird, kannst du dich vorbereiten:

- Erstelle eine Mindmap oder Liste für jede Art von möglichem Impuls.

- Sammle darin Wörter oder ganze Sätze, um über die verschiedenen Impulse zu sprechen. Dies hilft dir, deinen Vortrag zu strukturieren, und deinem Gegenüber, ihm zu folgen. Lerne diese Redewendungen – wenn du sie sicher beherrschst, kannst du dich in der Prüfungssituation auf die Inhalte konzentrieren.
  (➜ *SMC 21, 22, 23, 24*)

PRÄSENTATION/MÜNDLICHER VORTRAG ZU EINEM THEMA

Wenn du für deine Prüfung eine Präsentation/einen mündlichen Vortrag zu einem Thema vorbereiten sollst, gehe dabei vor wie bei anderen Präsentationen auch (➡ *SMC 29, 30*). Einige Punkte solltest du aber besonders beachten:

· Struktur: Stelle sicher, dass die Zuhörer deiner Präsentation gut folgen können. Lerne und verwende Redewendungen wie *first of all, finally, next, I would like to finish by saying …*

· Medien: Bereite alle Medien (Bilder, Präsentationen etc.) gut vor. Dazu gehören z. B auch deine Notizen, am besten auf Karteikarten.

· Zeitmanagement: Halte dich an die vorgegebene Zeit. Das schaffst du am besten, wenn du deine Präsentation ein paar Mal laut übst, z. B vor einem Partner/einer Partnerin oder deiner Familie.

· Vortrag: Sieh die Prüfer an, wenn du sprichst, nicht deine Notizen. Sprich langsam, deutlich und lass dir ruhig Zeit, zwischendurch mal tief Luft zu holen, besonders wenn du nervös bist. Mach das auch schon beim Üben.

DIALOGISCHES SPRECHEN – AN GESPRÄCHEN TEILNEHMEN

Oft beinhaltet eine mündliche Prüfung auch einen dialogischen Teil, in dem du mit einem Partner oder den Prüfern kommunizierst.

Dies kann z. B ein Gespräch zu einem Thema sein, aber auch eine Diskussion, ein Interview oder ein Rollenspiel. Auch wenn du nicht genau weißt, mit was du in der Prüfung konfrontiert wirst, kannst du dich auf die Situation vorbereiten.

Step 1: Überlege dir, evtl. mit einem Partner/einer Partnerin, im Vorfeld für jede der möglichen Formen – Gespräch, Diskussion, Interview, Rollenspiel – worauf du dabei achten musst.

Step 2: Notiere dir, was du an Phrasen und Redewendungen für die einzelnen Phasen eines Dialoges brauchst und lerne sie. (➡ *SMC 22*)

· Anfang einer Diskussion: Today we're talking about … · Let me start with … · …

· Zustimmen/widersprechen: What a great/… idea. · My point exactly. · … / That's not how I see it. · I don't agree with …

· Nachfragen: Can you give an example of that? · Do you mean …?

· Eine/n Partner/in einbeziehen: How about you? · What do you think/How do you feel about that?

· Unterbrechen: May I interrupt? · Excuse me, can I just say that …?

· Zeit zum Überlegen gewinnen: Can I repeat what we said before? · Well, now let me see … · Let me think about that for a second.

· Zusammenfassen: We've seen that … · To come to a conclusion …

TIPP

Beachte auch diese allgemeinen Tipps für die Prüfungssituation:

· Erstelle deine Notizen so, dass du sie schnell finden und auf einen Blick entziffern kannst.
· Sei gut ausgeschlafen. Trage angemessene Kleidung, in der du dich auch wohlfühlst. Sei pünktlich.
· Sei höflich und freundlich. Bedenke auch, dass du in einer dialogischen Prüfungssituation nicht für deine eigene Note arbeitest, sondern auch für deine/n Partner/in.

44 Preparing for a listening exam

Auf Hörverstehensprüfungen kannst du dich ebenso vorbereiten wie auf schriftliche oder mündliche Prüfungen.

WAS WIRD GEPRÜFT?

Ein *listening exam* überprüft deine Hörverstehenskompetenz. Dabei sollst du zeigen, dass du

- Gesprächen folgen kannst,
- Gesprächen und längeren Hörtexten Hauptpunkte und wichtige Details entnehmen kannst *(gist and detail)*,
- die wesentlichen Einstellungen der Sprechenden identifizieren kannst, also z.B. sagen kannst, wie jemand auf etwas reagiert, das im Hörtext passiert.

WIE SIEHT DIE PRÜFUNG AUS?

Du wirst in einer Prüfung zwei Arten von Aufgaben begegnen: geschlossenen Aufgaben und halboffenen Aufgaben. Meist wird deine Prüfung aus einer Mischung aus beidem bestehen.

Geschlossene Aufgaben

Multiple Choice

Matching

Halboffene Aufgaben

Fill in

Short answers

Beispiele für die vier Aufgabenformate findest du auf der nächsten Seite.

VORBEREITUNG

Hier sind einige Dinge, die du im Vorfeld der Prüfung zur Vorbereitung klären kannst:

- Dauer: Besteht die Prüfung aus mehreren Teilen? Wenn ja, wieviele Teile sind es? Wie lange dauert die Prüfung/die einzelnen Teile?
- Format: Sieh dir die möglichen Aufgabenformate an und mache dich mit ihnen vertraut.
- Benotung: Wie wird die Prüfung benotet? Haben die unterschiedlichen Aufgabenformate in der Prüfung eine unterschiedliche Gewichtung?

Sammle alle Informationen wie z.B auch Musterprüfungen und Informationen zur Benotung z.B. in einem Ordner "Prüfungsvorbereitung" auf deinem PC oder in einer Mappe, so dass du schnell darauf Zugriff hast.

DURCHFÜHRUNG

- Lies die Arbeitsanweisungen gut durch, am besten vor dem ersten Hören. Stelle sicher, dass du genau verstanden hast, was du tun sollst.
- Konzentriere dich auf die Informationen, die du benötigst, um die Aufgaben zu bearbeiten und mache dir kurze, stichwortartige Notizen dazu (➡ *SMC 41*).
- Versuche so viel wie möglich beim ersten Hören zu verstehen und nutze das zweite Hören, um deine Informationen zu vervollständigen. (➡ *SMC 26*)
- Beantworte immer alle Aufgaben. Wenn du die Antwort nicht weißt, versuche die Antwort zu erschließen.

AUFGABENFORMATE

Generell können alle genannten Formate alle Aspekte des Hörverstehens überprüfen (*gist, detail*, Einstellungen der Sprechenden). Im Folgenden findest du ein paar Beispielaufgaben, damit du ein Gespür dafür bekommst, welche Fragestellung auf welche Informationen abzielt.

GESCHLOSSENE AUFGABENFORMATE

Multiple Choice

Multiple Choice-Aufgaben bestehen in der Regel aus einer Frage oder Aussage sowie mehreren Möglichkeiten, die Frage zu beantworten bzw. die Aussage zu vervollständigen.

1 Peter talks to Fred about …

  a) his hobbies.
  b) Fred's hobbies.
  c) his dad's hobbies.

2 How does Fred react to Peter's plans?

  a) He is surprised.
  b) He is angry.
  c) He is confused.

Beispiel 1 überprüft, ob du spezifische Details korrekt heraushören kannst (über wessen Hobbies wird gesprochen?). Beispiel 2 überprüft, ob du Aussagen im Zusammenhang erfassen kannst (Kannst du aus dem Gesagten erschließen, was der Sprecher/die Sprecherin denkt/meint/fühlt?).

Matching

Bei Matching-Aufgaben musst du Dinge einander zuordnen.

Who says what?

1	Jack	a) thinks climate change isn't a problem at all.
2	Peter	b) thinks climate change is a problem but not a big one.
3	Fred	c) thinks climate change is a really big problem.
4	Simon	d) thinks climate change is the biggest problem we have today.

Bei diesem Beispiel oben sollst du aus dem Gesagten heraushören, was die Sprecher genau sagen/meinen.

HALBOFFENE AUFGABENFORMATE

Fill in

Bei diesem Format sollst du Infomationen mithilfe des Hörtextes ergänzen.

People in New York City are afraid that _____ .

Dieses Beispiel überprüft, ob du spezifische Details korrekt heraushören kannst.

Short answers

Bei diesem Format musst du Fragen beantworten. Hier hilft es, wenn du dir beim Hören Notizen gemacht hast.

Why do many people think that New York is the most exciting city in the world?

_____ .

Dieses Beispiel überprüft, ob du die Gesamtaussage des Textes verstanden hast.

Das <u>Vocabulary</u> (S. 202 – 227) enthält alle Wörter und Wendungen deines Englischbuches, die du lernen musst.
Sie stehen in der Reihenfolge, in der sie im Buch zum ersten Mal vorkommen.

Hier siehst du, wie das **Vocabulary** aufgebaut ist:

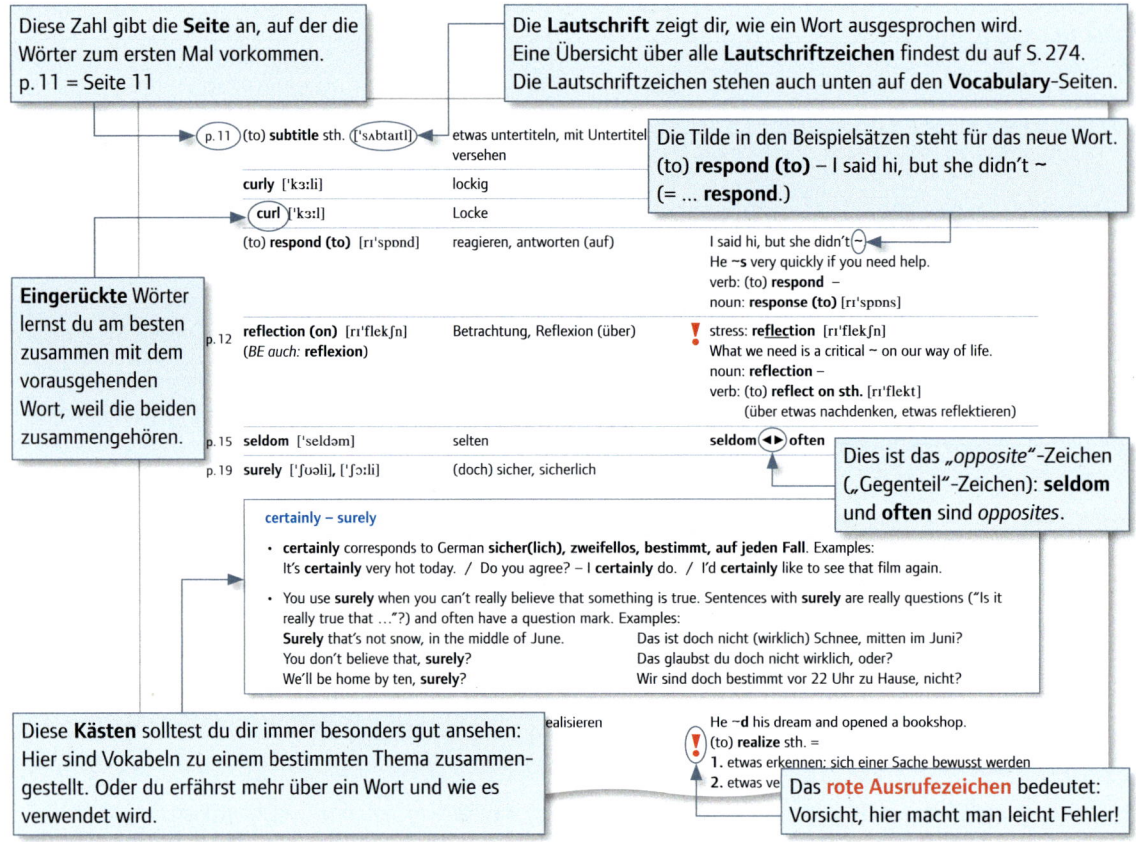

Diese Zahl gibt die **Seite** an, auf der die Wörter zum ersten Mal vorkommen.
p. 11 = Seite 11

Die **Lautschrift** zeigt dir, wie ein Wort ausgesprochen wird.
Eine Übersicht über alle **Lautschriftzeichen** findest du auf S. 274.
Die Lautschriftzeichen stehen auch unten auf den **Vocabulary**-Seiten.

Die Tilde in den Beispielsätzen steht für das neue Wort.
(to) **respond (to)** – I said hi, but she didn't ~
(= ... **respond**.)

Eingerückte Wörter lernst du am besten zusammen mit dem vorausgehenden Wort, weil die beiden zusammengehören.

p. 11 (to) **subtitle** sth. [ˈsʌbtaɪtl]	etwas untertiteln, mit Untertitel versehen	
curly [ˈkɜːli]	lockig	
curl [ˈkɜːl]	Locke	
(to) **respond (to)** [rɪˈspɒnd]	reagieren, antworten (auf)	I said hi, but she didn't ~ He ~s very quickly if you need help. verb: (to) **respond** – noun: **response (to)** [rɪˈspɒns]
p. 12 **reflection (on)** [rɪˈflekʃn] (*BE auch:* **reflexion**)	Betrachtung, Reflexion (über)	❗ stress: <u>re</u>flection [rɪˈflekʃn] What we need is a critical ~ on our way of life. noun: **reflection** – verb: (to) **reflect on** sth. [rɪˈflekt] (über etwas nachdenken, etwas reflektieren)
p. 15 **seldom** [ˈseldəm]	selten	**seldom** ◀▶ **often**
p. 19 **surely** [ˈʃʊəli], [ˈʃɔːli]	(doch) sicher, sicherlich	

Dies ist das „*opposite*"-Zeichen („Gegenteil"-Zeichen): **seldom** und **often** sind *opposites*.

certainly – surely

- **certainly** corresponds to German **sicher(lich), zweifellos, bestimmt, auf jeden Fall**. Examples:
  It's **certainly** very hot today. / Do you agree? – I **certainly** do. / I'd **certainly** like to see that film again.

- You use **surely** when you can't really believe that something is true. Sentences with **surely** are really questions ("Is it really true that ...?") and often have a question mark. Examples:
  Surely that's not snow, in the middle of June.   Das ist doch nicht (wirklich) Schnee, mitten im Juni?
  You don't believe that, **surely**?   Das glaubst du doch nicht wirklich, oder?
  We'll be home by ten, **surely**?   Wir sind doch bestimmt vor 22 Uhr zu Hause, nicht?

Diese **Kästen** solltest du dir immer besonders gut ansehen: Hier sind Vokabeln zu einem bestimmten Thema zusammengestellt. Oder du erfährst mehr über ein Wort und wie es verwendet wird.

...ealisieren

He ~d his dream and opened a bookshop.
❗ (to) **realize** sth. =
1. etwas erkennen; sich einer Sache bewusst werden
2. etwas ve...

Das **rote Ausrufezeichen** bedeutet: Vorsicht, hier macht man leicht Fehler!

Im **Vocabulary** werden folgende **Abkürzungen** verwendet:

p. = page • pp. = pages

sth. = something • sb. = somebody

jd. = jemand • jn. = jemanden • jm. = jemandem

pl = *plural* • *adj* = *adjective* • *adv* = *adverb* • *conj* = *conjunction* • *prep* = *preposition*

BE = *British English* • *AE* = *American English*

infml = *informal* (umgangssprachlich) • *fml* = *formal* (formell, förmlich)

Ⓕ = *verwandtes Wort im Französischen* • Ⓛ = *verwandtes Wort im Lateinischen*

Wenn du **nachschlagen** möchtest, was ein englisches Wort bedeutet oder wie man es ausspricht,
dann verwende das **English – German Dictionary** auf den Seiten 228 – 274.

[iː] green · [i] happy · [ɪ] big · [e] red · [æ] cat · [ɑː] class · [ɒ] song ·
[ɔː] door · [uː] blue · [ʊ] book · [ʌ] mum · [ɜː] girl · [ə] a partner

Unit 1   Who are you?

op. 10/11 **in their (late) teens**	im (späten) Teenageralter	
dreadlocks *(pl)* [ˈdredlɒks]	Rasta-Locken	

dreadlocks

She has **curly** hair.

curly [ˈkɜːli]	lockig	
curl [kɜːl]	Locke	**curls**

kinky [ˈkɪŋki] *(AE)*	kraus, gekräuselt *(Haare)*	

She has **kinky** hair.

(to) **be dressed** [drest]	angezogen sein	(to) **be dressed** angezogen sein (to) **get dressed** sich anziehen
casually [ˈkæʒuəli]	leger, lässig *(gekleidet)*	

casually dressed   **formally** dressed

blazer [ˈbleɪzə]	Sakko, Blazer *(sportliches Jackett)*	
denim [ˈdenɪm]	Jeansstoff	
paint [peɪnt]	Farbe, Lack	verb: (to) **paint** – noun: **paint** Ⓕ la peinture

headscarves

headscarf, *pl* **headscarves** [ˈhedskɑːf, ˈhedskɑːvz]	Kopftuch	
tie [taɪ]	Krawatte, Schlips	

tie

patriotic [ˌpeɪtriˈɒtɪk]	patriotisch, vaterlandsliebend	Ⓕ patriotique Ⓛ patria *(Vaterland, Heimat)*
hairstyle [ˈheəstaɪl]	Frisur	
(to) **suggest** sth. [səˈdʒest]	auf etwas hindeuten, etwas nahelegen	New research ~**s** that students learn better if they are in a good mood. ❗ (to) **suggest** sth. = 1. etwas vorschlagen; 2. auf etwas hindeuten, etwas nahelegen
conservative [kənˈsɜːvətɪv]	konservativ; Konservative(r)	❗ stress: con**se**rvative [kənˈsɜːvətɪv] Ⓛ conservare *(bewahren)*
original [əˈrɪdʒənl]	originell	❗ **original** = 1. Original-, ursprüngliche(r, s); 2. originell Ⓕ original, e Ⓛ origo, inis f *(Ursprung)*
(to) **prefer** sb. **to do** sth. [prɪˈfɜː]	(es) vorziehen, wenn jd. etwas täte/tun würde	*English:* I'd prefer you to pay cash. Ⓛ praeferre *German:* Ich würde es vorziehen, wenn Sie bar bezahlen würden.

[eɪ] **name** · [aɪ] **time** · [ɔɪ] **boy** · [əʊ] **old** ·
[aʊ] **town** · [ɪə] **here** · [eə] **where** · [ʊə] **tour**

Part A

p. 12	**award-winning** [əˈwɔːd wɪnɪŋ]	preisgekrönt	
	poet [ˈpəʊɪt]	Dichter/in, Poet/in	❗ stress: **poet** [ˈpəʊɪt] (F) le poète, la poétesse (L) poeta *m*
	playwright [ˈpleɪraɪt]	Dramatiker/in, Bühnenautor/in	
	novelist [ˈnɒvəlɪst]	Romanautor/in	❗ **novel** = Roman, Novelle = **short story**
	(to) **picture** sb./sth. [ˈpɪktʃə]	sich jn./etwas vorstellen	Her photo surprised me – I had ~**d** her as much older.
	desire [dɪˈzaɪə]	Wunsch, Verlangen	After reading Robinson Crusoe, he felt a strong ~ to explore the world. (F) le désir (L) desiderium
	awkward [ˈɔːkwəd]	plump; peinlich, unangenehm	We felt rather ~ when Jake found out we hadn't invited him to the party.
	painfully [ˈpeɪnfəli]	furchtbar, äußerst, schmerzlich	~ slow/hard/clear/… This new software is ~ slow.
	pain [peɪn]	Schmerz(en)	noun: **pain**　Schmerz(en) adj: **painful**　schmerzhaft, qualvoll adv: **painfully**　furchtbar, äußerst, schmerzlich
	(to) **cope** [kəʊp]	zurechtkommen, klarkommen	It's a bit of a problem, but don't worry – we'll ~.
	alarm [əˈlɑːm] (*kurz für:* **alarm clock**)	Wecker	
	(to) **wink (at** sb.**)** [wɪŋk]	(jm. zu)zwinkern	My face turned red when I noticed he was ~**ing at** me.
	(to) **shave** [ʃeɪv]	(sich) rasieren	

He's **shaving**.　　a **shaved** head (ein kahlgeschorener Kopf)

	headphones (*pl*) [ˈhedfəʊnz]	Kopfhörer	*English:*　a **pair of headphones** *German:*　ein **Kopfhörer**
	hood [hʊd]	Kapuze	
p. 13	**instructor** [ɪnˈstrʌktə]	Lehrer/in, Ausbilder/in	(F) l'instructeur (*m*) (L) instruere (*ausrüsten; unterrichten*)
	simple [ˈsɪmpl]	einfach, unkompliziert	Anyone can make this cake – it's a really ~ recipe. (L) simplex
	branch [brɑːntʃ]	Ast, Zweig; Zweigstelle, Filiale	After the storm, the road was covered with fallen ~**es**. As more and more people bank online, banks have closed ~**es** all over the country.
	record [ˈrekɔːd]	Schallplatte	(L) recordari (*sich erinnern*)
	(to) **make** sb. **do** sth.	jn. dazu bringen, etwas zu tun; jn. veranlassen, etwas zu tun	Sad films always ~ **me cry**.

(to) make sb. do sth. – (to) let sb. do sth.

(to) **make** sb. **do** sth. = jn. dazu bringen/jn. veranlassen, etwas zu tun　　Mum tried to **make me talk** about my feelings.

(to) **let** sb. **do** sth. = jn. etwas tun lassen; jm. erlauben, etwas zu tun; zulassen, dass jemand etwas tut　　Our teacher **lets us talk** to our neighbours in class.

---

[b] **b**oat · [p] **p**ool · [d] **d**ad · [t] **t**en · [g] **g**ood · [k] **c**at ·
[m] **m**um · [n] **n**o · [ŋ] so**ng** · [l] he**ll**o · [r] **r**ed · [w] **w**e · [j] **y**ou

yet [jet]	trotzdem, dennoch	

> **yet**
>
> 1. Have you packed your bags **yet**?   **schon**
>   – No, I haven't. I have**n't** decided what to take with me **yet**.   **noch nicht**
>
> 2. We live in the country and **yet** we are quite close to the city.   **trotzdem, dennoch**

nor do I want to … [nɔː]	und ich will auch nicht …	Jack doesn't want to sit next to me, ~ **do I want to** sit next to him.

> **English "nor" – German "auch nicht"**
>
> **She doesn't like pop music, and nor do I.** (… ich auch nicht.)   Vergleiche: **She likes jazz, and so do I.** (… ich auch.)
>
> Mit **nor** + Hilfsverb + (Pro-)Nomen kann man zum Ausdruck bringen,
> dass etwas <u>auch nicht</u> für jemand anders gilt. Weitere Beispiele:
>
> John **isn't** interested in jazz.   **Nor is** Joanna.   He **hasn't** been abroad.   **Nor has** Joanna.
> He **can't** dance very well.   **Nor can** Joanna.   He **didn't** leave school last year.   **Nor did** Joanna.
> He **hasn't** got a CD player.   **Nor has** Joanna.   He **wouldn't** want to live in Spain. **Nor would** Joanna.
> He **doesn't** earn a lot of money.   **Nor does** Joanna.
>
> Mit **not … either** kann man dasselbe ausdrücken: John **isn't** interested in jazz. – Joanna **isn't either**
>   He **can't** dance very well. – Joanna **can't either**.

somewhat (adv) [ˈsʌmwɒt]	etwas, ein wenig	He felt ~ uncomfortable wearing a suit.
p. 14 **perspective** [pəˈspektɪv]	Perspektive, Blickwinkel	❗ stress: **perspective** [pəˈspektɪv] Ⓕ la perspective Ⓛ perspicere
aggressive [əˈgresɪv]	aggressiv	❗ stress: **aggressive** [əˈgresɪv]
depressed [dɪˈprest]	depri(miert)	
light-hearted [ˌlaɪt ˈhɑːtɪd]	fröhlich, heiter	
melancholic [ˌmelənˈkɒlɪk]	trübsinnig	Ⓕ mélancolique
nostalgic [nɒˈstældʒɪk]	nostalgisch	When I saw my old school, I felt very ~.
uplifting [ʌpˈlɪftɪŋ]	erhebend, aufmunternd	~ music; an ~ moment/experience
poetry [ˈpəʊətri]	Gedichte, Lyrik	
(to) **reflect** [rɪˈflekt]	reflektieren, (wider)spiegeln	A poem can ~ emotions like a mirror ~s images. Ⓕ refléter
(to) **realize sth.** [ˈriːəlaɪz]	etwas erkennen; sich einer Sache bewusst werden	When I got home, I ~d that I had left my bag on the train.
p. 15 **imagery** [ˈɪmɪdʒəri]	bildhafte Sprache; Sprachbilder	Ⓛ imago, inis f
simile [ˈsɪməli]	Vergleich	~**s** compare things, usually with as or like: *She was as white as a ghost.* Ⓛ simile, is n
metaphor [ˈmetəfɔː]	Metapher	~**s** compare things without as or like: *He had eyes of fire.* Ⓕ la métaphore ❗ stress: **metaphor** [ˈmetəfɔː] Ⓛ metaphora
device [dɪˈvaɪs]	Mittel; Gerät, Apparat	Similes and metaphors are **stylistic** ~**s**. (Stilmittel) A thermometer is a ~ that tells you the temperature.
gentle [ˈdʒentl]	sanft(mütig)	The dog looks dangerous, but he's really very ~.

---

[f] **f**ather · [v] **r**i**v**er · [s] **s**ister · [z] plea**s**e · [ʃ] **sh**op · [ʒ] televi**s**ion ·
[tʃ] **t**ea**ch**er · [dʒ] **G**ermany · [θ] **th**anks · [ð] **th**is · [h] **h**ere

two hundred and five   205

dove [dʌv]	Taube	❗ • pronunciation: **dove** [dʌv] • There is no biological difference between **doves** and **pigeons**. However, when people hear the word **pigeon** they picture the grey bird found everywhere in cities. When they hear the word **dove** they picture the white bird that is often used as a symbol of peace.
(to) **be considered** sth. [kən'sɪdəd]	als etwas betrachtet werden; für etwas gehalten werden	They**'re** ~ (to be) one of the best new bands around.

a **hawk**   an **owl**

hawk [hɔːk]	Habicht; (im übertragenen Sinn:) Falke	
owl [aʊl]	Eule	
blind [blaɪnd]	blind	❗ pronunciation: **blind** [blaɪnd]
peaceful ['piːsfl]	friedlich, friedfertig	
p. 16 **athletic** [æθ'letɪk]	athletisch, sportlich	❗ stress: noun: **ath**lete ['æθliːt] – adj: ath**let**ic [æθ'letɪk]
gay [geɪ]	schwul, lesbisch	
straight [streɪt]	hetero	
conventional [kən'venʃənl]	konventionell	❗ stress: con**ven**tional [kən'venʃənl] Ⓛ conventio, -onis f (Vereinbarung)
liberal ['lɪbərəl]	liberal	❗ stress: **lib**eral ['lɪbərəl]
religious [rɪ'lɪdʒəs]	religiös; gläubig	❗ stress: re**lig**ious [rɪ'lɪdʒəs] noun: **religion** – adj: **religious**
African-American [ˌæfrɪkən_ə'merɪkən]	Afroamerikaner/in; afroamerikanisch	
upbringing ['ʌpbrɪŋɪŋ]	Erziehung	My ~ has influenced the way I view the world.
dialect ['daɪəlekt]	Dialekt	❗ stress: **di**alect ['daɪəlekt]
particularly [pə'tɪkjələli]	besonders; vor allem	She loves history. She's ~ interested in Roman Britain. I'm ~ looking forward to seeing John again.

> **Intensifying adverbs** [ɪn'tensɪfaɪɪŋ] **(Verstärkende Adverbien)**
>
> | | | | |
> |---|---|---|---|
> | **absolutely** thrilled | völlig begeistert | **particularly** beautiful | besonders schön |
> | **completely** normal | völlig normal, ganz normal | **terribly** tired | schrecklich müde |
> | **especially** helpful | besonders hilfreich | **totally** wrong | völlig falsch |
> | **extremely** hot | äußerst heiß | **very** confused | sehr verwirrt |

(to) **modify** ['mɒdɪfaɪ]	näher bestimmen	You can use adverbs to ~ adjectives.
search engine ['sɜːtʃ_ˌendʒɪn]	(Internet-)Suchmaschine	
p. 17 (to) **format** ['fɔːmæt]	formatieren (Text am Computer)	❗ stress: **for**mat ['fɔːmæt]
electronic [ɪˌlek'trɒnɪk]	elektronisch	
visual ['vɪʒuəl]	optisch, visuell	❗ stress: **vis**ual ['vɪʒuəl] adj: **visual** – adv: **visually** Ⓕ visuel, le Ⓛ videre (sehen)

[iː] green · [i] happy · [ɪ] big · [e] red · [æ] cat · [ɑː] class · [ɒ] song · [ɔː] door · [uː] blue · [ʊ] book · [ʌ] mum · [ɜː] girl · [ə] a partner

proper [ˈprɒpə]	richtige(r, s), angemessene(r, s), ordentliche(r, s)	It's important to have a ~ breakfast, not just a cup of tea or coffee.
margin [ˈmɑːdʒɪn]	Rand	You can write any comments in the ~ on the right. (F) la marge (L) margo, inis *m/f*
(to) indent [ɪnˈdent]	(eine Zeile) einrücken	
neither … nor …	weder … noch …	
in relation to [rɪˈleɪʃn]	im Verhältnis zu	I think my ears are too big in ~ to my head. ❗ stress: **relation** [rɪˈleɪʃn]
source [sɔːs]	Quelle (auch: Textquelle)	I think books are better for research than online ~**s**.
font [fɒnt]	Schrift(art)	Arial, *Corsetta* and **STENCIL** are different ~**s**.
italics [ɪˈtælɪks]	Kursivschrift	I usually print book or song titles in *italics*.
bold (type) [bəʊld]	Fettdruck	And if a word is really important, I print it in **bold**.
clarity [ˈklærəti]	Klarheit	adj: **clear** – noun: **clarity** (L) claritas, atis f
untidy [ʌnˈtaɪdi]	unordentlich, unsauber	**tidy ◄► untidy**
legible [ˈledʒəbl]	lesbar, leserlich	**legible ◄► illegible** (unleserlich) (L) legere *(lesen)*
pt (*Abkürzung für* **point**)	Punkt *(Maßeinheit f. Schriftgrad, Zeilenabstände u.Ä.)*	
function [ˈfʌŋkʃn]	Funktion	Can you explain the ~ of the Bundesrat to me?
(to) type [taɪp]	tippen, Maschine schreiben	It's time I learned to ~ with ten fingers.

Part B

p. 18

equality [iˈkwɒləti]	Gleichheit, Gleichberechtigung	adjective: **equal** – noun: **equality**
opinion piece [əˈpɪnjən piːs]	Stellungnahme, Meinungsartikel	an article in which the writer expresses a personal opinion (L) opinio, onis f *(Meinung)*
(to) recognize [ˈrekəgnaɪz]	anerkennen	You need to ~ the fact that the world is changing. ❗ (to) **recognize** = 1. erkennen; 2. anerkennen
(to) make sth. up	etwas bilden	Girls ~ **up** 58 percent of the students at our school. This book is **made up** of three units.
percent [pəˈsent] *(AE)*, per cent *(BE)*	Prozent	
nonexistent [ˌnɒnɪgˈzɪstənt] (*BE meist:* **non-existent**)	nicht vorhanden, nicht existierend	**existent ◄► non-existent**
(to) exist [ɪgˈzɪst]	existieren	Some people believe that life ~**s** on Mars. (L) existere
(to) differ [ˈdɪfə]	sich unterscheiden, verschieden sein	verb: (to) **differ** – adj: **different** – noun: **difference** (L) differre
biological [ˌbaɪəˈlɒdʒɪkl]	biologisch	noun: **biology** – adj: **biological** – adv: **biologically**
when it comes to …	was … betrifft/anbelangt, …	I understand a lot of grammar, but I'm not so good **when it ~ to** everyday conversation.
representation [ˌreprɪzenˈteɪʃn]	Vertretung, Repräsentanz	❗ verb: (to) **represent** [ˌreprɪˈzent] It's an honour to ~ your country in the Olympic Games. (vertreten, repräsentieren) noun: **representation** [ˌreprɪzenˈteɪʃn] We want to improve the ~ of minorities in parliament. (Vertretung, Repräsentanz)

(to) **have** sb. **do** sth.	jn. etwas tun lassen; veranlassen, dass jemand etwas tut	

> **(to) have sb. do sth. – (to) have sth. done**
>
> (to) **have** <u>sb.</u> **do sth.** = jn. etwas tun lassen; veranlassen, dass jemand etwas tut
>
> We **had** <u>a friend</u> **check** our car.
> Wir haben einen Freund unser Auto checken lassen.
>
> (to) **have** <u>sth.</u> **done** = etwas machen/erledigen lassen
>
> We **had** <u>our car</u> **checked** last Friday.
> Wir haben letzten Freitag unser Auto checken lassen.

(to) **show up** *(infml)*	auftauchen, erscheinen	He said he'd come and help us, but he didn't **~ up**.
husband ['hʌzbənd]	Ehemann	
counselor ['kaʊnsələ] (*BE*: **counsellor**)	Berater/in; Betreuer/in	If you need advice, you can make an appointment with a **~**. (L) consilium (*Rat, Vorschlag*)
ridiculous [rɪ'dɪkjələs]	lächerlich	What a silly hat! It makes you look **~**. (F) ridicule (L) ridiculosus
contribution [ˌkɒntrɪ'bjuːʃn]	Beitrag	(F) la contribution (L) contribure (*beitragen*)
after all [ˌɑːftər_'ɔːl]	(schließlich) doch	I know him very well. **After ~**, we've been friends for more than ten years.
constantly ['kɒnstəntli]	ständig, dauernd	❗ stress: **constant(ly)** ['kɒnstənt(li)] • adj: **constant** – the **constant** noise of cars • adv: **constantly** – **constantly** changing prices (F) constamment (L) constanter (*adv*)
(to) **eliminate** [ɪ'lɪmɪneɪt]	abschaffen, beseitigen, eliminieren	Do you think we will ever be able to **~** disease? (F) éliminer
in the meantime ['miːntaɪm]	in der Zwischenzeit; inzwischen	The food is in the oven. **In the ~**, we could wash the dishes. Have you repaired your bike **in the ~**?
importance [ɪm'pɔːtəns]	Wichtigkeit, Bedeutung	These photos are of great **~** to me. adj: **important** – noun: **importance** (F) important, e – l'importance (f)
p. 19 (to) **produce** [prə'djuːs]	produzieren, erzeugen, herstellen	noun: **product** (Produkt) – verb: (to) **produce**
headline ['hedlaɪn]	Schlagzeile, Überschrift	
provocative [prə'vɒkətɪv]	provozierend, provokativ	❗ stress: **provocative** [prə'vɒkətɪv] (F) provocant, e
(to) **support** [sə'pɔːt]	unterstützen	verb: (to) **support** – My parents always **support** my dreams and plans. noun: **support** (Unterstützung) – My parents are a great **support**.
(to) **back** sth. **up**	etwas untermauern (*Argument*)	Have you got any facts to **~ up** this statement?
(to) **restate** sth. [ˌriː'steɪt]	etwas wiederholen, etwas noch einmal formulieren	I would like to **~** my support for this suggestion.
(to) **call for** sth.	etwas verlangen, etwas fordern; zu etwas auffordern	Many people are **~ing for** a change in the law.
sex [seks]	Geschlecht	What **~** is their new baby? (F) le sexe
marriage ['mærɪdʒ]	Ehe; Heirat	verb: (to) **marry** – adj: **married** – noun: **marriage** (F) le mariage
same-sex marriage	gleichgeschlechtliche Ehe	

[b] **b**oat · [p] **p**ool · [d] **d**ad · [t] **t**en · [g] **g**ood · [k] **c**at ·
[m] **m**um · [n] **n**o · [ŋ] so**ng** · [l] **h**ello · [r] **r**ed · [w] **w**e · [j] **y**ou

p. 20	**paragraph break** ['pærəgrɑːf breɪk]	Absatzumbruch
	pay [peɪ]	Bezahlung, Lohn
	(to) **discriminate against** sb. [dɪˈskrɪmɪneɪt]	jn. diskriminieren, jn. benachteiligen
	sadly [ˈsædli]	leider, bedauerlicherweise
	(to) **take time off**	sich frei nehmen
	(to) **raise your voice** [reɪz]	seine Stimme erheben
	fine [faɪn]	Geldstrafe
	(to) **take** sth./sb. **seriously** [ˈsɪəriəsli]	etwas/jn. ernst nehmen
	unequal [ʌnˈiːkwəl]	ungleich
p. 21	**persuasion** [pəˈsweɪʒn]	Überredung, Überzeugung
	(to) **persuade** [pəˈsweɪd]	überreden
	anecdote [ˈænɪkdəʊt]	Anekdote
	historical [hɪˈstɒrɪkl]	historisch, geschichtlich
	factual [ˈfæktʃʊəl]	sachlich; faktisch; den Tatsachen entsprechend
	expressive [ɪkˈspresɪv]	ausdrucksstark, aussagekräftig
	rhetorical [rɪˈtɒrɪkl]	rhetorisch
	(to) **deny** [dɪˈnaɪ]	bestreiten, abstreiten; leugnen
	emphatic [ɪmˈfætɪk]	nachdrücklich, eindringlich, emphatisch
	improvement [ɪmˈpruːvmənt]	Verbesserung

Right-hand examples:

- verb: (to) **pay (for)** – noun: **pay**
- *English:* (to) **discriminate against sb.**
  German: **jn. diskriminieren**
  English: (to) **discriminate on pay**
  German: **beim Lohn diskriminieren**
  Ⓕ discriminer Ⓛ discriminare (*unterscheiden*)
- ~, I never knew my grandmother.
  adj: **sad** (traurig) – adv: **sadly**
- We **took** ~ **off** and went to Devon for a few days.
- My mother got a ~ for driving through a red light.
- You should fly less if you ~ climate change **seriously**.
  ❗ *not:* ... take climate change ~~serious~~
- **equal** ◄► **unequal**
- Ⓕ la persuasion
- I didn't want to go at first, but Paul ~**d** me that it would be fun. Ⓕ persuader Ⓛ persuadere
- ❗ stress: **anecdote** [ˈænɪkdəʊt] Ⓕ l'anecdote (f)
- The town's main ~ attraction is a 12th century castle.
- You need more ~ information to back up your argument.
- The book is written in a very ~ style. Ⓛ expressus, a, um (*anschaulich*)
- When someone asks a ~ question, they usually want to stress a point, not get an answer. Ⓕ rhétorique Ⓛ rhetoricus, a, um
- He **denied** stealing the money.
  or: He **denied** that he had stolen the money.
- She answered with an ~ "yes" when we invited her to be on the team.
- verb: (to) **improve** – noun: **improvement**

Part C

p. 22	**cell** [sel]	Zelle

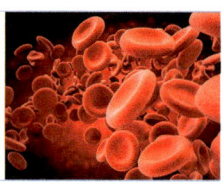
blood **cells**

	genetics [dʒəˈnetɪks]	Genetik
	gene [dʒiːn]	Gen
	genetic [dʒəˈnetɪk]	genetisch
	human race [ˌhjuːmən ˈreɪs]	Menschheit
	aid [eɪd]	Hilfe, Unterstützung

- Ⓕ la génétique Ⓛ genus, eris n (*Abstammung*)
- Ⓛ humanus, i m
- **First Aid** = Erste Hilfe

[f] **f**ather · [v] ri**v**er · [s] **s**i**s**ter · [z] plea**s**e · [ʃ] **sh**op · [ʒ] televi**s**ion ·
[tʃ] **t**ea**ch**er · [dʒ] **G**ermany · [θ] **th**anks · [ð] **th**is · [h] **h**ere

technology [tekˈnɒlədʒi]	Technik, Technologie	❗ stress: **techn<u>o</u>logy** [tekˈn<u>ɒ</u>lədʒi] Ⓕ la technologie
ancient [ˈeɪnʃənt]	(ur)alt; antik	Look at this coin I found in the garden! It must be ~. Ⓕ ancien, ne
(to) **rust** [rʌst]	rosten, verrosten	The old pipe has **rusted** through.
(to) **erode** [ɪˈrəʊd]	abtragen, erodieren, auswaschen *(Boden)*	The cliff has been ~**d** by the sea and could collapse.
earthquake [ˈɜːθkweɪk]	Erdbeben	destroyed by an **earthquake**
species [ˈspiːʃiːz], *pl* **species**	Art, Spezies	Ⓛ species, ei f
record [ˈrekɔːd]	Aufzeichnung(en)	❗ noun: **record** [ˈrekɔːd] **1.** Schallplatte; **2.** Rekord; **3.** Aufzeichnung(en) verb: (to) **record** [rɪˈkɔːd] aufzeichnen *(Musik, Daten)*; dokumentieren *(Daten)* Ⓛ recordari *(sich erinnern)*
(to) **be around** [əˈraʊnd]	da sein, dabei sein; in der Nähe sein	A friend is someone who **is** always ~ when you need them.
skeleton [ˈskelɪtn]	Skelett	a **skeleton**
astonishment [əˈstɒnɪʃmənt]	Erstaunen	adj: **astonished** [əˈstɒnɪʃt] (erstaunt) – noun: **astonishment**
excitement [ɪkˈsaɪtmənt]	Aufregung, Begeisterung	adj: **excited; exciting** – noun: **excitement** Ⓛ excitare *(begeistern)*
frustration [frʌˈstreɪʃn]	Frust; Enttäuschung	noun: **frustration** – adj: **frustrating, frustrated** We weren't successful – that's very **frustrating**. (frustrierend) We were very **frustrated**. (frustriert)
the ups and downs	die Höhen und Tiefen	You have to learn to live with the ~ **and downs** of life.
p.23 **compound** [ˈkɒmpaʊnd]	Verbindung	**chemical** ~ = chemische Verbindung
(to) **contain** [kənˈteɪn]	enthalten, beinhalten	I don't want to eat this. It ~**s** meat, and I'm a vegetarian. verb: (to) **contain** – noun: **content**
instruction [ɪnˈstrʌkʃn]	Anweisung	Before you use this machine, please read the ~**s** carefully. nouns: *(what you tell others)* **instruction**; *(person)* **instructor** – verb: (to) **instruct** sb. **to do** sth. (jn. anweisen, etwas zu tun)

[iː] green · [i] happy · [ɪ] big · [e] red · [æ] cat · [ɑː] class · [ɒ] song · [ɔː] door · [uː] blue · [ʊ] book · [ʌ] mum · [ɜː] girl · [ə] a partner

210   two hundred and ten

organism [ˈɔːɡənɪzəm]	Organismus	Ⓛ organum, i n. (Werkzeug, Instrument, Organ)
(to) **pack** [pæk]	packen; verpacken	
controversial [ˌkɒntrəˈvɜːʃl]	kontrovers, umstritten	Ⓛ controversia, -ae f. (Streit)
whereas [ˌweərˈæz]	während, wohingegen	
humanity [hjuːˈmænəti]	Menschheit; Menschlichkeit, Humanität	❗ humanity = 1. Menschheit – Climate change is one of the big challenges facing **humanity**. 2. Menschlichkeit – I think war is a crime against **humanity**.
bacteria *(pl)* [bækˈtɪəriə]	Bakterien	
(to) **be located (in …)** [ləʊˈkeɪtɪd]	(in …) liegen, sich (in …) befinden	verb: (to) **be located** (in …) – noun: **location**
(to) **remove** [rɪˈmuːv]	entfernen, beseitigen; ausziehen *(Kleidung)*	(to) take sth. away; (to) take (clothes) off
harmless [ˈhɑːmləs]	harmlos	This animal looks ~ but is very dangerous.
extraordinary [ɪkˈstrɔːdnri]	außergewöhnlich	Ⓛ extraordinarius Ⓕ extraordinair/e
breakthrough [ˈbreɪkθruː]	Durchbruch	
precise [prɪˈsaɪs]	genau, präzise	Ⓛ praecidere, -cidi, -cisum *(abschneiden)*
accurate [ˈækjərət]	genau, präzise	precise
method [ˈmeθəd]	Methode	Is this a reliable ~ of testing / testing ~? ❗ stress: **method** [ˈmeθəd]
cancer [ˈkænsə]	Krebs *(Erkrankung)*	
permanent [ˈpɜːmənənt]	permanent, dauerhaft	❗ stress: **permanent** [ˈpɜːmənənt]
pill [pɪl]	Pille, Tablette	
fear (of) [fɪə]	Angst (vor)	verb: (to) **fear** The workers ~**ed** their boss. – noun: **fear (of)** (Angst (vor)) I have a **fear of** rats.
so-called [ˌsəʊ ˈkɔːld]	sogenannt	
topping [ˈtɒpɪŋ]	Überzug, Belag; Soße	with a cheese **topping** = mit Käse überbacken
unethical [ʌnˈeθɪkl]	unethisch	
with regard to [rɪˈɡɑːd]	bezüglich	
(to) **acquire** [əˈkwaɪə]	erwerben, in den Besitz gelangen	Ⓛ acquirare, acquivisi, acquisitum
p.24 **newsreader** [ˈnjuːzriːdə]	Nachrichtensprecher/in	
power line [ˈpaʊə laɪn]	Überlandleitung	**power lines**
(to) **repair** [rɪˈpeə]	reparieren	verb: (to) **repair** – noun: **repair** Ⓛ reparare *(erneuern)*
high winds *(pl)*	starker Wind, starke Winde	
rail link [ˌreɪl ˈlɪŋk]	Bahnverbindung	

p.27	**applause** [əˈplɔːz]	Beifall, Applaus	The audience burst into wild/warm/loud/ spontaneous ~.
			There was only a little polite ~ from the audience.
			(F) les applaudissements (m; pl)
			(L) applaudere (Beifall klatschen)
	climax [ˈklaɪmæks]	Höhepunkt	The ~ of the show was Adele's performance of her latest hit.
	single [ˈsɪŋgl]	einzige(r, s)	There was not a ~ biscuit left.
			❗ **single** = **1.** einzige(r, s); **2.** ledig, alleinstehend
			(L) singulus, a, um

Unit 2   What makes a community?

pp.32/33	(to) **define** [dɪˈfaɪn]	definieren; charakterisieren, ausmachen	How would you ~ "tolerance"?
			Liberty, democracy and equal rights ~ us as a society.
			verb: (to) **define** – noun: **definition** [ˌdefɪˈnɪʃn]
			(F) définir (L) definire

Part A

p.34	**meeting** [ˈmiːtɪŋ]	Treffen; Besprechung, Versammlung	verb: (to) **meet** – noun: **meeting**
	jungle [ˈdʒʌŋgl]	Dschungel	(F) la jungle
	the locals (pl) [ˈləʊklz]	die Einheimischen	(L) locus (Ort, Platz)
	villager [ˈvɪlɪdʒə]	Dorfbewohner/in	(L) villa (Landhaus)
	(to) **observe** [əbˈzɜːv] (fml)	beobachten	The patient should stay in hospital and be ~**d** for a week.
			(F) observer (L) observare
	(to) **affect** [əˈfekt]	betreffen, sich auswirken auf; beeinflussen	Climate change will ~ all of us.
			(= Climate change will have an effect on all of us.)
			(L) afficere
	drunk [drʌŋk]	betrunken	If you drink too much beer, you'll get ~.
	(to) **save** [seɪv]	sparen; speichern	❗ (to) **save** = **1.** sparen; **2.** retten; **3.** speichern, sichern
	therefore [ˈðeəfɔː]	daher, deshalb	The village is remote and is ~ difficult to reach.
	(to) **infect** [ɪnˈfekt]	infizieren; anstecken	verb: (to) **infect** – adj: **infected** (infiziert; entzündet)
			(L) inficere (vergiften)
	cream [kriːm]	Creme; Salbe	
			cream
	liquid [ˈlɪkwɪd]	Flüssigkeit	
			a red **liquid** (F) le liquide (L) liquidum
	manners (pl) [ˈmænəz]	Manieren	Don't forget your ~. Take your feet off the seat.
	no matter if/whether; no matter what/who/ how/… [ˈmætə]	ganz gleich, ob; ganz gleich, was/wer/wie/…	The boss often bursts into my office, **no** ~ **whether** I'm busy or on the phone or anything.
			I don't want to see him again, **no** ~ **how** often he tells me he loves me.

[b] **b**oat · [p] **p**ool · [d] **d**ad · [t] **t**en · [g] **g**ood · [k] **c**at ·
[m] **m**um · [n] **n**o · [ŋ] so**ng** · [l] **h**ello · [r] **r**ed · [w] **w**e · [j] **y**ou

(to) **happen to do** sth. [ˈhæpn]	zufällig(erweise) etwas tun	Do you ~ **to** know the way to the post office? I met my class teacher last week. She ~**ed to** be in Paris at the same time as me.
(to) **teach** sb. **a lesson**	jm. eine Lektion erteilen	I made a mistake, but it **taught me an** important ~.
(to) **trade** [treɪd]	(ein)tauschen; Handel treiben	He ~**d** his sweets for a toy car. Germany ~**s** a lot with China. verb: (to) **trade** – noun: **trade** *(L)* tradere *(übergeben)*
bullet [ˈbʊlɪt]	(Gewehr-)Kugel	**bullets**
(to) **return** [rɪˈtɜːn]	zurückkehren, zurückkommen	verb: (to) **return** – noun: **return** (Rückkehr)
p. 35 **greeting** [ˈgriːtɪŋ]	Begrüßung	noun: **greeting** – verb: (to) **greet** (begrüßen) When we arrived, we were ~**ed** by the head teacher.
(to) **respond** [rɪˈspɒnd]	antworten, erwidern; reagieren	I said hi, but she didn't ~. (= she didn't answer) He ~**s** very quickly if you need help. (= he reacts) *(F)* répondre *(L)* respondere
post [pəʊst]	Pfosten	a **fence post**
turtle [ˈtɜːtl]	Wasserschildkröte	❗ **turtle** = Wasserschildkröte **tortoise** = Landschildkröte *(In den USA wird **turtle** umgangssprachlich für alle Arten von Schildkröten verwendet.)*
the other day	neulich	I met my old class teacher **the** ~ **day**.
sense [sens]	Vernunft, Verstand	Why did you do that? Don't you have any ~ at all? *(L)* sensus
pole [pəʊl]	Stange, Pfahl, Mast	**flagpole** (Flaggenmast, Fahnenmast) **tent poles** (Zeltstangen) **curtain pole** (Gardinenstange) **telegraph pole** (Telegrafenmast) **totem pole** (Totempfahl) **ski poles** (Skistöcke)
(to) **come to an understanding**	sich einigen; zu einer Übereinkunft kommen	They **came to an** ~ that she would work and he would stay at home.
none of us [nʌn]	keine/r von uns	He had 11 cousins but ~ **of them** lived near him.
stingy [ˈstɪndʒi] *(infml)*	knauserig, geizig	**generous ◀▶ stingy**

[f] **f**ather · [v] ri**v**er · [s] **s**ister · [z] plea**s**e · [ʃ] **sh**op · [ʒ] televi**s**ion ·
[tʃ] **t**ea**ch**er · [dʒ] **G**ermany · [θ] **th**anks · [ð] **th**is · [h] **h**ere

two hundred and thirteen   213

(to) **refuse** [rɪˈfjuːz]	sich weigern, ablehnen	(to) **refuse** = sich weigern, ablehnen · I asked him to help me, but he ~**d**. · She was very proud and ~**d** her friend's help. · (to) **refuse to do sth.** = sich weigern / es ablehnen, etwas zu tun He ~**d** to help his brother with his homework.	

p. 36 **mattress** [ˈmætrəs]	Matratze	❗ stress: <u>mattress</u>
		         [ˈmætrəs]
		
		      some **mattresses**	

(to) **reach for** sth.	nach etwas greifen	Remember your manners. Don't just ~ **for** the butter.	
(to) **unwrap** [ʌnˈræp]	auspacken, auswickeln	I just love ~**ping** my presents at Christmas.	
(to) **indicate** sth./sb. [ˈɪndɪkeɪt] *(fml)*	auf etwas/jn. zeigen, deuten, hinweisen	Pointing to the left, the police officer ~**d** the direction we should take. With a small movement of his hand, he ~**d** that we should sit down. Ⓕ indiquer Ⓛ indicare	
p. 37 **narrative** [ˈnærətɪv]	Erzählung, Geschichte	**first-person narrative** = Ich-Erzählung	
prose [prəʊz]	Prosa		
fiction [ˈfɪkʃn]	Belletristik, Prosa(literatur); Märchen, Fiktion	Do you only read history and science books? – No, I like ~ too, like the Harry Potter series. Don't believe him … everything he says is ~.	
graphic novel [ˌgræfɪk ˈnɒvl]	Bildroman, Comicroman		
non-fiction [ˌnɒn ˈfɪkʃn]	Sachliteratur	**fiction** ◄► **non-fiction**	
companion [kəmˈpænjən]	Begleiter/in, Gefährte/-in	Ⓕ compagnon	
sympathy [ˈsɪmpəθi]	Sympathie; Mitgefühl	❗ stress: <u>sympathy</u> [ˈsɪmpəθi]	
(to) succeed [səkˈsiːd]	Erfolg haben	(to) **succeed in doing** sth. = es schaffen, etwas zu tun verb: (to) **succeed** – noun: **success** – adj: **successful**	
observation [ˌɒbzəˈveɪʃn]	Beobachtung	verb: (to) **observe** – noun: **observation**	
omniscient [ɒmˈnɪsiənt]	allwissend	Ⓛ omnisciens	
p. 39 **messaging app** [ˈmesɪdʒɪŋ æp]	Chatprogramm		
p. 40 **footage** [ˈfʊtɪdʒ]	Bildmaterial, Film(material)		
p. 41 **cotton** [ˈkɒtn]	Baumwolle	Ⓕ coton	
reflection [rɪˈflekʃn] (*in BE auch:* **reflexion**)	Betrachtung, Reflexion	❗ stress: <u>ref</u>lection [rɪˈflekʃn]	

Part B

p. 42 **review** [rɪˈvjuː]	Rezension, Besprechung, Kritik	Before I buy a book, I try to read a few ~**s** of it.	
(to) **review** [rɪˈvjuː]	besprechen, rezensieren	That new play was ~**ed** in the paper this morning.	
fictional [ˈfɪkʃənl]	fiktiv, erfunden	❗ stress: <u>fic</u>tional [ˈfɪkʃənl] noun: **fiction** – adjective: **fictional** Ⓛ fingere, fictum *(sich ausdenken)*	
misunderstanding [ˌmɪsʌndəˈstændɪŋ]	Missverständnis	There was a ~ about my meal. I had ordered chicken but the waiter brought me a hamburger.	

214   two hundred and fourteen

[iː] **green** · [i] **happy** · [ɪ] **big** · [e] **red** · [æ] **cat** · [ɑː] **class** · [ɒ] **song** ·
[ɔː] **door** · [uː] **blue** · [ʊ] **book** · [ʌ] **mum** · [ɜː] **girl** · [ə] **a partner**

(to) **narrate** [nə'reɪt]	schildern, erzählen	The story is ~**d** by a teenage girl. verb: (to) **narrate** – noun: **narration** Ⓛ narrare
(to) **bathe** [beɪð] *(bes. AE)*	baden	I ~ once a week but take a shower every day.
ignorant ['ɪɡnərənt]	unwissend, nicht informiert, schlecht informiert	He is not stupid, just ~. Ⓛ ignorare *(nicht wissen)*
wife [waɪf], *pl* **wives**	Ehefrau	husband ◄► wife
(to) **put** sth. **off**	etwas aufschieben	We have to do something now. We can't ~ it **off** any longer.
for now	einstweilen, vorerst, fürs Erste	Let's stop for ~ and continue at 2 o'clock.
(to) **abandon** sb. [ə'bændən]	jn. verlassen, im Stich lassen; aussetzen	I think it's terrible how people ~ dogs on busy roads. Ⓕ abandonner
(to) **breastfeed** ['brestfiːd], -fed, -fed	stillen	
eventually [ɪ'ventʃuəli]	schließlich, letzten Endes	We had to wait a long time, but ~ we saw them getting off the train. ❗ false friends: *English* **eventually** = *German* schließlich *English* **perhaps** = *German* eventuell
literally ['lɪtərəli]	im wahrsten Sinne des Wortes; buchstäblich	There was so much noise that it was ~ impossible to concentrate. Ⓕ littéralement Ⓛ littera *(Buchstabe)*
(to) **grow** smaller/old/…, grew, grown	(allmählich) kleiner/alt/… werden	I love you. I want to ~ old with you.

(to) grow

1. Orange trees don't **grow** in cold countries.   wachsen
   I **grew up** in a small village in Cornwall.   aufwachsen
   She wants to be a doctor when she **grows up**.   erwachsen werden

2. You can't **grow** orange trees in cold countries.   anbauen, anpflanzen

3. The sun went down and it **grew** colder.   (allmählich) werden
   Over time, Alicia **grew closer to** Joanna.   jm. näherkommen

---

enormous [ɪ'nɔːməs]	riesig, gewaltig, enorm	My uncle lives in an ~ house with six bathrooms. Ⓕ énorme
credible ['kredəbl]	glaubwürdig, glaubhaft	
informative [ɪn'fɔːmətɪv]	informativ, lehrreich	❗ stress: **informative** [ɪn'fɔːmətɪv] Ⓕ informatif, ve Ⓛ informare *(unterrichten)*
strongly ['strɒŋli]	nachdrücklich, entschieden, eindringlich	I'm ~ against the new plan. We appeal ~ to everyone to give us their support.
engaging [ɪn'ɡeɪdʒɪŋ]	fesselnd *(Literatur, Film u.Ä.)*	I found the book so ~ that I read it in one night.
distant ['dɪstənt]	(weit) entfernt, fern	It will take you a long time to get to such a ~ place. The Romans ruled Britain in the ~ past. adj: **distant** – noun: **distance**
p. 43 (to) **inform** sb. [ɪn'fɔːm]	jn. informieren	Ⓕ informer Ⓛ informare
plot [plɒt]	Handlung(sverlauf) *(eines Films/einer Geschichte)*	the story that a book/film/play tells us

---

[eɪ] name · [aɪ] time · [ɔɪ] boy · [əʊ] old ·
[aʊ] town · [ɪə] here · [eə] where · [ʊə] tour

(to) **hint (at sth.)** [hɪnt]	(etwas) andeuten, durchblicken lassen	She didn't actually say she wanted more money, but she ~**ed at** it. "Oh, it's almost midnight." – "Are you ~**ing** that you'd like to go home now?"
(to) **summarize** [ˈsʌməraɪz]	zusammenfassen	Can you ~ the main points of the book? verb: **summarize** – noun: **summary**
suitable [ˈsuːtəbl]	geeignet, passend	I don't have any ~ clothes for the job interview.
p.44 (to) **appeal to** sb. [əˈpiːl]	für jn. attraktiv sein, jn. ansprechen	She found his style very ~**ing**. noun: **appeal** – verb: (to) **appeal**
ladder [ˈlædə]	Leiter	a **ladder**
p.45 **genre** [ˈʒɑːnrə]	Gattung, Genre	(F) le genre (L) genus, eris n (Gattung, Art)
semi- [ˈsemi]	halb-; Halb-	**semi**-professional; **semi**-official; **semi**-circle; **semi**-final
autobiographical [ˌɔːtəˌbaɪəˈgræfɪkl]	autobiografisch	
intended [ɪnˈtendɪd]	beabsichtigt, gemeint	(L) intendere
powerful [ˈpaʊəfl]	mächtig, kräftig, stark	a ~ country/computer/car/storm
lover [ˈlʌvə]	Liebhaber/in	
(to) **be set in** [set]	spielen in	The film **is** ~ **in** Mexico but filmed in Spain.
hilarious [hɪˈleəriəs]	urkomisch, unheimlich witzig	It wasn't just funny, it was absolutely ~. (L) hilarus, a, um
account [əˈkaʊnt]	Bericht, Schilderung, Darstellung	❗ **account** = 1. Konto; 2. Bericht, Schilderung, Darstellung
emphasis [ˈemfəsɪs]	Betonung, Hervorhebung	
(to) **emphasize** [ˈemfəsaɪz]	betonen, hervorheben	Why did you highlight that word? – I wanted to ~ it.
entertaining [ˌentəˈteɪnɪŋ]	unterhaltsam, amüsant, kurzweilig	
read [riːd]	Lektüre	Her latest novel is a highly entertaining ~.
enjoyable [ɪnˈdʒɔɪəbl]	angenehm, unterhaltsam	verb: (to) **enjoy** – adj: **enjoyable**
lifelike [ˈlaɪflaɪk]	lebensecht, realistisch	a ~ painting/portrait/statue/account/description
gripping [ˈgrɪpɪŋ]	spannend, fesselnd	
meaningful [ˈmiːnɪŋfl]	aussagekräftig	a ~ example/message/statement; ~ statistics
(to) **quote** [kwəʊt]	zitieren	verb: (to) **quote** – noun: **quotation**, **quote** (infml)

Part C

p.46 **diversity** [daɪˈvɜːsəti]	Vielfalt, Verschiedenartigkeit	Our lively discussion has produced a great ~ of ideas. (F) la diversité (L) diversitas, atis f
display [dɪˈspleɪ]	Ausstellung, Vorführung, Schau	❗ stress: **display** [dɪˈspleɪ] His latest paintings are now **on** ~ in our art gallery. (… sind jetzt ausgestellt …)
(to) **title** [ˈtaɪtl]	betiteln, benennen	(to) give sth. a title, a name

[b] **b**oat · [p] **p**ool · [d] **d**ad · [t] **t**en · [g] **g**ood · [k] **c**at · [m] **m**um · [n] **n**o · [ŋ] so**ng** · [l] **h**ello · [r] **r**ed · [w] **w**e · [j] **y**ou

harmony [ˈhɑːməni]	Harmonie, Eintracht	Why can't we live in ~ with nature? ❗ stress: **harmony** [ˈhɑːməni] Ⓕ l'harmonie (f) Ⓛ harmonia
(to) **embrace** [ɪmˈbreɪs]	annehmen, mit offenen Armen begrüßen; (sich) umarmen	For some people it's not easy to ~ new ideas. They said goodbye and ~**d**. Ⓕ s'embrasser
derogatory [dɪˈrɒɡətri] (fml)	abfällig, abwertend	I consider that a very ~ comment. Ⓛ derogare (jm. etwas absprechen)
stereotype [ˈsteriətaɪp]	Klischee(vorstellung), Stereotyp	The film's main character doesn't seem real to me. She's just the ~ of a schoolgirl in love. Ⓕ le stéréotype
(to) **be present** [ˈpreznt]	vorhanden sein; anwesend sein	The 17th century furniture **is** still ~ in this castle. **Was** your dad ~ at your birth? Ⓕ être présent, e Ⓛ praesens
(to) **capture** [ˈkæptʃə]	(ein)fangen (auch im übertragenen Sinne)	The animals were ~**d** about 15 km from the zoo. The first sentence of the book immediately ~**d** my interest. Ⓛ capere, captum
(to) **paste** [peɪst]	(an)kleben; (Computer) einfügen	He was caught **pasting** posters on public buildings.
(to) **install** [ɪnˈstɔːl]	installieren, einrichten	Ⓕ installer
p. 47 (to) **take a stand (on** sth.**/ against** sth.**)**	Stellung beziehen (zu etwas); ein Zeichen setzen	I'm **taking a** ~ **on** pollution by using cotton bags. I think it's important to **take a** ~ **against** bullying. (= to make it very clear that you are against bullying)
collective [kəˈlektɪv]	gemeinschaftlich, vereint	Ⓛ colligere, collegi, collectum
awareness [əˈweənəs]	Bewusstsein, Aufmerksamkeit	
flash mob	Flashmob	
(to) **rise up, rose, risen**	sich erheben, aufstehen	(to) **rise up** = **1.** aufragen, emporragen (Berge, Säulen, Türme, …); **2.** sich erheben, aufstehen
(to) **make a difference**	etwas bewirken, etwas bewegen	
disruption [dɪsˈrʌpʃn]	Störung, Beeinträchtigung; Zusammenbruch	The terrorist attacks caused a ~ of the power supply. **social disruption** = soziale Spannungen, sozialer Zerfall
(to) **frighten sb.** [ˈfraɪtn]	jm. Angst machen	
seldom [ˈseldəm]	selten	not very often
aim [eɪm]	Ziel	noun: **aim** – verb: (to) **aim at** (zielen auf)
crisis [ˈkraɪsɪs], pl **crises**	Krise	an economic / a financial / a political ~
p. 48 **particular** [pəˈtɪkjələ]	bestimmte(r, s), spezielle(r, s)	Are you looking for a ~ kind of bike? **particularly** or **in particular** = insbesondere
option [ˈɒpʃn]	Option, (Wahl-)Möglichkeit	You have two ~**s**: you can wash the dishes or clean the bathroom. ❗ stress: **option** [ˈɒpʃn] Ⓕ l'option (f) Ⓛ optio, onis f (Wunsch, Belieben)
(to) **be committed to** sth. [kəˈmɪtɪd]	sich für etwas verpflichten, sich zu etwas bekennen	Our school is ~ to inclusion and equality.
p. 49 **convinced** [kənˈvɪnst]	überzeugt	
rarely [ˈreəli]	selten; kaum je	adj: **rare** (selten) – adv: **rarely** (selten, kaum je)

[f] **f**ather · [v] **r**i**v**er · [s] **s**i**s**ter · [z] plea**s**e · [ʃ] **sh**op · [ʒ] televi**s**ion ·
[tʃ] **t**ea**ch**er · [dʒ] **G**ermany · [θ] **th**anks · [ð] **th**is · [h] **h**ere

exercise *(no pl)* ['eksəsaɪz]	Bewegung, *(körperliches)* Training	❗	**1. exercise** *(no pl)* = Bewegung – My parents say I need more exercise. **2. exercise(s)** = Übung(en) – I couldn't do **exercises** 4 and 5. ⓛ exercitium *(milit. Übung)*
p. 52 **refine** [rɪ'faɪn]	verfeinern, weiterentwickeln		Ⓕ raffiner
opener ['əʊpnə]	Eröffnung		
ironic [aɪ'rɒnɪk]	ironisch		
dinosaur ['daɪnəsɔː]	Dinosaurier	❗	stress: <u>di</u>nosaur ['daɪnəsɔː]
the United Nations (UN) [juˌnaɪtɪd 'neɪʃnz]	die Vereinten Nationen		
statistic [stə'tɪstɪk]	statistische Tatsache, statistische Größe	❗	**statistic** = statistische Tatsache, statistische Größe; **statistics** *(pl)* [stə'tɪstɪks] = Statistik(en)
carbon ['kɑːbən]	Kohlenstoff		
(to) release [rɪ'liːs]	abgeben, freisetzen		· verb: (to) **release** – 1000 balloons were **~d** in Hyde Park this morning to celebrate the anniversary. We should stop **releasing** greenhouse gases into the atmosphere. (to) **release a prisoner** (eine/n Gefangene/n freilassen) · noun: **release** (Austritt, Freisetzung; Freilassung) ❗ **release** = 1. abgeben, freisetzen / Austritt, Freisetzung; 2. veröffentlichen, herausbringen / Veröffentlichung
bang [bæŋ]	Knall		
memorable ['memərəbl]	einprägsam; unvergesslich		nouns: **memory** (Erinnerung); **memorial** (Denkmal) – adj: **memorable**

Unit 3   How is the world changing?

pp. 56/57 **technological** [ˌteknə'lɒdʒɪkl]	technologisch		noun: **technology** [tek'nɒlədʒi] – adj: **technological** [ˌteknə'lɒdʒɪkl] Ⓕ la technologie – technologique
progress *(no pl)* ['prəʊgres]	Fortschritt(e)		I've made good ~ since I started learning the piano. Ⓕ le progrès ⓛ progredi *(voranschreiten)*
delivery [dɪ'lɪvəri]	Lieferung		~ is free on orders worth ten pounds or more. verb: (to) **deliver** – noun: **delivery**
package ['pækɪdʒ]	Paket		
automation [ˌɔːtə'meɪʃn]	Automatisierung		
drone [drəʊn]	Drohne		
robot ['rəʊbɒt]	Roboter		
artificial [ˌɑːtɪ'fɪʃl]	künstlich, Kunst-		real ◄► **artificial** ~ **intelligence (AI)** = künstliche Intelligenz Ⓕ artificiel,le ⓛ artificium *(Kunstwerk)*
bee [biː]	Biene		a **bee**

[iː] green · [i] happy · [ɪ] big · [e] red · [æ] cat · [ɑː] class · [ɒ] song · [ɔː] door · [uː] blue · [ʊ] book · [ʌ] mum · [ɜː] girl · [ə] a partner

218   two hundred and eighteen

(to) **pollinate** ['pɒləneɪt]	bestäuben	Insects that ~ plants include bees and butterflies.
pollen ['pɒlən]	Blütenstaub	He's sneezing because he's allergic to ~. (L) pollen, inis *n* (Staubmehl)
production [prəˈdʌkʃn]	Produktion, Herstellung	verb: (to) **produce** [prəˈdjuːs] – nouns: **producer** [prəˈdjuːsə], **product** ['prɒdʌkt], **production** [prəˈdʌkʃn] (F) la production (L) producere (herstellen)
panel discussion ['pænl dɪskʌʃn]	Podiumsdiskussion	

Part A

p. 58	(to) **exaggerate** [ɪgˈzædʒəreɪt]	übertreiben	When he says she owns millions and millions, I'm sure he's **exaggerating**. She can't be so rich!
	(to) **be likely to do** sth. ['laɪkli]	wahrscheinlich etwas tun (werden)	I would take an umbrella. It'**s ~ to** rain at this time of the year.
	breakdown ['breɪkdaʊn]	Zusammenbruch	She had so much stress at work that she had/ suffered a **nervous ~**. **nervous breakdown** = Nervenzusammenbruch
	electricity [ɪˌlekˈtrɪsəti]	Elektrizität, Strom	❗ stress: elec**tri**city [ɪˌlekˈtrɪsəti] (F) l'électricité f
	electric [ɪˈlektrɪk]	elektrisch	I play the ~ guitar in our rock band.
	social networking [ˌsəʊʃl ˈnetwɜːkɪŋ]	Kommunikation über Online-Plattformen	Be careful with information about yourself when you're online. Here are some tips for safe **social ~**.
	radical ['rædɪkl]	radikal	❗ stress: **ra**dical ['rædɪkl] (L) radix (Wurzel)
	corporation [ˌkɔːpəˈreɪʃn]	(Handels-)Gesellschaft, Konzern; Körperschaft	How can big international ~s earn lots of money, but often manage to avoid paying their fair share of tax?
	reality [riˈæləti]	Realität, Wirklichkeit	❗ stress: re**a**lity [riˈæləti] noun: **reality** – adjective: **real** (F) réalité
	(to) **claim** [kleɪm]	angeben, behaupten	He looks about 15, but ~s he's 18. verb: (to) **claim** – noun: **claim** (Behauptung)
	obvious ['ɒbviəs]	offensichtlich	adj: **obvious** – It's **obvious** that this will help a lot. adv: **obviously** – It's **obviously** a good idea.
	radiologist [ˌreɪdiˈɒlədʒɪst]	Radiologe/-in	❗ stress: radi**o**logist [ˌreɪdiˈɒlədʒɪst]
	(to) **feature** sth. ['fiːtʃə]	featuren, über etwas berichten	I watched an interesting documentary that ~d the story of how this corporation became so big and successful. verb: (to) **feature** – noun: **feature**
	elsewhere [ˌelsˈweə]	anderswo	Times are over when we can sit back and think that climate change only happens ~.
	fluent ['fluːənt]	fließend, flüssig (Sprache)	adj: **fluent** – noun: **fluency** ['fluːənsi] (Flüssigkeit, Gewandtheit) (L) fluens
	capacity [kəˈpæsəti]	Fähigkeit, Leistungsvermögen	As an actor, you should have a good ~ for learning a lot of text in a short time.
	disconnection [ˌdɪskəˈnekʃn]	Abkopplung, Trennung	There is often a ~ between politicians and ordinary people, which is why many people completely lose interest in politics.

[eɪ] **name** · [aɪ] **time** · [ɔɪ] **boy** · [əʊ] **old** ·
[aʊ] **town** · [ɪə] **here** · [eə] **where** · [ʊə] **tour**

two hundred and nineteen 219

(to) **meditate** [ˈmedɪteɪt]	meditieren	verb: (to) **meditate** – noun: **meditation** [ˌmedɪˈteɪʃn]
basis [ˈbeɪsɪs], *pl* **bases** [ˈbeɪsiːz]	Basis, Grundlage	**on the basis of** sth. ▶ **based on** sth. ⓁＬ basis ⒻＦ base
brain [breɪn]	Gehirn	The ~ is in your head. Without it, you couldn't move, think, remember things or feel anything.
(to) **alter** [ˈɔːltə]	verändern, abändern	(to) change sth. ⓁＬ alterare
current [ˈkʌrənt]	aktuelle(r,s), gegenwärtige(r,s)	**current affairs** *(pl)* = Tagespolitik, aktuelle Ereignisse **current account** = Girokonto
(to) **generate** [ˈdʒenəreɪt]	generieren, erzeugen	(to) produce *(especially energy, electricity, etc.)*
misinformation *(no pl)* [ˌmɪsɪnfəˈmeɪʃn]	Fehlinformation(en), Falschinformation(en)	information that is incorrect
toxic [ˈtɒksɪk]	toxisch, schädlich	poisonous; very bad and unhealthy ⓁＬ toxicum *(Gift)*
database [ˈdeɪtəbeɪs]	Datenbank	We have all our customers' addresses in a ~.
threat [θret]	(Be-)Drohung	noun: **threat** – verb: (to) **threaten**
sentient [ˈsentiənt], [ˈsenʃnt]	empfindungsfähig	able to feel things through the senses **sense** = Sinn, Gefühl, Bewusstsein ⓁＬ sentire *(fühlen)*
p. 59 **collection** [kəˈlekʃn]	Sammlung	noun: **collection** – verb: (to) **collect**
distinct [dɪˈstɪŋkt]	verschieden, unterschiedlich; deutlich	I had the ~ impression that something was wrong. These substances are not the same – they come from two ~ groups of chemicals.
unqualified [ˌʌnˈkwɒlɪfaɪd]	unqualifiziert	not qualified ⒻＦ qualifié
morality [məˈræləti]	Moral, Anstand, gute Sitten	Be careful when you travel abroad. Rules of ~ may vary from culture to culture.
physics [ˈfɪzɪks]	Physik	You cannot create or destroy energy: that's one of the basic laws of ~.
vehicle [ˈviːəkl]	Fahrzeug	Cars and buses, for example, are ~**s**. ❗ stress: <u>ve</u>hicle [ˈviːəkl] ⒻＦ véhicule *m*
traffic [ˈtræfɪk]	Verkehr	There is so much ~ on the roads! I prefer to go by train. There was a lot of ~, so it took us an hour to drive home.
(to) **generalize** [ˈdʒenrəlaɪz]	verallgemeinern	You know a few people from a group, and then you ~ about the whole group? That's called prejudice!
a bunch of … *(infml)* [bʌntʃ]	eine Menge …, ein Bündel …	I learned a whole ~ **of** interesting new things on the course. Don't listen to them. They're a ~ **of** losers.
sceptical [ˈskeptɪkl]	skeptisch	I'm ~ that he'll keep his promise. (= I'm not sure that he'll keep his promise.)
tight [taɪt]	fest, eng; knapp, eng anliegend *(Kleidung)*	We were a very ~ team from the beginning. This dress is too ~. I need a bigger size.
regulation [ˌregjuˈleɪʃn]	Vorschrift; Regulierung	**tight** ~ = strenge Regelung
unpredicted [ˌʌnprɪˈdɪktɪd]	unvorhergesehen	not predicted ⓁＬ praedicere *(vorhersagen)*

[b] **b**oat · [p] **p**ool · [d] **d**ad · [t] **t**en · [g] **g**ood · [k] **c**at · [m] **m**um · [n] **n**o · [ŋ] so**ng** · [l] **h**ello · [r] **r**ed · [w] **w**e · [j] **y**ou

consequence ['kɒnsɪkwəns]	Folge, Konsequenz	Think of the ~**s** before you do that!
polarization [ˌpəʊlərai'zeɪʃn]	Polarisierung	a situation where there are two distinct groups of people with completely opposite opinions; causing such a situation
(to) **stem from** sth. [stem]	von etwas herrühren; etwas entspringen	(to) be a result or consequence of sth.
think tank ['θɪŋk tæŋk]	Expertenkommission, Denkfabrik	a group of experts, e.g. in economy or politics
potential [pə'tenʃl]	potenziell, möglich	❗ stress: po**ten**tial [pə'tenʃl] adj: **potential** – noun: **potential** (Potenzial)
(to) **have** sb's. **best interests at heart**	jds. Bestes wollen	Parents often say they only have their children's **best ~ at heart**.
deliberate [dɪ'lɪbərət]	absichtlich, vorsätzlich	Was it a ~ act? = Did you do this ~**ly**? Or did you do it **by accident**? (aus Versehen) **deliberately ◄► by accident** (aus Versehen) Ⓛ deliberare *(abwägen)*

p. 60 (to) **last** [lɑːst]	(an)dauern; halten	(to) **take** – (to) **last**
		1. *(Zeit benötigen)* **take**
		   It usually **takes** 15 minutes to get home, but this evening it **took** (us) an hour.
		2. *(andauern; halten)* **last**
		   A football match **lasts** 90 minutes.
		   Cheap toys often don't **last** very long.

strike [straɪk]	Streik	*English:* (to) **go on strike** *German:* **streiken, in den Streik treten** *English:* (to) **be on strike** *German:* **streiken, sich im Streik befinden**
sequence ['siːkwəns]	Abfolge, Reihenfolge	Police are investigating the ~ of events on the night of the crime. Ⓛ sequentia
isle [aɪl]	(kleine) Insel, Eiland	the **British Isles** *(pl)* = die Britischen Inseln
frequency ['friːkwənsi]	Häufigkeit	Scientists believe that climate change is behind the growing ~ of autumn storms. Ⓕ la fréquence Ⓛ frequentia
manner ['mænə]	Art und Weise	He was very friendly and spoke to us in a relaxed ~.
p. 61 (to) **manage** sth. ['mænɪdʒ]	etwas handhaben, bedienen; mit etwas umgehen	You need to ~ your money better. ❗ (to) **manage** sth. = **1.** etwas schaffen; etwas zustande bringen; **2.** etwas handhaben, etwas bedienen
(to) **charge** [tʃɑːdʒ]	(auf)laden	I can't make any calls right now – I have to ~ my mobile first. Ⓕ charger
(to) **swipe** [swaɪp]	*(am Touchscreen)* wischen, *(mit dem Finger)* streichen/fahren; *(Kreditkarte u.Ä.)* durchziehen	To view the next picture, ~ left. We had to ~ a card at the door to get into our hotel room.
button ['bʌtn]	Knopf; Taste	some **buttons** Ⓕ le bouton

[f] **f**ather · [v] **r**i**v**er · [s] **s**i**s**ter · [z] plea**s**e · [ʃ] **sh**op · [ʒ] televi**s**ion ·
[tʃ] **t**ea**ch**er · [dʒ] **G**ermany · [θ] **th**anks · [ð] **th**is · [h] **h**ere

two hundred and twenty-one   221

icon [ˈaɪkən]	Symbol, Icon	some **icons**
menu [ˈmenjuː]	(Computer) Menü	❗ **menu** = 1. Speisekarte; 2. (Computer) Menü
search bar [ˈsɜːtʃ bɑː]	(Computer) Suchfeld, Suchleiste	Enter the word or phrase in the **search** ~.
tab [tæb]	Tab, Reiter (Karteikarte, Browser)	Click here to open a new ~.
(to) navigate [ˈnævɪgeɪt]	navigieren, steuern	It's an interesting website, but it's difficult to ~. ⓕ naviguer ⓛ navigare (ein Schiff steuern)
data [ˈdeɪtə]	Daten	❗ English: The **data** shows that … / The **data** was collected in … German: Die **Daten** zeigen, dass … / Die **Daten** wurden in … gesammelt.
(to) download sth. [ˌdaʊnˈləʊd]	etwas herunterladen	
memory [ˈmeməri]	(Computer) Speicher	❗ **memory** = 1. Erinnerung; Gedächtnis; 2. (Computer) Speicher ⓕ la mémoire ⓛ memoria (Erinnerung)
(to) run [rʌn], ran, run	ausführen (Computerprogramm)	
(to) browse [braʊz]	(durch)stöbern; (durch)blättern; browsen, (im Internet) surfen	(to) **browse** around a shop/museum (to) **browse** through a magazine/book (to) **browse** the internet/a website
(to) customize [ˈkʌstəmaɪz]	anpassen, individuell einrichten	You can ~ the app by clicking on "Options".
settings (pl) [ˈsetɪŋz]	Einstellungen	
attachment [əˈtætʃmənt]	Anhang (einer E-Mail)	(to) add/send/download/delete an **attachment**
friend request [ˈfrend rɪˌkwest]	Freundschaftsanfrage	When someone accepts your **friend** ~, their name appears in your list of friends.

Part B

p. 62 feature article [ˈfiːtʃər ˌɑːtɪkl]	Sonderbericht, Sonderbeitrag	
(to) buzz off [ˌbʌzˈɒf] (infml)	abschwirren, einen Abflug machen	
trap [træp]	Falle	a **trap**
(to) sting [stɪŋ], stung, stung [stʌŋ]	stechen; brennen	Some insects can ~. These eyedrops will ~ a little, but not for long.
crop [krɒp]	(Feld-)Frucht	What kinds of ~s do you grow on your farm?
colony [ˈkɒləni]	Kolonie	
factor [ˈfæktə]	Faktor	
use [juːs]	Gebrauch, Verwendung	❗ pronunciation: (to) **use** (verb) [juːz] **use** (noun) [juːs] ⓛ usus, us m
pesticide [ˈpestɪsaɪd]	Schädlingsbekämpfungsmittel, Pestizid	ⓕ le pesticide
varied [ˈveərid]	abwechslungsreich; verschiedenartig, vielfältig	Doctors say it's important to have a ~ diet. Public opinion on the issue was ~.
diet [ˈdaɪət]	Ernährung(sweise), Speiseplan; Diät	
(to) rely on sth. [rɪˈlaɪ]	auf etwas angewiesen sein	

[iː] green · [i] happy · [ɪ] big · [e] red · [æ] cat · [ɑː] class · [ɒ] song · [ɔː] door · [uː] blue · [ʊ] book · [ʌ] mum · [ɜː] girl · [ə] a partner

parasite [ˈpærəsaɪt]	Parasit	❗ stress: **parasite** [ˈpærəsaɪt] Ⓕ le parasite
mite [maɪt]	Milbe	
(to) **weaken** [ˈwiːkən]	schwächen	adj: **weak** – verb: (to) **weaken**
immune system [ɪˈmjuːn sɪstəm]	Immunsystem	Ⓛ immunis, e (befreit, verschont)
(to) **be prone to** sth. [prəʊn]	anfällig sein für etwas; zu etwas neigen	Human beings **are ~ to** making mistakes.
hibernation [ˌhaɪbəˈneɪʃn]	Winterschlaf	In winter, bears go into ~. Ⓛ hibernare (überwintern)
habitat [ˈhæbɪtæt]	Lebensraum	The natural ~ of the panda is China.
(to) **shrink** [ʃrɪŋk], **shrank** [ʃræŋk], **shrunk** [ʃrʌŋk]	schrumpfen	If you wash this pullover too hot, it will ~. The population of eastern Germany **shrank** from 17 million in 1990 to 14 million in the 2010s.
(to) **compensate** [ˈkɒmpenseɪt]	kompensieren, ausgleichen; entschädigen	How do vegetarians ~ for not eating meat? The company will ~ customers for poor service. ❗ stress: **compensate** [ˈkɒmpenseɪt] Ⓕ compenser Ⓛ compensare
worrying [ˈwʌriɪŋ]	beunruhigend	verb: (to) **worry** – adj: **worrying**
(to) **lay** [leɪ], **laid, laid** [leɪd]	legen	❗ (to) **lie, lay, lain** = liegen – Our dog is not allowed to **lie** on the sofa. (to) **lay, laid, laid** = legen – You can **lay** your jacket on the sofa.
(to) **ensure** [ɪnˈʃʊə, ɪnˈʃɔː]	gewährleisten, sicherstellen	(to) make sure
survival [səˈvaɪvl]	Überleben	noun: **survival** – verb: (to) **survive**
muesli [ˈmjuːzli]	Müsli	
p. 63 (to) **announce** [əˈnaʊns]	bekanntgeben; verkünden	The winner will be **~d** tomorrow. verb: (to) **announce** – noun: **announcement** Ⓕ annoncer Ⓛ annuntiare
generation [ˌdʒenəˈreɪʃn]	Erzeugung	Innovation will lead to the ~ of new jobs. ❗ **generation** = 1. Generation; 2. Erzeugung Ⓕ la génération Ⓛ generare (erzeugen)
pilot [ˈpaɪlət]	Pilot/in	❗ stress / pronunciation: **pilot** [ˈpaɪlət] Ⓕ le/la pilote
p. 64 **overall** [ˌəʊvəˈrɔːl]	Gesamt-; allgemeine(r, s)	What is the ~ cost of buying a house?
effectiveness [ɪˈfektɪvnəs]	Wirksamkeit, Effektivität	adj: **effective** – noun: **effectiveness** Ⓛ efficere (etwas bewirken)
disappearance [ˌdɪsəˈpɪərəns]	Verschwinden; Aussterben	verb: (to) **disappear** – noun: **disappearance**
(to) **damage** [ˈdæmɪdʒ]	(be)schädigen, schaden	Smoking **~s** your health. The car had hit a tree. It was badly **~d**. Ⓛ damnum (Schaden)
infrastructure [ˈɪnfrəstrʌktʃə]	Infrastruktur	We need to spend a lot more money on our education ~.
polar bear [ˈpəʊlə beə]	Eisbär	
organic [ɔːˈɡænɪk]	biologisch angebaut, Bio-	
p. 65 **concise** [kənˈsaɪs]	knapp, kurz, prägnant	Give a ~ explanation without going into too much detail. Ⓛ concisus, a, um

[eɪ] n**a**me · [aɪ] t**i**me · [ɔɪ] b**oy** · [əʊ] **o**ld ·
[aʊ] t**own** · [ɪə] h**ere** · [eə] wh**ere** · [ʊə] t**our**

nightmare [ˈnaɪtmeə]	Albtraum	
(to) **pinch** [pɪntʃ]	kneifen	Please ~ me so I know I'm not dreaming!
p. 66 **viewer** [ˈvjuːə]	Zuschauer/in	

Part C

p. 68 **imagination** [ɪˌmædʒɪˈneɪʃn]	Fantasie, Vorstellung(skraft)	verb: (to) **imagine** – noun: **imagination**
		(F) imaginer – l'imagination f
		(L) imaginatio, onis f
bookstore [ˈbʊkʃɒp]	Buchladen, Buchhandlung	
bankrupt [ˈbæŋkrʌpt]	bankrott	❗ stress: **bankrupt** [ˈbæŋkrʌpt]
clerk [klɑːk]	(Büro-)Angestellte(r)	
for sale [seil]	zum Verkauf, zu verkaufen	
identical [aɪˈdentɪkl]	identisch	The two versions are very similar but not totally ~.
		(F) identique
alternative [ɔːlˈtɜːnətɪv]	Alternative	❗ stress: **alternative** [ɔːlˈtɜːnətɪv]
		(F) l'alternative f (L) alternare (abwechseln)
hypothetical [ˌhaɪpəˈθetɪkl]	hypothetisch	a **hypothetical** question
vertical [ˈvɜːtɪkl]	vertikal, senkrecht	**vertical** ◄► **horizontal** [ˌhɒrɪˈzɒntl] (horizontal, waagerecht)
civilization [ˌsɪvəlaɪˈzeɪʃn]	Zivilisation	(F) la civilisation
		(L) civis, is m/f (Bürger/in, Stadtbewohner/in)
smart [smɑːt]	schlau, intelligent	clever
ratio [ˈreɪʃiəʊ]	(Größen-, Zahlen-)Verhältnis	The ~ of boys to girls in class 10 is 3 : 4.
		(L) ratio, onis f
(to) **program** [ˈprəʊgræm]	programmieren	verb: (to) **program** – noun: **program** ((Computer-) Programm)
		❗ · **programme** (BE) / **program** (AE) = 1. Programm; 2. (Fernseh-/Radio-)Sendung · **program** (BE, AE) = (Computer-)Programm
band [bænd]	Gruppe, Bande, Gang	A ~ of youths threatened us in the city centre last night.
(to) **rule** [ruːl]	herrschen, beherrschen	
immortality [ˌɪmɔːˈtæləti]	Unsterblichkeit, Unvergänglichkeit	**immortality** ◄► **mortality** [ˌmɔːˈtæləti]
		(F) la mortalité – l'immortalité f
		(L) immortalitas, atis f
(to) **put** sth. (+ adv)	etwas (auf eine bestimmte Art) ausdrücken, formulieren	

(to) put sth. politely/simply/… (etwas höflich/einfach/… ausdrücken)	
I don't understand. Can you **put it more simply**?	… Kannst du es einfacher ausdrücken?
Let me **put it (in) a different way**: …	Lass es mich anders sagen/formulieren: …
The food was … **how shall I put it?** … a bit disappointing.	Das Essen war … wie soll ich sagen? …
As my brother put it, "You can't have everything."	Wie mein Bruder es ausdrückte, …
I often find it difficult to **put my feelings into words**.	… meine Gefühle in Worte zu fassen.

[b] **b**oat · [p] **p**ool · [d] **d**ad · [t] **t**en · [g] **g**ood · [k] **c**at ·
[m] **m**um · [n] **n**o · [ŋ] so**ng** · [l] **h**ello · [r] **r**ed · [w] **w**e · [j] **y**ou

(to) **accomplish** sth. [əˈkʌmplɪʃ]	etwas erreichen, vollbringen, bewirken	You'll have to work hard to ~ your goals. *(F) accomplir*
charming [ˈtʃɑːmɪŋ]	charmant, bezaubernd	
(to) **glance (at)** [glɑːns]	einen (kurzen) Blick werfen (auf)	He ~d shyly **at** the girl, and then looked away again.
p. 69 (to) **straighten** sth. [ˈstreɪtn]	etwas gerade rücken, biegen; etwas strecken, straffen	(to) **straighten** one's body/legs/shoulders (aufrichten / ausstrecken / straffen) (to) **straighten** the chairs (gerade rücken)
nuclear [ˈnjuːklɪə]	Kern-, Atom-	
anywhere [ˈeniweə]	überall, überallhin	**where** = wo, wohin **somewhere** = irgendwo(hin) **anywhere** = überall(hin) *(an einen/einem beliebigen Ort)* **everywhere** = überall(hin) *(an jeden/jedem Ort)* **not anywhere** = nirgendwo(hin)
analogy [əˈnælədʒi]	Analogie, Vergleich	❗ stress: an**a**logy [əˈnælədʒi] *(F) l'analogie f*
decent [ˈdiːsnt]	anständig; angemessen	
physical [ˈfɪzɪkl]	physisch, körperlich	Grandpa was ~**ly** weak, but his mind was still active.
cushion [ˈkʊʃn]	Kissen	

some **cushions**

loose [luːs]	lose, locker	She went to the dentist about her ~ tooth.
romance [rəʊˈmæns]	Romantik, romantische Liebe	
romantic [rəʊˈmæntɪk]	romantisch; Liebes-	
(to) **occur to** sb. [əˈkɜː]	jm. einfallen, in den Sinn kommen	The idea ~**red to** me in a dream. *(L) occurrere*
familiar (to sb. / **with** sth.**)** [fəˈmɪlɪə]	(jm. / mit etwas) vertraut	Who's that guy over there? He looks ~, but I can't think of how I might know him.
dozen [ˈdʌzn]	Dutzend	❗ • two **dozen** eggs (zwei Dutzend Eier) • **dozens** of people *(infml)* (Dutzende von Leuten)
somehow [ˈsʌmhaʊ]	irgendwie	~ I'll have to get out of this difficult situation. ~ they managed to escape from prison.
cheek [tʃiːk]	Wange	
p. 70 **reasonable** [ˈriːznəbl]	vernünftig, akzeptabel	Most people find it hard to refuse a ~ request. *(F) raisonnable*
sincerity [sɪnˈserəti]	Ernsthaftigkeit, Aufrichtigkeit	*(F) la sincérité*
sincere [sɪnˈsɪə]	aufrichtig, ehrlich	It is my ~ hope that we'll reach an agreement. *(F) sincerus, a, um*
bright [braɪt]	klug, gescheit, „hell"	❗ **bright** = 1. strahlend, leuchtend, hell; 2. klug, gescheit, „hell"
beneath [bɪˈniːθ]	unterhalb (von)	under
addicted (to) [əˈdɪktɪd]	süchtig (nach), abhängig (von)	adj: **addicted** – They're ~ **to** drugs. noun: **addict** – They're drug **addicts**. [ˈædɪkt] Abhängige/r, Süchtige/r noun: **addiction** – Their **addiction to** drugs is terrible. [əˈdɪkʃn] (Sucht nach, Abhängigkeit von)

[f] **f**ather · [v] **r**iver · [s] **s**ister · [z] plea**s**e · [ʃ] **sh**op · [ʒ] televi**s**ion · [tʃ] **t**eacher · [dʒ] **G**ermany · [θ] **th**anks · [ð] **th**is · [h] **h**ere

two hundred and twenty-five 225

p. 71	**straightforward** [ˌstreɪtˈfɔːwəd]	einfach, klar *(ausgedrückt)*	not complicated
	(to) **lose one's temper**	die Beherrschung verlieren	Even if patients are difficult sometimes, a doctor should not lose their ~. (= should not get angry)
	inner [ˈɪnə]	innere(r, s)	I sometimes wish an ~ voice would give me advice and tell me how to decide.
	motivation [məʊtɪˈveɪʃn]	Motivation	noun: **motivation** – verb: (to) **motivate** sb. **(to do** sth.**)**
	(to) **slam** [slæm]	schlagen; zuknallen *(Tür)*	When I'm angry, I sometimes leave the room, ~**ming** the door behind me.
	surroundings *(pl)* [səˈraʊndɪŋz]	Umgebung	Visit our quiet hotel in beautiful ~ on the shore of Loch Carron!
	(to) **convey** [kənˈveɪ]	vermitteln, übermitteln	The advert tries to ~ the message that this expensive product is a must-have.
	pace [peɪs]	Tempo, Geschwindigkeit; Schritt	Traffic moved at a terribly slow ~. **at a … pace** = mit … Geschwindigkeit Ⓕ pas *m*
	evidence *(no pl)* [ˈevɪdəns]	Nachweis, Beleg, Beweis	The police arrested a man, but there was no ~ that he was the thief they were looking for. Ⓕ évidence *f*
	sensitive [ˈsensətɪv]	einfühlsam, sensibel	❗ *English:* **sensitive** – *German:* **sensibel, einfühlsam** *English:* **sensible** – *German:* **vernünftig; praktisch**
	stylistic [staɪˈlɪstɪk]	stilistisch, Stil-	adjective: **stylistic** – adverb: **stylistically** [staɪˈlɪstɪkli] – noun: **style** – verb: (to) **style** (*(Haare)* stylen; *(Kleidung)* schneiden)
p. 72	**completion** [kəmˈpliːʃn]	Vervollständigung; Abschluss; Fertigstellung	Ⓛ complere, complevi, completum
p. 73	(to) **activate** [ˈæktɪveɪt]	aktivieren	Ⓕ activer
	survey [ˈsɜːveɪ]	Umfrage, Studie	
	(to) **predict** [prɪˈdɪkt]	vorhersagen, voraussagen	verb: (to) **predict** – noun: **prediction** Ⓕ prédire Ⓛ praedicere
	(to) **be concerned about** sth. [kənˈsɜːnd]	über/um/wegen etw. besorgt sein	We could ~ **from** his tone of voice that he didn't like the idea.
	despite [dɪˈspaɪt]	trotz, obwohl	**despite** the dangers = **although** it is/was dangerous
	(to) **view oneself as** sth. [vjuː]	sich als jd./etwas betrachten	verb: (to) **view** – noun: **view**
	confident [ˈkɒnfɪdənt]	selbstsicher; zuversichtlich	Ⓕ confiant Ⓛ confidens
	overwhelming [ˌəʊvəˈwelmɪŋ]	überwältigend	
p. 74	(to) **chair** [tʃeə]	den Vorsitz führen, innehaben	Who's going to ~ our team meeting today?
	moderator [ˈmɒdəreɪtə]	Moderator/in	❗ stress: **moderator** [ˈmɒdəreɪtə]
	(to) **research** [rɪˈsɜːtʃ]	recherchieren	verb: (to) **research** [rɪˈsɜːtʃ] – noun: **research** [ˈriːsɜːtʃ, rɪˈsɜːtʃ]
	(to) **ban** sth. [bæn]	verbieten; für unzulässig erklären	Eating in class is ~**ned** at my school. You can only eat in the break.
	(to) **concern** sb. [kənˈsɜːn]	jn. betreffen, angehen; jn. beunruhigen	Climate change is an issue that ~**s** all of us. Her father's health ~**s** her a lot. Ⓛ concernere *(betreffen)*

[b] **b**oat · [p] **p**ool · [d] **d**ad · [t] **t**en · [g] **g**ood · [k] **c**at · [m] **m**um · [n] **n**o · [ŋ] so**ng** · [l] **h**ello · [r] **r**ed · [w] **w**e · [j] **y**ou

aspect [ˈæspekt]	Aspekt, Gesichtspunkt	There are many ~**s** to think about before you go on a student exchange. ❗ Betonung auf der 1. Silbe: <u>**aspect**</u> [ˈespekt]
(to) **take sides**	Partei ergreifen	As a moderator, you shouldn't ~ **sides** in a discussion.
firmly [ˈfɜːmli]	bestimmt, entschieden, nachdrücklich	"I'm not going to accept that," she said ~. Ⓛ firmus *(fest, stark)*
thorough [ˈθʌrə]	gründlich, sorgfältig	• adj: **thorough** – We were give a **thorough** lesson in how to use the new equipment. • adv: **thoroughly** – You should wash fruit **thoroughly** before eating it.
(to) **rank sth.** [ræŋk]	etwas einstufen, etwas anordnen	Iga Swiatek is ~**ed** number 1 in the world.
counter-argument [ˈkaʊntər‿ˌɑːgjumənt]	Gegenargument	

[f] **f**ather · [v] ri**v**er · [s] **s**i**s**ter · [z] plea**s**e · [ʃ] **sh**op · [ʒ] televi**s**ion ·
[tʃ] **t**ea**ch**er · [dʒ] **G**ermany · [θ] **th**anks · [ð] **th**is · [h] **h**ere

two hundred and twenty-seven   227

Dictionary

Im **English – German Dictionary** kannst du nachschlagen, wenn du wissen möchtest, was ein englisches Wort bedeutet, wie man es ausspricht oder wie es geschrieben wird.

Im **Dictionary** werden folgende **Abkürzungen und Symbole** verwendet:

sth. = something (etwas)   sb. = somebody (jemand)
jd. = jemand   jn. = jemanden   jm. = jemandem
pl = *plural* (Mehrzahl)   *infml* = *informal* (umgangssprachlich)
BE = British English   *AE* = American English
° Mit diesem Kringel sind Wörter markiert, die nicht zum Lernwortschatz gehören.

▶ Der Pfeil weist auf Kästen im **Vocabulary** (S. 202 – 227) hin, in denen du weitere Informationen zu diesem Wort findest.

Die **Fundstellenangaben** zeigen, wo ein Wort zum ersten Mal vorkommt.
I = Band 1;   II = Band 2;   III = Band 3;   IV = Band 4;   V = Band 5;   VI 1 (15) = Band 6, Unit 1, Seite 15

Tipps zur Arbeit mit einem Wörterbuch findest du im Teil Skills & Media Competence auf Seite 190.

A

a [ə] ein, eine I   **once/twice a week** einmal/zweimal pro Woche II
A level (= advanced level) ['eɪ levl] *Prüfungen zur Hochschulzulassungsberechtigung (etwa wie Abitur)* V
abandon sb. [ə'bændən] jn. verlassen, im Stich lassen; aussetzen VI 2 (42)
abbreviation [ə,briːvi'eɪʃn] Abkürzung II
ability [ə'bɪlɪti] Fähigkeit, Können V
able ['eɪbl]: **be able to do sth.** etwas tun können; fähig sein / in der Lage sein, etwas zu tun III
Aboriginal [,æbə'rɪdʒənl] Aborigine- *(die Ureinwohner/- innen Australiens betreffend)* V
Aborigine [,æbə'rɪdʒəni] *Ureinwohner/in Australiens* V
°**abortion** [ə'bɔːʃn] Abtreibung, Schwangerschaftsabbruch
about [ə'baʊt]:
1. über, von I
about me/you/... über mich/dich/... I   **It's about a seagull.** Es geht um eine Möwe. / Es handelt von einer Möwe. I   **the best thing about ...** das Beste an ... III   **What about you?** Und du? / Und was ist mit dir? Und ihr? / Und was ist mit euch? I   **What is the poster about?** Wovon handelt dein Poster? / Worum geht es bei deinem Poster? I
2. ungefähr II
3. **be about to do sth.** im Begriff sein, etwas zu tun; kurz davor sein, etwas zu tun IV

above [ə'bʌv] oben, darüber; über, oberhalb (von) III
abroad [ə'brɔːd] im/ins Ausland V
absolutely ['æbsəluːtli] völlig, absolut III
abstract ['æbstrækt] abstrakt IV
academic [,ækə'demɪk] wissenschaftlich, akademisch V   **academic credits** *(pl)* Anrechnungspunkte (für das Studium); Leistungsnachweis V
academy [ə'kædəmi] Akademie, (Fach-)Hochschule; *(in GB:) unabhängige, direkt von der Regierung finanzierte Schule* V
accent ['æksənt] Akzent III
accept [ək'sept] akzeptieren, annehmen V
acceptable [ək'septəbl] akzeptable, hinnehmbar VI 3 (66)
access ['ækses] Zugang, Zutritt I   **access sth.** auf etwas zugreifen V
accessible [ək'sesəbl] zugänglich, erreichbar V
accident ['æksɪdənt] Unfall III   **by accident** aus Versehen VI 3 (59)
accommodation *(no pl)* [ə,kɒmə'deɪʃn] Unterkunft V
accomplish sth. [ə'kʌmplɪʃ] etwas erreichen, vollbringen, bewirken VI 3 (68)
according to [ə'kɔːdɪŋ tə] laut, zufolge V
account [ə'kaʊnt]:
1. Konto, Account V
2. Bericht, Schilderung, Darstellung VI 2 (45)
accumulate sth. [ə'kjuːmjəleɪt] etwas ansammeln V
°**accuracy** ['ækjərəsi] Genauigkeit
accurate ['ækjərət] genau, präzise VI 1 (23)

°**accuse sb. of sth.** [ə'kjuːz] jdm. etwas vorwerfen
achieve [ə'tʃiːv] erreichen *(Ziel)*, erzielen *(Resultat)*; zustande bringen V
acquaintance [ə'kweɪntəns] Bekannte(r) V
acquire [ə'kwaɪə] erwerben, in den Besitz gelangen VI 1 (23)
across [ə'krɒs]: **across the moor/the street** (quer) über das Moor/die Straße II   **across the world** weltweit; über die ganze Welt V   **come across sb./sth.** stoßen auf, (zufällig) treffen III   **get a message across** eine Botschaft rüberbringen, sich verständlich machen V
act [ækt] schauspielern II   **act out** vorspielen I
action ['ækʃn] Action; Handlung, Tat I
activate ['æktɪveɪt] VI 3 (73)
active ['æktɪv] aktiv V
activist ['æktɪvɪst] Aktivist/in V
activity [æk'tɪvəti] Aktivität I   **free-time activities** Freizeitaktivitäten I
actor ['æktə] Schauspieler/in III
actually ['æktʃuəli] eigentlich; übrigens; tatsächlich III
ad [æd] *kurz für* **advertisement** Werbespot, Werbung; Anzeige, Inserat V
add (to) [æd] hinzufügen, ergänzen, addieren (zu) III
adder ['ædə] Kreuzotter II
addict ['ædɪkt] Abhängige/r, Süchtige/r VI 3 (70)
addicted (to) [ə'dɪktɪd] süchtig (nach), abhängig (von) VI 3 (70)

addition [ə'dɪʃn]: **in addition to …** neben …; außer …; zusätzlich zu … V

address [ə'dres]:
1. Adresse, Anschrift I
2. address sb. zu jm. sprechen; jn. ansprechen; das Wort an jn. richten V

admire [əd'maɪə] bewundern V

adolescent [ˌædə'lesnt] Heranwachsende(r), Jugendliche(r) V

adopt [ə'dɒpt]:
1. adoptieren VI 2 (42)
°**2.** annehmen, übernehmen (Brauch, Religion, Methode u.Ä.)

adult ['ædʌlt] Erwachsene(r) III

°**advance** [əd'vɑːns] (adj) Vor-

advanced [əd'vɑːnst] fortgeschritten; für Fortgeschrittene V
advanced level (A level) (entspricht etwa) Abitur V

advantage [əd'vɑːntɪdʒ] Vorteil III

adventure [əd'ventʃə] Abenteuer II

adventurer [əd'ventʃərə] Abenteurer/in V

adverb ['ædvɜːb] Adverb II

advert ['ædvɜːt] Werbespot, Werbung II

advertise ['ædvətaɪz] Werbung machen (für); inserieren V

advertisement [əd'vɜːtɪsmənt] Werbespot, Werbung; Anzeige, Inserat IV

advertising (no pl) ['ædvətaɪzɪŋ] Werbung; Werbe- V

advice (no pl) [əd'vaɪs] Rat, Ratschlag, Ratschläge IV

advise sb. to do sth. [əd'vaɪz] jm. raten, etwas zu tun IV

affect [ə'fekt] betreffen, sich auswirken auf; beeinflussen VI 2 (34)

afraid [ə'freɪd]: **be afraid (of sth./ sb.)** Angst haben (vor etwas/jm.) IV
I'm afraid … Leider … V

African-American [ˌæfrɪkən_ə'merɪkən] Afroamerikaner/in; afroamerikanisch VI 1 (16)

after ['ɑːftə]:
1. nachdem I
2. nach (zeitlich) I
after all (schließlich) doch VI 1 (18)
after breakfast nach dem Frühstück I **after that** danach III
3. run after sb. hinter jm. herrennen I

afternoon [ˌɑːftə'nuːn] Nachmittag I **in the afternoon** nachmittags, am Nachmittag I **on Saturday afternoon** am Samstagnachmittag I

afterwards ['ɑːftəwədz] nachher, danach IV

again [ə'gen] wieder; noch einmal I
again and again immer wieder II
once again erneut, wieder (einmal), einmal mehr V

against [ə'genst] gegen II

age [eɪdʒ] Alter I **ages ago** vor einer Ewigkeit III **for ages** unendlich lange Zeit III

aged [eɪdʒd] im Alter von V

agent ['eɪdʒnt]: **travel agent** Reisebürokaufmann/-frau V

aggressive [ə'gresɪv] aggressiv VI 1 (14)

ago [ə'gəʊ]: **a week ago** vor einer Woche II

agree [ə'griː]: **agree on sth.** sich auf etwas einigen I **agree to differ** sich darauf einigen, dass man verschiedener Ansicht ist; einsehen, dass man sich nicht einigen kann V
agree with sb. jm. zustimmen I

agreement [ə'griːmənt] Einigung; Vereinbarung I

agriculture ['ægrɪkʌltʃə] Landwirtschaft V

ahead [ə'hed]: **Go ahead.** Leg los. / Fang an. / Nur zu. V

AI (artificial intelligence) [ˌeɪ 'aɪ] künstliche Intelligenz VI 3 (56/57)

aid [eɪd] Hilfe, Unterstützung VI 1 (22)

aim [eɪm] Ziel VI 2 (47)

aim (at) [eɪm] zielen (auf) VI 2 (47)

air [eə] Luft II

airport ['eəpɔːt] Flughafen III **(airport) terminal** Terminal, Abfertigungsgebäude V

alarm (clock) [ə'lɑːm] Wecker VI 1 (12)

alive [ə'laɪv]: **be alive** leben, am Leben sein IV

all [ɔːl] alles; alle I **all alone** ganz allein II **all of Plymouth** ganz Plymouth, das ganze Plymouth I **all over the city / the world** in der ganzen Stadt / auf der ganzen Welt IV **all right** okay; in Ordnung I **all-star team/player** Auswahlmannschaft/-spieler/in V **not … at all** überhaupt nicht(s), gar nicht(s); überhaupt kein/e, gar kein/e II

allergic (to sth.) [ə'lɜːdʒɪk] allergisch (gegen etwas) IV

alligator ['ælɪgeɪtə] Alligator IV

alliteration [əˌlɪtə'reɪʃn] Alliteration, Stabreim, Anlautreim V

allow [ə'laʊ] erlauben, zulassen III
be allowed to do sth. etwas tun dürfen II

allowance [ə'laʊəns] Taschengeld V

almost ['ɔːlməʊst] fast, beinahe I

alone [ə'ləʊn] allein I

along [ə'lɒŋ]: **along the street/the river/...** die Straße/den Fluss/... entlang I **sing along (with sb.)** (mit jm.) mitsingen III

aloud [ə'laʊd]: **read aloud** laut (vor)lesen II

°**alphabetical** [ˌælfə'betɪkl] alphabetisch

already [ɔːl'redi] schon, bereits II

also ['ɔːlsəʊ] auch I

alter ['ɔːltə] verändern, abändern VI 3 (58)

alternative [ɔːl'tɜːnətɪv] Alternative VI 3 (68)

although [ɔːl'ðəʊ] obwohl III

altogether [ˌɔːltə'geðə] insgesamt, alles in allem III

always ['ɔːlweɪz] immer I

am [ˌeɪ_'em]: **4 am** 4 Uhr morgens I

amaze sb. [ə'meɪz] jn. erstaunen, verblüffen V

amazing [ə'meɪzɪŋ] erstaunlich, unglaublich III

ambition [æm'bɪʃn] Ehrgeiz, Bestreben V

ambitious [æm'bɪʃəs] ehrgeizig V

among [ə'mʌŋ] zwischen, unter (mehreren Personen, Tieren, Dingen) V

amount (of) [ə'maʊnt] Betrag, Menge; Höhe (von Gehalt, Taschengeld) V

an [æn], [ən]: **an elephant** ein Elefant I

analogy [ə'nælədʒi] Analogie, Vergleich VI 3 (69)

analyse ['ænəlaɪz] analysieren, auswerten, untersuchen V

analysis [ə'næləsɪs], pl **analyses** Analyse, Auswertung V

ancestor ['ænsestə] Vorfahr/in V

ancient ['eɪnʃənt] (ur)alt; antik VI 1 (22)

and [ænd], [ənd] und I

anecdote ['ænɪkdəʊt] Anekdote VI 1 (21)

angel ['eɪndʒl] Engel V

angry ['æŋgri] wütend I

animal ['ænɪml] Tier I

anniversary [ˌænɪ'vɜːsəri] Jahrestag IV

announce [ə'naʊns] bekanntgeben; verkünden VI 3 (63)

Dictionary

announcement [ə'naʊnsmənt]
Durchsage, Ansage III
annoyed (with sb./about sth.)
[ə'nɔɪd] verärgert (über jn./etwas),
irritiert V
another [ə'nʌðə] ein(e) andere(r, s);
noch ein(e) II
answer ['ɑːnsə]:
1. Antwort I
2. antworten; beantworten I
3. answer the phone ans Telefon
gehen II
ant [ænt] Ameise I
anthem ['ænθəm]: **national anthem**
Nationalhymne IV
antonym ['æntənɪm] Antonym (Ge-
gensatzwort) IV
any ['eni]: **Are there any …?** Gibt
es (irgendwelche) …? I **more than
in any other place** mehr als an
jedem anderen Ort IV **not (…) any
longer** nicht länger; nicht mehr IV
not … any more nicht mehr II
There aren't any … Es gibt/sind
keine … I
anybody? ['enibɒdi] (irgend)je-
mand? II **not … anybody** niemand II
anyone? ['eniwʌn] (irgend)jemand?
II **not … anyone** niemand II
anything? ['eniθɪŋ] (irgend)etwas?
II **anything else?** sonst noch
etwas? III **not … anything** nichts
II
Anyway, … ['eniweɪ] Jedenfalls,
… / Wie dem auch sei, … / Aber egal,
… II **And anyway, …** Und überhaupt, … III
anywhere ['eniweə] überall, überall-
hin VI 3 (69)
apart [ə'pɑːt] auseinander, voneinan-
der entfernt IV
apartment [ə'pɑːtmənt] Wohnung II
app [æp] App III
appeal [ə'piːl]:
1. appeal (to) Appell, Aufruf (an) V
2. appeal to sb. für jn. attraktiv
sein, jn. ansprechen VI 2 (44)
appealing [ə'piːlɪŋ] ansprechend
VI 2 (44)
appear [ə'pɪə] erscheinen, auftauchen II
appearance [ə'pɪərəns]
Erscheinung(sbild), Aussehen V
applause [ə'plɔːz] Beifall, Applaus
VI 1 (27)
apple ['æpl] Apfel II
applicant ['æplɪkənt] Bewerber/in V

application [ˌæplɪ'keɪʃn] Bewerbung
V **letter of application** Bewer-
bungsschreiben V
apply (for sth.) [ə'plaɪ] sich (um/für
etwas) bewerben V
appointment [ə'pɔɪntmənt] Verab-
redung, Termin I
appreciate sb./sth. [ə'priːʃieɪt]
etwas schätzen, etwas zu schätzen
wissen IV
appropriate [ə'prəʊpriət] angemessen, passend, geeignet V
April ['eɪprəl] April I
aquarium [ə'kweəriəm] Aquarium;
Aquarienhaus I
architect ['ɑːkɪtekt] Architekt/in III
are [ɑː] bist; sind; seid I **Are you
…?** Bist du …? I **The DVDs are
…** Die DVDs kosten … I
area ['eəriə] Bereich; Gebiet, Gegend
I
aren't [ɑːnt]: **you aren't … (= you
are not …)** du bist nicht …; du bist
kein/e …; ihr seid nicht …; ihr seid
kein/e … I
argue ['ɑːgjuː]:
1. (sich) streiten; (sich) zanken III
2. argumentieren; behaupten V
argument ['ɑːgjumənt]:
1. Argument III
2. Streit, Auseinandersetzung III
argumentative [ˌɑːgju'mentətɪv]
argumentativ; streitsüchtig V **argumentative writing** Erörterung, Ar-
gumentation V
arm [ɑːm] Arm II
armchair ['ɑːmtʃeə] Sessel I
army ['ɑːmi] Armee III
around … [ə'raʊnd] um … (herum)
II **all around her** überall um sie
herum III **around the library/the
beach** in der Bücherei / auf dem
Strand umher II **be around** da
sein, dabei sein; in der Nähe sein
VI 1 (22) **look around** sich umsehen,
sich umdrehen; sich umschauen II
look around sich umsehen III **turn
around** sich umdrehen I **walk
around** herumlaufen II
arrange [ə'reɪndʒ]:
1. anordnen III
2. organisieren, vereinbaren IV
°**arrangements** (pl) [ə'reɪndʒmənts]
Vorbereitungen; Regelungen V
arrest [ə'rest] verhaften, festnehmen
IV
arrive [ə'raɪv] ankommen, eintreffen
I

art [ɑːt] Kunst I **work of art**
Kunstwerk IV
article ['ɑːtɪkl] Artikel II **feature
article** Sonderbericht, Sonderbeitrag
VI 3 (62)
artificial [ˌɑːtɪ'fɪʃl] künstlich, Kunst-
VI 3 (56/57) **artificial intelligence
(AI)** künstliche Intelligenz VI 3 (56/57)
artist ['ɑːtɪst] Künstler/in II
street artist Straßenkünstler/in II
as [æz], [əz]:
1. als, während II
as if als ob IV
2. as a child als Kind II
as kung fu master als Kung Fu-
Master II
3. (not) as big as (nicht) so groß
wie II
4. as he said wie er (einmal) sagte
III
5. as soon as sobald, sowie III
ashes (pl) ['æʃɪz] Asche (sterbliche
Überreste) III
ask [ɑːsk] fragen I **ask a question**
eine Frage stellen I **ask for sth.**
um etwas bitten II **ask sb. the way**
jn. nach dem Weg fragen II **ask sb.
to do sth.** jemanden bitten, etwas zu
tun I
asleep [ə'sliːp]: **be asleep** schlafen
II
aspect ['æspekt] Aspekt, Gesichts-
punkt VI 3 (74)
°**assess** [ə'ses] einschätzen, beurteilen
assessment [ə'sesmənt] Beurteilung,
Bewertung V
assignment [ə'saɪnmənt] Aufgabe,
Arbeitsauftrag (in der Schule oder daheim zu erledigen) IV
assist (with) [ə'sɪst] assistieren, helfen (bei) V **How may we assist?**
(im Geschäft:) Wie können wir Ihnen
helfen/behilflich sein? V
assistant [ə'sɪstənt] Verkäufer/in II
shop assistant Verkäufer/in II
astonishment [ə'stɒnɪʃmənt] Erstaunen VI 1 (22)
°**astounding** [ə'staʊndɪŋ] verblüf-
fend, erstaunlich
astronaut ['æstrənɔːt] Astronaut/in
III
at [æt], [ət] (in Ortsangaben) an, bei,
in I **at any time** jederzeit, zu jeder
Zeit IV **at Dad's** bei Papa/Vati II
at first zuerst, anfangs, am Anfang
II **at home** daheim, zu Hause I
at last endlich, schließlich I **at
least** zumindest, wenigstens II **at
no time** nie IV **at school** in der

Schule I **at the moment** gerade, im Moment I

ate [et], [eɪt] *siehe* **eat**

athletic [æθ'letɪk] athletisch, sportlich VI 1 (16)

Atlantic [ət'læntɪk]: **the Atlantic (Ocean)** der Atlantik, der Atlantische Ozean III

atmosphere ['ætməsfɪə] Atmosphäre; Stimmung III

atom ['ætəm] Atom V **atom bomb** Atombombe V

attachment [ə'tætʃmənt] Anhang *(einer E-Mail)* VI 3 (61)

attack [ə'tæk]:
1. angreifen II
2. Angriff IV

attend [ə'tend]: **attend (a course)** einen Kurs besuchen, an einem Kurs teilnehmen IV

attendant [ə'tendənt]: **flight attendant** Flugbegleiter/in V

attention [ə'tenʃn] Aufmerksamkeit V **attract/catch/grab sb.'s attention** jemandes Aufmerksamkeit erregen; jemandes Aufmerksamkeit gewinnen V **draw attention to sth.** auf etwas aufmerksam machen; die Aufmerksamkeit auf etwas lenken V **pay attention (to)** achten (auf), aufpassen (auf) V

attic ['ætɪk] Dachboden I

°**attitude** ['ætɪtjuːd] Haltung V

attract [ə'trækt] anziehen, anlocken IV **attract sb.'s attention** jemandes Aufmerksamkeit erregen; jemandes Aufmerksamkeit gewinnen V **be attracted to sb.** sich zu jm. hingezogen fühlen V

attraction [ə'trækʃn] Attraktion; Anziehungspunkt III

attractive [ə'træktɪv] attraktiv, verlockend V

audience ['ɔːdiəns] Publikum, Zuschauer/innen, Zuhörer/innen II

audition [ɔː'dɪʃn] Vorsprechen, Vorsingen, Vorspielen II

August ['ɔːgəst] August I

aunt [ɑːnt] Tante I

Aussie ['ɒzi] Australier/in; australisch V

author ['ɔːθə] Autor/in I

autobiographical [ˌɔːtəˌbaɪə'græfɪkl] autobiografisch VI 2 (45)

autograph ['ɔːtəɡrɑːf] Autogramm IV

automation [ˌɔːtə'meɪʃn] Automatisierung VI 3 (56/57)

autumn ['ɔːtəm] Herbst II

available [ə'veɪləbl] erhältlich, verfügbar; erreichbar *(am Telefon)* III

avenue ['ævənjuː] Allee, Boulevard IV

average ['ævərɪdʒ] durchschnittlich; Durchschnitt V

avoid sth./doing sth. [ə'vɔɪd] etwas vermeiden / vermeiden, etwas zu tun V

awake [ə'weɪk] wach III

award-winning [ə'wɔːd wɪnɪŋ] preisgekrönt VI 1 (12)

awareness [ə'weənəs] Bewusstsein, Aufmerksamkeit VI 2 (47)

away [ə'weɪ] weg, fort I

awe-inspiring ['ɔː_ˌɪnspaɪərɪŋ] ehrfurchtgebietend V

awesome ['ɔːsəm] *(AE, infml)* klasse, großartig IV

awful ['ɔːfl] schrecklich, fürchterlich II

awfully ['ɔːfli] furchtbar, außerordentlich IV

awkward ['ɔːkwəd] peinlich, unangenehm; schwierig VI 1 (12)

B

back [bæk]:
1. zurück I
back and forth hin und her; hin und zurück; auf und ab V
2. Rücken II
Rückseite, hintere Seite II
3. **back sth. up** etwas untermauern *(Argument)* VI 1 (19)

background ['bækgraʊnd] Hintergrund II **background file** Hintergrundinformation(en) I

backpack ['bækpæk] Rucksack IV

backup file ['bækʌp faɪl] Sicherungskopie VI 3 (61)

backyard [ˌbæk'jɑːd] BE: Hinterhof; AE: Garten hinter dem Haus V

bacon ['beɪkən] Schinkenspeck II

bacteria *(pl)* [bæk'tɪəriə] Bakterien VI 1 (23)

bad [bæd] schlecht, schlimm II

baddie ['bædi] Bösewicht, Schurke/Schurkin V

bag [bæɡ]: **sleeping bag** Schlafsack V

baggage ['bæɡɪdʒ] *(bes. AE)* Gepäck V

bagpiper ['bæɡpaɪpə] Dudelsackpfeifer/in, Dudelsackspieler/in, Sackpfeifer/in III

bagpipes *(pl)* ['bæɡpaɪps] Dudelsack, Sackpfeife III

bake [beɪk] backen IV

balance sth. out [ˌbæləns_'aʊt] etwas ausbalancieren, etwas ins Gleichgewicht bringen V

balcony ['bælkəni] Balkon IV

ball [bɔːl] Ball I

ban [bæn] verbieten; für unzulässig erklären VI 3 (74)

banana [bə'nɑːnə] Banane III

band [bænd]:
1. Band, (Musik-)Gruppe II
2. Gruppe, Bande, Gang VI 3 (68)

bandage ['bændɪdʒ] Bandage, Verband V

bang [bæŋ] Knall VI 2 (52)

bank [bæŋk] Bank *(Geldinstitut)* V **piggy bank** Sparschwein V

bankrupt ['bæŋkrʌpt] bankrott VI 3 (68)

banner ['bænə] Spruchband V

bar [bɑː]:
1. Riegel *(Schokolade, Müsli)*, Tafel *(Schokolade)* III
2. Bar III

bar chart ['bɑː tʃɑːt] Balkendiagramm V

barbecue ['bɑːbɪkjuː] Grill; Grillfest, Grillparty V

barbie ['bɑːbi] *(infml) siehe* **barbecue**

bark [bɑːk] bellen I

barman ['bɑːmən], *pl* **barmen** Barkeeper III

barn [bɑːn] Scheune II

baseball ['beɪsbɔːl] Baseball V

based [beɪst]: **...-based** ...-basiert V

bases ['beɪsiːz] *plural of* **basis**

basic ['beɪsɪk] elementar, Grund- IV

basis ['beɪsɪs], *pl* **bases** Basis, Grundlage VI 3 (58)

basket ['bɑːskɪt] Korb I

basketball ['bɑːskɪtbɔːl] Basketball I

bat [bæt] Schläger, Schlagholz *(Baseball, Kricket, Tischtennis)* V

bath [bɑːθ] Bad II **have/take a bath** baden, ein Bad nehmen II

bathe [beɪð] baden VI 2 (42)

bathroom ['bɑːθruːm] Badezimmer I

battery ['bætəri] Batterie, Akku V

battle ['bætl] Schlacht; Kampf V

BBQ ['bɑːbɪkjuː] *siehe* **barbecue**

be [bi], **was/were, been** sein I **be into sth.** *(infml)* etwas mögen, auf etwas stehen III

beach [biːtʃ] Strand I

bean [biːn] Bohne IV

bear [beə] Bär | **polar bear** Eisbär VI 3 (64)

beard [bɪəd] Bart II

beat [biːt], **beat, beaten** schlagen; besiegen III **beat sb. up** jn. zusammenschlagen IV

beaten [ˈbiːtn] *siehe* **beat**

beautiful [ˈbjuːtɪfl] schön II

beauty [ˈbjuːti] Schönheit V

became [bɪˈkeɪm] *siehe* **become**

because [bɪˈkɒz] weil I

become [bɪˈkʌm], **became, become** werden II

bed [bed] Bett I **bed and breakfast (B&B)** Frühstückspension (*wörtlich:* Bett und Frühstück) III

bedroom [ˈbedruːm] Schlafzimmer I

bee [biː] Biene VI 3 (56/57)

beef [biːf] Rindfleisch IV **roast beef** Rinderbraten I

been [biːn] *siehe* **be Have you ever been to …?** Bist du schon (einmal) in … gewesen? II

beep [biːp] piepen II

before [bɪˈfɔː]:
  1. bevor I
  2. **before school/lessons** vor der Schule (*vor Schulbeginn*) / vorm Unterricht I
  3. (vorher) schon mal II **not/never before** (vorher) noch nie II **the week before** die Woche zuvor; in der Woche davor IV
  4. **before long** schon bald III

beg (for) [beg] betteln (um) V

began [bɪˈgæn] *siehe* **begin**

begin [bɪˈgɪn], **began, begun** beginnen, anfangen II

beginning [bɪˈgɪnɪŋ] Anfang, Beginn III

begun [bɪˈgʌn] *siehe* **begin**

behalf [bɪˈhɑːf]: **on behalf of sb. / on sb.'s behalf** im Namen/im Auftrag von jm.; für jn. V

behave [bɪˈheɪv] sich verhalten, sich benehmen III **well-behaved** brav IV

behaviour [bɪˈheɪvjə] Verhalten; Benehmen V

behind [bɪˈhaɪnd] hinter I

being [ˈbiːɪŋ]: **human being** Mensch V

believe [bɪˈliːv] glauben II

bell [bel] Klingel, Glocke II

belong [bɪˈlɒŋ]: **belong to sb.** jm. gehören; zu jm. gehören IV

below [bɪˈləʊ] unten, darunter; unter, unterhalb (von) III

bend down [bend], **bent, bent** sich hinunterbeugen, sich bücken III

beneath [bɪˈniːθ] unterhalb (von) VI 3 (70)

°**benefit** [ˈbenɪfɪt]:
  1. profitieren
  2. Nutzen, Vorteil

bent [bent] *siehe* **bend**

best [best]: **the best …** der/die/das beste …; die besten … I **the best thing about …** das Beste an … III

bestseller [ˌbestˈselə] Bestseller VI 2 (44)

bet [bet], **bet, bet** wetten III

better [ˈbetə] besser I **I'd better … (= I had better)** Ich sollte lieber … IV

between [bɪˈtwiːn] zwischen I

beyond [bɪˈjɒnd] jenseits (von), über … hinaus/hinweg III

big [bɪg] groß I **big wheel** Riesenrad I **the biggest …** der/die/das größte … I

bike [baɪk]:
  1. Fahrrad I
  °2. Rad fahren
  3. **ride a bike** Fahrrad fahren I

bilingual [baɪˈlɪŋgwəl] zweisprachig IV

bill [bɪl] Rechnung V

billboard [ˈbɪlbɔːd] Plakatwand, Werbetafel V

billion [ˈbɪljən] Milliarde (*tausend Millionen*) V

bin [bɪn]: **rubbish bin** Mülltonne, Abfalleimer IV

°**bind** [baɪnd], **bound, bound** binden

biological [ˌbaɪəˈlɒdʒɪkl] biologisch VI 1 (18)

biology [baɪˈɒlədʒi] Biologie VI 3 (58)

°**bipartisan** [ˌbaɪpɑːˈtɪzæn] überparteilich

bird [bɜːd] Vogel I

birthday [ˈbɜːθdeɪ] Geburtstag I **My birthday is in May.** Ich habe im Mai Geburtstag. I **When's your birthday?** Wann hast du Geburtstag? I

biscuit [ˈbɪskɪt] Keks, Plätzchen I

bison [ˈbaɪsn], *pl* **bison** Amerikanischer Bison IV

bit [bɪt] *siehe* **bite a bit** ein bisschen, etwas II

bite [baɪt]:
  1. (**bit, bitten**) beißen II
  2. Biss, Bissen III

bitten [bɪtn] *siehe* **bite**

bitter [ˈbɪtə] bitter IV

bitterness [ˈbɪtənəs] Bitterkeit IV

black [blæk] schwarz I

blazer [ˈbleɪzə] Sakko, Blazer (*sportliches Jackett*) VI 1 (10/11)

blew [bluː] *siehe* **blow**

blind [blaɪnd] blind VI 1 (15)

block [blɒk]:
  1. (Häuser-, Wohn-)Block IV
  2. blockieren, sperren IV

blog [blɒg] Blog (*Weblog, digitales Tagebuch*) IV

blogger [ˈblɒgə] Blogschreiber/in III

blond [blɒnd] (*bei Frauen oft:* **blonde**) blond I

blood [blʌd] Blut III

°**blood pressure** [ˈblʌd preʃə] Blutdruck

bloom [bluːm] blühen IV

blow [bləʊ], **blew, blown**:
  1. **blow sth. out** etwas auspusten, ausblasen II
  2. **blow the whistle** pfeifen (*auf der Trillerpfeife*) III

blown [bləʊn] *siehe* **blow**

blue [bluː] blau I

board [bɔːd]:
  1. (Wand-)Tafel I **bulletin board** (AE) Schwarzes Brett (*auch elektronisch*) V
  2. **on board (the ship)** an Bord (des Schiffes) III

boarding school [ˈbɔːdɪŋ skuːl] Internat II

boat [bəʊt] Boot I **sailing boat** Segelboot I

body [ˈbɒdi]:
  1. Körper II
  2. Hauptteil (*eines Textes*) III
  3. Leiche III

boil [bɔɪl] kochen; zum Kochen bringen IV

bold (type) [bəʊld] Fettdruck VI 1 (17)

bomb [bɒm]: **atom bomb** Atombombe V

book [bʊk]:
  1. Buch I
  2. buchen, reservieren V

bookstore [ˈbʊkstɔː] Buchladen, Buchhandlung VI 3 (68)

boot [buːt] Stiefel II

border [ˈbɔːdə] Grenze III

bored [bɔːd]: **be/feel bored** gelangweilt sein, sich langweilen II

boring [ˈbɔːrɪŋ] langweilig I

born [bɔːn]: **be born** geboren sein/werden III

borrow sth. (from sb.) [ˈbɒrəʊ] sich etwas (aus)leihen (vom jm.), etwas entleihen IV

boss [bɒs] Chef/in, Boss III

bossy [ˈbɒsi] herrisch, rechthaberisch V

bot [bɒt] Bot *(Computerprogramm, das automatisch sich wiederholende Aufgaben abarbeitet)* VI 3 (68)

botanic [bəˈtænɪk] botanisch V

both [bəʊθ] beide II **both ... and ...** sowohl … als auch … IV

bottle [ˈbɒtl] Flasche I

bottom [ˈbɒtəm]: **at the bottom (of)** unten, am unteren Ende (von) II

bought [bɔːt] *siehe* **buy**

°**bound** [baʊnd] *siehe* **bind**

bow [baʊ] sich verbeugen, sich verneigen II

bowl [bəʊl] Schüssel II

box [bɒks] Kasten, Kiste, Kästchen I

boy [bɔɪ] Junge I

boyfriend [ˈbɔɪfrend] Freund III

°**bracket** [ˈbrækɪt] Klammer *(in Texten)*

brain [breɪn] Gehirn VI 3 (58)

brainstorm [ˈbreɪnstɔːm] brainstormen *(so viele Ideen wie möglich sammeln)* V

branch [brɑːntʃ] Ast, Zweig; Zweigstelle, Filiale VI 1 (13)

brass band [ˌbrɑːs ˈbænd] Blaskapelle IV

brave [breɪv] mutig, tapfer IV

bread [bred] Brot I

break [breɪk] Pause I **commercial break** Werbepause V **paragraph break** Absatzumbruch VI 1 (20)

break [breɪk]**, broke, broken** zerbrechen, kaputt machen; brechen, kaputt gehen II **break up (with sb.)** Schluss machen (mit jm.), sich trennen (von jm.) V

breakdown [ˈbreɪkdaʊn] Zusammenbruch VI 3 (58) **nervous breakdown** Nervenzusammenbruch VI 3 (58)

breakfast [ˈbrekfəst] Frühstück I **bed and breakfast (B&B)** Frühstückspension *(wörtlich: Bett und Frühstück)* III **have breakfast** frühstücken I

breakthrough [ˈbreɪkθruː] Durchbruch VI 1 (23)

breastfed [ˈbrestfed] *siehe* breastfeed VI 2 (42)

breastfeed [ˈbrestfiːd]**, breastfed, breastfed** stillen VI 2 (42)

breath [breθ] Atem, Atemzug II **…, he said under his breath.** …, sagte er flüsternd / murmelte er. III

breathe [briːð] atmen V

breeze [briːz] Brise III

bridge [brɪdʒ] Brücke II

brief [briːf] kurz (gefasst), knapp, von kurzer Dauer V

briefly [ˈbriːfli] in Kürze, in wenigen Worten V

bright [braɪt]:
1. strahlend, leuchtend, hell I
2. klug, gescheit, „hell" VI 3 (70)

brilliant [ˈbrɪliənt] glänzend, großartig, genial II

bring [brɪŋ]**, brought, brought** (mit-, her)bringen II **bring in** *(hay)* einbringen *(Heu)* II

British [ˈbrɪtɪʃ] britisch I

brochure [ˈbrəʊʃə] Broschüre, Prospekt II

broke [brəʊk] *siehe* **break**

broken [ˈbrəʊkən]:
1. *siehe* **break**
2. zerbrochen, kaputt; gebrochen II

brother [ˈbrʌðə] Bruder I

brought [brɔːt] *siehe* **bring**

brown [braʊn] braun I

browse [braʊz] (durch)stöbern; (durch)blättern; browsen, *(im Internet)* surfen VI 3 (61)

buck [bʌk] *(infml)* Dollar IV

bucket [ˈbʌkɪt] Eimer II

buddy [ˈbʌdi] *(infml)* Kumpel, Freund/in V

budget [ˈbʌdʒɪt]:
1. Budget V
2. haushalten V

build [bɪld]**, built, built** bauen III

building [ˈbɪldɪŋ] Gebäude II

built [bɪlt] *siehe* **build**

bullet [ˈbʊlɪt] (Gewehr-)Kugel VI 2 (34)

bulletin board [ˈbʊlətɪn bɔːd] *(AE)* Schwarzes Brett *(auch elektronisch)* V

bully [ˈbʊli]:
1. (Schul-)Tyrann III
2. **bully sb.** jn. tyrannisieren, mobben V

bump into sb. [bʌmp] jn. zufällig treffen, jm. zufällig begegnen V

bunch [bʌntʃ] *(infml)*: **a bunch of ...** eine Menge …, ein Bündel … VI 3 (59)

burger [ˈbɜːgə] Hamburger II

burn [bɜːn] brennen; verbrennen III

burnt [bɜːnt] verbrannt IV

burst into tears [bɜːst]**, burst, burst** in Tränen ausbrechen III

bury [ˈberi] begraben, beerdigen IV

bus [bʌs] Bus I **bus stop** Bushaltestelle III **go by bus** mit dem Bus fahren I

bush [bʊʃ] Busch, Strauch *(auch: unerschlossenes, „wildes" Land in Australien u. Afrika)* V

business [ˈbɪznəs] Geschäft, Geschäfts-; Unternehmen, Betrieb V

busy [ˈbɪzi] belebt, geschäftig, hektisch III **busy season** Hauptsaison V **be busy** beschäftigt sein; viel zu tun haben II

but [bʌt], [bət] aber I

butter [ˈbʌtə] Butter III

butterfly [ˈbʌtəflaɪ] Schmetterling I

button [ˈbʌtn] Knopf, Taste VI 3 (61)

buy [baɪ]**, bought, bought** kaufen I

buzz off [ˌbʌz ˈɒf] abschwirren, einen Abflug machen VI 3 (62)

by [baɪ]:
1. von … II
2. **by the sea** am Meer I
3. **go by car/bus/…** mit dem Auto/Bus/… fahren I
4. **by 8 pm** bis (spätestens) 20 Uhr III

Bye. [baɪ] Tschüs. I

C

café [ˈkæfeɪ] Café I

cafeteria [ˌkæfəˈtɪəriə] Cafeteria IV

cake [keɪk] Kuchen I

calendar [ˈkælɪndə] Kalender V

calf [kɑːf], *pl* **calves** Kalb; Wade V

call [kɔːl]:
1. rufen; anrufen; nennen I **call for sth.** etwas verlangen, etwas fordern; zu etwas auffordern VI 1 (19) **call out the names** die Namen aufrufen II **call sb. names** jn. beschimpfen, jm. Schimpfwörter nachrufen IV
2. Anruf; Telefongespräch II

called [kɔːld]: **be called** heißen, genannt werden I

caller [ˈkɔːlə] Anrufer/in II

calm [kɑːm] ruhig III

°**calory** [ˈkæləri] Kalorie

calves [kɑːvz] *siehe* **calf**

came [keɪm] *siehe* **come**

camel [ˈkæml] Kamel V

camera [ˈkæmərə] Kamera, Fotoapparat I

camp (out) [kæmp] zelten, im Freien kampieren V

campaign [kæmˈpeɪn]:
1. Kampagne V
2. **campaign for/against sth.** sich einsetzen, kämpfen für/gegen V

°**campaigner** [kæmˈpeɪnə] Aktivist/in

campfire [ˈkæmpfaɪə] Lagerfeuer IV

campsite [ˈkæmpsaɪt] Zeltplatz II

Dictionary

can [kæn], [kən]**:**
1. können I
we cannot wir können nicht … I
we can't … wir können nicht … I
2. Dose IV
3. trash can (AE) Mülltonne, Abfall-eimer IV
canal [kə'næl] Kanal III
cancer ['kænsə] Krebs (Erkrankung) VI 1 (23)
°**candidate** ['kændɪdət] Bewerber/in, Kandidat/in
candle ['kændl] Kerze II
candy ['kændi] (AE) Süßigkeiten IV
cannon ['kænən] Kanone, Geschütz V
cannot ['kænɒt]**: we cannot** wir können nicht … I
canteen [kæn'tiːn] Kantine, (Schul-)Mensa I
canyon ['kænjən] Cañon IV
cap [kæp] Mütze, Kappe II
capacity [kə'pæsəti] Fähigkeit, Leis-tungsvermögen VI 3 (58)
cape [keɪp] Kap V
capital ['kæpɪtl] Hauptstadt III
captain ['kæptɪn] Kapitän/in I
caption ['kæpʃn] Bildunterschrift I
capture ['kæptʃə] (ein)fangen (auch im übertragenen Sinne) VI 2 (46)
car [kɑː] Auto I **car park** (BE) Parkplatz IV **go by car** mit dem Auto fahren I
caravan ['kærəvæn] Wohnwagen II
carbon ['kɑːbən] Kohlenstoff VI 2 (52)
carbon dioxide (CO₂) Kohlendioxid V
card [kɑːd] Karte I
care [keə]**: care (about sth.)** etwas ernst nehmen, etwas wichtig nehmen V **take care of sth.** sich (gut) um etwas kümmern; sorgfältig mit etwas umgehen IV
career [kə'rɪə] Karriere III
careful ['keəfl] vorsichtig II
carnival ['kɑːnɪvl] Karneval, Fasching III
°**carol** ['kærəl] Weihnachtslied
carpenter ['kɑːpəntə] Tischler/in, Zimmerer/Zimmerin III
carrot ['kærət] Möhre, Karotte III
carry ['kæri] tragen I
cart [kɑːt] Karren I
cartoon [kɑː'tuːn] Cartoon, Witz-zeichnung VI 3 (68)
carve [kɑːv] meißeln; schnitzen IV
case [keɪs]**:**
1. Fall V

in case falls V
2. pencil case Federmäppchen I
cash [kæʃ] Bargeld; (infml auch) Geld V **cash desk** Kasse (in Geschäften) II **cash flow** Cashflow (die finanzi-elle Situation) V **pay cash** bar be-zahlen V
cashier [kæ'ʃɪə] Kassierer/in V
°**cast (a vote/your vote)** [kɑːst]**, cast, cast** abstimmen, seine Stimme abgeben
castle ['kɑːsl] Burg, Schloss I
casually ['kæʒuəli] leger, lässig (ge-kleidet) VI 1 (10/11)
cat [kæt] Katze I
catch [kætʃ]**, caught, caught** fan-gen I **catch sb.'s attention** je-mandes Aufmerksamkeit erregen; je-mandes Aufmerksamkeit gewinnen V
catchy ['kætʃi] eingängig (Melodie, Slogan) IV
category ['kætəgəri] Kategorie V
cathedral [kə'θiːdrəl] Kathedrale, Dom III
caught [kɔːt] siehe **catch**
cause [kɔːz]**:**
1. verursachen IV
2. Ursache IV
3. Anliegen, Sache, Zweck V
°**4. 'cause** weil (= because)
Caution! ['kɔːʃn] Achtung! Vorsicht! V
cautious ['kɔːʃəs] vorsichtig V
celebrate ['selɪbreɪt] feiern II
celebration [ˌselɪ'breɪʃn] Feier II
celebrity [sə'lebrəti] Berühmtheit (berühmte Person) IV
cell [sel] Zelle VI 1 (22) **cell (phone)** (bes. AE) Mobiltelefon, Handy IV
Celsius (C) ['selsiəs] Celsius IV
cemetery ['semətri] Friedhof IV
cent [sent] Cent III
center ['sentə] (AE) Zentrum IV
central ['sentrəl] zentral, Zentral-, Mittel- IV
centre ['sentə] Zentrum; Mitte I
century ['sentʃəri] Jahrhundert II
ceremony ['serəməni] Zeremonie IV
certain ['sɜːtn] bestimmte(r, s), gewisse(r, s) IV
certainly ['sɜːtnli] sicher(lich), auf jeden Fall V
certificate [sə'tɪfɪkət] Urkunde, Be-scheinigung; Zeugnis V
certification [ˌsɜːtɪfɪ'keɪʃn]**: organic certification** etwa: Bio-Zertifizie-rung V
chair [tʃeə]**:**
1. Stuhl I

2. den Vorsitz führen, innehaben VI 3 (74)
challenge ['tʃælɪndʒ]**:**
1. Herausforderung III
2. challenge sb. (to sth.) jn. her-ausfordern (zu etwas) III
champion ['tʃæmpiən] Meister/in, Champion II
chance [tʃɑːns] Gelegenheit, Mög-lichkeit, Chance III
change [tʃeɪndʒ]**:**
1. (ver)ändern; sich (ver)ändern II
change your mind seine Meinung ändern IV
2. wechseln, umtauschen (Geld) III
3. umsteigen III
4. Änderung, Veränderung II
climate change Klimawandel IV
for a change zur Abwechslung IV
5. Wechselgeld II
channel ['tʃænl] Kanal, Sender IV
chant [tʃɑːnt] singen (Sprechge-sang); skandieren V
chanting ['tʃɑːntɪŋ] (Sprech-)Ge-sang V
chaos ['keɪɒs] Chaos I
character ['kærəktə] Figur, Person (in Roman, Film, Theaterstück usw.) I
°**characteristics (pl)** [ˌkærəktə'rɪstɪks] Eigenschaften
characterization [ˌkærəktəraɪ'zeɪʃn] Charakterisierung, Beschreibung V
characterize ['kærəktəraɪz] charak-terisieren, beschreiben V
charge [tʃɑːdʒ] (auf)laden VI 3 (61)
charity ['tʃærəti] Wohlfahrtsorgani-sation; Wohltätigkeit, wohltätige Zwecke II
charming ['tʃɑːmɪŋ] charmant, bezaubernd VI 3 (68)
chart [tʃɑːt] Tabelle, Schaubild V
bar chart Balkendiagramm V
pie chart Tortendiagramm V
chat [tʃæt]**:**
1. Chat III
2. chatten III
cheap [tʃiːp] billig, preiswert II
check [tʃek]**:**
1. (über)prüfen, kontrollieren I
2. Überprüfung, Kontrolle I
cheek [tʃiːk] Wange VI 3 (69)
cheer [tʃɪə] jubeln II
cheese [tʃiːz] Käse I
chemical ['kemɪkl] Chemikalie V
chess [tʃes] Schach I
chest [tʃest] Brust, Brustkorb II
chicken ['tʃɪkɪn] Huhn; (Brat-)Hähn-chen IV
child [tʃaɪld], pl **children** Kind I

childhood [ˈtʃaɪldhʊd] Kindheit V

children [ˈtʃɪldrən] *siehe* **child**

chill [tʃɪl] sich entspannen, chillen; sich abregen V

chip [tʃɪp] Chip VI 3 (56/57) **chips** *(pl)* Pommes frites II

chocolate [ˈtʃɒklət] **:**
1. Schokolade I
2. Praline II

choice [tʃɔɪs] Wahl; Auswahl III

choir [ˈkwaɪə] Chor II

choose [tʃuːz]**, chose, chosen** aussuchen, (aus)wählen; sich aussuchen I

chore [tʃɔː] (Haus-)Arbeit; *(lästige)* Pflicht V

chorus [ˈkɔːrəs] Refrain II

chose [tʃəʊz] *siehe* **choose**

chosen [ˈtʃəʊzn] *siehe* **choose**

Christmas [ˈkrɪsməs] Weihnachten III

chunk [tʃʌŋk] (dickes, großes) Stück V

church [tʃɜːtʃ] Kirche II

cigarette [ˌsɪgəˈret] Zigarette IV

cinema [ˈsɪnəmə] Kino II

circle [ˈsɜːkl] Kreis II

circular [ˈsɜːkjələ] kreisförmig, rund V

citizen [ˈsɪtɪzn] (Staats-)Bürger/in V

city [ˈsɪti] Stadt, Großstadt I

civil rights *(pl)* [ˌsɪvl ˈraɪts] Bürgerrechte IV

civil war [ˌsɪvl ˈwɔː] Bürgerkrieg V

civilization [ˌsɪvəlaɪˈzeɪʃn] Zivilisation VI 3 (68)

claim [kleɪm]**:**
1. angeben, behaupten VI 3 (58)
2. Behauptung VI 3 (58)

clap [klæp] (Beifall) klatschen II
Clap your hands. Klatscht in die Hände. II

clarity [ˈklærəti] Klarheit VI 1 (17)

class [klɑːs] (Schul-)Klasse I

classical [ˈklæsɪkl] klassisch III

classmate [ˈklɑːsmeɪt] Mitschüler/in, Klassenkamerad/in I

classroom [ˈklɑːsruːm] Klassenzimmer I

clean [kliːn]**:**
1. sauber machen, putzen I
2. sauber II

clear [klɪə]**:**
1. klar, deutlich II
2. räumen; abräumen III

clerk [klɑːk] (Büro-)Angestellte(r) VI 3 (68)

clever [ˈklevə] klug, schlau III

click [klɪk] klicken IV

cliff [klɪf] Klippe III

climate [ˈklaɪmət] Klima IV

climate change Klimawandel IV

climax [ˈklaɪmæks] Höhepunkt VI 1 (27)

climb [klaɪm]**:**
1. klettern; hinaufklettern (auf) II
2. Aufstieg, Anstieg III

clinic [ˈklɪnɪk] Klinik V

clip [klɪp] Kurzfilm, Clip V

clock [klɒk] (Wand-, Stand-, Turm-) Uhr I

close [kləʊz] schließen II

close (to) [kləʊs] nah, dicht (bei, an) II **look closely** genau hinschauen II

close-up [ˈkləʊs ˌʌp] Nahaufnahme IV

closet [ˈklɒzɪt] Wandschrank *(oft begehbar)* IV

clothes *(pl)* [kləʊðz] Kleidung, Kleidungsstücke I

cloud [klaʊd] Wolke II

cloudless [ˈklaʊdləs] wolkenlos IV

cloudy [ˈklaʊdi] bewölkt II

clown [klaʊn] Clown/in II

club [klʌb] Klub I **join a club** in einen Klub eintreten; sich einem Klub anschließen I

clue [kluː] (Lösungs-)Hinweis; Anhaltspunkt III

coach [kəʊtʃ] Trainer/in IV

coal [kəʊl] Kohle III

°**coalition** [ˌkəʊəˈlɪʃn] Bündnis, Zusammenschluss; Koalition

coast [kəʊst] Küste I

coastal [ˈkəʊstl] Küsten- V

coastline [ˈkəʊstlaɪn] Küste, Küstenlinie V

coat [kəʊt] Mantel II

cocoa [ˈkəʊkəʊ] Kakao II

coffee [ˈkɒfi] Kaffee III **make coffee** Kaffee kochen IV

coin [kɔɪn] Münze I

cold [kəʊld]**:**
1. kalt I
be cold frieren II
2. Erkältung II
have a cold eine Erkältung haben, erkältet sein II

collapse [kəˈlæps] einstürzen; zusammenbrechen IV

collect [kəˈlekt] sammeln I

collection [kəˈlekʃn] Sammlung VI 3 (59)

collective [kəˈlektɪv] gemeinschaftlich, vereint VI 2 (47)

college [ˈkɒlɪdʒ] Hochschule IV

collocation [ˌkɒləˈkeɪʃn] Kollokation *(Wörter, die oft zusammen vorkommen)* V

colon [ˈkəʊlən] Doppelpunkt II

colonize [ˈkɒlənaɪz] besiedeln, kolonisieren V

colony [ˈkɒləni] Kolonie VI 3 (62)

colour [ˈkʌlə] **(**AE: **color)** Farbe I

coloured [ˈkʌləd] farbig VI 1 (13)

colourful [ˈkʌləfl] bunt, farbenfreudig IV

column [ˈkɒləm] Säule III

combine [kəmˈbaɪn] kombinieren, verbinden IV

come [kʌm]**, came, come** kommen I **come across sb./sth.** stoßen auf, (zufällig) treffen III **come down with sth.** bekommen *(Krankheit)*, erkranken an III **Come on, Dad.** Na los, Dad! / Komm, Dad! I **come over** herüberkommen, vorbeikommen III **come over (to)** herüberkommen (zu/nach), vorbeikommen (bei) III **come to an understanding** sich einigen; zu einer Übereinkunft kommen VI 2 (35) **come up to sb.** auf jn. zukommen IV **come up with sth.** haben, kommen auf *(Idee, Vorschlag)* III **when it comes to …** was … betrifft/anbelangt, … VI 1 (18)

comedy [ˈkɒmədi] Comedyshow, Komödie II

comfortable [ˈkʌmftəbl] bequem; angenehm III

comma [ˈkɒmə] Komma II

°**command** [kəˈmɑːnd] Anordnung; Befehl

commemorate sth. [kəˈmeməreɪt] einer Sache gedenken, an etwas erinnern V

comment [ˈkɒment]**:**
1. Bemerkung, Kommentar III
2. **comment on sth.** etwas kommentieren, sich zu etwas äußern V

commercial [kəˈmɜːʃl] kommerziell, gewerblich V **commercial break** Werbepause V

committed [kəˈmɪtɪd]**: be committed to sth.** sich für etwas verpflichten, sich zu etwas bekennen VI 2 (48)

common [ˈkɒmən]**:**
1. häufig; weit verbreitet IV
°**the House of Commons** das Unterhaus *(des britischen Parlaments)*
2. gemeinsame(r, s) V
3. **have sth. in common** etwas miteinander gemein haben IV

communicate (with) [kəˈmjuːnɪkeɪt] kommunizieren (mit), sich verständigen (mit) V

communication [kəˌmjuːnɪˈkeɪʃn] Kommunikation, Verständigung V community [kə'mjuːnəti] Gemeinde; Gemeinschaft V

companion [kəm'pænjən] Begleiter/in, Gefährte/-in VI 2 (37)

company ['kʌmpəni] Firma V

compare [kəm'peə] vergleichen IV

comparison [kəm'pærɪsn] Vergleich V **make comparisons** Vergleiche anstellen; vergleichen V

compensate ['kɒmpenseɪt] kompensieren, ausgleichen; entschädigen VI 3 (62)

competition [ˌkɒmpə'tɪʃn] Wettbewerb II

competitive [kəm'petətɪv] leistungsorientiert, ehrgeizig; wettbewerbsorientiert V

complain [kəm'pleɪn] sich beschweren, sich beklagen IV

complete [kəm'pliːt]:
1. abschließen, vollenden; vervollständigen IV
2. komplett, vollständig IV

completion [kəm'pliːʃn] Vervollständigung; Abschluss; Fertigstellung VI 3 (72)

complex ['kɒmpleks] komplex V

complicated ['kɒmplɪkeɪtɪd] kompliziert III

compliment ['kɒmplɪmənt] Kompliment V **pay/give sb. a compliment** jm. ein Kompliment machen V

compound ['kɒmpaʊnd] Verbindung VI 1 (23)

comprehension [ˌkɒmprɪ'henʃn] Verständnis V

comprehensive school [ˌkɒmprɪ'hensɪv skuːl] *einer deutschen Gesamtschule vergleichbare Schulform in GB* V

computer [kəm'pjuːtə] Computer I

concentrate (on sth.) ['kɒnsntreɪt] sich konzentrieren (auf etwas) V

concept ['kɒnsept] Vorstellung, Begriff, Konzept V

°concern [kən'sɜːn] Befürchtung, Bedenken, Sorge

concern sb. [kən'sɜːn] jn. betreffen, angehen; jn. beunruhigen VI 3 (74)

concerned [kən'sɜːnd] **be concerned about sth.** über/um/wegen etw. besorgt sein VI 3 (73)

concert ['kɒnsət] Konzert II

concise [kən'saɪs] knapp, kurz, prägnant VI 3 (65)

conclusion [kən'kluːʒn] Schluss(folgerung) III

concrete ['kɒŋkriːt] konkret IV

°conference ['kɒnfərəns] Konferenz, Besprechung, Tagung

confidence ['kɒnfɪdəns] (Selbst-)Vertrauen, Zuversicht V

confident ['kɒnfɪdənt] selbstsicher; zuversichtlich VI 3 (73)

°confirm [kən'fɜːm] bestätigen

conflict ['kɒnflɪkt] Konflikt, Auseinandersetzung V

confused [kən'fjuːzd] verwirrt V

confusing [kən'fjuːzɪŋ] verwirrend V

connect [kə'nekt] verbinden, verknüpfen V

°connection [kə'nekʃn] Verbindung

°cons [kɒnz]: **pros and cons** Vor- und Nachteile, Für und Wider

consent [kən'sent] Einverständnis, Einwilligung V

consequence ['kɒnsɪkwəns] Folge, Konsequenz VI 3 (59)

conservation [ˌkɒnsə'veɪʃn] Umweltschutz III

conservative [kən'sɜːvətɪv] konservativ; Konservative(r) VI 1 (10/11)

consider [kən'sɪdə]:
1. erwägen, in Betracht/in Erwägung ziehen; berücksichtigen V
2. nachdenken über; bedenken, abwägen V
3. betrachten als, halten für V
be considered sth. als etwas betrachtet werden; für etwas gehalten werden VI 1 (15)

consist of [kən'sɪst] bestehen aus V

consonant ['kɒnsənənt] Konsonant, Mitlaut II

constant ['kɒnstənt] ständig, dauernd VI 1 (18)

contact ['kɒntækt]:
1. Kontakt V
2. **contact sb.** Kontakt zu jm. aufnehmen, sich bei jm. melden V

contain [kən'teɪn] enthalten, beinhalten VI 1 (23)

contemporary [kən'temprəri] zeitgenössisch V

content ['kɒntent] Inhalt III

°contest ['kɒntest] Wettbewerb

context ['kɒntekst] (Satz-, Text-)Zusammenhang, Kontext II

continent ['kɒntɪnənt] Kontinent V

continue sth. [kən'tɪnjuː] etwas fortsetzen III

contrast ['kɒntrɑːst] Kontrast, Gegensatz IV

contribute sth. (to) [kən'trɪbjuːt] etwas beitragen, beisteuern (zu) V

contribution [ˌkɒntrɪ'bjuːʃn] Beitrag VI 1 (18)

control [kən'trəʊl]:
1. kontrollieren, beherrschen; unter Kontrolle halten/bekommen III
2. Kontrolle IV
remote control Fernbedienung III
take control Kontrolle übernehmen IV

controversial [ˌkɒntrə'vɜːʃl] kontrovers, umstritten VI 1 (23)

°controversy ['kɒntrəvɜːsi] Kontroverse, Auseinandersetzung

conventional [kən'venʃənl] konventionell VI 1 (16)

conversation [ˌkɒnvə'seɪʃn] Gespräch, Unterhaltung II

convey [kən'veɪ] vermitteln, übermitteln VI 3 (71)

convict ['kɒnvɪkt] Sträfling, Strafgefangene(r) V

°convince [kən'vɪns] überzeugen

convinced [kən'vɪnst] überzeugt VI 2 (49)

cook [kʊk]:
1. kochen, zubereiten III
2. Koch, Köchin IV

cookie ['kʊki] (AE) Keks IV

cool [kuːl]:
1. cool I
2. kühl II

cooperation [kəʊˌɒpə'reɪʃn] Zusammenarbeit V

°coordinate [kəʊ'ɔːdɪneɪt] koordinieren

coordinator [kəʊ'ɔːdɪneɪtə] Koordinator/in III

cope [kəʊp] zurechtkommen, klarkommen VI 1 (12)

copy ['kɒpi] kopieren, abschreiben I

coral ['kɒrəl] Koralle; Korallen- V

corner ['kɔːnə] Ecke I **corner shop** Laden an der Ecke; Tante-Emma-Laden I **on the corner of Church Road and London Road** Church Road, Ecke London Road II

cornflakes ['kɔːnfleɪks] Cornflakes I

corporation [ˌkɔːpə'reɪʃn] (Handels-)Gesellschaft, Konzern; Körperschaft VI 3 (58)

correct [kə'rekt]:
1. richtig, korrekt II
2. korrigieren, verbessern II

correctness [kə'rektnəs] Korrektheit, Fehlerfreiheit V

corridor ['kɒrɪdɔː] Gang, Korridor III

cost [kɒst]**, cost, cost** kosten II

costume ['kɒstjuːm] Kostüm, Verkleidung II

cottage [ˈkɒtɪdʒ] Häuschen, Cottage II

cotton [ˈkɒtn] Baumwolle VI 2 (41)

cough [kɒf]: **have a cough** Husten haben II

could [kʊd], [kəd]:
1. She could feel the tears. Sie konnte die Tränen spüren. II
2. What could be better? Was könnte besser sein? II

council [ˈkaʊnsl] Ausschuss; Rat (Stadtrat, Gemeinderat u.Ä.) IV

counsellor [ˈkaʊnsələ] Berater/in; Betreuer/in VI 1 (18)

count (to) [kaʊnt] zählen (bis) I

counter(top) [ˈkaʊntə], [ˈkaʊntətɒp] Theke; Ladentisch IV

counter-argument [ˈkaʊntərˌɑːgjumənt] Gegenargument VI 3 (74)

country [ˈkʌntri]:
1. Land (Staat) II
2. Land (im Gegensatz zur Stadt) III

countryside [ˈkʌntrisaɪd] Landschaft, (ländliche) Gegend II

county [ˈkaʊnti] Grafschaft (in Großbritannien) I

couple [ˈkʌpl]: **a couple** ein Paar; ein paar IV

courage [ˈkʌrɪdʒ] Mut, Courage IV

course [kɔːs] Kurs, Lehrgang I
attend a course einen Kurs besuchen, an einem Kurs teilnehmen IV

court [kɔːt] Spielfeld V

courteous [ˈkɜːtiəs] höflich V

cousin [ˈkʌzn] Cousin, Cousine I

cover [ˈkʌvə] behandeln, abdecken IV

cow [kaʊ] Kuh II

crab [kræb] Krebs I

°**crack** [kræk]: **crack sth. in two** etwas in zwei Hälften brechen

craft [krɑːft] Können, Kunst; (Kunst-)Handwerk V

cranberry [ˈkrænbəri] Preiselbeere IV

crash [kræʃ] abstürzen (Flugzeug; Computer) IV **crash into sth.** (Flugzeug) in etwas stürzen; (Auto) gegen etwas fahren IV

crazy [ˈkreɪzi] verrückt IV

cream [kriːm]:
1. Sahne I
2. Creme; Salbe VI 2 (34)
3. ice cream (Speise-)Eis I

create [kriˈeɪt] (er)schaffen, kreieren IV

creative [kriˈeɪtɪv] kreativ VI 1 (16)

credible [ˈkredəbl] glaubwürdig, glaubhaft VI 2 (42)

°**crescendo** [krəˈʃendəʊ] Crescendo (Anwachsen der Lautstärke)

crib sheet [ˈkrɪb ʃiːt] (infml) Spickzettel, Merkzettel II

cricket [ˈkrɪkɪt] Cricket I

crime [kraɪm] Verbrechen; Kriminalität V

crises [ˈkraɪsiːz] plural of **crisis**

crisis [ˈkraɪsɪs], pl **crises** Krise VI 2 (47)

°**criteria** (pl) [kraɪˈtɪəriə] Kriterien

critical [ˈkrɪtɪkl] kritisch V

°**criticism** [ˈkrɪtɪsɪzəm] Kritik

criticize sb. (for) [ˈkrɪtɪsaɪz] jn. kritisieren (wegen) I

crocodile [ˈkrɒkədaɪl] Krokodil V

crop [krɒp] (Feld-)Frucht VI 3 (62)

cross [krɒs]:
1. überqueren, kreuzen; sich kreuzen II
2. cross (with sb.) böse, sauer (auf jn.) V

cross-cultural [ˌkrɒs ˈkʌltʃərəl] interkulturell V

crossword [ˈkrɒswɜːd] Kreuzworträtsel III

crowd [kraʊd] (Menschen-)Menge II

crowded [ˈkraʊdɪd] voller Menschen; überfüllt III

crown [kraʊn] Krone III

cruel [kruːəl] grausam IV

cruise [kruːz] Kreuzfahrt, Schiffsreise, Bootsfahrt III

cry [kraɪ] schreien; weinen II

cultural [ˈkʌltʃərəl] kulturell V

culture [ˈkʌltʃə] Kultur III

cup [kʌp] Tasse I **a cup of tea** eine Tasse Tee I

cupboard [ˈkʌbəd] Schrank I

curious [ˈkjʊəriəs] wissbegierig, neugierig III

curl [kɜːl] Locke VI 1 (10/11)

curly [ˈkɜːli] lockig VI 1 (10/11)

currency [ˈkʌrənsi] Währung III

current [ˈkʌrənt] aktuelle(r,s), gegenwärtige(r, s) VI 3 (58)

current account [ˈkʌrənt əkaʊnt] Girokonto VI 3 (58)

current affairs (pl) [ˌkʌrənt əˈfeəz] Tagespolitik, aktuelle Ereignisse VI 3 (58)

curriculum [kəˈrɪkjələm], pl **curriculums** or **curricula** Lehrplan, Kurrikulum V

curriculum vitae (CV) [kəˌrɪkjələm ˈviːtaɪ] Lebenslauf V

curry [ˈkʌri] Curry(gericht) III

cushion [ˈkʊʃn] Kissen VI 3 (69)

customer [ˈkʌstəmə] Kunde/Kundin V

customize [ˈkʌstəmaɪz] anpassen, individuell einrichten VI 3 (61)

customs (pl) [ˈkʌstəmz] Bräuche, Gebräuche, Sitten V

cut [kʌt], **cut, cut** schneiden II **be cut off from sth.** von etwas abgeschnitten/abgetrennt sein IV

Cut! [kʌt] Schnitt! (beim Filmen) II

cute [kjuːt] niedlich, süß IV

CV (curriculum vitae) [ˌsiː ˈviː] Lebenslauf V

cyberbullying [ˈsaɪbəbʊliɪŋ] Cyber-Mobbing (Verleumdung oder Belästigung anderer im Internet) V

cycle [ˈsaɪkl] Rad fahren, mit dem Rad fahren IV

cyclist [ˈsaɪklɪst] Radfahrer/in VI 2 (55)

cyclone [ˈsaɪkləʊn] Zyklon, Wirbelsturm V

D

dad [dæd] Papa, Vati I

daily [ˈdeɪli] täglich V

dairy products (pl) [ˈdeəri prɒdʌkts] Milchprodukte, Molkereiprodukte IV

damage [ˈdæmɪdʒ] (be)schädigen, schaden VI 3 (64)

dance [dɑːns]:
1. tanzen I
2. Tanz II
dance floor Tanzfläche II

dancer [ˈdɑːnsə] Tänzer/in II

danger [ˈdeɪndʒə] Gefahr III

dangerous [ˈdeɪndʒərəs] gefährlich I

dark [dɑːk] dunkel I

darkness [ˈdɑːknəs] Dunkelheit, Finsternis III

data [ˈdeɪtə] Daten VI 3 (61)

database [ˈdeɪtəbeɪs] Datenbank VI 3 (58)

date [deɪt]:
1. Datum I
2. date sb. mit jm. gehen, mit jm. zusammen sein V

daughter [ˈdɔːtə] Tochter II

day [deɪ] Tag I **day of the week** Wochentag I

dead [ded] tot I

deal with sth. [diːl], **dealt, dealt** sich mit etwas beschäftigen; von etwas handeln IV

dealt [delt] siehe **deal**

Dictionary

dear [dɪə]: **Oh dear!** Oje! II
Dear Sir or Madam, ... [dɪə] (BE) Sehr geehrte Damen und Herren, ... V
death [deθ] Tod IV
debacle [dɪˈbɑːkl] Debakel VI 3 (58)
debate [dɪˈbeɪt] Debatte V
debate sth. [dɪˈbeɪt] über etwas debattieren V
decade [ˈdekeɪd] Jahrzehnt VI 1 (23)
December [dɪˈsembə] Dezember I
decent [ˈdiːsnt] anständig; angemessen VI 3 (69)
decide [dɪˈsaɪd] beschließen, sich entscheiden II
decision [dɪˈsɪʒn] Entscheidung III
deck [dek] Deck (eines Schiffes) I
dedicated [ˈdedɪkeɪtɪd]: **be dedicated to** gewidmet sein (einer Sache/Person) IV
deep [diːp] tief II
deer [dɪə], pl **deer** Reh, Hirsch II
defence [dɪˈfens] Verteidigung V
defend sb./sth. (against sb./sth.) [dɪˈfend] jn./etwas verteidigen (gegen jn./etwas) II
defense [dɪˈfens] (AE) Verteidigung V
define [dɪˈfaɪn] definieren; charakterisieren, ausmachen VI 2 (32/33)
definite [ˈdefɪnət] bestimmte(r, s); definitiv, endgültig, eindeutig V
definitely [ˈdefɪnətli] sicher, bestimmt IV
definition [ˌdefɪˈnɪʃn] Definition VI 2 (32/33)
degree [dɪˈɡriː] Grad IV
delayed [dɪˈleɪd] verspätet VI 2 (39)
delete [dɪˈliːt] löschen; streichen III
deliberate [dɪˈlɪbərət] absichtlich, vorsätzlich VI 3 (59)
delicious [dɪˈlɪʃəs] köstlich, lecker II
delighted [dɪˈlaɪtɪd] hocherfreut, begeistert
deliver [dɪˈlɪvə]:
1. liefern, ausliefern V
2. zustellen, überbringen V
delivery [dɪˈlɪvəri]:
1. Vortrag(sweise) V
2. Lieferung VI 3 (56/57)
demand [dɪˈmɑːnd]:
1. fordern, verlangen V
2. Forderung V
dementia [dɪˈmenʃə] Demenz
democracy [dɪˈmɒkrəsi] Demokratie V
democratic [ˌdeməˈkrætɪk] demokratisch

demonstrate [ˈdemənstreɪt]: **demonstrate for/against sth.** für/gegen etwas demonstrieren V
demonstrate sth. etwas zeigen, demonstrieren, nachweisen V
demonstration [ˌdemənˈstreɪʃn] Demonstration, Vorführung II
denim [ˈdenɪm] Jeansstoff VI 1 (10/11)
dentist [ˈdentɪst] Zahnarzt/-ärztin II
deny [dɪˈnaɪ] bestreiten, abstreiten; leugnen VI 1 (21)
depend on [dɪˈpend] abhängen von; angewiesen sein auf V
dependency [dɪˈpendənsi] Schutzgebiet, Kolonie V
depict [dɪˈpɪk] darstellen, abbilden
depressed [dɪˈprest] depri(miert) VI 1 (14)
depressing [dɪˈpresɪŋ] deprimierend IV
derogatory [dɪˈrɒɡətri] abfällig, abwertend VI 2 (46)
descended [dɪˈsendɪd]: **be descended from** abstammen von V
describe sth. (to sb.) [dɪˈskraɪb] (jm.) etwas beschreiben II
description [dɪˈskrɪpʃn] Beschreibung V
descriptive [dɪˈskrɪptɪv] beschreibend V
desert [ˈdezət] Wüste IV
deserve [dɪˈzɜːv] verdienen (zu Recht bekommen) V
design and technology [dɪˌzaɪn ənd tekˈnɒlədʒi] Design und Technik I
designer [dɪˈzaɪnə] Designer/in II
desire [dɪˈzaɪə] Wunsch, Verlangen VI 1 (12)
desk [desk] Schreibtisch I **cash desk** Kasse (in Geschäften) II
despite [dɪˈspaɪt] trotz, obwohl VI 3 (73)
dessert [dɪˈzɜːt] Nachtisch, Nachspeise I
destination [ˌdestɪˈneɪʃn] (Reise-)Ziel, Bestimmungsort V
destroy [dɪˈstrɔɪ] zerstören II
detail [ˈdiːteɪl] Detail, Einzelheit III
detailed [ˈdiːteɪld] ausführlich, detailliert V
determined [dɪˈtɜːmɪnd]: **be determined to do sth.** (fest) entschlossen sein, etwas zu tun V
devastation [ˌdevəˈsteɪʃn] Verwüstung, Zerstörung V
develop [dɪˈveləp] entwickeln, weiterentwickeln; sich entwickeln V

development [dɪˈveləpmənt] Entwicklung V
device [dɪˈvaɪs] Mittel; Gerät, Apparat VI 1 (15)
diabetes [ˌdaɪəˈbiːtiːz] Diabetes
diagonal [daɪˈæɡənl] diagonal
diagram [ˈdaɪəɡræm] Diagramm VI 1 (14)
dial [ˈdaɪəl] wählen (Telefonnummer) III
dialect [ˈdaɪəlekt] Dialekt VI 1 (16)
dialogue [ˈdaɪəlɒɡ] Dialog II
diary [ˈdaɪəri] Tagebuch; Kalender I
dictionary [ˈdɪkʃənri] alphabetisches Wörterverzeichnis, Wörterbuch I
did [dɪd] siehe **do**
die [daɪ] sterben II
diet [ˈdaɪət] Ernährung(sweise), Speiseplan; Diät VI 3 (62)
differ [ˈdɪfə] sich unterscheiden, verschieden sein VI 1 (18)
difference [ˈdɪfrəns] Unterschied III **make a difference** etwas bewirken, etwas bewegen VI 2 (47)
different [ˈdɪfrənt] verschieden; anders I **take a different view** einen anderen Standpunkt vertreten; anderer Ansicht sein V
difficult [ˈdɪfɪkəlt] schwierig II
difficulty [ˈdɪfɪkəlti] Schwierigkeit(en) V
dig (for sth.) [dɪɡ], **dug, dug** (nach etwas) graben V
digital [ˈdɪdʒɪtl] digital III
diner [ˈdaɪnə] (AE) (kleines, preiswertes) Restaurant IV
dining room [ˈdaɪnɪŋ ruːm] Esszimmer I
dinner [ˈdɪnə] Abendessen, Abendbrot I
dinosaur [ˈdaɪnəsɔː] Dinosaurier VI 2 (52)
diploma [dɪˈpləʊmə]: **High School Diploma** Schulabschluss in den USA (mit Hochschulzugangsberechtigung) V
diplomacy [dɪˈpləʊməsi] Diplomatie V
diplomat [ˈdɪpləmæt] Diplomat/in VI 2 (54)
direct [dəˈrekt], [daɪˈrekt] direkt V **direct marketing** Direktvertrieb, Direktmarketing V
direction [dəˈrekʃn] Richtung III **ask for directions** nach dem Weg fragen IV **give sb. directions (to)** jm. den Weg beschreiben (zu/nach) IV
director [dəˈrektə] Regisseur/in II

dirty ['dɜːti] schmutzig II

disadvantage [ˌdɪsəd'vɑːntɪdʒ] Nachteil III

disagree (with) [ˌdɪsə'griː] anderer Meinung sein (als); nicht übereinstimmen (mit); nicht zustimmen V

disagreement [ˌdɪsə'griːmənt] Uneinigkeit, Zerwürfnis, Streit V

disappear [ˌdɪsə'pɪə] verschwinden II

disappearance [ˌdɪsə'pɪərəns] Verschwinden; Aussterben VI 3 (64)

disappointed (with) [ˌdɪsə'pɔɪntɪd] enttäuscht (von) IV

disco ['dɪskəʊ] Disko II

disconnection [ˌdɪskə'nekʃn] Abkopplung, Trennung VI 3 (58)

discourage [dɪs'kʌrɪdʒ] unterbinden, zu verhindern suchen; abschrecken V **discourage sb. from doing sth.** jn. davon abhalten, etwas zu tun V

discover [dɪ'skʌvə] entdecken; herausfinden IV

discovery [dɪ'skʌvəri] Entdeckung IV

discriminate against sb. [dɪ'skrɪmɪneɪt] jn. diskriminieren, jn. benachteiligen VI 1 (20)

discrimination (against) [dɪˌskrɪmɪ'neɪʃn] Diskriminierung (von) IV

discuss sth. [dɪ'skʌs] über etwas diskutieren, etwas besprechen V

discussion [dɪ'skʌʃn] Diskussion III **panel discussion** Podiumsdiskussion VI 3 (56/57)

disease [dɪ'ziːz] (ansteckende) Krankheit V

disgusting [dɪs'gʌstɪŋ] ekelhaft, widerlich IV

dish [dɪʃ] Gericht (Speise) IV **wash the dishes (pl)** das Geschirr abwaschen, spülen II

dishonest [dɪs'ɒnɪst] unehrlich V

dishonesty [dɪs'ɒnɪsti] Unehrlichkeit, Unredlichkeit V

dishwasher ['dɪʃwɒʃə] Geschirrspüler III

dislike [dɪs'laɪk]:
1. nicht mögen V
2. likes and dislikes (pl) Vorlieben und Abneigungen I

°**disorder** [dɪs'ɔːdə] Störung; Krankheit

display [dɪ'spleɪ] Ausstellung, Vorführung, Schau VI 2 (46) **be on display** ausgestellt sein VI 2 (46)

disrespectful [ˌdɪsrɪ'spektfl] respektlos V

disruption [dɪs'rʌpʃn] Störung, Beeinträchtigung; Zusammenbruch VI 2 (47) **social disruption** soziale Spannungen, sozialer Zerfall VI 2 (47)

distance ['dɪstəns] Ferne; Entfernung III

distant ['dɪstənt] (weit) entfernt, fern VI 2 (42)

distinct [dɪ'stɪŋkt] verschieden, unterschiedlich; deutlich VI 3 (59)

distract [dɪ'strækt] ablenken V

distraction [dɪ'strækʃn] Ablenkung V

°**distribution** [ˌdɪstrɪ'bjuːʃn] Verteilung

district ['dɪstrɪkt] Gegend, Bezirk, Viertel III

°**disturbing** [dɪ'stɜːbɪŋ] verstörend, erschütternd

ditch [dɪtʃ] Graben III

dive in [daɪv‿'ɪn] hineinspringen III

diversity [daɪ'vɜːsəti] Vielfalt, Verschiedenartigkeit VI 2 (46)

divide (into) [dɪ'vaɪd] (sich) teilen (in), (sich) aufteilen (in) IV

°**division** [dɪ'vɪʒn] Teilung, Spaltung

divorced [dɪ'vɔːst] geschieden I

dizzy ['dɪzi] schwindlig III

°**DNA** [ˌdiː en 'eɪ] DNS

do [duː], **did, done** machen, tun I **do sport** Sport treiben I **Don't go.** Geh nicht. I **he doesn't have time** er hat keine Zeit I

dock [dɒk] Hafen III

doctor ['dɒktə] Arzt/Ärztin, Doktor II

document ['dɒkjumənt] Dokument V

documentary [ˌdɒkju'mentri] Dokumentarfilm V

dog [dɒg] Hund I

dollar ($) ['dɒlə] Dollar IV

dominate ['dɒmɪneɪt] dominieren, beherrschen V

done [dʌn] siehe **do**

°**doom and gloom** [ˌduːm ən 'gluːm] Schwarzmalerei, Untergangsszenario

door [dɔː] Tür I

doorbell ['dɔːbel] Türklingel, Türglocke II

°**dot** [dɒt] Pünktchen

double ['dʌbl] Doppel- I

dove [dʌv] Taube VI 1 (15)

down [daʊn] hinunter, herunter; nach unten I **down there** dort unten II **the ups and downs** die Höhen und Tiefen VI 1 (22)

downhill [ˌdaʊn'hɪl] bergab III

download sth. [ˌdaʊn'ləʊd] etwas herunterladen VI 3 (61)

°**downside** ['daʊnsaɪd] Kehrseite, Nachteil

downstairs [ˌdaʊn'steəz] unten; nach unten I

downstream [ˌdaʊn'striːm] flussabwärts III

downtown ['daʊntaʊn] (AE) im Zentrum IV

dozen ['dʌzn] Dutzend VI 3 (69)

draft [drɑːft] Entwurf II

drain [dreɪn] entwässern, trockenlegen V

drama ['drɑːmə] Schauspiel; darstellende Kunst II

dramatic [drə'mætɪk] dramatisch IV

drank [dræŋk] siehe **drink**

drastic ['dræstɪk] drastisch V

draw [drɔː], **drew, drawn** zeichnen II **draw attention to sth.** auf etwas aufmerksam machen; die Aufmerksamkeit auf etwas lenken V

°**drawback** ['drɔːbæk] Schattenseite, Nachteil

drawing ['drɔːɪŋ] Zeichnung II

drawn [drɔːn] siehe **draw**

dreadlocks (pl) ['dredlɒks] Rasta-Locken VI 1 (10/11)

dream [driːm]:
1. Traum I
2. träumen V

dress [dres] Kleid I

dress up [ˌdres‿'ʌp] sich verkleiden; sich schick anziehen II

dressed [drest]: **be dressed** angezogen sein VI 1 (10/11)

drew [druː] siehe **draw**

drink [drɪŋk]:
1. Getränk I
2. (drank, drunk) trinken I

drive [draɪv]:
1. Fahrt IV
2. (drove, driven) (mit dem Auto) fahren II **driving licence** (BE) Führerschein, Fahrerlaubnis IV

driven [drɪvn] siehe **drive**

driver ['draɪvə] Fahrer/in III **driver's license** (AE) Führerschein, Fahrerlaubnis IV

drone [drəʊn] Drohne VI 3 (56/57)

drop sth. [drɒp] etwas fallen lassen II

drought [draʊt] Dürre, Trockenheit IV

drove [drəʊv] siehe **drive**

drown [draʊn] ertrinken III

drum [drʌm] Trommel ı **drums** (pl)
Schlagzeug ı **play the drums**
Schlagzeug spielen ı

drunk [drʌŋk]:
1. siehe **drink**
2. betrunken VI 2 (34)

dry [draɪ] trocken III

due to [djuː] aufgrund, infolge V

dug [dʌg] siehe **dig**

during [ˈdjʊərɪŋ] während III

dust [dʌst] Staub IV

dusty [ˈdʌsti] staubig VI 3 (68)

duty [ˈdjuːti] Aufgabe, Pflicht V
be off duty außer Dienst sein, keinen Dienst haben V **be on duty** im
Dienst sein, Dienst haben V

DVD [ˌdiːviːˈdiː] DVD ı

E

each [iːtʃ] jeder, jede, jedes (einzelne) II **each other** sich (gegensei-
tig), einander III

ear [ɪə] Ohr II

early [ˈɜːli] früh ı

earn [ɜːn] verdienen (Geld) III

earphones (pl) [ˈɪəfəʊnz] Ohrhörer,
Kopfhörer II

earring [ˈɪərɪŋ] Ohrring IV

earth [ɜːθ]: **(the) earth** (die) Erde
(der Planet) II **on earth** auf der
Erde II

earthquake [ˈɜːθkweɪk] Erdbeben
VI 1 (22)

east [iːst] Osten; nach Osten; östlich
III

eastbound [ˈiːstbaʊnd] Richtung
Osten III

easy [ˈiːzi] leicht, einfach II **easy-
going** locker, unbeschwert, gelassen
V

eat [iːt]**, ate, eaten** essen ı

eaten [ˈiːtn] siehe **eat**

°**economical** [ˌiːkəˈnɒmɪkl] ökono-
misch, sparsam

economy [ɪˈkɒnəmi] (Volks-)Wirt-
schaft, Ökonomie V

edge [edʒ] Rand, Kante III

edit [ˈedɪt] bearbeiten; schneiden
(Film, Video) ı

editor [ˈedɪtə] Redakteur/in; Heraus-
geber/in III

education [ˌedʒuˈkeɪʃn] (Schul-,
Aus-)Bildung; Erziehung III

educational [ˌedʒuˈkeɪʃənl] lehrreich, informativ; Bildungs- V

effect (on) [ɪˈfekt] (Aus-)Wirkung
(auf) IV

effective [ɪˈfektɪv] effektiv, wir-
kungsvoll V

effectiveness [ɪˈfektɪvnəs] Wirk-
samkeit, Effektivität VI 3 (64)

effort [ˈefət] Anstrengung; Bemü-
hung, Mühe V **make an effort**
sich Mühe geben; Anstrengungen unternehmen V

e.g. [ˌiː ˈdʒiː] z.B. (zum Beispiel) II

egg [eg] Ei ı

eight [eɪt] acht ı

either [ˈaɪðə], [ˈiːðə]: **not ... either**
auch nicht ı

elderly [ˈeldəli] ältere(r, s) V **the
elderly** (pl) ältere Menschen V

elect sb. [ɪˈlekt] jn. wählen V

election [ɪˈlekʃn] Wahl V
°**presidential election** Präsidentschaftswahl

electric [ɪˈlektrɪk] elektrisch VI 3 (58)

electricity [ɪˌlekˈtrɪsəti] Elektrizität,
Strom VI 3 (58)

electronic [ɪˌlekˈtrɒnɪk] elektronisch
VI 1 (17)

element [ˈelɪmənt] Element VI 2 (40)

elephant [ˈelɪfənt] Elefant ı

elevator [ˈelɪveɪtə] (bes. AE) Fahrstuhl, Aufzug, Lift IV

eleven [ɪˈlevn] elf ı

eliminate [ɪˈlɪmɪneɪt] abschaffen,
beseitigen, eliminieren VI 1 (18)

else [els] sonst III **anything else?**
sonst noch etwas? III **everybody
else** alle anderen; sonst jeder III
someone else jemand anders III
What else can you do? Was kannst
du (sonst) noch tun? III **what else?**
was (sonst) noch? III **who else?**
wer (sonst) noch? III

elsewhere [ˌelsˈweə] anderswo
VI 3 (58)

email [ˈiːmeɪl]:
1. E-Mail ı
2. **email (sb. sth.)** (jm. etwas) mai-
len VI 2 (49)

embarrass sb. [ɪmˈbærəs] jn. in Verlegenheit bringen IV

embarrassed [ɪmˈbærəst] verlegen;
peinlich berührt IV

embrace [ɪmˈbreɪs] annehmen, mit
offenen Armen begrüßen; (sich) umarmen VI 2 (46)

emergency [ɪˈmɜːdʒənsi] Notfall,
Not- IV

emotion [ɪˈməʊʃn] Gefühl, Emotion
III

emotional [ɪˈməʊʃənl] emotional;
gefühlsbetont IV

emphasis [ˈemfəsɪs] Betonung, Hervorhebung VI 2 (45)

emphasize [ˈemfəsaɪz] betonen,
hervorheben VI 2 (45)

emphatic [ɪmˈfætɪk] nachdrücklich,
eindringlich, emphatisch VI 1 (21)

empire [ˈempaɪə] Reich, Imperium V

employ sb. [ɪmˈplɔɪ] jn. anstellen, jn.
beschäftigen V **self-employed**
selbstständig V

employee [ɪmˈplɔɪiː] Arbeitnehmer/in
V

employer [ɪmˈplɔɪə] Arbeitgeber/in
V

employment [ɪmˈplɔɪmənt] Anstel-
lung, Arbeit V

empower sb. [ɪmˈpaʊə] jn. stärken;
jn. befähigen/in die Lage versetzen
(, etwas zu tun) V

empty [ˈempti] leer III

encore [ˈɒŋkɔː] Zugabe II

encourage sb. [ɪnˈkʌrɪdʒ] jn. ermu-
tigen, jn. ermuntern V

end [end]:
1. Ende, Schluss ı
2. enden; beenden II

ending [ˈendɪŋ] Ende, (Ab-)Schluss
II

°**endless** [ˈendləs] endlos

endorsement [ɪnˈdɔːsmənt]
Endorsement (Produktempfehlung
durch eine berühmte Person) V

enemy [ˈenəmi] Feind/in II

energy [ˈenədʒi] Energie, Kraft III
solar energy Solarenergie, Sonnenenergie V

°**enforcement** (fml.) [ɪnˈfɔːsmənt]:
law enforcement Rechtsdurchsetzung, Vollzug

engaging [ɪnˈgeɪdʒɪŋ] fesselnd (Literatur, Film u.Ä.) VI 2 (42)

engine [endʒɪn]: **search engine** (In-
ternet-)Suchmaschine VI 1 (16)

engineer [ˌendʒɪˈnɪə] Ingenieur/in
III

engineering [ˌendʒɪˈnɪərɪŋ] Ingeni-
eurwesen, Maschinenbau V

English [ˈɪŋglɪʃ] Englisch; englisch ı
in English auf Englisch ı

enjoy [ɪnˈdʒɔɪ] genießen III
I enjoyed myself. Ich habe mich
amüsiert. / Ich hatte Spaß. III

enjoyable [ɪnˈdʒɔɪəbl] angenehm,
unterhaltsam VI 2 (45)

enormous [ɪˈnɔːməs] riesig, gewaltig, enorm VI 2 (42)

enough [ɪˈnʌf] genug ı

ensure [ɪnˈʃʊə], [ɪnˈʃɔː] gewährleisten, sicherstellen VI 3 (62)

enter [ˈentə] betreten, hineingehen in; eintreten III

entertaining [ˌentəˈteɪnɪŋ] unterhaltsam, amüsant, kurzweilig VI 2 (45)

entertainment [ˌentəˈteɪnmənt] Unterhaltung (Belustigung, Vergnügen) V

enthusiastic (about) [ɪnˌθjuːziˈæstɪk] begeistert (von) V

entire [ɪnˈtaɪə] ganze(r,s) V

entirely [ɪnˈtaɪəli] völlig, gänzlich V

entry [ˈentri]:
1. Eintrag, Eintragung (im Tagebuch, Wörterbuch) II
2. Eintritt, Zutritt III

environment [ɪnˈvaɪrənmənt] Umwelt IV

environmentally friendly [ɪnvaɪrənˌmentəli ˈfrendli] umweltfreundlich, umweltverträglich VI 3 (72)

episode [ˈepɪsəʊd] Episode IV

equal [ˈiːkwəl] gleich V

equality [iˈkwɒləti] Gleichheit, Gleichberechtigung VI 1 (18)

equipment (no pl) [ɪˈkwɪpmənt] Ausrüstung III

erode [ɪˈrəʊd] abtragen, erodieren, auswaschen (Boden) VI 1 (22)

escape [ɪˈskeɪp]:
1. fliehen III
2. Flucht III

especially [ɪˈspeʃli] besonders, vor allem V

essay [ˈeseɪ] Aufsatz V

etc. (et cetera) [etˈsetərə] usw. (und so weiter) II

ethical [ˈeθɪkl] ethisch VI 1 (23)

EU [ˌiː ˈjuː]: **the EU** die EU III

euro (€) [ˈjʊərəʊ] Euro III

Europe [ˈjʊərəp] Europa III

European Union [ˌjʊərəpiːən ˈjuːnɪən]: **the European Union** die Europäische Union III

evacuate [ɪˈvækjueɪt] evakuieren IV

°**evaluate** [ɪˈvæljueɪt] bewerten, einschätzen

°**evaluation** [ɪˌvæljuˈeɪʃn] Bewertung, Beurteilung

eve [iːv]: **New Year's Eve** Silvester II

even [ˈiːvn] sogar II **even if** selbst wenn II **even though** auch wenn; obwohl IV **not even** (noch) nicht einmal II

evening [ˈiːvnɪŋ] Abend I **in the evening** abends, am Abend I

event [ɪˈvent] Ereignis II

eventually [ɪˈventʃuəli] schließlich, letzten Endes VI 2 (42)

ever [ˈevə] jemals I **better than ever** besser als je zuvor II **for ever** (für) immer; ewig II **Have you ever been to …?** Bist du schon (einmal) in … gewesen? I

every day / colour / boat [ˈevri] jeder Tag / jede Farbe / jedes Boot I

everybody [ˈevribɒdi] jeder; alle I **everybody else** alle anderen; sonst jeder III

everyday [ˈevrideɪ] Alltags- I

everyone [ˈevriwʌn] jeder; alle I

everything [ˈevriθɪŋ] alles II

everywhere [ˈevriweə] überall II

evidence [ˈevɪdəns] Nachweis, Beleg, Beweis VI 3 (71)

ex- [eks] Ex-; ehemalige(r, s) V

exact [ɪgˈzækt] genau III

exaggerate [ɪgˈzædʒəreɪt] übertreiben VI 3 (58)

exam [ɪgˈzæm] Prüfung IV

examine [ɪgˈzæmɪn] untersuchen V

example [ɪgˈzɑːmpl] Beispiel II **for example** zum Beispiel II

excellent [ˈeksələnt] ausgezeichnet, hervorragend IV

except [ɪkˈsept] außer, bis auf II

exception [ɪkˈsepʃn] Ausnahme V

excerpt (from) [ˈeksɜːpt] Auszug (aus) IV

exchange [ɪksˈtʃeɪndʒ] Austausch III

excited [ɪkˈsaɪtɪd] aufgeregt, gespannt I

excitement [ɪkˈsaɪtmənt] Aufregung, Begeisterung VI 1 (22)

exciting [ɪkˈsaɪtɪŋ] aufregend, spannend I

exclamation mark [ˌekskləˈmeɪʃn mɑːk] Ausrufezeichen II

excursion [ɪkˈskɜːʃn] Ausflug, Exkursion V

Excuse me, … [ɪkˈskjuːz miː] Entschuldigung, … / Entschuldigen Sie, … II

exercise [ˈeksəsaɪz]:
1. Übung I
exercise book Schulheft, Übungsheft I
2. (no pl) Bewegung, (körperliches) Training VI 2 (49)

exhibition [ˌeksɪˈbɪʃn] Ausstellung; Messe V

exist [ɪgˈzɪst] existieren VI 1 (18)

existent [ɪgˈzɪstənt] existent VI 1 (18)

exotic [ɪgˈzɒtɪk] exotisch IV

expect sth. [ɪkˈspekt] etwas erwarten III

expense [ɪkˈspens] Ausgabe V

expensive [ɪkˈspensɪv] teuer II

experience [ɪkˈspɪəriəns]:
1. erfahren, erleben IV
2. **experience** (no pl) Erfahrung(en) III
work experience (no pl) Arbeitserfahrung(en), Praxiserfahrung(en); Praktikum V

°**experimental (exp)** [ɪkˌsperɪˈmentl] experimentell

expert [ˈekspɜːt] Experte/Expertin IV

explain sth. to sb. [ɪkˈspleɪn] jm. etwas erklären, erläutern I

explanation [ˌekspləˈneɪʃn] Erklärung V

explore [ɪkˈsplɔː] erkunden, erforschen III

explorer [ɪkˈsplɔːrə] Forscher/in, Forschungsreisende(r) V

°**explosive** [ɪkˈspləʊsɪv] explosiv

export [ɪkˈspɔːt] ausführen, exportieren V

export [ˈekspɔːt] Export, Ausfuhr V

express [ɪkˈspres] ausdrücken, zum Ausdruck bringen V

expression [ɪkˈspreʃn]: **facial expression** Gesichtsausdruck, Mimik III

expressive [ɪkˈspresɪv] ausdrucksstark, aussagekräftig VI 1 (21)

extinct [ɪkˈstɪŋkt] ausgestorben V

extinction [ɪkˈstɪŋkʃn] Aussterben V

extra [ˈekstrə] zusätzlich IV

°**extract** [ˈekstrækt] Auszug, Extrakt

extraordinary [ɪkˈstrɔːdnri] außergewöhnlich VI 1 (23)

extremely [ɪkˈstriːmli] äußerst, höchst IV

eye [aɪ] Auge I

F

face [feɪs] Gesicht I **face-to-face** von Angesicht zu Angesicht V

facial [ˈfeɪʃl]: **facial expression** Gesichtsausdruck, Mimik III °**facial recognition** Gesichtserkennung

facilities (pl) [fəˈsɪlətiz] Einrichtungen, Ausstattung, Anlage(n), Angebot(e) V

fact [fækt] Tatsache, Fakt III **in fact** eigentlich, in Wirklichkeit III

factor [ˈfæktə] Faktor VI 3 (62)

factory [ˈfæktri] Fabrik IV

factual ['fæktʃʊəl] sachlich; faktisch; den Tatsachen entsprechend VI 1 (21)

Fahrenheit (F) ['færənhaɪt] Fahrenheit IV

fail (a test) [feɪl] nicht bestehen *(Test, Prüfung)*; durchfallen IV

faint [feɪnt]: **she feels faint** ihr ist schwindelig IV

fair [feə] fair, gerecht IV

fairly ['feəli] ziemlich IV

°**fake** [feɪk] Fälschung; gefälscht

fall [fɔːl]:
1. (fell, fallen) fallen, stürzen; hinfallen I
fall asleep einschlafen I **fall in love (with sb.)** sich (in jn.) verlieben V
2. fall *(AE)* Herbst IV

fallen ['fɔːlən] *siehe* **fall**

false [fɔːls] falsch I

fame [feɪm] Ruhm IV

familiar [fəˈmɪliə] vertraut VI 3 (69)

family ['fæməli] Familie I **family tree** (Familien-)Stammbaum I **a family of four** eine vierköpfige Familie III **host family** Gastfamilie II **the Blackwell family** (die) Familie Blackwell I

famous (for) ['feɪməs] berühmt (für, wegen) II

fan [fæn] Fan, Anhänger/in VI 1 (16)

fancy sth. ['fænsi] *(infml)* Lust auf etwas/zu etwas haben IV

fantastic [fænˈtæstɪk] fantastisch II

fantasy ['fæntəsi] Fantasy *(Genre)*, fantastische Literatur VI 2 (45)

far [fɑː] weit (entfernt) I

faraway ['fɑːrəweɪ] fern, abgelegen, entlegen V

farm [fɑːm] Bauernhof, Farm I

farmer ['fɑːmə] Bauer/Bäuerin, Landwirt/in I

farmhouse ['fɑːmhaʊs] Bauernhaus III

farming ['fɑːmɪŋ] Landwirtschaft V

farmland ['fɑːmlænd] Ackerland; landwirtschaftlich genutzte Fläche V

fashion ['fæʃn] Mode II

fast [fɑːst] schnell I

fasten sth. ['fɑːsn] etwas zumachen, festmachen, befestigen V

fat [fæt] dick, fett II

father ['fɑːðə] Vater I

favourite *(AE: favorite)* ['feɪvərɪt]: **my favourite colour** meine Lieblingsfarbe I

fear [fɪə]:
1. fürchten, befürchten VI 1 (23)
2. fear (of) Angst (vor) VI 1 (23)

feast [fiːst] Festessen V

feature ['fiːtʃə]:
1. Merkmal, Eigenschaft, Kennzeichen V
2. feature sth. etwas featuren, über etwas berichten VI 3 (58)
feature article Sonderbericht, Sonderbeitrag VI 3 (62)

February ['februəri] Februar I

fed [fed] *siehe* **feed**

federal ['fedərəl] Bundes-, bundesstaatlich V **federal republic** Bundesrepublik V

feed [fiːd], **fed, fed** füttern I **feed on** sich ernähren (von) V **feeding time** Fütterungszeit I

feedback ['fiːdbæk] Rückmeldung, Feedback I

feel [fiːl], **felt, felt** fühlen; sich fühlen I **I don't feel well.** Ich fühle mich nicht gut. II **I feel sick.** Mir ist schlecht. II

feeling ['fiːlɪŋ] Gefühl I

feet [fiːt] *siehe* **foot**

fell [fel] *siehe* **fall**

fellow ['feləʊ] *(vor Nomen)* Mit- V

felt [felt] *siehe* **feel**

felt pen [felt 'pen] Filzstift II

female ['fiːmeɪl] weiblich; weibliche Person; Weibchen V

fence [fens] Zaun II

ferry ['feri] Fähre I

festival ['festɪvl] Fest, Festival II

few [ə 'fjuː]: **a few** ein paar, einige II **quite a few** ziemlich viele IV

fewest ['fjuːəst]: **the fewest** die wenigsten V

fiction ['fɪkʃn] Belletristik, Prosa(literatur); Märchen, Fiktion VI 2 (37)

fictional ['fɪkʃənl] fiktiv, erfunden VI 2 (42)

field [fiːld] Feld, Acker, Weide II

fight [faɪt]:
1. Kampf, Schlägerei III
2. (fought, fought) kämpfen I **fight sb.** jn. bekämpfen; gegen jmd. kämpfen II

fighter ['faɪtə] Kämpfer/in II

figure ['fɪgə]:
1. Zahl, Ziffer III
2. Figur, Gestalt III

file [faɪl] Datei, File V

fill [fɪl] füllen III

film [fɪlm]:
1. filmen I
2. Film I

final ['faɪnl]:
1. letzte(r, s), End- III
2. Finale, Endspiel IV

finally ['faɪnəli] endlich, schließlich III

°**finance** ['faɪnæns], [faɪ'næns] finanzieren

find [faɪnd], **found, found** finden I **find sth. out** etwas herausfinden II

fine [faɪn]:
1. fein I
Fine, thanks. Gut, danke. I
2. Geldstrafe VI 1 (20)

finger ['fɪŋgə] Finger II

°**fingernail** ['fɪŋgəneɪl] Fingernagel

finish ['fɪnɪʃ]:
1. enden I
2. finish sth. etwas beenden; mit etwas fertig werden/sein I
We're finished. Wir sind fertig. I

fire ['faɪə] Feuer II

firefighter ['faɪəfaɪtə] Feuerwehrmann/-frau IV

fireplace ['faɪəpleɪs] Kamin II

firework ['faɪəwɜːk] Feuerwerkskörper II

fireworks *(pl)* ['faɪəwɜːks] Feuerwerk II

firmly ['fɜːmli] bestimmt, entschieden, nachdrücklich VI 3 (74)

first [fɜːst]:
1. zuerst, als Erstes I
first-person narrative Ich-Erzählung VI 2 (37) **at first** zuerst, anfangs, am Anfang II **In the first place, ...** Erstens ...; Zunächst ... V
2. the first day der erste Tag I

Firstly, ... ['fɜːstli] Erstens ... V

fish [fɪʃ], *pl* **fish** Fisch I

°**fission** ['fɪʃn] Spaltung **nuclear fission** Kernspaltung

fit [fɪt] passen III

five [faɪv] fünf I

°**fix sth.** [fɪks] festlegen, in Ordnung bringen

flag [flæg] Fahne, Flagge II

flame [fleɪm] Flamme IV

flash [flæʃ]:
1. Lichtblitz II
flash mob Flashmob VI 2 (47)
2. flash through sb.'s mind jm. durch den Kopf schießen IV

flashlight ['flæʃlaɪt] *(AE)* Taschenlampe IV

flat [flæt]:
1. Wohnung I
2. flach, eben IV

flew [fluː] *siehe* **fly**

flexible ['fleksəbl] flexibel V

flight [flaɪt] Flug V **flight attendant** Flugbegleiter/in V **in-flight magazine/meal** Bordmagazin/ Bordmahlzeit V

°**float** [fləʊt] treiben, schwimmen (auf dem Wasser)

flock [flɒk]: **flock of birds** Vogelschar III **flock of sheep/goats** Schaf-/Ziegenherde III

flood [flʌd]:
1. überfluten, überschwemmen IV
2. Flut, Überschwemmung IV

floodlight [ˈflʌdlaɪt] Flutlicht(lampe) IV

floor [flɔː]:
1. Fußboden I
2. Geschoss, Etage, Stockwerk IV

flour [ˈflaʊə] Mehl IV

flow [fləʊ] fließen III **cash flow** Cashflow (die finanzielle Situation) V

flower [ˈflaʊə] Blume; Blüte II

flown [fləʊn] siehe **fly**

fluency [ˈfluːənsi] Flüssigkeit, Gewandtheit VI 3 (58)

fluent [ˈfluːənt] fließend, flüssig (Sprache) VI 3 (58)

flute [fluːt] Querflöte III

fly [flaɪ], **flew, flown** fliegen II

flying fox [ˌflaɪɪŋ ˈfɒks] Flughund V

focus [ˈfəʊkəs] Mittelpunkt, Schwerpunkt III **focus on** fokussieren auf, abzielen auf V

folk [ˈfəʊk mjuːzɪk]: **folk music** Volksmusik III

folk [fəʊk] (pl, infml) Leute V

follow [ˈfɒləʊ miː] folgen I **Follow me.** Folg mir. / Folgt mir. I

follower [ˈfɒləʊə] Follower (Anhänger/in, Fan) VI 2 (47)

font [fɒnt] Schrift(art) VI 1 (17)

food [fuːd] Essen; Lebensmittel; Futter I

foot [fʊt], pl **feet** Fuß (auch Längenmaß; ca. 30 cm) I **a 9,740-foot swimming pool** ein 9.740 Fuß langes Schwimmbad IV

footage [ˈfʊtɪdʒ] Bildmaterial, Film(material) VI 2 (40)

footprint [ˈfʊtprɪnt] Fußabdruck II

footstep [ˈfʊtstep] Schritt IV

for [fɔː], [fə]:
1. für I
for ever (für) immer; ewig II **for example** zum Beispiel II **for now** einstweilen, vorerst, fürs Erste VI 2 (42) **for sale** zum Verkauf, zu verkaufen VI 3 (68) **What's for homework?** Was haben wir als Hausaufgabe auf? I **What's for lunch?** Was gibt es zum Mittagessen? I

2. **for hours/weeks/...** seit Stunden/Wochen/... III
3. **for sure** klar; ganz bestimmt IV

force [fɔːs] zwingen IV **force your way into sth.** sich in etwas eindrängen IV

foreground [ˈfɔːgraʊnd] Vordergrund II

foreign [ˈfɒrən] fremd, ausländisch IV

forest [ˈfɒrɪst] Wald II

forget [fəˈget], **forgot, forgotten** vergessen I

forgot [fəˈgɒt] siehe **forget**

forgotten [fəˈgɒtn] siehe **forget**

fork [fɔːk] Gabel II

form [fɔːm]:
1. bilden, formen III
2. **form (of)** Form (von) I

formal [ˈfɔːml] formell, förmlich V

format [ˈfɔːmæt] formatieren (Text am Computer) VI 1 (17)

forth [fɔːθ]: **back and forth** hin und her; hin und zurück; auf und ab V

fortunately [ˈfɔːtʃənətli] glücklicherweise IV

forward [ˈfɔːwəd]: **look forward to sth.** sich auf etwas freuen II

fossil [ˈfɒsl] Fossilie VI 2 (52) **fossil fuel** fossiler Brennstoff V

fought [fɔːt] siehe **fight**

found [faʊnd]:
1. siehe **find**
2. gründen V

four [fɔː] vier I

fourth [fɔːθ] (AE) Viertel V

fox [fɒks] Fuchs V

°**fraud** [frɔːd]: **voter fraud** Wahlbetrug V

free [friː]:
1. frei I
free kick Freistoß III **free-time activities** Freizeitaktivitäten I **be free** frei haben IV
2. kostenlos II

French [frentʃ] Französisch I

frequency [ˈfriːkwənsi] Häufigkeit VI 3 (60)

frequent [ˈfriːkwənt] häufig IV

fresh [freʃ] frisch II

Friday [ˈfraɪdeɪ], [ˈfraɪdi] Freitag I

friend [frend] Freund/in I **friend request** Freundschaftsanfrage VI 3 (61)

friendly [ˈfrendli] freundlich I

friendship [ˈfrendʃɪp] Freundschaft V

fries [fraɪz] (pl, AE) Pommes frites II

frighten sb. [ˈfraɪtn] jm. Angst machen VI 2 (47)

frightened [ˈfraɪtnd] verängstigt V

frog [frɒg] Frosch I

from [frɒm], [frəm] aus, von I **from ... to ...** von ... bis ... I

front [frʌnt] Vorderseite, vordere Seite II **in front of** vor I

frown [fraʊn] die Stirn runzeln II

frozen [ˈfrəʊzn] tiefgekühlt IV

fruit [fruːt] Obst, Früchte; Frucht I **fruit salad** Obstsalat I **fruits** (pl) Obstarten VI 3 (62)

frustrated [frʌˈstreɪtɪd] frustriert VI 1 (22)

frustrating [frʌˈstreɪtɪŋ] frustrierend VI 1 (22)

frustration [frʌˈstreɪʃn] Frust; Enttäuschung VI 1 (22)

fry [fraɪ] braten (in der Pfanne) IV

frying pan [ˈfraɪɪŋ pæn] Bratpfanne IV

fuel [ˈfjuːəl] Brennstoff V **fossil fuel** fossiler Brennstoff V

full [fʊl]:
1. voll II
full (of) voll (von) II **full sentence** ganzer Satz II **full-time** (Vollzeit-, Ganztags-) V **full-time job** Vollzeitbeschäftigung V
2. **full stop** Punkt II

fun [fʌn] Spaß I **fun park** Vergnügungspark II **have fun** Spaß haben, sich amüsieren I **make fun of sb./sth.** sich über jn./etwas lustig machen III **That sounds fun.** Das klingt nach Spaß. I

function [ˈfʌŋkʃn] Funktion VI 1 (17)

fund [fʌnd] finanzieren V

funeral [ˈfjuːnərəl] Trauerfeier III

funny [ˈfʌni] witzig, komisch I

furious (with/at sb.) [ˈfjʊəriəs] wütend, zornig (auf jn.), wutentbrannt V

furniture (no pl) [ˈfɜːnɪtʃə] Möbel III

further [ˈfɜːðə] weiter II

furthermore [ˌfɜːðəˈmɔː] außerdem, ferner; des Weiteren V

furthest [ˈfɜːðɪst] am weitesten II

°**fusion** [ˈfjuːʒn]: **nuclear fusion** Kernfusion

fuss [fʌs]: **make a fuss about sth.** großen Wirbel um etwas machen III

future [ˈfjuːtʃə]:
1. Zukunft II
2. zukünftige(r, s) II

futuristic [ˌfjuːtʃəˈrɪstɪk] futuristisch VI 3 (71)

G

°**gadget** ['gædʒɪt] Gerät, technischer Krimskrams

gain [geɪn] bekommen; gewinnen V

gallery ['gæləri] Galerie III

gallop ['gæləp] galoppieren III

game [geɪm] Spiel I

°**gap** [gæp] Lücke

garbage ['gɑːbɪdʒ] (AE) Müll, Abfall IV

garden ['gɑːdn] Garten I

gardening ['gɑːdnɪŋ] Gärtnern, Gartenarbeit I

garlic ['gɑːlɪk] Knoblauch IV

gas [gæs]: **greenhouse gas** Treibhausgas V

gas [gæs] (AE) Benzin V

gas station Tankstelle V

gate [geɪt] Tor, Pforte, Gatter II

gather ['gæðə] (sich) versammeln V

gave [geɪv] siehe **give**

gay [geɪ] schwul, lesbisch VI 1 (16)

gaze [geɪz] blicken, starren IV

GCSE (= General Certificate of Secondary Education) [ˌdʒiː siː ˏes 'iː] Prüfung für Schüler/innen ab 15, mittlerer Schulabschluss V

gel [dʒel] Gel I

gender ['dʒendə] (soziales) Geschlecht, Gender V

gene [dʒiːn] Gen VI 1 (22)

general ['dʒenrəl] allgemeine(r, s) V

generalize ['dʒenrəlaɪz] verallgemeinern VI 3 (59)

generate ['dʒenəreɪt] generieren, erzeugen VI 3 (58)

generation [ˌdʒenə'reɪʃn]:
1. Generation IV
2. Erzeugung VI 3 (63)

generous ['dʒenərəs] großzügig V

genetic [dʒə'netɪk] genetisch VI 1 (22)

genetics [dʒə'netɪks] Genetik VI 1 (22)

genre ['ʒɑːnrə] Gattung, Genre VI 2 (45)

gentle ['dʒentl] sanft(mütig) VI 1 (15)

gently ['dʒentli] behutsam, sanft III

geography [dʒi'ɒgrəfi] Geografie I

°**geothermal energy** [dʒiːˌəʊˌθɜːml ˈenədʒi] Erdwärme, Geothermie

gesture ['dʒestʃə] Geste, Gebärde V

get [get], **got, got:**
1. bekommen II
get in touch (with sb.) (mit jm.) Kontakt aufnehmen; sich (mit jm.) in Verbindung setzen II **Did you get it?** (infml) Hast du es verstanden/kapiert/ mitbekommen? II
2. **get sth.** (sich) etwas besorgen, (sich) etwas holen II
3. gelangen, (hin)kommen I
get in(to) a car/taxi (in ein Auto/ Taxi) einsteigen II **get off (the boat)** (aus dem Boot) aussteigen I **get on a bus/train/plane** (in einen Bus/Zug, in ein Flugzeug) einsteigen II **get out (of a car)** (aus einem Auto) aussteigen II **get ready (for)** sich fertig machen (für); sich vorbereiten (auf) II **get to know sb.** jn. kennenlernen V
4. **get angry/cold/...** wütend/ kalt/... werden I
Get lost! Verzieh dich! III
5. **get on** vorankommen, zurechtkommen II
6. **get up** aufstehen I

ghost [gəʊst] Geist, Gespenst I

giant ['dʒaɪənt]:
1. Riese I
2. riesig, Riesen- IV

gift [gɪft] Geschenk; Gabe V **gift voucher** Geschenkgutschein V

giraffe [dʒə'rɑːf] Giraffe I

girl [gɜːl] Mädchen I

girlfriend ['gɜːlfrend] Freundin III

give [gɪv], **gave, given:**
1. geben I
give up aufgeben III
2. **give a talk (about)** einen Vortrag/eine Rede halten (über) I
3. angeben (nennen) IV
4. **give sb. directions (to)** jm. den Weg beschreiben (zu/nach) IV

given ['gɪvn] siehe **give**

glad [glæd] froh, dankbar IV

glance (at) [glɑːns] einen (kurzen) Blick werfen (auf) VI 3 (68)

glass [glɑːs] Glas II **glasses** (pl) (eine) Brille II **a glass of milk** ein Glas Milch II

global ['gləʊbl] global V **global warming** Erderwärmung V

globalization [ˌgləʊbəlaɪ'zeɪʃn] Globalisierung V

globe [gləʊb] Welt, Erdball; Globus; Kugel V

°**gloom** [ˌduːm ən 'gluːm]: **doom and gloom** Schwarzmalerei, Untergangsszenario

glove [glʌv] Handschuh II

glue [gluː] Klebstoff I **glue stick** Klebstift I

glum [glʌm] niedergeschlagen IV

go [gəʊ], **went, gone:**
1. gehen; fahren I
Go ahead. Leg los. / Fang an. / Nur zu. V **go by** vergehen, vorübergehen (Zeit) III **go by car/bus/...** mit dem Auto/Bus/... fahren I **go camping** zelten gehen II **go for a walk** spazieren gehen, einen Spaziergang machen I **go home** nach Hause gehen I **go in** hineingehen II **go into detail** ins Detail gehen, auf Einzelheiten eingehen III **go on** weiterreden, fortfahren, weitermachen I **go on day trips** Tagesausflüge machen II **go on holiday** in Urlaub fahren II **go sailing** segeln; segeln gehen I **go shopping** einkaufen gehen I **go together** zusammenpassen, zueinander passen III **go with sth.** zu etwas passen; zu etwas gehören I **Here we go.** Los geht's. / Jetzt geht's los. I **How's it going?** Wie geht's? / Wie läuft's? IV **My heart goes out to ...** Ich fühle mit ... / Mein Mitgefühl gilt ... IV
2. **go red** rot werden, erröten II
3. **I'm going to sing a song.** Ich werde ein Lied singen. / Ich habe vor ein Lied zu singen. II
4. **Have a go.** Versuch's mal. I

goal [gəʊl] Tor III **save a goal** ein Tor halten, abwehren III

goalkeeper ['gəʊlkiːpə] Torwart, Torfrau III

goat [gəʊt] Ziege II

god, God [gɒd] Gott III

goddess ['gɒdes] Göttin III

gold [gəʊld]:
1. Gold I
2. golden, Gold- II

gone [gɒn] siehe **go**

°**gonna** ['gɒnə] = going to

good [gʊd]:
1. gut I
Good luck! Viel Glück! I **Good morning.** Guten Morgen. I **good-looking** gutaussehend II **be good at kung fu** gut sein in Kung-Fu; gut Kung-Fu können I
2. brav II

Goodbye. [ˌgʊd'baɪ] Auf Wiedersehen. I

goods (pl) [gʊdz] Waren, Güter V

gossip ['gɒsɪp]:
1. Klatsch, Tratsch V
2. klatschen, tratschen V

got [gɒt] siehe **get**

govern ['gʌvən] regieren V

government [ˈɡʌvənmənt] Regierung III

grab [ɡræb] schnappen, packen III
grab sb.'s attention jemandes Aufmerksamkeit erregen; jemandes Aufmerksamkeit gewinnen V

grade [ɡreɪd] (AE) Jahrgangsstufe, Klasse IV **grade (bes. AE)** (Schul-)Note, Zensur IV

graffiti [ɡrəˈfiːti] Graffiti IV

°**grain** [ɡreɪn] Korn, Getreide V

gram [ɡræm] Gramm II

grammar school [ˈɡræmə skuːl] einem deutschen Gymnasium vergleichbare Schulform in GB V

grandfather [ˈɡrænfɑːðə] Großvater I

grandma [ˈɡrænmɑː] Oma I

grandmother [ˈɡrænmʌðə] Großmutter I

grandpa [ˈɡrænpɑː] Opa I

grandparents [ˈɡrænpeərənts] Großeltern II

granite [ˈɡrænɪt] Granit IV

graphic novel [ˌɡræfɪk ˈnɒvl] Bildroman, Comicroman VI 2 (37)

graphics (pl) [ˈɡræfɪks] Grafiken IV

grass [ɡrɑːs] Gras; Rasen II

grave [ɡreɪv] Grab II

great [ɡreɪt] großartig I

great-grandfather [ˌɡreɪt ˈɡrænfɑːðə] Urgroßvater IV

great-grandmother [ˌɡreɪt ˈɡrænmʌðə] Urgroßmutter IV

greatly [ˈɡreɪtli] außerordentlich, sehr VI 3 (62)

green [ɡriːn] grün I

greenhouse [ˈɡriːnhaʊs] Gewächshaus, Treibhaus V **greenhouse gas** Treibhausgas V

greet sb. [ɡriːt] jn. begrüßen V

greeting [ˈɡriːtɪŋ] Begrüßung VI 2 (35)

Greetings, ... (pl) [ˈɡriːtɪŋz] Grüße V

grew [ɡruː] siehe **grow**

grey [ɡreɪ] grau I

gripping [ˈɡrɪpɪŋ] spannend, fesselnd VI 2 (45)

groan [ɡrəʊn]:
1. stöhnen II
2. Stöhnen II

groceries (pl) [ˈɡrəʊsəriz] Lebensmittel V

grocery (store) [ˈɡrəʊsəri] Lebensmittelgeschäft V

ground [ɡraʊnd]:
1. (Erd-)Boden II
grounds (pl) Gelände IV

2. **ground sb.** jm. Hausarrest/Ausgehverbot erteilen III

group (of) [ɡruːp] Gruppe I **pressure group** Pressuregroup, Lobby V

grow [ɡrəʊ]**, grew, grown:**
1. wachsen II
grow smaller/old/... (allmählich) kleiner/alt/... werden VI 2 (42)
grow up erwachsen werden; aufwachsen III
2. anbauen, anpflanzen I
▶ S. 215 (to) grow

grown [ɡrəʊn] siehe **grow**

°**growth** [ɡrəʊθ] Wachstum V

grub [ɡrʌb]: (infml) Essen V

guard [ɡɑːd]:
1. bewachen III
2. Wachposten, Wache IV

guess [ɡes] raten, erraten I **And guess what!** Und stell dir / stellt euch vor! Und weißt du / wisst ihr was? II **I guess ...** Ich nehme an, ... / Ich denke, ... IV

guest [ɡest] Gast III

guide [ɡaɪd]:
1. Fremdenführer/in; Reiseleiter/in II
2. führen V
guided tour Führung V

guidebook [ˈɡaɪdbʊk] Reiseführer III

guideline [ˈɡaɪdlaɪn] Richtlinie, Richtschnur V

guinea pig [ˈɡɪni pɪɡ] Meerschweinchen I

guitar [ɡɪˈtɑː] Gitarre I **play the guitar** Gitarre spielen I

gun [ɡʌn] Schusswaffe V

guy [ɡaɪ] Mann; Junge III **guys** (pl) Leute III

gym [dʒɪm] Turnhalle I

gymnastics [dʒɪmˈnæstɪks] Gymnastik, Turnen I

H

habit [ˈhæbɪt] (An-)Gewohnheit IV

habitat [ˈhæbɪtæt] Lebensraum VI 3 (62)

hacker [ˈhækə] Hacker/in V

had [hæd] siehe **have**

hair [heə] Haar, Haare I

hairdresser [ˈheədresə] Friseur/in III

hairstyle [ˈheəstaɪl] Frisur VI 1 (10/11)

half [hɑːf], pl **halves:**
1. Hälfte V
2. **half past ten** halb elf (10.30 / 22.30) I

hall [hɔːl]: **sports hall** Sporthalle VI 1 (25) **town hall** Rathaus II °**school hall** Aula

halves [hɑːvz] siehe **half**

hammer [ˈhæmə] Hammer III

hamster [ˈhæmstə] Hamster II

hand [hænd]:
1. Hand I
On the one hand, ... On the other hand, ... Einerseits ... Andererseits ... V
2. **hand sth. down** weitergeben; vererben V
hand sth. in etwas abgeben; etwas einreichen II

handball [ˈhændbɔːl] Handball VI 2 (38)

handful [ˈhændfʊl]: **a handful of ...** eine Handvoll ... VI 1 (22)

handle sth. [ˈhændl] etwas handhaben, mit etwas umgehen (können), mit etwas fertig werden V

handy [ˈhændi] (infml) nützlich, praktisch, hilfreich; griffbereit, zur Hand; geschickt V **come in handy** sich als nützlich erweisen V

hang [hæŋ]**, hung, hung:**
1. **hang out** abhängen, rumhängen III
2. **hang sth. up** etwas aufhängen II

happen (to) [ˈhæpən] geschehen, passieren (mit) II

happen to do sth. [ˈhæpn] zufällig(erweise) etwas tun VI 2 (34)

happiness [ˈhæpinəs] Glück IV

happy [ˈhæpi] glücklich, froh I

harbour [ˈhɑːbə] Hafen I

hard [hɑːd] schwer, schwierig; hart I **hard-working** fleißig V **be hard on sb.** streng mit jm. sein; hart mit jm. umgehen V

hardly [ˈhɑːdli] kaum IV

hardware [ˈhɑːdweə] Hardware VI 3 (69)

harmful [ˈhɑːmfl] schädlich VI 1 (23)

harmless [ˈhɑːmləs] harmlos VI 1 (23)

harmonica [hɑːˈmɒnɪkə] Mundharmonika IV

°**harmonized** [ˈhɑːmənaɪzd] angeglichen, in/im Einklang

harmony [ˈhɑːməni] Harmonie, Eintracht VI 2 (46)

harvest [ˈhɑːvɪst] Ernte V

has [hæz]: **he/she has** er/sie hat I

hat [hæt] Hut II

hate [heɪt] hassen III

have [hæv], [həv], **had, had** haben I **Have a go.** Versuch's mal. I **have a look (at sth.)** nachschauen; einen

Blick auf etwas werfen III **have a shower** (sich) duschen III **have a toothache/a headache/asore throat** Zahnschmerzen/Kopfschmerzen/Halsschmerzen haben II **have breakfast** frühstücken I **have dinner** zu Abend essen I **have lunch** zu Mittag essen I **have sb. do sth.** jn. etwas tun lassen; veranlassen, dass jemand etwas tut VI 1 (18) **have sth. done** etwas machen *(erledigen)* lassen VI 1 (18) **have to go/work/...** gehen/arbeiten/... müssen I **Have you got ...?** Haben Sie ...? / Hast du ...? / Habt ihr ...? II **I'll have a tea/pizza/...** Ich nehme einen Tee/eine Pizza/... *(beim Essen, im Restaurant)* II **May I have a word with you?** Kann ich Sie/dich kurz sprechen? II

▶ S. 208 (to) have sb. do sth. – (to) have sth. done

hawk [hɔːk] Habicht; *(im übertragenen Sinn:)* Falke VI 1 (15)

hay [heɪ] Heu II

he [hiː] er I

head [hed]:
1. Kopf II
head teacher Schulleiter/in III
2. head for sth. auf etwas zusteuern/zugehen/zufahren IV

headache ['hedeɪk] Kopfschmerzen II

heading ['hedɪŋ] Überschrift IV

headline ['hedlaɪn] Schlagzeile, Überschrift VI 1 (19)

headphones *(pl)* ['hedfəʊnz] Kopfhörer VI 1 (12)

headscarf ['hedskɑːf], *pl* **headscarves** Kopftuch VI 1 (10/11)

headword ['hedwɜːd] Stichwort *(im Wörterbuch)* III

health [helθ] Gesundheit V **mental health** psychische Gesundheit V °**health insurance** Krankenversicherung

healthy ['helθi] gesund IV

hear [hɪə], **heard, heard** hören I

heard [hɜːd] *siehe* **hear**

heart [hɑːt] Herz II **have sb's. best interests at heart** jds. Bestes wollen VI 3 (59) **My heart goes out to ...** Ich fühle mit ... / Mein Mitgefühl gilt ... IV

heartbreaking ['hɑːtbreɪkɪŋ] herzzerreißend VI 2 (45)

heartbroken ['hɑːtbrəʊkən] todunglücklich, untröstlich V

heat [hiːt]:
1. erhitzen; heizen V
2. Hitze, Wärme V

heather ['heðə] Heide(kraut) III

heavy ['hevi] schwer *(von Gewicht)* II **heavy rain** starker Regen, heftiger Regen II

°**hedge fund** ['hedʒ fʌnd] *stark spekulierender Investmentfonds*

height [haɪt] Höhe, (Körper-)Größe V

held [held] *siehe* **hold**

helicopter ['helɪkɒptə] Hubschrauber, Helikopter IV

Hello. [hə'ləʊ] Hallo. / Guten Tag. I **Say hello to ... for me.** Grüß ... von mir. II

help [help]:
1. helfen I
Help yourselves. Greift zu! / Bedient euch! III
2. Hilfe I

helper ['helpə] Helfer/in II

helpful ['helpfl] hilfreich IV

her [hɜː]:
1. sie; ihr I
2. ihr, ihre I
her best friend ihr bester Freund / ihre beste Freundin I

herb [hɜːb] (Gewürz-)Kraut IV

herd [hɜːd] Herde V

here [hɪə] hier; hierher I **Here we go.** Los geht's. / Jetzt geht's los. I **Here you are.** Bitte sehr. / Hier bitte. II **near here** (hier) in der Nähe I **up here** hier oben; nach hier oben II

hero ['hɪərəʊ], *pl* **heroes** Held/in III

hers [hɜːz] ihrer, ihre, ihrs II

herself [hɜː'self] sich III

hesitate ['hezɪteɪt] zögern V

hibernation [ˌhaɪbə'neɪʃn] Winterschlaf VI 3 (62)

hid [hɪd] *siehe* **hide**

hidden [hɪdn] *siehe* **hide**

hide [haɪd], **hid, hidden** (sich) verstecken I

high [haɪ] hoch II **high winds** *(pl)* starker Wind, starke Winde VI 1 (24) **a high-quality translation** eine qualitativ hochwertige Übersetzung V

high school ['haɪ skuːl] (USA) Schule für 14- bis 18-Jährige IV **High School Diploma** *Schulabschluss in den USA (mit Hochschulzugangsberechtigung)* V

Highlands *(pl)* ['haɪləndz]: **the Highlands** das schottische Hochland III

highlight ['haɪlaɪt] hervorheben, markieren *(mit Textmarker)* II

highly ['haɪli] sehr, höchst, äußerst, ausgesprochen V

hiking ['haɪkɪŋ] (das) Wandern V **go hiking** (berg)wandern gehen V

hilarious [hɪ'leəriəs] urkomisch, unheimlich witzig VI 2 (45)

hill [hɪl] Hügel V

him [hɪm] ihn; ihm I

himself [hɪm'self] sich IV **He killed the alligator himself.** Er hat den Alligator selbst getötet. IV **The director himself welcomed us.** Der Regisseur selbst hieß uns willkommen. IV

Hindi ['hɪndi] Hindi V

hint (at sth.) [hɪnt] (etwas) andeuten, durchblicken lassen VI 2 (43)

hip [hɪp] Hüfte III

hire ['haɪə] *(Person)* einstellen; mieten, leihen V

his [hɪz]:
1. his mum seine Mama I
2. seiner, seine, seins II

historic [hɪ'stɒrɪk] historisch *(geschichtlich bedeutsam)* IV

historical [hɪ'stɒrɪkl] historisch, geschichtlich VI 1 (21)

history ['hɪstri] Geschichte I **natural history** Naturkunde III

hit [hɪt], **hit, hit** schlagen; treffen (auf); *(Ball)* schlagen gegen II

hobby ['hɒbi], *pl* **hobbies** Hobby I

hold [həʊld], **held, held** abhalten *(Veranstaltung)* V **Hold on a minute.** Bleib / Bleiben Sie am Apparat. *(am Telefon)* II **hold onto sth.** sich an etwas festhalten III

hole [həʊl] Loch II

holiday ['hɒlədeɪ] Urlaub II **holidays** *(pl)* Ferien I **be on holiday** in Urlaub sein II **go on holiday** in Urlaub fahren II

holidaymaker ['hɒlədeɪmeɪkə] Urlauber/in I

home [həʊm] Heim, Zuhause I **be home to sth.** Heimat sein für etwas; etwas beheimaten III **go home** nach Hause gehen I

°**home-made** [həʊm 'meɪd] hausgemacht, selbstgemacht

homesick ['həʊmsɪk]: **be homesick** Heimweh haben V **get homesick** Heimweh bekommen V

hometown [ˌhəʊm'taʊn] Heimatstadt I

homework ['həʊmwɜːk] Hausaufgabe(n) I **Do your homework.** Mach deine Hausaufgaben. I **What's for homework?** Was haben wir als Hausaufgabe auf? I

honest ['ɒnɪst] ehrlich V

honesty ['ɒnəsti] Ehrlichkeit V

honey ['hʌni]:
1. Honig IV
2. *(infml, als Anrede:)* Schatz, Schätzchen IV

honk [hɒŋk] hupen IV

honour ['ɒnə] Ehre II

hood [hʊd] Kapuze VI 1 (12)

hook [hʊk]:
1. Haken IV
2. an den Haken / an die Angel bekommen IV

hope [həʊp] hoffen I

hopeful ['həʊpfl] zuversichtlich, hoffnungsvoll V

hopefully ['həʊpfəli] hoffnungsvoll, voller Hoffnung; hoffentlich V

°**horizontal** [ˌhɒrɪ'zɒntl] horizontal V

horror ['hɒrə] **in horror** entsetzt III

horse [hɔːs] Pferd I

hospital ['hɒspɪtl] Krankenhaus II

host [həʊst] Gastgeber/in; Moderator/in V **host family** Gastfamilie II

hostel ['hɒstl] Herberge, Wohnheim III

hostess ['həʊstəs] Gastgeberin *(in USA auch: Frau, die in einem Restaurant die Gäste in Empfang nimmt)* IV

hot [hɒt]:
1. heiß I
2. scharf *(gewürzt)* IV

hour ['aʊə] Stunde I **a 24-hour supermarket** ein Supermarkt, der 24 Stunden geöffnet ist IV **a two-hour lesson** eine zweistündige Unterrichtsstunde IV

house [haʊs]:
1. Haus I
°**the House of Lords** das Oberhaus *(des britischen Parlaments)*
°**2. the House of Commons** das Unterhaus *(des britischen Parlaments)*

household ['haʊshəʊld] Haushalt; Haushalts- V

how [haʊ] wie I **How are you?** Wie geht's? / Wie geht es dir/euch? I **How do you know …?** Woher weißt/kennst du …? III **How do you like it?** Wie findest du es (sie/

ihn)? / Wie gefällt es (sie/er) dir? I

how many wie viele I **how much** wie viel I **How much are …?** Was kosten …? I **How much is …?** Was kostet …? I **How old are you?** Wie alt bist du? I **how to do sth.** wie man etwas macht / machen kann / machen soll III **How's it going?** Wie geht's? / Wie läuft's? IV

however [haʊ'evə] aber; allerdings; jedoch IV

hug [hʌg]:
1. **hug sb.** jn. umarmen II
2. **give sb. a hug** jn. umarmen II

huge [hjuːdʒ] riesig, sehr groß III

human ['hjuːmən] Mensch; menschlich V **human being** Mensch V **human race** Menschheit VI 1 (22)

humanity [hjuː'mænəti] Menschheit; Menschlichkeit, Humanität VI 1 (23)

humid ['hjuːmɪd] feucht, feuchtwarm V

humour ['hjuːmə]: **sense of humour** (Sinn für) Humor III

hundred ['hʌndrəd]: **a/one hundred** einhundert I

hung [hʌŋ] *siehe* **hang**

hungry ['hʌŋgri]: **be hungry** hungrig sein, Hunger haben II

hunt [hʌnt] jagen IV

hurricane ['hʌrɪkən] Hurrikan, Orkan IV

hurry ['hʌri] eilen; sich beeilen II **hurry up** sich beeilen I

hurt [hɜːt]:
1. **(hurt, hurt)** schmerzen, wehtun; verletzen II
2. verletzt II

hurtful ['hɜːtfl] verletzend V

husband ['hʌzbənd] Ehemann VI 1 (18)

°**hydro energy** [ˌhaɪdrəʊ_'enədʒi] Wasserkraft

°**hydrogen** ['haɪdrədʒən] Wasserstoff

hyphen ['haɪfən] Bindestrich II

hypothetical [ˌhaɪpə'θetɪkl] hypothetisch VI 3 (68)

I

I [aɪ] ich I **I'm from Plymouth.** Ich bin aus Plymouth. / Ich komme aus Plymouth. I **I'm … (= I am …)** Ich bin … I **I'm afraid …** Leider … V

ice [aɪs] Eis II **ice cream** (Speise-) Eis I

icon ['aɪkɒn] Symbol, Icon VI 3 (61)

ICT [ˌaɪ siː 'tiː] Informations- und Kommunikationstechnologie I

ID card [ˌaɪ 'diː kɑːd] Personalausweis III

idea [aɪ'dɪə] Idee; Vorstellung I **We had no idea where to go.** Wir hatten keine Ahnung, wohin wir gehen sollten. III

ideal [aɪ'dɪəl] ideal V

identical [aɪ'dentɪkl] identisch VI 3 (68)

identify sb./sth. (by sth.) [aɪ'dentɪfaɪ] jn./etwas identifizieren (anhand von etwas) V

identity [aɪ'dentəti] Identität V

if [ɪf]:
1. wenn, falls II
even if selbst wenn II
2. ob IV
as if als ob IV

ignorant ['ɪgnərənt] unwissend, nicht informiert, schlecht informiert VI 2 (42)

ignore [ɪg'nɔː] nicht beachten, ignorieren V

ill [ɪl] krank II

illegal [ɪ'liːgl] illegal, ungesetzlich IV

illegible [ɪ'ledʒəbl] unleserlich VI 1 (17)

illness ['ɪlnəs] Krankheit V

illogical [ɪ'lɒdʒɪkl] unlogisch V

°**illustrate** ['ɪləstraɪt] illustrieren

illustration [ˌɪlə'streɪʃn] Illustration, Abbildung V

image ['ɪmɪdʒ] Bild, Abbild; Vorstellung IV

imagery ['ɪmɪdʒəri] bildhafte Sprache; Sprachbilder VI 1 (15)

imagination [ɪˌmædʒɪ'neɪʃn] Vorstellung(skraft), Fantasie VI 3 (68)

imagine sth. [ɪ'mædʒɪn] sich etwas vorstellen I

immediately [ɪ'miːdiətli] sofort III

immigrant ['ɪmɪgrənt] Einwanderer/Einwanderin IV

°**immigration** [ˌɪmɪ'greɪʃn] Einwanderung

immortality [ˌɪmɔː'tæləti] Unsterblichkeit, Unvergänglichkeit VI 3 (68)

immune system [ɪ'mjuːn ˌsɪstəm] Immunsystem VI 3 (62)

impact ['ɪmpækt] Auswirkung, Effekt V

impatience [ɪm'peɪʃns] Ungeduld V

impatient [ɪm'peɪʃnt] ungeduldig IV

impolite [ˌɪmpə'laɪt] unhöflich III

import [ɪmˈpɔːt] importieren V

import [ˈɪmpɔːt] Import, Einfuhr V

importance [ɪmˈpɔːtəns] Wichtigkeit, Bedeutung VI 1 (18)

important [ɪmˈpɔːtnt] wichtig I

impossible [ɪmˈpɒsəbl] unmöglich II

impractical [ɪmˈpræktɪkl] unpraktisch V

impression [ɪmˈpreʃn] Eindruck III

impressive [ɪmˈpresɪv] beeindruckend IV

improve [ɪmˈpruːv] verbessern; sich verbessern III

improvement [ɪmˈpruːvmənt] Verbesserung VI 1 (21)

in [ɪn]: **in 1580** im Jahr 1580 I **in a loud/soft voice** mit lauter/sanfter Stimme II **in England** in England I **in English / in German** auf Englisch / auf Deutsch I **in front of** vor I **in the afternoon** nachmittags, am Nachmittag I **in the attic** auf dem Dachboden I **in the photo/picture** auf dem Foto/Bild I **be in** zu Hause sein II **come in** hereinkommen I

in-flight magazine/meal [ˌɪn ˈflaɪt] Bordmagazin/Bordmahlzeit V

inch [ɪntʃ] Zoll *(Längenmaß; 2,54 cm)* IV

include [ɪnˈkluːd] einschließen; beinhalten IV

including [ɪnˈkluːdɪŋ] einschließlich; darunter (auch) III

incorrect [ˌɪnkəˈrekt] falsch V

increase [ɪnˈkriːs] erhöhen, steigern, vergrößern; (an)steigen, zunehmen V

incredible [ɪnˈkredəbl] unglaublich V

indent [ɪnˈdent] *(eine Zeile)* einrücken VI 1 (17)

°**independence** [ˌɪndɪˈpendəns] Unabhängigkeit

independent [ˌɪndɪˈpendənt] unabhängig V

Indian [ˈɪndiən] Inder/in; indisch II

indicate sth./sb. [ˈɪndɪkeɪt] auf etwas/jn. zeigen, deuten, hinweisen VI 2 (36)

indigenous [ɪnˈdɪdʒənəs] indigen, einheimisch; Ur- V

indirect [ˌɪndəˈrekt], [ˌɪndaɪˈrekt] indirekt V

indirectly [ˌɪndəˈrektli] indirekt; auf indirekte Weise V

individual [ˌɪndɪˈvɪdʒuəl] Individuum, Einzelperson; einzelne(r, s), individuelle(r, s) V

industrial [ɪnˈdʌstriəl] industriell VI 3 (62)

industry [ˈɪndəstri] Industrie VI 3 (72)

infect [ɪnˈfekt] infizieren; anstecken VI 2 (34)

infected [ɪnˈfektɪd] infiziert; entzündet VI 2 (34)

influence [ˈɪnfluəns] beeinflussen V

influencer [ˈɪnfluənsə] Influencer/in V **influencer marketing** Multiplikatoren-Marketing *(der Einsatz von Social-Media Meinungsführer/innen zu Werbezwecken)* V

influential [ˌɪnfluˈenʃl] einflussreich V

inform sb. [ɪnˈfɔːm] jn. informieren VI 2 (43)

informal [ɪnˈfɔːml] informell; umgangssprachlich V

information (about/on) *(no pl)* [ˌɪnfəˈmeɪʃn] Information(en) (über) I **Information and Communications Technology** Informations- und Kommunikationstechnologie I

informative [ɪnˈfɔːmətɪv] informativ, lehrreich VI 2 (42)

infrastructure [ˈɪnfrəstrʌktʃə] Infrastruktur VI 3 (64)

ingredient [ɪnˈgriːdiənt] Zutat IV

°**initial** [ɪˈnɪʃl] anfänglich

°**initiative** [ɪˈnɪʃətɪv] Initiative, Aktion V

injure sb. [ˈɪndʒə] jn. verletzen V

inland [ˈɪnlænd] Binnen-; im Landesinneren V

inner [ˈɪnə] innere(r, s) VI 3 (71)

insect [ˈɪnsekt] Insekt V

°**insert** [ɪnˈsɜːt] einsetzen, (hin)einstecken

inside [ˌɪnˈsaɪd] drinnen; nach drinnen I

°**insight** [ˈɪnsaɪt] Einsicht, Erkenntnis

insist on sth. [ɪnˈsɪst] auf etwas bestehen V

inspire sb. [ɪnˈspaɪə] jn. inspirieren, jn. beflügeln, jn. anspornen V **awe-inspiring** ehrfurchtgebietend V

°**instability** [ˌɪnstəˈbɪləti] Instabilität, Unbeständigkeit

install [ɪnˈstɔːl] installieren, einrichten VI 2 (46)

instantly [ˈɪnstəntli] sofort V

instead [ɪnˈsted] stattdessen II **instead of** anstelle von, statt III

°**institution** [ˌɪnstɪˈtjuːʃn] Einrichtung, Institution

instruct sb. to do sth. [ɪnˈstrʌkt] jn. anweisen, etwas zu tun VI 1 (23)

instruction [ɪnˈstrʌkʃn] Anweisung VI 1 (23)

instructor [ɪnˈstrʌktə] Lehrer/in, Ausbilder/in VI 1 (13)

instrument [ˈɪnstrəmənt] Instrument I **musical instrument** Musikinstrument III

insult (to) [ˈɪnsʌlt] Beleidigung (für) IV

insulted [ɪnˈsʌltɪd] beleidigt IV

°**insurance** [ɪnˈʃʊərəns]: **health insurance** Krankenversicherung

intelligence [ɪnˈtelɪdʒəns] Intelligenz VI 1 (23) **artificial intelligence (AI)** künstliche Intelligenz VI 3 (56/57)

intended [ɪnˈtendɪd] beabsichtigt, gemeint VI 2 (45)

intensification [ɪnˌtensɪfɪˈkeɪʃn] Verstärkung, Intensivierung V

intensify [ɪnˈtensɪfaɪ] verstärken, intensivieren V

intensive [ɪnˈtensɪv] intensiv V

intention [ɪnˈtenʃn] Absicht, Vorsatz V

°**interact** [ˌɪntərˈækt] (miteinander) interagieren, kommunizieren

interaction [ˌɪntərˈækʃn] Interaktion, Umgang III

interactive [ˌɪntərˈæktɪv] interaktiv V

interest sb. [ˈɪntrəst] jn. interessieren III

interested [ˈɪntrəstɪd]: **be interested in** interessiert sein (an), sich interessieren (für) II

interesting [ˈɪntrəstɪŋ] interessant I

international [ˌɪntəˈnæʃnəl] international V

internship [ˈɪntɜːnʃɪp] Praktikum V

interrupt [ˌɪntəˈrʌpt] unterbrechen II

interruption [ˌɪntəˈrʌpʃn] Unterbrechung V

interview [ˈɪntəvjuː]:
1. Interview V
2. interview sb. jn. interviewen, jn. befragen I

interviewee [ˌɪntəvjuːˈiː] Interviewpartner/in, Befragte(r) V

interviewer [ˈɪntəvjuːə] Leiter/in des Vorstellungsgesprächs V

into [ˈɪntʊ]: **into the kitchen** in die Küche (hinein) I **be into sth.** *(infml)* etwas mögen, auf etwas stehen III

intolerant [ɪnˈtɒlərənt] intolerant V

intonation [ˌɪntəˈneɪʃn] Intonation; Satzmelodie V

introduce sth./sb. (to sb.) [ˌɪntrəˈdjuːs] etwas/jn. (jm.) vorstellen II

introduction [ˌɪntrə'dʌkʃn] Einleitung, Einführung III
invade (a country) [ɪn'veɪd] (in ein Land) einmarschieren II
invent [ɪn'vent] erfinden III
invest [ɪn'vest] investieren V
investigate [ɪn'vestɪgeɪt] (polizeilich) untersuchen; ermitteln IV
investment [ɪn'vestmənt] Investition, (Geld-)Anlage V
invitation (to) [ˌɪnvɪ'teɪʃn] Einladung (zu, nach) II
invite sb. (to) [ɪn'vaɪt] jn. einladen (zu) II
involve [ɪn'vɒlv] bestehen aus, beinhalten, mit sich bringen; einbeziehen, beteiligen V
involved [ɪn'vɒlvd]:
  1. be involved (in) beteiligt sein (an); etwas zu tun haben (mit) V
  2. get involved (in) sich engagieren (für, bei); sich beteiligen (an) V
involvement (in) [ɪn'vɒlvmənt] Engagement (für); Beteiligung (an) V
ironic [aɪ'rɒnɪk] ironisch VI 2 (52)
irony ['aɪrəni] Ironie V
irregular [ɪ'regjələ] unregelmäßig II
irrelevant (to sb.) [ɪ'reləvənt] irrelevant (für jn.) VI 1 (18)
irresponsible [ˌɪrɪ'spɒnsəbl] unverantwortlich V
is [ɪz]: **Is it Monday?** Ist es Montag? I **Is that you?** Bist du's? / Bist du das? I **The camera is …** Die Kamera kostet … I
island ['aɪlənd] Insel II
isle [aɪl] (kleine) Insel, Eiland VI 3 (60) **the British Isles** die Britischen Inseln VI 3 (60)
isn't ['ɪznt]: **he/she/it isn't … (= is not)** er/sie/es ist nicht …; er/sie/es ist kein/e … I
issue ['ɪʃuː] Thema, (Streit-)Frage, Angelegenheit V
it [ɪt] er, sie, es I **it's … (= it is)** er/sie/es ist … I
italics [ɪ'tælɪks] Kursivschrift VI 1 (17)
item ['aɪtəm] Posten, Artikel, Punkt (auf einer Liste) V
itinerary [aɪ'tɪnərəri] Reiseroute V
its name [ɪts] sein Name / ihr Name I
itself [ɪt'self] sich III **The room itself was OK, …** Das Zimmer selbst war in Ordnung, … IV

J

jacket ['dʒækɪt] Jacke, Jackett II

jam [dʒæm] Marmelade I
January ['dʒænjuəri] Januar I
jealous (of) ['dʒeləs] neidisch (auf); eifersüchtig (auf) III
jealousy ['dʒeləsi] Eifersucht V
jeans (pl) [dʒiːnz] Jeans I
jelly ['dʒeli] (AE) Marmelade IV
jet [dʒet] Düsenflugzeug, Jet VI 3 (59)
jewellery (no pl) ['dʒuːəlri] Schmuck IV
jewelry ['dʒuːəlri] (AE) (no pl) Schmuck IV
jewels (pl) ['dʒuːəlz] Juwelen III
jigsaw ['dʒɪgsɔː] Puzzle II
job [dʒɒb] Job, (Arbeits-)Stelle I
join [dʒɔɪn]:
  1. join a club in einen Klub eintreten; sich einem Klub anschließen I
  2. join in (sth.) (bei etwas) mitmachen III
joke [dʒəʊk]:
  1. Witz I
  2. scherzen, Witze machen III
jolt [dʒəʊlt] Ruck, Stoß III
journalist ['dʒɜːnəlɪst] Journalist/in V
journey ['dʒɜːni] Reise, Fahrt II
judge [dʒʌdʒ] Richter III
judo ['dʒuːdəʊ] Judo I
juggle sth. ['dʒʌgl] mit etwas jonglieren II
juggler ['dʒʌglə] Jongleur/in II
juice [dʒuːs] Saft II
July [dʒu'laɪ] Juli I
jump [dʒʌmp]:
  1. springen I
  jump up aufspringen, hochspringen II
  2. Sprung I
June [dʒuːn] Juni I
jungle ['dʒʌŋgl] Dschungel VI 2 (34)
junior year ['dʒuːniə jɪə] 10. Klasse der High School V
just [dʒʌst]:
  1. (einfach) nur, bloß I
  2. gerade (eben), soeben II
  just after … gleich nachdem …; kurz nachdem … II **just then** genau in dem Moment; gerade dann II
  3. just as good/bad/… genauso gut/schlecht/… III
  just like … genau wie … II

K

kangaroo [ˌkæŋgə'ruː] Känguru V
kayak ['kaɪæk] Kajak III
keen [kiːn]: **be keen on doing sth.** wild darauf sein, etwas zu tun IV **be keen on sth.** wild auf etwas sein IV
keep [kiːp]**, kept, kept:**
  1. aufheben; behalten; aufbewahren III
  2. keep (on) doing sth. etwas immer wieder/immer weiter/ständig tun III
  3. halten; erhalten III
  keep sth. up etwas aufrechterhalten, etwas fortsetzen IV **keep sth. warm/fresh/…** etwas warm/frisch/… halten III **keep to sth.** sich an etwas halten IV
  4. aufsparen IV
kept [kept] siehe **keep**
ketchup ['ketʃəp] Ketchup III
key [kiː] Schlüssel II
  a key statistic eine statistische Schlüsselkennzahl V
keyword ['kiːwɜːd] Schlüsselwort V
kick [kɪk] treten III **free kick** Freistoß III **take a free kick** einen Freistoß ausführen III
kid [kɪd] (infml) Kind; Jugendliche(r) I
kill [kɪl] töten I
kilogram, kilo (kg) ['kiːləʊ], ['kɪləgræm] Kilogramm, Kilo I **a 150-kilogram bear** ein 150 Kilogramm schwerer Bär IV
kilometre (km) ['kɪləmiːtə], [kɪ'lɒmɪtə] Kilometer I **a ten-kilometre walk** eine Zehn-Kilometer-Wanderung IV **square kilometre (sq km)** Quadratkilometer (km²) II
kind [kaɪnd] freundlich, nett II
kind [kaɪnd]: **a kind of …** eine Art (von) … I
kinda (= kind of) ['kaɪndə] (infml) irgendwie IV
kindergarten ['kɪndəgɑːtn] BE: Kindergarten; AE: Vorschule V
king [kɪŋ] König III
kinky ['kɪŋki] kraus, gekräuselt (Haare) VI 1 (10/11)
°**kinsman, kinswomen** ['kɪnzmən], ['kɪnzwʊmən] (veraltet) Verwandte/r
kit [kɪt] Ausrüstung I
kitchen ['kɪtʃɪn] Küche I
knee [niː] Knie II

knew [njuː] *siehe* **know**

knife [naɪf], *pl* **knives** Messer II

knight [naɪt] Ritter II

knock (on sth.) [nɒk] (an)klopfen (an etwas) III

know [nəʊ], **knew, known** wissen; kennen I **know about sth.** sich mit etwas auskennen; über etwas Bescheid wissen II **…, you know.** …, weißt du. / …, wissen Sie. I **get to know sb.** jn. kennenlernen V **I don't know what to do.** Ich weiß nicht, was ich tun soll. III **I don't know.** Ich weiß (es) nicht. I

knowledge *(no pl)* [ˈnɒlɪdʒ] Wissen; Kenntnis(se) V

known [nəʊn] *siehe* **know** **well-known** bekannt, wohlbekannt III

koala [kəʊˈɑːlə] Koala V

kung fu [ˌkʌŋ ˈfuː] Kung Fu I

L

lab [læb] *(infml)* Labor V

label [ˈleɪbl]:
1. beschriften; etikettieren II
2. Beschriftung; Schild, Etikett II

laboratory [ləˈbɒrətri] Labor V

labour [ˈleɪbə] Arbeit V

lack [læk]:
1. **lack of** Mangel an V
2. **sb. lacks sth.** jm. fehlt es an etwas V

ladder [ˈlædə] Leiter VI 2 (44)

Ladies and gentlemen [ˌleɪdiz‿ən ˈdʒentlmən] Meine Damen und Herren / Sehr geehrte Damen und Herren IV

lady [ˈleɪdi] Dame VI 2 (36)

laid [leɪd] *siehe* **lay**

lain [leɪn] *siehe* **lie**

lake [leɪk] (Binnen-)See II

lamb [læm] Lamm II

lamp [læmp] Lampe I

land [lænd]:
1. Land II
2. landen, ans Land gehen II

landmark [ˈlændmɑːk] Wahrzeichen V

landscape [ˈlandskeɪp] Landschaft V

language [ˈlæŋgwɪdʒ] Sprache I

large [lɑːdʒ] groß II

last [lɑːst] (an)dauern; halten VI 3 (60)
▶ S. 221 (to) take – (to) last

last [lɑːst]: **the last …** der/die/das letzte … I

late [leɪtɪst]: **the latest** das Neueste IV **You're late.** Du bist spät dran. / Du bist zu spät. I

later [ˈleɪtə] später I

laugh [lɑːf] lachen I

laughter [ˈlɑːftə] Gelächter III

launch [lɔːntʃ] starten, einleiten, einführen, auf den Markt bringen V

law [lɔː] Gesetz III °**law enforcement** Rechtsdurchsetzung, Vollzug

lawn [lɔːn] Rasen IV

lay [leɪ] *siehe* **lie**

lay [leɪ], **laid, laid** legen VI 3 (62) °**lay out** planen, entwerfen, anlegen

layout [ˈleɪaʊt] Layout, Gestaltung III

lazy [ˈleɪzi] faul V

lead [liːd], **led, led** führen, leiten III

leader [ˈliːdə] Leiter/in III

leaf [liːf], *pl* **leaves** Blatt IV

league [liːg] Liga V

lean [liːn] sich lehnen; sich beugen IV

learn [lɜːn] lernen I

least [liːst]: **the least** der/die/das wenigste V

leather [ˈleðə] Leder IV

leave [liːv], **left, left:**
1. verlassen; zurücklassen I
2. (weg)gehen; abfahren II
3. lassen II
leave a message eine Nachricht hinterlassen II **leave sth.** etwas übrig lassen II

led [led] *siehe* **lead**

left [left]:
1. *siehe* **leave**
2. linke(r, s); (nach) links II
on the left links/auf der linken Seite II **turn left** (nach) links abbiegen II
3. **be left** übrig sein III

leg [leg] Bein II

legal [ˈliːgl] legal, gesetzlich IV

°**legalize** [ˈliːgəlaɪz] legalisieren

legend [ˈledʒənd] Legende, Sage III

legendary [ˈledʒəndri] legendär, berühmt IV

legible [ˈledʒəbl] lesbar, leserlich VI 1 (17)

°**legislature** [ˈledʒɪslətʃə] *(fml)* Legislative, Gesetzgebung

lemon [ˈlemən] Zitrone IV

lend [lend], **lent, lent** jm. etwas leihen IV

length [leŋθ] Länge; Dauer V

lent [lent] *siehe* **lend**

lentil [ˈlentl] Linse *(Gemüse)* IV

less (than) [les] weniger (als) III

lesson [ˈlesn] (Unterrichts-)Stunde I **teach sb. a lesson** jm. eine Lektion erteilen VI 2 (34)

let [let], **let, let** lassen I **Let's go.** Auf geht's I

letter [ˈletə]:
1. Buchstabe I
2. Brief I
letter of reference Empfehlungsschreiben, Referenz(schreiben) V

letterbox [ˈletəbɒks] Briefkasten III

level [ˈlevl] Grad, Niveau; (Lern-)Stand V **A level (= advanced level)** *Prüfungen zur Hochschulzulassungsberechtigung (etwa wie Abitur)* V

liberal [ˈlɪbərəl] liberal VI 1 (16)

liberty [ˈlɪbəti] Freiheit IV

library [ˈlaɪbrəri] Bibliothek, Bücherei I

lie [laɪ], **lay, lain** liegen II **lie down** sich hinlegen III

life [laɪf], *pl* **lives** Leben I **way of life** Lebensweise, Lebensart V

lifelike [ˈlaɪflaɪk] lebensecht, realistisch VI 2 (45)

lifestyle [ˈlaɪfstaɪl] Lebensstil VI 2 (34)

lift [lɪft]:
1. Mitfahrgelegenheit II
2. Fahrstuhl, Aufzug III

light [laɪt]:
1. Licht I
2. **light green/blue/…** hellgrün/-blau/… IV
3. **(lit, lit)** anzünden II
light sth. up etwas erhellen *(aufleuchten lassen)* II

light-hearted [ˌlaɪt ˈhɑːtɪd] fröhlich, heiter VI 1 (14)

lightning *(no pl)* [ˈlaɪtnɪŋ] Blitz II

like [laɪk]:
1. mögen, gernhaben I
I like … Ich mag … I **I'd like …** (= I would like …) Ich hätte gern … / Ich möchte … I **What would you like to eat?** Was möchtest du essen? I
2. **like boys** wie Jungen I
like that / like this so *(auf diese Weise)* I **What's she like?** Wie ist sie? / Wie ist sie so? I
3. **likes and dislikes** *(pl)* Vorlieben und Abneigungen I
4. *(infml)* als ob III

likely ['laɪkli]: **be likely to do sth.** wahrscheinlich etwas tun (werden) VI 3 (58)

limit ['lɪmɪt]: **speed limit** Geschwindigkeitsbegrenzung, -beschränkung III

limited ['lɪmɪtɪd] beschränkt, begrenzt IV

limousine [ˌlɪməˈziːn], ['lɪməziːn] Luxuslimousine, Straßenkreuzer IV

line [laɪn]:
1. Zeile I
2. (U-Bahn-)Linie III
3. Leine, (Angel-)Schnur IV
power line Überlandleitung VI 1 (24)
4. (AE) Schlange, Reihe (wartender Menschen) IV
stand/wait in line (AE) Schlange stehen, sich anstellen IV

lingua franca [ˌlɪŋgwə ˈfræŋkə] Verkehrssprache, Lingua franca V

linguistics [lɪŋˈgwɪstɪks] Sprachwissenschaft, Linguistik V

link [lɪŋk]:
1. verbinden, verknüpfen III
linking word Bindewort III **be linked** verbunden sein III
2. Link, Verknüpfung, Verbindung IV
rail link Bahnverbindung VI 1 (24)

lion ['laɪən] Löwe I
lip [lɪp] Lippe II
liquid ['lɪkwɪd] Flüssigkeit VI 2 (34)
list [lɪst]:
1. Liste I
°**2.** auflisten

listen ['lɪsn] zuhören, horchen I
Listen, Justin. Hör zu, Justin. I
listen to sb. jm. zuhören I **listen to sth.** sich etwas anhören I

listener ['lɪsənə] Zuhörer/in II

lit [lɪt] siehe **light**

literally ['lɪtərəli] im wahrsten Sinne des Wortes; buchstäblich VI 2 (42)

literature ['lɪtrətʃə] Literatur IV

litter ['lɪtə]:
1. Abfall V
2. Abfälle zurücklassen (Müll einfach wegwerfen) V

litter bin ['lɪtə bɪn] Abfalleimer II

little ['lɪtl] klein I **a little** ein bisschen, ein wenig, etwas IV

live [lɪv] leben; wohnen I
lively ['laɪvli] lebendig, lebhaft IV
lives [laɪvz] siehe **life**
living room ['lɪvɪŋ ruːm] Wohnzimmer I

local ['ləʊkl] örtlich, Lokal-; am/vom Ort III

locals ['ləʊklz]: **the locals** (pl) die Einheimischen VI 2 (34)

located [ləʊˈkeɪtɪd]: **be located (in ...)** (in ...) liegen, sich (in ...) befinden VI 1 (23)

location [ləʊˈkeɪʃn] Ort, Standort; Drehort IV

°**lock** [lɒk] verschließen, absperren
locker ['lɒkə] Schließfach, Spind IV
log in/out [lɒg] sich ein-/ausloggen VI 3 (61)

logical ['lɒdʒɪkl] logisch V
°**logistics** [ləˈdʒɪstɪks] Logistik
loneliness ['ləʊnlinəs] Einsamkeit VI 1 (14)

lonely ['ləʊnli] einsam II
long [lɒŋ]:
1. lang I
before long schon bald III **not (...) any longer** nicht länger; nicht mehr IV
2. long shot Totale, Totalaufnahme IV

look [lʊk]:
1. schauen I
look after sb. auf jn. aufpassen; sich um jn. kümmern II **look around** sich umsehen, sich umdrehen; sich umschauen II **look at sth.** etwas anschauen, ansehen I **look closely** genau hinschauen II **look for sth.** etwas suchen I **look into sth.** untersuchen, prüfen III **look out for sb./sth.** nach jm./etwas Ausschau halten IV **look sth. up** nachschlagen (Wörter, Informationen) III **look up** hochsehen, aufschauen III
2. look happy/angry/... glücklich/wütend/... aussehen I
good-looking gutaussehend II
3. have a look (at sth.) nachschauen; einen Blick auf etwas werfen III

loose [luːs] lose, locker VI 3 (69)
°**lord** [lɔːd]: **the House of Lords** das Oberhaus (des britischen Parlaments)
lorry ['lɒri] Lastwagen, LKW III
lose [luːz], lost, lost verlieren II
lose one's temper die Beherrschung verlieren VI 3 (71)

lost [lɒst]:
1. siehe **lose**
2. Get lost! Verzieh dich! III
lot [lɒt]:
1. lots of .../a lot of ... viel ..., viele ... I
I like her a lot. Ich mag sie sehr. II
2. parking lot (AE) Parkplatz IV

loud [laʊd] laut I **in a loud voice** mit lauter Stimme II

loudspeaker [ˌlaʊdˈspiːkə] Lautsprecher; Megaphon III

love [lʌv]:
1. lieben, sehr mögen I
I'd love to ... Ich würde sehr gern ... II
2. Liebe V
Love, ... Alles Liebe, ... (Briefschluss) II **fall in love (with sb.)** sich (in jn.) verlieben V

lovely ['lʌvli] schön, hübsch, herrlich II

lover ['lʌvə] Liebhaber/in VI 2 (45)
low [ləʊ] niedrig V
°**lower** ['ləʊə] senken, herabsetzen
loyal ['lɔɪəl] loyal V
luckily ['lʌkɪli] glücklicherweise; zum Glück V
lucky ['lʌki]:
1. be lucky Glück haben II
2. Lucky you. Du Glückspilz. II
luggage ['lʌgɪdʒ] Gepäck V
lunch [lʌntʃ] Mittagessen I
What's for lunch? Was gibt es zum Mittagessen? I
lunchtime ['lʌntʃtaɪm] Mittagszeit I **at lunchtime** mittags I

M

machine [məˈʃiːn] Maschine, Gerät IV

mad [mæd] verrückt I
madam ['mædəm] (BE): **Dear Sir or Madam, ...** Sehr geehrte Damen und Herren, ... V

made [meɪd]:
1. siehe **make**
2. be made of sth. aus etwas (gemacht) sein II

magazine [ˌmægəˈziːn] Zeitschrift I
magic ['mædʒɪk] magisch, Zauber- II

magical ['mædʒɪkl] zauberhaft, wundervoll; magisch III
mail [meɪl] E-Mail II
main [meɪn] Haupt- II
mainly ['meɪnli] hauptsächlich, vorwiegend I

maintain [meɪnˈteɪn] beibehalten, aufrecht erhalten; instand halten, unterhalten V

°**major** ['meɪdʒə] bedeutende(r, s), wichtige(r, s)

majority [məˈdʒɒrəti] Mehrheit V

make [meɪk]**, made, made** machen; herstellen I **make comparisons** Vergleiche anstellen; vergleichen V **make friends** Freunde finden I **make sb. do sth.** jn. dazu bringen, etwas zu tun; jn. veranlassen, etwas zu tun VI 1 (13) **make sb. sth.** jn. zu etwas machen II **make sth. up** sich etwas ausdenken III **make sth. up** etwas bilden VI 1 (18) **make sure that …** sich vergewissern, dass …; darauf achten, dass …; dafür sorgen, dass … II **make tea/coffee/soup** Tee/Kaffee/Suppe kochen IV

▶ S. 204 (to) make sb. do sth. – (to) let sb. do sth.

make-up [ˈmeɪk_ʌp] Make-up II
malaria [məˈleəriə] Malaria III
male [meɪl] männlich; männliche Person; Männchen V
mall [mɔːl]: **(shopping) mall** (großes) Einkaufszentrum II
mammal [ˈmæml] Säugetier V
man [mæn], pl **men** Mann I
manage sth. [ˈmænɪdʒ]:
1. etwas schaffen; etwas zustande bringen III
2. etwas handhaben, bedienen; mit etwas umgehen VI 3 (61)
°**manipulate** [məˈnɪpjuleɪt] manipulieren, beeinflussen; bedienen, handhaben, bearbeiten
°**manipulation** [mənɪpjuˈleɪʃn] Beeinflussung, Bearbeitung
manner [ˈmænə] Art und Weise VI 3 (60)
manners (pl) [ˈmænəz] Manieren VI 2 (34)
many [ˈmeni] viele I
Maori [ˈmaʊri] Maori (Ureinwohner/in Neuseelands); maorisch V
map [mæp] Landkarte; Stadtplan I **on the map** auf der Landkarte; auf dem Stadtplan I
March [mɑːtʃ] März I
march [mɑːtʃ] Marsch, Demonstration III
marcher [ˈmɑːtʃə] Demonstrant/in III
Mardi Gras [ˌmɑːdi ˈɡrɑː] Faschingsdienstag (auch: die Karnevalsfeiern in New Orleans) IV
margin [ˈmɑːdʒɪn] Rand VI 1 (17)
marine [məˈriːn] Meeres- IV
mark [mɑːk]:
1. markieren II
mark sth. up etwas markieren, kennzeichnen II
2. (BE) (Schul-)Note, Zensur IV
3. **exclamation mark** Ausrufezei-

chen II
question mark Fragezeichen II
stress mark Betonungszeichen III
market [ˈmɑːkɪt] Markt I
marketing [ˈmɑːkɪtɪŋ] Marketing, Vermarktung, Vertrieb V **direct marketing** Direktvertrieb, Direktmarketing V **influencer marketing** Multiplikatoren-Marketing (der Einsatz von Social-Media Meinungsführer/innen zu Werbezwecken) V
marriage [ˈmærɪdʒ] Ehe; Heirat VI 1 (19) **same-sex marriage** gleichgeschlechtliche Ehe VI 1 (19)
marry sb. [ˈmæri] jn. heiraten III
married (to) verheiratet (mit) I
marvellous [ˈmɑːvələs] wunderbar, fabelhaft V
master [ˈmɑːstə] Meister/in I
°**match** [mætʃ]: **match with/to** zuordnen
mate [meɪt] Kumpel, Freund III **No worries, mate.** Kein Problem! / Alles OK! / Alles gut! V
material [məˈtɪəriəl] Material, Stoff III
mathematical [ˌmæθəˈmætɪkl] mathematisch VI 3 (59)
maths [mæθs] Mathematik I
matter [ˈmætə] Angelegenheit, Sache V **no matter if/whether** ganz gleich, ob VI 2 (34) **no matter what/who/how/…** ganz gleich, was/wer/wie/… VI 2 (34) **What's the matter?** Was ist denn? / Was ist los? I
mattress [ˈmætrəs] Matratze VI 2 (36)
maximum [ˈmæksɪməm] Maximum V
May [meɪ] Mai I
may [meɪ] dürfen II **May I have a word with you?** Kann ich Sie/dich kurz sprechen? II
maybe [ˈmeɪbi] vielleicht I
mayor [meə] Bürgermeister/in II
me [miː] mich; mir I **Me too.** Ich auch. I
meal [miːl] Mahlzeit, Essen III
mean [miːn]:
1. (**meant, meant**) bedeuten II meinen, sagen wollen II
2. gemein, fies; geizig V
meaning [ˈmiːnɪŋ] Bedeutung II
meaningful [ˈmiːnɪŋfl] aussagekräftig VI 2 (45)
meanness [ˈmiːnnəs] Geiz; Gemeinheit V
meant [ment] siehe **mean**

meantime [ˈmiːntaɪm]: **in the meantime** in der Zwischenzeit; inzwischen VI 1 (18)
°**measure** [ˈmeʒə] messen
meat [miːt] Fleisch I
medal [ˈmedl] Medaille V
media (pl) [ˈmiːdiə] Medien III **social media** (pl) soziale Medien III
mediation [ˌmiːdiˈeɪʃn] Sprachmittlung, Mediation I
°**medical** [ˈmedɪkl] medizinisch
medicine [ˈmedsn], [ˈmedɪsn] Medizin; Arznei VI 1 (23)
meditate [ˈmedɪteɪt] meditieren VI 3 (58)
°**medium** [ˈmiːdiəm] Kommunikationsmedium
medium shot [ˈmiːdiəm ʃɒt] Halbtotale IV
meet [miːt], **met, met**:
1. sich treffen I
Meet your classmates. Triff deine Mitschüler/innen. / Lerne deine Mitschüler/innen kennen. I **Nice to meet you.** Freut mich, dich/euch/Sie kennenzulernen. I
2. einhalten, erfüllen (Kriterien, Bedingungen, Anforderungen) V
meeting [ˈmiːtɪŋ] Treffen; Besprechung, Versammlung VI 2 (34)
melancholic [ˌmelənˈkɒlɪk] trübsinnig VI 1 (14)
melt [melt] schmelzen II
member [ˈmembə] Mitglied V **Members only!** nur für Mitglieder! V **MP (= Member of Parliament)** Parlamentsmitglied, Abgeordnete(r) V
memorable [ˈmemərəbl] einprägsam; unvergesslich VI 2 (52)
memorial [məˈmɔːriəl] Denkmal; Gedenk- III
memory [ˈmeməri]:
1. Erinnerung II
2. (Computer) Speicher VI 3 (61)
men [men] siehe **man**
mental health [ˌmentl ˈhelθ] psychische Gesundheit V
mention [ˈmenʃn] erwähnen IV
menu [ˈmenjuː]:
1. Speisekarte IV
2. (Computer) Menü VI 3 (61)
message [ˈmesɪdʒ]:
1. Nachricht II
leave a message eine Nachricht hinterlassen II **text message** SMS II
2. Botschaft, Aussage III
get a message across eine Bot-

schaft rüberbringen, sich verständlich machen V

messaging app ['mesɪdʒɪŋ æp] Chatprogramm VI 2 (39)

°**messy** ['mesi] unordentlich; dreckig

met [met] *siehe* **meet**

metal ['metl] Metall; Metall- IV

metaphor ['metəfɔː] Metapher VI 1 (15)

metaphorical [ˌmetə'fɒrɪkl] metaphorisch VI 3 (71)

meter ['miːtə] *(AE)* Meter IV

method ['meθəd] Methode VI 1 (23)

metre ['miːtə] Meter I

microphone ['maɪkrəfəʊn] Mikrofon V

middle ['mɪdl] Mitte I   **in the middle** in der Mitte I

midnight ['mɪdnaɪt] Mitternacht I

might [maɪt]: **someone might like it** jemand könnte es mögen III

mild [maɪld] mild V

mile [maɪl] Meile *(ca. 1,6 km)* II   **miles per hour** Meilen pro Stunde IV   **for miles** meilenweit II

milk [mɪlk]:
1. Milch I
2. melken V

million ['mɪljən] Million II

mind [maɪnd]:
1. Verstand, Sinn, Geist IV   **change your mind** seine Meinung ändern IV   **flash through sb.'s mind** jm. durch den Kopf schießen IV   **read sb.'s mind** jemandes Gedanken lesen III
2. **mind sth.** etwas dagegen haben III

minded ['maɪndɪd]: **open-minded** aufgeschlossen, unvoreingenommen V

mine [maɪn]:
1. meiner, meine, meins II
2. Bergwerk III

minimum ['mɪnɪməm] Minimum V   **minimum wage** Mindestlohn V

minister ['mɪnɪstə] Minister/in VI 1 (25)   °**prime minister** Premierminister/in, Ministerpräsident/in

minor ['maɪnə] Minderjährige(r) V

minority [maɪ'nɒrəti] Minderheit V

minute ['mɪnɪt] Minute I   **a 30-minute ride** eine 30-minütige Fahrt IV   **Hold on a minute.** Bleib / Bleiben Sie am Apparat. *(am Telefon)* II   **Wait a minute.** Warte einen Moment. / Moment mal. I

mirror ['mɪrə] Spiegel II

misinformation [ˌmɪsɪnfə'meɪʃn] Fehlinformation(en), Falschinformation(en) VI 3 (58)

Miss [mɪs] Fräulein, junge Frau *(Anrede für eine Unbekannte)* IV

miss [mɪs] verpassen II

Miss: Miss Bell Frau Bell *(übliche Anrede von Lehrerinnen)* I

miss [mɪs] vermissen III

missing ['mɪsɪŋ]:
1. verschollen, vermisst III
2. **be missing** fehlen II

°**missionary** ['mɪʃənri] Missionar/in

mist [mɪst] (leichter) Nebel, Dunst(schleier) II

mistake [mɪ'steɪk] Fehler II

mistaken [mɪ'steɪkən]: **be mistaken** sich irren, sich täuschen V

mistreatment [ˌmɪs'triːtmənt] Misshandlung V

misunderstanding [ˌmɪsʌndə'stændɪŋ] Missverständnis VI 2 (42)

mite [maɪt] Milbe VI 3 (62)

°**mix** [mɪks] Mischung

mixed [mɪkst] gemischt V

mob [mɒb]: **flash mob** Flashmob VI 2 (47)

mobile (phone) [ˌməʊbaɪl 'fəʊn] Mobiltelefon, Handy I

model ['mɒdl] Model II   **role model** Vorbild V

moderator ['mɒdəreɪtə] Moderator/in VI 3 (74)

modern ['mɒdən] modern III

modify ['mɒdɪfaɪ] näher bestimmen VI 1 (16)

°**molecule** ['mɒlɪkjuːl] Molekül

mom [mɑːm] *(AE)* Mama, Mutti IV

Monday ['mʌndeɪ], ['mʌndi] Montag I

money ['mʌni] Geld I

monitor ['mɒnɪtə] Monitor, Bildschirm V

monkey ['mʌŋki] Affe I

monster ['mɒnstə] Monster I

month [mʌnθ] Monat I

monument (to) ['mɒnjumənt] Denkmal, Monument (für/zum Gedenken an) III

mood [muːd] Laune, Stimmung IV   **be in a good/bad mood** gute/ schlechte Laune haben IV

moon [muːn] Mond I   **at full moon** bei Vollmond II

moonlight ['muːnlaɪt] Mondlicht III

moor [mɔː], [mʊə] Hochmoor II

mop [mɒp]:
1. wischen III
2. Wischmopp III

morality [mə'ræləti] Moral, Anstand, gute Sitten VI 3 (59)

more [mɔː] mehr I   **more and more frequent/beautiful** immer häufiger/schöner IV   **more beautiful (than)** schöner (als) II   **one more photo** noch ein Foto; ein weiteres Foto II   **one more time** noch einmal, noch ein Mal II

morning ['mɔːnɪŋ] Morgen I   **Good morning.** Guten Morgen. I   **in the morning** morgens, vormittags, am Morgen/Vormittag I

most [məʊst]: **most of them** die meisten von ihnen II   **most people** die meisten Menschen II   **(the) most beautiful** der/die/das schönste …; am schönsten II

mostly ['məʊstli] hauptsächlich, überwiegend, meistens V

motel [məʊ'tel] Motel *(Hotel mit Zimmern und Garagen an einer Autostraße)* IV

moth [mɒθ] Nachtfalter; Motte V

mother ['mʌðə] Mutter I

motion ['məʊʃn]: **slow motion** Zeitlupe III

motivate sb. to do sth. ['məʊtɪveɪt] jn. motivieren (etwas zu tun) VI 3 (71)

motivated ['məʊtɪveɪtɪd] motiviert V

motivation [məʊtɪ'veɪʃn] Motivation VI 3 (71)

motor ['məʊtə] Motor III

mountain ['maʊntən] Berg II

mountainous ['maʊntənəs] bergig, gebirgig V

mouth [maʊθ] Mund; Maul I

move [muːv]:
1. bewegen; sich bewegen I   **move (to)** umziehen (nach) II   **move in** einziehen II   **moving** bewegend VI 2 (45)
2. Zug *(bei Brettspielen)* IV

movement ['muːvmənt] Bewegung III

movie ['muːvi] Film IV   **movie theater** *(AE)* Kino IV

MP (= Member of Parliament) [ˌem'piː] Parlamentsmitglied, Abgeordnete(r) V

mph (miles per hour) [ˌem piː ˈeɪtʃ] Meilen pro Stunde IV

Mr Brown ['mɪstə] Herr Brown I

°**MRI** [ˌem,ɑːr'eɪ] *(magnetic resonance imaging)* MRT

Dictionary

Mrs Brown [ˈmɪsɪz] Frau Brown I

Ms Miller [mɪz], [məz] Frau Miller IV

much [mʌtʃ] viel I

mud [mʌd] Schlamm, Matsch II

muddy [ˈmʌdi] schlammig, matschig III

muesli [ˈmjuːzli] Müsli VI 3 (62)

mug [mʌg] Becher I

multi- [ˈmʌlti] multi, Multi; viel-, mehr- V

multilingualism [ˌmʌltiˈlɪŋgwəlɪzm] Mehrsprachigkeit V

mum [mʌm] Mama, Mutti I

°**mummy** [ˈmʌmi] Mumie IV

murder [ˈden]

museum [mjuˈziːəm] Museum I

mushroom [ˈmʌʃrʊm], [ˈmʌʃruːm] Pilz IV

music [ˈmjuːzɪk] Musik I

musical [ˈmjuːzɪkl]:
1. Musical II
2. musikalisch VI 1 (16)
musical instrument Musikinstrument III

musician [mjuˈzɪʃn] Musiker/in III

must [mʌst] müssen II   **we mustn't do it** wir dürfen es nicht tun II

my [maɪ] mein/e I   **my name is …** ich heiße … I

myself [maɪˈself] mich, mir III

mysterious [mɪˈstɪəriəs] mysteriös, geheimnisvoll V

N

name [neɪm]:
1. Name I
My name is Justin. Ich heiße Justin (wörtlich: Mein Name ist Justin.) I
What's your name? Wie heißt du? / Wie heißt ihr? I
2. **call sb. names** jn. beschimpfen, jm. Schimpfwörter nachrufen IV
3. (be)nennen III

narrate [nəˈreɪt] schildern, erzählen VI 2 (42)

narration [nəˈreɪʃn] Erzählung, Schilderung V

narrative [ˈnærətɪv] Erzählung, Geschichte VI 2 (37)

narrator [nəˈreɪtə] Erzähler/in; Sprecher/in IV

narrow [ˈnærəʊ] schmal, eng III

nation [ˈneɪʃn] Nation, Volk III

national [ˈnæʃnəl] national, National- III

national anthem [ˌnæʃnəl ˈænθəm] Nationalhymne IV

Native American [ˌneɪtɪv əˈmerɪkən] amerikanischer Ureinwohner / amerikanische Ureinwohnerin IV

native speaker [ˌneɪtɪv ˈspiːkə] Muttersprachler/in IV

natural [ˈnætʃrəl] natürlich III
natural history Naturkunde III

nature [ˈneɪtʃə] Natur III

navigate [ˈnævɪgeɪt] navigieren, steuern VI 3 (61)

navy [ˈneɪvi] Marine I

near [nɪə] in der Nähe von, nahe (bei) I   **near here** (hier) in der Nähe I

nearby [ˈnɪəbaɪ]: **a nearby town** eine nahegelegene Stadt II

nearly [ˈnɪəli] fast, beinahe III

necessary [ˈnesəsəri] notwendig IV

neck [nek] Hals II

need [niːd] brauchen, benötigen I
need to do sth. etwas tun müssen II   **I need help, but I don't know who to ask.** Ich brauche Hilfe, aber ich weiß nicht, wen ich fragen kann/soll. III   **we needn't do it** wir müssen es nicht tun, wir brauchen es nicht zu tun II

negative [ˈnegətɪv] negativ V

neighbour [ˈneɪbə] (AE: **neighbor**) Nachbar/in II

neighbourhood [ˈneɪbəhʊd] Viertel, Gegend, Umgebung; Nachbarschaft IV

neither [ˈnaɪðə], [ˈniːðə]: **neither … nor …** weder … noch … VI 1 (17)
Me neither. Ich auch nicht. III

nerd [nɜːd] Nerd, Freak V

nervous [ˈnɜːvəs] nervös, aufgeregt II   **nervous breakdown** Nervenzusammenbruch VI 3 (58)

network [ˈnetwɜːk] Netz, Netzwerk IV

neutral [ˈnjuːtrəl] neutral IV

never [ˈnevə] nie, niemals I

°**nevertheless** [ˌnevəðəˈles] trotzdem, dennoch I

new [njuː] neu I

New Year's Eve [ˌnjuː jɪəz ˈiːv] Silvester II

news (no pl) [njuːz] Nachrichten; Neuigkeiten II

newspaper [ˈnjuːzpeɪpə] (kurz auch: **paper**) Zeitung IV

newsreader [ˈnjuːzriːdə] Nachrichtensprecher/in VI 1 (24)

next to [ˈnekst] neben II   **the next picture/question** das nächste Bild / die nächste Frage I

nice [naɪs] nett, schön I   **Nice to meet you.** Freut mich, dich/euch/Sie kennenzulernen. I

night [ət ˈnaɪt]: **at night** nachts, in der Nacht I

nightmare [ˈnaɪtmeə] Albtraum VI 3 (65)

nil [nɪl] null, Null III

nine [naɪn] neun I

no [nəʊ]:
1. nein I
2. **no …** kein …, keine … I
at no time nie IV   **it was no different** es war nicht anders III   **We had no idea where to go.** Wir hatten keine Ahnung, wohin wir gehen sollten. III

no one [ˈnəʊ wʌn] niemand I

nobody [ˈnəʊbədi] niemand I

nod [nɒd] nicken II

noise [nɔɪz] Geräusch; Lärm III

noisy [ˈnɔɪzi] laut, lärmend, voller Lärm III

non- [nɒn] nicht-; Nicht- V

non-fiction [ˌnɒn ˈfɪkʃn] Sachliteratur VI 2 (37)

none [nʌn] **none of us** keine/r von uns VI 2 (35)

nonexistent [ˌnɒnɪgˈzɪstənt] nicht vorhanden, nicht existierend VI 1 (18)

nonsense [ˈnɒnsns] Unsinn, dummes Zeug V

noon [nuːn] Mittag IV

nor [nɔː]: **nor do I want to …** und ich will auch nicht … VI 1 (13) II   **neither … nor …** weder … noch … VI 1 (17)
▶ S. 205 English "nor" – German "auch nicht"

normal [ˈnɔːml] normal III

north [nɔːθ] Norden; nach Norden; nördlich III

north-east [ˌnɔːθ ˈiːst] Nordosten; nach Nordosten; nordöstlich III

north-west [ˌnɔːθ ˈwest] Nordwesten; nach Nordwesten; nordwestlich III

northbound [ˈnɔːθbaʊnd] Richtung Norden III

northern [ˈnɔːðən] nördlich, Nord- III

nose [nəʊz] Nase II

nostalgic [nɒˈstældʒɪk] nostalgisch VI 1 (14)

not [nɒt] nicht I   **not … at all** überhaupt nicht(s), gar nicht(s);

überhaupt kein/e, gar kein/e II
not … yet noch nicht I **not …
any more** nicht mehr II **not …
either** auch nicht II **not even**
(noch) nicht einmal II **not till
three** erst um drei, nicht vor drei II
note [nəʊt]:
  1. Notiz, Mitteilung II
  make notes (on sth.) (sich) Notizen machen (über/zu etwas) (zur
Vorbereitung) II **take notes** (sich)
Notizen machen *(beim Lesen oder
Zuhören)* II °**note down** aufschreiben, notieren
  2. Note, Ton *(Musik)* III
nothing [ˈnʌθɪŋ] (gar) nichts I
notice [ˈnəʊtɪs] merken, bemerken
IV
noticeboard [ˈnəʊtɪsbɔːd] Schwarzes Brett *(auch elektronisch)* V
novel [ˈnɒvl] Roman VI 1 (12)
novelist [ˈnɒvəlɪst] Romanautor/in
VI 1 (12)
November [nəʊ'vembə] November I
now [naʊ] nun, jetzt I **for now**
einstweilen, vorerst, fürs Erste
VI 2 (42)
nowhere [ˈnəʊweə] nirgendwo; nir-
gendwohin III **out of nowhere**
(wie) aus dem Nichts III
nuclear [ˈnjuːkliə] Kern-, Atom-
VI 3 (69) °**nuclear fission** Kernspaltung °**nuclear fusion** Kernfusion
number [ˈnʌmbə] Zahl, Nummer,
Ziffer I
nurse [nɜːs] Krankenpfleger/in III
nut [nʌt] Nuss IV

O

o [əʊ] Null *(in Telefonnummern)* I
object [ˈɒbdʒekt] Objekt II
observation [ˌɒbzə'veɪʃn] Beobach-
tung VI 2 (37)
observe [əb'zɜːv] beobachten
VI 2 (34)
°**obtain** [əb'teɪn] erhalten, bekommen
obvious [ˈɒbviəs] offensichtlich
VI 3 (58)
occasion [ə'keɪʒn] Gelegenheit; Ereignis, Anlass V
occur to sb. [ə'kɜː] jm. einfallen, in
den Sinn kommen VI 3 (69)
ocean [ˈəʊʃn] Ozean I

o'clock [ə'klɒk]: **at 1 o'clock** um 1
Uhr / um 13 Uhr I
October [ɒk'təʊbə] Oktober I
octopus [ˈɒktəpəs] Krake III
of [ɒv], [əv] von I **a family of
four** eine vierköpfige Familie III
of course [əv 'kɔːs] natürlich,
selbstverständlich I
off [ɒf]: **be off** ausgeschaltet sein
(Radio, Licht usw.) III **get/have a
day off** einen Tag frei bekommen/
haben III
offensive [ə'fensɪv] beleidigend,
Anstoß erregend IV
offer [ˈɒfə] anbieten II
office [ˈɒfɪs] Büro III
official [ə'fɪʃl]:
  1. amtlich, Amts- III
  2. Beamte(r), Beamtin III
officially [ə'fɪʃəli] offiziell V
often [ˈɒfn], [ˈɒftən] oft I
oh [əʊ]: **Oh, it's you.** Ach, du bist
es. I **Oh dear!** Oje! II
oil [ɔɪl] Öl I
old [əʊld]: **old-fashioned** altmo-
disch V **a 70-year-old teacher**
ein 70-jähriger Lehrer IV **How old
are you?** Wie alt bist du? I
Olympic Games [ə,lɪmpɪk 'geɪmz]:
the Olympic Games *(pl)* die Olym-
pischen Spiele V
omniscient [ɒm'nɪsiənt] allwissend
VI 2 (37)
on [ɒn]:
  1. auf I
on earth auf der Erde II **on Monday** am Montag I **on Mondays**
montags, an Montagen I **on Saturday afternoon** am Samstagnachmittag I **on the map** auf der
Landkarte; auf dem Stadtplan I **On
the one hand, … On the other
hand, …** Einerseits … Andererseits
… V **on the phone** am Telefon II
on the plane im Flugzeug II **on
the radio** im Radio I
  2. walk/run/sail/… on
weitergehen/-laufen/-segeln/… II
  3. be on eingeschaltet sein, an sein
(Radio, Licht usw.); laufen, übertragen werden *(Programm, Sendung)* III
once [wʌns] einmal II **once again**
erneut, wieder (einmal), einmal mehr
V **once/twice a week** einmal/
zweimal pro Woche II
one [wʌn]:
  1. eins I
one by one einer nach dem anderen
II **one more time** noch einmal,

noch ein Mal II **one night/day**
eines Nachts/Tages II **a one-hour
concert** ein einstündiges Konzert III
at one time zur selben Zeit, gleichzeitig III **On the one hand, … On
the other hand, …** Einerseits …
Andererseits … V
  2. a white one ein weißer / eine
weiße / ein weißes II
two black ones zwei schwarze II
Which one? Welche(r, s)? II
  3. no one niemand I
onion [ˈʌnjən] Zwiebel IV
only [ˈəʊnli]:
  1. nur, bloß I
Members only! nur für Mitglieder!
V
  2. erst II
  3. the only … der/die/das einzige
…; die einzigen… II
onto [ˈɒntʊ]:
  1. auf (… hinauf) I
  2. hold onto sth. sich an etwas
festhalten III
opal [ˈəʊpl] Opal V
open [ˈəʊpən]:
  1. öffnen, aufmachen I
  2. sich öffnen I
  3. geöffnet, offen I
open-minded aufgeschlossen, unvoreingenommen V
opener [ˈəʊpnə] Eröffnung VI 2 (52)
openness [ˈəʊpənnəs] Offenheit,
Aufgeschlossenheit V
opera [ˈɒprə] Oper V
°**operate** [ˈɒpəreɪt] *(geschäftlich)*
tätig sein
opinion [ə'pɪnjən] Meinung III
opinion piece Stellungnahme, Meinungsartikel VI 1 (18) **opinion poll**
Meinungsumfrage V **In my opinion …** Meiner Meinung nach … III
opportunity [ˌɒpə'tjuːnəti] Gelegenheit, Möglichkeit, Chance V
oppose sth. [ə'pəʊz] etwas ablehn-
en, gegen etwas sein V
opposite [ˈɒpəzɪt]:
  1. gegenüber (von) II
  2. Gegenteil IV
optimist [ˈɒptɪmɪst] Optimist/in
VI 3 (68)
optimistic [ˌɒptɪ'mɪstɪk] optimis-
tisch V
option [ˈɒpʃn] Option, (Wahl-)Mög-
lichkeit VI 2 (48)
or [ɔː] oder I
orange [ˈɒrɪndʒ]:
  1. orange I
  2. Orange, Apfelsine I

order [ˈɔːdə]:
1. bestellen II
2. ordnen III
3. Reihenfolge II
4. **in order to do sth.** um etwas zu tun V

organic [ɔːˈɡænɪk] biologisch angebaut, Bio- VI 3 (64)

organic certification [ɔːˌɡænɪk sɜːtɪfɪˈkeɪʃn] etwa: Bio-Zertifizierung V

organism [ˈɔːɡənɪzəm] Organismus VI 1 (23)

organization [ˌɔːɡənaɪˈzeɪʃn] Organisation V

organize [ˈɔːɡənaɪz] organisieren; ordnen III

°**organizer** [ˈɔːɡənaɪzə] Organisator/in

original [əˈrɪdʒənl] originell VI 1 (10/11)

originally [əˈrɪdʒənəli] ursprünglich III

other [ˈʌðə] andere(r, s) I **otherworldly** (welt)entrückt; überirdisch (nicht von dieser Welt) V **On the one hand, … On the other hand, …** Einerseits … Andererseits … V **the other day** neulich VI 2 (35)

otter [ˈɒtə] Otter II

ought [ɔːt]: **you ought to …** du solltest … V

our [ˈaʊə] unser/e I

ours [ˈaʊəz] unserer, unsere, unseres II

ourselves [ɑːˈselvz], [aʊəˈselvz] uns III **We painted the room ourselves.** Wir haben das Zimmer selbst gestrichen. IV

out [aʊt] aus, hinaus I **out and about** unterwegs II **out of …** aus … (heraus/hinaus) I **be out** nicht zu Hause sein, nicht da sein II

outback [ˈaʊtbæk]: **the outback** das Hinterland Australiens V

outdoor [ˈaʊtdɔː] Außen-, im Freien II

outdoors [ˌaʊtˈdɔːz] im Freien, draußen V

outline [ˈaʊtlaɪn] Gliederung IV

outside [ˌaʊtˈsaɪd]:
1. draußen; nach draußen I
2. **outside Rosie's Diner** vor Rosie's Diner, außerhalb von Rosie's Diner II

outspoken [aʊtˈspəʊkən] direkt, geradeheraus, offen und ehrlich V

outstanding [aʊtˈstændɪŋ] hervorragend, außergewöhnlich V

oval [ˈəʊvl] oval IV

oven [ˈʌvn] Backofen IV

over [ˈəʊvə]:
1. über II **over 400 years** über 400 Jahre; mehr als 400 Jahre I **over here** hier herüber II **over there** da drüben, dort drüben II **over to …** hinüber zu/nach … II **all over the city / the world** in der ganzen Stadt / auf der ganzen Welt IV
2. **be over** vorbei sein, zu Ende sein I

overall [ˌəʊvəˈrɔːl] Gesamt-; allgemeine(r, s) VI 3 (64)

overcrowded [ˌəʊvəˈkraʊdɪd] überfüllt V

overpopulation [ˌəʊvəˌpɒpjuˈleɪʃn] Überbevölkerung VI 3 (74)

overreact [ˌəʊvəriˈækt] überreagieren V

overridden [ˌəʊvəˈrɪdn] siehe **override**

override [ˌəʊvəˈraɪd], **overrode**, **overridden** aufheben, außer Kraft setzen V

overrode [ˌəʊvəˈrəʊd] siehe **override**

overwhelming [ˌəʊvəˈwelmɪŋ] überwältigend VI 3 (73)

owl [aʊl] Eule VI 1 (15)

own [əʊn]:
1. besitzen II
2. **my own film/room/…** mein eigener Film / mein eigenes Zimmer / … II
3. **on my/your/their/… own** allein II

owner [ˈəʊnə] Besitzer/in III

P

p [piː] Abkürzung für pence, penny I

pace [peɪs] Tempo, Geschwindigkeit; Schritt VI 3 (71) **at a … pace** mit … Geschwindigkeit VI 3 (71)

Pacific [pəˈsɪfɪk]: **the Pacific (Ocean)** der Pazifische Ozean V

pack [pæk] packen; verpacken VI 1 (23)

package [ˈpækɪdʒ] Paket VI 3 (56/57)

packet [ˈpækɪt] Packung, Päckchen II

page [peɪdʒ] Seite I **What page are we on?** Auf welcher Seite sind wir? I

°**page-turner** [ˈpeɪdʒ tɜːnə] spannendes Buch

paid [peɪd] siehe **pay**

pain [peɪn] Schmerz(en) VI 1 (12)

painfully [ˈpeɪnfəli] furchtbar, äußerst, schmerzlich VI 1 (12)

paint [peɪnt]:
1. (an)streichen; (an)malen II
2. Farbe, Lack VI 1 (10/11)

painted [ˈpeɪntɪd] bemalt, angemalt II

painter [ˈpeɪntə] Maler/in III

painting [ˈpeɪntɪŋ] Gemälde, Bild V

pair [peə] Paar II **a pair of …** ein Paar … II

palace [ˈpæləs] Palast, Schloss III

palm tree [ˈpɑːm triː] Palme IV

pan [pæn]: **frying pan** Bratpfanne IV

pancake [ˈpænkeɪk] Pfannkuchen, Eierkuchen II

pandemic [pænˈdemɪk] Pandemie (weltweite Epidemie) V

panel discussion [ˈpænl dɪˌskʌʃn] Podiumsdiskussion VI 3 (56/57)

panellist [ˈpænəlɪst] Diskussionsteilnehmer (eines Podiumsdiskussion) VI 3 (74)

panic [ˈpænɪk] in Panik geraten III

pants [pænts] (pl, AE) Hose IV

paper [ˈpeɪpə]:
1. Papier I
2. kurz für: **newspaper** Zeitung IV

parade [pəˈreɪd] Parade, Umzug II

paradise [ˈpærədaɪs] Paradies V

paragraph [ˈpærəɡrɑːf] Absatz (in einem Text) II **paragraph break** Absatzumbruch VI 1 (20)

paraphrase [ˈpærəfreɪz] umschreiben, anders ausdrücken IV

parasite [ˈpærəsaɪt] Parasit VI 3 (62)

parent [ˈpeərənt] Elternteil II

parenting [ˈpeərəntɪŋ] (Kindes-)Erziehung V

parents [ˈpeərənts] Eltern II

park [pɑːk]:
1. Park I
2. parken VI 3 (59)
3. **car park** (BE) Parkplatz IV

parking lot [ˈpɑːkɪŋ lɒt] (AE) Parkplatz IV

parliament [ˈpɑːləmənt] Parlament III **MP (= Member of Parliament)** Parlamentsmitglied, Abgeordnete(r) V

parsley [ˈpɑːsli] Petersilie IV

part [pɑːt] Teil I **part of speech** Wortart III

part-time [ˈpɑːt taɪm] Teilzeit-, Halbtags- V **part-time job** Halbtagsjob, Teilzeitbeschäftigung V

participant (in) [pɑːˈtɪsɪpənt] Teilnehmer/in (an) V
participate (in) [pɑːˈtɪsɪpeɪt] *(fml)* teilnehmen (an), sich beteiligen (an) V
particular [pəˈtɪkjələ] bestimmte(r, s), spezielle(r, s) VI 2 (48) **in particular** insbesondere VI 2 (48)
particularly [pəˈtɪkjələli] besonders; vor allem VI 1 (16)
▶ S. 206 Intensifying adverbs
partner [ˈpɑːtnə] Partner/in I
party [ˈpɑːti] Partei V
pass [pɑːs]:
  1. pass sth./sb. an etwas/jm. vorbeigehen/vorbeifahren II
  2. pass sth. around etwas herumgeben, herumreichen II
  pass sth. on (to sb.) etwas weitergeben (an jn.) V
  3. pass *(a test)* bestehen *(Test, Prüfung)* IV
passenger [ˈpæsɪndʒə] Passagier/in, Fahrgast, Fluggast V
passion [ˈpæʃn] Passion, Leidenschaft V
passionate [ˈpæʃənət] leidenschaftlich V
passport [ˈpɑːspɔːt] (Reise-)Pass III
password [ˈpɑːswɜːd] Passwort III
past [pɑːst]:
  1. Vergangenheit II
  2. vorbei (an), vorüber (an) II
  quarter past ten Viertel nach zehn (10.15 / 22.15) I
paste [peɪst] (an)kleben; *(Computer)* einfügen VI 2 (46)
pasture [ˈpɑːstʃə] Weide V
pat [pæt] tätscheln IV
path [pɑːθ] Pfad, Weg II
patience [ˈpeɪʃns] Geduld V
patient [ˈpeɪʃnt] Patient/in V
patriotic [ˌpeɪtriˈɒtɪk] patriotisch, vaterlandsliebend VI 1 (10/11)
patriotism [ˈpeɪtriətɪzəm] Patriotismus IV
pattern [ˈpætn] Muster IV
pause [pɔːz] innehalten, pausieren; eine Pause einlegen II
pavement [ˈpeɪvmənt] Gehweg, Bürgersteig III
paw [pɔː] Pfote, Tatze II
pay [peɪ] Bezahlung, Lohn VI 1 (20)
  °**pay rise** Lohnerhöhung, Gehaltserhöhung
pay [peɪ], **paid, paid:**
  1. pay (for sth.) (etwas) bezahlen II
  pay cash bar bezahlen V

  2. pay attention (to) achten (auf), aufpassen (auf) V
  3. pay sb. a compliment jm. ein Kompliment machen V
PE [ˌpiːˈiː] Sportunterricht, Turnen I
peace [piːs] Friede, Frieden III
peaceful [ˈpiːsfl] friedlich, friedfertig VI 1 (15)
peak [piːk] Gipfel, Spitze; Höhepunkt V
pedestrian [pəˈdestriən] Fußgänger II **pedestrian zone** Fußgängerzone II
peer [pɪə] *Angehörige(r) derselben Alters- oder Berufsgruppe* V
pen [pen] Kugelschreiber, Stift, Füller I
pence [pens] Pence *(Plural von penny)* I
pencil [ˈpensl] Bleistift I **pencil case** Federmäppchen I
penguin [ˈpeŋgwɪn] Pinguin V
people [ˈpiːpl] Leute, Menschen I
pepper [ˈpepə]:
  1. Pfeffer I
  2. Paprika(schote) IV
per [pə], [pɜː] pro IV **miles per hour** Meilen pro Stunde IV
percent [pəˈsent]: **percent, per cent** Prozent VI 1 (18)
percentage [pəˈsentɪdʒ] Prozentsatz; prozentualer Anteil V
perfect [ˈpɜːfɪkt] perfekt, ideal I
°**perfect sth.** [pəˈfekt] perfektionieren
perform [pəˈfɔːm] auftreten *(Künstler/in)* III
performance [pəˈfɔːməns] Aufführung, Vorstellung, Auftritt IV
performer [pəˈfɔːmə] Künstler/in, Performer/in III
perhaps [pəˈhæps] vielleicht V
period [ˈpɪəriəd] Unterrichtsstunde, Schulstunde IV
permanent [ˈpɜːmənənt] permanent, dauerhaft VI 1 (23)
permission [pəˈmɪʃn] Erlaubnis III
  You need permission to … Man benötigt eine Erlaubnis, … III
permit [ˈpɜːmɪt] Genehmigung, Erlaubnis(schein) IV
person [ˈpɜːsn] Person I
  in person persönlich V
personal [ˈpɜːsənl] persönlich V
personality [ˌpɜːsəˈnæləti] Persönlichkeit V
personally [ˈpɜːsənəli] persönlich V

perspective [pəˈspektɪv] Perspektive, Blickwinkel VI 1 (14)
persuade [pəˈsweɪd] überreden VI 1 (21)
persuasion [pəˈsweɪʒn] Überredung, Überzeugung VI 1 (21)
pessimistic [ˌpesɪˈmɪstɪk] pessimistisch V
pesticide [ˈpestɪsaɪd] Schädlingsbekämpfungsmittel, Pestizid VI 3 (62)
pet [pet] Haustier I **… isn't a good pet (= is not)** … ist kein gutes Haustier. I
petition [pəˈtɪʃn] Petition, Eingabe, Unterschriftensammlung V
petrol [ˈpetrəl] Benzin V **petrol station** Tankstelle V
phone [fəʊn]:
  1. Telefon I
  phone call Anruf; Telefongespräch II **answer the phone** ans Telefon gehen II **cell phone** *(AE)* Mobiltelefon, Handy IV **mobile phone** Mobiltelefon, Handy I **on the phone** am Telefon II
  2. phone sb. jn. anrufen II
photo [ˈfəʊtəʊ] Foto I **in the photo** auf dem Foto I **take photos** fotografieren, Fotos machen II
photograph [ˈfəʊtəɡrɑːf] fotografieren III
photographer [fəˈtɒɡrəfə] Fotograf/in V
photography [fəˈtɒɡrəfi] Fotografie V
phrase [freɪz] Ausdruck, (Rede-)Wendung I
physical [ˈfɪzɪkl] physisch, körperlich VI 3 (69) **Physical Education** Sportunterricht, Turnen I
physics [ˈfɪzɪks] Physik VI 3 (59)
piano [piˈænəʊ] Klavier, Piano I
  play the piano Klavier spielen I
pick up [ˌpɪkˈʌp] **pick sb. up** jn. abholen II **pick sth. up** etwas aufheben (vom Boden), etwas hochheben II
picnic [ˈpɪknɪk] Picknick I
picture [ˈpɪktʃə]:
  1. Bild I
  2. picture sb./sth. sich jn./etwas vorstellen VI 1 (12)
pie [ˈpaɪ] Obstkuchen; Pastete IV
pie chart Tortendiagramm V
piece [piːs]: **a piece of …** ein Stück … III **opinion piece** Stellungnahme, Meinungsartikel VI 1 (18)
pig [pɪɡ] Schwein I
pigeon [ˈpɪdʒɪn] (Stadt-)Taube IV

piggy bank [ˈpɪgi bæŋk] Sparschwein V
pile [paɪl] Stapel, Haufen IV
pill [pɪl] Pille, Tablette VI 1 (23)
pilot [ˈpaɪlət] Pilot/in VI 3 (63)
°**PIN (personal identification number)** [pɪn] PIN
pinch [pɪntʃ] kneifen VI 3 (65)
pink [pɪŋk] pink, rosa I
pipe [paɪp] Pfeife III
pit [pɪt] Grube V
pitch [pɪtʃ]:
1. (Sport-)Platz, Spielfeld III
2. Tonlage, Tonhöhe V
pity [ˈpɪti]: **It was a pity that …** Es
war schade, dass … III
pizza [ˈpiːtsə] Pizza I
place [pleɪs] Ort, Platz, Stelle I **in
second place** auf dem zweiten
Platz; an zweiter Stelle III **In the
first place, …** Erstens …; Zunächst
… V **take place** stattfinden III
°**placemat** [ˈpleɪsmæt] Platzdeckchen
placement [ˈpleɪsmənt]: **product
placement** Produktplatzierung
(Schleichwerbung) V
plan [plæn]:
1. Plan I
2. planen II
plane [pleɪn] Flugzeug II **on the
plane** im Flugzeug II
planet [ˈplænɪt] Planet I
plant [plɑːnt]:
1. Pflanze II
2. pflanzen II
plaster [ˈplɑːstə] (Heft-)Pflaster II
plastic [ˈplæstɪk] Plastik, Kunststoff
II
plate [pleɪt]: **a plate of …** ein Teller
… I
platform [ˈplætfɔːm] Bahnsteig,
Gleis III
play [pleɪ]:
1. spielen I
play the drums/the guitar/…
Schlagzeug/Gitarre/… spielen I
2. abspielen (CD, DVD) I
3. Theaterstück I
player [ˈpleɪə] Spieler/in I
playground [ˈpleɪgraʊnd] Spielplatz;
Schulhof V
playwright [ˈpleɪraɪt]
Dramatiker(in), Bühnenautor(in)
VI 1 (12)
please [pliːz] bitte I
pleased [pliːzd] froh, erfreut, zufrie-
den V

pleasure [ˈpleʒə] Vergnügen V **It
is my pleasure …** Es ist mir ein Vergnügen … V
plot [plɒt] Handlung(sverlauf) (eines
Films/einer Geschichte) VI 2 (43)
plus [plʌs] (infml) Plus, Vorteil V
pm [ˌpiːˈem]: **4 pm** 4 Uhr nachmittags / 16 Uhr I
pocket [ˈpɒkɪt] Tasche (Manteltas-
sche, Hosentasche) II
podcast [ˈpɒdkɑːst] Podcast V
poem [ˈpəʊɪm] Gedicht II
poet [ˈpəʊɪt] Dichter/in, Poet/in
VI 1 (12)
poetic [pəʊˈetɪk] poetisch V
poetry [ˈpəʊətri] Gedichte, Lyrik
VI 1 (14)
point [pɔɪnt]:
1. Punkt I
point of view Standpunkt III
(auch **pt.**) Maßeinheit für Schrift-
grad, Zeilenabstände u.Ä. VI 1 (17)
three point five (3.5) drei Komma
fünf (3,5) III
2. **point sth. at sb.** etwas auf jn.
richten I
point sth. out (to sb.) (jn.) auf
etwas hinweisen III **point to sth.**
auf etwas zeigen, deuten I
3. **have a point** nicht ganz Unrecht
haben V
poisonous [ˈpɔɪzənəs] giftig V
polar bear [ˈpəʊlə beə] Eisbär
VI 3 (64)
polarization [ˌpəʊləraɪˈzeɪʃn] Pola-
risierung VI 3 (59)
polarized [ˈpəʊləraɪzd] polarisiert
VI 3 (59)
pole [pəʊl] Stange, Pfahl, Mast
VI 2 (35)
police (pl) [pəˈliːs] Polizei III
police officer Polizist/in I
policeman [pəˈliːsmən] Polizist I
policewoman [pəˈliːswʊmən] Poli-
zistin I
policy [ˈpɒləsi] Politik (politische
Linie), Richtlinie(n) V
°**policymaker** [ˈpɒləsimeɪkə]
politische/r Entscheidungsträger/in
polite [pəˈlaɪt] höflich III
politeness [pəˈlaɪtnəs] Höflichkeit
V
political [pəˈlɪtɪkl] politisch V
politician [ˌpɒləˈtɪʃn] Politiker/in V
politics (no pl) [ˈpɒlətɪks] Politik
(politisches Leben, Geschehen) V
poll [pəʊl]: **opinion poll** Meinungsumfrage V

pollen [ˈpɒlən] Blütenstaub
VI 3 (56/57)
pollinate [ˈpɒləneɪt] bestäuben
VI 3 (56/57)
polluter [pəˈluːtə] Umweltver-
schmutzer/in VI 2 (48)
pollution [pəˈluːʃn] (Umwelt-)Ver-
schmutzung V
pony [ˈpəʊni] Pony II
pool [puːl] Schwimmbad, Schwimmbecken I
poor [pɔː], [pʊə] arm I
popular (with) [ˈpɒpjələ] populär,
beliebt (bei) III
population [ˌpɒpjuˈleɪʃn] Bevölke-
rung, Einwohner(zahl) III
populous [ˈpɒpjələs] bevölkerungs-
reich; dicht besiedelt V
porch [pɔːtʃ] Veranda (AE); Vorbau,
Vordach (BE) IV
pork [pɔːk] Schweinefleisch IV
portion [ˈpɔːʃn] Portion III
portrait [ˈpɔːtreɪt], [ˈpɔːtrət] Porträt
VI 2 (46)
pose a risk/a problem [pəʊz] ein
Risiko/ein Problem darstellen V
position [pəˈzɪʃn] Platz, Position IV
positive [ˈpɒzətɪv] positiv V
°**possession** [pəˈzeʃn] Besitz
possible [ˈpɒsəbl] möglich IV
possibly möglicherweise, vielleicht
IV
post [pəʊst]:
1. Posting (auf Blog), Blog-Eintrag
III
2. Pfosten VI 2 (35)
3. posten, bekanntgeben III
4. **Stay posted.** Bleib(t) auf dem
Laufenden! IV
post office [ˈpəʊst ˌɒfɪs] Postamt II
poster [ˈpəʊstə] Poster II **study
poster** Lernposter II
pot [pɒt] Gefäß; Topf III **pot of
tea** Kännchen III
potato [pəˈteɪtəʊ], pl **potatoes** Kar-
toffel I **roast potatoes** (pl) (im
Backofen in Fett) gebackene Kartoffeln I **sweet potato** Süßkartoffel
IV
potential [pəˈtenʃl]:
1. Potenzial VI 3 (59)
2. potenziell, möglich VI 3 (59)
pound [paʊnd] Pfund (Gewicht und
britische Währung) I **a three-
pound ball** ein drei Pfund schwerer
Ball IV
pour [pɔː] gießen II
poverty [ˈpɒvəti] Armut V
powder [ˈpaʊdə] Pulver IV

power ['paʊə]:
1. Energie, Strom; Kraft, Stärke; Macht IV
2. antreiben, betreiben, mit Energie versorgen V
3. power line Überlandleitung VI 1 (24)

powerful ['paʊəfl] mächtig, kräftig, stark VI 2 (45)

practical ['præktɪkl] praktisch IV

practice ['præktɪs] Übung I **it takes practice** es erfordert Übung IV

practise ['præktɪs] **(**AE: **practice)** üben, trainieren I

prairie ['preəri] Prärie, Grasland IV

precise [prɪ'saɪs] genau, präzise VI 1 (23)

predict [prɪ'dɪkt] vorhersagen, voraussagen VI 3 (73)

prediction [prɪ'dɪkʃn] Vorhersage, Voraussage IV

prefer [prɪ'fɜː]: **prefer sb. to do sth.** (es) vorziehen, wenn jd. etwas täte/tun würde VI 1 (10/11) **prefer sth. (to sth.)** etwas (einer anderen Sache) vorziehen; etwas lieber tun (als etwas) III

prefix ['priːfɪks] Präfix, Vorsilbe IV

prejudice (against) ['predʒudɪs] Vorurteil (gegen), Voreingenommenheit (gegenüber) IV

prepare sth. [prɪ'peə] etwas vorbereiten I

present ['preznt]:
1. Geschenk I
be present vorhanden sein; anwesend sein VI 2 (46)
2. Gegenwart II

present sth. (to sb.) [prɪ'zent] (jm.) etwas präsentieren, vorstellen II

presentation [ˌprezn'teɪʃn] Präsentation, Vorstellung II

president ['prezɪdənt] Präsident/in III

°**presidential election** [prezɪˌdenʃl ɪ'lekʃn] Präsidentschaftswahl

press [pres] drücken III

°**pressure** ['preʃə]: **blood pressure** Blutdruck

pressure group ['preʃə gruːp] Pressuregroup, Lobby V

prestigious [pre'stɪdʒəs] angesehen, renommiert, prestigeträchtig V

pretend [prɪ'tend] so tun, als ob III

pretty ['prɪti] hübsch II

price [praɪs] (Kauf-)Preis I

pride (in sth.) [praɪd] Stolz (auf etwas) IV

priest [priːst] Priester/in V

°**primaries** ['praɪməriz] pl Vorwahlen (in den USA)

primary school ['praɪməri skuːl] Grundschule V

°**prime minister** [ˌpraɪm 'mɪnɪstə] Premierminister/in, Ministerpräsident/in

principal ['prɪnsəpl] Schulleiter/in IV

print [prɪnt]:
1. in print gedruckt VI 2 (43)
°**2. print sth. (out)** etwas (aus) drucken

prison ['prɪzn] Gefängnis I

privacy ['prɪvəsi] Privatsphäre V

private ['praɪvət] privat V

prize [praɪz] Preis, Gewinn II

pro [prəʊ] Profi- V

probably ['prɒbəbli] wahrscheinlich II

problem ['prɒbləm] Problem II

process ['prəʊses] Prozess, Vorgang IV

produce [prə'djuːs] produzieren, erzeugen, herstellen VI 1 (19)

product ['prɒdʌkt] Produkt V
product placement Produktplatzierung (Schleichwerbung) V

production [prə'dʌkʃn] Produktion, Herstellung VI 3 (56/57)

professional [prə'feʃənl] professionell, Profi- V

profile ['prəʊfaɪl] Profil; Beschreibung, Porträt I

program ['prəʊgræm] programmieren VI 3 (68)

programme ['prəʊgræm] Programm (auch im Theater usw.), (Radio-, Fernseh-)Sendung I **What programmes ...?** Welche Programme ...? / Welche Art von Programmen ...? I

programmer ['prəʊgræmə] Programmierer/in VI 3 (69)

progress (no pl) ['prəʊgres] Fortschritt(e) VI 3 (56/57) **in progress** im Gange, im Verlauf V

project ['prɒdʒekt] Projekt II

°**prologue** ['prəʊlɒg] Vorwort

promise ['prɒmɪs] versprechen II

promote [prə'məʊt] fördern V
promote sb. jn. befördern V **promote sth.** etwas bewerben, Werbung machen für etwas V

prone [prəʊn]: **be prone to sth.** anfällig sein für etwas; zu etwas neigen VI 3 (62)

°**pronoun** ['prəʊnaʊn] Pronomen

pronounce [prə'naʊns] aussprechen III

pronunciation [prəˌnʌnsi'eɪʃn] Aussprache I

°**proofread** ['pruːfriːd], **-read,- read** Korrektur lesen

proper ['prɒpə] richtige(r,s), angemessene(r, s), ordentliche(r,s) VI 1 (17)

property ['prɒpəti] Eigentum IV

°**proposal** [prə'pəʊzl] Vorschlag

°**propose** [prə'pəʊz] vorschlagen

°**pros and cons** [ˌprəʊz ənd 'kɒnz] Vor- und Nachteile, Für und Wider

prose [prəʊz] Prosa VI 2 (37)

°**protagonist** [prə'tægənɪst] (fml) Protagonist/in VI 2 (37)

protect sb./sth. (from sb./sth.) [prə'tekt] jn./etwas (be)schützen (vor jm./etwas) III

protest ['prəʊtest] Protest IV

protest [prə'test] protestieren IV

protester [prə'testə] Demonstrant/in IV

proud (of) [praʊd] stolz (auf) III

prove [pruːv] nachweisen, beweisen V

provide [prə'vaɪd] (an)bieten, zur Verfügung stellen V **provide sb. with sth.** jn. mit etwas versorgen, jm. etwas zur Verfügung stellen V

provocative [prə'vɒkətɪv] provozierend, provokativ VI 1 (19)

provoke [prə'vəʊk] provozieren V

psychologist [saɪ'kɒlədʒɪst] Psychologe/Psychologin V

pt [pɔɪnt] siehe point VI 1 (17)

pub [pʌb] Kneipe, Lokal III

public ['pʌblɪk] öffentliche(r, s) III
public transport (BE) **/ public transportation** (AE) öffentliche Verkehrsmittel V **(the) public** die Öffentlichkeit III **Don't do that in public.** Tu das nicht in der Öffentlichkeit. III

°**publication** [ˌpʌblɪ'keɪʃn] Veröffentlichung

publish ['pʌblɪʃ] veröffentlichen III

pull [pʊl] ziehen II **pull sth. out** etwas herausziehen II

pullover [pə'fɔːm] Pullover II

pumpkin ['pʌmpkɪn] Kürbis IV

punctuation [ˌpʌŋktʃu'eɪʃn] Zeichensetzung II

punish ['pʌnɪʃ] bestrafen V

punishment ['pʌnɪʃmənt] Bestrafung, Strafe III

puppet ['pʌpɪt] Marionette, Handpuppe II

purple ['pɜːpl] violett, lila I

purpose ['pɜːpəs] Absicht, Sinn, Zweck, Ziel V **on purpose** mit Absicht, absichtlich V

purse [pɜːs] Portemonnaie, Geldbörse III

push [pʊʃ] drücken, schieben, stoßen I

put [pʊt]**, put, put** legen, stellen, (etwas wohin) tun I **put sth.** (+ adv) etwas (auf eine bestimmte Art) ausdrücken, formulieren VI 3 (68) **put sth. off** etwas aufschieben VI 2 (42) **put sth. on** etwas anziehen (Kleidung); etwas aufsetzen (Hut, Helm) II

▶ S. 224 (to) put sth. politely/simply/…

python ['paɪθən] Python V

Q

qualification [ˌkwɒlɪfɪ'keɪʃn] Qualifikation V

qualify ['kwɒlɪfaɪ] sich qualifizieren IV

quality ['kwɒləti] Eigenschaft, Qualität V **a high-quality translation** eine qualitativ hochwertige Übersetzung V

quarter ['kwɔːtə] Viertel (auch: Stadtviertel) IV **quarter past ten** Viertel nach zehn (10.15 / 22.15) I **quarter to eleven** Viertel vor elf (10.45 / 22.45) I

quay [kiː] Kai V

quayside ['kiːsaɪd] Kai V

queen [kwiːn] Königin II

question ['kwestʃən] Frage I **ask a question** eine Frage stellen I

question mark ['kwestʃən mɑːk] Fragezeichen II

queue [kjuː]:
1. Schlange stehen, sich anstellen II
2. Schlange, Reihe (wartender Menschen) III

quick [kwɪk] schnell II

quiet ['kwaɪət] ruhig, still, leise I

quite [kwaɪt] ziemlich; ganz III **quite a few** ziemlich viele IV

quiz [kwɪz] Quiz, Ratespiel I

quotation [kwəʊ'teɪʃn] Zitat IV **quotation marks** (pl) Anführungszeichen, -striche VI 1 (21)

quote [kwəʊt]:
1. Zitat IV
2. zitieren VI 2 (45)

R

rabbit ['ræbɪt] Kaninchen I

race [reɪs]:
1. Rennen, (Wett-)Lauf II
2. rasen III
3. **human race** Menschheit VI 1 (22)

racism ['reɪsɪzm] Rassismus V

racist ['reɪsɪst] Rassist/in; rassistisch V

radical ['rædɪkl] radikal VI 3 (58)

radio ['reɪdiəʊ] Radio I **on the radio** im Radio I

°**radioactive** [ˌreɪdiəʊ'æktɪv] radioaktiv

radiologist [ˌreɪdi'ɒlədʒɪst] Radiologe/-in VI 3 (58)

rail link [ˌreɪl 'lɪŋk] Bahnverbindung VI 1 (24)

railroad ['reɪlrəʊd] (AE) Eisenbahn IV

railway ['reɪlweɪ] (BE) Eisenbahn IV

rain [reɪn]:
1. Regen II
2. regnen II

rainbow ['reɪnbəʊ] Regenbogen III

raincoat ['reɪnkəʊt] Regenmantel II

rainforest ['reɪnfɒrɪst] Regenwald II

rainy ['reɪni] regnerisch II

raise [reɪz]: **raise money (for sth.)** Geld sammeln (für etwas) (für wohltätige Zwecke) II **raise one's voice** seine Stimme erheben VI 1 (20)

rally ['ræli] Rallye II

ran [ræn] siehe **run**

rang [ræŋ] siehe **ring**

range [reɪndʒ] Bereich, Bandbreite, Palette V

rank sth. [ræŋk] etwas einstufen, etwas anordnen VI 3 (74)

rare [reə] selten VI 2 (49)

rarely ['reəli] selten; kaum je VI 2 (49)

rat [ræt] Ratte I

rate [reɪt] Rate, Quote V **flat rate** Flatrate, Pauschalpreis V

rather (…) than ['rɑːðə] eher (…) als, lieber (…) als, statt V

ratio ['reɪʃiəʊ] (Größen-, Zahlen-) Verhältnis VI 3 (68)

raven ['reɪvn] Rabe III

reach [riːtʃ] erreichen III **reach for sth.** nach etwas greifen VI 2 (36) **reach over** die Hand ausstrecken III

react (to) [ri'ækt] reagieren (auf) III

reaction (to) [ri'ækʃn] Reaktion (auf) IV

°**reactor** [ri'æktə] Reaktor

read [red] siehe **read**

read [riːd]:
1. **(read, read)** lesen I **read aloud** laut (vor)lesen II **read sb.'s mind** jemandes Gedanken lesen III
2. Lektüre VI 2 (45)

readable ['riːdəbl] lesenswert, lesbar VI 2 (45)

reader ['riːdə] Leser/in II

ready ['redi] bereit, fertig I

real ['riːəl] echt, wirklich III

°**realistic** [ˌriːə'lɪstɪk] realistisch

reality [ri'æləti] Realität, Wirklichkeit VI 3 (58)

realize sth. ['riːəlaɪz] etwas erkennen; sich einer Sache bewusst werden VI 1 (14)

really ['rɪəli] echt, wirklich I

reason ['riːzn] Grund, Begründung II **for this reason** aus diesem Grund IV

reasonable ['riːznəbl] vernünftig, akzeptabel VI 3 (70)

reboot [ˌriː'buːt] neu booten, neu starten VI 3 (68)

receive [rɪ'siːv] erhalten, empfangen V

recent ['riːsnt] aktuell, neu; kürzlich geschehen/erfolgt V **in recent months** in den letzten Monaten V

recently ['riːsntli] vor Kurzem, neulich; in letzter Zeit V

reception [rɪ'sepʃn] Empfang (Hotel u.Ä.) V

receptionist [rɪ'sepʃənɪst] Empfangschef/in V

recess ['riːses] (AE) Pause (zwischen Schulstunden) V

recipe ['resəpi] (Koch-)Rezept II

°**recognition** [ˌrekəg'nɪʃn]: **facial recognition** Gesichtserkennung

recognize ['rekəgnaɪz]:
1. erkennen III
2. anerkennen VI 1 (18)

recommend sth. (to sb.) [ˌrekə'mend] (jm.) etwas empfehlen IV

record ['rekɔːd]:
1. Rekord V
2. Schallplatte VI 1 (13)
3. aufzeichnen (Musik, Daten); dokumentieren (Daten) VI 1 (22)
4. Aufzeichnung(en) VI 1 (22)

recorder [rɪ'kɔːdə] Blockflöte II

°**recording** [rɪ'kɔːdɪŋ] Aufnahme, Aufzeichnung

recover (from) [rɪ'kʌvə] sich erholen (von) V

°**recreation** [ˌriːkri'eɪʃn] Freizeit(beschäftigung); Erholung

recycle [ˌriːˈsaɪkl] recyceln, wiederverwerten V

recycling [ˌriːˈsaɪklɪŋ] Recycling, Wiederverwertung V

red [red] rot I

reduce (to) [rɪˈdjuːs] reduzieren, verkleinern (auf) V

reef [riːf] Riff V

refer to [rɪˈfɜː] verweisen auf; sich beziehen auf V

referee [ˌrefəˈriː] Schiedsrichter/in III

reference [ˈrefrəns] Verweis (auf), Bezug (auf) V **letter of reference** Empfehlungsschreiben, Referenz(schreiben) V

referendum [ˌrefəˈrendəm]**,** *pl* **referendums** *or* **referenda** Volksentscheid V

refine [rɪˈfaɪn] verfeinern, weiterentwickeln VI 2 (52)

reflect [rɪˈflekt] reflektieren, (wider)spiegeln VI 1 (14)

reflection [rɪˈflekʃn] Betrachtung, Reflexion VI 2 (41)

refuse [rɪˈfjuːz] sich weigern, ablehnen VI 2 (35)

regard [rɪˈgɑːd]**: with regard to** bezüglich VI 1 (23)

regardless (of) [rɪˈgɑːdləs] ungeachtet V

region [ˈriːdʒən] Region IV

regional [ˈriːdʒənl] regional III

register [ˈredʒɪstə] Klassenbuch; Register, Verzeichnis IV

regular [ˈregjələ] regelmäßig II

regulation [ˌregjuˈleɪʃn] Vorschrift; Regulierung VI 3 (59)

rehearse [rɪˈhɜːs] proben; einüben *(sich leise vorsprechen)* V

reins *(pl)* [reɪnz] Zügel III

relate sth. to sth. [rɪˈleɪt] etwas mit etwas verknüpfen, etwas zu etwas in Beziehung setzen V

relation [rɪˈleɪʃn]**: in relation to** im Verhältnis zu VI 1 (17)

relationship [rɪˈleɪʃnʃɪp] Beziehung, Verhältnis IV

relative [ˈrelətɪv] Verwandte(r) V

relax [rɪˈlæks] sich entspannen, sich ausruhen III

relaxed [rɪˈlækst] entspannt IV

release [rɪˈliːs] abgeben, freisetzen VI 2 (52) **release a prisoner** eine/n Gefangene/n freilassen VI 2 (52)

relevant (to sth.) [ˈreləvənt] relevant, wichtig (für etwas) IV

reliability [rɪˌlaɪəˈbɪləti]:
1. Verlässlichkeit V
2. Zuverlässigkeit V

reliable [rɪˈlaɪəbl] verlässlich, zuverlässig V

religion [rɪˈlɪdʒən] Religion I

religious [rɪˈlɪdʒəs] religiös; gläubig VI 1 (16)

rely on sth. [rɪˈlaɪ] auf etwas angewiesen sein VI 3 (62)

°**remain** [rɪˈmeɪn] (ver)bleiben

remember [rɪˈmembə] sich erinnern (an) I **remember sth.** an etwas denken; sich etwas merken III

remind sb. [rɪˈmaɪnd] jn. erinnern IV

remote [rɪˈməʊt] abgelegen, abgeschieden V **remote control (***kurz auch:* **remote)** Fernbedienung III

remove [rɪˈmuːv] entfernen, beseitigen; ausziehen *(Kleidung)* VI 1 (23)

repair [rɪˈpeə]:
1. Reparatur VI 1 (24)
2. reparieren VI 1 (24)

repeat [rɪˈpiːt] wiederholen II

repetition [ˌrepəˈtɪʃn] Wiederholung V

replace sb./sth. (with) [rɪˈpleɪs] jn./etwas ersetzen (durch); austauschen V

reply (to) [rɪˈplaɪ] antworten (auf); erwidern, entgegnen III

report [rɪˈpɔːt]:
1. Bericht, Reportage II
2. berichten IV

reporter [rɪˈpɔːtə] Reporter/in VI 3 (66)

represent [ˌreprɪˈzent] vertreten, repräsentieren; verkörpern, symbolisieren V

representation [ˌreprɪzenˈteɪʃn] Vertretung, Repräsentanz VI 1 (18)

°**representative** [ˌreprɪˈzentətɪv] Repräsentant/in, Abgeordnete(r)

republic [rɪˈpʌblɪk] Republik III **federal republic** Bundesrepublik V

reputation [ˌrepjuˈteɪʃn] Ruf, Reputation V

request [rɪˈkwest] Bitte, Wunsch V **friend request** Freundschaftsanfrage VI 3 (61)

requirement [rɪˈkwaɪəmənt] Voraussetzung, Anforderung V

rescue [ˈreskjuː] retten II

research [rɪˈsɜːtʃ]:
1. Recherche, Forschung(en) III
2. recherchieren VI 3 (74)

researcher [rɪˈsɜːtʃə] Forscher/in V

reservation [ˌrezəˈveɪʃn] **(***kurz auch:* **rez)** Reservat, Reservation IV

reserve [rɪˈzɜːv]:
1. reservieren, buchen III
2. Schutzgebiet, Reservat IV

residence [ˈrezɪdəns] Wohnung, Wohnsitz V

resident [ˈrezɪdənt] Bewohner/in, Anwohner/in IV

°**resolve** [rɪˈzɒlv] lösen, auflösen, *(Streit)* schlichten

resources *(pl)* [rɪˈsɔːsɪz], [rɪˈzɔːsɪz] Mittel, Ressourcen V

respect sb./sth. (for) [rɪˈspekt] jn./etwas respektieren, achten (wegen) V

respectful [rɪˈspektfl] respektvoll V

respond [rɪˈspɒnd] antworten, erwidern; reagieren VI 2 (35)

°**response** [rɪˈspɒns] Antwort, Reaktion

responsibility [rɪˌspɒnsəˈbɪləti] Verantwortung V

responsible [rɪˈspɒnsəbl] verantwortlich II

rest [rest]:
1. ruhen, sich ausruhen III
2. Rest III
3. Pause; Ruhe, Erholung VI 2 (38)

restate sth. [ˌriːˈsteɪt] etwas wiederholen, etwas noch einmal formulieren VI 1 (19)

restaurant [ˈrestrɒnt] Restaurant III

restroom [ˈrestruːm] *(AE) (öffentliche)* Toilette, WC IV

result [rɪˈzʌlt]:
1. Ergebnis, Resultat III
as a result folglich III
2. **result in sth.** zu etwas führen, etwas zur Folge haben V

résumé [ˈrezəmeɪ] Lebenslauf V

return [rɪˈtɜːn]:
1. **in return** als Gegenleistung V
2. zurückkehren, zurückkommen VI 2 (34)

reveal [rɪˈviːl] offenbaren, preisgeben, verraten IV

review [rɪˈvjuː]:
1. besprechen, rezensieren VI 2 (42)
2. Rezension, Besprechung, Kritik VI 2 (42)

revise [rɪˈvaɪz] überarbeiten; *(Lernstoff)* wiederholen III

revision [rɪˈvɪʒn] Wiederholung *(des Lernstoffs)* II

revolutionize [ˌrevəˈluːʃənaɪz] revolutionieren VI 1 (23)

rewrite [ˌriːˈraɪt] neu schreiben, umarbeiten VI 1 (23)

rhetorical [rɪˈtɒrɪkl] rhetorisch VI 1 (21)

rhyme [raɪm] Reim; Vers I

rhythm [ˈrɪðəm] Rhythmus III

rice [raɪs] Reis IV

rich [rɪtʃ] reich I
ridden ['rɪdn] *siehe* **ride**
ride [raɪd]:
1. **(rode, ridden)** reiten II
ride a bike Fahrrad fahren I
2. Fahrt *(auch Karussellfahrt u.Ä.)* II
rider ['raɪdə] Reiter/in V
ridiculous [rɪ'dɪkjələs] lächerlich
VI 1 (18)
riding ['raɪdɪŋ] Reiten I
right [raɪt]:
1. richtig I
..., right? ..., nicht wahr? II **all
right** okay; in Ordnung I **someone is right** jemand hat Recht I
Yes, that's right. Ja, das ist richtig. / Ja, das stimmt. I
2. rechte(r, s); (nach) rechts II
on the right rechts/auf der rechten
Seite II **turn right** (nach) rechts
abbiegen II
3. **right behind you** direkt hinter
dir, genau hinter dir II
right now jetzt gerade II
4. **rights** *(pl)* Rechte IV
civil rights *(pl)* Bürgerrechte IV
ring [rɪŋ]:
1. Ring II
2. **(rang, rung)** klingeln, läuten II
°**rise** [raɪz]: **pay rise** Lohnerhöhung,
Gehaltserhöhung
rise [raɪz], **rose, risen**:
1. (an)steigen, aufsteigen; (sich) erhöhen V
2. **rise up** sich erheben VI 2 (47)
aufragen, emporragen *(Berge, Säulen,
Türme, …)* III
risen ['rɪzn] *siehe* **rise**
risk [rɪsk] Risiko V **at risk** in Gefahr, gefährdet V **pose a risk** ein
Risiko darstellen V
°**ritual** ['rɪtʃuəl] Ritual V
river ['rɪvə] Fluss I
road [rəʊd] Straße *(Landstraße zwischen Orten; Straße in Orten)* I
road trip Autoreise, *(lange)* Autofahrt V **at 8 Beach Road** in der
Beach Road (Nummer) 8 I **in
Beach Road** in der Beach Road I
roar [rɔː]:
1. brüllen III
2. tosen, dröhnen IV
roast [rəʊst] braten *(im Backofen)*
IV **roast beef** Rinderbraten I
roast potatoes *(pl)* *(im Backofen in
Fett)* gebackene Kartoffeln I
robot ['rəʊbɒt] Roboter VI 3 (56/57)

rock [rɒk]:
1. Fels, Felsen I
2. **rock (music)** Rockmusik II
rocky ['rɒki] felsig, steinig II
rode [rəʊd] *siehe* **ride**
rodeo ['rəʊdiəʊ] Rodeo IV
role [rəʊl] Rolle *(in einem Theaterstück, Film)* II **role model** Vorbild
V
roll [rəʊl] rollen II
roller coaster ['rəʊlə kəʊstə] Ach-
terbahn IV
romance [rəʊ'mæns] Romantik, romantische Liebe VI 3 (69)
romantic [rəʊ'mæntɪk] romantisch;
Liebes- III
roof [ruːf] Dach II
room [ruːm] Zimmer, Raum I
°**root** [ruːt] Wurzel I
rope [rəʊp] Seil III
rose [rəʊz]:
1. Rose IV
2. *siehe* **rise**
rotten ['rɒtn] verfault, faul, verdor-
ben V
round [raʊnd]:
1. **round the world** um die Welt II
2. **round sth. off (with sth.)**
etwas (mit etwas) abschließen, vervollständigen IV
roundabout ['raʊndəbaʊt] Kreisver-
kehr II
route [ruːt] Strecke, Route III
routine [ruːˈtiːn] Routine II
row [rəʊ] Reihe VI 3 (56/57) **in a
row** in Folge, hintereinander, nachei-
nander V
royal ['rɔɪəl] königlich III
rubber ['rʌbə] Radiergummi I
rubbish ['rʌbɪʃ] Müll, Abfall II
rubbish bin Mülltonne, Abfalleimer
IV
rucksack ['rʌksæk] Rucksack IV
rude [ruːd] unhöflich; unverschämt
III
rudeness ['ruːdnəs] Unhöflichkeit V
rugby ['rʌgbi] Rugby V
ruin ['ruːɪn] Ruine II
rule [ruːl]:
1. Regel, Vorschrift II
2. herrschen, beherrschen VI 3 (68)
ruler ['ruːlə] Lineal I
run [rʌn], **ran, run**:
1. rennen, laufen I
run after sb. hinter jm. herrennen I
run for your life um sein Leben
rennen IV
2. ausführen *(Computerprogramm)*
VI 3 (61)

**run a school / a company / a
hotel** eine Schule / eine Firma / ein
Hotel leiten, führen V
3. **run out** knapp werden; zu Ende
gehen V
They run out of money. Ihnen
geht das Geld aus. / Bei ihnen wird
das Geld knapp. V
rung [rʌŋ] *siehe* ring II
runner ['rʌnə] Läufer/in II
rural ['rʊərəl] ländlich, Land- V
rust [rʌst] rosten, verrosten VI 1 (22)

S

sacred ['seɪkrɪd] heilig IV
sad [sæd] traurig I
saddle ['sædl] Sattel III
sadly ['sædli] leider, bedauerlicher-
weise VI 1 (20)
sadness ['sædnəs] Traurigkeit IV
safe [seɪf] sicher, in Sicherheit III
safety ['seɪfti] Sicherheit V
said [sed] *siehe* **say**
sailing ['seɪlɪŋ]: **sailing boat** Segelboot I **go sailing** segeln; segeln
gehen I
sailor ['seɪlə] Seemann, Matrose,
Matrosin III
salad ['sæləd] Salat I **fruit salad**
Obstsalat I
sale [seɪl]: **for sale** zum Verkauf, zu
verkaufen VI 3 (68)
°**saliva** *(no pl)* [sə'laɪvə] Speichel I
salt [sɔːlt] Salz IV
°**salty** ['sɔːlti] salzig I
samba ['sæmbə] Samba I
same [seɪm]: **the same as ...** der-/
die-/dasselbe wie ... I
°**sample** ['saːmpl] Probe V
sand [sænd] Sand I
sandcastle ['sændkaːsl] Sandburg V
sandwich ['sænwɪtʃ], ['sænwɪdʒ]
Sandwich, *(zusammengeklapptes)*
belegtes Brot I
sandy ['sændi] sandig V
sang [sæŋ] *siehe* **sing**
sank [sæŋk] *siehe* **sink**
sarcasm ['saːkæzəm] Sarkasmus V
sarcastic [saːˈkæstɪk] sarkastisch V
sat [sæt] *siehe* **sit**
Saturday ['sætədeɪ], ['sætədi]
Samstag, Sonnabend I
sauce [sɔːs] Soße IV
saucepan ['sɔːspən] Kochtopf, Stiel-
topf IV

sausage [ˈsɒsɪdʒ] Wurst, Würstchen IV

save [seɪv]:
1. retten III
2. sparen; speichern VI 2 (34)
save a goal ein Tor halten, abwehren III **save sb. from sth.** jn. von/vor etwas retten III

saw [sɔː] *siehe* **see**

say [seɪ], **said, said** sagen I **Say hello to … for me.** Grüß … von mir. II

saying [ˈseɪɪŋ] Sprichwort, Redensart IV

scan sth. (for sth.) [skæn] etwas (nach etwas) absuchen III **scan a text** einen Text schnell *(nach bestimmten Wörtern/Informationen)* absuchen II

scanner [ˈskænə] Scanner *(med)* VI 1 (24) **security scanner** Sicherheitsscanner V

scare sb. [skeə] jn. erschrecken; jm. Angst machen III

scared [skeəd] verängstigt II

scarf [skɑːf], *pl* **scarves** Schal III

scarves [skɑːvz] *siehe* **scarf**

scary [ˈskeəri] unheimlich, gruselig I

scene [siːn] Szene I

scenic [ˈsiːnɪk] *(landschaftlich)* schön V

sceptical [ˈskeptɪkl] skeptisch VI 3 (59)

schedule [ˈʃedjuːl], [ˈskedʒuːl] (Zeit-)Plan, Programm III

scholar [ˈskɒlə] Gelehrte(r), Wissenschaftler/in V

school [skuːl] Schule I **school bag** Schultasche I **at school** in der Schule I **before school** vor der Schule *(vor Schulbeginn)* I **°school hall** Aula

schoolbook [ˈskuːlbʊk] Schulbuch VI 2 (39)

schoolyard [ˈskuːljɑːd] Schulhof I

science [ˈsaɪəns] Naturwissenschaft I

scientific [ˌsaɪənˈtɪfɪk] (natur)wissenschaftlich V

scientist [ˈsaɪəntɪst] Naturwissenschaftler/in III

scone [skɒn] *kleines rundes Milchbrötchen, leicht süß, oft mit Rosinen* I

score [skɔː]:
1. Spielstand; Punktestand III **What's the score?** Wie steht es? III
2. Treffer erzielen, Tor schießen III

scratch [skrætʃ] kratzen V

scream [skriːm] schreien III

screen [skriːn] Bildschirm II **split screen** geteilter Bildschirm; Bildschirm(auf)teilung III

script [skrɪpt] Drehbuch; Manuskript IV

scroll [skrəʊl] scrollen III

°scuff [skʌf] abnutzen; schlurfen

sculpture [ˈskʌlptʃə] Skulptur IV

sea [siː] Meer I

seagull [ˈsiːgʌl] Möwe I

seal [əˈsiːl] Robbe I

search (for) [sɜːtʃ]:
1. (durch)suchen (nach) III
2. Durchsuchung; Suche (nach) III
search bar *(Computer)* Suchfeld, Suchleiste VI 3 (61) **search engine** (Internet-)Suchmaschine VI 1 (16)

season [ˈsiːzn]:
1. Jahreszeit; Saison V
busy season Hauptsaison V
2. *(AE)* Staffel *(einer Fernsehserie)* IV

seat [siːt] Sitz, Platz II **seat belt** Sicherheitsgurt V

seatbelt [ˈsiːtbelt] Sicherheitsgurt V

°seating [ˈsiːtɪŋ] Bestuhlung

°seawater [ˈsiːwɔːtə] Meerwasser

second [ˈsekənd]:
1. zweite(r, s) I
in second place auf dem zweiten Platz; an zweiter Stelle III
2. Sekunde II

secondary [ˈsekəndri]: **secondary school** weiterführende Schule *(in GB)* V

secondly, … [ˈsekəndli] zweitens … V

secret [ˈsiːkrət] geheim V

section [ˈsekʃn] Teil(stück), Abschnitt V

°secure [sɪˈkjuə] sicher, gesichert

security [sɪˈkjʊərəti] Sicherheit, Sicherheits- IV **security scanner** Sicherheitsscanner V

see [siː], **saw, seen**:
1. sehen I
2. besuchen I
see a doctor einen Arzt/eine Ärztin aufsuchen; zum Arzt gehen II
3. be seeing sb. mit jm. zusammen sein V
4. …, you see. …, weißt du. II
I see. Aha! / Verstehe. III
5. See you. Bis gleich. / Bis bald. I

seed [siːd] Samen IV

seem (to be/do) [siːm] (zu sein/zu tun) scheinen III

seen [siːn] *siehe* **see**

segregation [ˌsegrɪˈgeɪʃn] Trennung *(nach Hautfarbe, Religion oder Geschlecht)* IV

seldom [ˈseldəm] selten VI 2 (47)

self [self]: **self-confidence** Selbstbewusstsein V **self-confident** selbstbewusst, (selbst)sicher V **self-employed** selbstständig V

selfie [ˈselfi] Selfie III

sell [sel], **sold, sold** verkaufen I

semester [sɪˈmestə] *(bes. AE)* Semester; Schulhalbjahr V

semi- [ˈsemi] halb-; Halb- VI 2 (45)

send sth. to sb. [send], **sent, sent** jm. etwas schicken, senden I

senior year [ˈsiːniə jɪə] Abschlussklasse, -jahr V

sense [sens]:
1. Vernunft, Verstand VI 2 (35)
2. Sinn, Gefühl, Bewusstsein VI 3 (58)

sense of humour [ˌsens əv ˈhjuːmə] (Sinn für) Humor III

sensible [ˈsensəbl] vernünftig; praktisch VI 3 (71)

sensitive [ˈsensətɪv] einfühlsam, sensibel VI 3 (71)

°sensor [ˈsensə] Sensor

sent [sent] *siehe* **send**

sentence [ˈsentəns] Satz I

sentient [ˈsentiənt], [ˈsenʃnt] empfindungsfähig VI 3 (58)

separate [ˈseprət]:
1. getrennt IV
2. trennen V

separately [ˈseprətli] einzeln, separat IV

September [sepˈtembə] September I

sequence [ˈsiːkwəns] Abfolge, Reihenfolge VI 3 (60)

series [ˈsɪəriːz], *pl* **series** (Sende-)Reihe, Serie V

serious [ˈsɪəriəs] ernst; ernsthaft III **take sth./sb. seriously** etwas/jn. ernst nehmen VI 1 (20)

serve [sɜːv] servieren; bedienen V

service [ˈsɜːvɪs]:
1. Gottesdienst III
2. Dienst, Service IV

session [ˈseʃn] Sitzung, Einheit IV

set [set] Satz, Set II

set [set], **set, set: set sth. up** etwas errichten, aufbauen; etwas arrangieren IV **be set in** spielen in VI 2 (45)

settings *(pl)* [ˈsetɪŋz] Einstellungen VI 3 (61)

settle [ˈsetl] sich niederlassen, sich ansiedeln V

settlement ['setlmənt] Siedlung v

settler ['setlə] Siedler/in v

seven ['sevn] sieben I

several ['sevrəl] mehrere, verschiedene v

sex [seks] Geschlecht VI 1 (19)
 same-sex marriage gleichgeschlechtliche Ehe VI 1 (19)

sexism ['seksɪzəm] Sexismus v

sexist ['seksɪst] sexistisch v

shadow ['ʃædəʊ] Schatten II

shake [ʃeɪk], **shook, shaken** schütteln II

shaken ['ʃeɪkən] *siehe* **shake**

Shall I ...? [ʃæl] Soll ich ...? III

shallow ['ʃæləʊ] flach, nicht tief III

°**shame sb.** [ʃeɪm] jn. beschämen, jn. bloßstellen

°**shape** [ʃeɪp] formen

share sth. [ʃeə] (sich) etwas teilen III

shark [ʃɑːk] Hai I

sharp [ʃɑːp] scharf IV

sharpener ['ʃɑːpnə] Anspitzer I

shave [ʃeɪv] (sich) rasieren VI 1 (12)

she [ʃiː] sie I

sheep [ʃiːp], pl **sheep** Schaf II

sheepdog ['ʃiːpdɒg] Hütehund III

shelf [ʃelf], pl **shelves** Regal I

shell [ʃel] Muschel(schale) IV

shelves [ʃelvz] *siehe* **shelf**

shepherd ['ʃepəd] Schäfer/in, Schafhirte/-hirtin III

shine [ʃaɪn], **shone, shone** scheinen (Sonne) III

shiny ['ʃaɪni] glänzend IV

ship [ʃɪp] Schiff I

shirt [ʃɜːt] Hemd II

shock [ʃɒk] schockieren v

shocked [ʃɒkt] schockiert, entsetzt II

shoe [ʃuː] Schuh I

shone [ʃɒn] *siehe* **shine**

shook [ʃʊk] *siehe* **shake**

shoot [ʃuːt], **shot, shot** schießen; erschießen IV **shoot a film** einen Film drehen IV

shop [ʃɒp] einkaufen II **shop assistant** Verkäufer/in II **corner shop** Laden an der Ecke; Tante-Emma-Laden I

shopper ['ʃɒpə] (Ein-)Käufer/in II

shopping ['ʃɒpɪŋ sentə]: **shopping centre** Einkaufszentrum II **shopping mall** (*kurz auch:* **mall**) (großes) Einkaufszentrum II **do the/ some shopping** einkaufen gehen; Einkäufe erledigen II **go shopping** einkaufen gehen I

shore [ʃɔː] Ufer (eines Sees), Strand II

short [ʃɔːt] kurz I

shorten ['ʃɔːtn] (ver)kürzen v

shortly ['ʃɔːtli] in Kürze, bald; kurz, gleich v

shot [ʃɒt]:
 1. *siehe* **shoot**
 2. Aufnahme, Foto; (Film) Einstellung, Szene IV
 long shot Totale, Totalaufnahme IV
 medium shot Halbtotale IV

should [ʃʊd], [ʃəd]: **You should ...** Du solltest ... / Ihr solltet ... II

shoulder ['ʃəʊldə] Schulter II

shout [ʃaʊt] schreien, rufen I

show [ʃəʊ]:
 1. Show, Vorstellung II
 2. **(showed, shown /** (*seltener*) **showed)** zeigen I
 3. **show up** (infml) auftauchen, erscheinen VI 1 (18)

shower ['ʃaʊə] Dusche III **have a shower** (sich) duschen III

shown [ʃəʊn] *siehe* **show**

shrank [ʃræŋk] *siehe* **shrink**

shrimp [ʃrɪmp], pl **shrimp** or **shrimps** Garnele IV

shrink [ʃrɪŋk], **shrank, shrunk** schrumpfen VI 3 (62)

shrub [ʃrʌb] Strauch, Busch IV

shrunk [ʃrʌŋk] *siehe* **shrink**

shy [ʃaɪ] schüchtern, scheu II

sick [sɪk] krank I **I feel sick.** Mir ist schlecht. II **I'm going to be sick.** Ich muss mich übergeben. II

side [saɪd] Seite II **take sides** Partei ergreifen VI 3 (74)

sidewalk ['saɪdwɔːk] (AE) Gehweg, Bürgersteig IV

sigh [saɪ] seufzen III

sights (pl) [saɪts] Sehenswürdigkeiten II

sightseeing ['saɪtsiːɪŋ] Sightseeing; das Besichtigen von Sehenswürdigkeiten v **go sightseeing** sich Sehenswürdigkeiten ansehen v

sign [saɪn]:
 1. Schild; Zeichen I
 no sign of ... keine Spur von ... II
 2. unterschreiben v

signal ['sɪgnəl] Signal, Zeichen III

signature ['sɪgnətʃə] Unterschrift v

°**signpost** ['saɪnpəʊst] beschildern; aufzeigen; den Weg weisen v

silent ['saɪlənt] still, leise III
 silently lautlos; schweigend III

silliness ['sɪlinəs] Albernheit, Blödheit IV

silly ['sɪli]:
 1. albern; blöd I
 2. Dummerchen I

silver ['sɪlvə] Silber; silbern, Silber- v

similar (to sth./sb.) ['sɪmələ] (etwas/jm.) ähnlich II

°**similarity** [ˌsɪmə'lærəti] Ähnlichkeit v

simile ['sɪməli] Vergleich VI 1 (15)

simple ['sɪmpl] einfach, unkompliziert VI 1 (13)

since 10 o'clock [sɪns] seit 10 Uhr III

sincere [sɪn'sɪə] aufrichtig, ehrlich VI 3 (70)

sincerely [sɪn'sɪəli]: **Yours sincerely** Mit freundlichen Grüßen (Briefschluss) v

sincerity [sɪn'serəti] Ernsthaftigkeit, Aufrichtigkeit VI 3 (70)

sing [sɪŋ], **sang, sung** singen I **sing along (with sb.)** (mit jm.) mitsingen III

singer ['sɪŋə] Sänger/in II

single ['sɪŋgl]:
 1. ledig, alleinstehend I
 2. einzige(r,s) VI 1 (27)
 3. Single (alleinstehende Person) I

sink [sɪŋk], **sank, sunk** sinken III

sir [sɜː] (BE): **Dear Sir or Madam, ...** Sehr geehrte Damen und Herren, ... v

sister ['sɪstə] Schwester I

sit [sɪt], **sat, sat** sitzen; sich setzen I **sit down** sich hinsetzen I **sit up** sich aufsetzen III

site [saɪt]: **internet site** Site, Website v

situation [ˌsɪtʃu'eɪʃn] Situation III

six [sɪks] sechs I

sixties ['sɪkstiz]:
 1. **the sixties** die Sechzigerjahre v
 in the 1960s in den 60er-Jahren (des 20. Jahrhunderts) IV

size [saɪz] Größe II

skates ['skeɪts] Inlineskates I

skating ['skeɪtɪŋ] Inlineskaten, Rollschuhlaufen I

skeleton ['skelɪtn] Skelett VI 1 (22)

skill [skɪl] Fertigkeit II

skilled [skɪld] geschickt v

skim (a text) [skɪm] (einen Text) überfliegen (um den Inhalt grob zu erfassen) IV

skin [skɪn] Haut v

skirt [skɜːt] Rock II

sky [skaɪ] Himmel II **in the sky** am Himmel II

skyline ['skaɪlaɪn] Skyline; Horizont III

skyscraper ['skaɪskreɪpə] Wolkenkratzer IV

slam [slæm] schlagen; zuknallen *(Tür)* VI 3 (71)

slang [slæŋ] Slang V

slap [slæp] knallen, klatschen IV

slave [sleɪv] Sklave, Sklavin IV

slavery ['sleɪvəri] Sklaverei IV

sleep [sliːp]**, slept, slept** schlafen I

sleeping bag ['sliːpɪŋ bæg] Schlafsack V

sleepover ['sliːpəʊvə] Schlafparty I

slept [slept] *siehe* **sleep**

slide [slaɪd] Folie *(für Präsentationsprogramme)* III

sling [slɪŋ] Schlinge V

slip [slɪp] (aus)rutschen III

slow [sləʊ]:
   1. langsam I
   slow motion Zeitlupe III
   2. slow down langsamer werden; (sich) verlangsamen V

small [smɔːl] klein I **small talk** Smalltalk *(spontan geführtes Gespräch in umgangssprachlichem Ton)* III

smart [smɑːt]:
   1. elegant, schick; gepflegt V
   2. schlau, intelligent VI 3 (68)

smartphone ['smɑːtfəʊn] Smartphone VI 3 (58)

smell [smel] riechen I **smell sth.** an etwas riechen I

smile [smaɪl]:
   1. lächeln I
   smile at sb. jn. anlächeln I
   2. Lächeln I

smiley ['smaɪli] Smiley I

smoke [sməʊk] rauchen III

smoothie ['smuːði] Smoothie, Fruchtshake III

smuggle ['smʌgl] schmuggeln I

smuggler ['smʌglə] Schmuggler/in I

smuggling ['smʌglɪŋ] der Schmuggel, das Schmuggeln I

snack [snæk] Snack, Imbiss I

snake [sneɪk] Schlange I

sneakers *(pl)* [sniːks] Turnschuhe IV

sneeze [sniːz] niesen I

snorkel ['snɔːkl] schnorcheln V

snow [snəʊ] Schnee I

so [səʊ]:
   1. also; deshalb, daher I
   2. so cool/nice/… so cool/ nett/… I
   so far bis jetzt; bis hierher II

3. so that … (oft auch kurz: **so …)** sodass, damit II

4. So what? Na und? IV
So? Und? / Na und? I

5. auch V
John is really clever. So is Joanna. … Joanna auch. V

so-called [ˌsəʊ ˈkɔːld] sogenannt VI 1 (23)

soccer ['sɒkə] Fußball IV

social ['səʊʃl] sozial, Sozial-, gesellschaftlich IV **social media** *(pl)* soziale Medien III **social studies** Sozialkunde IV

social networking [ˌsəʊʃl ˈnetwɜːkɪŋ] Kommunikation über Online-Plattformen VI 3 (58)

socialize ['səʊʃəlaɪz] sich treffen, Kontakt pflegen V

society [sə'saɪəti] (die) Gesellschaft V

sock [sɒk] Socke II

sofa ['səʊfə] Sofa I

soft [sɒft] weich II **in a soft voice** mit sanfter Stimme II

solar energy [ˌsəʊlər ˈenədʒi] Solarenergie, Sonnenenergie V

sold [səʊld] *siehe* **sell**

soldier ['səʊldʒə] Soldat/in III

solidarity [ˌsɒlɪ'dærəti] Solidarität V

solo ['səʊləʊ] Solo- II

solution (to) [sə'luːʃn] Lösung (für) *(Problem; Aufgabe)* V

solve [sɒlv] lösen III

some [sʌm,] einige, ein paar; etwas I

somebody ['sʌmbədi] jemand I

somehow ['sʌmhaʊ] irgendwie VI 3 (69)

someone ['sʌmwʌn] jemand I

something ['sʌmθɪŋ] etwas I

sometimes ['sʌmtaɪmz] manchmal I

somewhat ['sʌmwɒt] etwas, ein wenig VI 1 (13)

somewhere ['sʌmweə] irgendwo, irgendwohin IV

son [sʌn] Sohn II

song [sɒŋ] Lied, Song I

soon [suːn] bald I

sophomore ['sɒfəmɔː] *Schüler/in in der 10. Klasse der High School; Student/in im zweiten Studienjahr* V

sore [sɔː]: **be sore** wund sein; wehtun II **have a sore throat** Halsschmerzen haben II

sorry ['sɒri]:
   1. (I'm) sorry. Tut mir leid. / Entschuldigung. I

I'm sorry about … Es tut mir leid wegen … II **Sorry?** Wie bitte? IV

sort (of) [sɔːt] Art, Sorte V

sound [saʊnd]:
   1. Geräusch; Klang I
   2. klingen, sich *(gut usw.)* anhören I

soup [suːp] Suppe I **make soup** Suppe kochen IV

sour ['saʊə] sauer, säuerlich IV

source [sɔːs] Quelle *(auch:* Textquelle*)* VI 1 (17)

south [saʊθ] Süden; nach Süden; südlich III

south-east [ˌsaʊθ ˈiːst] Südosten; nach Südosten; südöstlich III

south-west [ˌsaʊθ ˈwest] Südwesten; nach Südwesten; südwestlich III

southbound ['saʊθbaʊnd] Richtung Süden III

southern ['sʌðən] südlich, Süd- V

souvenir [ˌsuːvə'nɪə] Andenken, Souvenir II

space [speɪs]:
   1. Platz, Raum IV
   °**2.** Weltraum

spaceship ['speɪsʃɪp] Raumschiff VI 3 (69)

spaghetti [spə'geti] Spagetti I

Spanish ['spænɪʃ] spanisch II

speak [spiːk]**, spoke, spoken** sprechen I **speak out** den Mund aufmachen; sich (kritisch) äußern IV

speaker ['spiːkə] Sprecher/in I

special ['speʃl] besondere(r, s) II

species ['spiːʃiːz]**,** *pl* **species** Art, Spezies VI 1 (22)

°**speculate** ['spekjuleɪt] spekulieren, Vermutungen anstellen

speech [spiːtʃ] *(offizielle)* Rede II **part of speech** Wortart III

speed [spiːd]:
   1. Geschwindigkeit III
   speed limit Geschwindigkeitsbegrenzung, -beschränkung III
   2. speed up beschleunigen, schneller werden IV

spell [spel] buchstabieren I

spelling ['spelɪŋ] Rechtschreibung; Schreibweise III

spend time/money (on) [spend]**, spent, spent** Zeit verbringen (mit); Geld ausgeben (für) III

spent [spent] *siehe* **spend**

spice [spaɪs] Gewürz IV

spicy ['spaɪsi] würzig, pikant IV

spider ['spaɪdə] Spinne V

spinach ['spɪnɪtʃ] Spinat IV

splash sb. [splæʃ] jn. nass spritzen III

Dictionary

°**split** [splɪt], **split, split** aufteilen; (sich) trennen; spalten

split screen [splɪt 'skriːn] geteilter Bildschirm; Bildschirm(auf)teilung III °**2.** geteilter Bildschirm; Bildschirm(auf)teilung

spoke [spəʊk] *siehe* **speak**

spoken [spəʊkən] *siehe* **speak**

spoon [spuːn] Löffel II

sport [spɔːt] Sport; Sportart I **sports hall** Turnhalle, Sporthalle VI 1 (25) **do sport** Sport treiben I

sportsperson ['spɔːtspɜːsn] Sportler/in V

spot [spɒt]:
1. Fleck, Punkt I
2. **spot sb./sth.** jn./etwas entdecken, erblicken IV

spray [spreɪ] (be)sprühen, sprayen IV

spread [spred], **spread, spread** (sich) ausbreiten, verbreiten III

spring [sprɪŋ] Frühling II

square [skweə]:
1. Platz *(in der Stadt)* IV
2. **square kilometre (sq km)** Quadratkilometer (km²) II

squash sth. [skwɒʃ] etwas zerdrücken, zerquetschen IV

stable ['steɪbl] (Pferde-, Kuh)Stall III

stadium ['steɪdiəm] Stadion III

staff [staːf] Personal, Mitarbeiter/innen VI 2 (54)

stage [steɪdʒ] Bühne II

stairs *(pl)* [steəz] Treppe; Treppenstufen II

stall [stɔːl] (Markt-)Stand II

stamp [stæmp] Stempel II

stand [stænd]:
1. **(stood, stood)** stehen; sich (hin)stellen II **stand in line** *(AE)* Schlange stehen, sich anstellen IV
2. **take a stand (on sth./ against sth.)** Stellung beziehen (zu etwas); ein Zeichen setzen VI 2 (47)

standard ['stændəd] Standard; Standard- III

°**stanza** ['stænzə] Strophe

star [staː]:
1. (Film-, Pop-)Star I
2. Stern III

stare (at sb./sth.) [steə] (jn./etwas an)starren III

start [staːt] anfangen, beginnen I

starving ['staːvɪŋ]: **be starving** einen Riesenhunger haben III

state [steɪt]:
1. Staat III

2. Zustand IV
3. **state sth.** etwas äußern, etwas angeben V

statement ['steɪtmənt] Aussage; Erklärung; Aussagesatz V

station ['steɪʃn]:
1. Bahnhof II
2. **petrol station** *(BE)* / **gas station** *(AE)* Tankstelle V

statistic [stə'tɪstɪk]:
1. statistische Tatsache, statistische Größe VI 2 (52) **a key statistic** eine statistische Schlüsselkennzahl V
2. **statistics** *(pl)* Statistik V

statue ['stætʃuː] Statue IV

status ['steɪtəs] Status V

stay [steɪ]:
1. bleiben II **stay in touch (with sb.)** (mit jm.) Kontakt halten; (mit jm.) in Verbindung bleiben II **stay up late** lang aufbleiben II
2. **stay (at/with)** (vorübergehend) wohnen, übernachten (in/bei) III
3. Aufenthalt V

steal [stiːl], **stole, stolen** stehlen IV

steep [stiːp] steil III

steering wheel ['stɪərɪŋ wiːl] Lenkrad IV

stem from sth. [stem] von etwas herrühren; etwas entspringen VI 3 (59)

step [step]:
1. Schritt I
2. Stufe III

stereotype ['steriətaɪp] Klischee(vorstellung), Stereotyp VI 2 (46)

stew [stjuː] Eintopf IV

stick [stɪk]:
1. Stock III
2. **(stuck, stuck)** bleiben; kleben IV
3. **stick sth. into sth.** etwas in etwas stechen, stecken II

sticker ['stɪkə] Aufkleber V

still [stɪl]:
1. (immer) noch I
°**2.** Standbild *(Film)*

sting [stɪŋ], **stung, stung** stechen; brennen VI 3 (62)

stingy ['stɪndʒi] knauserig, geizig VI 2 (35)

°**stock** [stɒk] Aktie **stock market** Aktienmarkt, Börse

stole [stəʊl] *siehe* **steal**

stolen [stəʊlən] *siehe* **steal**

stomach ['stʌmək] Magen II

stone [stəʊn] Stein III

stood [stʊd] *siehe* **stand**

stop [stɒp]:
1. anhalten, stoppen I **full stop** Punkt II
2. Halt; Station, Haltestelle II **bus stop** Bushaltestelle III

store [stɔː] *(AE)* Laden, Geschäft IV

storm [stɔːm] Sturm, Unwetter, Gewitter II

story ['stɔːri] Geschichte, Erzählung I

straight [streɪt]:
1. direkt, geradewegs III
2. hetero VI 1 (16)
3. **straight on** geradeaus weiter II

straighten sth. ['streɪtn] etwas gerade rücken, biegen; etwas strecken, straffen VI 3 (69)

straightforward [ˌstreɪt'fɔːwəd] einfach, klar *(ausgedrückt)* VI 3 (71)

strange [streɪndʒ] seltsam, komisch I

stranger ['streɪndʒə] Fremde(r), Unbekannte(r) IV

°**strategy** ['strætədʒi] Strategie

strawberry ['strɔːbəri] Erdbeere II

stream [striːm] Bach III

street [striːt] Straße I **street artist** Straßenkünstler/in II **at 14 Dean Street** in der Dean Street 14 I **in Dean Street** in der Dean Street I

streetcar ['striːtkaː] *(AE)* Straßenbahn IV

strength [streŋθ] Stärke, Kraft V

stress [stres]:
1. betonen III
2. Betonung III **stress mark** Betonungszeichen III
3. Stress IV

stretch [stretʃ] sich dehnen, sich strecken IV **stretch sth. out** etwas ausstrecken III

strict [strɪkt] streng IV

strike [straɪk] Streik VI 3 (60)

string [strɪŋ] Saite IV

strong [strɒŋ] stark, kräftig II

strongly ['strɒŋli] nachdrücklich, entschieden, eindringlich VI 2 (42)

structure ['strʌktʃə]:
1. Struktur, Gliederung III
2. strukturieren, gliedern III

struggle ['strʌgl] Ringen, Kampf V

stuck [stʌk] *siehe* **stick**

student ['stjuːdənt] Schüler/in; Student/in I

studio ['stjuːdiəʊ] Studio I

study ['stʌdi]:
1. studieren; untersuchen, beobach-

ten; lernen III

2. social studies Sozialkunde IV

stuff [stʌf] Zeug, Kram III

stung [stʌŋ] *siehe* **sting**

stunning ['stʌnɪŋ] atemberaubend, überwältigend, umwerfend V

stupid ['stjuːpɪd] dumm, blöd III

style [staɪl] Stil IV

stylistic [staɪ'lɪstɪk] stilistisch, Stil- VI 3 (71)

sub- [sʌb]: **sub-clause** Nebensatz I **sub-heading** Zwischenüberschrift; Kapitelüberschrift IV

subject ['sʌbdʒɪkt], ['sʌbdʒekt] Subjekt II **(school) subject** Schulfach I

submarine [ˌsʌbmə'riːn] U-Boot III

subtitle ['sʌbtaɪtl] Untertitel I

suburb ['sʌbɜːb] Vorort V

suburban [sə'bɜːbən] Vorort-, Vorstadt-; vorstädtisch V

subway ['sʌbweɪ] *(AE)* U-Bahn IV

succeed [sək'siːd] Erfolg haben VI 2 (37) **succeed in doing sth.** es schaffen, etwas zu tun VI 2 (37)

success [sək'ses] Erfolg III

successful [sək'sesfl] erfolgreich V

such [sʌtʃ]: **such a ...** so ein/e ...; solch ein/e ... III **such as** wie etwa V

suddenly ['sʌdnli] plötzlich, auf einmal I

suffer (from) ['sʌfə] leiden (an, unter) V

suffix ['sʌfɪks] Suffix, Nachsilbe IV

sugar ['ʃʊgə] Zucker IV

suggest sth. [sə'dʒest] auf etwas hindeuten, etwas nahelegen VI 1 (10/11) **suggest sth. (to sb.)** (jm.) etwas vorschlagen III

suggestion [sə'dʒestʃən] Vorschlag IV

suit [suːt] Anzug III

suitable ['suːtəbl] geeignet, passend VI 2 (43)

suitcase ['suːtkeɪs] Koffer V

sum sth. up [ˌsʌm_'ʌp] etwas zusammenfassen III

summarize ['sʌməraɪz] zusammenfassen VI 2 (43)

summary ['sʌməri] Zusammenfassung III

summer ['sʌmə] Sommer II

summit ['sʌmɪt] Gipfel III

sun [sʌn] Sonne I

sunburn ['sʌnbɜːn] Sonnenbrand V

Sunday ['sʌndeɪ], ['sʌndi] Sonntag I

sunflower ['sʌnflaʊə] Sonnenblume VI 3 (62)

sung [sʌŋ] *siehe* **sing**

sunglasses *(pl)* ['sʌnglɑːsɪz] (eine) Sonnenbrille II

sunk [sʌŋk] *siehe* **sink**

sunny ['sʌni] sonnig II

sunscreen ['sʌnskriːn] Sonnenschutzmittel V

sunset ['sʌnset] Sonnenuntergang III

supermarket ['suːpəmɑːkɪt] Supermarkt IV **a 24-hour supermarket** ein Supermarkt, der 24 Stunden geöffnet ist IV

supply [sə'plaɪ] Vorrat; Versorgung, Lieferung IV

support [sə'pɔːt]: **1.** unterstützen III **support a team** Ein Team/eine Mannschaft unterstützen, Fan eines Teams/einer Mannschaft sein III **2.** Unterstützung VI 1 (19)

°**supportive** [sə'pɔːtɪv] (unter)stützend, verständnisvoll

suppose [sə'pəʊz] annehmen, vermuten III **be supposed to do sth.** etwas tun sollen V

sure [ʃʊə], [ʃɔː] sicher II **for sure** klar; ganz bestimmt IV **make sure that ...** sich vergewissern, dass ...; darauf achten, dass ...; dafür sorgen, dass ... II

surface ['sɜːfɪs] Oberfläche III

surfing ['sɜːfɪŋ]: **go surfing** wellenreiten gehen, surfen gehen V

surprise [sə'praɪz] Überraschung IV

surprised [sə'praɪzd] überrascht I

surprising [sə'praɪzɪŋ] überraschend IV

surrounded by [sə'raʊndɪd] umgeben von V

surroundings *(pl)* [sə'raʊndɪŋz] Umgebung VI 3 (71)

survey ['sɜːveɪ] Umfrage, Studie VI 3 (73)

survival [sə'vaɪvl] Überleben VI 3 (62)

survive [sə'vaɪv] überleben III

sustainability [səˌsteɪnə'bɪləti] Nachhaltigkeit, Zukunftsfähigkeit V

sustainable [sə'steɪnəbl] nachhaltig, umweltverträglich; zukunftsfähig V

swallow ['swɒləʊ] schlucken; verschlucken V

swam [swæm] *siehe* **swim**

swamp [swɒmp] Sumpf IV

sweater ['swetə] *(bes. AE)* Pullover IV

sweet [swiːt]: **1.** süß II **sweet potato** Süßkartoffel IV **2.** Süßigkeit II

swim [swɪm]**, swam, swum** schwimmen I

swimmer ['swɪmə] Schwimmer/in I

swimming pool ['swɪmɪŋ puːl] Schwimmbad, Schwimmbecken I

swing [swɪŋ]**, swung, swung** schwingen V

swipe [swaɪp] *(am Touchscreen)* wischen, *(mit dem Finger)* streichen/fahren; *(Kreditkarte u.Ä.)* durchziehen VI 3 (61)

switch [swɪtʃ] wechseln IV

sword [sɔːd] Schwert I

swum [swʌm] *siehe* **swim**

swung [swʌŋ] *siehe* **swing**

syllable ['sɪləbl] Silbe II

symbol ['sɪmbl] Symbol II

sympathy ['sɪmpəθi] Sympathie VI 2 (37)

synonym ['sɪnənɪm] Synonym *(bedeutungsgleiches Wort)* IV

system ['sɪstəm] System IV

T

T-shirt ['tiːʃɜːt] T-Shirt I

tab [tæb] Tab, Reiter *(Karteikarte, Browser)* VI 3 (61)

table ['teɪbl]: **1.** Tisch I **2.** Tabelle I

tablet ['tæblət] Tablet III

take [teɪk]: **1.** Take *(Einstellung beim Film)* IV **2. take (on sth.)** Einstellung, Meinung (zu etwas) V **3. (took, taken)** nehmen, mitnehmen; (weg-, hin)bringen I **take (time)** (Zeit) brauchen; dauern II **take a different view** einen anderen Standpunkt vertreten; anderer Ansicht sein V **take a free kick** einen Freistoß ausführen III **take a walk** *(bes. AE)* spazieren gehen, einen Spaziergang machen IV **take care of sth.** sich (gut) um etwas kümmern; sorgfältig mit etwas umgehen IV **take control** Kontrolle übernehmen IV **take notes** (sich) Notizen machen *(beim Lesen oder Zuhören)* II **take part in sth.** an etwas teilnehmen II **take photos** fotografieren, Fotos machen II **take place** stattfinden III **take sides** Partei ergreifen VI 3 (74) **take sth. off** etwas ausziehen *(Kleidung)*; etwas absetzen *(Hut, Helm)* II **take time off** sich frei nehmen VI 1 (20) **it takes practice** es erfordert Übung IV

▶ S. 221 (to) take – (to) last

takeaway ['teɪkəweɪ]:
1. *Restaurant/Imbissgeschäft, das auch Essen zum Mitnehmen verkauft* II
2. Essen zum Mitnehmen II

taken [taken] *siehe* **take**

takeout ['teɪkaʊt] *(AE)* Essen zum Mitnehmen IV

talent ['tælənt] Talent, Begabung VI 1 (18)

talented ['tæləntɪd] begabt, talentiert II

talk [tɔːk]:
1. Vortrag, Referat, Rede I
give a talk (about) einen Vortrag/eine Rede halten (über) I
2. **talk (to)** reden (mit), sich unterhalten (mit) I

talkative ['tɔːkətɪv] gesprächig V

tall [tɔːl] groß *(Person)*; hoch *(Gebäude, Baum)* II

tank [tæŋk]: **think tank** Expertenkommission, Denkfabrik VI 3 (59)

tap [tæp] tippen, (vorsichtig) klopfen II

target ['tɑːgɪt] Ziel, Zielscheibe IV

task [tɑːsk] Aufgabe I

taste [teɪst]:
1. schmecken I
2. Geschmack IV

tasty ['teɪsti] lecker II

taught [tɔːt] *siehe* **teach**

tax [tæks] (die) Steuer IV

taxpayer ['tækspeɪə] Steuerzahler/in IV

tea [tiː]:
1. Tee I
2. *leichte Nachmittags- oder Abendmahlzeit* II

teach [tiːtʃ], **taught, taught** unterrichten, lehren III **teach sb. a lesson** jm. eine Lektion erteilen VI 2 (34)

teacher ['tiːtʃə] Lehrer/in I **head teacher** Schulleiter/in III

team [tiːm] Team, Mannschaft III

tear [tɪə] Träne II

tear [teə]:
1. Riss V

2. **tear sth. down, tore, torn** etwas abreißen IV

teaspoon ['tiːspuːn] Teelöffel II

°**tech** [tek] Technologie

tech nerd [tek nɜːd] Technikfreak V

technique [tek'niːk] Technik, Methode IV

technological [ˌteknə'lɒdʒɪkl] technologisch VI 3 (56/57)

technology [tek'nɒlədʒi] Technik, Technologie VI 1 (22)

teen [tiːn] Teenager/in III

teenage ['tiːneɪdʒ]: **a teenage girl** ein Mädchen im Teenageralter VI 2 (42)

teenager ['tiːneɪdʒə] Teenager VI 1 (25)

teens [tiːnz]: **in their teens** im Teenageralter VI 1 (10/11)

teeth [tiːθ] *siehe* **tooth**

telephone ['telɪfəʊn] Telefon I

television ['telɪvɪʒn] Fernsehen V

tell [tel], **told, told** sagen, erzählen I **tell sb. (not) to do sth.** jn. auffordern, etwas (nicht) zu tun; jm. sagen, dass er/sie etwas (nicht) tun soll III **tell sb. about sth.** jm. von etwas erzählen; jm. über etwas berichten I **tell sb. the way (to …)** jm. den Weg (nach …) beschreiben II **Can you tell me how to get to the station?** Können Sie mir sagen, wie ich zum Bahnhof komme/kommen kann? III

temper ['tempə]: **lose one's temper** die Beherrschung verlieren VI 3 (71)

temperature ['temprətʃə] Temperatur, Fieber II **have a temperature** Fieber haben II

ten [ten] zehn I

tend to be/do sth. [tend] dazu neigen etwas zu tun/sein, meistens etwas tun/sein V

tennis ['tenɪs] Tennis I

tension ['tenʃn] Spannung, Anspannung III

tent [tent] Zelt II

term [tɜːm]:
1. Trimester II
2. Ausdruck, Begriff III

terminal ['tɜːmɪnl] Terminal, Abfertigungsgebäude V

terrible ['terəbl] schrecklich, furchtbar II

terrified ['terɪfaɪd] entsetzt V

territory ['terətri] Territorium, Revier II

terrorist ['terərɪst] terroristische(r, s); Terrorist/in IV

test [test]:
1. Test III
2. testen, prüfen III

testimonial [ˌtestɪ'məʊniəl] Erfahrungsbericht; Zeugnis V

text [tekst]:
1. Text I
2. **text message** *(kurz auch:* **text**) SMS II
3. **text a friend** einem Freund / einer Freundin eine SMS schicken I

than [ðæn], [ðən]: **bigger than** größer als II

thank sb. [θæŋk] jm. danken VI 3 (72)

Thank you. ['θæŋk juː] Danke. I **Thank you for listening.** Danke, dass ihr zugehört habt. / Danke für eure Aufmerksamkeit. II

Thanks. ['θæŋks] Danke. I **thanks to Maya** dank Maya II

Thanksgiving [θæŋks'gɪvɪŋ] Erntedankfest *(amerikanischer Feiertag am vierten Donnerstag im November)* IV

that [ðæt]:
1. der/die/das; die *(Relativpronomen)* II
2. dass I
it shows that … es zeigt, dass … I
3. **that group** die Gruppe (dort), jene Gruppe II
that way dort entlang; in die Richtung II
4. **that's why** deshalb, darum II

the [ðə] der, die, das; die I

theatre ['θɪətə] *(AE:* **theater)** Theater II

their [ðeə] ihr I **their first day** ihr erster Tag I

theirs [ðeəz] ihrer, ihre, ihrs II

them [ðem], [ðəm] sie; ihnen I

theme [θiːm] Thema II

themselves [ðəm'selvz] sich III

then [ðen] dann I

°**theory** ['θɪəri] Theorie **in theory** theoretisch

therapy ['θerəpi] Therapie VI 1 (23)

there [ðeə] da, dort; dahin, dorthin I **There are …** Es sind … / Es gibt … I **There's …** Es ist … / Es gibt … I **down there** dort unten II **over there** da drüben, dort drüben II

therefore ['ðeəfɔː] daher, deshalb VI 2 (34)

thermometer [θə'mɒmɪtə] Thermometer II

these [ðiːz] diese, die (hier) I

they [ðeɪ] sie (pl) ı **they're (= they are)** sie sind … ı

thick [θɪk] dick ıv

thief [θiːf], pl **thieves** Dieb/in ı

thieves [θiːvz] siehe **thief**

thing [θɪŋ] Sache, Ding ı

think [θɪŋk], **thought, thought** denken, glauben ı **think of sth.** sich etwas ausdenken; an etwas denken ıı **think sth. of sth./sb.** etwas von etwas/jm. halten ııı **think tank** Expertenkommission, Denkfabrik vı 3 (59)

third [θɜːd] dritte(r, s) ı **one third** ein Drittel v

thirdly, … [ˈθɜːdli] drittens … v

thirsty [ˈθɜːsti] **be thirsty** durstig sein, Durst haben ı

this [ðɪs]:
1. This is … Dies ist … / Das ist … ı
this year's musical das diesjährige Musical ıı
2. this afternoon/evening/… heute Nachmittag/Abend/… ıı
this place/break/subject dieser Ort / diese Pause / dieses Fach ı
3. like this so ıı

thorough [ˈθʌrə] gründlich, sorgfältig vı 3 (74)

those … [ðəʊz] die … dort; jene … ı

though [ðəʊ] obwohl v **…** **though** (adv) allerdings; trotzdem v **even though** auch wenn; obwohl ıv

thought [θɔːt]:
1. siehe **think**
2. Gedanke ııı

thoughtful [ˈθɔːtfl] nachdenklich v

thousand [ˈθaʊznd] tausend, Tausend ıv

threat [θret] (Be-)Drohung vı 3 (58)

threaten [ˈθretn] (be)drohen v

three [θriː] drei ı

threw [θruː] siehe **throw**

thrilled [θrɪld] begeistert v

thriller [ˈθrɪlə] Thriller (spannendes Buch) vı 2 (45)

throat [θrəʊt] Hals, Kehle ıı **have a sore throat** Halsschmerzen haben ıı

through [θruː] durch ı

throughout … [θruːˈaʊt] überall in …, in ganz … v

throw [θrəʊ], **threw, thrown** werfen ı

thrown [θrəʊn] siehe **throw**

thunder [ˈθʌndə] Donner ıı

Thursday [ˈθɜːzdeɪ], [ˈθɜːzdi] Donnerstag ı

ticket [ˈtɪkɪt]:
1. Eintrittskarte ı
2. Fahrkarte ııı
3. ticket office Fahrkartenschalter; Kasse (für den Verkauf von Eintrittskarten) ııı

°**tidal** [ˈɡrævəti] Gezeiten-

tide [taɪd] Gezeiten, Ebbe und Flut ııı

tidy [ˈtaɪdi] ordentlich, sauber vı 1 (17)

tie [taɪ] Krawatte, Schlips vı 1 (10/11)

tiger [ˈtaɪɡə] Tiger vı 1 (14)

tight [taɪt] fest, eng; knapp, eng anliegend (Kleidung) vı 3 (59)

tighten [ˈtaɪtn] spannen, festziehen, nachziehen ıv

till [tɪl]: **till 12 o'clock** bis 12 Uhr ı **not till three** erst um drei, nicht vor drei ıı

time [taɪm]:
1. Zeit; Uhrzeit ı
at any time jederzeit, zu jeder Zeit ıv **at no time** nie ıv **at one time** zur selben Zeit, gleichzeitig ııı **part-time** Teilzeit-, Halbtags- v **take time off** sich frei nehmen vı 1 (20) **What time is it?** Wie spät ist es? ı
2. Mal ıı
one more time noch einmal, noch ein Mal ıı

timeline [ˈtaɪmlaɪn] Zeitstrahl, Zeitleiste ıv

timer [ˈtaɪmə] Zeitmesser ıv

timetable [ˈtaɪmteɪbl]:
1. Stundenplan ı
2. Fahrplan ııı

tin [tɪn] Dose ıı

tinned [tɪnd] Dosen-; in Dosen ıv

tiny [ˈtaɪni] winzig v

tip [tɪp] Tipp ı

tired [ˈtaɪəd] müde ı

title [ˈtaɪtl]:
1. Titel, Überschrift ı
2. betiteln, benennen vı 2 (46)

to [tu], [tə]:
1. in; an; zu, nach ı
2. um zu ıı
3. from … to … von … bis … ı
4. quarter to eleven Viertel vor elf (10.45 / 22.45) ı

toast [təʊst] Toast(brot) ııı

today [təˈdeɪ] heute ı

toe [təʊ] Zeh ıı

together [təˈɡeðə] zusammen ı

toilet [ˈtɔɪlət] Toilette ı

told [təʊld] siehe **tell**

tolerance [ˈtɒlərəns] Toleranz v

tolerant (of) [ˈtɒlərənt] tolerant (gegenüber) v

tomato [təˈmɑːtəʊ], pl **tomatoes** Tomate ıı

tomorrow [təˈmɒrəʊ] morgen ıı **tomorrow morning** morgen früh ıı

ton [tʌn] Tonne (Gewicht) v **tons of ice cream** jede Menge Eis v

tone [təʊn] Ton v

tongue [tʌŋ] Zunge ıı **tongue-twister** Zungenbrecher ıı

tonight [təˈnaɪt] heute Nacht, heute Abend ııı

too [tuː]:
1. auch ı
2. too late/cold/big/… zu spät/ kalt/groß/… ı

took [tʊk] siehe **take**

tool [tuːl] Werkzeug; (Hilfs-)Mittel v

tooth [tuːθ], pl **teeth** Zahn ıı

toothache [ˈtuːθeɪk]: **have a toothache** Zahnschmerzen haben ıı

top [tɒp]:
1. Top, Oberteil ı
2. Spitze; oberes Ende ıı
at the top (of) oben, am oberen Ende, an der Spitze (von) ıı
3. Spitzen-, oberste(r, s) ıı

topic [ˈtɒpɪk] Thema, Themengebiet ıı **topic sentence** Satz, der in das Thema eines Absatzes einführt ııı

topping [ˈtɒpɪŋ] Überzug, Belag; Soße vı 1 (23) **with a cheese topping** mit Käse überbacken vı 1 (23)

torch [tɔːtʃ]:
1. Taschenlampe ıı
2. Fackel ıı

tore [tɔː] siehe **tear**

torn [tɔːn] siehe **tear**

tortoise [ˈtɔːtəs] (Land-)Schildkröte ııı

total [ˈtəʊtəl] Gesamt- ıv **a total of …** eine Gesamtsumme von …; insgesamt ııı

totally [ˈtəʊtəli] völlig, total ıv

touch [tʌtʃ]:
1. berühren, anfassen ı
2. get in touch (with sb.) (mit jm.) Kontakt aufnehmen; sich (mit jm.) in Verbindung setzen ıı
stay in touch (with sb.) (mit jm.) Kontakt halten; (mit jm.) in Verbindung bleiben ıı

tough [tʌf] (knall)hart, schwierig ıv

tour [tʊə]: **a tour of my house** ein Rundgang durch mein Haus I **guided tour** Führung V

tourism ['tʊərɪzəm], ['tɔːrɪzəm] Tourismus V

tourist ['tʊərɪst] Tourist/in I

tournament ['tʊənəmənt], ['tɔːnəmənt] Turnier, Wettkampf V

towards the station/Mr Bell [təˈwɔːdz] auf den Bahnhof / Mr Bell zu, in Richtung Bahnhof / Mr Bell III

tower ['taʊə] Turm I

town [taʊn] Stadt I **town hall** Rathaus II

toxic ['tɒksɪk] toxisch, schädlich VI 3 (58)

toy [tɔɪ] Spielzeug I

track [træk] (Bahn-)Gleis IV

°**track sth.** [træk] etwas verfolgen

tractor ['træktə] Traktor II

trade [treɪd]:
1. Handel V
2. handeln V
3. (ein)tauschen; Handel treiben VI 2 (34)

trader ['treɪdə] Händler/in V

tradition [trəˈdɪʃn] Tradition III

traditional [trəˈdɪʃənl] traditionell II

traffic ['træfɪk] Verkehr VI 3 (59)

trail [treɪl] Weg, Pfad III

train [treɪn]:
1. Zug II
2. trainieren II

trainer ['treɪnə] Turnschuh I

training ['treɪnɪŋ] Training(sstunde) I

tram [træm] Straßenbahn IV

transform [trænsˈfɔːm] verwandeln; umwandeln V

°**transition** [trænˈzɪʃn] Überleitung

translate [trænsˈleɪt] übersetzen II

translation [trænsˈleɪʃn] Übersetzung III

translator [trænsˈleɪtə] Übersetzer/in V

transport ['trænspɔːt] Transport(wesen); Verkehrsmittel V **public transport** (BE) öffentliche Verkehrsmittel V

transport [trænˈspɔːt] transportieren, befördern V

transportation [ˌtrænspɔːˈteɪʃn] (AE): **public transportion** öffentliche Verkehrsmittel V

transporter [trænˈspɔːtə] Transporter VI 3 (69)

trap [træp] Falle VI 3 (62)

trash can ['træʃ kæn] (AE) Mülltonne, Abfalleimer IV

travel ['trævl] reisen I

travel agent ['trævl ˌeɪdʒnt] Reisebürokaufmann/-frau I **travel agent's** Reisebüro V

traveller ['trævələ] Reisende(r) I

treat [triːt] behandeln V

treatment ['triːtmənt] Behandlung V

treaty ['triːti] Vertrag, Abkommen V

tree [triː] Baum I

°**tremendous** [trɪˈmendəs] gewaltig

trendy ['trendi] modisch, angesagt, „in" V

trials (pl) ['traɪəlz] Turnier, Wettkampf III

tribe [traɪb] (Volks-)Stamm V

trick [trɪk] Kunststück, Trick II

tricky ['trɪki] heikel, verzwickt, knifflig V

trip [trɪp] Ausflug; Reise I **road trip** Autoreise, (lange) Autofahrt V

troll [trɒl], [trəʊl] sachlich falsche Dinge im Internet behaupten V

trophy ['trəʊfi] Pokal; Trophäe I

tropical ['trɒpɪkl] tropisch, Tropen- IV

tropics ['trɒpɪks]: **the tropics** (pl) die Tropen V

trouble ['trʌbl]: **be in trouble** in Schwierigkeiten sein; Ärger kriegen I

trousers (pl) ['traʊzəz] Hose II **a pair of trousers** (eine) Hose II

truck [trʌk] Lastwagen, LKW III

true [truː] wahr I

trumpet ['trʌmpɪt] Trompete III

trust [trʌst] trauen, vertrauen V

truth [truːθ] Wahrheit II

try [traɪ] (aus)probieren; versuchen I

tube [tjuːb]: **the Tube** (no pl) die U-Bahn (in London) III

tuck [tʌk] stecken, klemmen IV

Tuesday ['tjuːzdeɪ], ['tjuːzdi] Dienstag I

tulip ['tjuːlɪp] Tulpe II

tune [tjuːn] stimmen (Instrument) IV

turkey ['tɜːki] Pute, Truthahn IV

turn [tɜːn]:
1. sich (um)drehen III
turn around sich umdrehen I **turn left/right** (nach) links/rechts abbiegen II **turn sth. off** etwas ausschalten II **turn sth. on** etwas einschalten I **turn sth. up/down** etwas lauter/leiser stellen III **turn to sb.** sich jm. zuwenden; sich an jn. wenden II

2. **(It's) my turn.** Ich bin dran / an der Reihe. I

turtle ['tɜːtl] Wasserschildkröte VI 2 (35)

tutor sb. ['tjuːtə] jn. unterrichten, jm. Stunden geben IV

TV [ˌtiːˈviː] Fernsehen, Fernsehgerät I

twelve [twelv] zwölf I

twenty ['twenti] zwanzig I

twice [twaɪs] zweimal II

twins (pl) [twɪnz] Zwillinge I

two [tuː] zwei I

type [taɪp] tippen, Maschine schreiben VI 1 (17)

type (of) [taɪp] Art, Sorte, Typ IV

typical (of) ['tɪpɪkl] typisch (für) III

°**typo** ['taɪpəʊ] Tippfehler

U

UK [ˌjuːˈkeɪ]: **the UK (the United Kingdom)** das Vereinigte Königreich (Großbritannien und Nordirland) I

umbrella [ʌmˈbrelə] Schirm, Regenschirm I

UN [juːˈen]: **United Nations (UN)** die Vereinten Nationen VI 2 (52)

uncle ['ʌŋkl] Onkel I

unclean [ˌʌnˈkliːn] schmutzig, unrein VI 2 (42)

uncomfortable [ʌnˈkʌmftəbl] unbehaglich; unbequem VI 2 (35)

uncrowded [ʌnˈkraʊdɪd] nicht überfüllt VI 2 (54)

under ['ʌndə] unter I

underground ['ʌndəgraʊnd]: **the underground** (no pl) die U-Bahn III

underline [ˌʌndəˈlaɪn] unterstreichen II

understand [ˌʌndəˈstænd], **-stood, -stood** verstehen I

understanding [ˌʌndəˈstændɪŋ]: **come to an understanding** sich einigen; zu einer Übereinkunft kommen VI 2 (35)

understood [ˌʌndəˈstʊd] siehe **understand**

unemployed [ˌʌnɪmˈplɔɪd] arbeitslos V

unemployment [ˌʌnɪmˈplɔɪmənt] Arbeitslosigkeit V

unequal [ʌnˈiːkwəl] ungleich VI 1 (20)

unethical [ʌnˈeθɪkl] unethisch VI 1 (23)

unexpected [ˌʌnɪkˈspektɪd] unerwartet VI 1 (21)

unfortunately [ʌnˈfɔːtʃənətli] leider, unglücklicherweise IV

unfriendly [ʌnˈfrendli] unfreundlich V

unhappy [ʌnˈhæpi] unglücklich II

unhealthy [ʌnˈhelθi] ungesund V

uniform [ˈjuːnɪfɔːm] (Schul-)Uniform I

°**unique** [juˈniːk] einmalig, einzigartig

unit [ˈjuːnɪt] Kapitel, Lektion I

unite [juˈnaɪt] (sich) vereinen, vereinigen V

united [juˈnaɪtɪd] vereinigt III **the United Kingdom** das Vereinigte Königreich I

United Nations (UN) [juˌnaɪtɪd ˈneɪʃnz] die Vereinten Nationen VI 2 (52)

university [ˌjuːnɪˈvɜːsəti] Universität V

university [ˌjuːnɪˈvɜːsəti], *short:* **uni** Universität VI 3 (64)

unkind [ˌʌnˈkaɪnd] unfreundlich, wenig nett, herzlos V

unknown [ˌʌnˈnəʊn] unbekannt, nicht bekannt V

unlearn sth. [ˌʌnˈlɜːn] etwas verlernen; etwas ablegen *(Angewohnheit)* V

unless [ənˈles] es sei denn; außer (wenn) V

unlike [ˌʌnˈlaɪk] im Gegensatz zu V

unmute [ˌʌnˈmjuːt] die Stummschaltung aufheben, deaktivieren V

unofficially [ˌʌnəˈfɪʃəli] inoffiziell V

unpack [ˌʌnˈpæk] auspacken III

unpredicted [ˌʌnprɪˈdɪktɪd] unvorhergesehen VI 3 (59)

unqualified [ˌʌnˈkwɒlɪfaɪd] unqualifiziert VI 3 (59)

unreliable [ˌʌnrɪˈlaɪəbl] unzuverlässig V

°**unrest** [ʌnˈrest] Unruhen

unstoppable [ʌnˈstɒpəbl] unaufhaltsam, unaufhaltbar IV

unsure [ˌʌnˈʃʊə], [ˌʌnˈʃɔː] unsicher V

untidy [ʌnˈtaɪdi] unordentlich, unsauber VI 1 (17)

until [ənˈtɪl] bis II **not until three** erst um drei, nicht vor drei III

unusual [ʌnˈjuːʒuəl] ungewöhnlich III

unwrap [ʌnˈræp] auspacken, auswickeln VI 2 (36)

up [ʌp] hinauf, herauf; (nach) oben I **up and down** auf und ab; rauf und runter II **up here** hier oben; nach hier oben II **up to** bis (zu) II **the ups and downs** die Höhen und Tiefen VI 1 (22)

upbringing [ˈʌpbrɪŋɪŋ] Erziehung VI 1 (16)

uplifting [ʌpˈlɪftɪŋ] erhebend, aufmunternd VI 1 (14)

upload sth. [ˌʌpˈləʊd] etwas hochladen V

upset [ˌʌpˈset] aufgebracht, gekränkt, mitgenommen III

upstairs [ˌʌpˈsteəz] oben; nach oben I

urban [ˈɜːbən] städtisch, Stadt- V

urge sb. [ɜːdʒ] jn. drängen; jn. eindringlich bitten V

°**urgent** [ˈɜːdʒənt] dringend, eilig V

us [ʌs], [əs] uns I

USA [ˌjuː ˌes ˈeɪ]: **the USA (the United States of America)** die USA (die Vereinigten Staaten von Amerika) II

usage [ˈjuːsɪdʒ], [ˈjuːzɪdʒ] Gebrauch *(insbes. Sprachgebrauch)* V

use [juːz] benutzen, verwenden I

use [juːs] Gebrauch, Verwendung VI 3 (62)

used to [ˈjuːst tə]: **the library is more modern than it used to be** die Bibliothek ist moderner als früher / als sie früher war V

useful [ˈjuːsfl] nützlich V

user [ˈjuːzə] Nutzer/in, Benutzer/in V

username [ˈjuːzəneɪm] Benutzername VI 3 (61)

usual [ˈjuːʒuəl] gewöhnlich, üblich III

usually [ˈjuːʒuəli] meistens, normalerweise, gewöhnlich I

V

vacation [vəˈkeɪʃn] *(AE)* Urlaub IV

°**valid** [ˈvælɪd] gültig

valley [ˈvæli] Tal II

valuable [ˈvæljuəbl] wertvoll V

value [ˈvæljuː]:
1. Wert V
2. **value sth.** etwas schätzen, wertschätzen; auf etwas Wert legen V

van [væn] Transporter, Lieferwagen V

variety [vəˈraɪəti] Vielzahl, Auswahl V

vary [ˈveəri] variieren, schwanken V **varied** abwechslungsreich; verschiedenartig, vielfältig VI 3 (62)

vase [vɑːz], [veɪz] Vase V

vast [vɑːst] riesig IV

vegetables *(pl)* [ˈvedʒtəblz] Gemüse I

vegetarian [ˌvedʒəˈteəriən] Vegetarier/in; vegetarisch IV

vehicle [ˈviːəkl] Fahrzeug VI 3 (59)

°**venue** [ˈvenjuː] Veranstaltungsort

verse [vɜːs] Vers, Strophe II

version [ˈvɜːʃn], [ˈvɜːʒn] Version, Fassung V

°**versus** [ˈvɜːsəs] **(v.** or **vs.)** gegenüber; gegen *(bei Wettkämpfen)*

vertical [ˈvɜːtɪkl] vertikal, senkrecht VI 3 (68)

very [ˈveri]:
1. **very funny/wet/…** sehr witzig, komisch I
2. genau V
about this very subject über genau dieses Thema V

°**victim** [ˈvɪktɪm] Opfer

video [ˈvɪdiəʊ] Video I **video camera** Videokamera I

view [vjuː]:
1. **view (of)** Aussicht, Blick (auf) II **in my view** meiner Ansicht nach, meiner Meinung nach V **point of view** Standpunkt III **take a different view** einen anderen Standpunkt vertreten; anderer Ansicht sein V
2. **view oneself as sb./sth.** sich als jd./etwas betrachten VI 3 (73)

viewer [ˈvjuːə] Zuschauer/in VI 3 (66)

village [ˈvɪlɪdʒ] Dorf I

villager [ˈvɪlɪdʒə] Dorfbewohner/in VI 2 (34)

°**violence** [ˈvaɪələns] Gewalt, Gewalttätigkeit

violent [ˈvaɪələnt] gewalttätig; gewaltsam V

violin [vaɪəˈlɪn] Violine, Geige III

VIP (very important person) [ˌviː ˌaɪ ˈpiː] Prominente(r) IV

viral [ˈvaɪrəl]: **go viral** sich wie ein Virus ausbreiten / sich wie ein Lauffeuer verbreiten IV

virus [ˈvaɪrəs], [ˈvaɪrəsɪz], *pl* **viruses** Virus VI 1 (23)

visa [ˈviːzə] Visum V

°**visible** [ˈvɪzəbl] sichtbar

visit ['vɪzɪt]:
1. besuchen I
2. Besuch II
visitor ['vɪzɪtə] Besucher/in, Gast II
visual ['vɪʒuəl] optisch, visuell
VI 1 (17)
vital ['vaɪtl] unerlässlich; unverzichtbar; (lebens)wichtig V
vocabulary [və'kæbjələri] Vokabelverzeichnis, Wörterverzeichnis I
voice [vɔɪs] Stimme I **in a loud voice** mit lauter Stimme II
volcanic [vɒl'kænɪk] vulkanisch V
volcano [vɒl'keɪnəʊ] Vulkan III
volleyball ['vɒlibɔːl] Volleyball I
volunteer [vɒlən'tɪə]:
1. Freiwillige(r), Ehrenamtliche(r) III
2. ehrenamtliche Arbeit leisten; sich freiwillig melden, sich bereit erklären V
volunteer work ehrenamtliche Arbeit V
vote [vəʊt]:
1. vote for/against sb./sth. für/gegen jn./etwas stimmen VI 2 (50)
°**2.** Abstimmung V
°**3.** Stimme (bei Wahlen) V
°**voter fraud** [ˌvəʊtə 'frɔːd] Wahlbetrug V
voucher ['vaʊtʃə]: **gift voucher** Geschenkgutschein V
vowel ['vaʊəl] Vokal, Selbstlaut II
°**vs** ['vɜːsəs] siehe **versus**

W

wage [weɪdʒ] Lohn V **minimum wage** Mindestlohn V
waist [weɪst] Taille II
wait (for) [weɪt] warten (auf) I
Wait a minute. Warte einen Moment./ Moment mal. I **wait in line** (AE) Schlange stehen, sich anstellen IV **I can't wait to see ...** Ich kann es kaum erwarten, ... zu sehen II
waiter ['weɪtə] Kellner IV
waitress ['weɪtrəs] Kellnerin IV
wake up [ˌweɪk‿'ʌp]**, woke, woke:**
1. aufwachen I
2. wake sb. up jn. (auf)wecken II
walk [wɔːk]:
1. (zu Fuß) gehen I
walk around herumlaufen II
2. go for a walk spazieren gehen, einen Spaziergang machen I
take a walk (bes. AE) spazieren gehen, einen Spaziergang machen IV

wall [wɔːl] Mauer; Wand II
wallet ['wɒlɪt] Portemonnaie, Geldbörse III
wander ['wɒndə] herumlaufen; herumirren II
want [wɒnt]: **want sth.** etwas (haben) wollen I **want to do sth.** etwas tun wollen I
war ['wɔː]: **civil war** Bürgerkrieg V
warm [wɔːm] warm II
warn sb. [wɔːn] jn. warnen V
warn sb. not to do sth. jn. davor warnen, etwas zu tun V
warning ['wɔːnɪŋ] Warnung III
was [wɒz], [wəz] siehe **be**
wash [wɒʃ] waschen VI 2 (42)
waste [weɪst]:
1. Abfall, Müll V
2. Verschwendung V
3. waste sth. (on) etwas verschwenden, vergeuden (für) V
watch [wɒtʃ]:
1. sich etwas anschauen; beobachten I
Watch out! Pass auf!/Vorsicht! I
watch TV fernsehen I
2. Armbanduhr I
water ['wɔːtə] Wasser I
waterfall ['wɔːtəfɔːl] Wasserfall II
waterfront ['wɔːtəfrʌnt] Hafenviertel (oft modernisiert und zum Wohnviertel umgebaut) V
wave [weɪv]:
1. Welle II
2. wave (at sb.) (jm. zu)winken III
wave a flag eine Fahne schwenken III
way [weɪ]:
1. Weg II
by the way übrigens III **force your way into sth.** sich in etwas eindrängen IV **No way!** Auf keinen Fall!/Kommt nicht in Frage! III **on the way to ...** auf dem Weg zu/nach ... I **tell sb. the way (to ...)** jm. den Weg (nach ...) beschreiben II **that way** dort entlang; in die Richtung II
2. Art und Weise IV
way of life Lebensweise, Lebensart V
we [wiː] wir I
weak [wiːk] schwach V
weaken ['wiːkən] schwächen VI 3 (62)
weakness ['wiːknəs] Schwäche; Schwachstelle V
weapon ['wepən] Waffe V

wear [weə]**, wore, worn** tragen (Kleidung) I
weather ['weðə] Wetter II
web [web] (Spinnen-)Netz; das Web (Internet) VI 3 (61)
website ['websaɪt] Website I
wedding ['wedɪŋ] Hochzeit, Trauung III
Wednesday ['wenzdeɪ], ['wenzdi] Mittwoch I
wee [wiː] (bes. Scottish English, infml) klein III
week [wiːk] Woche I **a three-week holiday** ein dreiwöchiger Urlaub IV
weekend [ˌwiːk'end] Wochenende I **at the weekend** am Wochenende I **on the weekend** (AE) am Wochenende IV
weigh [weɪ] wiegen I
weird [wɪəd] seltsam, komisch III
weirdo ['wɪədəʊ] (infml) Spinner/in IV
welcome ['welkəm]: **welcome sb. (to)** jn. begrüßen (in), jn. willkommen heißen (in) III **Welcome to Plymouth.** Willkommen in Plymouth. I
well [wel]:
1. gut II
well-behaved brav IV **well-known** bekannt, wohlbekannt III
2. gesund, gut II
I don't feel well. Ich fühle mich nicht gut. II
3. Well, ... Nun, .../Also, .../Na ja, ... I
Welsh [welʃ] Walisisch; walisisch III
went [went] siehe **go**
were [wɜː], [wə] siehe **be**
west [west] Westen; nach Westen; westlich III
westbound ['westbaʊnd] Richtung Westen III
western ['westən] westlich, West- III
wet [wet]:
1. nass I
2. Nässe V
wetland, auch: **wetlands** (pl) ['wetlənd] Feuchtgebiet(e), Sumpfgebiet(e) V
wetsuit ['wetsuːt] Surfanzug, Taucheranzug V
whale [weɪl] Wal I
wharf [wɔːf] Kai, Anlegeplatz V
what? [wɒt] was? I **What about you?** Und du?/Und was ist mit dir? Und ihr?/Und was ist mit euch? I

What colour is/are …? Welche Farbe hat/haben …? | **what else?** was (sonst) noch? ||| **What is the poster about?** Wovon handelt dein Poster? / Worum geht es bei deinem Poster? | **What programmes …?** Welche Programme …? / Welche Art von Programmen …? | **What time is it?** Wie spät ist es? | **What's up?** Was gibt's? / Was ist los? ||| **What's she like?** Wie ist sie? / Wie ist sie so? | **What's your name?** Wie heißt du? / Wie heißt ihr? | **And guess what!** Und stell dir / stellt euch vor! Und weißt du / wisst ihr was? || **I don't know what to do.** Ich weiß nicht, was ich tun soll. ||| **So what?** Na und? |v

whatever [ˌwɒt'evə] was immer |v
wheat [wiːt] Weizen |v
wheel [wiːl] Rad |v **(kurz für steering wheel)** Lenkrad |v **big wheel** Riesenrad |
when [wen]:
  1. wenn |
  2. als ||
  3. when? wann? |
whenever [ˌwen'evə] wann (auch) immer; egal, wann |v
where? [weə] wo? / wohin? |
Where are you from? Woher kommst du? |
whereas [ˌweər'æz] während, wohingegen |v 1 (23)
wherever [weər'evə] wo immer |v
whether ['weðə] ob |v
which [wɪtʃ]:
  1. der/die/das; die (Relativpronomen) ||
  2. Which clubs/jokes/…? Welche Klubs/Witze/…? |
Which one? Welche(r, s)? ||
while [waɪl] während ||
whisper ['wɪspə] flüstern ||
whistle ['wɪsl]:
  1. pfeifen ||
  2. (Triller-)Pfeife |||
  3. Pfiff |||
white [waɪt] weiß |
who [huː]:
  1. wer |
Who danced with you? Wer hat mit dir getanzt? || **who else?** wer (sonst) noch? |||
  2. wem/wen ||
Who did you dance with? Mit wem hast du getanzt? ||
  3. der/die/das; die (Relativpronomen) ||

Find someone who … Finde jemanden, der … |
whoever [huː'evə] wer immer |v
whole [həʊl] ganze(r, s), gesamte(r, s) ||
whose [huːz]:
  1. whose? wessen? ||
  2. the men whose homes … die Männer, deren Wohnungen … |v
why? [waɪ]:
  1. warum? |
  2. that's why deshalb, darum ||
Wi-Fi ['waɪ faɪ] Wi-Fi, WLAN |v
wide [waɪd] weit; breit |||
°**widely** ['waɪdli] weit (verbreitet), in großem Umfang
widespread ['waɪdspred] weit verbreitet, groß(flächig) |v
wife [waɪf], pl **wives** Ehefrau |v 2 (42)
wild [waɪld] wild ||
wildfire ['waɪldfaɪə] Waldbrand, Buschbrand |v
wildlife ['waɪldlaɪf] Tierwelt, frei lebende Tiere |v
will [wɪl]: **we'll go (= we will go)** wir werden gehen ||
win [wɪn], **won, won** gewinnen |
wind [wɪnd] Wind || **high winds** (pl) starker Wind, starke Winde |v 1 (24)
window ['wɪndəʊ] Fenster |
windy ['wɪndi] windig ||
wing [wɪŋ] Flügel |||
wink (at sb.) [wɪŋk] (jm. zu)zwinkern |v 1 (12)
winner ['wɪnə] Gewinner/in, Sieger/in |
winter ['wɪntə] Winter ||
wisdom ['wɪzdəm] Weisheit |v
wise [waɪz] weise |v
wish [wɪʃ] wünschen || **I wish it was warmer.** Ich wünschte, es wäre wärmer. ||
with [wɪð]:
  1. mit |
  2. bei |
within [wɪ'ðɪn] innerhalb (von) |v
without [wɪ'ðaʊt] ohne |
wives [waɪvz] siehe **wife**
woke [wəʊk] siehe **wake up**
woken ['wəʊkən] siehe **wake up**
wolf [wʊlf], pl **wolves** Wolf |v
woman ['wʊmən], pl **women** Frau |
women ['wɪmɪn] siehe **woman**
won [wʌn] siehe **win**
won't [wəʊnt]: **she won't come (=she will not come)** sie wird nicht kommen ||

wonder ['wʌndə]:
  1. sich fragen, gern wissen wollen |||
  2. Wunder |||
No wonder … Kein Wunder … |v
wonderful ['wʌndəfəl] wunderbar |v
wood [wʊd] Holz ||
wooden ['wʊdn] hölzern; Holz- |||
word [wɜːd] Wort | **word order** Wortstellung | **May I have a word with you?** Kann ich Sie/dich kurz sprechen? ||
°**wordy** ['wɜːdi] langatmig, wortreich
wore [wɔː] siehe **wear**
work [wɜːk]:
  1. arbeiten |
  2. Arbeit |
work experience (no pl) Arbeitserfahrung(en), Praxiserfahrung(en); Praktikum |v
work of art Kunstwerk |v
workbook ['wɜːkbʊk] Arbeitsheft |
worker ['wɜːkə] Arbeiter/in ||
°**workload** ['wɜːkləʊd] Arbeitsbelastung, Pensum
workplace ['wɜːkpleɪs] Arbeitsplatz |v
worksheet ['wɜːkʃiːt] Arbeitsblatt ||
workshop ['wɜːkʃɒp]:
  1. Workshop, Lehrgang ||
  2. Werkstatt |||
worktop ['wɜːktɒp] Theke; Ladentisch |v
world [wɜːld] Welt || **in the world** auf der Welt ||
worldwide ['wɜːldwaɪd] weltweit |v 2 (46)
worm [wɜːm] Wurm |
worn [wɔːn] siehe **wear**
worried ['wʌrid] besorgt, beunruhigt |
worry ['wʌri]:
  1. Sorge |v
No worries, mate. Kein Problem! / Alles OK! / Alles gut! |v
  2. worry (about) sich Sorgen machen (wegen, um) ||
worrying ['wʌriɪŋ] beunruhigend |v 3 (62)
worse [wɜːs] schlechter, schlimmer ||
worst [wɜːst] der/die/das schlechteste/schlimmste …; am schlechtesten/schlimmsten ||
worth [wɜːθ] wert |||
would [wʊd]: **Grandma would take us to the zoo.** Oma ging (früher) mit uns in den Zoo. |v **I would have screamed too.** Ich hätte auch

Dictionary

geschrien. IV **I'd like … (= I would like …)** Ich hätte gern … / Ich möchte … I **I'd love to … (= I would love to)** Ich würde sehr gern … II **What would you like to eat?** Was möchtest du essen? I **What would you like?** Was hättest du gern? / Was möchtest du? I

°**wrist** [rɪst] Handgelenk

write [raɪt]**, wrote, written** schreiben I **write sth. down** etwas aufschreiben II

writer ['raɪtə] Schreiber/in; Schriftsteller/in VI 1 (15)

wrong [rɒŋ]:
1. falsch, verkehrt I
What's wrong with you/Sam? Was fehlt dir/Sam? Was ist los mit dir/Sam? II
2. **someone is wrong** jemand irrt sich; jemand hat Unrecht I

wrote [rəʊt] *siehe* **write**

Y

yard [jɑːd] *(AE)* Garten IV
year [jɪə]:
1. Jahr I **I'm 12 years old.** Ich bin zwölf Jahre alt. I **this year's musical** das diesjährige Musical II
2. Jahrgang(sstufe) I
yell [jel] schreien V
yellow ['jeləʊ] gelb I
yes [jes] ja I
yesterday ['jestədeɪ], ['jestədi] gestern I
yet [jet] trotzdem, dennoch VI 1 (13) **Have you … yet?** Hast du schon …? II **not … yet** noch nicht I
▶ S. 205 yet
yoga ['jəʊgə] Yoga I
yoghurt ['jɒgət] Joghurt I
you [juː]:
1. du/dich/dir, ihr/euch, Sie/Ihnen I
2. man III

young [jʌŋ] jung I
your [jɔː], [jə] dein/e; euer/eure; Ihr/Ihre I
yours [jɔːz] deiner, deine, deins; eurer, eure, eures II **Yours sincerely** Mit freundlichen Grüßen *(Briefschluss)* V
yourself [jɔː'self], [jə'self] selbst IV **about yourself** über dich selbst I
yourselves [jɔː'selvz], [jə'selvz] euch; sich *(bei „Sie")* III
yummy ['jʌmi] *(infml)* lecker I

Z

zero ['zɪərəʊ] Null I
zone [zəʊn] Zone II **pedestrian zone** Fußgängerzone II
zoo [zuː] Zoo I
zoom in/out [zuːm] rein-/herauszoomen III

English sounds

[iː]	gr**ee**n, h**e**, s**ea**
[i]	happ**y**, monk**ey**
[ɪ]	b**i**g, **i**n, **e**xpensive
[e]	r**e**d, y**e**s, ag**ai**n, br**ea**kfast
[æ]	c**a**t, **a**nimal, **a**pple, bl**a**ck
[ɑː]	cl**a**ss, **a**sk, c**a**r, p**a**rk
[ɒ]	s**o**ng, **o**n, d**o**g, wh**a**t
[ɔː]	d**oo**r, **or**, b**a**ll, f**our**, m**or**ning
[uː]	bl**ue**, r**u**ler, t**oo**, tw**o**, y**ou**
[ʊ]	b**oo**k, g**oo**d, p**u**llover
[ʌ]	m**u**m, b**u**s, c**o**lour
[ɜː]	g**ir**l, **ear**ly, h**er**, w**or**k, T-sh**ir**t
[ə]	**a** partner, **a**gain, t**o**day
[eɪ]	n**a**me, **eigh**t, pl**ay**, gr**ea**t
[aɪ]	t**i**me, r**igh**t, m**y**, **I**
[ɔɪ]	b**oy**, t**oi**let, n**oi**se
[əʊ]	**o**ld, n**o**, r**oa**d, yell**ow**
[aʊ]	t**ow**n, n**ow**, h**ou**se
[ɪə]	h**ere**, y**ear**, id**ea**
[eə]	wh**ere**, p**air**, sh**are**, th**eir**
[ʊə]	t**our**

[b]	**b**oat, ta**b**le, ver**b**
[p]	**p**ool, **p**a**p**er, sho**p**
[d]	**d**ad, win**d**ow, goo**d**
[t]	**t**en, le**tt**er, a**t**
[g]	**g**ood, a**g**ain, ba**g**
[k]	**c**at, **k**itchen, ba**ck**
[m]	**m**um, **m**an, re**m**ember
[n]	**n**o, o**n**e, te**n**
[ŋ]	so**ng**, you**ng**, u**n**cle, tha**n**ks
[l]	he**ll**o, **l**ike, o**l**d, sma**ll**
[r]	**r**ed, **r**uler, f**r**iend, so**rr**y
[w]	**w**e, **wh**ere, **o**ne
[j]	**y**ou, **y**es, **u**niform
[f]	**f**amily, a**f**ter, laug**h**
[v]	ri**v**er, **v**ery, se**v**en, ha**v**e
[s]	**s**ister, po**s**ter, ye**s**
[z]	plea**s**e, **z**oo, qui**z**, hi**s**, mu**s**ic
[ʃ]	**sh**op, sta**ti**on, Engli**sh**
[ʒ]	televi**s**ion, u**s**ually
[tʃ]	**t**eacher, **ch**ild, wa**tch**
[dʒ]	**G**ermany, **j**ob, pro**j**ect, oran**ge**
[θ]	**th**anks, **th**ree, bath**r**oom
[ð]	**th**e, **th**is, fa**th**er, wi**th**
[h]	**h**ere, **wh**o, be**h**ind
[x]	lo**ch**

Am besten kannst du dir die Aussprache der einzelnen Lautzeichen einprägen, wenn du dir zu jedem Zeichen ein einfaches Wort merkst – das [iː] ist der **green**-Laut, das [eɪ] ist der **name**-Laut usw.

Place names
Boulder [ˈbəʊldə]
Colorado [ˌkɒləˈrɑːdəʊ]
Dakota [dəˈkəʊtə]
Des Moines [də ˈmɔɪn]
Dumfries [dʌmˈfriːs]
Durham [ˈdʌrəm]
Lochinver [lɒxˈɪnvə]
Mount Rainier [ˈreɪnɪə], [rəˈnɪər]
Winston-Salem [ˌwɪnstənˈseɪləm]

First names
Alicia [əˈlɪʃə]
Brianna [briˈænə]
Clay [kleɪ]
Hugh [hjuː]
Jake [dʒeɪk]
Jamal [dʒəˈmɑːl]
Joanna [dʒəʊˈænə]
Lauren [ˈlɔːrən], [ˈlɒrən]
Rahel [ˈrɑːhel]
Shari [ˈʃɑːri]
Sherman [ˈʃɜːmən]
Shireen [ʃəˈriːn]
Zach [zæk]

Family names
Abelove [ˈeɪbəlʌv]
Alexie [əˈleksi]
Ambachew [ˈæmbətʃuː]
Boiskin [ˈbɔɪskɪn]
Cady [ˈkeɪdi]
Harrison [ˈhærɪsən]
Hughes [hjuːz]
Ingraham [ˈɪngrəhəm]
Jannon [ˈdʒænən]
Ludington [luːdɪŋtn]
McMillan [məkˈmɪlən]
Penumbra [pəˈnʌmbrə]
Potente [pəˈtenteɪ]
Revere [rəˈvɪə]
Rowling [ˈrəʊlɪŋ]
Sykes [saɪks]
Tubman [ˈtʌbmən]
Weasley [ˈwiːzli]

Other names
Amnesty [ˈæmnəsti]
Greenpeace [ˈgriːnˌpiːs]
Isabo [iːˈsɑːbəʊ]
Tiresias [taɪˈriːsiəs]

False friends

⚠ Leider gibt es einige Wörter, die im Englischen und Deutschen ähnlich klingen oder aussehen, aber eine ganz andere Bedeutung haben. Hier sind einige Beispiele für *false friends*:

English	German	German	English
also	= auch	also	= **so; Well …**
bald	= glatzköpfig	bald	= **soon**
become	= werden	bekommen	= **get**
boot	= Stiefel	Boot	= **boat**
brave	= mutig	brav	= **good, well-behaved**
build	= bauen	bilden	= **make, form**
chips	= Pommes frites	Kartoffelchips	= **crisps**
fire	= Feuer	Feier	= **celebration**
gift	= Geschenk	Gift	= **poison**
grade	= Jahrgangsstufe, Klasse	Grad	= **degree**
kind	= freundlich	Kind	= **child**
handy	= praktisch	Handy	= **mobile**
listen	= zuhören	Listen	= **lists**
map	= Landkarte	Mappe	= **folder**
mist	= Nebel	Mist *(Unsinn)*	= **rubbish**
mode	= Methode, Modus	Mode	= **fashion**
Roman	= römisch	Roman	= **novel**
snake	= Schlange	Schnecke	= **snail**
stay	= bleiben	stehen	= **stand**
where	= wo	wer	= **who**
while	= während	weil	= **because**

Countries and continents

Country/Continent	Adjective	Person	People
Marco is from Italy.	*Pizza is Italian.*	*Marco is an Italian.*	*The Italians invented pizza.*
Africa ['æfrɪkə] *Afrika*	African ['æfrɪkən]	an African	the Africans
Asia ['eɪʒə, 'eɪʃə] *Asien*	Asian ['eɪʃn, 'eɪʒn]	an Asian	the Asians
Australia [ɒ'streɪliə] *Australien*	Australian [ɒ'streɪliən]	an Australian	the Australians
Austria ['ɒstriə] *Österreich*	Austrian ['ɒstriən]	an Austrian	the Austrians
Belarus [ˌbelə'ruːs] *Weißrussland*	Belarusian [ˌbelə'ruːsiən]	a Belarusian	the Belarusians
Belgium ['beldʒəm] *Belgien*	Belgian ['beldʒən]	a Belgian	the Belgians
Bosnia and Herzegovina ['bɒzniə ən ˌhɜːtsəgə'viːnə] *Bosnien und Herzegowina*	Bosnian ['bɒzniən]; Herzegovinian [ˌhɜːtsəgə'vɪniən]	a Bosnian; a Herzegovinian	the Bosnians; the Herzegovinians
Canada ['kænədə] *Kanada*	Canadian [kə'neɪdiən]	a Canadian	the Canadians
China ['tʃaɪnə]	Chinese [ˌtʃaɪ'niːz]	a Chinese	the Chinese
Croatia [krəʊ'eɪʃə] *Kroatien*	Croatian [krəʊ'eɪʃn]	a Croatian	the Croatians
the **Czech Republic** [ˌtʃek rɪ'pʌblɪk] *Tschechien, die Tschechische Republik*	Czech [tʃek]	a Czech	the Czechs
Denmark ['denmɑːk] *Dänemark*	Danish ['deɪnɪʃ]	a Dane [deɪn]	the Danes
England ['ɪŋglənd]	English ['ɪŋglɪʃ]	an Englishman / -woman	the English
Estonia [e'stəʊniə] *Estland*	Estonian [e'stəʊniən]	an Estonian	the Estonians
Europe ['jʊərəp] *Europa*	European [ˌjʊərə'piːən]	a European	the Europeans
Finland ['fɪnlənd] *Finnland*	Finnish ['fɪnɪʃ]	a Finn [fɪn]	the Finns
France [frɑːns] *Frankreich*	French [frentʃ]	a Frenchman / -woman	the French
Germany ['dʒɜːməni] *Deutschland*	German ['dʒɜːmən]	a German	the Germans
(Great) Britain ['brɪtn] *Großbritannien*	British ['brɪtɪʃ]	a Briton ['brɪtn]	the British
Greece [griːs] *Griechenland*	Greek [griːk]	a Greek	the Greeks
Hungary ['hʌŋgəri] *Ungarn*	Hungarian [hʌŋ'geəriən]	a Hungarian	the Hungarians
Iceland ['aɪslənd] *Island*	Icelandic [aɪs'lændɪk]	an Icelander ['aɪsləndə]	the Icelanders
India ['ɪndiə] *Indien*	Indian ['ɪndiən]	an Indian	the Indians
Ireland ['aɪələnd] *Irland*	Irish ['aɪrɪʃ]	an Irishman / -woman	the Irish
Israel ['ɪzreɪl]	Israeli [ɪz'reɪli]	an Israeli	the Israelis
Italy ['ɪtəli] *Italien*	Italian [ɪ'tæliən]	an Italian	the Italians
Kosovo ['kɒsəvəʊ]	Kosovan ['kɒsəvən]	a Kosovan	the Kosovans
Latvia ['lætviə] *Lettland*	Latvian ['lætviən]	a Latvian	the Latvians
Lithuania [ˌlɪθju'eɪniə] *Litauen*	Lithuanian [ˌlɪθju'eɪniən]	a Lithuanian	the Lithuanians
Luxembourg ['lʌksəmbɜːg] *Luxemburg*	Luxembourg	a Luxembourger ['lʌksəmbɜːgə]	the Luxembourgers

Country/Continent	Adjective	Person	People
Marco is from Italy.	*Pizza is Italian.*	*Marco is an Italian.*	*The Italians invented pizza.*
Macedonia [ˌmæsəˈdəʊniə] *Mazedonien*	Macedonian [ˌmæsəˈdəʊniən]	a Macedonian	the Macedonians
Malta [ˈmɔːltə]	Maltese [mɔːlˈtiːz]	a Maltese	the Maltese
Moldova [mɒlˈdəʊvə] *Moldawien*	Moldovan [mɒlˈdəʊvən]	a Moldovan	the Moldovans
Montenegro [ˌmɒntɪˈniːgrəʊ] *Montenegro*	Montenegrin [ˌmɒntɪˈniːgrɪn]	a Montenegrin	the Montenegrins
the **Netherlands** [ˈneðələndz] *die Niederlande*	Dutch [dʌtʃ]	a Dutchman / a Dutchwoman	the Dutch
New Zealand [ˌnjuːˈziːlənd] *Neuseeland*	New Zealand	a New Zealander	the New Zealanders
Northern Ireland [ˌnɔːðən ˈaɪələnd] *Nordirland*	Northern Irish [ˌnɔːðən ˈaɪrɪʃ]	a Northern Irishman / a Northern Irishwoman	the Northern Irish
Norway [ˈnɔːweɪ] *Norwegen*	Norwegian [nɔːˈwiːdʒən]	a Norwegian	the Norwegians
Peru [pəˈruː]	Peruvian [pəˈruːviən]	a Peruvian	the Peruvians
Poland [ˈpəʊlənd] *Polen*	Polish [ˈpəʊlɪʃ]	a Pole [pəʊl]	the Poles
Portugal [ˈpɔːtʃʊgl]	Portuguese [ˌpɔːtʃʊˈgiːz]	a Portuguese	the Portuguese
Romania [ruˈmeɪniə] *Rumänien*	Romanian [ruˈmeɪniən]	a Romanian	the Romanians
Russia [ˈrʌʃə] *Russland*	Russian [ˈrʌʃn]	a Russian	the Russians
Scotland [ˈskɒtlənd] *Schottland*	Scottish [ˈskɒtɪʃ]	a Scot [skɒt]; a Scotsman / a Scotswoman	the Scots, the Scottish
Serbia [ˈsɜːbiə] *Serbien*	Serbian [ˈsɜːbiən]	a Serbian	the Serbians
Slovakia [sləʊˈvækiə] *die Slowakei*	Slovak [ˈsləʊvæk]	a Slovak	the Slovaks
Slovenia [sləʊˈviːniə] *Slowenien*	Slovenian [sləʊˈviːniən]	a Slovenian	the Slovenians
South Africa [ˌsaʊθˈæfrɪkən]	South African	a South African	the South Africans
South America [ˌsaʊθ_əˈmerɪkə] *Südamerika*	South American [ˌsaʊθ_əˈmerɪkən]	a South American	the South Americans
Spain [speɪn] *Spanien*	Spanish [ˈspænɪʃ]	a Spaniard [ˈspæniəd]	the Spanish
Sweden [ˈswiːdn] *Schweden*	Swedish [ˈswiːdɪʃ]	a Swede [swiːd]	the Swedes
Switzerland [ˈswɪtsələnd] *die Schweiz*	Swiss [swɪs]	a Swiss	the Swiss
Turkey [ˈtɜːki] *die Türkei*	Turkish [ˈtɜːkɪʃ]	a Turk [tɜːk]	the Turks
Ukraine [juːˈkreɪn] *die Ukraine*	Ukrainian [juːˈkreɪniən]	a Ukrainian	the Ukrainians
the **United Kingdom** [juˌnaɪtɪd ˈkɪŋdəm] *das Vereinigte Königreich*	British [ˈbrɪtɪʃ]	a Briton [ˈbrɪtn]	the British
the **United States of America** [juˌnaɪtɪd ˌsteɪts_əv_əˈmerɪkə] *die Vereinigten Staaten von Amerika*	American [əˈmerɪkən]	an American	the Americans
Wales [weɪlz]	Welsh [welʃ]	a Welshman /-woman	the Welsh

Irregular verbs

infinitive	simple past	past participle	
(to) **be**	**was; were**	**been**	sein
(to) **beat**	**beat**	**beaten**	schlagen; besiegen
(to) **become**	**became**	**become**	werden
(to) **begin**	**began**	**begun**	beginnen, anfangen
(to) **bend**	**bent**	**bent**	sich bücken, sich beugen
(to) **bet**	**bet**	**bet**	wetten
(to) **bind**	**bound** [aʊ]	**bound**	binden
(to) **bite** [aɪ]	**bit** [ɪ]	**bitten** [ɪ]	beißen
(to) **blow sth. out**	**blew**	**blown**	etwas auspusten, ausblasen
(to) **break** [eɪ]	**broke**	**broken**	brechen; zerbrechen
(to) **bring**	**brought**	**brought**	(mit-, her)bringen
(to) **build**	**built**	**built**	bauen
(to) **burst**	**burst**	**burst**	platzen
(to) **buy**	**bought**	**bought**	kaufen
(to) **cast a vote**	**cast**	**cast**	abstimmen, seine Stimme abgeben
(to) **catch**	**caught**	**caught**	fangen
(to) **choose** [uː]	**chose** [əʊ]	**chosen** [əʊ]	aussuchen, (aus)wählen; sich aussuchen
(to) **come**	**came**	**come**	kommen
(to) **cost**	**cost**	**cost**	kosten
(to) **cut**	**cut**	**cut**	schneiden
(to) **deal with** [iː]	**dealt** [e]	**dealt** [e]	sich beschäftigen mit; handeln von
(to) **dig**	**dug**	**dug**	graben
(to) **do**	**did**	**done** [ʌ]	tun, machen
(to) **draw**	**drew**	**drawn**	zeichnen
(to) **drive** [aɪ]	**drove** [əʊ]	**driven** [ɪ]	(mit dem Auto) fahren
(to) **drink**	**drank**	**drunk**	trinken
(to) **eat**	**ate** [et, eɪt]	**eaten**	essen
(to) **fall**	**fell**	**fallen**	fallen, stürzen; hinfallen
(to) **feed**	**fed**	**fed**	füttern
(to) **feel**	**felt**	**felt**	fühlen; sich fühlen
(to) **fight**	**fought**	**fought**	(be)kämpfen
(to) **find**	**found**	**found**	finden
(to) **fly**	**flew**	**flown**	fliegen
(to) **forget**	**forgot**	**forgotten**	vergessen
(to) **get**	**got**	**got**	bekommen; holen; werden; gelangen
(to) **give**	**gave**	**given**	geben
(to) **go**	**went**	**gone** [ɒ]	gehen
(to) **grow**	**grew**	**grown**	wachsen; anbauen, anpflanzen; werden
(to) **hang**	**hung**	**hung**	hängen
(to) **have**	**had**	**had**	haben
(to) **hear** [ɪə]	**heard** [ɜː]	**heard** [ɜː]	hören
(to) **hide** [aɪ]	**hid** [ɪ]	**hidden** [ɪ]	verstecken; sich verstecken
(to) **hit**	**hit**	**hit**	schlagen
(to) **hold**	**held**	**held**	halten
(to) **hurt**	**hurt**	**hurt**	schmerzen, wehtun; verletzen
(to) **keep**	**kept**	**kept**	behalten; aufheben, aufsparen; aufbewahren
(to) **know** [nəʊ]	**knew** [njuː]	**known** [nəʊn]	wissen; kennen
(to) **lay**	**laid**	**laid**	legen
(to) **lead** [iː]	**led**	**led**	führen, leiten

infinitive	simple past	past participle	
(to) **leave** [iː]	**left**	**left**	(weg)gehen; abfahren; (zurück)lassen; verlassen
(to) **lend sb. sth.**	**lent**	**lent**	jm. etwas leihen
(to) **let**	**let**	**let**	lassen
(to) **lie**	**lay**	**lain**	liegen
(to) **light** [aɪ]	**lit** [ɪ]	**lit** [ɪ]	anzünden
(to) **lose** [uː]	**lost** [ɒ]	**lost** [ɒ]	verlieren
(to) **make**	**made**	**made**	machen; herstellen
(to) **mean** [iː]	**meant** [e]	**meant** [e]	bedeuten; meinen
(to) **meet** [iː]	**met** [e]	**met**	treffen; sich treffen; kennenlernen
(to) **pay**	**paid**	**paid**	bezahlen
(to) **put**	**put**	**put**	(etwas wohin) tun, legen, stellen
(to) **read** [iː]	**read** [e]	**read** [e]	lesen
(to) **ride** [aɪ]	**rode**	**ridden** [ɪ]	reiten; (Rad) fahren
(to) **ring**	**rang**	**rung**	klingeln, läuten
(to) **rise** [aɪ]	**rose**	**risen** [ɪ]	(an-, auf)steigen
(to) **run**	**ran**	**run**	rennen, laufen
(to) **say** [eɪ]	**said** [e]	**said** [e]	sagen
(to) **see**	**saw**	**seen**	sehen
(to) **sell**	**sold**	**sold**	verkaufen
(to) **send**	**sent**	**sent**	schicken, senden
(to) **set sth. up**	**set**	**set**	etwas errichten, aufbauen; etwas arrangieren
(to) **shake**	**shook**	**shaken**	schütteln; zittern
(to) **shine**	**shone** [BE: ɒ, AE: əʊ]	**shone** [ɒ, əʊ]	scheinen (Sonne)
(to) **shoot** [uː]	**shot** [ɒ]	**shot** [ɒ]	schießen; erschießen
(to) **shrink**	**shrank**	**shrunk**	schrumpfen
(to) **sing**	**sang**	**sung**	singen
(to) **sink**	**sank**	**sunk**	sinken
(to) **sit**	**sat**	**sat**	sitzen; sich setzen
(to) **sleep**	**slept**	**slept**	schlafen
(to) **speak** [iː]	**spoke**	**spoken**	sprechen
(to) **spend**	**spent**	**spent**	(Zeit) verbringen; (Geld) ausgeben
(to) **split**	**split**	**split**	aufteilen; (sich) trennen; spalten
(to) **spread** [e]	**spread** [e]	**spread** [e]	ausbreiten, verbreiten; sich ausbreiten, verbreiten
(to) **stand**	**stood**	**stood**	stehen; sich (hin)stellen
(to) **steal**	**stole**	**stolen**	stehlen
(to) **stick**	**stuck**	**stuck**	stechen, stecken
(to) **sting**	**stung**	**stung**	stechen; brennen
(to) **swim**	**swam**	**swum**	schwimmen
(to) **swing**	**swang**	**swung**	schwingen
(to) **take**	**took**	**taken**	(mit)nehmen; (weg-, hin)bringen; dauern
(to) **teach**	**taught**	**taught**	unterrichten, lehren
(to) **tear** [teə]	**tore**	**torn**	reißen, zerreißen
(to) **tell**	**told**	**told**	erzählen, berichten
(to) **think**	**thought**	**thought**	denken, glauben
(to) **throw**	**threw**	**thrown**	werfen
(to) **understand**	**understood**	**understood**	verstehen
(to) **wake up**	**woke up**	**woken up**	aufwachen; (auf)wecken
(to) **wear** [eə]	**wore** [ɔː]	**worn** [ɔː]	tragen (Kleidung)
(to) **win**	**won** [ʌ]	**won** [ʌ]	gewinnen
(to) **write**	**wrote**	**written**	schreiben

Writing a limerick
← p. 94

a) There are 8 syllables in lines 1,2 and 5. There are 5 syllables in lines 3 and 4.

b) The correct order is:
There was a young man from Cologne
Who called his best friend on his phone:
Let's go for a walk,
And have a good talk
It's much better than being alone.

c) Individual answers.

Similes
← p. 94

1 like a cat on a hot tin roof   2 like a bull in a china shop   3 as stubborn as a mule   4 as bold as brass
5 as cool as a cucumber   6 as easy as pie   7 as good as gold

DNA manipulation
← p. 95

1 New methods of manipulating DNA are being discovered by scientists every day, it seems. **Picture E**
2 Here, genetic material is being extracted from a human cell. **Picture A**
3 DNA sequences are being examined by a scientist looking for damaged genes that can lead to disease.
   Picture C
4 The disease-causing gene is being replaced with a good copy from a healthy cell. **Picture B**
5 The question of whether we should change our genetic code is still being discussed today. **Picture D**

Advertising slogans
← p. 95

a) 1   Fresh breath leads to success **Picture F**
   2   A journey is more than just getting from A to B **Picture A**
   3   Keep your whole life in your pocket **Picture B**
   4   Start your day the healthy way **Picture C**
b) Individual answers for **Pictures D and E.**

Where was it said?
← p. 96

a) A + 3, B + 1, C + 7, D + 6, E + 4, F + 5, G + 2, H + 9, I + 8
b) Minor variations are possible
   2   The store offers/offered/is offering €50 cashback on old smartphones.
   3   The referee warned the player not to do it again.
   4   They announced a ten minute delay for the London train.
   5   The doctor advised the patient to take some medicine and rest at home.
   6   The teacher told the boys to concentrate.
   7   The child refused to give the toy to another child.
   8   The teacher suggested extra maths lessons for Tim.
   9   The waiter recommended the pasta (to the customer).

Presentation tips ← p. 96

1+20	4+15	6+12	8+2	9+14	10+3
11+22	13+19	16+24	17+7	23+18	

Adjectives to adverbs ← p. 97

Suggested answers:
2 Luckily, the weather is very good for the football match.
3 Normally, we watch two films in a row on Saturdays.
4 Frank gently told Sally the bad news. / (Very) gently, Frank told Sally the bad news.
5 Ben and Kevin both react allergically to nuts and milk.
6 Try not to speak so glumly when you're giving your presentation.
7 Anish's classmates think highly of him.
8 He came into the room and smiled awkwardly at us.
9 She always plays the piano so passionately.
10 Try to speak more respectfully to your parents.
11 It rained so heavily that it caused serious flooding.

Communication and social media ← p. 97

Individual answers

Change one letter ← p. 97

1 JOB	2 RISE	3 EAT	4 SEA	5 MEAT	6 GROW
7 HUGE	8 CAUSE	9 POINT	10 SOME	11 LEVEL	

Three word sentence: BEES ARE COOL.

English G Access **uses the same special vocabulary** *('Operatoren')* **that is used in standard tests.**
Make sure you understand what you need to do when you read one of the verbs below.

The task says	German	Example
ANFORDERUNGSBEREICH I (Comprehension)		
Complete/Finish sth.	Vervollständige etwas.	*Use the words in brackets to complete the sentences. Finish three sentences in a different way.*
Describe sth.	Beschreibe etwas.	*Describe the atmosphere in the park.*
Imagine.	Stelle dir vor.	*Imagine you live in New York.*
List things.	Liste/ Führe Sachen auf.	*List the reasons the two writers give.*
Look sth. up.	Schlage etwas nach.	*Look up the words in a dictionary.*
Make notes (on/about sth.).	Mache (dir) Notizen (über/zu etwas) (zur Vorbereitung)	*Make notes on what you see in the photos.*
Match sth.	Ordne etwas zu.	*Match the definitions to the pictures.*
Outline sth.	Skizziere etwas.	*Outline the author's main ideas.*
Scan a text (for sth.).	Suche einen Text (nach etwas) ab.	*Scan the article for these numbers.*
Skim a text.	Überfliege einen Text, um den Inhalt grob zu erfassen.	*Go to page 177. Skim the three texts there and decide which one you should read.*
Structure sth.	Strukturiere etwas.	*Structure the vocabulary in the box.*
Summarize (sth.) / Sum (sth.) up.	Fasse (etwas) zusammen.	*Sum up / Summarize the main points of your presentation.*
Take notes (on/about sth.).	Mache (dir) Notizen (über/zu etwas) beim Lesen oder Zuhören.	*Listen to the woman and take notes on what she tells you.*
Work sth. out.	Finde etwas heraus.	*In each situation, there is something you can't hear. Work out from the context what it is.*
Write (+ text type).	Schreibe (+ Texttyp).	*Choose five words from box 1 and write sentences with them.*
ANFORDERUNGSBEREICH I/II (Comprehension/Analysis)		
Present sth.	Stelle etwas vor.	*Discuss your ideas and present them to the class.*
Report sth. (to sb.).	Berichte (jm.) (von) etwas.	*Report your ideas to the class.*

The task says	German	Example
ANFORDERUNGSBEREICH II (Analysis)		
Check sth.	Prüfe etwas.	*Check that you have all the special vocabulary you need.*
Compare two things.	Vergleiche zwei Sachen.	*Compare your tables and correct them if necessary.*
Decide.	Entscheide dich.	*Decide if the people in the dialogues speak British or American English.*
Explain sth.	Erkläre etwas.	*Explain what decision she has made and why.*
Give reasons for sth.	Begründe etwas.	*Give reasons for your answer.*

The task says	German	Example
ANFORDERUNGSBEREICH III (Discussion and comment)		
Agree on sth.	Einigt euch auf etwas.	*Use a placemat to agree on five places to visit.*
Assess sth.	Beurteile etwas.	*Use the feedback sheet to assess each other's report.*
Comment on sth.	Kommentiere etwas.	*Comment on what went wrong.*
Discuss sth.	Diskutiert über etwas. / Besprecht etwas.	*Discuss your alternative titles and choose the best one.*
Give (sb.) feedback.	*Gib (jm.) Feedback/Rückmeldung.*	*Take notes on your partner's talk and give them feedback.*
Share sth. (with sb.).	*Teile etwas (mit jm.).*	*Share your ideas and give each other feedback.*

Quellenverzeichnis

Titelbild

S.I & IV: Cornelsen/Hintergrund: mauritius images/ Novarc Images; Wanderer: Shutterstock.com/Dudarev Mikhail

Fotos & Filmstills

akg-images (S. 18 mi.: Pictures From History; S. 103: un.re.); **Cornelsen** (S. 69 mi. Cover: Shutterstock/ dobrohotovo , S. 76 ob.li. Cover: Fotolia/Irochka, S. 76 ob.mi. Cover: Jane Leon/Photonica/Getty Images); **Crooked Letter Films, NY** (S. 181 mitte rechts, S. 181 mitte links, S.181 oben rechts); **ddp images** (S. 4 un.li.: dapd/INTERTOPICS/Empics/Yui Mok); **dpa Picture-Alliance** (S. 47 ob.li.: /REUTERS/X02348/AP); **Dr. Eijiro Miyako** (S. 6 mi.li., S. 57 mi.li.); **F1online** (S. 76 mi.re.: Westend61/Walter Allgöwer); **Imago Stock & People GmbH** (S. 12 oben rechts, mitte rechts: Dafydd Owen / Avalon/Photosho, S. 17 oben rechts, mitte rechts: Dafydd Owen / Avalon/Photosho, S. 24 mitte rechts: xWilliamxMeyerx, S. 26 oben rechts: Hannelore Förster, S. 26 mitte rechts: Huntstock, S. 33 mitte links: PAN-IMAGES/Nordmann, S. 76 mitte: ZUMA Press, S. 102 mitte rechts: StockTrek Images,); **interfoto e.k.** (S. 13 ob.mi., S. 26 A: JTB PHOTO/Loop Images); **Started by the French artist JR** (S. 46 mi.re.: Amanual Begna, S. 46 mi.: Rahel Ambachew, S. 46 un.re.: Rebekah Janway); **mauritius images GmbH**(S. 4 : Alamy/andrew sadler, S. 4 : Anthony Collins, S. 10 oben rechts: Loop Images, S. 10 oben links: Alamy/andrew sadler, S. 32 mitte rechts: Alamy/Guy Corbishley, S. 33 oben rechts: Alamy/JOHN BRACEGIRDLE, S. 50 mitte rechts: Alamy/Anthony Collins, S. 53 unten rechts: Shakeyjon, S. 57 unten links: Alamy /Kathryn Truepenny, S. 176 oben rechts: Picture Partners); **MOMONDO** (S. 27 A-D: The DNA Journey); **Picture-Alliance** (S. 33: C, S. 51 mi.+un.re.: dpa /AP Photo, S. 13 ob.re.: dpa/Everett Collection); **Sapna Richter, Berlin** (S. 21 unten rechts, S. 48 unten rechts, unten mitte, S. 56 mitte rechts, S. 65 unten rechts, S. 177 mitte rechts, S. 188 oben rechts);**Shutterstock.com** (S. 1 mitte rechts: Dudarev Mikhail, S. 8 mitte, unten mitte: Mendo Wong, S. 8 unten mitte: Interior Design, S. 10 unten rechts: Kseniia Perminova, S. 11 mitte rechts: Jacob Lund, S. 15 mitte rechts: DVARG, S. 20 unten rechts: Popartic, S. 23 oben rechts: Panuwach, S. 26 unten mitte: Carboxylase, S. 28 mitte rechts: Corepics VOF, S. 28 unten rechts: Maxx-Studio, S. 32 oben mitte: Rawpixel.com, S. 32 oben rechts: CREATISTA, S. 32 mitte: Kristin F. Ruhs, S. 33 mitte rechts: Leszek Glasner, S. 47 oben rechts: Zenza Flarini, S. 50 mitte rechts: cbies, S. 50 oben rechts: Vlad G, S. 51 oben rechts: Giraphics, S. 55 oben rechts: Maksym Kapliuk, S. 56 unten mitte: Andrey_Popov, S. 56 unten links: Interior Design, S. 61 unten rechts: MJTH, S. 62 oben rechts: Daniel Prudek, S. 62 oben rechts: Lane V. Erickson, S. 67 oben mitte: VectorMine, S.69 mitte:dobrohotovo, S. 70 oben rechts: Sergey Nivens, S. 72 mitte rechts: Travel and Learn, S. 73 mitte rechts: , S. 76 mitte links: Teresa Prokhoryan, S. 76 mitte: T. Lesia, S. 89 oben rechts: Thai Breeze, S. 95 unten rechts: p_ saranya, S. 95 mitte: Elnur, S. 95 oben mitte: vchal, S. 95 unten links: zentilia, S. 95 oben links: koya979, S. 95 unten links: veryulissa, S. 95 unten mitte: Kostenko Maxim, S. 95 unten mitte: eranicle, S. 95 mitte: Golden Pixels LLC, S. 95 unten rechts: Africa Studio, S. 95 oben rechts: gopixa, S. 98 mitte rechts: pixs4u, S. 98 unten rechts: Maksym Kapliuk, S. 100 oben rechts: Nataliia K, S. 100 oben rechts: Sven Hoppe, S. 102 mitte rechts: alexmillos, S. 103 mitte rechts: yui, S. 163 unten rechts: sarahdesign, S. 185 oben rechts: Creaktiva, S. 203 mitte rechts: Odua Images, S. 203 oben rechts: ostill, S. 203 mitte: JPC-PROD, S. 203 mitte rechts: michaeljung, S. 203 mitte: George Rudy, S. 203 mitte rechts: Aila Images, S. 203 oben rechts: Daniel M Ernst, S. 203 oben rechts: DiversityStudio, S. 204 mitte rechts: Maksym Bondarchuk, S. 204 mitte: Goodluz, S. 204 mitte rechts: fototip, S. 206 oben rechts: Alan Tunnicliffe, S. 206 oben mitte: Collins93, S. 209 unten rechts: Phonlamai Photo, S. 210 mitte rechts: Christopher Elwell, S. 210 oben rechts: A_Lesik, S. 210 oben rechts: deepspace, S. 211 unten rechts: wxin, S. 212 unten mitte: studiovin, S. 212 unten rechts: jprom, S. 212 unten rechts: carlosdelacalle, S. 213 unten rechts: Richard Peterson, S. 213 unten rechts: frantic00, S. 213 mitte rechts: Pause08, S. 213 unten mitte: GDM, S. 213 mitte: Sunflowerr, S. 213 mitte rechts: SnelsonStock, S. 213 mitte rechts: 3drenderings, S. 213 oben rechts: Dario Lo Presti, S. 214 oben rechts: Maxx-Studio, S. 215 mitte rechts: sripfoto, S. 216 oben rechts: Ewa Studio, S. 218 unten rechts: Daniel Prudek, S. 221 unten mitte: Alex Leo, S. 221 unten rechts: foxie, S. 221 unten mitte: USBFCO, S. 222 mitte rechts: solar22, S. 222 oben rechts: notbad, S. 222 oben rechts: notbad, S. 222 oben rechts: notbad, S. 223 unten rechts: Gecko1968, S. 225 mitte rechts: Africa Studio), **Sky News** (S. 93 A-H, S. 66 A-D); **stock.adobe.com** (S. 10 mitte rechts: Jürgen Fälchle, S. 10 mitte links: djma, S. 10 unten links: chanawit, S. 11 oben rechts: Krakenimages. com, S. 28 oben rechts: Sashkin, S. 28 mitte rechts: Andrey Popov, S. 42 oben rechts: Matyas Rehak, S. 56 mitte: mipan, S. 56 mitte links: adimas, S. 56 unten rechts: bokan, S. 76 mitte: Orlando Bellini, S. 97 oben rechts: Irina K., S. 100 mitte rechts: 12ee12, S. 170 oben rechts: structuresxx, S. 174 oben rechts: undrey, S. 176 mitte rechts: Miriam Dörr, S. 188 mitte rechts: pressmaster);

The Cinema Guild/Kahane Cooperman (S. 40 A-F: Kahane Cooperman); **The Ocean Cleanup** (S. 84 ob.mi.; S. 86 mi.: Yuri van Geenen); **Walker Books Australia** (S. 79 mi.re. Cover)

Illustrationen

Roland Beier (S. 114 un.re.); **Carlos Borell, Berlin** (S. 2); **Tobias Dahmen, Utrecht, NL** (S. 15 ob., S. 16 ob., S. 24 un.re., S. 29 ob., S. 44 un.re., S. 64 un.re., S. 91 un.re., S. 108 mi.+un.re., S. 110 un.re., S. 112 mi., S. 116 ob.mi., S. 138 ob.re., S. 150 re.); **M.B.Schulz, Düsseldorf** (S. 130 mi.re.); **Michael Fleischmann** (S. 126 mi., S. 134 mi.re., S. 142 un.re.); **Eric Gira** (S. 11 un.li., S. 22 ob.re., S. 30 ob.re., S. 56 mi.re., S. 74 un.re., S.137 mitte links, S. 153 ob.li., S. 186 mi.re.); **Bonnie Glänzer** (S. 165 un.re., S. 173 mi.re.); **Bernd Kissel** (S. 76 ob.re.)

Texte & Graphic Novel

S. 12: © 2014, **Kae Tempest** (previously Kate Tempest) Excerpts from "Hold Your Own / Tiresias" Publisher: Picador, London; **S.13** : "Theme for English B " from **Langston Hughes** © 1994 by The Estate of Langston Hughes, Harold Ober Associates, New York and Liepman AG, Zurich; **S.14** : Excerpt from the text "Roar" from Katy Perry; **S.14** : „I come from", **Dean Atta**, _https://www. intotheoutside.org.uk/voices/dean-atta/i-come_.; **S. 18** : "Women need to be recognized as a part of our history" **Shari Boiskin**, Eastside-Online.org 2016; **S. 22** : Excerpts from "The Seven Daughters of Eve" by **Bryan Sykes**, pages 1-2, W.W. Norton & Company, 2001; **S. 34-36** : Adapted Excerpts from "Go and Come Back", DK, a division of Penguin Random House LLC. by **Joan Abelove**, 1998., **S 58-59**: Excerpt from "Siri or Skynet: How to separate artificial intelligence fact from fiction" from **Gary Marcus**, 07 Aug.2022, Observer/The Guardian News and Media Ltd; **S. 68-69** : Excerpts from "Maximum Happy Imagination" from "MR. PENUMBRA'S 24-HOUR BOOKSTORE" © 2012 by **Robin Sloan;** Farrar, Straus and Giroux; **S.77-79** : Excerpts from "Finding Nevo" © 2017 by **Nevo Zisin**, Walker Books Australia; **S. 80-83**: 2000 word text excerpt from „Messy Roots: A Graphic Memoir of a Wuhanese American", by **Laura Gao**, illustrated by Laura Gao, Used by permission of HarperCollins Publishers; **S. 99** mi.li.: **die Urbanisten,** Youth Projects in Germany, Excerpt from "Create your Skateplaza 2.0", e.V./Lukas Seelwische.

Giving feedback to your classmates

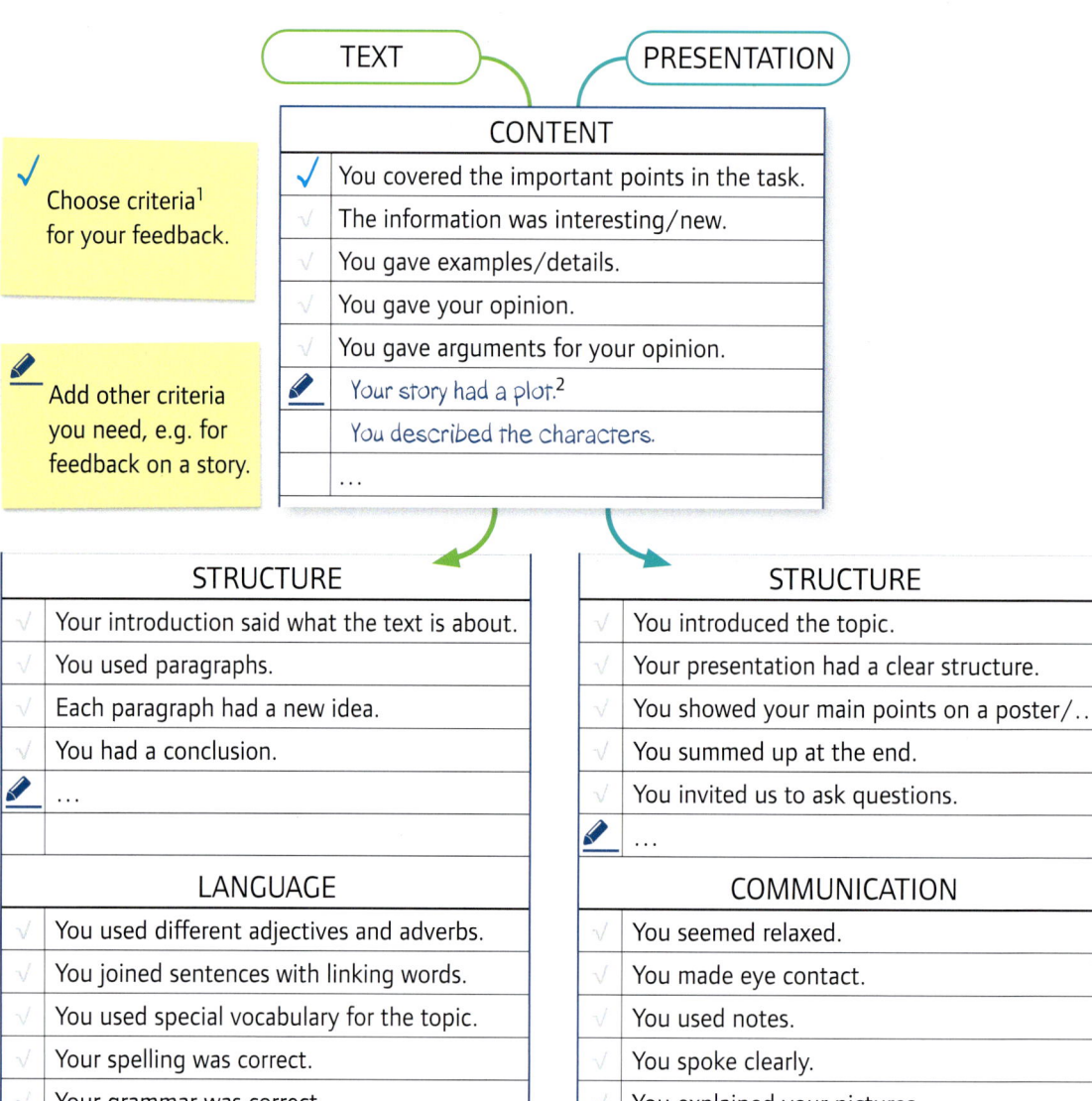

TEXT   PRESENTATION

CONTENT

✓	You covered the important points in the task.
√	The information was interesting/new.
√	You gave examples/details.
√	You gave your opinion.
√	You gave arguments for your opinion.
✎	Your story had a plot.[2]
	You described the characters.
	…

✓ Choose criteria[1] for your feedback.

✎ Add other criteria you need, e.g. for feedback on a story.

STRUCTURE

√	Your introduction said what the text is about.
√	You used paragraphs.
√	Each paragraph had a new idea.
√	You had a conclusion.
✎	…

LANGUAGE

√	You used different adjectives and adverbs.
√	You joined sentences with linking words.
√	You used special vocabulary for the topic.
√	Your spelling was correct.
√	Your grammar was correct.
✎	…

STRUCTURE

√	You introduced the topic.
√	Your presentation had a clear structure.
√	You showed your main points on a poster/…
√	You summed up at the end.
√	You invited us to ask questions.
✎	…

COMMUNICATION

√	You seemed relaxed.
√	You made eye contact.
√	You used notes.
√	You spoke clearly.
√	You explained your pictures.
✎	…

TIPS

1 Use the criteria you chose to assess[3] your classmate's work.

2 Give details when you say what a classmate did/didn't do well.
   Always start with something positive.

Where	What
In the first paragraph you	wrote a good introduction ….
At the end of your presentation you	didn't ask if we had questions /…

3 Suggest how the classmate could do better.
   You could try to use more linking words like and or because /use more pictures / …

---

[1] **criteria** (pl) [kraɪˈtɪəriə] Kriterien   [2]**plot** [plɒt] Handlung   [3](to) **assess** [əˈses] einschätzen

TIPS

1 Use the criteria you chose to assess[4] your classmates' work.

2 Using emoticons can help you with your assessment.   ☹

3 Give details of what your classmates did well/didn't do well.

4 Always start with something positive. When you criticize something, suggest what your classmates could improve

The phrases below can help you when you give feedback and make suggestions.

😃

| Your | introduction ideas visuals[5] ... | was were | clever! interesting! helpful! ... |

| I really liked the way you | introduced your topic. structured your ideas. summed up at the end. explained your visuals. .... |

Here's an example of what I liked.

🙂

| Your | introduction ideas visuals ... | was were | quite good. quite interesting. mostly OK. ... |

| You | structured your ideas explained your visuals summed up ... | quite well. |

| Here's an example of what you | did well. could improve. |

😐

| Some of your | ideas examples visuals ... | were | quite good. interesting. all right. ... |

| Your | introduction grammar ... | was OK, but ... |

| You didn't (always) | use linking words. speak very clearly. ... |

| I don't think you | checked your text very carefully. gave very good examples. used enough adjectives. ... |

| Maybe you could | join up these sentences. use captions under your visuals. ... |

☹

| You forgot to You didn't | cover the important points. use paragraphs. introduce your subject. sum up at the end. ... |

| You almost never | used linking words. gave examples. made eye contact with us. ... |

| I don't think you | did enough research. spent much time on your text. had a good conclusion. ... |

| If I were you I would | start a new paragraph here. write the conclusion again. ... |

---

[4] (to) **assess** [ə'ses] einschätzen   [5] **visuals** (pl) ['vɪʒuəlz] Bildmaterialien, Anschauungsmaterialien